CW01185474

Pulsed Neural Networks

Pulsed Neural Networks

edited by
Wolfgang Maass
Christopher M. Bishop

A Bradford Book
The MIT Press
Cambridge, Massachusetts
London, England

©1999 Massachusetts Institute of Technology

All rights reserved. No part of this book may be reproduced in any form by any electronic or mechanical means (including photocopying, recording, or information storage and retrieval) without permission in writing from the publisher.

This book was set in LaTeX by Heike Graf and was printed and bound in the United States of America.

Library of Congress Cataloging-in-Publication Data

Pulsed neural networks / edited by

Wolfgang Maass, Christopher M. Bishop

    p. cm.

  Includes bibliographical references.

  ISBN 0-262-13350-4 (hc. : alk. paper)

  1. Neural networks (Computer science)

  I. Maass, Wolfgang, 1949 August 21, II. Bishop, Christopher M.

QA76.87.P85   1998

006.3'2–dc21   98-38511

                                                                               CIP

Contents

Foreword by Terrence J. Sejnowski   xiii

Preface   xxv

Contributors to the book   xxvii

Basic Concepts and Models   1

1 Spiking Neurons   3
- 1.1 The Problem of Neural Coding   3
  - 1.1.1 Motivation   3
  - 1.1.2 Rate Codes   7
  - 1.1.3 Candidate Pulse Codes   11
  - 1.1.4 Discussion: Spikes or Rates?   15
- 1.2 Neuron Models   16
  - 1.2.1 Simple Spiking Neuron Model   17
  - 1.2.2 First Steps towards Coding by Spikes   20
  - 1.2.3 Threshold-Fire Models   23
  - 1.2.4 Conductance-Based Models   34
  - 1.2.5 Rate Models   45
- 1.3 Conclusions   47
- References   48

2 Computing with Spiking Neurons   55
- 2.1 Introduction   55
- 2.2 A Formal Computational Model for a Network of Spiking Neurons   55
- 2.3 McCulloch-Pitts Neurons versus Spiking Neurons   57
- 2.4 Computing with Temporal Patterns   59
  - 2.4.1 Conincidence Detection   59
  - 2.4.2 RBF-Units in the Temporal Domain   62
  - 2.4.3 Computing a Weighted Sum in Temporal Coding   63
  - 2.4.4 Universal Approximation of Continuous Functions with Spiking Neurons   65

		2.4.5 Other Computations with Temporal Patterns in Networks of Spiking Neurons	67
	2.5	Computing with a Space-Rate Code	68
	2.6	Computing with Firing Rates	73
	2.7	Firing Rates and Temporal Correlations	74
	2.8	Networks of Spiking Neurons for Storing and Retrieving Information	79
	2.9	Computing on Spike Trains	80
	2.10	Conclusions	80
		References	81
3	**Pulse-Based Computation in VLSI Neural Networks**		**87**
	3.1	Background	87
	3.2	Pulsed Coding: A VLSI Perspective	88
		3.2.1 Pulse Amplitude Modulation	90
		3.2.2 Pulse Width Modulation	90
		3.2.3 Pulse Frequency Modulation	91
		3.2.4 Phase or Delay Modulation	91
		3.2.5 Noise, Robustness, Accuracy and Speed	92
	3.3	A MOSFET Introduction	93
		3.3.1 Subthreshold Circuits for Neural Networks	96
	3.4	Pulse Generation in VLSI	97
		3.4.1 Pulse Intercommunication	99
	3.5	Pulsed Arithmetic in VLSI	99
		3.5.1 Addition of Pulse Stream Signals	99
		3.5.2 Multiplication of Pulse Stream Signals	101
		3.5.3 MOS Transconductance Multiplier	102
		3.5.4 MOSFET Analog Multiplier	102
	3.6	Learning in Pulsed Systems	104
	3.7	Summary and Issues Raised	105
		References	107
4	**Encoding Information in Neuronal Activity**		**111**
	4.1	Introduction	111
	4.2	Synchronization and Oscillations	114
	4.3	Temporal Binding	116
	4.4	Phase Coding	118

4.5		Dynamic Range and Firing Rate Codes	119
4.6		Interspike Interval Variability	120
4.7		Synapses and Rate Coding	124
4.8		Summary and Implications	125
		References	127

Implementations 133

5 Building Silicon Nervous Systems with Dendritic Tree Neuromorphs 135

5.1		Introduction	135
	5.1.1	Why Spikes?	135
	5.1.2	Dendritic Processing of Spikes	136
	5.1.3	Tunability	137
5.2		Implementation in VLSI	138
	5.2.1	Artificial Dendrites	138
	5.2.2	Synapses	139
	5.2.3	Dendritic Non-Linearities	141
	5.2.4	Spike-Generating Soma	142
	5.2.5	Excitability Control	143
	5.2.6	Spike Distribution - Virtual Wires	144
5.3		Neuromorphs in Action	146
	5.3.1	Feedback to Threshold-Setting Synapses	147
	5.3.2	Discrimination of Complex Spatio-Temporal Patterns	147
	5.3.3	Processing of Temporally Encoded Information	149
5.4		Conclusions	153
		References	154

6 A Pulse-Coded Communications Infrastructure 157

6.1		Introduction	157
6.2		Neuromorphic Computational Nodes	158
6.3		Neuromorphic aVLSI Neurons	158
6.4		Address Event Representation (AER)	162
6.5		Implementations of AER	165
6.6		Silicon Cortex	166
	6.6.1	Basic Layout	168

	6.7	Functional Tests of Silicon Cortex	170
		6.7.1	An Example Neuronal Network	170
		6.7.2	An Example of Sensory Input to SCX	172
	6.8	Future Research on AER Neuromorphic Systems	174
		References	176
7	**Analog VLSI Pulsed Networks for Perceptive Processing**	**179**
	7.1	Introduction	179
	7.2	Analog Perceptive Nets Communication Requirements	180
		7.2.1	Coding Information with Pulses	180
		7.2.2	Multiplexing of the Signals Issued by Each Neuron	181
		7.2.3	Non-Arbitered PFM Communication	182
	7.3	Analysis of the NAPFM Communication Systems	183
		7.3.1	Statistical Assumptions	183
		7.3.2	Detection	184
		7.3.3	Performance	186
		7.3.4	Data Dependency of System Performance	189
		7.3.5	Discussion	191
	7.4	Address Coding	193
	7.5	Silicon Retina Equipped with the NAPFM Communication System	194
		7.5.1	Circuit Description	194
		7.5.2	Noise Measurement Results	197
	7.6	Projective Field Generation	199
		7.6.1	Overview	199
		7.6.2	Anisotropic Current Pulse Spreading in a Nonlinear Network	201
		7.6.3	Analysis of the Spatial Response of the Nonlinear Network	202
		7.6.4	Analysis of the Size and Shape of the Bubbles Generable by the Nonlinear Network	204
	7.7	Description of the Integrated Circuit for Orientation Enhancement	207
		7.7.1	Overview	207
		7.7.2	Circuit Description	207
		7.7.3	System Measurement Results	208
		7.7.4	Other Applications	209

	7.8		Display Interface	211
	7.9		Conclusion	214
			References	215
8	**Preprocessing for Pulsed Neural VLSI Systems**			**217**
	8.1		Introduction	217
	8.2		A Sound Segmentation System	217
	8.3		Signal Processing in Analog VLSI	219
		8.3.1	Continuous Time Active Filters	220
		8.3.2	Sampled Data Active Switched Capacitor (SC) Filters	220
		8.3.3	Sampled Data Active Switched Current (SI) Filters	221
		8.3.4	Discussion	223
	8.4		Palmo - Pulse Based Signal Processing	224
		8.4.1	Basic Palmo Concepts	224
		8.4.2	A CMOS Analog Palmo Cell Implementation	226
		8.4.3	Interconnecting Analog Palmo Cells	228
		8.4.4	Results from a Palmo VLSI Device	231
		8.4.5	Digital Processing of Palmo Signals	232
		8.4.6	CMOS Analog Palmo Cell: Performance	233
	8.5		Conclusions	233
	8.6		Further Work	234
	8.7		Acknowledgements	234
			References	235
9	**Digital Simulation of Spiking Neural Networks**			**237**
	9.1		Introduction	237
	9.2		Implementation Issues of Pulse-Coded Neural Networks	238
		9.2.1	Discrete-Time Simulation	239
		9.2.2	Requisite Arithmetic Precision	240
		9.2.3	Basic Procedures of Network Computation	242
	9.3		Programming Environment	242
	9.4		Concepts of Efficient Simulation	244
	9.5		Mapping Neural Networks on Parallel Computers	247
		9.5.1	Neuron-Parallelism	248
		9.5.2	Synapse-Parallelism	248
		9.5.3	Pattern-Parallelism	249

		9.5.4	Partitioning of the Network	249
	9.6	Performance Study		251
		9.6.1	Single PE Workstations	251
		9.6.2	Neurocomputer	251
		9.6.3	Parallel Computers	253
		9.6.4	Results of the Performance Study	254
		9.6.5	Conclusions	255
		References		256

Design and Analysis of Pulsed Neural Systems   259

10 Populations of Spiking Neurons   261

10.1	Introduction		261
10.2	Model		263
10.3	Population Activity Equation		265
	10.3.1	Integral Equation for the Dynamics	265
	10.3.2	Normalization	267
10.4	Noise-Free Population Dynamics		268
10.5	Locking		269
	10.5.1	Locking Condition	270
	10.5.2	Graphical Interpretation	273
10.6	Transients		276
10.7	Incoherent Firing		279
	10.7.1	Determination of the Activity	280
	10.7.2	Stability of Asynchronous Firing	283
10.8	Conclusions		291
	References		293

11 Collective Excitation Phenomena and Their Applications   297

11.1	Introduction	297
	11.1.1 Two Variable Formulation of IAF Neurons	298
11.2	Synchronization of Pulse Coupled Oscillators	299
11.3	Clustering via Temporal Segmentation	302
11.4	Limits on Temporal Segmentation	304
11.5	Image Analysis	307
	11.5.1 Image Segmentation	308

	11.5.2 Edge Detection	309
11.6	Solitary Waves	311
11.7	The Importance of Noise	314
11.8	Conclusions	315
	References	317

12 Computing and Learning with Dynamic Synapses — 321

12.1	Introduction	321
12.2	Biological Data on Dynamic Synapses	322
12.3	Quantitative Models	326
12.4	On the Computational Role of Dynamic Synapses	329
12.5	Implications for Learning in Pulsed Neural Nets	333
12.6	Conclusions	334
	References	335

13 Stochastic Bit-Stream Neural Networks — 337

13.1	Introduction	338
13.2	Basic Neural Modelling	338
13.3	Feedforward Networks and Learning	341
	13.3.1 Probability Level Learning	341
	13.3.2 Bit-Stream Level Learning	342
13.4	Generalization Analysis	343
13.5	Recurrent Networks	344
13.6	Applications to Graph Colouring	344
13.7	Hardware Implementation	346
	13.7.1 The Stochastic Neuron	346
	13.7.2 Calculating Output Derivatives	348
	13.7.3 Generating Stochastic Bit-Streams	348
	13.7.4 Recurrent Networks	349
13.8	Conclusions	349
	References	351

14 Hebbian Learning of Pulse Timing in the *Barn Owl* Auditory System — 353

14.1	Introduction	353
14.2	Hebbian Learning	354
	14.2.1 Review of Standard Formulations	354

	14.2.2 Spike-Based Learning	355
	14.2.3 Example	358
	14.2.4 Learning Window	359
14.3	Barn Owl Auditory System	361
	14.3.1 The Localization Task	361
	14.3.2 Auditory Localization Pathway	362
14.4	Phase Locking	364
	14.4.1 Neuron Model	364
	14.4.2 Phase Locking – Schematic	365
	14.4.3 Simulation Results	366
14.5	Delay Tuning by Hebbian Learning	368
	14.5.1 Motivation	368
	14.5.2 Selection of Delays	369
14.6	Conclusions	371
	References	373

Foreword

Neural Pulse Coding

Terrence J. Sejnowski

Neurons use action potentials to signal over long distances, as summarized in Chapter 1 by Gerstner. The all-or-none nature of the action potential means that it codes information by its presence or absence, but not by its size or shape. In this respect, an action potential can be considered a pulse. This is an important fact about how brains are built, but it is equally important as a theoretical challenge to understanding the function of the brain. How do action potentials represent sensory states? How is information contained in the firing patterns of action potentials stored and retrieved? These are old questions that have been the focus of much research, but recent advances in experimental techniques are opening new ways to test theories for how information is encoded and decoded by spiking neurons in neural systems [Rieke et al., 1997]. The papers in the collection provide a window into the current state of theoretical and computational thinking based on spikes.

Spike Timing

The timing of spikes is already well established as a means for coding information in the electrosensory system of electric fish [Heiligenberg, 1991], in the auditory system of echolocating bats [Kuwabara, 1993], and in the visual system of flies [Bialek et al., 1991]. The relative spike timing between auditory inputs to the brain can be used to determine the location of a sound source [AgmonSnir, Carr and Rinzel, 1998] and Chapter 14 by Gerstner et al. provides a model for how the pulse timing could be learned. There are many possible ways that spike timing could be used in the nervous system, and papers in the collection explore some of the theoretical possibilities. Does the timing of spikes mean anything in cerebral cortex? If so, then there must be a sophisticated system in the cortex to organize the coding and decoding of spike timing.

Although some of the earliest theoretical models of neural networks, such as the McCulloch-Pitts model based on binary units, captured the all-or-none character of signaling by action potentials, many of the recent network models rely on continuous variables such as the average firing rate and input-output functions such as sigmoids. Although the average firing rate for a single neuron is well defined under stationary conditions and over a long enough time period to achieve statistical significance, none of these conditions obtain in the brain during most behaviors. Visual object recognition takes around 100 ms and the motor system has an even faster time scale. As the time interval for averaging gets shorter, the coding becomes discrete and a more general statistical framework is needed that takes into account joint probability distributions in the population of neurons. One exciting possibility is that the timing of the spikes in a population of neurons represents the probability distributions directly [Anderson, 1994; Zhang et al., 1998; Zhang and Sejnowski, 1999; Hinton, personal communication]. A concrete example will be given below for neurons in the rat hippocampus.

Another issue that is closely tied to spike coding is the issue of spike reliability. Averages of spike trains are presented because of the variability observed in recordings from neurons in the central nervous system. For example, the spike trains of sensory neurons elicited by the same stimulus presented repeatedly display a high degree of variability [Schiller et al., 1976; Britten et al., 1993; O'Keefe et al., 1997; Gur et al., 1997]. For cortical neurons, the intervals between spikes has an approximately Poisson distribution in response to a constant stimulus [O'Keefe, Bair and Movshon, 1997]. The Poisson firing rate can itself be a stochastic variable and may vary rapidly on the scale of the interspike interval [Sejnowski, 1976; Buracas et al., 1998]. This modulated Poisson model is a good compromise between models that are entirely based on average quantities like the firing rate and spike timing variables.

There is growing evidence that the variability observed in cortical spike trains cannot be attributed to unreliability in spike initiation [Mainen and Sejnowski, 1995; Berry et al., 1997; Nowak et al., 1997; Tang, 1997; de Ruyter van Steveninck et al., 1997]. Another possible explanation is that the variability reflects fluctuation in the inputs. This might occur if the dynamic operating point of a neuron is kept near its threshold, which is a region where a neuron is most sensitive to input correlations. This condition can be maintained by balancing the excitatory and inhibitory inputs to the neuron [Amit and Tsodyks, 1992; Tsodyks and Sejnowski, 1995; Shadlen and Newsome, 1994, 1998; van Vreeswijk and Sompolinsky, 1996]. When the inputs to a neuron are balanced, its firing rate can be increased by increasing the variance of the fluctuations without increasing the net excitation to the neuron.

In thinking about the distinctions between rate codes and pulse codes, it is important to keep in mind that the time a spike occurs can be used both to represent external time-varying stimuli and internal states. Often, many trials are presented and the poststimulus time (PST) histogram is computed to average out the variability, a form of ensemble averaging. On any given trial, however, the precise timing of a spike is an additional degree of freedom that could be used for many different purposes. For example, spike timing could be used to encode additional information about the sensory stimulus [Dan et al., 1997; Berry et al., 1997; de Ruyter van Steveninck et al., 1997].

The relative timing of spikes in a population of neurons could also encode information in addition to that conveyed by each spike train independently [Ritz and Sejnowski, 1997]. It has been suggested that the synchronous firing of neurons in a population can carry information about the global significance of the stimulus for the animal [Gray et al., 1989] or to organize information together in packets [Jeffreys, Traub and Whittington, 1996]. Learning may also depend on relative spike timing [Stopfer et al., 1997]. Changing the relative timing of presynaptic and postsynaptic spikes in a cortical neuron by as little as 10 msec can determine whether a synapse is potentiated or depressed [Markram et al., 1997]. This suggests that the relative timing of spikes may be highly regulated in order to control the conditions when synaptic plasticity occurs.

A neural coding strategy that depends on precise temporal coincidences requires precise mechanisms for decoding the temporal code. The biophysics of neuronal spike integration, especially in dendrites, is therefore as important as the neural coding [Murthy et al., 1994; Mel, 1992]. Local computation in dendritic trees is accomplished by active membrane conductances. Cortical neurons receive information at thousands of synapses at rates ranging from zero to several hundred hertz (Hz). It has been suggested that a neuron performs computations involving smaller numbers of synaptic inputs on localized regions of its dendritic tree [Mel, 1992]. Correlations between sets of afferent spike trains could also play an important role in generating responses. For example, sets of afferents with highly synchronized action potentials might be particularly effective at generating a postsynaptic response [Murthy et al., 1994]. Short-term synaptic depression could make a postsynaptic neuron more sensitive to correlated inputs by reducing the impact of the average firing rates of the inputs [Markram and Tsodyks, 1996; Abbott et al., 1997]. Furthermore, single synapses can be quite unreliable, since on average an excitatory synapse in the cortex or hippocampus releases less than a single vesicle in response to a stimulus. Thus, decoding schemes are likely to be probabilistic. The consequences of synaptic unreliability for pulse coded systems is explored by Maass and Zador in Chapter 12.

Population Codes

A sensory stimulus gives rise to action potentials in a large number of cortical neurons, which represent different aspects of the stimulus. The central question how different aspects of the stimulus are represented in the population of responding neurons [Lehky and Sejnowski, 1990; Konishi, 1991; Seung and Sompolinsky, 1993; Foldiak, 1993; Abbott, 1994; Salinas and Abbott, 1994; Sanger, 1996; Abbott and Dayan, 1999; Zhang et al., 1998]. New experimental techniques, such as simultaneous recordings from the spike trains of over 100 neurons [Gray et al., 1995; Meister, 1996], provide a glimpse of the large-scale population codes in different parts of the brain. The goal is to decipher the coding schemes by recording spike trains from a large number of neurons and try to reconstruct from those spike trains physical and psychological properties of the stimulus. In the case of the motor system, the goal is to predict the movement of the animal from the pattern of spikes recorded from the motor system.

Many neurons in the motor cortex of the monkey fire at rates that are correlated with the direction of arm reaching [Schwartz et al., 1988]. The average firing rate of a given neuron is maximal when the arm movement is in a particular direction known as the preferred direction for that neuron. A popular reconstruction method is called the population vector scheme, which estimates the direction of arm movement by summing the preferred direction vectors weighted by the firing rate of each neuron (Georgopoulos et al., 1988]. A similar coding strategy has been found among the interneurons responsible for the bending reflex of the leech (Lewis and Kristan, 1998; Abbott, 1998]. A more general approach to reconstruction is to allow the neurons to represent more general basis functions of the physical variables [Girosi and Poggio, 1990; Pouget and Sejnowski, 1997; Zhang et al., 1998]. Each neuron contributes a basis function in this space of variables whenever it fires, and the best estimate of the physical variables can be computed from the sum of these functions weighted by the number of spike occurring in each neuron during a time interval.

An alternative method for decoding a population code is based on Bayesian reconstruction and maximum likelihood estimation. These are probabilistic methods that take into account prior probabilities and attempt to reconstruct the entire probability distribution. Instead of adding together the kernels, as in the basis function method, the probabilistic approach multiplies them, assuming that the spikes in each neuron are independent. This method can be used to establish limits on the accuracy of a neural code. The Fisher information, which is the variance of the maximum likelihood estimate of a stimulus, sets a limit for any unbiased estimator of a stimulus based on the neural responses it evokes [Paradiso, 1988; Seung and Sompolinsky, 1993; Abbott and Dayan, 1999; Zhang et al., 1998].

Although these reconstruction methods may be useful for telling us what information could be available in a population of neurons, it does not tell us what information is actually used by the brain. In particular, it is not clear whether these reconstruction methods could be implemented with neurons. Pouget [Pouget et al., 1998] show how maximum likelihood decoding can be performed using the highly recurrent architecture of cortical circuits, and thus establishes that the theoretical limit corresponding to the Fisher information is achievable. Zhang [Zhang et al., 1998] show how a feedforward network with one layer of weights could in principle read out a Bayesian code. Thus, optimal decoding is well within the capability of the network mechanisms known to exist in the cortex. However, an explicit readout of a population code may not be needed until the final common pathway of the motor system since projections between cortical areas may simply perform transformations between different population codes.

Foreword   xvii

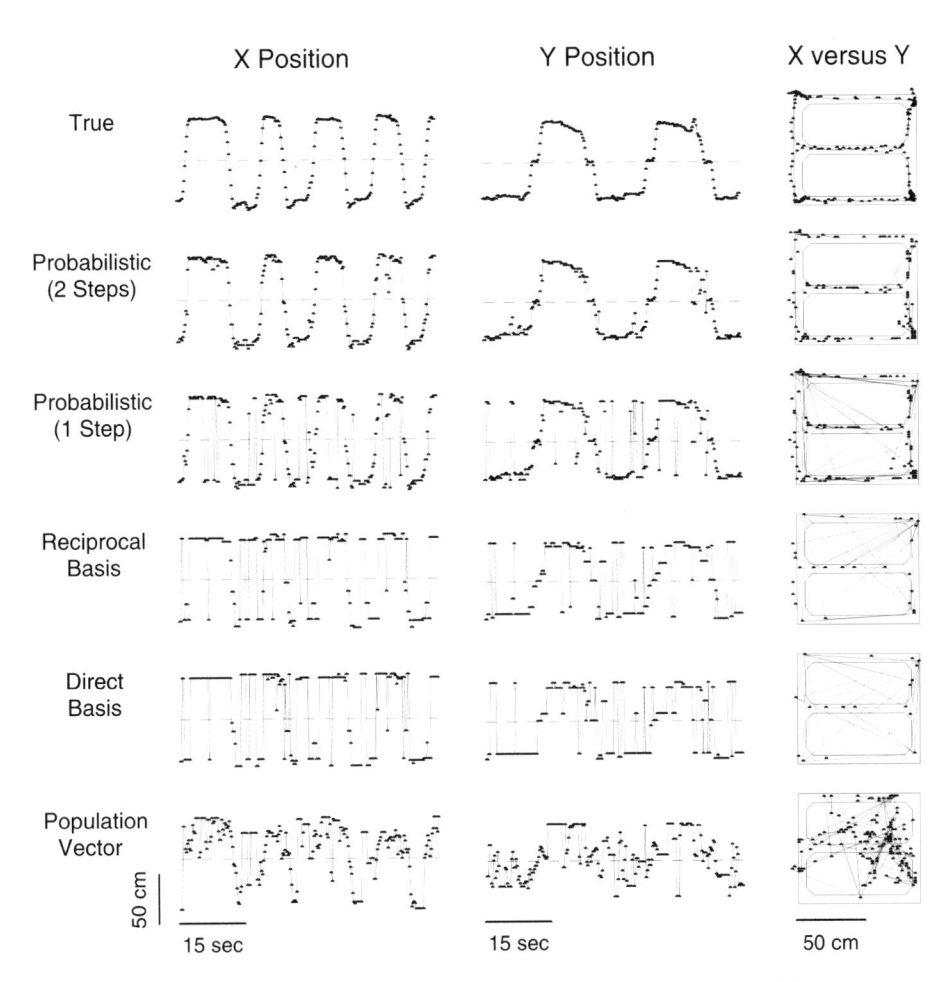

Figure 1. True X and Y positions of a rat running on an elevated figure-8 maze as compared with the positions reconstructed by different methods using 25 place cells and a sliding time window of 0.5 sec. The same 60-second segment is shown in all plots. The probabilistic or Bayesian methods were especially accurate, and the erratic jumps in the reconstructed trajectory were reduced by a continuity constraint using information from 2 consecutive time steps. By contrast, the population vector method often yielded implausible positions. From [Zhang et al., 1998].

Hippocampal Place Fields

An example of how the timing of spikes in a population of neurons can be used to reconstruct a physical variable is the reconstruction of the location of a rat in its environment from the place fields of neurons in the hippocampus of the rat. In the experiment reported here, the firing patterns of 25 cells were simultaneously recorded from a freely moving rat [Zhang et al., 1998]. The place cells were silent most of the time, and they fired maximally only when the animal's head was within restricted region in the environment called its place field [Wilson et al., 1993]. The reconstruction problem was to determine the rat's position based on the spike firing times of the place cells.

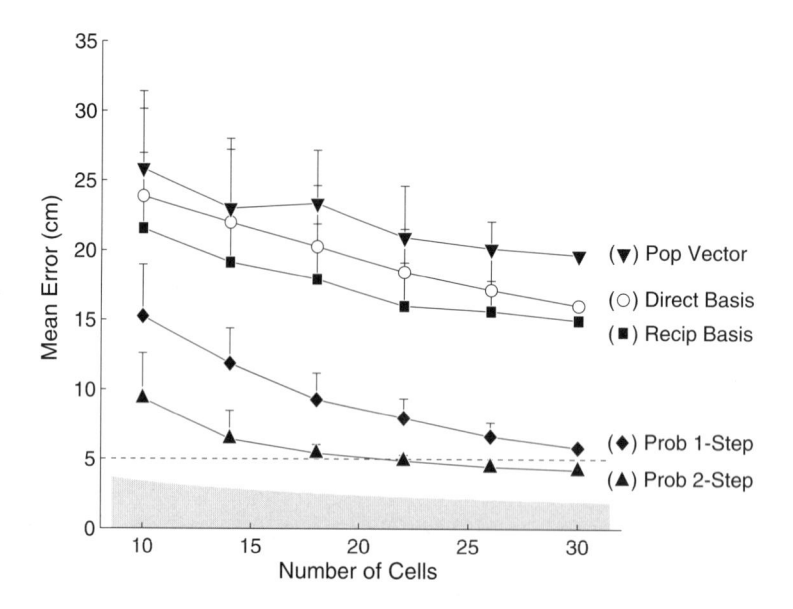

Figure 2. All reconstruction methods became more accurate when more cells were used, shown here for a rat running on a rectangular maze. Each data point represents the mean error of 40 repetitive trials in which a subset of cells were drawn randomly from the whole sample. The shaded region represents reconstruction errors excluded by the Cramér-Rao bound based on Fisher information. From [Zhang et al., 1998].

Bayesian reconstruction was used to estimate the position of the rat in the figure-8 maze shown in Figure 1 [Zhang et al., 1998]. Assume that a population of N neurons encodes several variables $(x_1, x_2, \ldots)$, which will be written as vector **x**. From the number of spikes $\mathbf{n} = (n_1, n_2, \ldots, n_N)$ fired by the N neurons within a time interval τ, we want to estimate the value of **x** using the Bayes rule for conditional probability:

$$P(\mathbf{x}|\mathbf{n}) = P(\mathbf{n}|\mathbf{x})P(\mathbf{x})/P(\mathbf{n}) \qquad (1)$$

assuming independent Poisson spike statistics. The final formula reads

$$P(\mathbf{x}|\mathbf{n}) = kP(\mathbf{x}) \left(\prod_{i=1}^{N} f_i(\mathbf{x})^{n_i} \right) \exp\left(-\tau \sum_{i=1}^{N} f_i(\mathbf{x}) \right) \qquad (2)$$

where k is a normalization constant, $P(\mathbf{x})$ is the prior probability, and $f_i(\mathbf{x})$ is the measured tuning function, i.e., the average firing rate of neuron i for each variable value **x**. The most probable value of **x** can thus be obtained by finding the **x** that maximizes $P(\mathbf{x}|\mathbf{n})$, namely,

$$\hat{\mathbf{x}} = \arg\max_{\mathbf{x}} P(\mathbf{x}|\mathbf{n}) \qquad (3)$$

By sliding the time window forward, the entire time course of **x** can be reconstructed from the time varying-activity of the neural population.

A comparison of several different reconstruction methods is shown in Figure 1. The Bayesian reconstruction method was the most accurate. As the number of neurons included in the reconstruction is increased, the accuracy of all the methods increased, as shown in Figure 2. The best mean error was about 5 cm, in the range of the intrinsic error of the infrared position tracking system. There are thousands of place cells in the hippocampus of a rat that respond in any given environment. However, it is not known how this information is used by the rat in solving navigational problems.

There is evidence for information in the relative timing of neurons in the rat hippocampus. As a rat moves through the preferred place of a hippocampal neuron, the timing of the spikes relative to a background 4-6 Hz theta rhythm changes from phase lag to phase lead [O'Keefe and Recce, 1993]. Thus, the relative timing of spikes in the population of hippocampal place neurons carry information about relative location (Chapter 5 by Recce provides more details about this form of phase coding). Hopfield [Hopfield, 1996] has suggested a general method by which vectors can be encoded by the relative timing of impulses and decoded by neurons using time delays.

Hardware Models

The technology that makes possible digital computers can also be used for implementing large networks of spiking neurons. Several of the chapters in this book illustrate how very large scale integrated (VLSI) technology can be used to emulate the integration in dendrites (Chapter 5 by Northmore and Elias) and recurrent cortical networks (Chapter 6 by Whatley, Deiss and Douglas). Scaling up from a single chip to a system of chips requires a complex communications system that corresponds to the major tracts that connect different brain areas. Most of the brain volume is composed of fiber bundles called white matter, which are composed of axons that carry spikes over long distances. Even within the neuropil of the cortex, a significant fraction of the volume is taken up with axons used for local communication. Thus, it should be expected that any hardware system based on the brain would make a major commitment of resources to communication.

Computing with spikes is not easy. The precision of the hardware required for most spike timing codes is much greater than that required for schemes based on average firing rates. Another important consideration is the amount of power required to generate pulses and charge up long wires. Finally, the high precision must be maintained over varying conditions which, in the case of the cortex, means a range of temperatures and ionic concentrations. Homeostatic mechanisms could be used to stabilize timing circuits, which suggests that calibration is also an important function that needs to be implemented in the cortex

As more evidence is found for the importance of spike timing in the cortex, the question shifts from whether spike timing carries information to how it is used. This volume provides a rich source of ideas that will serve as the starting point for many research directions.

References

[Abbott, 1994] Abbott, L. F. (1994). Decoding neuronal firing and modeling neural networks. *Quarterly Review of Biophysics*, 27:291-331.

[Abbott, 1998] Abbott, L. F. (1998). The analytical bend of the leech. *Nature*, 391: 18-9.

[Abbott and Dayan, 1999] Abbott, L. F., and Dayan, P. (1999). The effect of correlated variability on the accuracy of a population code. *Neural Computation*, 11 (1).

[Abbott et al., 1997] Abbott, L. F., Varela, J. A., Sen, K., and Nelson, S. B. (1997). Synaptic depression and cortical gain control. *Science*, 275:220–224.

[AgmonSnir et al., 1998] AgmonSnir, H., Carr, C. E., and Rinzel, J. (1998). The role of dendrites in auditory coincidence detection. *Nature*, 393: 268-272.

[Amit and Tsodyks, 1992] Amit, D. and Tsodyks, M. (1992). Effective neurons and attractor neural networks in cortical environments. *Network*, 3:121-137.

[Anderson, 1994] Anderson, C. H. (1994). Basic elements of biological computational systems. *International Journal of Modern Physics C*, 5:135-137.

[Berry et al., 1997] Berry, M. J., Warland, D. K., Meister, M. (1997). The structure and precision of retinal spike trains. *Proceedings of the National Academy of Sciences of the United States of America*, 94:5411-6.

[Bialek et al., 1991] Bialek, W., Rieke, F., de Ruyter, R., van Steveninck, R.R. and Warland, D. Reading a neural code. Science 252, 1854-7 (1991).

[Britten et al., 1993] Britten, K. H., Shadlen, M., Newsome, W. T., and Movshon, J. A. (1993). Response of neurons in macaque MT to stochastic motion signals. *Visual Neuroscience*, 10:1157-1169.

[Buracas et al., 1998] Buracas, G., Zador, A., DeWeese, M. and Albright, T. (1998). Efficient discrimination of temporal patterns by motion-sensitive neurons in primate visual cortex. *Neuron*, 20:959-969.

[Dan et al., 1996] Dan, Y., Atick, J. J., Reid, R. C. (1996). Efficient coding of natural scenes in the lateral geniculate nucleus: experimental test of a computational theory. *Journal of Neuroscience* 16:3351-62.

[Foldiak, 1993] Foldiak, P. (1993). The 'ideal homunculus': Statistical inference from neural population responses. In *Computation and Neural Systems*, F. H. Eeckman and J. Bower, eds., Norwell, MA: Kluwer Academic Publishers, 55-60.

[Georgopoulos et al., 1988] Georgopoulos, A. P., Kettner, R. E., and Schwartz, A. B. (1988). Primate motor cortex and free arm movements to visual targets in three-dimensional space. II. Coding of the direction of movement by a neuronal population. *Neuroscience*, 8:2928-2937.

[Girosi and Poggio, 1990] Girosi, F., and Poggio, T. (1990). Networks and the best approximation property. *Biological Cybernetics*, 63:169-176.

[Gray et al., 1989] Gray, C. M., König, P., Engel, A. K., and Singer, W. (1989). Oscillatory responses in cat visual cortex exhibit intercolumnar synchronization which reflects global stimulus properties. *Nature*, 338:334–337.

[Gray et al., 1995] Gray, C. M., Maldonado, P. E., Wilson, M., McNaughton, B. (1995). Tetrodes markedly improve the reliability and yield of multiple single-unit isolation from multi-unit recordings in cat striate cortex. *Journal of Neuroscience Methods*, 63: 43-54.

[Gur et al., 1997] Gur, M., Beylin, A., and Snodderly, D. M (1997). Response variability of neurons in primary visual cortex (V1) of alert monkeys. *Journal of Neuroscience*, 17:2914-2920.

[Heiligenberg, 1991] Heiligenberg, W. (1991). *Neural Nets in Electric Fish*, MIT Press, Cambridge, MA.

[Hopfield, 1996] Hopfield, J. J. (1996). Transforming neural computations and representing time. *Proceedings of the National Academy of Sciences of the United States of America*, 93:15440-4.

[Jefferys et al., 1996] Jefferys, J. G., Traub, R. D., Whittington, M. A. (1996) Neuronal networks for induced '40 Hz' rhythms. *Trends in Neurosciences*, 19(5):202-8.

[Konishi, 1991] Konishi, M. (1991). Deciphering the Brain's Codes. *Neural Computation*, 3(1), 1-18

[Kuwabara and Suga, 1993] Kuwabara, N., and Suga, N. (1993). Delay lines and amplitude selectivity are created in subthalamic auditory nuclei: the brachium of the inferior colliculus of the mustached bat. *Journal of Neurophysiology 69*, 1713-1724.

[Lehky and Sejnowski, 1990] Lehky, S. R., and Sejnowski, T. J. (1990). Neural model of stereoacuity and depth interpolation based on a distributed representation of stereo disparity. *Journal of Neuroscience*, 10:2281-2299.

[Lewis and Kristan] Lewis, J. E., and Kristan, W. B. (1998). A neuronal network for computing population vectors in the leech. *Nature*, 391: 76-9.

[Mainen and Sejnowski, 1995] Mainen, Z. F., and Sejnowski, T. J. (1995). Reliability of spike timing in neocortical neurons. *Science*, 268:1503-1506.

[Markram and Tsodyks, 1996] Markram, H., and Tsodyks, M. (1996). Redistribution of synaptic efficacy between neocortical pyramidal neurons. *Nature*, 382: 807-10.

[Markram et al., 1997] Markram, H., Lübke, J., Frotscher, M., and Sakman, B. (1997).. Physiology and anatomy of synaptic connections between thick tufted pyramidal neurones in the developing rat neocortex., *Journal of Physiology*, 500: 409-40.

[Meister, 1996] Meister, M. (1996). Multineuronal codes in retinal signaling. *Proceedings of the National Academy of Sciences of the United States of America*, 93:609-14.

[Mel, 1992] Mel, B., (1992). NMDA-Based Pattern Discrimination in a Modeled Cortical Neuron, *Neural Computation*, 4(4), 502-517.

[Murthy and Fetz, 1994] Murthy, V. N., and Fetz, E. E. (1994). Effects of Input Synchrony on the Firing Rate of a Three-Conductance Cortical Neuron Model. *Neural Computation*, 6(6) 1111-1126.

[O'Keefe and Recce, 1993] O'Keefe, J., and Recce, M. L. (1993). Phase relationship between hippocampal place units and the EEG theta rhythm. *Hippocampus*, 3:317-330.

[O'Keefe et al., 1997] O'Keefe, L. P., Bair, W., and Movshon, J. A. (1997). Response variability of MT neurons in macaque monkey. *Society for Neuroscience Abstracts*, 23:1125.

[Paradiso, 1988] Paradiso, M. A. (1988). A theory for the use of visual orientation information which exploits the columnar structure of striate cortex. *Biological Cybernetics*, 58:35-49.

[Pouget, 1997] Pouget, A. and Sejnowski, T. J. (1997). Spatial transformations in the parietal cortex using basis functions. *Journal of Cognitive Neuroscience* 9(2), 222-237.

[Pouget et al., 1997] Pouget, A., Zhang, K., Deneve, S., and Latham, P. (1997). Statistically Efficient Estimation Using Population Coding, *Neural Computation*, 10: 373-401, 1998.

[Rieke et al., 1997] Rieke, F., Warland, D., de Ruyter van Stevelinck, R. R., and Bialek, W. (1997). *Spikes – Exploring the Neural Code*. MIT Press, Cambridge, MA.

[Ritz and Sejnowski, 1997] Ritz, R., and Sejnowski, T. J. (1997). Synchronous oscillatory activity in sensory systems: new vistas on mechanisms. *Current Opinion in Neurobiology*, 7(4):536-46.

[de Ruyter van Stevenick et al., 1997] de Ruyter van Stevenick, R. R., Lewen, G. D., Strong, S. P., Koberle, R., Bialek, W. (1997). Reproducibility and variability in neural spike trains. *Science*, 275:1805-8.

[Salinas and Abbott, 1994] Salinas, E., and Abbott, L. F. (1994) Vector reconstruction from firing rates. *Journal of Computational Neuroscience*. 1:89-107.

[Sanger, 1996] Sanger, T. D. (1996). Probability density estimation for the interpretation of neural population codes. *Journal of Neurophysiology*, 76:2790-2793.

[Schiller et al., 1976] Schiller, P. H., Finlay, B. L., and Volman, S. F. (1976). Short-term response variability of monkey striate neurons. *Brain Research*, 105:347-349.

[Schwartz et al., 1988] Schwartz, A., Kettner, R. E., and Georgopoulos, A. P. (1988). Primate motor cortex and free arm movements to visual targets in three-dimensional space. I. Relations between single cell discharge and direction of movement. *Neuroscience*, 8:2913-2927.

[Sejnowski, 1976] Sejnowski, T. J. (1976). On the stochastic dynamics of neuronal interaction. *Biological Cybernetics*, 22:203-11.

[Sejnowski, 1996] Sejnowski, T. J. (1996). Pattern recognition. Time for a new neural code? *Nature*, 376:21-2.

[Seung and Sompolinsky, 1993] Seung, H. S., and Sompolinsky, H. (1993). Simple models for reading neuronal population codes. *Proceedings of the National Academy of Sciences*, 90:10749-10753.

[Shadlen and Newsome, 1994] Shadlen, M. N., and Newsome, W. T. (1994). Noise, neural codes and cortical organization. *Current Opinion in Neurobiology*, 4:569-579.

[Shadlen and Newsome, 1998] Shadlen, M. N., and Newsome, W. T. (1998). The variable discharge of cortical neurons: implications for connectivity, computation, and information coding. *Journal of Neuroscience*, 18(10):3870-96.

[Stopfer, 1997] Stopfer, M., Bhagavan, S., Smith, B. H, Laurent, G. (1997). Impaired odour discrimination on desynchronization of odour-encoding neural assemblies. *Nature*, 390:70-4.

[Tang et al., 1997] Tang, A. C., Bartels, A. M., Sejnowski, T. J. (1997). Effects of cholinergic modulation on responses of neocortical neurons to fluctuating input. *Cerebral Cortex*, 7:502-9.

[Tsodyks and Sejnowski, 1995] Tsodyks, M., and Sejnowski, T. J. (1995). Rapid switching in balanced cortical network models. *Network*, 6:1-14.

[van Vreeswijk and Sompolinsky, 1996] van Vreeswijk, C., and Sompolinsky, H. (1996). Chaos in neuronal networks with balanced excitatory and inhibitory activity. *Science*, 274:1724-1726.

[Wilson and McNaughton, 1993] Wilson, M. A., and McNaughton B. L. (1993). Dynamics of the hippocampal ensemble code for space. *Science*, 261:1055-8.

[Zhang et al., 1998] Zhang, K., Ginzburg, I., McNaughton, B. L., and Sejnowski, T. J. (1998). Interpreting neuronal population activity by reconstruction: unified framework with application to hippocampal place cells. *Journal of Neurophysiology*, 79:1017-44.

[Zhang and Sejnowski, 1999] Zhang, K., and Sejnowski, T. J. (1999). Neuronal tuning: to sharpen or broaden? *Neural Computation*, 11 (1).

Preface

The majority of artificial neural network models are based on a computational paradigm involving the propagation of continuous variables from one processing unit to the next. In recent years, however, data from neurobiological experiments have made it increasingly clear that biological neural networks, which communicate through pulses, use the timing of these pulses to transmit information and to perform computation. This realization has stimulated a significant growth of research activity in the area of pulsed neural networks ranging from neurobiological modeling and theoretical analyses, to algorithm development and hardware implementations. Such research is motivated both by the desire to enhance our understanding of information processing in biological networks, as well as by the goal of developing new information processing technologies.

Our aim in producing this book has been to provide a comprehensive treatment of the field of pulsed neural networks, which will be accessible to researchers from diverse disciplines such as electrical engineering, signal processing, computer science, physics, and computational neuroscience. By virtue of its pedagogical emphasis, it will also find a place in many of the advanced undergraduate and graduate courses in neural networks now taught in many universities.

The Isaac Newton Institute

This book originated from a two-day workshop entitled *Pulsed Neural Networks* that we organized in August 1997 at the Isaac Newton Institute for Mathematical Sciences in Cambridge.[1] The workshop formed part of the six-month Newton Institute program *Neural Networks and Machine Learning*, organized by Chris Bishop, David Haussler, Geoffrey Hinton, Mahesan Niranjan and Leslie Valiant. This research program was the largest international event of its kind to have taken place in the field of neural computing, and attracted several hundred participants for visits ranging from one or two weeks up to six months.

The workshop on *Pulsed Neural Networks* comprised two days of invited presentations by many of the foremost researchers in the field, and proved to be a very timely event. In view of the interdisciplinary nature of this subject, the workshop included a number of tutorials that introduced pulsed neural networks from the point of view of different disciplines. As a result of the success of the workshop, there was considerable enthusiasm to capture the highlights of the meeting in book form and thereby make the workshop contributions, including both tutorials and research presentations, accessible to a much wider audience. All contributions were rewritten to take into account the special context of this book, and to use consistent terminology and notation across the different disciplines. We hope

---

[1] Further information about the Isaac Newton Institute can be found at http://www.newton.cam.ac.uk/.

this book will convey some of the excitement of the workshop and of the field of pulsed neural networks.

Overview of the Book

The *Foreword* by Terry Sejnowski sets the stage for the book. The core of the book consists of three parts. The first part (*Basic Concepts and Models*) comprises four tutorial chapters. The tutorial *Spiking Neurons* (Chapter 1) by Wulfram Gerstner introduces the neurophysiological background and motivations for computing with pulses. It discusses a simple mathematical model for a spiking neuron, the spike response model, that provides the basis for later chapters. The tutorial *Computing with Spiking Neurons* (Chapter 2) by Wolfgang Maass analyzes the computational power of networks of spiking neurons, and compares them with traditional neural network models. Hardware implementations of pulsed neural nets are discussed in the tutorial *Pulsed-Based Computations in VLSI Neural Networks* (Chapter 3) by Alan Murray. The tutorial *Encoding Information in Neural Activity* (Chapter 4) by Michael Recce surveys results about the way in which biological systems encode information in spatial-temporal patterns of pulses.

The chapters in the second part of the book (*Implementations*) review a number of options for implementing pulsed neural nets in electronic hardware. Chapters 5 to 8 discuss approaches, and first results, for implementing artificial pulsed neural nets in analog VLSI. Chapter 9 reviews the state of the art regarding digital simulations of pulsed neural nets.

The third part of the book (*Design and Analysis of Pulsed Neural Systems*) surveys current research on the design and analysis of pulsed neural networks, in both biological and artificial systems.

Each of the chapters in the second and third part should be comprehensible to anyone who has worked through the four tutorials in the first part of the book. Together these chapters constitute a survey of current research issues across all aspects of pulsed neural networks including mathematical analyses, algorithms, hardware and software implementations, and neurobiology.

Acknowledgments

We would like to express our sincere appreciation to the staff of the Isaac Newton Institute for the tremendous assistance they provided not only in helping to organize the workshop on *Pulsed Neural Networks* but also for their unfailing energy and enthusiasm throughout the six month research program. We are grateful to Heike Graf and Ingrid Preininger from the Technische Universität Graz for their dedication and skill in creating the camera-ready copy for this book. Finally we would like to thank the staff of MIT Press for their help in the preparation of this book.

Christopher M. Bishop and Wolfgang Maass

Cambridge and Graz, February 1998

Contributors

Christopher M. Bishop *Preface*
Microsoft Research, Cambridge
Cambridge CB2 3NH, England, UK
cmbishop@microsoft.com

Peter S. Burge *Chapter 13*
Department of Computer Science
Royal Holloway, University of London
Egham, England, UK
peter@neurocolt.com

Max R. van Daalen *Chapter 13*
Department of Computer Science
Royal Holloway, University of London
Egham, England, UK
max@dcs.rhbnc.ac.uk

Stephen R. Deiss *Chapter 6*
Applied Neurodynamics
Encinitas, CA, 92024-5354, USA
deiss@sba.cerf.net

Rodney J. Douglas *Chapter 6*
Institut für Neuroinformatik
Universität Zürich & ETH Zürich
Zürich, Switzerland
rjd@ini.phys.ethz.ch

John G. Elias *Chapter 5*
Department of Electrical and Computer Engineering
University of Delaware
Newark, Delaware 19716, USA
elias@udel.edu

Wulfram Gerstner *Chapters 1, 10, 14*
Center for Neuromimetic Systems
Swiss Federal Institute of Technology, EPFL
CH-1015 Lausanne, Switzerland
Wulfram.Gerstner@di.epfl.ch

Alister Hamilton *Chapter 8*
Department of Electrical Engineering
University of Edinburgh
Edinburgh, Scotland, UK
Alister.Hamilton@ee.ed.ac.uk

J. Leo van Hemmen *Chapter 14*
Physik Department, TU München
D-85747 Garching bei München
München, Germany
Leo.van.Hemmen@Physik.TU-München.de

David Horn *Chapter 11*
School of Physics and Astronomy
Tel Aviv University
Tel Aviv, Israel
horn@neuron.tau.ac.il

Axel Jahnke *Chapter 9*
Institut of Microelectronics
TU Berlin
Berlin, Germany
jahnke@mikro.ee.tu-berlin.de

Richard Kempter *Chapter 14*
Institut für Theoretische Physik
Physik-Department der TU München
München, Germany
Richard.Kempter@Physik.TU-Muenchen.DE

Wolfgang Maass *Preface, Chapters 2, 12*
Institute for Theoretical Computer Science
Technische Universität Graz
A-8010 Graz, Austria
maass@igi.tu-graz.ac.at

Alessandro Mortara *Chapter 7*
Advanced Microelectronics Division
Centre Suisse d'Electronique et de Microtechnique
Neuchatel, Switzerland
mortara@csemne.ch

Alan F. Murray *Chapter 3*
Dept. of Electrical Engineering
University of Edinburgh
Edinburgh, EH9 3JL., England, UK
Alan.Murray@ee.ed.ac.uk

David P. M. Northmore *Chapter 5*
Department of Psychology
University of Delaware
Newark, Delaware 19716, USA
northmor@udel.edu

Irit Opher *Chapter 11*
School of Physics and Astronomy
Tel Aviv University
Tel Aviv, Israel
irit@neuron.tau.ac.il

Kostas A. Papathanasiou *Chapter 8*
Department of Electrical Engineering
University of Edinburgh
Edinburgh, Scotland, UK
Kostas.Papathanasiou@ee.ed.ac.uk

Michael Recce — *Chapter 4*
Department of Computer and Information Science
New Jersey Institute of Technology
Newark, NJ 07102, USA
recce@homer.njit.edu

Barry J. P. Rising — *Chapter 13*
Department of Computer Science
Royal Holloway, University of London
Egham, England, UK
barry@dcs.rhbnc.ac.uk

Ulrich Roth — *Chapter 9*
Institut of Microelectronics
TU Berlin
Berlin, Germany
roth@mikro.ee.tu-berlin.de

Tim Schönauer — *Chapter 9*
Institut of Microelectronics
TU Berlin
Berlin, Germany
tim@mikro.ee.tu-berlin.de

Terrence J. Sejnowski — *Foreword*
The Salk Institute
La Jolla, CA 92037, USA
terry@salk.edu

John S. Shawe-Taylor — *Chapter 13*
Department of Computer Science
Royal Holloway, University of London
Egham, UK
john@dcs.rhbnc.ac.uk

Philippe Venier — *Chapter 7*
Advanced Microelectronics Division
Centre Suisse d'Electronique et de Microtechnique
Neuchatel, Switzerland
venier@csemne.ch

Hermann Wagner — *Chapter 14*
Institut für Biologie
Lehrstuhl für Zoologie/Tierphysiologie
RWTH Aachen
D-52074 Aachen, Germany
wagner@tyto.bio2.rwth-aachen.de

Adrian M. Whatley — *Chapter 6*
Institut für Neuroinformatik
Universität Zürich & ETH Zürich
Zürich, Switzerland
amw@ini.phys.ethz.ch

Anthony M. Zador — *Chapter 12*
The Salk Institute
La Jolla, CA 92037, USA
zador@salk.edu

Part I
Basic Concepts and Models

1 Spiking Neurons

Wulfram Gerstner

An organism which interacts with its environment must be capable of receiving sensory input from the environment. It has to process the sensory information, recognize food sources or predators, and take appropriate actions. The difficulty of these tasks is appreciated, if one tries to program a small robot to do the same thing: It turns out to be a challenging endeavor. Yet animals perform these tasks with apparent ease.

Their astonishingly good performance is due to a neural system or 'brain' which has been optimized over the time courses of evolution. Even though a lot of detailed information about neurons and their connections is available by now, one of the fundamental questions of neuroscience is unsolved: What is the code used by the neurons? Do neurons communicate by a 'rate code' or a 'pulse code'?

In the first part of this chapter, different potential coding schemes are discussed. Various interpretations of rate coding are contrasted with some pulse coding schemes. Pulse coded neural networks require appropriate neuron models. In the second part of the chapter, several neuron models that are used throughout the book are introduced. Special emphasis has been put on spiking neurons models of the 'integrate-and-fire' type, but the Hodgkin-Huxley model, compartmental models, and rate models are reviewed as well.

1.1 The Problem of Neural Coding

1.1.1 Motivation

Over the past hundred years, biological research has accumulated an enormous amount of detailed knowledge about the structure and the function of the brain see, e.g., [Kandel and Schwartz, 1991]. The elementary processing units in the brain are neurons which are connected to each other in an intricate pattern. A portion of such a network of neurons in the mammalian cortex is sketched in Figure 1.1. It is a reproduction of a famous drawing by Ramón y Cajal, one of the pioneers of neuroscience around the turn of the century. We can distinguish several neurons with triangular or circular cell bodies and long wire-like extensions. This drawing gives a glimpse of the network of neurons in the cortex. Only a few of the neurons present in the sample have been made visible by the staining procedure. In reality the neurons and their connections form a dense network with more than 10^4 cell bodies and several kilometers of 'wires' per cubic millimeter.

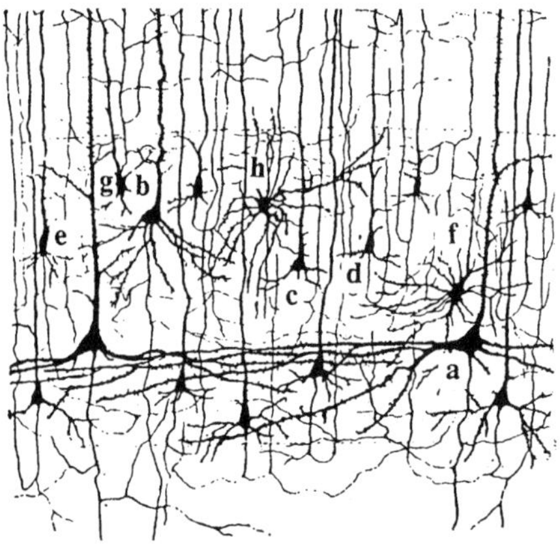

1. Spiking Neurons

Figure 1.1. This reproduction of a drawing of Ramón y Cajal shows a few neurons in the cortex. Only a small portion of the neurons are shown; the density of neurons is in reality much higher. Cell b is a nice example of a pyramidal cell with a triangularly shaped cell body. Dendrites, which leave the cell laterally and upwards, can be recognized by their rough surface. The axon extends downwards with a few branches to the left and right. From Ramón y Cajal.

In other areas of the brain the wiring pattern looks different. In all areas, however, neurons of different sizes and shapes form the basic elements.

A typical neuron has three parts, called dendritic tree, soma, and axon; see Figure 1.2. Roughly speaking, signals from other neurons arrive onto the dendritic tree and are transmitted to the soma and the axon. The transition zone between the soma and the axon is of special interest. In this area the the essential non-linear processing step occurs. If the total excitation caused by the input is sufficient, an output signal is emitted which is propagated along the axon and its branches to other neurons. The junction between an axonal branch and the dendrite (or the soma) of a receiving neuron is called a synapse. It is common to refer to a sending neuron as the presynaptic neuron and to the receiving neuron as a postsynaptic neuron. A neuron in the cortex often makes connections to more than 10^4 postsynaptic neurons. Many of its axonal branches end in the direct neighborhood of the neuron, but the axon can also stretch over several millimeters and connect to neurons in other areas of the brain.

So far, we have stated that neurons transmit signals along the axon to thousands of other neurons – but what do these signals look like? The neuronal signals can be observed by placing a fine electrode close to the soma or axon of a neuron; see Figure 1.2. The voltage trace in a typical recording shows a sequence of short pulses, called action potentials or spikes. A chain of pulses emitted by a single neuron is usually called a spike train – a sequence of stereotyped events which occur at regular or irregular intervals. The duration of an action potential is typically in the range of 1-2 ms. Since all spikes of a given neuron look alike, the form of the action potential does not carry any information. Rather, it is the number and the timing of spikes which matter.

Throughout this book, we will refer to the moment when a given neuron emits an action potential as the firing time of that neuron. The firing time

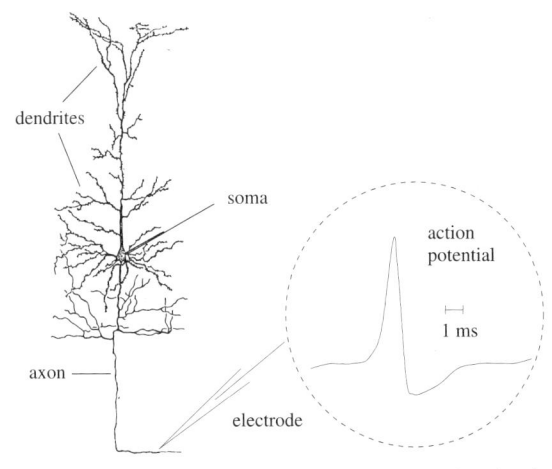

Figure 1.2. A single neuron. Dendrite, soma, and axon can be clearly distinguished. The inset shows an example of a neuronal action potential (schematic). Neuron drawing after Ramón y Cajal. The action potential is a short voltage pulse of 1-2 ms duration.

of neuron i will be denoted by $t_i^{(f)}$. The spike train of a neuron i is fully characterized by the set of firing times

$$\mathcal{F}_i = \{t_i^{(1)}, \ldots, t_i^{(n)}\} \tag{1.1}$$

where $t_i^{(n)}$ is the most recent spike of neuron i.

In an experimental setting, firing times are measured with some resolution Δt. A spike train may be described as a sequence of ones and zeros for 'spike' and 'no spike' at times $\Delta t, 2\Delta t \ldots$, respectively. The choice of ones and zeros is, of course arbitrary. We may just as well take the number $1/\Delta t$ instead of unity to denote the occurrence of a spike. With this definition, the spike train of a neuron i corresponds to a sequence of numbers $S_i(\Delta t), S_i(2\Delta t), \ldots$ with

$$S_i(n\,\Delta t) = \begin{cases} 1/\Delta t & \text{if } n\,\Delta t \leq t_i^{(f)} < (n+1)\,\Delta t \\ 0 & \text{otherwise.} \end{cases} \tag{1.2}$$

Formally we may take the limit $\Delta t \to 0$ and write the spike train as a sequence of δ-functions

$$S_i(t) = \sum_{t_i^{(f)} \in \mathcal{F}_i}^{n} \delta(t - t_i^{(f)}) \tag{1.3}$$

where $\delta(.)$ denotes the Dirac δ function with $\delta(s) = 0$ for $s \neq 0$ and $\int_{-\infty}^{\infty} \delta(s)ds = 1$.

So far we have focused on the spike train of a single neuron. Since there are so many neurons in the brain, thousands of spike trains are emitted constantly by different neurons; see Figure 1.3. What is the information contained in such a spatio-temporal pattern of pulses? What is the code used by the neurons to transmit that information? How might other neurons decode the signal? As external observers, can we read the code, and understand the message of the neuronal activity pattern?

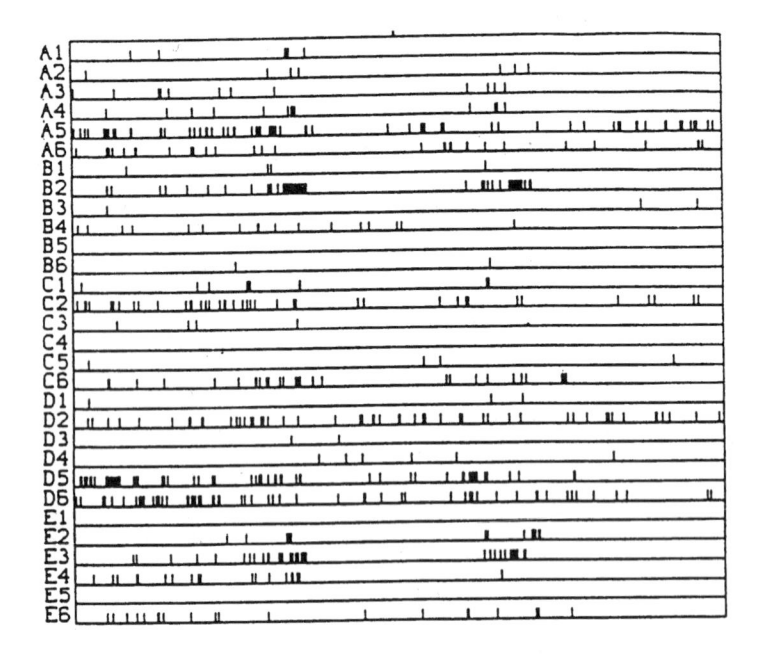

Figure 1.3. Spatio-temporal pulse pattern. The spikes of 30 neurons (A1-E6, plotted along the vertical axes) are shown as a function of time (horizontal axis, total time is 4 000 ms). The firing times are marked by short vertical bars. From [Krüger and Aiple, 1988].

At present, a definite answer to these questions is not known. Traditionally it has been thought that most, if not all, of the relevant information was contained in the mean firing rate of the neuron. The firing rate is usually defined by a temporal average; see Figure 1.4. The experimentalist sets a time window of, let us say, $T = 100$ ms or $T = 500$ ms and counts the number of spikes $n_{\rm sp}(T)$ that occur in this time window. Division by the length of the time window gives the mean firing rate

$$\nu = \frac{n_{\rm sp}(T)}{T} \qquad (1.4)$$

usually reported in units of s^{-1} or Hz.

The concept of mean firing rates has been successfully applied during the last 80 years. It dates back to the pioneering work of Adrian [Adrian, 1926, 1928] who showed that the firing rate of stretch receptor neurons in the muscles is related to the force applied to the muscle. In the following decades, measurement of firing rates became a standard tool for describing the properties of all types of sensory or cortical neurons [Mountcastle, 1957; Hubel and Wiesel, 1959], partly due to the relative ease of measuring rates experimentally. It is clear, however, that an approach based on a temporal average neglects all the information possibly contained in the exact timing of the spikes. It is therefore no surprise that the firing rate concept has been repeatedly criticized and is subject of an ongoing debate [Abeles, 1994; Bialek et al., 1991; Hopfield, 1995; Shadlen and Newsome, 1994; Softky, 1995; Rieke et al., 1996].

During recent years, more and more experimental evidence has accumulated which suggests that a straightforward firing rate concept based on temporal averaging may be too simple for describing brain activity. One of the main arguments is that reaction times in behavioral experiments are often too short to allow slow temporal averaging [Thorpe et al., 1996]. Moreover, in experiments on a visual neuron in the fly, it was possible to 'read the neural code' and reconstruct the time-dependent stimulus based on the neurons firing times [Bialek et al., 1991]. There is evidence of precise temporal correlations between pulses of different neurons [Abeles, 1994; Lestienne, 1996] and stimulus dependent synchronization of the activity in populations of neurons [Eckhorn et al., 1988; Gray and Singer, 1989; Gray et al., 1989; Engel et al., 1991; Singer, 1994]. Most of these data are inconsistent with a naïve concept of coding by mean firing rates where the exact timing of spikes should play no role. In this book we will explore some of the possibilities of coding by pulses. Before we can do so, we have to lay the foundations which will be the topic of this and the next three chapters.

We start in the next subsection with a review of some potential coding schemes. What exactly is a pulse code – and what is a rate code? We then turn to models of spiking neurons (Section 2). How can we describe the process of spike generation? What is the effect of a spike on a postsynaptic neuron? Can we mathematically analyze models of spiking neurons?

The following Chapters 2 and 3 in the 'Foundation' part of the book will focus on the computational power of spiking neurons and their hardware implementations. Can we build a Turing machine with spiking neurons? How many elements do we need? How fast is the processing? How can pulses be generated in hardware? Many of these questions outlined in the Foundation chapters will be revisited in the detailed studies contained in the parts II and III of the book. Chapter 4, the last chapter in the Foundation part, will discuss some of the biological evidence for temporal codes in more detail.

1.1.2   Rate Codes

A quick glance at the experimental literature reveals that there is no unique and well-defined concept of 'mean firing rate'. In fact, there are at least three different notions of rate which are often confused and used simultaneously. The three definitions refer to three different averaging procedures: either an average over time, or an average over several repetitions of the experiment, or an average over a population of neurons. The following three subsections will reconsider the three concepts. An excellent discussion of rate codes can also be found in [Rieke et al., 1996].

1.1.2.1 Rate as a Spike Count (Average over Time)

The first and most commonly used definition of a firing rate refers to a temporal average. As discussed in the preceding section, this is essentially the spike count in an interval T divided by T; see Figure 1.4. The length of the

1. Spiking Neurons

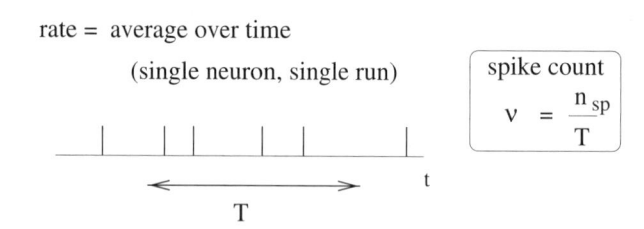

Figure 1.4. Definition of the mean firing rate via a temporal average.

time window is set by the experimenter and depends on the type of neuron recorded from and the stimulus. In practice, to get sensible averages, several spikes should occur within the time window. Values of $T = 100$ ms or $T = 500$ ms are typical, but the duration may also be longer or shorter.

This definition of rate has been successfully used in many preparations, particularly in experiments on sensory or motor systems. A classical example is the stretch receptor in a muscle spindle [Adrian, 1926]. The number of spikes emitted by the receptor neuron increases with the force applied to the muscle. Another textbook example is the touch receptor in the leech [Kandel and Schwartz, 1991]. The stronger the touch stimulus, the more spikes occur during a stimulation period of 500 ms.

These classical results show that the experimenter as an external observer can evaluate and classify neuronal firing by a spike count measure – but is this really the code used by neurons in the brain? In other words, is a neuron which receives signals from a sensory neuron only looking at and reacting to the numbers of spikes it receives in a time window of, say, 500 ms? We will approach this question from a modeling point of view later on in the book. Here we discuss some critical experimental evidence.

From behavioral experiments it is known that reaction times are often rather short. A fly can react to new stimulus and change the direction of flight within 30-40 ms; see the discussion in [Rieke et al., 1996]. This is not long enough for counting spikes and averaging over some long time window. It follows that the fly has to react to single spikes. Humans can recognize visual scenes in just a few hundred milliseconds [Thorpe et al., 1996], even though recognition is believed to involve several processing steps. Again, this leaves not enough time to perform temporal averages on each level.

Temporal averaging can work well where the stimulus is constant or slowly moving and does not require a fast reaction of the organism - and this is the situation usually encountered in experimental protocols. Real-world input, however, is hardly stationary, but often changing on a fast time scale. For example, even when viewing a static image, we perform saccades, rapid changes of the direction of gaze. The retinal photo receptors receive therefore every few hundred milliseconds a new input.

Despite its shortcomings, the concept of a firing rate code is widely used not only in experiments, but also in models of neural networks. It has led to the idea that a neuron transforms information about a single input variable (the stimulus strength) into a single continuous output variable (the firing rate). In this view, spikes are just a convenient way to transmit the analog output over long distances. In fact, the best coding scheme to transmit

1.1 The Problem of Neural Coding

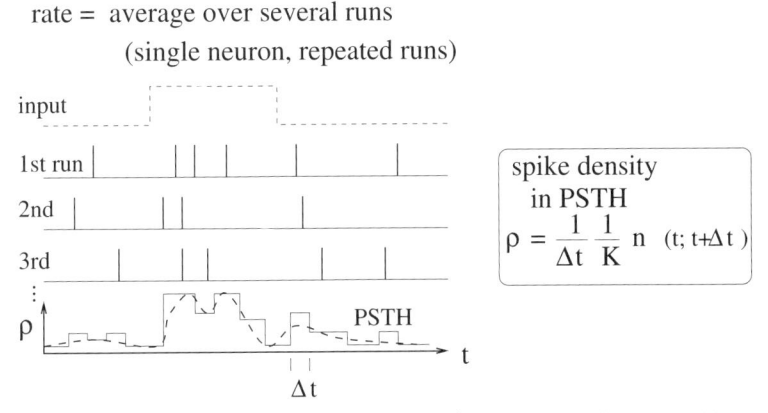

Figure 1.5. Definition of the spike density in the Peri-Stimulus-Time Histogram (PSTH).

the value of the rate ν would be by a regular spike train with intervals $1/\nu$. In this case, the rate could be reliably measured after only two spikes. From the point of view of rate coding, the irregularities encountered in real spike trains of neurons in the cortex must therefore be considered as noise. In order to get rid of the noise and arrive at a reliable estimate of the rate, the experimenter (or the postsynaptic neuron) has to average over a larger number of spikes. A critical discussion of the temporal averaging concept can be found in [Shadlen and Newsome, 1994; Softky, 1995; Rieke et al., 1996].

1.1.2.2 Rate as a Spike Density (Average over Several Runs)

There is a second definition of rate which works for stationary as well as for time-dependent stimuli. The experimenter records from a neuron while stimulating with some input sequence. The same stimulation sequence is repeated many times and the results are reported in a Peri-Stimulus-Time Histogram (PSTH); see Figure 1.5. For each short interval of time $[t, t + \Delta t]$, before, during, and after the stimulation sequence, the experimenter counts the number of times that a spike has occurred and sums them over all repetitions of the experiment. The time t is measured with respect to the start of the stimulation sequence and Δt is typically in the range of one or a few milliseconds. The number of occurrences of spikes $n(t; t + \Delta t)$ divided by the number K of repetitions is a measure of the typical activity of the neuron between time t and $t + \Delta t$. A further division by the interval length Δt yields the spike density of the PSTH

$$\rho(t) = \frac{1}{\Delta t} \frac{n(t; t + \Delta t)}{K}. \tag{1.5}$$

Sometimes the result is smoothed to get a continuous 'rate' variable. The spike density of the PSTH is usually reported in units of Hz and often called the (time-dependent) firing rate of the neuron.

As an experimental procedure, the spike density measure is a useful method to evaluate neuronal activity, in particular in the case of time-dependent

rate = average over pool of equivalent neurons
(several neurons, single run)

activity
$$A = \frac{1}{\Delta t} \frac{n_{act}(\Delta t)}{N}$$

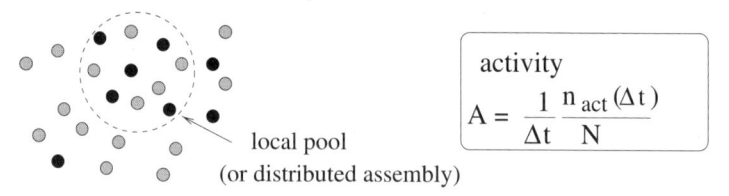

local pool
(or distributed assembly)

Figure 1.6. Definition of the population activity.

stimuli. The obvious problem with this approach is that it can not be the decoding scheme used by neurons in the brain. Consider for example a frog which wants to catch a fly. It can not wait for the insect to fly repeatedly along exactly the same trajectory. The frog has to base its decision on a single 'run' – each fly and each trajectory is different.

Nevertheless, the experimental spike density measure can make sense, if there are large populations of neurons which are independent of each other and sensitive to the same stimulus. Instead of recording from a population of N neurons in a single run, it is experimentally easier to record from a single neuron and average over N repeated runs. Thus, the spike density coding relies on the implicit assumption that there are always populations of neurons and therefore leads to the third notion of a firing rate, viz., a rate defined as a population average.

1.1.2.3 Rate as Population Activity (Average over Several Neurons)

The number of neurons in the brain is huge. Often many neurons have similar properties and respond to the same stimuli. For example, neurons in the primary visual cortex of cats and monkeys are arranged in columns of cells with similar properties [Hubel and Wiesel, 1962, 1977; Hubel, 1988]. Let us idealize the situation and consider a population of neurons with identical properties. In particular, all neurons in the population should have the same pattern of input and output connections. The spikes of the neurons in a population j are sent off to another population k. In our idealized picture, each neuron in population k receives input from all neurons in population j. The relevant quantity, from the point of view of the receiving neuron, is the proportion of active neurons in the presynaptic population j; see Figure 1.6. Formally, we define the population activity

$$A(t) = \frac{1}{\Delta t} \frac{n_{\text{act}}(t; t + \Delta t)}{N} \tag{1.6}$$

where N is the size of the population, Δt a small time interval, and $n_{\text{act}}(t; t + \Delta t)$ the number of spikes (summed over all neurons in the population) that occur between t and $t + \Delta t$. If the population is large, we can consider the limit $N \to \infty$ and take then $\Delta t \to 0$. This yields again a continuous quantity with units s^{-1} – in other words, a rate.

The population activity may vary rapidly and can reflect changes in the stimulus conditions nearly instantaneously [Tsodyks and Sejnowsky, 1995].

Thus the population activity does not suffer the disadvantages of a firing rate defined by temporal averaging at the single-unit level. The problem with the definition (1.6) is that we have formally required a homogeneous population of neurons with identical connections which is hardly realistic. Real populations will always have a certain degree of heterogeneity both in their internal parameters and in their connectivity pattern. Nevertheless, rate as a population activity (of suitably defined pools of neurons) may be a useful coding principle in many areas of the brain. For inhomogeneous populations, the definition (1.6) may be replaced by a weighted average over the population. A related scheme has been used successfully for an interpretation of neuronal activity in primate motor cortex [Georgopoulos et al., 1986].

1.1.3 Candidate Pulse Codes

In this subsection, we will briefly introduce some potential coding strategies based on spike timing. All codes will be discussed in more detail later on and will be referred to throughout the book.

1.1.3.1 Time-to-First-Spike

Let us study a neuron which abruptly receives a new input at time t_0. For example, a neuron might be driven by an external stimulus which is suddenly switched on at time t_0. This seems to be somewhat academic, but even in a realistic situation abrupt changes in the input are quite common. When we look at a picture, our gaze jumps from one point to the next. After each saccade, there is a new visual input at the photo receptors in the retina. Information about the time t_0 of a saccade would easily be available in the brain. We can then imagine a code where for each neuron the timing of the first spike to follow t_0 contains all information about the new stimulus. A neuron which fires shortly after t_0 could signal a strong stimulation, firing somewhat later would signal a weaker stimulation; see Figure 1.7.

In a pure version of this coding scheme, only the first spike of each neuron counts. All following spikes would be irrelevant. Alternatively, we can also assume that each neuron emits exactly one spike per saccade and is shut off by inhibitory input afterwards. It is clear that in such a scenario, only the timing conveys information and not the number of spikes.

A coding scheme based on the time-to-first-spike is certainly an idealization. In Chapter 2 it will be formally analyzed by Wolfgang Maass. In a slightly different context coding by first spikes has also been discussed by S. Thorpe [Thorpe et al., 1996]. Thorpe argues that the brain does not have time to evaluate more than one spike from each neuron per processing step. Therefore the first spike should contain most of the relevant information. Using information-theoretic measures on their experimental data, several groups have shown that most of the information about a new stimulus is indeed conveyed during the first 20 or 50 milliseconds after the onset of the neuronal response [Optican and Richmond, 1987; Kjaer et al., 1994; Tovee et al., 1993; Tovee and Rolls, 1995]. Rapid computation during the

12   1. Spiking Neurons

A)   time to first spike

B)   phase

background oscillation

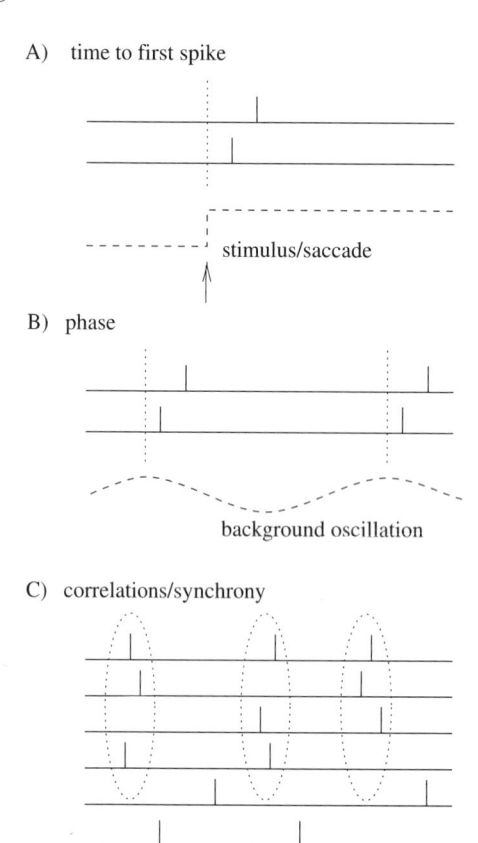

C)   correlations/synchrony

Figure 1.7. Three examples of pulse codes. A) Time-to-first spike. The second neuron responds faster to a change in the stimulus than the first one. Stimulus onset marked by arrow. B) Phase. The two neurons fire at different phases with respect to the background oscillation (dashed). C) Synchrony. The upper four neurons are nearly synchronous, two other neurons at the bottom are not synchronized with the others.

transients after a new stimulus has also been discussed in model studies [Hopfield and Herz, 1995; Tsodyks and Sejnowsky, 1995; van Vreeswijk and Sompolinsky, 1997].

1.1.3.2 Phase

We can apply a coding by 'time-to-first-spike' also in the situation where the reference signal is not a single event, but a periodic signal. In the hippocampus, in the olfactory system, and also in other areas of the brain, oscillations of some global variable (for example the population activity) are quite common. These oscillations could serve as an internal reference signal. Neuronal spike trains could then encode information in the phase of a pulse with respect to the background oscillation. If the input does not change between one cycle and the next, then the same pattern of phases repeats periodically; see Figure 1.7 B.

The concept of coding by phases has been studied by several different groups, not only in model studies [Hopfield, 1995; Jensen and Lisman,

1996; Maass, 1996], but also experimentally [O'Keefe and Recce, 1993]. There is for example evidence that the phase of a spike during an oscillation in the hippocampus of the rat conveys information on the spatial location of the animal which is not accounted for by the firing rate of the neuron alone [O'Keefe and Recce, 1993].

1.1.3.3 Correlations and Synchrony

We can also use spikes from other neurons as the reference signal for a pulse code. For example, synchrony between a pair or a group of neurons could signify special events and convey information which is not contained in the firing rate of the neurons; see Figure 1.7 C. One famous idea is that synchrony could mean 'belonging together' [Milner, 1974; Malsburg, 1981]. Consider for example a complex scene consisting of several objects. It is represented in the brain by the activity of a large number of neurons. Neurons which represent the same object could be 'labeled' by the fact that they fire synchronously [Malsburg, 1981; Malsburg and Buhmann, 1992; Eckhorn et al., 1988; Gray et al., 1989]. Coding by synchrony has been studied extensively both experimentally [Eckhorn et al., 1988; Gray et al., 1989; Gray and Singer, 1989; Singer, 1994; Engel et al., 1991ab; Kreiter and Singer, 1992] and in models [Wang et al., 1990; Malsburg and Buhmann, 1992; Eckhorn, 1990; Aertsen and Arndt, 1993; Koenig and Schillen, 1991; Schillen and Koenig, 1991; Gerstner et al., 1993; Ritz et al. 1993; Terman and Wang, 1995; Wang, 1995]. For a review of potential mechanism, see [Ritz and Sejnowski, 1997]. Coding by synchrony is discussed in Chapter 11.

More generally, not only synchrony but any precise spatio-temporal pulse pattern could be a meaningful event. For example, a spike pattern of three neurons, where neuron 1 fires at some arbitrary time t_1 followed by neuron 2 at time $t_1 + \delta_{12}$ and by neuron 3 at $t_1 + \delta_{13}$, might represent a certain stimulus condition. The same three neurons firing with different relative delays might signify a different stimulus. The relevance of precise spatio-temporal spike patterns has been studied intensively by Abeles [Abeles, 1991; Abeles et al., 1993; Abeles, 1994]. Similarly, but on a somewhat coarse time scale, correlations of auditory neurons are stimulus dependent and might convey information beyond the firing rate [deCharms and Merzenich, 1996].

1.1.3.4 Stimulus Reconstruction and Reverse Correlation

Let us consider a neuron which is driven by a time dependent stimulus $s(t)$. Every time a spike occurs, we note the time course of the stimulus in a time window of about 100 ms immediately before the spike. Averaging the results for several spikes yields the typical time course of the stimulus just before a spike. Such a procedure is called a 'reverse correlation' approach; see Figure 1.8. In contrast to the PSTH experiment sketched in Section 2.2 where the experimenter averages the neuron's response over several trials with the same stimulus, reverse correlation means that the experimenter averages the input under the condition of an identical response, viz., a spike. In other words, it is a spike-triggered average; see,

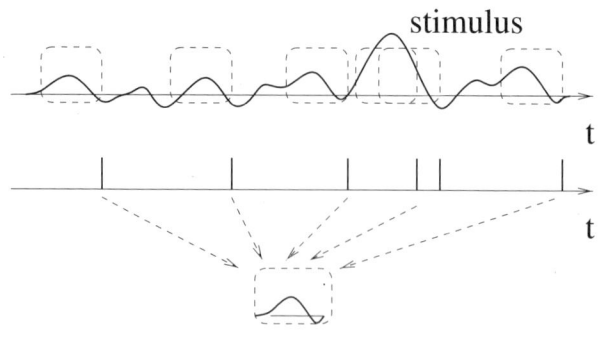

Figure 1.8. Reverse correlation technique (schematic). The stimulus in the top trace has caused the spike train shown immediately below. The time course of the stimulus just before the spikes (dashed boxes) has been averaged to yield the typical time course (bottom).

e.g., [de Ruyter van Steveninck and Bialek, 1988; Rieke et al., 1996]. The results of the reverse correlation, i.e., the typical time course of the stimulus which has triggered the spike, can be interpreted as the 'meaning' of a single spike. Reverse correlation techniques have made it possible for example to measure the spatio-temporal characteristics of neurons in the visual cortex [Eckhorn et al., 1993; DeAngelis et al., 1995].

With a somewhat more elaborate version of this approach, W. Bialek and his co-workers have been able to 'read' the neural code of the H1 neuron in the fly and to reconstruct a time-dependent stimulus [Bialek et al., 1991; Rieke et al., 1996]. Here we give a simplified version of the argument.

Results from reverse correlation analysis suggest, that each spike signifies the time course of the stimulus preceding the spike. If this is correct, a reconstruction of the complete time course of the stimulus $s(t)$ from the set of firing times $\mathcal{F} = \{t^{(1)}, \ldots t^{(n)}\}$ should be possible; see Figure 1.9.

As a simple test of this hypothesis, Bialek and coworkers have studied a linear reconstruction. A spike at time $t^{(f)}$ gives a contribution $\kappa(t - t^{(f)})$ to the estimation $s^{\text{est}}(t)$ of the time course of the stimulus. Here, $t^{(f)} \in \mathcal{F}$ is one of the firing times and $\kappa(t - t^{(f)})$ is a kernel which is nonzero during some time before and around $t^{(f)}$; see inset of Figure 1.9. A linear estimate of the stimulus is

$$s^{\text{est}}(t) = \sum_{f=1}^{n} \kappa(t - t^{(f)}). \qquad (1.7)$$

The form of the kernel κ was determined through optimization so that the average reconstruction error $\int dt [s(t) - s^{\text{est}}(t)]^2$ was minimal. The quality of the reconstruction was then tested on additional data which was not used for the optimization. Surprisingly enough, the simple linear reconstruction (1.7) gave a fair estimate of the time course of the stimulus [Bialek et al., 1991; Bialek and Rieke, 1992; Rieke et al., 1996]. These results show nicely that information about a time dependent input can indeed be conveyed by spike timing.

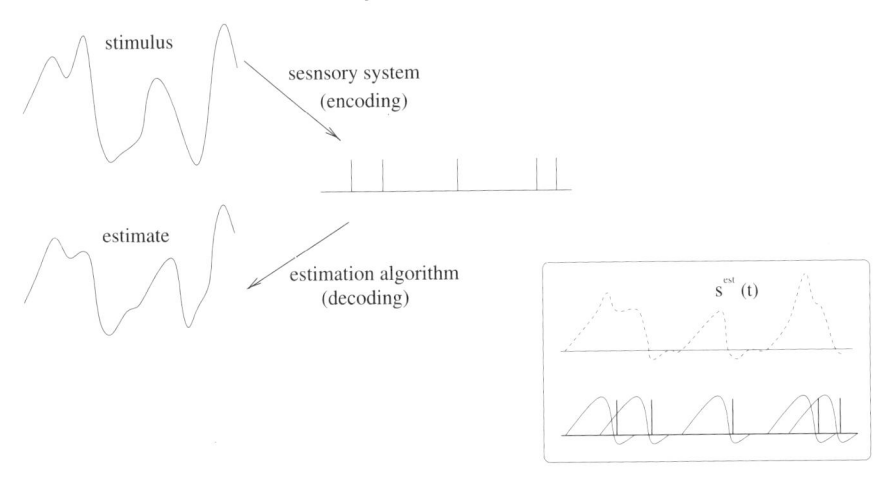

Figure 1.9. Reconstruction of a stimulus (schematic). A stimulus evokes a spike train of a neuron. The time course of the stimulus may be estimated from the spike train. The inset shows the principle of linear stimulus reconstruction. The estimation $s^{\text{est}}(t)$ (dashed) is the sum of the contributions (solid lines) of all spikes. Main figure redrawn after [Rieke et al., 1996].

1.1.4 Discussion: Spikes or Rates?

The dividing line between pulse codes and firing rates is not always as clearly drawn as it may seem at first sight. Some codes which were first proposed as pure examples of pulse codes have later been interpreted as variations of rate codes.

For example the stimulus reconstruction (1.7) with kernels seems to be a clear example of a pulse code. Nevertheless, it is also not so far from a rate code based on spike counts [Theunissen and Miller, 1995]. To see this, consider a spike count measure with a running time window $K(.)$. We can estimate the rate ν at time t by

$$\nu(t) = \frac{\int K(\tau)\, S(t-\tau)\, d\tau}{\int K(\tau)\, d\tau} \tag{1.8}$$

where $S(t) = \sum_{f=1}^{n} \delta(t - t^{(f)})$ is the spike train under consideration. The integrals run from minus to plus infinity. For a rectangular time window $K(\tau) = 1$ for $-T/2 < \tau < T/2$ and zero otherwise, (1.8) reduces exactly to our definition (1.4) of a rate as a spike count measure.

The time window in (1.8) can be made rather short so that at most a few spikes fall into the interval T. Furthermore, there is no need that the window $K(.)$ be symmetric and rectangular. We may just as well take an asymmetric time window with smooth borders. Moreover, we can perform the integration over the δ function which yields

$$\nu(t) = c \sum_{f=1}^{n} K(t - t^{(f)}) \tag{1.9}$$

where $c = [\int K(s)\, ds]^{-1}$ is a constant. Except for the normalization, the generalized rate formula (1.9) is now identical to the reconstruction formula (1.7). In other words, the linear reconstruction is just the firing rate measured with a cleverly optimized time window.

Similarly, a code based on the 'time-to-first-spike' is also consistent with a rate code. If, for example, the mean firing rate of neuron is high for a given stimulus, then the first spike is expected to occur early. If the rate is low, the first spike is expected to occur later. Thus the timing of the first spike contains a lot of information about the underlying rate.

Finally, a code based on population activities introduced in Section 1.1.2 as an example of a rate code may be used for very fast temporal coding schemes [Tsodyks and Sejnowski, 1995]. As discussed later in Chapter 10 the population activity reacts quickly to any change in the stimulus. Thus rate coding in the sense of a population average is consistent with fast temporal information processing, whereas rate coding in the sense of a naïve spike count measure is not.

We do not want to go into the details of the discussion whether or not to call a given code a rate code [Theunissen and Miller, 1995]. What is important, in our opinion, is to have a coding scheme which allows neurons to quickly respond to stimulus changes. A naïve spike count code with a long time window is unable to do this, but many of the other codes are. The name of such a code, whether it is deemed a rate code or not is of minor importance.

In this book, we will explore some of the possibilities of coding and computation by spikes. As modelers – mathematicians, physicists, and engineers – our aim is not to give a definite answer to the problem of neural coding in the brain. The final answers have to come from experiments. One possible task of modeling may be to discuss candidate coding schemes, study their computational potential, exemplify their utility, point out their limitations – and this is what we will attempt to do in the course of the following chapters.

1.2 Neuron Models

Neural activity may be described at several levels of abstraction. On a microscopic level, there are a large number of ion channels, pores in the cell membrane which open and close depending on the voltage and the presence (or absence) of various chemical messenger molecules. Compartmental models, where each small segment of a neuron is described by a set of ionic equations, aim at a description of these processes. A short introduction to this model class can be found in section 1.2.4.

On a higher level of abstraction, we do not worry about the spatial structure of a neuron nor about the exact ionic mechanisms. We consider the neuron as a homogeneous unit which generates spikes if the total excitation is sufficiently large. This is the level of the so-called integrate-and-fire models. In Section 1.2.3, we will discuss this model class in the framework of the 'spike response model'.

The spiking neuron models should be contrasted with the rate models reviewed in Section 1.2.5. Rate models neglect the pulse structure of the neuronal output, and are therefore higher up in the level of abstraction. On a yet coarser level would be models which describe the activity in and interaction between whole brain areas.

Most chapters in the book will make use of a generic neuron model on the intermediate description level. We therefore devote most of the space to the discussion in Section 1.2.3. For those readers who are not interested in the details, we present the basic concepts of our generic neuron model in a compressed version in the following section 1.2.1.

1.2.1 Simple Spiking Neuron Model

Spike Response Model - definitions

The state of neuron i is described by a state variable u_i. The neuron is said to fire, if u_i reaches a threshold ϑ. The moment of threshold crossing defines the firing time $t_i^{(f)}$; see Figure 1.10. The set of all firing times of neuron i is denoted by

$$\mathcal{F}_i = \{t_i^{(f)}; 1 \leq f \leq n\} = \{t \mid u_i(t) = \vartheta\}. \tag{1.10}$$

For the most recent spike $t_i^{(f)} < t$ of neuron i we write either $t_i^{(n)}$ or, shorter, $\hat{t}$.

Two different processes contribute to the value of the state variable u_i.

First, immediately after firing an output spike at $t_i^{(f)}$, the variable u_i is lowered or 'reset'. Mathematically, this is done by adding a negative contribution $\eta_i(t - t_i^{(f)})$ to the state variable u_i. An example of a refractory function η_i is shown in Figure 1.10. The kernel $\eta_i(s)$ vanishes for $s \leq 0$ and decays to zero for $s \to \infty$.

Second, the model neuron may receive input from presynaptic neurons $j \in \Gamma_i$ where

$$\Gamma_i = \{j \mid j \text{ presynaptic to } i\}. \tag{1.11}$$

A presynaptic spike at time $t_j^{(f)}$ increases (or decreases) the state u_i of neuron i for $t > t_j^{(f)}$ by an amount $w_{ij}\,\epsilon_{ij}(t - t_j^{(f)})$. The weight w_{ij} is a factor which accounts for the strength of the connection. An example of an ϵ_{ij} function is shown in Figure 1.10b. The effect of a presynaptic spike may be positive (excitatory) or negative (inhibitory). Because of causality, the kernel $\epsilon_{ij}(s)$ must vanish for $s \leq 0$. A transmission delay may be included in the definition of ϵ_{ij}; see Figure 1.10.

The state $u_i(t)$ of model neuron i at time t is given by the linear superposition of all contributions,

$$u_i(t) = \sum_{t_i^{(f)} \in \mathcal{F}_i} \eta_i(t - t_i^{(f)}) + \sum_{j \in \Gamma_i} \sum_{t_j^{(f)} \in \mathcal{F}_j} w_{ij}\,\epsilon_{ij}(t - t_j^{(f)}). \tag{1.12}$$

An interpretation of the terms on the right-hand side of (1.12) is straightforward. The η_i contributions describe the response of neuron i to its own spikes. The ϵ_{ij} kernels model the neurons response to presynaptic spikes.

18   1. Spiking Neurons

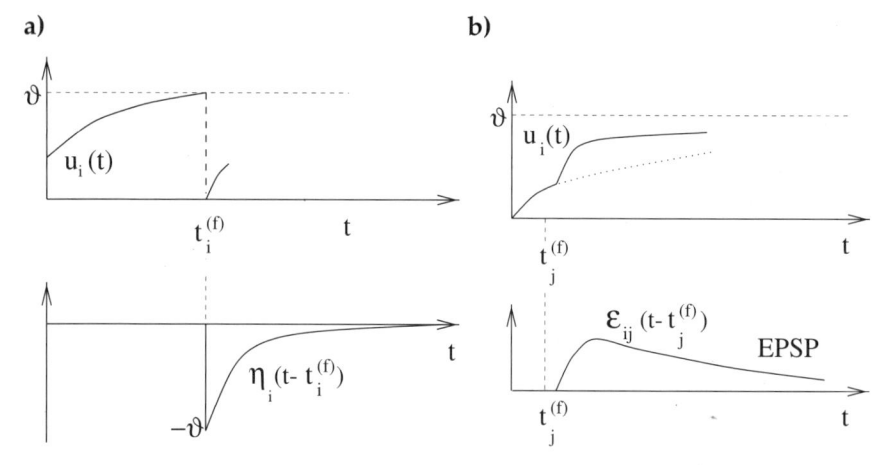

Figure 1.10. *a)* The state variable $u_i(t)$ reaches the threshold ϑ at time $t_i^{(f)}$. Immediately afterwards $u_i(t)$ is reset to zero. The reset is performed by adding a kernel $\eta_i(t - t_i^{(f)})$. The function $\eta_i(s)$ takes care of refractoriness after a spike emitted at $s = 0$. *b)* The state variable $u_i(t)$ changes after a presynaptic spike has occured at $t_j^{(f)}$. The kernels ϵ_{ij} describes the response of u_i to a presynaptic spike at $s = 0$. The postsynaptic potential can either be excitatory (EPSP) or inhibitory (IPSP).

We will refer to (1.10) - (1.12) as the Spike Response Model (SRM). In a biological context, the state variable u_i may be interpreted as the electrical membrane potential. The kernels ϵ_{ij} are the postsynaptic potentials and η_i accounts for neuronal refractoriness.

To be more specific, let us consider some examples of suitable functions η_i and ϵ_{ij}. The kernel $\eta_i(s)$ is usually nonpositive for $s > 0$. A typical form of η_i is shown in Figure 1.10a). A specific mathematical formulation is

$$\eta_i(s) = -\vartheta \exp\left(-\frac{s}{\tau}\right) \mathcal{H}(s) \qquad (1.13)$$

where τ is a time constant and $\mathcal{H}(s)$ is the Heaviside step function which vanishes for $s \leq 0$ and takes a value of 1 for $s > 0$. Note that at the moment of firing $u_i(t) = \vartheta$. The effect of (1.13) is that after each firing the state variable u_i is reset to zero. If the factor ϑ on the right-hand side of (1.13) is replaced by a parameter $\eta_0 \neq \vartheta$, then the state variable would be reset to a value $\vartheta - \eta_0 \neq 0$. For a further discussion of the η-kernel, the reader is referred to section 1.2.3.1.

The kernels ϵ_{ij} describe the response to presynaptic spikes; see Figure 1.10b). For excitatory synapses ϵ_{ij} is non-negative and is called the excitatory postsynaptic potential (EPSP). For inhibitory synapses, the kernel takes non-positive values and is called the inhibitory postsynaptic potential (IPSP). One of several potential mathematical formulations is

$$\epsilon_{ij}(s) = \left[\exp\left(-\frac{s - \Delta^{\text{ax}}}{\tau_m}\right) - \exp\left(-\frac{s - \Delta^{\text{ax}}}{\tau_s}\right)\right] \mathcal{H}(s - \Delta^{\text{ax}}). \qquad (1.14)$$

where τ_s, τ_m are time constants and Δ^{ax} is the axonal transmission delay. The amplitude of the response is scaled via the factor w_{ij} in (1.12). For

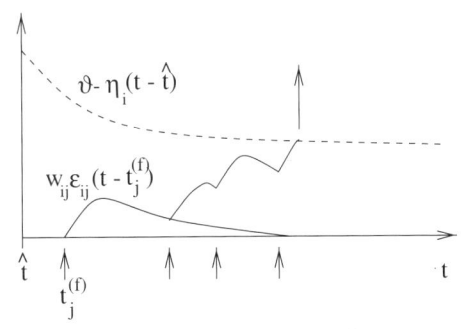

Figure 1.11. Dynamic threshold interpretation. The last firing of neuron i has occured at $t = \hat{t}$. Immediately after firing the dynamic threshold $\vartheta - \eta_i(t - \hat{t})$ (dashed) is high. The next output spike occurs, when the sum of the EPSPs $\sum_{t_j^{(f)} \in \mathcal{F}_j} w_{ij}\epsilon_{ij}(t - t_j^{(f)})$ caused by presynaptic spikes at times $t_j^{(f)}$ (arrows in the lower part of the figure) reaches the dynamic threshold again.

inhibitory synapses, the kernel ϵ_{ij} would have a negative sign in front of the expression on the right-hand side. Alternatively, we can put the sign in the synaptic efficacy and use $w_{ij} > 0$ for excitatiory synapses and $w_{ij} < 0$ for inhibitory synapses.

Equations (1.10) and (1.12) give a fairly general framework for the discussion of neuron models. We will show in Section 1.2.3., that the Spike Response Model (1.10) - (1.12) with kernels (1.13) and (1.14) is equivalent to the integrate-and-fire model. Furthermore, with a different choice of kernels, the Spike Response Model also approximates the Hodgkin-Huxley equations with time-dependent input; see Section 1.2.4. and [Kistler et al., 1997].

Dynamic threshold model

We note that (1.10) - (1.12) may also be formulated in terms of a dynamic threshold model. To see this, consider the threshold condition $u_i(t) = \vartheta$; see (1.10). With (1.12) we get

$$\sum_{j \in \Gamma_i} \sum_{t_j^{(f)} \in \mathcal{F}_j} w_{ij}\,\epsilon_{ij}(t - t_j^{(f)}) = \vartheta - \sum_{t_i^{(f)} \in \mathcal{F}_i} \eta_i(t - t_i^{(f)}) \qquad (1.15)$$

where we have moved the sum over the η_i's to the right-hand side of (1.15). We may consider the expression $\vartheta - \sum_{t_i^{(f)} \in \mathcal{F}_i} \eta(t - t_i^{(f)})$ as a dynamic threshold which increases after each firing and decays slowly back to its asymptotic value ϑ in case of no further firing of neuron i.

Short term memory

There is a variant of the Spike Response Model which is often useful to simplify the analytical treatment. We assume that only the last firing contributes to refractoriness. Hence, we simplify (1.12) slightly and only keep the influence of the *most recent* spike in the sum over the η contributions. Formally, we make the replacement

$$\sum_{t_i^{(f)} \in \mathcal{F}_i} \eta(t - t_i^{(f)}) \longrightarrow \eta(t - \hat{t}_i) \qquad (1.16)$$

20   1. Spiking Neurons

where $\hat{t}_i < t$ denotes the most recent firing of neuron i. We refer to this simplification as a neuron with short term memory. Instead of (1.12), the membrane potential of neuron i is now

$$u_i(t) = \eta_i(t - \hat{t}_i) + \sum_{j \in \Gamma_i} \sum_{t_j^{(f)} \in \mathcal{F}_j} w_{ij} \epsilon_{ij}(t - t_j^{(f)}). \quad (1.17)$$

The next spike occurs when

$$\sum_{j \in \Gamma_i} \sum_{t_j^{(f)} \in \mathcal{F}_j} w_{ij} \epsilon_{ij}(t - t_j^{(f)}) = \vartheta - \eta(t - \hat{t}_i). \quad (1.18)$$

A graphical interpretation of (1.18) is given in Fig. 1.11.

External input

A final modification concerns the possibility of external input. In addition to (or instead of) spike input from other neurons, a neuron may receive an analog input current $\mathcal{I}^{\text{ext}}(t)$, for example from a non-spiking sensory neuron. In this case, we add on the right-hand side of (1.12) a term

$$h^{\text{ext}}(t) = \int_0^\infty \tilde{\epsilon}(s) \mathcal{I}^{\text{ext}}(t - s) \, ds. \quad (1.19)$$

Here $\tilde{\epsilon}$ is another kernel, which discribes the response of the membrane potential to an external input pulse. As a notational convenience, we introduce a new variable h which summarizes all contributions from other neurons and from external sources

$$h(t) = \sum_{j \in \Gamma_i} w_{ij} \sum_{t_j^{(f)} \in \mathcal{F}_j} \epsilon_{ij}(t - t_j^{(f)}) + h^{\text{ext}}(t). \quad (1.20)$$

The membrane potential of a neuron with short term memory is then simply

$$u_i(t) = \eta(t - \hat{t}_i) + h(t). \quad (1.21)$$

We will make use of (1.21) repeatedly, since it allows us to analyze the neuronal dynamics in a transparent manner.

The equations (1.10) - (1.21) will be used in several chapters of this book. The following subsections 1.2.3-1.2.5 will put this generic neuron model in the context of other models of neural activity. Readers who are not interested in the details may proceed directly to Chapter 2 - or continue with the next subsection for a first introduction to coding by spikes in the framework of the above spiking neuron model.

1.2.2 First Steps towards Coding by Spikes

Before we proceed further with our discussion of neuron models, let us take a first glance at the type of computation we can do with such a model. To this end, we will reconsider some of the pulse codes introduced in Section 1.1.3. A full discussion of computation with spiking neurons follows

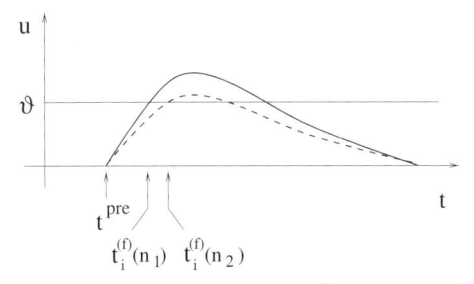

Figure 1.12. Time to first spike. The firing time $t^{(f)}$ encodes the number n_1 or n_2 of presynpatic spikes which have been fired synchronously at t^{pre}. If there are less presynaptic spikes, the potential u rises more slowly (dashed) and the firing occurs later. For the sake of simplicity, the axonal delay has been set to zero.

in Chapter 2 of this book. Here we use simple arguments from a graphical analysis to get a first understanding of how the model works.

Time-to-first-spike

Let us start with a coding scheme based on the 'time-to-first-spike'. In order to simplify the argument, let us consider a single neuron i which receives spikes from N presynaptic neurons j over synaptic connections which all have the same weight $w_{ij} = w_0$. There is no external input. We assume that the last spike of neuron i occurred long ago so that the spike afterpotential $\eta(.)$ in (1.12) may be neglected.

At $t = t^{\mathrm{pre}}$, a total number of $n_1 < N$ presynaptic spikes are simultaneously generated and transmitted to the postsynaptic neuron i. For $t > t^{\mathrm{pre}}$, the potential of i is

$$u_i(t) = n_1 \, w_0 \, \epsilon(t - t^{\mathrm{pre}}) \,. \tag{1.22}$$

An output spike of neuron i occurs whenever u_i reaches the threshold ϑ. We consider the firing time $t_i^{(f)}$ of the first output spike

$$t_i^{(f)} = \min\{t > t^{\mathrm{pre}} \,|\, u_i(t) = \vartheta\} \tag{1.23}$$

A graphical solution of (1.23) is shown in Figure 1.12. If there are less presynaptic spikes $n_2 < n_1$, then the postsynaptic potential is reduced and the firing occurs later as shown by the dashed line in Figure 1.12. It follows that the time difference $t_i^{(f)} - t^{\mathrm{pre}}$ is a measure of the number of presynaptic pulses. To put it differently, the timing of the first spike encodes the input strength.

Phase coding

Phase coding is possible if there is some periodic background signal which can serve as a reference. We include the background into the external input and write

$$h^{\mathrm{ext}}(t) = h_0 + h_1 \cos(2\pi \frac{t}{T}) \tag{1.24}$$

where h_0 is a constant and h_1 is the amplitude of the T-periodic signal.

Let us consider a single neuron driven by (1.24). There is no input from other neurons. We start from the simplified spike response mode (1.21)

22   1. Spiking Neurons

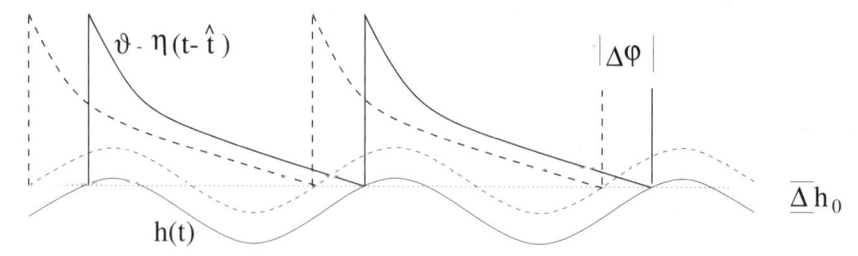

Figure 1.13. Phase coding. Firing occurs whenever the total input potential $h(t) = h_0 + h_1 \cos(2\pi t/T)$ hits the dynamic threshold $\vartheta - \eta(t-\hat{t})$ where $\hat{t}$ is the most recent firing time; cf. Fig. 1.11. In the presence of a periodic modulation $h_1 \neq 0$, a change Δh_0 in the level of (constant) stimulation results in a change $\Delta\varphi$ in the phase of firing.

which yields the membrane potential

$$u(t) = \eta(t - \hat{t}) + h^{\text{ext}}(t). \quad (1.25)$$

As usual $\hat{t}$ denotes the time of the most recent spike. To find the next firing time, (1.25) has to be combined with the threshold condition $u(t) = \vartheta$. We are interested in a solution where the neuron fires regularly and with the same period as the background signal. In this case the threshold condition reads

$$\vartheta - \eta(T) = h_0 + h_1 \cos(2\pi \frac{\hat{t}}{T}). \quad (1.26)$$

For a given period T, the left-hand side has a fixed value and we can solve for $\varphi = 2\pi\frac{\hat{t}}{T}$. For most combinations of parameters, there are two solutions but only one of them is stable. Thus the neuron has to fire at a certain phase φ with respect to the external signal. The value of φ depends on the level of the constant stimulation h_0. In other words, the strength h_0 of the stimulation is encoded in the phase of the spike. In (1.26) we have moved η to the left-hand side in order to suggest a dynamic threshold interpretation. A graphical illustration of equation (1.26) is given in Figure 1.13.

Correlation coding

Let us consider two identical uncoupled neurons. Both receive the same constant external stimulus $h^{\text{ext}}(t) = h_0$. As a result, they fire regularly with period T given by $\eta(T) = h_0$ as can be seen directly from (1.26) with $h_1 = 0$. Since the neurons are not coupled, they need not fire simultaneously. Let us assume that the firings of neuron 2 are shifted by an amount δ with respect to neuron 1.

Suppose that, at a given moment t^{pre}, both neurons receive input from a common presynaptic neuron j. This causes an additional contribution $\epsilon(t - t^{\text{pre}})$ to the membrane potential. If the synapse is excitatory, the two neurons will fire slightly sooner. More importantly, the spikes will also be closer together. In the situation sketched in Figure 1.14 the new firing time difference $\tilde{\delta}$ is reduced, $\tilde{\delta} < \delta$. In later chapters, we will analyze this phenomenon in more detail. Here we just note that this effect allows us to encode information using the time interval between the firings of two or more neurons. The reader who is interested in the computational aspects of coding by firing time differences may move directly to Chapter 2. The

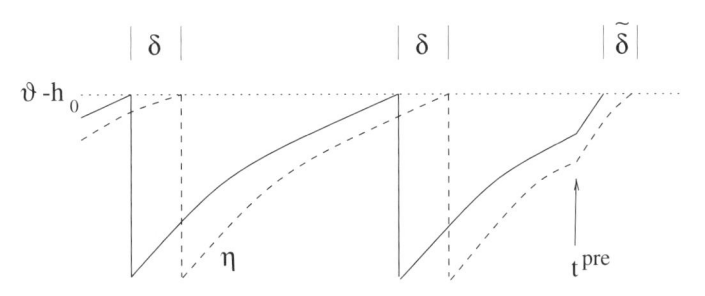

Figure 1.14. The firing time difference δ between two independent neurons is decreased to $\tilde{\delta} < \delta$, after both neurons receive a common excitatory input at time t^{pre}.

above argument also plays a major role in chapters 10 and 11 in the context of neuronal locking.

The remainder of Chapter 1 continues with a discussion of neuron models. Before turning to conductance-based neuron models, we want to put our simple neuron model into a larger context.

1.2.3 Threshold-Fire Models

The simple spiking neuron model introduced in Section 1.2.1 is an instance of a 'threshold-fire model'. The firing occurs at the moment when the state variable u crosses the threshold. A famous example in this model class is the 'integrate-and-fire' model.

In this section we review the arguments that motivate our simple model of a spiking neuron the Spike Response Model introduced in Section 1.2.1. We show the relation of the model to the integrate-and-fire model and discuss several variants. Finally we discuss several noisy versions of the model.

1.2.3.1 Spike Response Model - Further Details

In this paragraph we want to motivate the simple model of a spiking neuron introduced in Section 1.2.1., give further details, and discuss it in a more general context. Let us start and review the arguments for the simple neuron model.

We aim for a simple model which captures some generic properties of neural activity without going into too much detail. The neuronal output should consist of pulses. In real spike trains, all action potentials of a given neuron look alike. The pulses of our model can therefore be treated as stereotyped events that occur at certain firing times $t_i^{(f)}$. The lower index i denotes the neuron, the upper index is the spike number. A spike train is fully characterized by the set of firing times

$$\mathcal{F}_i = \{t_i^{(1)}, \ldots, t_i^{(n)}\} \tag{1.27}$$

already introduced in Equation (1.1).

24   1. Spiking Neurons

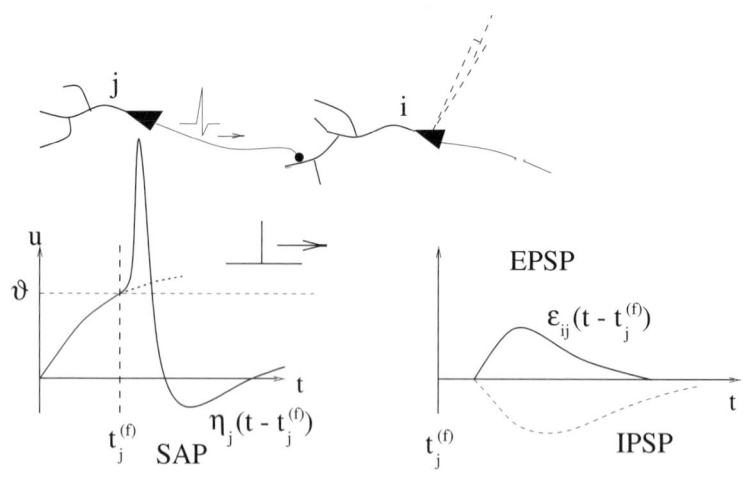

Figure 1.15. The Spike Response Model as a generic framework to describe the spike process. Spikes are generated by a threshold process whenever the membrane potential u crosses the threshold ϑ. The threshold crossing triggers the spike followed by a spike afterpotential (SAP), summarized in the function $\eta_j(t - t_j^{(f)})$. The spike evokes a response of the postsynaptic neuron described by the kernel $\epsilon_{ij}(t - t_j^{(f)})$. The voltage response to an input at an excitatory synapse is called the excitatory postsynaptic potential (EPSP) and can be measured with an electrode (schematically). Spike arrival at an inhibitory would cause an inhibitory postsynaptic potential (IPSP) which as a negative effect (dashed line).

The internal state of a model neuron is described by a single variable u. We will refer to u_i as the membrane potential of neuron i. Spikes are generated when the membrane potential crosses a threshold ϑ from below. The moment of threshold crossing can be used to formally define the firing times. If $u_i(t) = \vartheta$ and $u_i'(t) > 0$, then $t = t_i^{(f)}$. As always, the prime denotes a derivative. The set of firing times therefore is

$$\mathcal{F}_i = \{t \,|\, u_i(t) = \vartheta \wedge u_i'(t) > 0\}. \tag{1.28}$$

In contrast to (1.10) we have included here explicitly that the threshold must be reached from below ($u_i' > 0$). In the simple model of Section 1.2.1, this condition was automatically fulfilled, since the state variable could never pass threshold: as soon as u_i reached ϑ, the state variable was reset to a value below threshold. In the following we want to be slightly more general.

After a spike is triggered by the threshold process, a whole sequence of events is initiated. Ion channels open and close, some ions flow through the cell membrane into the neuron, others flow out. The result of these ionic processes is the action potential, a sharp peak of the voltage followed by a long lasting negative afterpotential. As mentioned before, the forms of the spike and its afterpotential are always roughly the same. Their generic time course will be described in our model by a function $\eta_i(s)$, where $s = t - t_i^{(f)} > 0$ is the time since the threshold crossing at $t_i^{(f)}$. A typical form of $\eta_i(.)$ is sketched in Figures 1.15 and 1.16a. Also, information about the spike event is transmitted to other postsynaptic neurons; see

Figure 1.15. The response of these neurons is described by another function $\epsilon_{ij}(s)$ which will be discussed further below. Let us concentrate on the function η_i first.

Since the form of the pulse itself does not carry any information, the exact time course during the positive part of the spike is irrelevant. Notice, however, that while the action potential is quickly rising or steeply falling, emission of a further spike is impossible. This effect is called absolute refractoriness. Important for refractoriness is also the spike afterpotential (SAP). A negative spike afterpotential means that the emission of a second spike immediately after the first pulse is more difficult. The time of reduced sensitivity after a spike is called the relative refractory period.

In an attempt to simplify the neuron model, we may therefore replace the initial segment of η_i by an absolute refractory period and concentrate on the negative spike after potential only. This is shown in Figure 1.16b. Here the positive part of the spike is reduced to a pulse of negligible width. Its sole purpose is to mark the firing time $s = 0$. Absolute and negative refractoriness may be modeled by

$$\eta_i(s) = -\eta_0 \exp\left(-\frac{s - \delta^{\text{abs}}}{\tau}\right) \mathcal{H}(s - \delta^{\text{abs}}) - K\,\mathcal{H}(s)\mathcal{H}(\delta^{\text{abs}} - s) \quad (1.29)$$

with a constant $K \to \infty$ in order to ensure absolute refractoriness during the time δ^{abs} after the firing. The Heaviside step function $\mathcal{H}(s)$ is unity for $s > 0$ and vanishes for $s \leq 0$. The constant η_0 is a parameter which scales the amplitude of relative refractoriness. If we are interested in a question of spike timing (but not in the form of the action potential), then a model description with such a simplified kernel may be fully sufficient.

Let us now consider two neurons connected via a synapse. If the presynaptic neuron j fires at time $t_j^{(f)}$, a pulse travels along the axon to the synapse where it evokes some response of the postsynaptic neuron i. In our model, we disregard all details of the transmission process and concentrate on the effect that the pulse has on the membrane potential at the soma of neuron i. This response is a measurable function called the postsynaptic potential (PSP) and can be positive (excitatory) or negative (inhibitory). The typical time course of an excitatory postsynaptic potential (EPSP) is sketched in Figure 1.15. In our model, the time course is described by a function $\epsilon_{ij}(s)$ where $s = t - t_j^{(f)}$ is the time which has passed since the emission of the presynaptic pulse. The kernel $\epsilon_{ij}(s)$ vanishes for $s \leq \Delta^{\text{ax}}$. We refer to Δ^{ax} as the axonal transmission delay. We often approximate the time course for $t - t_j^{(f)} > \Delta^{\text{ax}}$ by a so-called α-function $\propto x\,e^{-x}$ where $x = (t - t_j^{(f)} - \Delta^{\text{ax}})/\tau_s$ and τ_s some time constant. Another possibility is to describe the form of the response by the double exponential introduced in (1.14).

So far we have restricted our discussion to a pair of neurons. In reality, each postsynaptic neuron i will receive input from many different presynaptic neurons $j \in \Gamma_i$. All inputs cause some postsynaptic response and contribute to the membrane potential of i. In our model, we assume that the total membrane potential u_i of neuron i is the linear superposition of

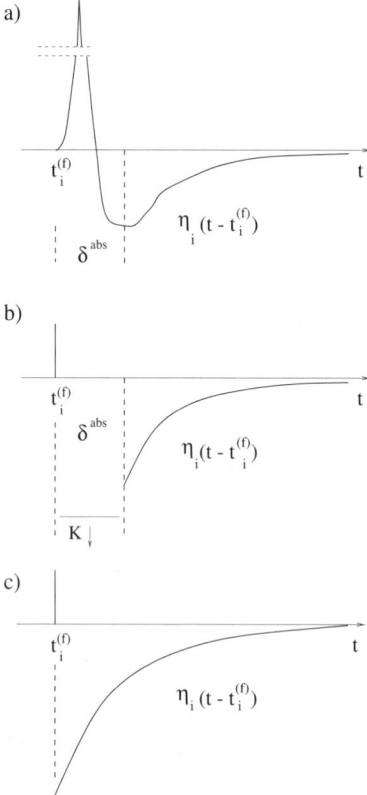

Figure 1.16. a) Action potential and spike after potential (schematic). The peak of the pulse is out of scale; cf. Fig.1.25. During the time δ^{abs}, emission of a further action potential is practically impossible. b) A simplified kernel η_i which includes an absolute refractory period of δ^{abs} followed by an exponential decay. The form of the action potential is not described explicitly. The firing time $t_i^{(f)}$ is marked by a vertical bar. c) As a further simplification of η_i, absolute refractoriness may be neglected.

all contributions

$$u_i(t) = \sum_{t_i^{(f)} \in \mathcal{F}_i} \eta_i(t - t_i^{(f)}) + \sum_{j \in \Gamma_i} \sum_{t_j^{(f)} \in \mathcal{F}_j} w_{ij} \epsilon_{ij}(t - t_j^{(f)}). \tag{1.30}$$

As above, the kernel η_i describes the neuron's response to its own firing. (In the following we often omit the subscript i.) The kernel ϵ_{ij} describes the generic response of neuron i to spikes from each presynaptic neurons $j \in \Gamma_i$. The weight w_{ij} gives the amplitude of the response. It corresponds to the synaptic efficacy of the connection from j to i. For the sake of simplicity, we often assume that the response has the same form for any pair ij of neurons, except for an amplitude factor w_{ij}. This means that we may suppress the index ij of ϵ_{ij} in (1.30) and write ϵ instead of ϵ_{ij}. Since the membrane potential in (1.30) is expressed in terms of response kernels, we will refer to the above description of neuronal activity as the Spike Response Model [Gerstner, 1991; Gerstner and van Hemmen, 1992; Gerstner et al., 1996]. Equation (1.30) is exactly the simplified neuron model introduced already in Section 1.2.1.

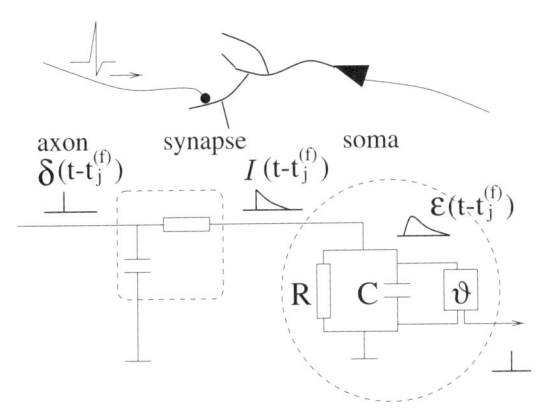

Figure 1.17. Integrate-and-fire neuron. The basic module is the RC circuit shown inside the circle on the right-hand side of the diagram. The circuit is charged by an input current I. If the voltage across the capacitor reaches a threshold ϑ the circuit is shunted and a δ-pulse is transmitted to other neurons (lower right). A δ-pulse sent out by a presynaptic neuron and travelling on the presynaptic axon (left), is low-pass filtered first (middle) before it is fed as a *current* pulse $I(t - t_j^{(f)})$ into the integrate-and-fire circuit. The voltage response of the RC circuit to the presynaptic pulse is the postsynaptic potential $\epsilon(t - t_j^{(f)})$

Equation (1.30) is a linear equation for the membrane potential. All contributions to u_i are caused by the firing events $t_i^{(f)}$ and $t_j^{(f)}$. The essential nonlinearity of the neuronal dynamics is given by the threshold condition (1.28) which defines the firing times. The Spike Response Model is defined by the combination of (1.28) and (1.30) and is the starting point for the analysis of spike based computation in Chapter 2. It is also used in some other chapters, e.g., Chapters 9 and 10.

1.2.3.2 Integrate-and-Fire Model

An important example in the class of 'threshold-fire models' is the integrate-and-fire neuron. The basic circuit of an integrate-and-fire model consists of a capacitor C in parallel with a resistor R driven by a current $I(t)$; see Figure 1.17. The driving current splits into two components, one charging the capacitor, the other going through the resistor. Conservation of charge yields the equation

$$I(t) = \frac{u(t)}{R} + C\frac{du}{dt} \tag{1.31}$$

where u is the voltage across the capacitor C. We introduce the time constant $\tau_m = RC$ of the 'leaky integrator' and write (1.31) in the standard form

$$\tau_m \frac{du}{dt} = -u(t) + R\,I(t). \tag{1.32}$$

We refer to u as the membrane potential and to τ_m as the membrane time constant of the neuron.

Equation (1.32) is a first-order linear differential equation and cannot describe full neuronal spiking behavior. To incorporate the essence of pulse emission, (1.32) is supplemented by a threshold condition. A threshold crossing $u(t^{(f)}) = \vartheta$ is used to define the firing time $t^{(f)}$. The form of the spike is not described explicitly. Immediately after $t^{(f)}$, the potential is reset to a new value u_r,

$$\lim_{\delta \to 0} u(t^{(f)} + \delta) = u_r. \tag{1.33}$$

For $t > t^{(f)}$ the dynamics is again given by (1.32), until the next threshold crossing occurs. The combination of leaky integration (1.32) and reset (1.33) defines the basic integrate-and-fire model.

To see how the model works, let us consider a model neuron with constant input current I_0 and reset potential $u_r = 0$. We assume that a first spike has occurred at $t = t^{(0)}$. The trajectory of the membrane potential can be found by integrating (1.32) with the initial condition $u(t^{(0)}) = u_r = 0$. The solution is

$$u(t) = R I_0 \left[1 - \exp\left(-\frac{t - t^{(0)}}{\tau_m}\right)\right]. \tag{1.34}$$

For $R I_0 < \vartheta$ no further spike can occur. For $R I_0 > \vartheta$, the membrane potential reaches the threshold ϑ at time $t^{(1)}$, which can be found from the threshold condition

$$\vartheta = R I_0 \left[1 - \exp\left(-\frac{t^{(1)} - t^{(0)}}{\tau_m}\right)\right]. \tag{1.35}$$

Solving (1.35) for the time interval $T = t^{(1)} - t^{(0)}$ yields

$$T = \tau_m \ln \frac{R I_0}{R I_0 - \vartheta}. \tag{1.36}$$

After the spike at $t^{(1)}$ the membrane potential is again reset to $u_r = 0$ and the integration process starts again. We conclude that for a constant input current I_0, the integrate-and-fire neuron fires regularly with period T given by (1.36).

Refractoriness

It is straightforward to include an absolute refractory period. After a spike at $t^{(f)}$, we force the membrane potential to a value $u = -K < 0$ and keep it there during a time δ^{abs}. At $t^{(f)} + \delta^{\text{abs}}$ we restart the integration (1.32) with the initial value $u = u_r$.

As before, we can solve the dynamics for a constant input current I_0. If $R I_0 > \vartheta$, the neuron will fire regularly. Due to the absolute refractory period the interval between firings is now longer by an amount δ^{abs} compared to the value in (1.36). Instead of giving the interval T between two spikes, the result is often stated in terms of the mean firing rate $\nu = 1/T$, viz.,

$$\nu = \left[\delta^{\text{abs}} + \tau_m \ln \frac{R I_0}{R I_0 - \vartheta}\right]^{-1}. \tag{1.37}$$

The firing rate of the integrate-and-fire neuron as a function of the constant input current is plotted in Figure 1.18.

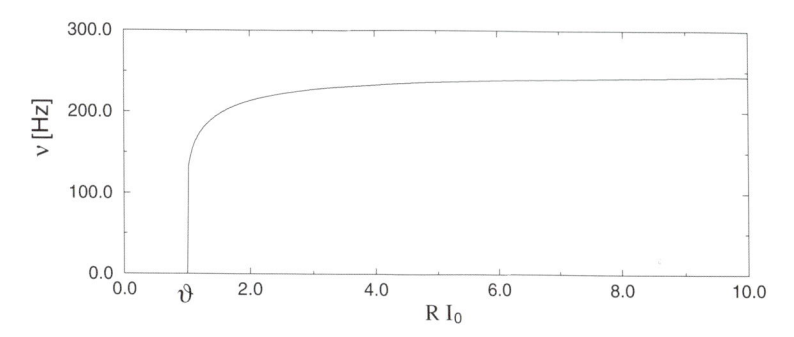

Figure 1.18. Gain function of an integrate-and-fire neuron with absolute refractoriness.

Synaptic currents

If the integrate-and-fire model is part of a network of spiking neurons, then the input current $I(t)$ must be generated somehow from the pulses of other neurons. A simple possibility is to describe the spikes of a presynaptic neuron j as Dirac δ-pulses and feed them directly into the postsynaptic neuron i. The input *current* to unit i is then

$$I_i(t) = \sum_{j \in \Gamma_i} c_{ij} \sum_{t_j^{(f)} \in \mathcal{F}_j} \delta(t - t_j^{(f)}). \tag{1.38}$$

The factor c_{ij} is a measure of the strength of the connection from j to i and corresponds directly to the charge deposited on the capacitor C by a single presynaptic pulse of neuron j. The parameter c_{ij} is, of course, proportional to the synaptic efficacy w_{ij} as we will see later on.

More generally, we can say that each presynaptic spike generates a current pulse of finite width and with time course $\alpha(t - t_j^{(f)})$ for $t > t_j^{(f)}$. In this case, the input current to neuron i should be written as

$$I_i(t) = \sum_{j \in \Gamma_i} c_{ij} \sum_{t_j^{(f)} \in \mathcal{F}_j} \alpha(t - t_j^{(f)}). \tag{1.39}$$

This is not too far from reality, since an input spike arriving at a synapse from j to i indeed evokes a current through the membrane of the postsynaptic neuron i. From measurements it is known that the form of the postsynaptic current (PSC) can often be approximated by

$$\alpha(s) = \frac{s - \Delta^{\text{ax}}}{\tau_s^2} \exp\left(-\frac{s - \Delta^{\text{ax}}}{\tau_s}\right) \mathcal{H}(s - \Delta^{\text{ax}}) \tag{1.40}$$

where τ_s is a synaptic time constant in the millisecond range and Δ^{ax} is the axonal transmission delay. As usual, $\mathcal{H}(x)$ denotes the Heaviside step function which vanishes for $x \leq 0$ and has a value of one for $x > 0$. For a yet more realistic description of the synaptic input current the reader should consult the Section 1.2.4 on conductance-based neuron models in this chapter. In passing we remark that in the literature, a function of the form $x \exp(-x)$ is often called an α-function. While this has motivated our

30   1. Spiking Neurons

choice of the symbol α for the synaptic input current, $\alpha(.)$ in (1.39) could in fact stand for any form of an input current pulse.

In Figure 1.17 we have sketched the situation where $\alpha(s)$ consists of a simple exponentially decaying pulse

$$\alpha(s) = \frac{1}{\tau_s} \exp(-\frac{s}{\tau_s}) \mathcal{H}(s) . \tag{1.41}$$

(1.41) is a first approximation to the low-pass characteristics of a synapse. Since the analytic expressions are simpler, (1.41) is often used instead of the more complicated expression (1.40). In simulations, it is convenient to generate the exponential pulse (1.41) by a differential equation for the *current*. The total postsynaptic current I_i into neuron i can be described by

$$\tau_s \frac{d}{dt} I_i(t) = -I_i + \sum_{j \in \Gamma_i} c_{ij} \sum_{t_j^{(f)} \in \mathcal{F}_j} \delta(t - t_j^{(f)}) . \tag{1.42}$$

The differential equation (1.42) replaces then the input current (1.39). In order to see the relation between (1.42) and (1.39) more clearly, we integrate (1.42), which yields

$$I_i(t) = \sum_{j \in \Gamma_i} c_{ij} \sum_{t_j^{(f)} \in \mathcal{F}_j} \frac{1}{\tau_s} \exp\left(-\frac{t - t_j^{(f)}}{\tau_s}\right) \mathcal{H}(t - t_j^{(f)}) . \tag{1.43}$$

Comparison of (1.43) with (1.39) and a current pulse according to (1.41) shows that the two formulations for the input current, the differential formulation (1.42) or the 'integrated' formulation (1.39) are indeed equivalent. In both cases, the resulting current is then put into (1.32) to get the voltage of the integrate-and-fire neuron.

Relation to the Spike Response Model
In this paragraph we show that the integrate-and-fire model discussed so far is in fact a special case of the Spike Response Model. To see this, we have to note two facts. First, (1.32) is a linear differential equation and can therefore easily be integrated. Second, the reset of the membrane potential after firing at time $t_i^{(f)}$ is equivalent to an outgoing current pulse of negligible width

$$I_i^{\text{out}}(t) = -C(\vartheta - u_r) \sum_{t_i^{(f)} \in \mathcal{F}_i} \delta(t - t_i^{(f)}) \tag{1.44}$$

where $\delta(.)$ denotes the Dirac δ-function. We add the current (1.44) on the right-hand side of (1.32)

$$\tau_m \frac{du_i}{dt} = -u_i(t) + R I_i(t) + R I_i^{\text{out}}(t) . \tag{1.45}$$

Let us check the effect of the last term. Integration of $\tau_m du/dt = R I_i^{\text{out}}$ yields at time $t_i^{(f)}$ indeed a reset of the potential from ϑ to u_r, as it should be.

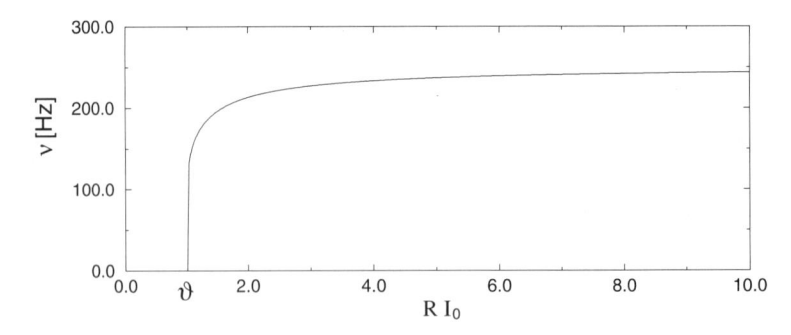

Figure 1.18. Gain function of an integrate-and-fire neuron with absolute refractoriness.

Synaptic currents

If the integrate-and-fire model is part of a network of spiking neurons, then the input current $I(t)$ must be generated somehow from the pulses of other neurons. A simple possibility is to describe the spikes of a presynaptic neuron j as Dirac δ-pulses and feed them directly into the postsynaptic neuron i. The input *current* to unit i is then

$$I_i(t) = \sum_{j \in \Gamma_i} c_{ij} \sum_{t_j^{(f)} \in \mathcal{F}_j} \delta(t - t_j^{(f)}). \tag{1.38}$$

The factor c_{ij} is a measure of the strength of the connection from j to i and corresponds directly to the charge deposited on the capacitor C by a single presynaptic pulse of neuron j. The parameter c_{ij} is, of course, proportional to the synaptic efficacy w_{ij} as we will see later on.

More generally, we can say that each presynaptic spike generates a *current* pulse of finite width and with time course $\alpha(t - t_j^{(f)})$ for $t > t_j^{(f)}$. In this case, the input current to neuron i should be written as

$$I_i(t) = \sum_{j \in \Gamma_i} c_{ij} \sum_{t_j^{(f)} \in \mathcal{F}_j} \alpha(t - t_j^{(f)}). \tag{1.39}$$

This is not too far from reality, since an input spike arriving at a synapse from j to i indeed evokes a current through the membrane of the postsynaptic neuron i. From measurements it is known that the form of the postsynaptic current (PSC) can often be approximated by

$$\alpha(s) = \frac{s - \Delta^{\text{ax}}}{\tau_s^2} \exp\left(-\frac{s - \Delta^{\text{ax}}}{\tau_s}\right) \mathcal{H}(s - \Delta^{\text{ax}}) \tag{1.40}$$

where τ_s is a synaptic time constant in the millisecond range and Δ^{ax} is the axonal transmission delay. As usual, $\mathcal{H}(x)$ denotes the Heaviside step function which vanishes for $x \leq 0$ and has a value of one for $x > 0$. For a yet more realistic description of the synaptic input current the reader should consult the Section 1.2.4 on conductance-based neuron models in this chapter. In passing we remark that in the literature, a function of the form $x \exp(-x)$ is often called an α-function. While this has motivated our

32   1. Spiking Neurons

$t + \Delta t$, given that the last spike occurred at $t^{(0)}$ and that the total input potential in the noiseless case is $h(t)$? For $\Delta t \to 0$, this defines the *probability density* for firing

$$P_h(t \mid t^{(0)}) \tag{1.50}$$

which we would like to calculate for each of the three noise models. We can interpret interpret $P_h(t \mid t^{(0)})$ as the distribution of interspike intervals in the presence of an input potential h. The lower index h is intended to remind the reader that the distribution depends on the time course of $h(t')$ for $t^{(0)} < t' < t$. We now discuss each of the three models of noise in turn.

A) Noisy threshold

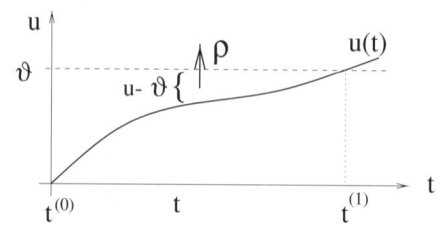

B) Noisy reset

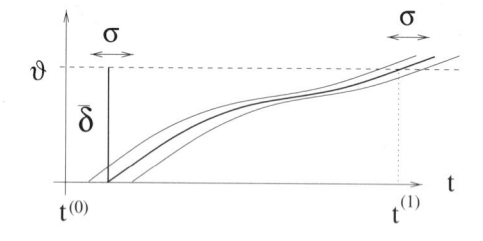

C) Noisy integration

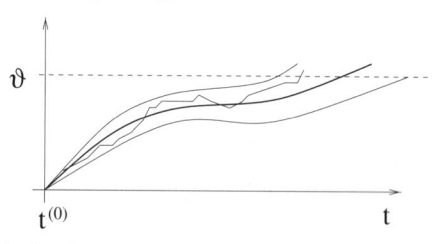

Figure 1.19. Noise in threshold neurons. a) Noisy threshold; a neuron may fire [with probability density $\rho(u - \vartheta)$] even though the membrane potential u has not yet reached the threshold ϑ. b) Noisy reset; a stochastic change in the absolute refractory period shifts the trajectory horizontally. c) Noisy integration; a stochastic contribution in the input *current* of an integrate-and-fire neuron causes the membrane potential to drift away from the reference trajectory.

Noisy threshold

In this first noise model, we assume the neuron can fire even though the formal threshold ϑ has not been reached yet. To do this consistently, we introduce an 'escape rate' ρ which depends on the distance between the momentary value of the membrane potential and the threshold,

$$\rho = f(u - \vartheta). \tag{1.51}$$

In the mathematical literature, the quantity ρ would be called a 'stochastic intensity'. The choice of the function f is arbitrary. A plausible assumption is an exponential dependence

$$\rho = \frac{1}{\tau_0} \exp[\beta (u - \vartheta)] \tag{1.52}$$

which can be motivated by the Arrhenius formula for chemical reaction rates. β and τ_0 are parameters. Note that the escape rate ρ is implicitly time-dependent, since the membrane potential $u(t) = \eta(t - t^{(0)}) + h(t)$ varies over time. In addition, we may also include an explicit time dependence, e.g., to account for a reduced spiking probability immediately after the spike at $t^{(0)}$.

Let us now calculate $P_h(t^{(1)} | t^{(0)})$, the probability density of having a spike at $t^{(1)}$ given that the last spike occurred at $t^{(0)}$, and in the presence of an input potential $h(t)$ for $t > t^{(0)}$. At each moment of time, the value $u(t)$ of the membrane potential determines the escape rate $\rho(t) = f[u(t) - \vartheta]$. In order to emit the next spike at $t^{(1)}$, the neuron has to 'survive' the interval $(t^{(0)}, t^{(1)})$ without firing and then fire at $t^{(1)}$. Given the escape rate $\rho(t)$, the probability of survival from $t^{(0)}$ to $t^{(1)}$ without a firing is

$$S_\rho(t^{(1)} | t^{(0)}) = \exp\left(-\int_{t^{(0)}}^{t^{(1)}} \rho(t)\, dt\right). \tag{1.53}$$

The probability density of firing at time $t^{(1)}$ is $\rho(t^{(1)})$, thus with (1.53) we have

$$P_h(t^{(1)} | t^{(0)}) = \rho(t^{(1)}) \exp\left(-\int_{t^{(0)}}^{t^{(1)}} \rho(t)\, dt\right) \tag{1.54}$$

which is the desired result. A more detailed derivation of (1.54) can be found in [Gerstner and van Hemmen, 1994].

Noisy Reset

In this noise model, firing is given by the exact threshold condition $u(t^{(f)}) = \vartheta$. Noise is included into the formulation of reset and refractoriness.

Let us consider the integrate-and-fire model with absolute refractoriness. The duration of refractoriness δ^{abs} is not fixed, but chosen stochastically from a distribution $p(\delta^{\text{abs}})$ with mean $\bar{\delta}$. Naturally we have to require that $p(x)$ vanishes for $x < 0$. In the formulation of the Spike Response Model, this procedure is equivalent to replacing the term $\eta(t - \hat{t})$ in (1.21) by $\eta(t - \hat{t} - \delta^{\text{abs}})$.

As with the preceding noise model, we are interested in calculating the firing density $P_h(t^{(1)} | t^{(0)})$ given some input potential $h(t)$. For the sake of simplicity, let us assume that the input is constant $h(t) = h_0$. The first spike has occurred at $t^{(0)}$. The firing time $t^{(1)}$ of the next spike can now be found from the threshold condition

$$\vartheta = \eta(t^{(1)} - t^{(0)} - \delta^{\text{abs}}) + h_0 . \tag{1.55}$$

In the absence of noise and for a refractory period $\bar{\delta}$ the next firing would occur at $t^{(1)} = t^{(0)} + T$ where T is the interspike interval. If, due to the noise, the value of the refractory period is $\delta^{\text{abs}} \neq \bar{\delta}$, then the interval is $t^{(1)} - t^{(0)} = T + \delta^{\text{abs}} - \bar{\delta}$. The firing *density* in the presence of noise is therefore

$$P_h(t^{(1)} \,|\, t^{(0)}) = p(t^{(1)} - t^{(0)} - T + \bar{\delta}) \tag{1.56}$$

where $p(.)$ is the distribution of the refractory period introduced above. Graphically, the result (1.56) is easy to understand. A change in the absolute refractory period shifts the trajectory horizontally. A stochastic component in the refractory period generates a stochastic shift of the firing time. Although a stochastic component in the refractoriness probably is not very realistic, it is a convenient way to introduce noise in a system. As shown in (1.56), noise can be treated analytically without causing too much problems.

Noisy integration

The final and most popular way of introducing noise into an integrate-and-fire model is by adding on the right-hand side of (1.32) a stochastic noise current I_{noise}

$$\tau_m \frac{du}{dt} = -u + R I(t) + R I_{noise} \tag{1.57}$$

with vanishing mean and finite variance. This choice of a noise term could be motivated either by spontaneous openings of ion channels, or else by stochastic arrival of excitatory and inhibitory inputs on dendrites of cortical neurons.

The noise causes the actual membrane trajectory to drift away from the noiseless reference trajectory. To get the distribution $P_h(t^{(1)} \,|\, t^{(0)})$ we have to solve the first passage time problem of (1.57) with initial value u_r and absorbing boundary condition at ϑ. Although (1.57) looks simple, it turns out that the first passage time problem for arbitrary input current $I(t)$ is rather difficult to solve analytically. Discussions of the first passage time problem for constant input $I(t) = I_0$ can be found in many textbooks; see, e.g., [Tuckwell, 1988].

1.2.4 Conductance-Based Models

In this section we briefly discuss a class of rather detailed neuron models which are known as conductance based models. At the origin of these models are the equations of Hodgkin and Huxley which we describe first. We then discuss the relation of the Hodgkin-Huxley model to the Spike Response Model introduced in the previous subsection. Finally, we mention the detailed compartmental models which focus on the spatial structure of the neuron as well as on the dynamics of various ion currents.

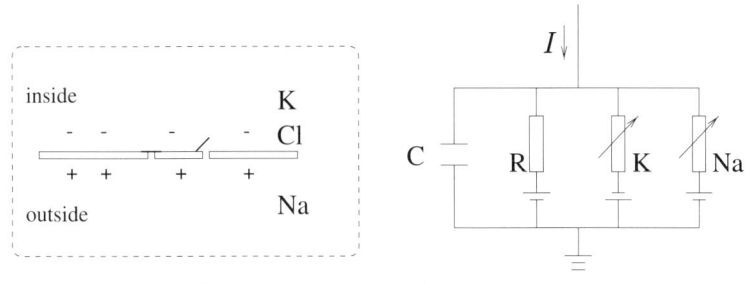

Figure 1.20. Schematic diagram for the Hodgkin-Huxley model.

1.2.4.1 Hodgkin-Huxley Model

The classic description of neuronal spiking dates back to Hodgkin and Huxley [1952] who summarized their extensive experimental studies on the giant axon of the squid with four differential equations. The first describes the conservation of electric charge on a piece of membrane of capacitance C under the influence of some charging currents

$$C\frac{du}{dt} = -\sum_k I_k + I(t) \qquad (1.58)$$

where u is the voltage, $I(t)$ is an external driving current and $\sum_k I_k$ is the sum of the ionic currents through the cell membrane. In the case of the Hodgkin-Huxley model, there are three types of ion current indexed respectively by Na, K, and L,

$$\sum_k I_k = g_{\text{Na}} m^3 h (u - V_{\text{Na}}) + g_K n^4 (u - V_K) + g_L (u - V_L). \qquad (1.59)$$

The parameters g are conductances and m, n, h are additional variables to be discussed below. Further parameters are the constants V_{Na}, V_K, and V_L. They are called reversal potentials since the direction of a current I_k changes when u crosses V_k.

To understand the two equations (1.58) and (1.59) consider the diagram in Figure 1.20. The semipermeable cell membrane separates the interior of the cell from the extracellular liquid. Due to the membrane's selective permeability and also because of active ion transport through the cell membrane, the ion concentrations inside and outside the cell are quite different. As a result, in the absence of external input the interior of the cell has a slightly negative potential with respect to the outside. The cell membrane acts like a capacitor which has been charged by a battery.

If an input current $I(t)$ is injected into the cell, it both charges the capacitor, and leaks through the channels in the cell membrane. This is the essence of (1.58). In the Hodgkin-Huxley model, three types of ion channels are accounted for. There is a sodium channel with subscript Na, a potassium channel with subscript K and an unspecific leakage channel with lower index L. The leakage channel is described by a voltage-independent conductance g_L; the conductances of the other other ion channels are voltage dependent. If the channels are fully open, they transmit currents with a

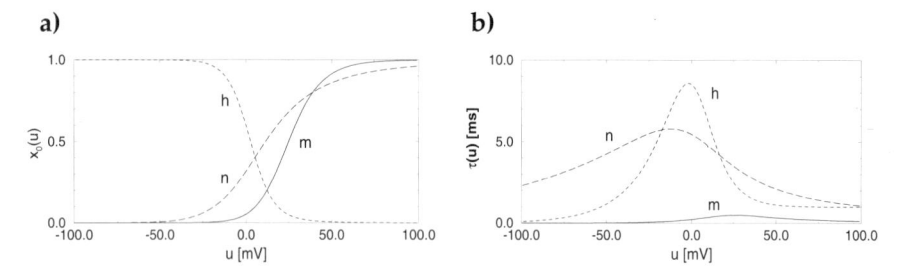

Figure 1.21. Equilibrium function (**a**) and time constant (**b**) for the three variables m, n, h in the Hodgkin-Huxley model.

maximum conductance g_{Na} or g_{K}, respectively. Normally, however, the channels are partially blocked. The removal of the block is voltage dependent and is described by the additional variables m, n, and h. The combined action of m and h controls the Na channels. The K gates are controlled by n.

The three variables m, n, and h evolve according to the differential equations

$$\begin{aligned} \dot{m} &= \alpha_m(u)(1-m) - \beta_m(u)m \\ \dot{n} &= \alpha_n(u)(1-n) - \beta_n(u)n \\ \dot{h} &= \alpha_h(u)(1-h) - \beta_h(u)h \end{aligned} \quad (1.60)$$

with $\dot{m} = dm/dt$, and so on. The α and β are empirical functions of u that have been adjusted to fit the data of the giant axon of the squid. Reversal potentials and conductances are also empirical parameters. In the appropriate units (of mS/cm^2), the factors are $g_{\text{Na}} = 120$, $g_{\text{K}} = 36$, and $g_L = 0.3$. The reversal potentials are $V_{\text{Na}} = 115$ mV, $V_{\text{K}} = -12$ mV, and $V_L = 10.6$ mV and the membrane capacity is $C = 1\ \mu\text{F}/\text{cm}^2$. Eqs. (1.58) - (1.60) define the Hodgkin-Huxley model.

To get an idea of how the model works it is more convenient to write (1.60) in the form

$$\dot{x} = -\frac{1}{\tau(u)}[x - x_0(u)] \quad (1.61)$$

where x stands for m, n, or h. If we force the voltage to a constant value u, the variable x would approach the value $x_0(u)$ with time constant $\tau(u)$. The asymptotic value $x_0(u)$ and the time constant $\tau(u)$ are given by the transformation $x_0(u) = \alpha_x(u)/[\alpha_x(u) + \beta_x(u)]$ and $\tau(u) = [\alpha_x(u) + \beta_x(u)]^{-1}$. Using the parameters given by Hodgkin and Huxley [1952], we have plotted the functions $x_0(u)$ and $\tau(u)$ in Figure 1.21. The function $x_0(u)$ has a sigmoidal shape with maximum slope at some 'threshold' θ_x; the time constant τ is significant only in a limited range around θ_x. Note that m and n increase with u whereas h decreases. Thus, if some external input causes the membrane voltage to rise, the ion conductance of sodium (Na) increases due to increasing m and sodium flows into the cell. This raises the membrane potential further and further and an action potential is initiated. At high values of u the sodium conductance is shut off due to the factor h. Also potassium (K) outflow sets in which lowers the potential. Due to the longer time constant $\tau_n(u)$, the potassium concentration reaches its

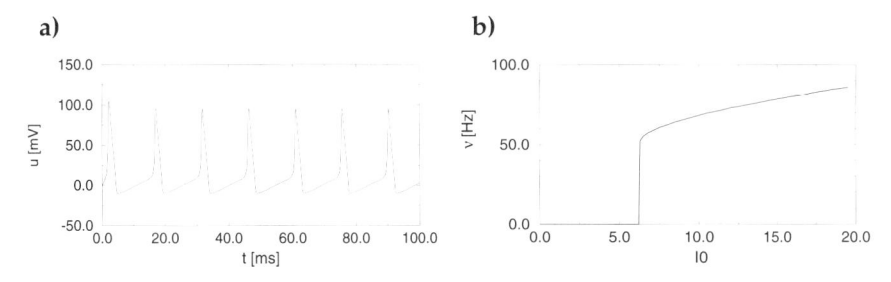

Figure 1.22. Spike train for constant input current (**a**) and gain function (**b**) of the Hodgkin-Huxley model.

equilibrium potential only slowly. The overall effect is a short action potential followed by a negative overshoot which decays slowly back to zero as shown in Figure 1.22a. Numerical integration of Eqs. (1.58)-(1.60) shows that a constant input $I(t) = I_0$ larger than a critical value I_θ results in a regular spike train. If the number of spikes during a large interval T is counted and divided by T, a firing *rate* results. The firing rate as a function of the input I_0 is called the *gain function* of the Hodgkin-Huxley model. It is plotted in Figure 1.22b.

Using the above equations and an appropriate set of parameters, Hodgkin and Huxley were able to describe an enormous amount of data from experiments on the giant axon of the squid. Due to its success in this special system, there have subsequently been several attempts to generalize the model in order to describe other experimental situations as well (for a review see, e.g., [Jack et al., 1975]).

Whereas the model had originally been designed to describe the form and temporal change of an action potential during *axonal* transmission, a set of equations completely analogous to Eqs. (1.58) to (1.60) has been also used to describe spike generation at the *soma* of the neuron [Bernander et al., 1991; Bush and Douglas, 1991 Ekeberg et al., 1991; Rapp et al., 1992; Traub et al., 1991; Wilson et al. 1989; Yamada et al., 1989]. The main difference is that additional ion channels have to be included, in particular those that account for Ca^{2+} and the slow components of the potassium current. For each type of ion channel i, a current $I_i = g_i x_i^{n_i}(u - V_i)$ is added. Here x is yet another variable with dynamics (1.61). The conductance parameters g_i, the exponents n_i, as well as the functions $x_0(u)$ and $\tau(u)$ are adjusted to fit experimental data. This approach leads to detailed compartmental models briefly discussed at the end of this section.

Signal transmission and integration on dendrites have traditionally been described by passive electric processes, most prominently in the dendritic cable theory of Rall; see e.g. [Rall, 1964]. Such an approach can even account for some nonlinear dendritic phenomena [Abbott, 1991; Bernander et al., 1991; Rapp et al., 1992]. A different approach to dendritic integration is based again on Hodgkin-Huxley type equations. The only change with respect to the theory of *axonal* signal transmission is that a different set of parameters for the conductivity of various channels are used on the dendrites. If a few spatial compartments of the neuron are put together, a set of more than 20 coupled nonlinear differential equations results (see

38   1. Spiking Neurons

e.g. [Traub et al., 1991]). Numerical solution of the system of equations shows good agreement with experiments. This is an important indication that a Hodgkin-Huxley type analysis is a useful tool in understanding the properties of single neurons. It is however obvious that such an approach is too detailed, if we want to describe large network of neurons.

1.2.4.2 Relation to the Spike Response Model

The system of equations proposed by Hodgkin and Huxley is rather complicated. It consists of four coupled nonlinear differential equations and as such is difficult to analyze mathematically. For this reason, several simplifications of the Hodgkin-Huxley equations have been proposed. The most common reduces the set of four differential equations to a system of two equations [FitzHugh, 1961; Nagumo, 1962; Rinzel and Ermentrout, 1989; Abbott and Kepler, 1990]. Two important approximations are made. First, the m dynamics which has a faster time course than the other variables (see the plot for τ_m in Figure 1.21b) is considered to be instantaneous, so that m can be replaced by its equilibrium value $m_0(u)$. Second, the equations for n and h which have according to Figure 1.21b roughly the same time constants are replaced by a single effective variable. [Rinzel and Ermentrout, 1989] and [Abbott and Kepler, 1990] have shown how to make such a reduction systematically. The resulting two-dimensional model is often called the Morris LeCar model or the FitzHugh-Nagumo Model. More generally, the two-dimensional set of equations is also called a Bonhoeffer/Van der Pol oscillator. The advantage of a two-dimensional set of equations is that it allows a systematic phase plane analysis. For a review of the methods and results see the article of [Rinzel and Ermentrout, 1989] in the review collection [Koch and Segev, 1989]. For a further reduction of the two-dimensional model to an integrate-and-fire model, see [Abbott and Kepler, 1990].

In this section, we will follow a somewhat different approach. We would like to relate the Hodgkin-Huxley equations to our generic threshold model, the Spike Response Model [Kistler et al., 1997]. To do so, we have to determine the following three terms which appear in the equations of the Spike Response Model (1.28) and (1.30): (i) the kernel ϵ which describes the response to incoming pulses, (ii) the kernel η which describes the response to spike emission, and (iii) the value of the threshold ϑ.

We start with the kernel ϵ. In the absence of input the membrane potential u is at some resting value u_{rest}. To find the kernel ϵ we perform a simulation with a short square current pulse as the input

$$I(t) = \frac{q}{\Delta} \quad \text{for } 0 < t < \Delta \tag{1.62}$$

and zero otherwise. Here q is some small unit charge and $\Delta \ll 1$ ms is the duration of the pulse. (Formally, we consider the limit $\Delta \to 0$.) The voltage response of the Hodgkin-Huxley model to this sub-threshold current pulse defines the kernel ϵ,

$$q\,\epsilon(t) = u(t) - u_{\text{rest}}\,. \tag{1.63}$$

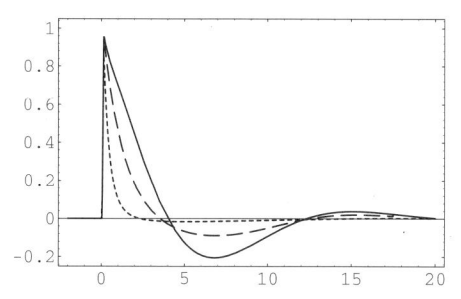

Figure 1.23. The voltage response of the Hodgkin-Huxley model to a short sub-threshold current pulse defines the kernel ϵ (solid line). If the same input current pulse occurs a few milliseconds after an output action potential, the duration of the response is reduced due to refractoriness (dashed line, input spike $\Delta t = 10.5$ ms after the output spike; dotted line $\Delta t = 6.5$ ms) x-axis, time in ms; y-axis voltage in mV; taken from [Kistler et al., 1997].

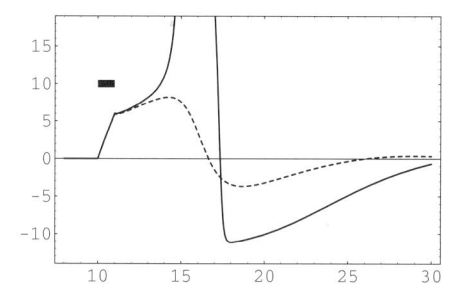

Figure 1.24. Threshold behavior of the Hodgkin-Huxley model. An input current pulse of 1 ms duration (thick bar) can evoke either an action potential (solid line) with amplitude 100 mV (out of scale) or a small response of about 10 mV (dashed) depending on the precise value of the input current. x-axis, time in ms; y-axis potential in mV. Solid line, input current 6.9 μAcm^{-2}; dashed line, input current 7.0 μAcm^{-2}; taken from [Kistler et al., 1997].

Here $t > 0$ is the time since the initiation of the pulse. The result is shown in Figure 1.23. Since the input current pulse delivers a unit charge during a very short amount of time $\Delta < 0.1$ ms, the ϵ-kernel jumps almost instantaneously at time $t = 0$ to a value of 1 mV. For synaptic input currents of finite width, the ϵ-kernel would have a finite rise time.

The kernel η is found by a similar procedure. We take a square current pulse as in (1.62) but with a charge q large enough to evoke a spike. The principle is indicated in Fig 1.24. We consider a series of current pulses of increasing q but the same duration of 1 ms. At a critical value of q the responses show an abrupt change from a response amplitude of about 10 mV to an amplitude of nearly 100 mV. If q is increased even further, the form of the pulse remains nearly the same. The kernel η allows us to describe the standard form of the spike and the spike afterpotential in a convenient manner. In order to define the kernel η, we set

$$\eta(s) = u(s) - u_{\text{rest}} \qquad (1.64)$$

where $u(s)$ is the voltage trajectory after the supra-threshold current pulse. The kernel $\eta(s)$ is shown in Figure 1.25. The time $s = 0$ denotes the moment of spike initiation.

40   1. Spiking Neurons

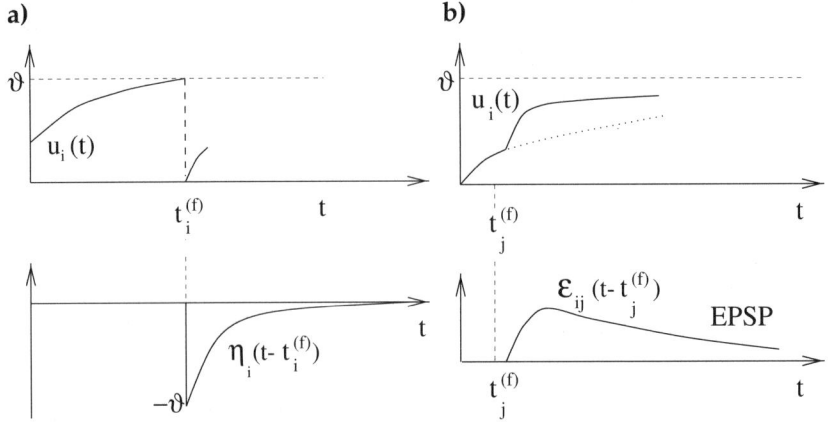

Figure 1.25. *a)* The state variable $u(t)$ reaches the threshold ϑ at time $t_i^{(f)}$. Immediately afterwards $u(t)$ is reset to zero. The reset is performed by adding a kernel $\eta_i(t - t_i^{(f)})$. The function $\eta_i(s)$ takes care of refractoriness after a spike emitted at $s = 0$. *b)* The state variable $u(t)$ changes after a presynaptic spike has occured at $t_j^{(f)}$. The kernels ϵ_{ij} describes the response of u_i to a presynaptic spike at $s = 0$. The figure shows an excitatory postsynaptic potential (EPSP). In case of an inhibitory postsynaptic potential (IPSP) the response would be negative. Note that the response occurs only after some delay.

The third term to be determined is the threshold ϑ. Even though Figure 1.24 suggests, that the Hodgkin-Huxley equation exhibits some type of threshold behavior, the threshold is not well-defined [Koch et al., 1995] and it is fairly difficult to estimate a voltage threshold directly from a single series of simulations. We therefore take the threshold as a parameter which will be adjusted by a procedure discussed below.

In Spike Response Model (SRM) approximation, we replace the full Hodgkin-Huxley model by the equation

$$u^{SRM}(t) = \eta(t - \hat{t}) + \int_0^\infty \epsilon(s) I(t - s) ds \qquad (1.65)$$

where $\hat{t}$ is the most recent firing time and the kernels ϵ and η are defined by (1.63) and (1.64), respectively. The next output spike occurs when the threshold ϑ is approached from below, i.e,. $u^{SRM}(t) = \vartheta$ and $\frac{d}{dt} u^{SRM}(t) > 0$.

To test the quality of the approximation (1.65) we compare the performance of the reduced model (1.65) with that of the full Hodgkin-Huxley model (1.58) - (1.60). Since it is our general assumption that timing is important, we study the difficult case of a time-dependent input current $I(t)$. The same current is applied to both models and we compare the firing times of the full Hodgkin-Huxley model with the spike times generated by (1.65). Whenever the firing times differ by more than 2 ms, we record an error in the performance of the SRM. Details may be found in [Kistler et al., 1997].

A time-dependent input current was generated stochastically by the following procedure. Every 2 ms a new target value for the input was drawn from a Gaussian distribution with zero mean and variance $\sigma = 3\mu A/cm^2$.

1.2 Neuron Models 41

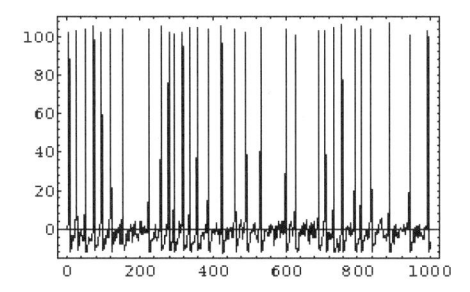

Figure 1.26. Spike train of the Hodgkin-Huxley model driven by a time dependent input current. The action potentials ocurr irregularly. x-axis, time in ms; y-axis, voltage in mV. Taken from [Kistler et al., 1997].

To get a continuous input current, a linear interpolation was used between the target values. The resulting time-dependent input current was then applied to the Hodgkin-Huxley model (1.58); a sample of the response is shown in Figure 1.26. The spike train looks irregular with a broad distribution of interspike intervals as is commonly found for cortical neurons.

The same input was then applied to the Spike Response Model (1.65). The value of the threshold ϑ was optimized so that the total number of spikes generated by (1.65) was roughly that of the Hodgkin-Huxley model; see [Kistler et al., 1997] for details. The spike times were then compared. About 70 per cent of the spikes of the Spike Response Model occurred within 2 ms of the action potentials of the Hodgkin-Huxley model. Moreover, the voltage trace is generally well approximated by (1.65) except just after a spike; see Figure 1.27. The inset in the lower left of Figure 1.27 shows that in an interval where there is no spike, the voltage of the Spike Response Model (dashed) closely follows that of the Hodgkin-Huxley model (solid line). Immediately after a spike, the approximation is poor (inset lower right).

Is there a simple way to improve the approximation? Obviously the problem is that (1.65) provides an incomplete description of refractoriness. In (1.65) refractoriness appears only in form of the spike afterpotential described by the kernel η. But refractoriness also has some other effects. During and immediately after a spike, the response to incoming current pulses is reduced. This is shown in Figure 1.23 by the dashed lines. To take this effect into account, we allow the kernel ϵ to depend on the time since the last output spike and replace (1.65) by

$$u^{SRM}(t) = \eta(t - \hat{t}) + \int_0^\infty \epsilon(t - \hat{t}, s)\, I(t - s)\, ds\,. \tag{1.66}$$

As before, $\hat{t}$ denotes the firing time of the most recent output spike. In order to find the kernel $\epsilon(t - \hat{t}, s)$ we determine numerically the response to a short input current pulse (1.62) under the condition that the last output spike was at $\hat{t}$. The original kernel ϵ in (1.65) corresponds to $\epsilon(\infty, s)$, that is, to the case in which the most recent output spike was long ago.

To test the performance of the improved approximation (1.66), we repeat the simulations with the same stochastic input current $I(t)$ as before and

42   1. Spiking Neurons

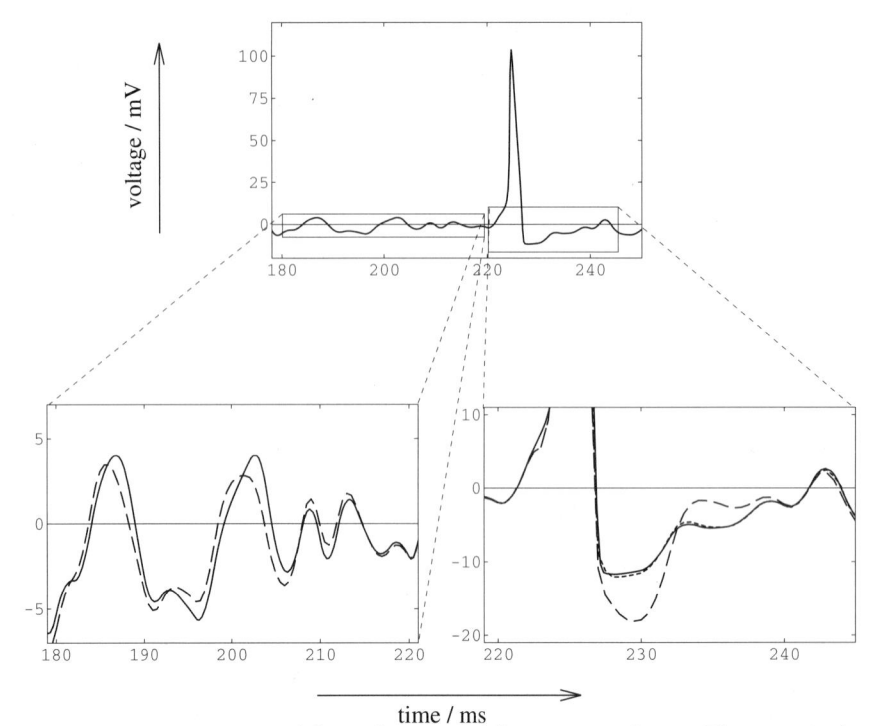

Figure 1.27. A segment of the spike train of the previous figure. The inset in the lower left corner shows the voltage of the Hodgkin-Huxley model (solid) together with the approximation of the Spike Response Model (dashed) during a period where no spike occurs. The inset on the lower right shows the situation during and after a spike. The approximation by the dashed line is not perfect, but the improved approximation (dotted) defined by (1.66) yields a very good fit; taken from [Kistler et al., 1997].

readjust the value of ϑ. The approximation (1.66) increased the percentage of firing times that coincided with the Hodgkin-Huxley action potentials from 70 to 90 percent. This shows that threshold-fire models like the (improved) Spike Response Model can indeed provide a simple and yet useful description of neuronal dynamics.

1.2.4.3 Compartmental Models

The neuron models described so far did not include any spatial structure. A neuron has been considered to be a point-like element and the main focus has been on the process of spike generation. Compartmental models provide a more detailed description of neuronal dynamics by explicitly taking into account the spatial structure of the dendritic tree and by modeling the synaptic transmission at a greater level of detail. Additionally, other ion currents beyond the Na and K currents incorporated in the Hodgkin-Huxley model are included in the description. Of particular interest have been slow currents like Ca^{2+} and Ca-mediated K currents which are related to neuronal adaptation [Yamada et al., 1989]. The basic idea of a compartmental model is indicated in Figure 1.28. Each small segment of the dendritic tree is characterized by ionic and electrical properties, de-

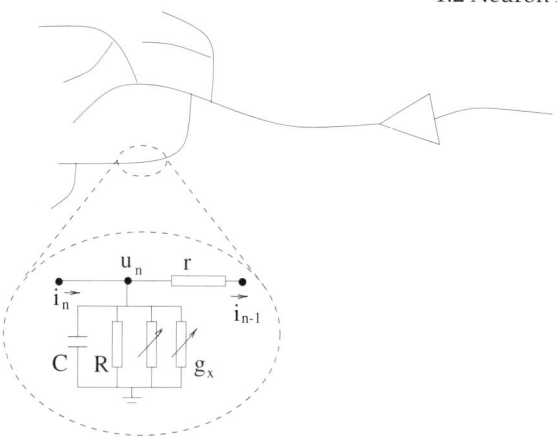

Figure 1.28. In a compartmental neuron model, each small segment of the dendritic tree is modelled by an equivalent electrical circuit. Many more ionic conductances g_x could be present. For the sake of simplicity, the batteries representing the reversal potentials have been suppressed in the drawing.

scribed by a capacitance C and a set of ionic conductances g_x with reversal potential V_x. Neighboring compartments are connected by a longitudinal resistance r. For details, we refer the reader to the vast literature on compartmental models [Bernander et al., 1991; Busch et al., 1991; Ekeberg et al., 1991; Rapp et al., 1992; Traub et al., 1991; Wilson et al., 1989; Yamada et al., 1989], in particular to the reviews in [Koch and Segev, 1989] and [Bower and Beeman, 1995].

Here we discuss a simplified linear model of dendritic structure as introduced by Rall [Rall, 1964, 1989]. The dendritic tree is described by a chain of compartments. In principle, we can allow for branching points, but for the sake of simplicity we focus on a single chain. Each compartment consists of a capacitor C in parallel with a resistor R which describe the linear properties of a patch of membrane. As we have seen above, a more detailed model would also contain non-linear conductances for various ionic currents – these are neglected in our simplified linear model. Each compartment is connected via the axial resistor r to adjacent compartments. The compartment with index $n = 1$ will be referred to as the somatic compartment.

In a chain of N neurons, conservation of current at each compartment yields the equations

$$\frac{u_{n+1} - u_n}{r} - \frac{u_n - u_{n-1}}{r} = C\frac{du_n}{dt} + \frac{u_n}{R} \quad (1.67)$$

for the interior compartments $2 \leq n \leq N - 1$ and similar equations for $n = 1$ and $n = N$. The terms on the left-hand side are the longitudinal currents i_n and i_{n-1} leading into and out of the compartment; see Fig 1.29. The difference between the two currents branches off into compartment n and either leaks through the membrane resistor R or charges the capacitor C. We introduce the membrane time constant $\tau_m = RC$ and reorder the terms yielding

$$\tau_m \frac{du_n}{dt} = -\left(1 + 2\frac{R}{r}\right) u_n + \frac{R}{r}(u_{n+1} + u_{n-1}) \quad (1.68)$$

44   1. Spiking Neurons

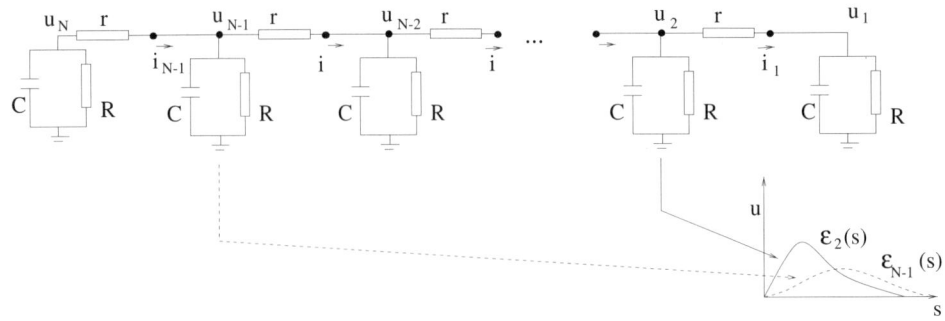

Figure 1.29. A linear compartmental model of the dendritic tree. A current input at compartment 2 at time $s = 0$ gives a strong and quickly rising voltage response ϵ_2 at the somatic compartment 1 (solid line); the same current injected at compartement $N - 1$ gives a weaker and broader response at the soma (ϵ_{N-1}, dashed line). Schematic drawing.

for the interior compartments $2 \leq n \leq N - 1$. At the two ends we have

$$\tau_m \frac{du_1}{dt} = -\left(1 + \frac{R}{r}\right) u_1 + \frac{R}{r} u_2 \qquad (1.69)$$

$$\tau_m \frac{du_N}{dt} = -\left(1 + \frac{R}{r}\right) u_N + \frac{R}{r} u_{N-1} \qquad (1.70)$$

Since (1.68) - (1.70) are linear equations, they can be solved exactly [Rall, 1989; Tuckwell, 1988; Abbott et al., 1991; Bressloff and Taylor, 1993]. For example we can ask the following important question. What is the voltage response of compartment number $n = 1$ (the soma) to a short input current pulse into compartment number n (somewhere on the dendritic tree)? If the input is close to the soma, e.g., $n = 2$, then the response is a fast rising function with a well pronounced maximum; see Figure 1.29. If the input is far away from the soma, the voltage at the soma rises more slowly. Thus the main effect of a linear dendritic tree is that the shape of the postsynaptic potential (as measured at the soma) depends on the location of the input. We can account for this effect in the generic Spike Response Model by making the form of the response kernel ϵ depend on the label of the compartment where the synapse is located.

The situation becomes more complicated if the synaptic currents are modeled at a greater level of detail. First, synaptic currents are not infinitely short but are pulses of finite width. If the dendrite were linear and described by (1.68) - (1.70) then the only difference would be that the postsynaptic potential $\epsilon(s)$ is somewhat broader. If the form and amplitude of the synaptic current were always identical, then we could simply add the individual postsynaptic potentials to get the total effect of the input as it is seen at the soma.

Reality is somewhat more difficult, however, since the amplitude of the synaptic input current itself depends on the voltage at the compartment where the synapse is located. In detailed models, each presynaptic action potential evokes a change in the synaptic *conductance* with standard time course $g(t - t^{(f)})$ where $t^{(f)}$ is the arrival time of the presynaptic pulse. The synaptic input current is modeled as

$$I(t - t^{(f)}) = g(t - t^{(f)}) \left[u_{syn}(t) - u_{rev}\right] \qquad (1.71)$$

where $u_{syn}(t)$ is the voltage at the location of the synapse and u_{rev} is called the reversal potential of the synapse.

The level of the reversal potential depends on the type of synapse. For excitatory synapses, u_{rev} is larger than the resting potential. The synaptic current then shows saturation. The higher the voltage u_{syn} at the synaptic compartment, the smaller the amplitude of the input current. A smaller input current, however, evokes a postsynaptic potential of reduced amplitude. The total postsynaptic potential is therefore not simply the sum of independent contributions. Nevertheless, since the reversal potential of excitatory synapses is usually significantly above the firing threshold, the factor $[u_{syn} - u_{rev}]$ is nearly constant and saturation can be neglected.

For inhibitory synapses, the reversal potential is close to the resting potential and saturation plays an important role. This is sometimes described as the 'shunting' phenomenon of inhibition. An action potential arriving at an inhibitory synapse pulls the membrane potential towards the reversal potential u_{rev} which is close to $u_{\rm rest}$. Thus, if the neuron is at rest, inhibitory input hardly has any effect. If the membrane potential is instead considerably above the resting potential, then the same input has a strong inhibitory effect.

1.2.5 Rate Models

Before we end the chapter, we want to mention the formal neuron model that is most widely used for the analysis of learning and memory in artificial neural networks - the sigmoidal unit. In standard neural network theory, neural activity is described in terms of rates. The rate ν_i of neuron i is an analog variable which depends nonlinearly upon the excitation u_i of the neuron,

$$\nu_i = g(u_i) \qquad (1.72)$$

where $g(.)$ is usually taken as a sigmoidal function with $g(u) \to 0$ for $u \to -\infty$ and $g(u) \to 1$ for $u \to \infty$; see Figure 1.30. The excitation is given by a linear sum over all input connections

$$u_i = \sum_{j \in \Gamma_i} w_{ij} \nu_j \qquad (1.73)$$

where ν_j is the output rate of a presynaptic neuron j. The sum runs over all neurons which send signals to neuron i. The paprameter w_{ij}, called synaptic efficacy, is the weight attributed to the connection from j to i.

Equations (1.72) and (1.73) can be summarized in a single equation

$$\nu_i = g\left(\sum_{j \in \Gamma_i} w_{ij} \nu_j\right) \qquad (1.74)$$

46   1. Spiking Neurons

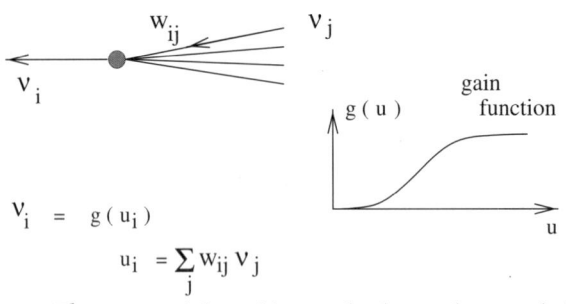

$$\nu_i = g(u_i)$$
$$u_i = \sum_j w_{ij}\nu_j$$

Figure 1.30. The rate model used in standard neural network theory.

which is the starting point of standard neural network theory [Hertz et al., 1991; Rojas, 1996; Haykin, 1994; Bishop, 1995].

Equation (1.74) is a static equation. It applies to situations where a stationary input (a set of firing rates ν_j) is mapped to a stationary output (the rate ν_i). Is it possible to make the equation time-dependent? A straightforward way to introduce dynamics into the rate equation (1.74) is to replace (1.74) by a differential equation [Cowan, 1968]

$$\tau \frac{d\nu_i}{dt} = -\nu_i + g\left(\sum_{j \in \Gamma_i} w_{ij}\nu_j\right) \quad (1.75)$$

with some time constant τ. For stationary input and output, the left-hand side of (1.75) vanishes and (1.75) reduces to (1.74). In other words, the fixed-point solutions of (1.75) are given by (1.74).

Equation (1.75) provides a convenient way to introduce some time dependence in the rate model (1.74), but can it be considered a realistic description of neuronal activity? As we have discussed in Section 1.1.2, an analog variable defined by a spike count measure requires a long temporal averaging window. It can therefore be used only if the input and the output change on a slow time scale. Considering the fact that, for example, the visual input changes due to saccades every 200-500 ms, a slowly changing input can not always be assumed.

It has therefore been argued that the rate equation (1.75) refers to a population average rather than to a temporal average. To make this clear in our notation, we rewrite (1.75) as

$$\tau \frac{dA_k}{dt} = -A_k + g\left(\sum_l J_{kl} A_l\right) \quad (1.76)$$

where A_k is the activity of a population k and the sum in the brackets runs over all other populations l which send signals to k. Again we may ask the question, whether (1.76) can be considered a realistic description of the population dynamics. More specifically, what determines the time constant τ which limits the response time of the system? Is it given by the membrane time constant of a neuron? It τ really a constant or does it depend on the input or activity of the system?

We will see later in the Chapter 10 on population dynamics that the population activity of a group of spiking model neurons can react instantaneously to changes in the input. This suggests that the 'time constant' τ in (1.76) is, at least in some cases, extremely short. The theory of population dynamics in Chapter 10 does not make use of the differential equation (1.76), but works in a more general setting.

We are now at the end of our review of neuron models. We will return to conductance based models and compartmental models in the context of hardware implementations in Chapters 5 and 6. Most of the other chapters will take one of the simple threshold-fire neurons as the computational unit of the neural network using either the integrate-and-fire neuron or the Spike Response Model. As we have seen, the two formulations are roughly equivalent. In the following chapter, we will study the computational capabilities of simple networks of spiking neurons. For this purpose a formulation with response kernels turns out to be most appropriate.

1.3 Conclusions

How do neurons encode information in a sequence of pulses? Even though it is a fundamental question the problem of neural coding is still not fully resolved. In this chapter, we have reviewed three concepts of rate codes, viz. spike count over some time window, spike density in a histogram, and population activity in an ensemble of neurons. All three concepts have been successfully used in experimental data analysis, but may be criticized on principal grounds. A constructive critic of rate codes may come from a presentation of some candidate pulse codes, if their usefulness in terms of computational power or ease of implementation can be shown. This endeavor is the program of the book.

We have seen that it is often difficult to draw a clear border line between pulse and rate codes. Whatever the name of the code, it should offer a neural system the possibility to react quickly to changes in the input. This seems to be a minimum requirement if fast behavioral reaction times are to be accounted for.

If pulse coding is relevant, neural network theory must be based on spiking neurons. Several pulsed neuron models have been reviewed in this chapter. Conductance based neurons models operate on a detailed level of description. If we want to investigate nonlinear interactions on the dendrite, conductance based neuron models are a suitable level of description.

The classic example of a conductance based neuron model is the Hodgkin-Huxley model. We have seen that the Hodgkin-Huxley model can be approximated by the Spike Response Model, if we use a suitable set of response kernels. This suggests that models in the class of threshold-fire models probably capture some important features of spiking neurons. Most of the theoretical investigations in chapters 10-14 will make use of this model class and use either the integrate-and-fire formulation or the formalism of the Spike Response Model.

References

[Abbott, 1991] Abbott, L. F. (1991). Realistic synaptic inputs for model neural networks. *Network*, 2:245–258.

[Abbott et al., 1991] Abbott, L. F., Fahri, E., and Gutmann, S. (1991). The path integral for dendritic trees. *Biol. Cybern.*, 66:49–60.

[Abbott and Kepler, 1990] Abbott, L. F., and Kepler, T. B. (1990). Model neurons: from Hodgkin-Huxley to Hopfield. *Statistical Mechanics of Neural Networks*. L. Garrido, ed., Springer, Berlin.

[Abeles, 1991] Abeles, M. (1991). *Corticonics*. Cambridge University Press, Cambridge.

[Abeles, 1994] Abeles, M. (1994). Firing rates and well-timed events. *Models of Neural Networks 2*, E. Domany, K. Schulten, and J. L. van Hemmen, eds., Springer, New York, chapter 3, 121–140.

[Abeles et al., 1993] Abeles, M., Bergman H., Margalit E., and Vaadia, E. (1993). Spatiotemporal firing patterns in the frontal cortex of behaving monkeys. *J. of Neurophysiology*, 70:1629–1638.

[Adrian, 1926] Adrian, E. D. (1926). The impulses produced by sensory nerve endings. *J. Physiol. (London)*, 61:49–72.

[Adrian, 1928] Adrian, E. D. (1928). *The Basis of Sensation*. W. W. Norton, New York.

[Aertsen, 1993] Aertsen, A., and Arndt, M. (1993). Response synchronization in the visual cortex. *Current Opinion in Neurobiology*, 3:586–594.

[Bernander et al., 1991] Bernander, Ö., Douglas, R. J., Martin, K. A. C., and Koch C. (1991). Synaptic background activity influences spatiotemporal integration in single pyramidal cells. *Proc. Natl. Acad. Sci. USA*, 88:11569–11573.

[Bialek et al., 1991] Bialek, W., Rieke, F., de Ruyter van Stevenick, R. R., and Warland, D. (1991). Reading a neural code. *Science*, 252:1854–1857.

[Bialek and Rieke, 1992] Bialek, W., and Rieke, F. (1992). Reliability and information transmission in spiking neurons. *Trends in Neurosciences*, 15(11):428–433.

[Bishop, 1995] Bishop, C. M. (1995). *Neural Networks for Pattern Recognition*. Clarendon Press, Oxford.

[Bower, 1995] Bower, J. M., and Beeman, D. (1995). *The Book of Genesis*. Springer, New York.

[Bressloff and Taylor, 1993] Bressloff, P. C., and Taylor, J. G. (1993). Compartmental-model response function for dendritic trees. *Biol. Cybern.*, 70:199–207.

[Bush and Douglas, 1991] Bush, R. C., and Douglas, R. J. (1991). Synchronization of bursting action potential discharge in a model network of neocortical neurons. *Neural Computation*, 3:19–30.

[Cowan, 1968] Cowan, J. D. (1968). Statistical Mechanics of Nervous Nets. *Proc. 1967 NATO conference on Neural Networks*, Springer, Berlin.

[de Ruyter van Stevenick and Bialek, 1988] de Ruyter van Stevenick, R. R., and Bialek, W. (1988). Real-time performance of a movement-sensitive neuron in the blowfly visual system: coding and information transfer in short spike sequences. *Proc. R. Soc. B*, 234:379–414.

[deCharms and Merzenich, 1996] deCharms, R. C., and Merzenich, M. M. (1996). Primary cortical representation of sounds by the coordination of action-potential timing. *Nature*, 381:610–613.

[DeAngelis et al., 1995] DeAngelis, G. C., Ohzwaw I., and Freeman, R. D. (1995). Receptive-field dynamics in the central visual pathways. *Trends in Neurosci.*, 18:451–458.

[Eckhorn et al., 1988] Eckhorn, R., Bauer, R., Jordan, W., Brosch, M., Kruse, W., Munk, M., and Reitboeck, H. J. (1988). Coherent oscillations: A mechanism of feature linking in the visual cortex? *Biol. Cybern.*, 60:121–130.

[Eckhorn et al., 1993] Eckhorn, R., Krause, F., and Nelson, J. L. (1993). The rf-cinematogram: a cross-correlation technique for mapping several visual fields at once. *Biol. Cybern.*, 69:37–55.

[Eckhorn et al., 1990] Eckhorn, R., Reitboeck, H. J., Arndt, M., and Dicke, P. (1990). Feature linking via synchronization among distributed assemblies: Simulations of results from cat visual cortex. *Neural Computation*, 2:293–307.

[Ekeberg et al., 1991] Ekeberg, O., Wallen, O., Lansner, A., Traven H., Brodin, L., and Grillner, S. (1991). A computer based model for realistic simulations of neural networks. *Biol. Cybern.*, 65:81–90.

[Engel et al., 1991a] Engel, A. K., König, P., and Singer, W. (1991). Direct physiological evidence for scene segmentation by temporal coding. *Proc. Natl. Acad. Sci. USA*, 88:9136–9140.

[Engel et al., 1991b] Engel, A. K., König, P., Kreiter, A. K., and Singer, W. (1991). Interhemispheric synchronization of oscillatory neural responses in cat visual cortex. *Science*, 252:1177–1179.

[FitzHugh, 1961] FitzHugh, R. (1961). Impulses and physiological states in models of nerve membrane. *Biophys. J.*, 1:445–466.

[Georgopoulos et al., 1986] Georgopoulos, A. P., Schwartz, A., and Kettner, R. E. (1986). Neuronal population coding of movement direction. *Science*, 233:1416–1419.

[Gerstner, 1991] Gerstner, W. (1991) Associative memory in a network of 'biological' neurons. *Advances in Neural Information Processing Systems, vol. 3*, Morgan Kaufmann Publishers, San Mateo, CA, 84–90.

[Gerstner and van Hemmen, 1992] Gerstner, W., and van Hemmen, J. L. (1992). Associative memory in a network of 'spiking' neurons. *Network*, 3:139–164.

[Gerstner et al., 1993] Gerstner, W., Ritz, R., and van Hemmen, J. L. (1993). A biologically motivated and analytically soluble model of collective oscillations in the cortex: I. theory of weak locking. *Biol. Cybern.*, 68:363–374.

[Gerstner and van Hemmen, 1994] Gerstner, W., and van Hemmen, J. L. (1994). Coding and information processing in neural networks. *Models of neural networks II*, E. Domany, J. L. van Hemmen, and K. Schulten, eds., Springer-Verlag, New York, 1–93.

[Gerstner et al., 1996] Gerstner, W., van Hemmen, J. L., and Cowan, J. D. (1996). What matters in neuronal locking. *Neural Computation*, 8:1689–1712.

[Gray and Singer, 1989] Gray, C. M., and Singer, W. (1989). Stimulus-specific neuronal oscillations in orientation columns of cat visual cortex. *Proc. Natl. Acad. Sci. USA*, 86:1698–1702.

[Gray et al., 1989b] Gray, C. M., König, P., Engel, A. K., and Singer, W. (1989). Oscillatory responses in cat visual cortex exhibit intercolumnar synchronization which reflects global stimulus properties. *Nature*, 338:334–337.

[Haykin, 1994] Haykin, S. (1994). *Neural Networks*. Prentice Hall, Upper Saddle River, NJ.

[Hertz et al., 1991] Hertz, J., Krogh, A., and Palmer, R. G. (1991). *Introduction to the Theory of Neural Computation*. Addison-Wesley, Redwood City CA.

[Hodgkin and Huxley, 1952] Hodgkin, A. L., and Huxley, A. F. (1952). A quantitative description of ion currents and its applications to conduction and excitation in nerve membranes. *J. Physiol. (London)*, 117:500–544.

[Hopfield, 1995] Hopfield, J. J. (1995). Pattern recognition computation using action potential timing for stimulus representation. *Nature*, 376:33–36.

[Hopfield and Herz, 1995] Hopfield, J. J., and Herz, A. V. M. (1995). Rapid local synchronization of action potentials: towards computation with coupled integrate-and-fire networks. *Proc. Natl. Acad. Sci. USA*, 92:6655.

[Hubel and Wiesel, 1959] Hubel, D. H. and Wiesel, T. N. (1959). Receptive fields of single neurons in the cat's striate cortex. *J. Physiol.*, 148:574–591.

[Hubel and Wiesel, 1962] Hubel, D. H., and Wiesel, T. N. (1962). Receptive fields, binocular interaction and functional architecture in the cat's visual cortex. *J. Physiol. (London)*, 160:106–154.

[Hubel and Wiesel, 1977] Hubel, D. H., and Wiesel, T. N. (1977). Functional architecture of macaque monkey visual cortex. *Proc. R. Soc. B*, 198:1–59.

[Hubel, 1988] Hubel, D. H. (1988). *Eye, Brain, and Vision*. W. H. Freeman, New York.

[Jack et al., 1975] Jack, J. J. B., Noble, D., and Tsien, R. W. (1975). *Electric Current Flow in Excitable Cells*. Clarendon Press, Oxford.

[Jensen and Lisman, 1996] Jensen, O., and Lisman, J. E. (1996). Hippocampal ca3 region predicts memory sequences: accounting for the phase precession of place cells. *Learning and Memory*, 3:279–287.

[O'Keefe and Recce, 1993] O'Keefe, J. and Recce, M. (1993). Phase relationship between hippocampal place units and the hippocampal theta rhythm. *Hippocampus*, 3:317–330.

[Kandel and Schwartz, 1991] Kandel, E. C., and Schwartz, J. H. (1991). *Principles of Neural Science*. Elsevier, New York, 3rd edition.

[Kistler et al., 1997] Kistler, W., Gerstner, W., and van Hemmen, J. L. (1997). Reduction of Hodgkin-Huxley equations to a single-variable threshold model. *Neural Computation*, 9:1015–1045.

[Kjaer et al., 1994] Kjaer, T. W., Hertz, J. A., and Richmond, B. J. (1994). Decoding cortical neuronal signals: network models, information estimation and spatial tuning. *J. Comput. Neuroscience*, 1:109–139.

[Koch et al., 1995] Koch, C., Bernander, Ö., and Douglas, R. J. (1995). Do neurons have a voltage or a current threshold for action potential initiation? *J. Comput. Neurosci.*, 2:63–82.

[Koch and Segev, 1989] Koch, C., and Segev, I. (1989). *Methods in Neuronal Modeling*. MIT Press.

[König and Schillen, 1991] König, P. and Schillen, T. B. (1991). Stimulus-dependent assembly formation of oscillatory responses: I. synchronization. *Neural Computation*, 3:155–166.

[Kreiter and Singer, 1992] Kreiter, A. K., and Singer, W. (1992). Oscillatory neuronal responses in the visual cortex of the awake macaque monkey. *Eur. J. Neurosci.*, 4:369–375.

[Lestienne, 1996] Lestienne, R. (1996). Determination of the precision of spike timing in the visual cortex of anaesthetised cats. *Biol. Cybern.*, 74:55–61.

[Maass, 1996] Maass, W. (1996). Lower bounds for the computational power of spiking neurons. *Neural Computation*, 8:1–40.

[Milner, 1974] Milner, P. M. (1974). A model for visual shape recognition. *Psychol. Rev.*, 81:521–535.

[Mountcastle, 19957] Mountcastle, V. B. (1957). Modality and topographic properties of single neurons of cat's somatosensory cortex. *J. Neurophysiol.*, 20:408–434.

[Nagumo et al., 1962] Nagumo, J., Arimoto, S., and Yoshizawa, S. (1962). An active pulse transmission line simulating nerve axon. *Proc. Institute of Radio Engineers (IRE)*, 50:2061–2070.

[Optican and Richmond, 1987] Optican, L. M., and Richmond, B. J. (1987). Temporal encoding of two-dimensional patterns by single units in primate inferior temporal cortex. 3. Information theoretic analysis. *J. Neurophysiol.*, 57:162–178.

[Rall, 1964] Rall, W. (1964). Theoretical significance of dendritic trees for neuronal input–output relations. *Neural Theory and Modeling*, R. F. Reiss, ed., Stanford University Press, Stanford CA, 73–97.

[Rall, 1989] Rall, W., (1989). Cable theory for dendritic neurons. *Methods in Neuronal Modeling*, C. Koch and I. Segev, eds., MIT Press, Cambridge, 9–62.

[Rapp et al., 1992] Rapp, M., Yarom, Y., and Segev, I. (1992). The impact of parallel fiber background activity in the cable properties of cerebellar purkinje cells. *Neural Computation*, 4:518–533, 1992.

[Rieke et al., 1996] Rieke, F., Warland, D., de Ruyter van Steveninck, R., and Bialek, W. (1996). *Spikes - Exploring the Neural Code*. MIT Press, Cambridge, MA.

[Rinzel and Ermentrout, 1989] Rinzel, J., and Ermentrout, B. B. (1989). Analysis of neural excitability and oscillations. *Methods in Neuronal Modeling*, C. Koch and I. Segev, eds., MIT Press, Cambridge, 135–169.

[Ritz et al., 1994] Ritz, R., Gerstner, W., and van Hemmen, J. L. (1994). A biologically motivated and analytically soluble model of collective oscillations in the cortex: II. Application to binding and pattern segmentation. *Biol. Cybern.*, 71:349–358.

[Ritz and Sejnowski, 1997] Ritz, R. and Sejnowski, T. J. (1997). Synchronous oscillatory activity in sensory systems: new vistas on mechanisms. *Current Opinion in Neurobiology*, 7:536–546.

[Rojas, 1996] Rojas, R. (1996). *Neural Networks: A Aystematic Introduction*. Springer, Berlin, Heidelberg.

[Schillen and König, 1991] Schillen, T. B., and König, P. (1991). Stimulus–dependent assembly formation of oscillatory responses: Ii. desynchronization. *Neural Computation*, 3:167–178.

[Shadlen and Newsome, 1994] Shadlen, M. N., and Newsome, W. T. (1994). Noise, neural codes and cortical organization. *Current Opininon in Neurobiology*, 4:569–579.

[Singer, 1994] Singer, W. (1994). *Models of Neural Networks 2*, Springer, Berlin Heidelberg New York, 141–173.

[Softky, 1995] Softky, W. R. (1995). Simple codes versus efficient codes. *Current Opinion in Neurobiology*, 5:239–247.

[Terman and Wang, 1995] Terman, D., and Wang, D. (1995). Global competition and local cooperation in a network of neural oscillators. *Physica D*, 81:148–176.

[Theunissen and Miller, 1995] Theunissen, F., and Miller, J. P. (1995). Temporal encoding in nervous systems: a rigorous definition. *J. Comput. Neurosci,*, 2:149–162.

[Thorpe et al., 1996] Thorpe, S., Fize, D., and Marlot, C. (1996). Speed of processing in the human visual system. *Nature*, 381:520–522.

[Tovee et al., 1993] Tovee, M. J., Rolls, E. T., Treves, A., and Belles, R. P. (1993). Information encoding and the responses of single neurons in the primate visual cortex. *J. Neurophysiol.*, 70:640–654.

[Tovee and Rolls, 1995] Tovee, M. J., and Rolls, E. T. (1995). Information encoding in short firing rate epochs by single neurons in the primate temporal visual cortex. *Visual Cognition*, 2(1):35–58.

[Traub et al., 1991] Traub, R. D., Wong, R. K. S., Miles, R., and Michelson, H. (1991). A model of a CA3 hippocampal pyramidal neuron incorporating voltage-clamp data on intrinsic conductances. *J. Neurophysiol.*, 66:635–650.

[Tsodyks and Sejnowski, 1995] Tsodyks, M. V., and Sejnowski, T. (1995). Rapid state switching in balanced cortical networks. *Network*, 6:111–124.

[Tuckwell, 1988a] Tuckwell, H. C. (1988). *Introduction to Theoretic Neurobiology*, volume 1, Cambridge Univ. Press, Cambridge.

[Tuckwell, 1988b] Tuckwell, H. C. (1988). *Introduction to Theoretic Neurobiology*, volume 2, Cambridge Univ. Press, Cambridge.

[Vreeswijk and Sompolinsky, 1997] van Vreeswijk, C., and Sompolinsky, H. (1997). Irregular firing in cortical circuits with inhibition/excitation balance. *Computational Neuroscience: Trends in Research, 1997*, J. Bower, ed., Plenum Press, New York, 209–213.

[von der Malsburg, 1981] von der Malsburg, C. (1981). The correlation theory of brain function. *Internal Report 81-2 of the Dept. of Neurobiology of the Max Planck Institute for Biophysical Chemistry in Göttingen*, Germany. Reprinted in *Models of Neural Networks II*, Domany et al., eds., Springer, 1994, 95–119.

[von der Malsburg and Buhmann, 1992] von der Malsburg, C., and Buhmann, J. (1992). Sensory segmentation with coupled neural oscillators. *Biol. Cybern.*, 67:233–242.

[Wang, 1995] D. Wang, D. (1995). Emergent synchrony in locally coupled neural oscillators. *IEEE Transactions on Neural Networks*, 6:941–948.

[Wang et al., 1990] Wang, D., Buhmann, J., and von der Malsburg, C. (1990). Pattern segmentation in associative memory. *Neural Computation*, 2:94–106.

[Wilson, et al., 1989] Wilson, M. A., Bhalla, U. S., Uhley, J. D., and Bower, J. M. (1989). Genesis: A system for simulating neural networks. In *Advances in Neural Information Processing Systems, vol. 1*, Morgan Kaufmann Publishers, San Mateo, CA, 485–492.

[Yamada et al., 1989] Yamada, W. M., Koch, C., and Adams, P. R. (1989). Multiple channels and calcium dynamics. *Methods in neuronal modeling, from synapses to networks*, C. Koch and I. Segev, eds., MIT Press, Cambridge.

2 Computing with Spiking Neurons

Wolfgang Maass

2.1 Introduction

In the preceding chapter a number of mathematical models for spiking neurons were introduced. Spiking neurons differ in essential aspects from the familiar computational units of common neural network models, such as McCulloch-Pitts neurons or sigmoidal gates. Therefore the question arises how one can *compute* with spiking neurons, or with related computational units in electronic hardware whose input and output consists of trains of pulses. Furthermore the question arises how the computational power of networks of such units relates to that of common reference models, such as threshold circuits or multi-layer perceptrons. Both of these questions will be addressed in this chapter.

2.2 A Formal Computational Model for a Network of Spiking Neurons

Our analysis will be based on the simplest one of the neuron models introduced in Chapter 1: the simple spiking neuron model defined in section 1.2.1. This simple version of a spiking neuron model has the advantage that it is relatively easy to analyze theoretically. On the other hand computer simulations (see e.g. [Maass and Natschläger, 1997]) have shown that various algorithms developed for this simple model carry over to the more complex Hodgin-Huxley model discussed in Section 1.2.4.1 of Chapter 1.

For the sake of completeness we quickly review the definition of the simple spiking neuron model from Section 1.2.1 in Chapter 1. Let I be a set of neurons, and assume that one has specified for each neuron $i \in I$ a set $\Gamma_i \subseteq I$ of immediate predecessors ("presynaptic neurons") in the network. The firing times $t_i^{(f)} \in \mathcal{F}_i$ for all neurons $i \in I$ are defined recursively (by simultaneous recursion along the time axis). According to equation (1.12) in Chapter 1 the neuron i fires whenever the state variable

$$u_i(t) = \sum_{t_i^{(f)} \in \mathcal{F}_i} \eta_i(t - t_i^{(f)}) + \sum_{j \in \Gamma_i} \sum_{t_j^{(f)} \in \mathcal{F}_j} w_{ij}\, \epsilon_{ij}(t - t_j^{(f)}) \qquad (2.1)$$

reaches the firing threshold ϑ of neuron i.

The response functions $\epsilon_{ij}(t - t_j^{(f)})$ model excitatory or inhibitory postsynaptic potentials (EPSP's and IPSP's, see Figure 2.1) at the soma of neuron i, which result from the firing of a presynaptic neuron j at time $t_j^{(f)}$. We will

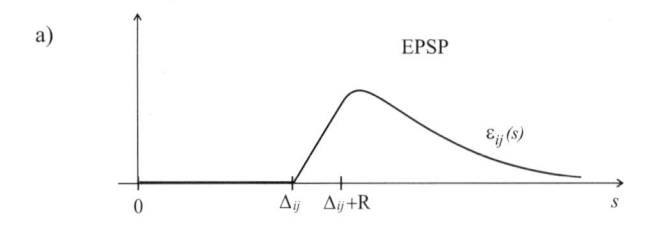

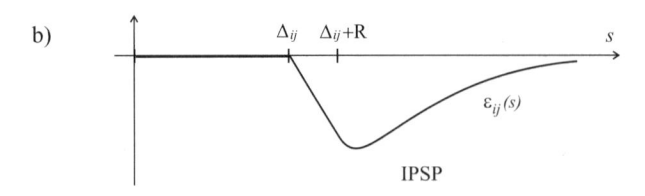

Figure 2.1. a) Typical shape of an excitatory postsynaptic potential (EPSP). b) Typical shape of an inhibitory postsynaptic potential (IPSP).

focus in the first part of this chapter on the case where the neuron i has not fired for a while, in which case the first summand with the refractory terms $\eta_i(t - t_i^{(f)})$ in (2.1) can be ignored.

In order to complete the definition of a network of spiking neurons as a formal computational model one has to specify its network input and output. We assume that subsets of neurons $I_{input} \subseteq I$ and $I_{output} \subseteq I$ have been fixed, and that the firing times $\mathcal{F}_i$ for the neurons $i \in I_{input}$ constitute the network input. Thus we assume that these firing times are determined through some external mechanism, rather than computed according to the previously described rules. The firing times $\mathcal{F}_i$ of the neurons $i \in I_{output}$ constitute the network output. These firing times are computed in the previously described way (like for all neurons $i \in I - I_{input}$) with the help of the state variable (2.1).

Thus from a mathematical point of view, a network of spiking neurons computes a function which maps a vector of several time series $\langle \mathcal{F}_i \rangle_{i \in I_{input}}$ on a vector of several other time series $\langle \mathcal{F}_i \rangle_{i \in I_{output}}$. It has often been argued that the fact that network input and output are vectors of *time series*, rather than vectors of numbers as in conventional neural network models, is essential for understanding computation in *biological* neural systems. After all, a biological organism has to be able to respond very fast in an online fashion to a constantly changing environment. Since artificial versions of pulsed neural nets are in a similar manner well-suited for computing in the time series domain, this application area is of particular interest for the design of artificial pulsed neural nets. In this chapter we will be more modest and survey existing models and results for computing with batch input, i.e., for a static vector of analog values that is presented to the network through the input $\langle \mathcal{F}_i \rangle_{i \in I_{input}}$.

2.3 McCulloch-Pitts Neurons versus Spiking Neurons

The simplest computational unit of traditional neural network models is a *McCulloch-Pitts neuron*, also referred to as *threshold gate* or *perceptron*. A McCulloch-Pitts neuron i with real valued weights α_{ij} and threshold ϑ receives as input n binary or real valued numbers $x_1, \ldots, x_n$. Its output has the value

$$\begin{cases} 1, & \text{if } \sum_{j=1}^{n} \alpha_{ij} \cdot x_j \geq \vartheta \\ 0, & \text{otherwise} . \end{cases} \qquad (2.2)$$

In multilayer networks one usually considers a variation of the threshold gate to which we will refer as a *sigmoidal gate* in the following. The output of a sigmoidal gate is defined with the help of some non-decreasing continuous *activation function* $g : \mathbf{R} \to \mathbf{R}$ with bounded range as

$$g(\sum_{j=1}^{n} \alpha_{ij} \cdot x_j - \vartheta) . \qquad (2.3)$$

By using sigmoidal gates instead of threshold gates one can not only compute functions with analog output, but also increase the computational power of neural nets for computing functions with boolean output [Maass et al, 1991; DasGupta and Schnitger, 1996].

In the following we will compare the computational capabilitites of these two computational units of traditional neural network models with that of the model for a spiking neuron discussed in Chapter 1. One immediately sees that a spiking neuron i can in principle simulate any given threshold gate (2.2) with positive threshold ϑ for binary input. For that we assume that the response functions $\epsilon_{ij}(x)$ are all identical except for their sign (which we choose to be positive if $\alpha_{ij} > 0$ and negative if $\alpha_{ij} \leq 0$), and that all presynaptic neurons j which fire, fire at the same time $t_j = T_{input}$. In this case the spiking neuron i fires if and only if

$$\sum_{j \text{ fires at time } T_{input}} w_{ij} \cdot \epsilon_{ij} \geq \vartheta , \qquad (2.4)$$

where ϵ_{ij} is the extremal value of $\epsilon_{ij}(s)$ (i.e., $e_{ij} = \max_s e_{ij}(s)$ if $e_{ij}(s)$ represents an EPSP, $e_{ij} = \min_s e_{ij}(s)$ if $e_{ij}(s)$ respresents an IPSP), $w_{ij} \geq 0$ is the synaptic weight, and $\vartheta > 0$ is the firing threshold of neuron i, see Figure 2.2. Then for $w_{ij} := \alpha_{ij}/e_{ij}$ the spiking neuron i can simulate any given threshold gate defined by (2.2) if the input bits $x_1, \ldots, x_n$ are encoded by the firing or nonfiring of presynaptic neurons $j = 1, \ldots, n$ at a common time T_{input}, and if the output bit of the threshold gate is encoded by the firing or nonfiring of the spiking neuron i during the relevant time window.

A closer look shows that it is substantially more difficult to simulate in the same manner a *multi-layer* network of threshold gates (i.e., a threshold circuit) by a network of spiking neurons. The exact firing time of the previously discussed spiking neuron i depends on its concrete input $x_1, \ldots, x_n$.

58   2. Computing with Spiking Neurons

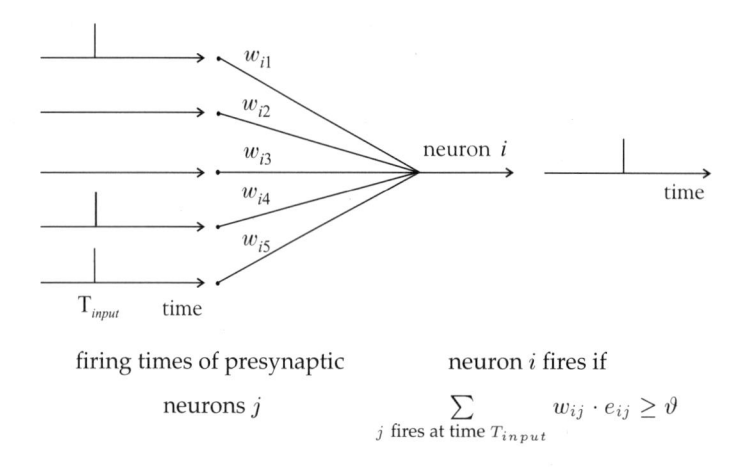

Figure 2.2. Simulation of a threshold gate by a spiking neuron.

If $\sum_{j \text{ fires at time } T_{input}} w_{ij} \cdot e_{ij} - \vartheta$ has a value well above 0, then the state variable $u_i(t) = \sum_{j \text{ fires at time } T_{input}} w_{ij} \cdot e_{ij}(t - T_{input})$ will cross the firing threshold ϑ earlier, yielding an *earlier* firing time of neuron i, compared with an input where $\sum_{j \text{ fires at time } T_{input}} w_{ij} \cdot e_{ij} - \vartheta$ is positive but close to 0. Therefore, if one employs several spiking neurons to simulate the threshold gates on the first layer[1] of a threshold circuit, those neurons on the first layer which do fire (corresponding to threshold gates with output 1) will in general fire at slightly different time points. This will occur even if all input neurons j of the network fired at the same time T_{input}. Therefore the timing of such straightforward simulation of a multi-layer threshold circuit is unstable: even if all firings in one layer occur synchronously, this synchronicity will in general get lost at the next layer. Similar problems arise in a simulation of other types of multi-layer boolean circuits by networks of spiking neurons.

Consequently one needs a separate *synchronization mechanism* in order to simulate a multi-layer boolean circuit – or any other common model for digital computation – by a network of spiking neurons with bits 1 and 0 encoded by firing and nonfiring. One can give a mathematically rigorous proof that such synchronization mechanism can in principle be provided by using some auxiliary spiking neurons [Maass, 1996]. This construction exploits the simple fact that the double-negation $\neg\neg b$ of a bit b has the same value as b. Therefore instead of making a spiking neuron i fire in the direct way described by equation (2.4), one can make sure that if $\sum_j \alpha_{ij} \cdot x_j \geq \vartheta$, then the spiking neuron i is *not prevented* from firing by auxiliary inhibitory neurons. These auxiliary inhibitory neurons are connected directly to the input neurons whose firing/nonfiring encodes the input bits $x_1, \ldots, x_n$, whereas the driving force for the firing of neuron i comes from input-independent excitatory neurons. With this method one

---
[1] We will not count the layer of input neurons in this chapter, and hence refer to the *first hidden layer* as the *first layer* of the network.

can simulate any given boolean circuit, and in the absence of noise even any Turing machine, by a finite network of spiking neurons [Maass, 1996] (we refer to [Judd and Aihara, 1993] for earlier work in this direction). On this basis one can also implement the constructions of [Valiant, 1994] in a network of spiking neurons.

Before we leave the issue of synchronization we would like to point out that in a practical context one can achieve a near-synchronization of firing times with the help of some common background excitation, for example an excitatory background oscillation $sin(\omega t)$ that is added to the membrane potential of all spiking neurons i [Hopfield, 1995]. With proper scaling of amplitudes and firing thresholds one can achieve that for all neurons i the state variable $u_i(t)$ can cross the firing threshold ϑ only when the background oscillation $sin(\omega t)$ is close to its peak. Thus it is no surprise that the strongest evidence for computations with digital coding occurs in those biological neural systems that have a strong oscillatory component, as for example in the olfactory system of the locust [Wehr and Laurent, 1996].

Our preceding discussion also points to a reason why it may be *less advantageous* for a network of spiking neurons to employ a forced synchronization. The small temporal differences in the firing times of the neurons i that simulate the first layer of a threshold circuit according to equation (2.4) contain valuable *additional information* that is destroyed by a forced synchronization: these temporal differences contain information about *how much* larger the weighted sum $\sum_j \alpha_{ij} \cdot x_j$ is compared with ϑ. Thus it appears to be advantageous for a network of spiking neurons to employ instead of a synchronized digital mode an asynchronous or loosely synchronized analog mode where subtle differences in firing times convey additional *analog* information. We will discuss in the next section computational operations which spiking neurons can execute in this quite different computational mode, where *analog* values are encoded in *temporal patterns* of firing times.

2.4 Computing with Temporal Patterns

2.4.1 Conincidence Detection

We will now consider the more typical scenario for a biological neuron, where preceding neurons do not fire in a synchronized manner, see Figure 2.3. In this case the computational operation of a spiking neuron cannot be easily described with the help of common computational operations or computational models.

We will show that in an asynchronous mode, with analog values encoded by a temporal pattern of firing times, a spiking neuron has in principle not only more computational power than a McCulloch-Pitts neuron, but also more computational power than a sigmoidal gate.

One new feature of a *spiking* neuron – which has no analog in the computational units of traditional neural network models – is that it can act as *coincidence detector* for incoming pulses [Abeles, 1982]. Hence if the arrival times of the incoming pulses encode *numbers*, a spiking neuron can

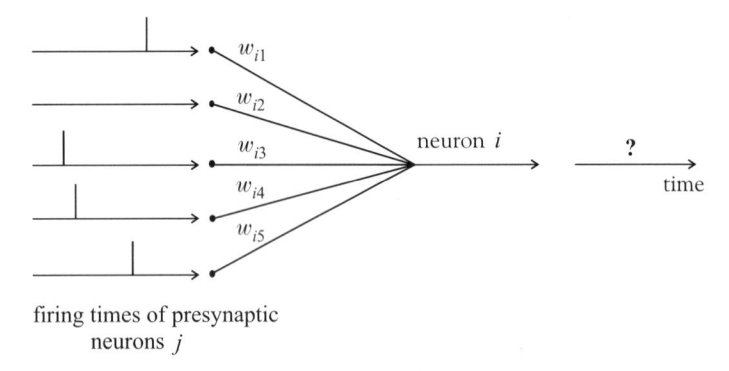

Figure 2.3. Typical input for a biological spiking neuron i, where its output cannot be easily described in terms of conventional computational units.

detect whether some of these numbers have (almost) equal value. On the other hand we will show below that this operation on numbers is a rather "expensive" computational operation from the point of view of traditional neural network models.

We will now make these statements more precise. Assume that $\{1,\ldots,n\} = \Gamma_i$ are the immediate predecessors of a spiking neuron i, that their connections to neuron i all have the same transmission delay Δ_{ij}, and that $w_{ij} = 1$ for all $j \in \Gamma_i$. Furthermore, assume that the response functions $\epsilon_{ij}(s)$ are defined as in equation (1.14) in Chapter 1 by

$$\epsilon_{ij}(s) = \frac{1}{1 - (\tau_s/\tau_m)} \left[\exp\left(-\frac{s - \Delta_{ij}}{\tau_m}\right) - \exp\left(-\frac{s - \Delta_{ij}}{\tau_s}\right) \right] \mathcal{H}(s - \Delta_{ij})$$

with time constants $0 < \tau_s < \tau_m$. A plot of an EPSP of such shape is shown in Figure 2.1a), see also Figure 1.10 b) and Figure 1.15 in Chapter 1. It consists of an almost linearly rising phase for small s, exponential decay for large s, and a smooth transition between both phases when it reaches its maximal value in between. For every given values of the time constants τ_s, τ_m with $\tau_s < \tau_m$ one can find values $0 < c_1 < c_2$ and ϑ so that $u_i(t) < \vartheta$ for any input consisting of an arbitrary number of EPSP's with distance $\geq c_2$, whereas $u_i(t)$ reaches a value $> \vartheta$ for two EPSP's in distance $\leq c_1$.

Then the spiking neuron i does not fire if the neurons $j \in \Gamma_i$ fire (each at most once) in temporal distance $\geq c_2$ (see Figure 2.4a)), but it fires whenever two presynaptic neurons $j \in \Gamma_i$ fire in temporal distance $\leq c_1$, see Figure 2.4.b)). Consequently, if for example one encodes n real numbers $x_1, \ldots, x_n$ through the firing times of the n neurons in Γ_i, and decodes the output of neuron i as "1" if it fires and "0" if it does not fire, the neuron i computes the following function $ED_n : \mathbf{R}^n \to \{0,1\}$:

$$ED_n(x_1, \ldots, x_n) = \begin{cases} 1 & , \text{ if there are } j \neq j' \text{ so that } |x_j - x_{j'}| \leq c_1 \\ 0 & , \text{ if } |x_j - x_{j'}| \geq c_2 \text{ for all } j \neq j' \end{cases}.$$

Note that this function $ED_n(x_1, \ldots, x_n)$ (where ED stands for "element distinctness") is in fact a partial function, which may output arbitrary val-

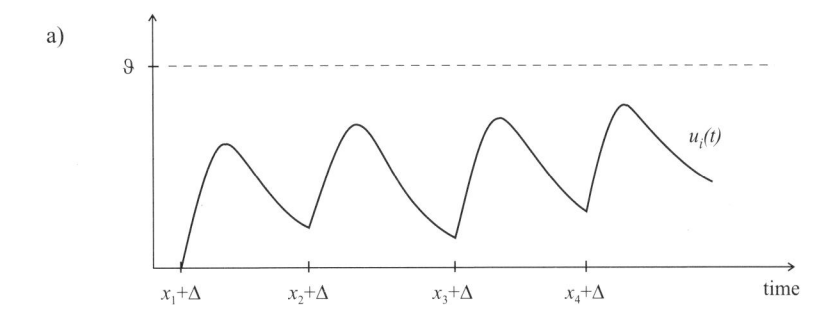

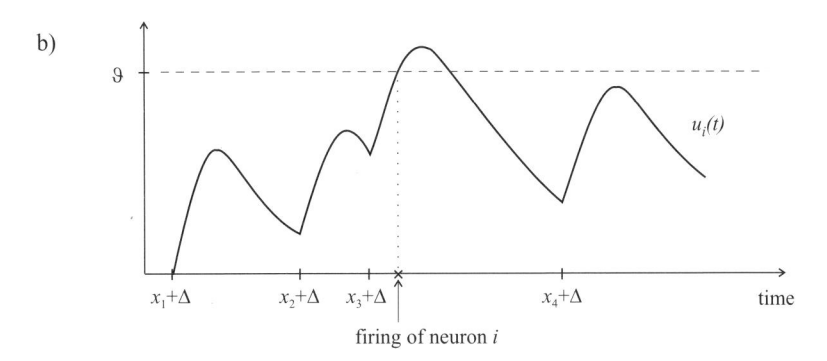

Figure 2.4. a) Typical time course of the state variable $u_i(t)$ if $ED_4(x_1, x_2, x_3, x_4) = 0$. b) Time course of $u_i(t)$ in the case where $ED_4(x_1, x_2, x_3, x_4) = 1$ because $|x_3 - x_2| \leq c_1$.

ues in case that $c_1 < \min\{|x_j - x_{j'}| : j \neq j' \text{ and } j, j' \in \Gamma_i\} < c_2$. Therefore hair-trigger situations can be avoided, and a single spiking neuron can compute this function ED_n even if there is a small amount of noise on its state variable $u_i(t)$.

On the other hand the following results show that the same partial function ED_n requires a substantial number of neurons if computed by neural networks consisting of McCulloch-Pitts neurons (threshold gates) or sigmoidal gates. These lower bounds hold for *arbitrary* feedforward architectures of the neural net, and *any values* of the weights and thresholds of the neurons. The inputs $x_1, \ldots, x_n$ are given to these neural nets in the usual manner as analog input variables.

Theorem 2.1 *Any layered threshold circuit that computes ED_n needs to have at least* $\log(n!) \geq \frac{n}{2} \cdot \log n$ *threshold gates on its first layer.*

The *proof* of Theorem 2.1 relies on a geometrical argument, see [Maass, 1997b].

Theorem 2.2 *Any feedforward neural net consisting of arbitrary sigmoidal gates needs to have at least $\frac{n-4}{2}$ gates in order to compute ED_n.*

The *proof* of Theorem 2.2 is more difficult, since the gates of a sigmoidal neural net (defined according to (2.3) with some smooth gain function g)

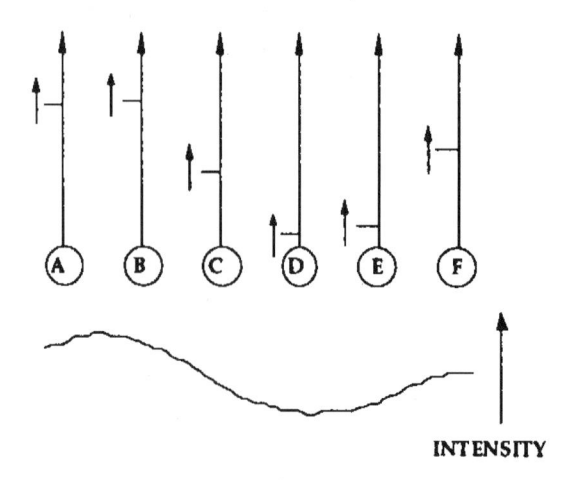

Figure 2.5. Coding by relative delay. Because of the intrinsic properties of neurons the most strongly activated neurons will fire first. Unit D has only just fired whereas the spike generated by unit A has already traveled a considerable distance along the afferent axon. From [Thorpe and Gautrais, 1997].

output *analog numbers* rather than *bits*. Therefore a multilayer circuit consisting of sigmoidal gates may have larger computational power than a circuit consisting of threshold gates. The proof procedes in an indirect fashion by showing that any sigmoidal neural net with m gates that computes ED_n can be transformed into another sigmoidal neural net that "shatters" *every* set of $n-1$ different inputs with the help of $m+1$ programmable parameters. According to [Sontag, 1997] this implies that $n-1 \leq 2(m+1)+1$. We refer to [Maass, 1997b] for further details. ∎

2.4.2 RBF-Units in the Temporal Domain

We have demonstrated in the preceding subsection that for some computational tasks a single spiking neuron has more computational power than a fairly large neural network of the conventional type. We will show in this subsection that the preceeding construction of a spiking neuron that detects coincidences among incoming pulses can be expanded to yield detectors for more complex temporal patterns.

Instead of a common delay Δ between presynaptic neurons $j \in \Gamma_i$ and neuron i (which appears in our formal model as the length of the initial flat part of the response function $\epsilon_{ij}(x)$) one can employ for different j *different* delays Δ_{ij} between neurons j and i. These delays Δ_{ij} represent a new set of parameters that have no counterpart in traditional neural network models[2]. There exists evidence that in some biological neural systems these delays Δ_{ij} can be tuned by "learning algorithms" (see Chapter 14). In addition one can tune the firing threshold ϑ and/or the weights w_{ij}

---

[2]Theoretical results about the Vapnik-Chervonenkis dimension (VC-dimension) of neural nets suggest that tuning of delays enhances the flexibility of spiking neurons for computations (i.e., the number of different functions they can compute) even more than tuning the weights [Maass and Schmitt, 1997].

of a spiking neuron to increase its ability to detect specific temporal patterns in the input. In the extreme case one can raise the firing threshold ϑ so high that *all* pulses from presynaptic neurons have to arrive nearly simultaneously at the soma of i to make it fire. In this case the spiking neuron can act in the temporal domain like an RBF-unit (i.e., radial basis function unit) in traditional neural network models: it will fire only if all presynaptic neurons $j \in \Gamma_i$ fire at times t_j so that for some constant T_{input} one has $t_j \approx T_{input} - \Delta_{ij}$ for all $j \in \Gamma_i$, where the vector $(\Delta_{ij})_{j \in \Gamma_i}$ of transmission delays plays now the role of the *center* of an RBF-unit. This possibility of using spiking neurons as RBF-like computational units in the temporal domain was first observed by Hopfield [Hopfield, 1995]. In the same article Hopfield demonstrates an advantageous consequence of employing a *logarithmic* encoding $x_j = \log y_j$ of external sensory input variables y_j through firing times $t_j = T_{input} - x_j$. Since spiking neurons have the ability to detect temporal patterns irrespective of a common additive constant in their arrival times, they can with the help of logarithmic encoding ignore constant *factors* λ in sensory input variables $\langle \lambda \cdot y_j \rangle_{j \in \Gamma_i}$. It has been argued that this useful mechanisms may be related to the amazing ability of biological organisms to classify patterns over a very large scale of intensities, such as for example visual patterns under drastically different lighting conditions.

In [Natschläger and Ruf, 1997] the previous construction of an RBF-unit for temporal patterns has been extended to a an RBF-network with the help of lateral inhibition between RBF-units (see Section 2.4.5). Alternatively one can add linear gates on the second layer of an RBF-network of spiking neurons with the help of the construction described in the following section.

2.4.3 Computing a Weighted Sum in Temporal Coding

A characteristic feature of the previously discussed computation of the function ED_n and the simulation of an RBF-unit is the *asymmetry* between coding schemes used for *input* and *output*. Whereas the input consisted of a vector of analog numbers, encoded through temporal delays, the output of the spiking neuron was just binary, encoded through firing or nonfiring of that neuron. Obviously for multilayer or recurrent computations with spiking neurons it is desirable to have mechanisms that enable a layer of spiking neurons to *output* a vector of analog numbers encoded in the same way as the input. For that purpose one needs mechanisms for *shifting* the firing time of a spiking neuron i in dependence of the firing times t_j of presynaptic neurons, in a manner that can be controlled through the internal parameters w_{ij} and Δ_{ij}. As an example for that we will now describe a simple mechanism for computing for arbitrary parameters $\alpha_{ij} \in \mathbf{R}$ and inputs $x_j \in [0, 1]$ the weighted sum $\sum_j \alpha_{ij} \cdot x_j$ through the firing time of neuron i.

We assume that each response function $\epsilon_{ij}(s)$ has a shape as shown in Figure 2.1: $e_{ij}(s)$ has value 0 for $s \leq \Delta_{ij}$ and then rises approximately lineary (in the case of an EPSP) or descends approximately lineary (in the case of an IPSP) with slope $\lambda_{ij} \in \mathbf{R}$ for an interval of length at least $R > 0$. Assume

64   2. Computing with Spiking Neurons

that the presynaptic neurons $j \in \Gamma_i$ fire at times $t_j = T_{input} - x_j$. If the state variable $u_i(t) = \sum_{j \in T_i} w_{ij} \cdot \epsilon_{ij}(t - t_j)$ of neuron i reaches the threshold ϑ at a time t_i when the response functions $\epsilon_{ij}(t - t_j)$ are all in their initial linear phase of length $\geq R$, then t_i is determined by the equation

$$\sum_{j \in \Gamma_i} w_{ij} \cdot \epsilon_{ij}(t_i - t_j) = \sum_{j \in \Gamma_i} w_{ij} \cdot \lambda_{ij} \cdot (t_i - t_j - \Delta_{ij}) = \vartheta \ . \tag{2.5}$$

Obviously (2.5) implies that

$$t_i = \frac{\vartheta}{\sum_{j \in \Gamma_i} w_{ij} \cdot \lambda_{ij}} + \frac{\sum_{j \in \Gamma_i} w_{ij} \cdot \lambda_{ij} \cdot (t_j + \Delta_{ij})}{\sum_{j \in \Gamma_i} w_{ij} \cdot \lambda_{ij}} \ . \tag{2.6}$$

Then by writing λ for $\sum_{j \in \Gamma_i} w_{ij} \cdot \lambda_{ij}$ and expressing t_j as $T_{input} - x_j$ we get

$$t_i = \frac{\vartheta}{\lambda} + \sum_{j \in \Gamma_i} \frac{w_{ij} \cdot \lambda_{ij}}{\lambda} \cdot (T_{input} - x_j + \Delta_{ij}) \ ,$$

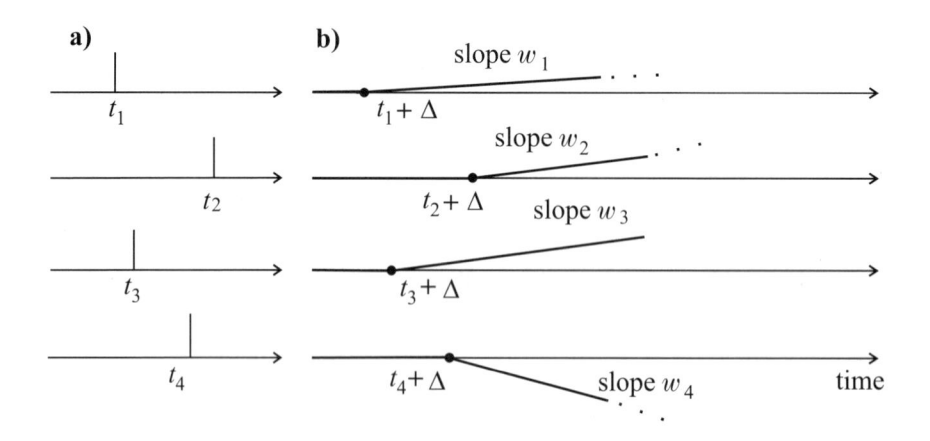

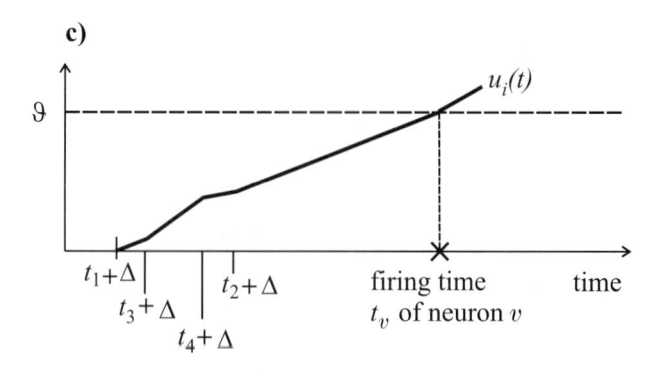

Figure 2.6. Mechanisms for computing a weighted sum in temporal coding according to equation (2.6). a) Firing times t_j of presynaptic neurons j. b) Initial linear segments of the weighted response functions $w_{ij} \cdot \epsilon_{ij}(t - t_j)$ at the soma of neuron i. c) State variable $u_i(t)$ and resulting firing time t_i of neuron i.

or equivalently

$$t_i = T_{output} - \sum_{j \in \Gamma_i} \alpha_{ij} \cdot x_j \qquad (2.7)$$

for some input-independent constant $T_{output} := \frac{\vartheta}{\lambda} + \sum_{j \in \Gamma_i} \frac{w_{ij} \cdot \lambda_{ij}}{\lambda}(T_{input} + \Delta_{ij})$, and formal "weights" α_{ij} defined by $\alpha_{ij} := \frac{w_{ij} \cdot \lambda_{ij}}{\lambda}$. These "weights" α_{ij} are automatically normalized: by the definition of λ they satisfy $\sum_{j \in \Gamma_i} \alpha_{ij} = 1$. Such automatic weight normalization may be desirable in some situations [Haefliger et al., 1997]. One can circumvent it by employing an auxiliary input neuron (see [Maass, 1997a]). In this way one can compute an arbitrary given weighted sum $\sum_{j \in T_i} \alpha_{ij} \cdot x_j$ in *temporal* coding by a *spiking* neuron. Note that in this construction the analog output $\sum_{j \in \Gamma_i} \alpha_{ij} \cdot x_j$ is encoded in exactly the same way as the analog inputs x_j.

2.4.4 Universal Approximation of Continuous Functions with Spiking Neurons

We will show in this subsection that on the basis of the computational mechanism described in the preceding subsection one can build networks of spiking neurons that can approximate arbitrary given bounded continuous functions in the temporal domain. We first observe that one can expand the previously described mechanism for computing a weighted sum $\sum_{j \in \Gamma_i} \alpha_{ij} \cdot x_j$ in the temporal domain to yield for *temporal coding* also a simulation of an arbitrary given sigmoidal neuron with the piecewise linear gain function

$$sat(x) = \begin{cases} x, & \text{if } 0 \leq x \leq 1 \\ 0, & \text{if } x \leq 0 \\ 1, & \text{if } x \geq 1 \end{cases}.$$

In this case we want that neuron i responds to firing of its presynaptic neurons at times $t_j = T_{input} - x_j$ by firing at time

$$t_i = T_{output} - sat(\sum_{j \in \Gamma_i} \alpha_{ij} \cdot x_j) \ .$$

For that purpose one just needs auxiliary mechanisms that support an approximation of the given sigmoidal neuron in the saturated regions of its gain function sat, i.e. for $x \leq 0$ and $x \geq 1$. Translated into the temporal domain this requires that the spiking neuron i does not fire before some fixed time T (simulating $sat(x) = 1$ for $x \geq 1$) and by the latest at some fixed time $T_{output} > T$ (simulating $sat(x) = 0$ for $x \leq 0$). This can easily be achieved with the help of auxiliary spiking neurons. Computer simulations suggest that in a practical situation such auxiliary neurons may not even be necessary [Maass and Natschläger, 1997].

According to the preceding construction one can simulate any sigmoidal neuron with the piecewise linear gain function *sat* by spiking neurons with analog inputs *and* outputs encoded by temporal delays of spikes. Since inputs and outputs employ the same coding scheme, the outputs from a first layer of spiking neurons (that simulate a first layer of sigmoidal gates) can be used as inputs for another layer of spiking neurons, simulating another layer of sigmoidal gates. Hence on the basis of the assumption that the initial segments of response functions $\epsilon_{ij}(s)$ are linear one can show with a rigorous mathematical proof [Maass, 1997a]:

Theorem 2.3 *Any feedforward or recurrent analog neural net (for example any multilayer perceptron), consisting of s sigmoidal neurons (where c is a small constant) that employ the gain function sat, can be simulated arbitrarily closely by a network of c spiking neurons with analog inputs and outputs encoded by temporal delays of spikes. This holds even if the spiking neurons are subject to noise.* ∎

Theorem 2.2 and 2.3 together exhibit an interesting *asymmetry* regarding the computational power of standard sigmoidal neural nets (multilayer perceptrons) and networks of spiking neurons: Whereas any sigmoidal neural net can be simulated by an insignificantly larger network of spiking neurons (with temporal coding), certain networks of spiking neurons can only be simulated by substantially larger sigmoidal neural nets.

It is wellknown that feedforward sigmoidal neural nets with gain function *sat* can approximate any given continuous function $F : [0,1]^n \to [0,1]^m$ with any desired degree of precision. Hence Theorem 2.3 implies:

Corollary 2.4 *Any given continuous function $F : [0,1]^n \to [0,1]^m$ can be approximated arbitrarily closely by a network of spiking neurons with inputs and outputs encoded by temporal delays.*

Remarks:

a) The construction that yields the proof of Theorem 2.3 shows that a network of spiking neurons can *change* the function: $F : [0,1]^n \to [0,1]^m$ that it computes in the same way as a traditional neural net: by changing the synaptic "weights" w_{ij} that scale the slopes of the initial segments of postsynaptic pulses. The delays Δ_{ij} between neurons need not be changed for that purpose (but they *could* be used to modulate the effective "weights" of the simulated sigmoidal neural net by additive constants). From that point of view this construction is complementary to the simulation of RBF-units by spiking neurons described in subsection 2.4.2: there the "program" of the encoded function was encoded exclusively in the delays Δ_{ij}.

b) It turns out that the network of spiking neurons constructed for the proof of Theorem 2.3 computes approximately the same function in rate-coding *and* in temporal coding.

2.4.5 Other Computations with Temporal Patterns in Networks of Spiking Neurons

The previously described method for emulating classical artificial neural networks in the temporal domain with spiking neurons can also be applied to Hopfield nets [Maass and Natschläger, 1997], Kohonen's self-organizing map [Ruf and Schmitt, 1997] and RBF-networks [Natschläger and Ruf, 1997]. The latter construction refines Hopfield's construction of an RBF-unit in the temporal domain. It simulates RBF-units by neurons that output an analog number (encoded in its firing time), rather than a single bit (encoded by firing/nonfiring). They implement a competition among different RBF-units through lateral inhibition. Furthermore they show through computer simulations that a variation of the Hebb-rule for spiking neurons with temporal coding that has been experimentally observed for biological neurons (see [Markram and Sakmann, 1995] and [Markram et al., 1997]), yields good performance for unsupervised learning of temporal input patterns. It is of interest for applications that their RBF-network also exhibits some robustness with regard to warping of temporal input patterns.

The theoretical results that support these simulations of classical neural networks by networks of spiking neurons with delay coding have been derived for the mathematically relatively simple spiking neuron model from Section 1.2.1 in Chapter 1. Computer simulations (employing the simulation system GENESIS described in [Bower and Beeman, 1995]) suggest that these results remain valid if one employs the mathematically more complex but biologically more realistic Hodgin-Huxley model from Section 1.2.4.1 as model for a spiking neuron ([Maass and Natschläger, 1997], [Natschläger and Ruf, 1997], [Ruf, 1997], [Ruf and Schmitt, 1997]). In fact, it is shown in [Maass and Natschläger, 1997] that often a simpler construction than the one needed for a rigorous mathematical verification yields already good performance. Furthermore it is shown that the length of the available time window for temporal coding (which is proportional to the parameter R from Section 2.4.3) can be enlarged by employing multiple synapses with different time delays (see Figure 2.7).

[Müller et al., 1996] suggest an alternative mechanism for simulating a sigmoidal gate by a spiking neuron with delay coding. This simulation employs effects that are reflected in the more complex Hodgkin-Huxley model (see Section 1.2.4.1), but not in the simple model for a spiking neuron. It exploits that in the case of excitatory input a *later* input spike raises the membrane potential by a *smaller* amount if earlier input spikes have moved the membrane potential already closer to the firing threshold (and thereby reduced the difference between the current membrane potential and the reversal potential for ion-channels that are relevant for these currents).

[Samuelides et al., 1997] have proposed yet another mechanism for classifying the *order* in which spikes arrive from different presynaptic neurons. This mechanism is based on a new type of synaptic dynamics that has so far not been observed in biological neural systems. The goal of their construction is that the output neurons of the net respond in a given way to the

68   2. Computing with Spiking Neurons

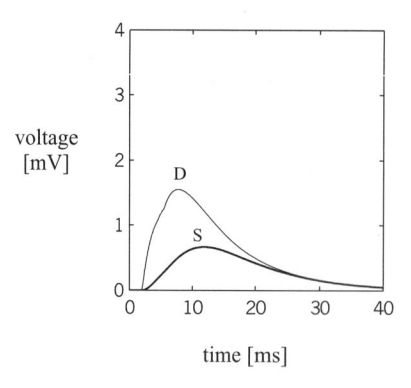

Figure 2.7. Superposition of several non-NMDA EPSP's caused by the firing of a single presynaptic neuron j which has three synapses with slightly different delays to the neuron i. The membrane voltage is measured at the dendrite (D) and at the soma (S) of neuron i in a computer simulation of the Hodgin-Huxley model (GENESIS). From [Maass and Natschläger, 1997].

firing *order* of the input neurons. This is a special case of the computations with spiking neurons considered in Sections 2.4.3 and 2.4.4. Obviously each firing order is naturally encoded in the vector $\underline{x}$ of delays of these spikes. Hence any classification task for spike orders can be viewed as a special case of a classification task for delay vectors $\underline{x}$. Theorem 2.3 shows that networks of spiking neurons can apply to this task the full classification power of multilayer perceptrons.

Finally we would like mention that [Watanabe and Aihara, 1997] have explored *chaos* in the temporal pattern of firing in a network of spiking neurons.

2.5 Computing with a Space-Rate Code

The second model for fast universal analog computation that we will discuss is more suitable for neural systems consisting of a large number of components which are not very reliable. In fact this model, which was recently developed in collaboration with Thomas Natschläger [Maass and Natschläger, 1998], *relies* on the assumption that individual synapses are "unreliable". It takes into account evidence from [Dobrunz and Stevens, 1997] and others, which shows that individual synaptic release sites are highly stochastic: they release a vesicle (filled with neurotransmitter) upon the arrival of a spike from the presynaptic neuron u with a certain probability (called *release probability*). This release probability varies among different synapses between values less than 0.1 and more than 0.9 (see Chapter 12).

This second model for fast universal analog computation is based on a space-rate encoding (also referred to as population coding, see section 1.1.2.3 in Chapter 1) of analog variables, i.e., an analog variable $x \in [0, 1]$ is encoded by the fraction of neurons in a population that fire within a short time window (say, of length 5 ms).

Although there exists substantial empirical evidence that many cortical systems encode relevant analog variables by such space-rate code, it has remained unclear how networks of spiking neurons can *compute* in terms of such a code. Some of the difficulties become apparent if one just wants to understand for example how the trivial linear function $f(x) = x/2$ can be computed by such a network if the input $x \in [0, 1]$ is encoded by a space-rate code in a pool U of neurons and the output $f(x) \in [0, 1/2]$ is supposed to be encoded by a space-rate code in another pool V of neurons. If one assumes that all neurons in V have the same firing threshold and that reliable synaptic connections from all neurons in U to all neurons in V exist with approximately equal weights, a firing of a percentage x of neurons in U during a short time interval will typically trigger *almost none* or *almost all* neurons in V to fire, since they all receive about the same input from U.

Several mechanisms have already been suggested that could in principle achieve a *smooth* graded response in terms of a space-rate code in V instead of a binary "all or none" firing, such as strongly varying firing thresholds or different numbers of synaptic connections from U for different neurons $v \in V$ [Wilson and Cowan, 1972]. Neither option is completely satisfactory, since firing thresholds of biological neurons appear to be rather homogeneous and a regulation of the response in V through the connectivity pattern would make it very difficult to implement changes of the gain through learning. Furthermore both of these options would fail to spread average activity over all neurons in V, and hence would make the computation less robust against failures of individual neurons.

We assume that n pools $U_1, \ldots, U_n$ consisting of N neurons each are given, and that all neurons in these pools have synaptic connections to all neurons in another pool V of N neurons.[3] We assume that for each pool U_j all neurons in U_j are excitatory, or all neurons in U_j are inhibitory. We will first investigate the question which functions $\langle x_1, \ldots, x_n \rangle \to y$ can be computed by such a network if x_j is the firing probability of each neuron in pool U_j during a short time interval I_{in} and y is the firing probability of each neuron in pool V during a slightly later time interval I_{out}.

In accordance with recent results from neurophysiology [Dobrunz and Stevens, 1997] we assume that an action potential ("spike") from a neuron $u \in U_j$ triggers with a certain probability r_{vu} ("release probability") the release of a vesicle filled with neurotransmitter at a release site of a synapse between neurons $u \in U_j$ and $v \in V$. The data from [Dobrunz and Stevens, 1997] strongly suggest that in the case of a release just one vesicle is released, but that in the case of a release the amplitude of the resulting EPSP in neuron v is stochastic. Consequently we model the amplitude of the EPSP (or IPSP) in the case of a release (i.e., the "potency" in the terminology of [Dobrunz and Stevens, 1997]) by a random variable a_{vu} with probability density function ϕ_{vu}. We will write $\bar{a}_{vu}$ for the mean amplitude $\int z \phi_{vu}(z) dz$ and $\hat{a}_{vu}$ for the second moment $\int z^2 \phi_{vu}(z) dz$.

Figure 2.8 shows the result of simulations of this model for $n = 8$ and $N = 200$, using compartmental model neurons according to chapter 15 of

---

[3]Our results remain valid if one considers instead connections by fixed random graphs with lower density between pools U_j and V.

70   2. Computing with Spiking Neurons

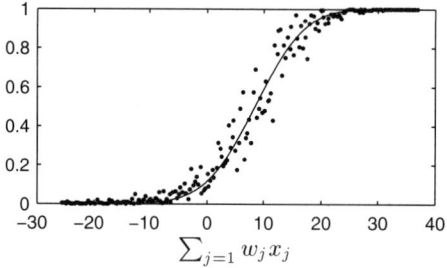

Figure 2.8. Each dot is the result of a GENESIS simulation of our model for $n = 8$, $N = 200$, $\langle w_1, \ldots, w_8 \rangle = \langle 5, -10, 14, 20, 18, -12, -10, -5 \rangle$. 200 inputs $\langle x_1, \ldots, x_8 \rangle$ were chosen randomly from $[0, 1]^8$ such that μ_v covers the range $[-20, 40]$ almost uniformly. The y-axis shows the fraction of neurons in pool V that fire during the interval I_{out}.

[Bower and Beeman, 1995]. The y-axis shows the fraction y of neurons in V that fire during a 5 ms time interval I_{out} in response to the firing of a fraction x_i of neurons in pool U_i during a 4 ms earlier time interval I_{in} of length 5 ms.

The x-axis shows the value of $\sum_{j=1}^{n} w_j x_j$, where $w_j = N \bar{a}_j r_j$, r_j is the average of the release probabilities r_{vu} for neurons $v \in V$ and $u \in U_j$, and $\bar{a}_j$ is the mean of the common amplitude distributions ϕ_{vu} for synapses between pools U_j and V. These simulations show that the output y given through the percentage of neurons in V that fire during a time interval I_{out} of length 5 ms approximates quite well the value $g(\sum_{j=1}^{n} w_j x_j)$ for a sigmoidal "activation function" g, see (2.1). Note that g has not been implemented explicitly in this set-up, but rather emerges *implicitly* through the large scale statistics of the firing activity – as will be explained in the next paragraphs.

We now consider an idealized mathematical model where the time intervals I_{in} and I_{out} are collapsed to two subsequent time points T_{in} and T_{out}, and the probability that a neuron $v \in V$ fires at time T_{out} can be described by the probability that the sum h_v of the amplitudes of EPSP's and IPSP's resulting from firing of neurons in presynaptic pools $U_1, \ldots, U_n$ exceeds at the trigger zone of v the firing threshold ϑ (which is assumed to be the same for all neurons $v \in V$).[4] This random variable h_v is the sum of random variables h_{vu} for all neurons $u \in \bigcup_{j=1}^{n} U_j$, where h_{vu} models the contribution of neuron u to h_v.

We assume that h_{vu} is nonzero only if neuron $u \in U_j$ fires at time T_{in} (which occurs with probability x_j) and the synapse between u and v releases a vesicle (which occurs with probability r_{vu} whenever u fires). If both events occur then the value of h_{vu} is chosen according to some probability density function $\phi_{vu}(z)$ that is nonzero only for positive z in the case of an excitatory synapse, and nonzero only for negative z in the case of an inhibitory synapse. For each neuron $v \in V$ we consider the sum $h_v = \sum_{j=1}^{n} \sum_{u \in U_j} h_{vu}$ of the random variables (r.v.'s) h_{vu} and we assume

---
[4]We assume here that the firing rates of neurons in pool V are relatively low, so that the impact of their refractory period can be neglected.

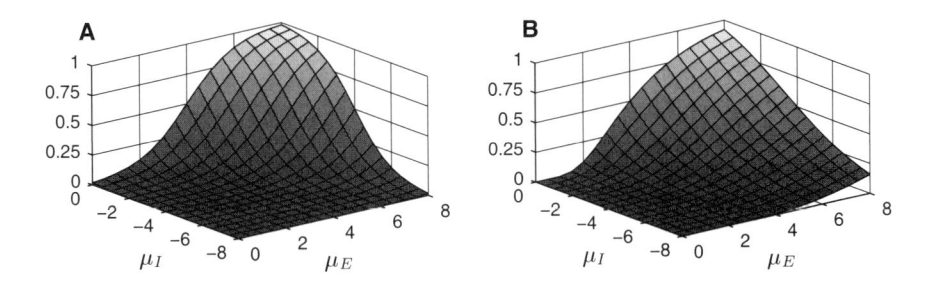

Figure 2.9. A) Plot of the function $\text{logsig}(\mu_E + \mu_I - \vartheta)$ with $\vartheta = 4$ where $\text{logsig}(z)$ is the logistic sigmoid function $1/(1 + \exp(-z))$. B) Plot of the function $1 - \Phi(\vartheta; \mu_E + \mu_I, \sqrt{|\mu_E| + |\mu_I|})$. Note that this function behaves qualitatively like $\text{logsig}(\mu_E + \mu_I - \vartheta)$.

that v fires at time T_{out} if and only if $h_v \geq \vartheta$ (where ϑ is the common firing threshold of all neurons $v \in V$). Although the r.v.'s h_{vu} have in general different distributions, their stochastic independence allows us to approximate the firing probability $P\{h_v \geq \vartheta\}$ through a normal distribution Φ. The Berry-Esseen Theorem [Petrov, 1995] implies that

$$|P\{h_v \geq \vartheta\} - (1 - \Phi(\vartheta; \mu_v, \sigma_v))| \leq 0.7915 \frac{\rho_v}{\sigma_v^3}, \tag{2.8}$$

where $\Phi(\vartheta; \mu_v, \sigma_v)$ denotes the probability that a normally distributed r.v. with mean μ_v and variance σ_v^2 has a value $< \vartheta$. In our case

$$\mu_v = \sum_{j=1}^{n} \sum_{u \in U_j} \text{E}[h_{vu}], \quad \sigma_v^2 = \sum_{j=1}^{n} \sum_{u \in U_j} \text{Var}[h_{vu}],$$

$$\text{and } \rho_v = \sum_{j=1}^{n} \sum_{u \in U_j} \text{E}\left[|h_{vu} - \text{E}[h_{vu}]|^3\right].$$

The right hand side of (2.8) scales like $N^{-1/2}$ if for all N the average value of the terms $\text{E}\left[|h_{vu} - \text{E}[h_{vu}]|^3\right]$ for $j \in \{1, \ldots, n\}$ and $u \in U_j$ is uniformly bounded from above and the average value of the terms $\text{Var}[h_{vu}]$ for $j \in \{1, \ldots, n\}$ and $u \in U_j$ is uniformly bounded from below by a constant > 0. According to the definition of the r.v. h_{vu} we have $\text{E}[h_{vu}] = x_j r_{vu} \bar{a}_{vu}$ and

$$\text{Var}[h_{vu}] = \text{E}[h_{vu}^2] - \text{E}[h_{vu}]^2 = x_j r_{vu} \hat{a}_{vu} - x_j^2 r_{vu}^2 \bar{a}_{vu}^2$$

for $u \in U_j$. Hence according to (2.8) the firing probability $y = P\{h_v \geq \vartheta\}$ of an arbitrary neuron v in pool V can be approximated by a smooth function of a weighted sum $\sum_{j=1}^{n} w_j x_j$ of the firing probabilities x_j in pools $U_1, \ldots, U_n$ if σ_v can also be approximated by a smooth function of $\sum_{j=1}^{n} w_j x_j$.

One can approximate σ_v by a smooth function of $\sum_{j=1}^{n} w_j x_j$ if r_{vu} and $\bar{a}_{vu}$ have common values $r_j, \bar{a}_j$ for all $v \in V$, $u \in U_j$ (which implies that

72   2. Computing with Spiking Neurons

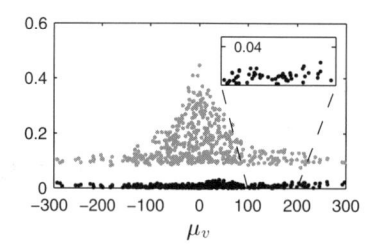

Figure 2.10. Comparison of the theoretical upper bound for the error in the approximation of $P\{h_v \geq \vartheta\}$ by (2.9) given by the Berry-Esseen Theorem, i.e. by the right hand side of (2.8) (gray dots), and the actual values (black dots) of the absolute values of their difference. We performed 1000 experiments with different randomly chosen parameters for the normal distributions of the r_{vu} and the uniform distributions of the a_{vu} for the set of synapses between any two pools U_j and V.

$r_j \bar{a}_j = w_j/|U_j| = w_j/N$), and if $\hat{a}_{vu} = \gamma \bar{a}_j$ with a common constant γ for all $j \in \{1,\ldots,n\}$, $u \in U_j$ and $v \in V$. According to (2.9) we can then write $\sigma_v^2 = \sum_{j=1}^n \sum_{u \in U_j} \text{Var}[h_{vu}] = \gamma \sum_{j=1}^n w_j x_j - \sum_{j=1}^n x_j^2 \sum_{u \in U_j} r_{vu}^2 \bar{a}_{vu}^2 = \gamma \sum_{j=1}^n w_j x_j - \sum_{j=1}^n x_j^2 N \left(\frac{w_j}{N}\right)^2$, which converges to $\gamma \sum_{j=1}^n w_j x_j$ for $N \to \infty$ if the weights w_j are bounded (or at least $w_j = o(N)$). Hence (2.8) implies that $y = P\{h_v \geq \vartheta\}$ can be approximated by a function of $\sum_{j=1}^n w_j x_j$ if N is sufficiently large, and at the same time the *release probabilities* r_{vu} are *sufficiently small* so that the *sum* $\sum_{u \in U_j} r_{vu} \bar{a}_{vu}$ has value w_j.

A complication arises if some of the "weights" w_j are positive and others are negative. Then $\mu_v = \mu_E + \mu_I$ for $\mu_E = \sum_{w_j > 0} w_j x_j$ and $\mu_I = \sum_{w_j < 0} w_j x_j$. It is then impossible to satisfy $\hat{a}_{vu} = \gamma \bar{a}_j$ with a common constant γ both for j with $w_j > 0$ (hence $\bar{a}_j > 0$) and $w_j < 0$ (hence $\bar{a}_j < 0$). However if $\hat{a}_{vu} = \gamma_E \bar{a}_j$ for all $u \in U_j$ with $w_j > 0$ and $\hat{a}_{vu} = \gamma_I \bar{a}_j$ for all $u \in U_j$ with $w_j < 0$, with two different constants $\gamma_E > 0$ and $\gamma_I < 0$, we can replace the term $1 - \Phi(\vartheta; \mu_v, \sigma_v)$ in (2.8) by

$$1 - \Phi\left(\vartheta; \mu_E + \mu_I, \sqrt{|\gamma_E \mu_E| + |\gamma_I \mu_I|}\right) . \tag{2.9}$$

This term does not just depend on $\mu_v = \mu_E + \mu_I$, but also on μ_E and μ_I. However Figure 2.9 shows that nevertheless the term (2.9) behaves qualitatively like a sigmoidal function of the single argument $\mu_v = \sum_{j=1}^n w_j x_j$. It is shown in Figure 2.10 that for the distributions we have considered the approximation of $P\{h_v \geq \vartheta\}$ by (2.9) is even better than guaranteed by (2.8).

The preceding arguments imply that an approximate computation of arbitrary functions of the form $\langle x_1, \ldots, x_n \rangle \to y = g(\sum_{j=1}^n w_j x_j)$, with inputs and output in space-rate code, can be carried out within 10 ms by a network of spiking neurons consisting of two layers. Hence according to the universal approximation theorem for multilayer perceptrons *arbitrary continuous functions* $f : [0,1]^n \to [0,1]^m$ can be approximated with a computation time of not more than 20 ms by a network of spiking neurons with 3 layers. An example of such a computation is shown in Figure 2.11.

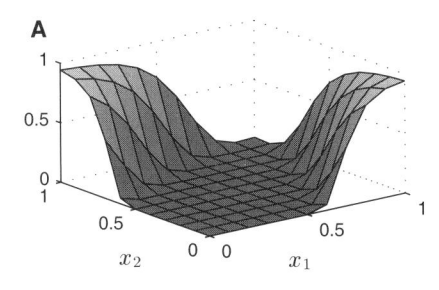

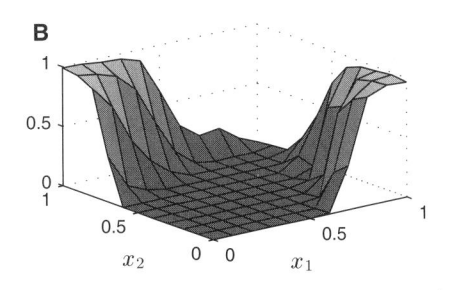

Figure 2.11. **A)** Plot of a function $f(x_1, x_2) : [0,1]^2 \to [0,1]$ which interpolates XOR. Hence f cannot be computed by a single sigmoid unit. **B)** Computation of f by a 3-layer network in space-rate coding with compartmental model neurons ($N = 200$) according to our model; simulations in GENESIS.

Remark 1 *The theoretical analysis of [Maass and Natschläger, 1998] suggests that for analog computing in a space-rate code it is advantageous to encode the "weigths" of a simulated sigmoidal gate in the release probabilities r_{vu} of synapses rather than in the mean amplitudes $\bar{a}_{vu}$ of postsynaptic potentials.*

Remark 2 *So far we have shown that arbitrary networks of sigmoidal neurons can be simulated by pools of spiking neurons with space-rate coding. This gives rise to the question whether the latter computational model is in a certain sense actually more powerful than the former one. A positive answer is given in [Maass and Natschläger, 1998] in the context of computations on time series. It is shown there that arbitrary linear filters can be approximated in the latter model. Hence it has the full power of the networks discussed in [Back and Tsoi, 1991] for computing on time series.*

2.6 Computing with Firing Rates

Traditionally a link between sigmoidal neural networks and biological neural systems is established by interpreting the firing rate (i.e., the spike count over time; see Sections 1.1.2.1 and 1.2.5) of a spiking neuron as an analog number between 0 and 1. In this interpretation one gets a plausible correspondence between the dependence of the output value $g(\sum_{j \in \Gamma_i} w_{ij} x_j)$ of a sigmoidal gate on its input values x_j on one hand, and the dependence of the firing rate of a spiking neuron i on the firing rates of presynaptic neurons $j \in \Gamma_i$ on the other hand.

There exists ample biological evidence that information about a stimulus is in many biological neural systems encoded in the firing rates of neurons. However recent empirical results from neurophysiology have raised doubts whether the firing rate of a biological neuron i does in fact depend on the firing rates x_j of presynaptic neurons $j \in \Gamma_i$ in a way that can be described by an expression of the form $g(\sum_{j \in \Gamma_i} w_{ij} x_j)$. Results of [Abbott et al., 1997] and others about the dynamic behavior of biological synapses show that for some neural systems above a "limiting frequency" of about 10 Hz the amplitudes of postsynaptic potentials are inversely proportional to the firing rate x_j of the presynaptic neuron $j \in \Gamma_i$. These results suggest that instead of a fixed parameter w_{ij} one has to model the "strength" of a biological synapse for rate coding by a quantity $w_{ij}(x_j)$ that *depends* on the firing rate x_j of the presynaptic neuron, and that this quantity $w_{ij}(x_j)$ is proportional to $\frac{1}{x_j}$. But then the weighted sum $\sum_{j \in \Gamma_i} w_{ij}(x_j) \cdot x_j$, which models the average membrane potential at the soma of a spiking neuron i, does no longer depend on the firing rates x_j of those presynaptic neurons j that fire above the limiting frequency. This issue will be discussed in more detail in Chapter 12.

A very interesting dual interpretation of the computational role of spiking neurons in the context of rate coding is due to [Srinivasan and Bernard, 1976]. They have pointed out that if a spiking neuron is working in the coincidence-detector-mode (i.e., with short integration time relative to the number and firing rates of presynaptic neurons), and the input spike trains are generated by stochastically independent Poisson processes, then its output firing rate is in a certain parameter range proportional to the *product* of the firing rates of the presynaptic neurons. If for example the spike trains from 3 presynaptic neurons j are generated by stochastically independent Poisson processes, then the probability that all of these three presynaptic neurons j fire within the same short time window A is proportional to the *product* of the firing probability of the individual neurons j. Hence if one assumes that a spiking neuron i fires if and only if these 3 presynaptic neurons j fire within a short time window A, its firing rate encodes (approximately) the product of the firing rates of the presynaptic neurons j.

This smart mechanism for *analog multiplication* is of substantial interest for possible applications of *artificial* pulsed neural nets. Chapter 13 discusses possible uses of this mechanism for carrying out complex optimization tasks with artificial pulsed neural nets.

2.7 Computing with Firing Rates and Temporal Correlations

We will discuss in this section computations that employ a quite different type of "temporal coding". Communication by spike trains offers a direct way to encode transient *relations* between different neurons: through coincidences (or near coincidences) in their firing times (see Section 1.1.3.3). Hence computations with spiking neurons may in principle also involve complex operations on *relations between computational objects*, a computational mode which has no parallel in traditional neural network models – or any other common computational model. This type of temporal coding need not necessarily take place on the microscopic level of coding by single spikes, but can also take place on a macroscopic level of statistical correlations between firing times of different neurons. We refer to Section 4.4 in Chapter 4 for further details on biological data involving firing correlations. Milner had conjectured already in 1974 that visual input might be encoded in the visual cortex in a way where "cells fired by the same figure fire together but not in synchrony with cells fired by other figures" ([Milner, 1974]). This conjecture (see also [von der Malsburg, 1981]) has been supported more recently by experimental data from several labs (see for example [Eckhorn et al., 1988; Gray et al., 1989; Kreiter and Singer, 1996; Vaadia et al., 1995]).

A variety of models have been proposed in order to shed light on the possible *organization* of *computing with firing correlations* in networks of spiking neurons. We have already shown in the preceding sections that spiking neurons are well-suited for *detecting* firing correlations among preceeding neurons. They also can *induce* firing correlations in other neurons k by sending the same output spike train to several other neurons k. But the question remains what exactly can be computed with firing correlations in a *network* of spiking neurons.

In [Eckhorn et al., 1990] a computational model was introduced whose computational units are modifications of integrate-and-fire neurons that receive two types of input: *feeding input* and *linking input*. Both types of inputs are processed in this model by leaky integrators with different time constants, and are then multiplied to produce the potential $u_i(t)$ of an integrate-and-fire neuron i. In networks of such computational units the feeding input typically is provided by feedforward connections, starting from the stimulus, whereas the linking input comes through feedback connections from higher layers of the network. These higher layers may represent information stored in an associative memory like in a Hopfield net. Computer simulations have shown that this model is quite successful in reproducing firing patterns in response to specific stimuli that match quite well firing patterns that have been experimentally observed in the visual cortex of cat and monkey. So far no theoretical results have been derived for this model.

A related model, but on a more abstract level – without spiking neurons – was proposed in [Kay and Phillips, 1996] (see also [Phillips and Singer, 1996] for a survey of this and related models). That model also involves two types of input, called RF and CF, where RF corresponds to "feeding input" and CF corresponds to "linking input". No computational model has been specified for the generation of the CF-values. A computational unit in their model outputs a continuous value $2 \cdot g(\frac{r}{2} \cdot (1 + e^{2r \cdot c})) - 1$ that ranges between -1 and 1. In this formula r is a weighted sum of RF-input, s is a weighted sum of CF-input to that unit, and g is the sigmoidal gain function from Section 1.2.2. In this computational unit the RF-input r determines the sign of the output. Furthermore $r = 0$ implies that the output has value 0, independently of the value of the CF-input c. However for $r \neq 0$ the size of the output is increased through the influence of the CF-input c if c has the same sign as r, and decreased otherwise. Computer simulations of large networks of such computational units have produced effects which are expected on the basis of psychological studies of visual perception in man [Phillips and Singer, 1996].

Other models aim directly at simulating effects of computing with firing correlations on an even more abstract conceptual level, see for example [von der Malsburg, 1981; Shastri and Ajjanagadde, 1993]. In

76 2. Computing with Spiking Neurons

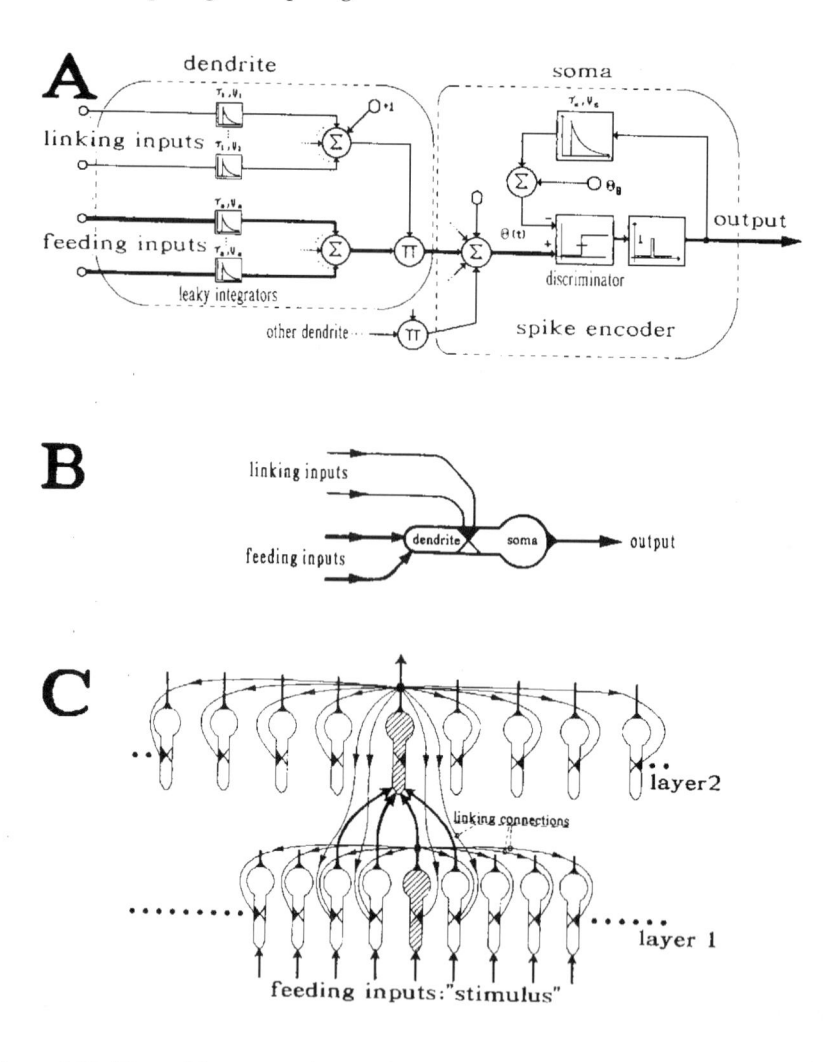

Figure 2.12. *The model neuron and network.* (A) Circuit diagram. Linking and feeding inputs with leaky integrators on a single "dendrite" interact multiplicatively. Signals from different "dendrites" are summed and fed to the "spike encoder" in the "soma". (B) Symbol for neuron in A. (C) Neural network. Thick lines: feeding connections; thin lines: linking connections. Full output connectivity is shown only for one layer 1 and one layer 2 neuron (hatched symbols). From [Eckhorn et al., 1990].

[Shastri and Ajjanagadde, 1993] a formal calculus is developed for exploiting the possibility to compute with *relations* encoded by precise temporal coincidences (rather than by statistical correlations in firing times).

No rigorous results are available so far which show that the previously described models have more computational power than conventional neural network models. In principle every function that is computed on any of the previously discussed models can also be approximated by a conventional sigmoidal neural net, i.e., by an abstract model for a network of spiking neurons that encode all information in their firing rates. This follows from the simple fact that a sigmoidal neural net has the "universal approximation property", i.e., it can approximate any given bounded continuous function. Thus the question about a possible increase in computational power through the use of firing correlations boils down to a *quantitative* rather than *qualitative* question: How much hardware, computation time, etc. can a neural network save by computing with firing correlations in addition to firing rates?

We will sketch a new model from [Maass, 1998] that provides some first results in this direction. We write $\nu(i)$ for the output of a sigmoidal gate i, which is assumed to range over $[0, 1]$. One may interpret $\nu(i)$ as the firing rate of a spiking neuron i. We now introduce for certain sets S of neurons a new variable $c(S)$, also ranging over $[0, 1]$, whose value models in an abstract way the current amount of *temporal correlation* in the firing times of the neurons $j \in S$. For example, for some time internal A of 5 msec one could demand that $c(S) = 0$ if

$$\frac{Pr[\text{ all } j \in S \text{ fire during } A]}{\Pi_{j \in S} \; Pr[j \text{ fires during } A]} \leq 1 \; ,$$

and that $c(S)$ approaches 1 when this quotient approaches infinity. Thus we have $c(S) = 0$ if all neurons $j \in S$ fire stochastically independently.

One then needs computational rules that extend the standard rule

$$\nu(i) = g(\sum_{j \in \Gamma_i} w_{ij} \cdot \nu(j))$$

for sigmoidal gates to rules that also involve the new variables $c(S)$ in a meaningful way. In particular, one wants to have that the firing rate $\nu(i)$ is increased if one or several subsets $S \subseteq \Gamma_i$ of preceding neurons fire with temporal correlation $c(S) > 0$. This motivates the first rule of our model:

$$\nu(i) = g(\sum_{j \in \Gamma_i} w_{ij} \cdot \nu(j) + \sum_{S \subseteq \Gamma_i} w_{iS} \cdot c(S) \cdot \Pi_{j \in S} \nu(j) + \vartheta) \; . \tag{2.10}$$

The products $c(S) \cdot \Pi_{j \in S} \nu(j)$ in the second summand of (2.10) reflect the fact that statistical correlations in the firing times of the neurons $j \in S$ can only increase the firing rate of neuron i by a significant amount if the firing rates $\nu(j)$ of all neurons $j \in S$ are sufficiently high. These products also arise naturally if $c(S)$ is interpreted as being proportional to

$$\frac{Pr[\text{ all } j \in S \text{ fire during } A]}{\Pi_{j \in S} \; Pr[j \text{ fires during } A]} \; , \tag{2.11}$$

and $\nu(j)$ is proportional to $Pr[j$ fires during $A]$. Multiplying (2.11) with $\Pi_{j \in S} \; \nu(j) \approx \Pi_{j \in S} \; Pr[j$ fires during $A]$ yields a term proportional to $Pr[\text{all } j \in S$ fire during $A]$. The latter term is the one that really determines by how much the firing rate of neuron i may increase through correlated firing of neurons in S: If the neurons $j \in S$ fire almost simultaneously, this will move the state variable $u_i(t)$ of neuron i to a larger peak value compared with a situation where the neurons $j \in S$ fire in a temporally dispersed manner.

78   2. Computing with Spiking Neurons

In order to complete the definition of our model for computing with firing rates $\nu(i)$ and firing correlations $c(S)$ one also has to specify how the correlation variable $c(S)$ is computed for a set S of "hidden" units i. Two effects have to be modelled:

(a) $c(S)$ increases if all neurons $i \in S$ receive common input from some other neuron k.

(b) $c(S)$ increases if there is a set S' of other neurons with significant correlation (i.e., $c(S') > 0$) so that each neuron $i \in S$ has some neuron $i' \in S'$ as predecessor (i.e., $\forall i \in S \ \exists i' \in S'(i' \in \Gamma_i)$).

These two effects give rise to the two terms in the following rule:

$$c(S) = g(\sum_k w_{Sk} \cdot \nu(k) + \sum_{S'} w_{SS'} \cdot c(S') \cdot \Pi_{i' \in S'} \ \nu(i') + \vartheta_S) \ . \quad (2.12)$$

From the point of view of computational complexity it is interesting to note that in a network of spiking neurons no additional units are needed to compute the value of $c(S)$ according to (2.12). The new parameters $w_{Sk}, w_{SS'}$ can be chosen so that they encode the relevant information about the connectivity structure of the net, for example $w_{Sk} = 0$ if not $\forall i \in S \ (k \in \Gamma_i)$ and $w_{SS'} = 0$ if not $\forall i \in S \ \exists i' \in S' \ (i' \in \Gamma_i)$. Under these assumptions the rule (2.12) models the previously described effects (a) and (b).

The rules (2.10) and (2.12) involve besides the familiar "synaptic weights" w_{ij} also new types of parameters w_{iS}, w_{Sk}, and $w_{SS'}$. The parameter w_{iS} scales the influence that correlated firing of the presynaptic neurons $j \in S$ has on the firing rate of neuron i. Thus for a biological neuron this parameter w_{iS} not only depends on the connectivity structure of the net, but also on the geometric and biochemical structure of the dendritic tree of neuron i and on the locations of the synapses from the neurons $j \in S$ on this dendritic tree. For example correlated firing of neurons $j \in S$ has a larger impact if these neurons either have synapses that are clustered together on a single subtree of the dendritic tree of i that contains voltage-gated channels ("hot spots"), or if they have synapses onto disjoint subtrees of the dendritic tree (thus avoiding sublinear summation of their EPSP's in the Hodgkin-Huxley model. Taking into account that frequently pairs of biological neurons are not connected just by one synapse, but by multiple synapses that may lie on different branches of their dendritic tree, one sees that in the context of computing with firing correlations the "program" of the computation can be encoded through these additional parameters w_{iS} in much more subtle and richer ways than just through the "synaptic weights" w_{ij}. Corresponding remarks apply to the other new parameters w_{Sk} and $w_{SS'}$ that arise in the context of computing with firing correlations.

The following result shows that a computational unit i that computes its output $\nu(i)$ according to rule (2.10) has more computational power than a sigmoidal gate (or even a small network of sigmoidal gates) that receives the same numerical variables $\nu(j), c(S)$ as input. This arises from the fact that the computational rule (2.10) involves a *product* of input variables.

Consider the boolean function $F : \{0,1\}^{n+\binom{n}{2}} \to \{0,1\}$ that outputs 1 for n boolean input variables $\nu(j)$, $j \in \{1,\ldots,n\}$, and $\binom{n}{2}$ boolean input variables $c(S)$ for all subsets $S \subseteq \{1,\ldots,n\}$ of size 2 *if and only if* $c(S) = 1$ and $\nu(j_1) = \nu(j_2) = 1$ for some subset $S = \{j_1, j_2\}$. It is obvious from equation (2.10) that if one takes as gain function the Heaviside function $\mathcal{H}$, then a *single* computational unit i of the type described by equation (2.10) can compute the function F_n. On the other hand the following result shows that a substantial number of threshold gates or sigmoidal gates are needed to compute the same function F_n. Its proof can be found in [Maass, 1998].

Theorem 2.5 *The function F_n can be computed by a single neuron that carries out computations with firing rates and firing correlations according to rule (2.10).*

On the other hand any feedforward threshold circuit that computes the function F_n needs to have on the order of $n^2 / \log n$ gates. Any feedforward circuit consisting of sigmoidal gates [5] *needs to have at least proportional to n many gates to compute F_n.* ∎

2.8 Networks of Spiking Neurons for Storing and Retrieving Information

Synfire chains [Abeles, 1991] are models for networks of spiking neurons that are well-suited for storing and retrieving information from a network of spiking neurons. A synfire chain is a chain of pools of neurons with a rich ("diverging/converging") pattern of excitatory feedforward connection from each pool to the next pool, that has a similar effect as complete connectivity between successive pools: an almost synchronous firing of most neurons in one pool in a synfire chain triggers an almost synchronous firing of most neurons in the next pool in the chain. Neurons may belong to different synfire chains, which has the consequence that the activation of one synfire chain may trigger the activation of another synfire chain (see [Bienenstock, 1995]). In this way a pointer from one memory item (implemented by one synfire chain) to another memory item (implemented by another synfire chain) can be realized by a network of spiking neurons. A remarkable property of synfire chains is that the temporal delay between the activation time of the first pool and the k-th pool in a synfire chain has a very small variance, even for large values of k. This is due to the temporal averaging of EPSP's from neurons in the preceding pool that is carried out through rich connectivity between successive pools.

An *analog* version of synfire chains results from the model for computing with space-rate coding discussed in section 2.6. If one takes synaptic unreliability into account for a synfire chain, one can achieve that the percentage of firing neurons of a later pool in the synfire chain becomes a smooth function of the percentage of firing neurons in the first pool. This variation of the synfire chain model predicts that precisely timed firing patterns of a fixed set of 2 or 3 neurons in different pools of a biological neural system occur more often than can be expected by chance, but not *every* time for

---
[5] with piecewise rational activation functions

the same stimulus. This prediction is consistent with experimental data [Abeles et al., 1993].

Other types of networks of spiking neurons that are useful for storing and retrieving information are various implementations of attractor neural networks with recurrent networks of spiking neurons, see for example [Fransen 1996; Gerstner and van Hemmen, 1992; Gerstner et al., 1993; Hopfield and Herz, 1995; Lanser and Fransén, 1992; Maass and Natschläger, 1997; Simmen et al.,1995].

2.9 Computing on Spike Trains

We still know very little about the power of networks of biological neurons for computations on spike trains, for example for spike trains that encode a time series of analog numbers as for example the spike trains from neuron $H1$ in the blowfly (see [Rieke et al., 1997] and the discussion in Section 4.5 of Chapter 4). One problem is that the previously discussed formal models for networks of spiking neurons are not really adequate for modeling computations by biological neural systems on *spike trains*, because they are based on the assumption that synaptic weights w_{ij} are *static* during a computation. This problem will be addressed in chapter 12. Another problem is the lack of empirical data about computing on time series in biological and artificial pulsed neural systems, and the lack of an adequate computational theory. Obviously this is an important topic for future research.

2.10 Conclusions

The results of this chapter show that networks of spiking neurons present a quite interesting new class of computational models. They can carry out computations under different modes for coding information in spike trains. In particular, they can carry out analog computation not only under a rate code, but also under temporal codes where the timing of spikes carries analog information. We have presented theoretical evidence which suggests that through the use of temporal coding a network of spiking neurons may gain for certain computational tasks more computational power than a traditional neural network of comparable size.

The models for networks of spiking neurons that we have discussed in this chapter originated in the investigation of biological neurons from Chapter 1. However it is obvious that many of the computational ideas and architectures presented in this chapter are of a more general nature, and can just as well be applied to implementations of pulsed neural nets in electronic hardware, such as those introduced in the following chapter.

References

[Abeles, 1982] Abeles, M. (1982). Role of the cortical neuron: integrator or coincidence detector? *Israel J. Med. Sci.*,18:83–92.

[Abeles, 1991] Abeles, M. (1991). *Corticonics*. Cambridge University Press, Cambridge.

[Abeles et al., 1993] Abeles, M., Bergmann, H., Margalit, E., and Vaadia, E. (1993). Spatiotemporal firing patterns in the frontal cortex of behaving monkeys. *J. of Neurophysiology*, 70(4), 1629–1638.

[Abbott et al., 1997] Abbott, L. F., Sen, K., Varela, J. A., and Nelson, S. B. (1997). Synaptic depression and cortical gain control. *Science*, 275:220–222.

[Back and Tsoi, 1991] Back, A. D. and Tsoi, A. C. (1991). FIR and IIR synapses, a new neural network architecture for time series modeling. *Neural Computation*, 3:375–385.

[Bienenstock, 1995] Bienenstock, E. (1995). A model of neocortex. *Network*, 6:179–224.

[Bernander et al., 1994] Bernander, Ö., Koch, C., and Usher, M. (1994). The effect of synchronized inputs at the single neuron level. *Neural Computation*, 6:622–641.

[Bower and Beeman, 1995] Bower, J. M. and Beeman, D. (1995). *The Book of GENESIS: Exploring Realistic Neural Models with the GEneral NEural SImulation System*. Springer-Verlag, Inc. Published by TELOS, New York.

[DasGupta and Schnitger, 1996] DasGupta, B. and Schnitger G. (1996). Analog versus discrete neural networks. *Neural Computation*, 8(4), 805–818.

[Dobrunz and Stevens, 1997] Dobrunz, L. and Stevens, C. (1997). Heterogenous release probabilities in hippocampal neurons. *Neuron*, 18:995–1008.

[Eckhorn et al., 1988] Eckhorn, R., Bauer, R., Jordan, W., Brosch, M., Kruse, W., Munk, M., and Reitboeck, H. J. (1988). Coherent oscillations: A mechanism of feature linking in the visual cortex? Multiple electrode and correlation analysis in the cat. *Biological Cybernetics*, 60:121–130.

[Eckhorn et al., 1990] Eckhorn, R., Reitboeck, H. J., Arndt, M., and Dicke, P. (1990). Feature linking via synchronization among distributed assemblies: simulations of results from cat visual cortex. *Neural Computation*, 2:293–307.

[Fransen, 1996] Fransén, E. (1996). *Biophysical Simulation of Cortical Associative Memory*. PhD thesis, Stockholm University.

[Gerstner and van Hemmen, 1992] Gerstner, W. and van Hemmen, J. L. (1992). Associative memory in a network of "spiking" neurons. *Network*, 3:139–164.

[Gerstner et al., 1993] Gerstner, W., Fuentes, U., van Hemmen, J. L., and Ritz, R. (1993). A biologically motivated and analytically soluble model of collective oscillations in the cortex. *Biological Cybernetics*, 71:349–358.

[Gray et al., 1989] Gray, C. M., König, P., Engel, A. K., and Singer, W. (1989). Oscillatory responses in cat visual cortex exhibit intercolumnar synchronization which reflects global stimulus properties. *Nature*, 338:334–337.

[Haefliger et al., 1997] Haefliger, P., Mahowald, M., and Watts, L. (1997). A spike based learning neuron in analog VLSI. *Advances in Neural Information Processing Systems, vol. 9*, MIT Press, Cambridge, 692–698.

[Hopfield, 1995] Hopfield, J. J. (1995). Pattern recognition computation using action potential timing for stimulus representation. *Nature*, 376:33–36.

[Hopfield and Herz, 1995] Hopfield, J. J., Herz, A. V. M. (1995). Rapid local synchronization of action potentials: Toward computation with coupled integrate-and-fire neurons. *Proc. Natl. Acad. Sci. USA*, 92:6655–6662.

[Judd and Aihara, 1993] Judd, K. T. and Aihara, K. (1993). Pulse propagation networks: A neural network model that uses temporal coding by action potentials. *Neural Networks*, 6:203–215.

[Kay and Phillips, 1996] Kay, J. and Phillips, W. A. (1997). Activation functions, computational goals, and learning rules for local processors with contextual guidance. *Neural Computation*, 9(4):895–910.

[Kreiter and Singer, 1996] Kreiter, A. K. and Singer, W. (1996). Stimulus-dependent synchronization of neuronal responses in the visual cortex of the awake macaque monkey. *The Journal of Neuroscience*, 16(7):2381–2396.

[Lanser and Fransén, 1992] Lanser, A. and Fransén, E. (1992). Modelling hebbian cell assemblies comprised of cortical neurons. *Network: Computation in Neural Systems*, 3:105–119.

[Maass, 1996] Maass, W. (1996). Lower bounds for the computational power of networks of spiking neurons. *Neural Computation*, 8(1):1–40.

[Maass, 1997a] Maass, W. (1997). Fast sigmoidal networks via spiking neurons. *Neural Computation*, 9:279–304.

[Maass, 1997b] Maass, W. (1997). Networks of spiking neurons: the third generation of neural network models. *Neural Networks*, 10(9):1659–1671. Extended abstract (with a different title) appeared in: *Advances in Neural Information Processing Systems, vol. 9*, MIT Press, Cambridge, 211–217.

[Maass, 1998] Maass, W. (1998). A simple model for neural computation with firing rates and firing correlations. *Network: Computation in Neural Systems*, 9(3), 381–397.

[Maass et al., 1991] Maass, W., Schnitger, G., and Sontag, E. (1991). On the computational power of sigmoid versus boolean threshold circuits. Proc. of the *32nd Annual IEEE Symposium on Foundations of Computer Science* 1991, 767–776; extended version appeared in: *Theoretical Advances in Neural Computation and Learning*, V. P. Roychowdhury, K. Y. Siu, A. Orlitsky, eds., Kluwer Academic Publishers (Boston, 1994), 127–151.

[Maass and Natschläger, 1997] Maass, W. and Natschläger, T. (1997). Networks of spiking neurons can emulate arbitrary Hopfield nets in temporal coding. *Network: Computation in Neural Systems*, 8(4):355–372.

[Maass and Natschläger, 1998] Maass, W. and Natschläger, T. (1998). A model for fast analog computation based on unreliable synapses. Submitted for publication.

[Maass and Schmitt, 1997] Maass, W. and Schmitt, M. (1997). Complexity of learning for networks of spiking neurons, submitted for publication; extended abstract appeared in *Proc. of the Tenth Annual Conference on Computational Learning Theory*, ACM, New York, 54–61.

[Markram et al., 1997] Markram, H., Lübke, J., Frotscher, M., and Sakman, B. (1997). Regulation of synaptic efficacy by coincidence of postsynaptic APs and EPSPs. *Science*, 275:213–215.

[Markram and Sakmann, 1995] Markram, H. and Sakmann, B. (1995). Action potentials propagating back into dendrites triggers changes in efficacy of single-axon synapses between layer V pyramidal neurons. *Society for Neuroscience Abstracts*, 21:2007.

[Milner, 1974] Milner, P. M. (1974). A model for visual shape recognition. *Psychological Review*, 81(6):521–535.

[Müller et al., 1996] Müller, R., MacKay, D. J. C., Herz, V. M. (1996). Associative memory using action potential timing. *Proc. BioNet '96, Bio-Informatics and Pulspropagating Networks* - Selected Contributions 3rd Workshop November 14-15, 1996, G. Heinz, ed., Berlin, 70–80.

[Natschläger and Ruf, 1997] Natschläger, T. and Ruf, B. (1997). Learning radial basis functions with spiking neurons using action potential timing. To appear in *Neuromorphic Systems: Engineering Silicon from Neurobiology*, World Scientific.

[Petrov, 1995] Petrov, V. V. (1995). *Limit Theorems of Probability Theory*. Oxford University Press.

[Phillips and Singer, 1996] Phillips, W. A. and Singer, W. (1996). In search of common foundations for cortical computation. *Behavioral and Brain Sciences*, in press.

[Rieke et al., 1997] Rieke, F., Warland, D., de Ruyter van Steveninck, R. R., and Bialek, W. (1997). *Spikes – Exploring the Neural Code*. MIT Press, Cambridge, MA.

[Ruf, 1997] Ruf, B. (1997). Computing functions with spiking neurons in temporal coding. In *Biological and Artificial Computation: From Neuroscience to Technology*, J. Mira, R. Moreno-Diaz, and J. Cabestany, eds., Lecture Note in Computer Science, Springer, Berlin, 1240:265–272.

[Ruf and Schmitt, 1997] Ruf, B., and Schmitt, M. (1997). Self-organizing maps of spiking neurons using temporal coding. In J. Bower, ed., *Computational Neuroscience: Trends in Research 1998*, Plenum Press, 1998 to appear.

[Samuelides et al., 1997] Samuelides, M. and Thorpe, S., Veneau, E. (1997). Implementing hebbian learning in a rank-based neural network. *Proc. 7th Int. Conference on Artificial Neural Networks - ICANN'97* in Lausanne, Switzerland, Springer, Berlin, 145–150.

[Shastri and Ajjanagadde, 1993] Shastri, L. and Ajjanagadde, V. (1993). From simple associations to systematic reasoning: a connectionist representation of rules, variables and dynamic bindings using temporal synchrony. *Behavioural and Brain Sciences*, 16:417–494.

[Simmen et al., 1995] Simmen, M. W., Rolls, E. T., and Treves, A. (1995). Rapid retrival in an autoassociative network of spiking neurons. *Computational Neuroscience*, Bower, J. M., ed., Academic Press, London New York, 273–278.

[Sontag, 1997] Sontag, E. D. (1997). Shattering all sets of 'k' points in "general position" requires $(k-1)/2$ parameters. *Neural Computation*, 9(2):337–348.

[Srinivasan and Bernard, 1976] Srinivasan, M. V. and Bernard, G. D. (1976). A proposed mechanism for multiplication of neural signals. *Biol. Cybernetics*, 21:227–236.

[Thorpe and Gautrais, 1997] Thorpe, S. J. and Gautrais, J. (1997). Rapid visual processing using spike asynchrony. *Advances in Neural Information Processing Systems, vol. 9*, MIT Press, Cambridge, MA, 901–907.

[Thorpe et al., 1996] Thorpe, S. J., Fize, D., and Marlot, C. (1996) Speed of processing in the human visual system. *Nature*, 381:520–522.

[Vaadia et al., 1995] Vaadia, E., Aertsen, A., and Nelken, I. (1995). Dynamics of neuronal interactions cannot be explained by neuronal transients. *Proc. Royal Soc. of London B*, 261:407–410.

[Valiant, 1994] Valiant, L. G. (1994). *Circuits of the Mind*, Oxford University Press, Oxford.

[von der Malsburg, 1981] von der Malsburg, C. (1981). The correlation theory of brain function. *Internal Report 81-2 of the Dept. of Neurobiology of the Max Planck Institute for Biophysical Chemistry in Göttingen*, Germany. Reprinted in *Models of Neural Networks II*, Domany et al., eds., Springer, 1994, 95–119.

[Watanabe and Aihara, 1997] Watanabe, M., and Aihara, K. (1997). Chaos in neural networks composed of coincidence detector neurons. *Neural Networks*, to appear.

[Wehr and Laurent, 1996] Wehr, M. and Laurent, G. (1996). Odour encoding by temporal sequences of firing in oscillating neural assemblies. *Nature*, 384:162–166.

[Wilson and Cowan, 1972] Wilson, H. R. and Cowan, J. D. (1972). Excitatory and inhibitory interactions in localized populations of model neurons. *Biophysics Journal*, 12:1–24.

3 Pulse-Based Computation in VLSI Neural Networks

Alan F. Murray

3.1 Background

This chapter sets out to describe the capabilities and limitations of Metal Oxide Silicon (MOS) Very Large Scale Integration (VLSI) technology with respect to pulsed computation - the use of spikes. Most VLSI systems use either binary voltages (e.g. 0V, 5V) to represent bits in binary numbers (digital VLSI) or continuously-variable voltages, currents and charges to represent numbers (analog VLSI). The aim here is not to provide an argument for or against digital, analog or hybrid coding schemes and circuits. It is, nevertheless, worth reviewing the received wisdom regarding the strengths and weaknesses of digital and analog approaches before concentrating on spiking circuit forms.

Digital technology and fabrication processes advance at alarming speed. As a result, digital processors become ever faster and more accurate and digital memories ever denser. Why, therefore, is analog computation in VLSI of any interest at all? Analog computation can also be fast, but is fundamentally inaccurate as analog noise cannot be eliminated from signals and therefore from computation (at temperatures above absolute zero!). Furthermore, analog design is error-prone and requires specialist skills. Worst of all in the neural context - analog memory is a major problem. Several attempts have been made to make non-volatile analog memory straightforward - for examples, see [Buchan et al., 1997, Holler et al., 1989, Holmes et al., 1995]. None has, as yet, been sufficiently reliable and convenient for use in serious neural "products".

At one time, the potential speed of analog computation was seen as its main advantage. Now, the niche that an analog approach targets is narrower and more carefully-defined. The justification for an analog approach must come from:

- Silicon area: a 12-bit digital multiplier comprises some 500-1000 transistors and is likely to occupy just under $1mm^2$ of silicon. A (two-quadrant[1]) analog multiplier can consist of 2 transistors and occupy a few tens of μm^2.

- Power: although low-power digital design is now a highly-developed art form, large circuits comprising arrays of synchronised digital circuits are fundamentally power-hungry. Low power can be achieved

---
[1] two quadrant – i.e. one multiplicand positive only, second multiplicand positive or negative

at the expense of reliability and/or speed. Analog circuits can also be designed to consume extremely low power, if the transistors are operated in sub-threshold mode (see below).

- Interfacing: the world is analog and analog chips can connect directly to signals from and to the analog outside world without power-hungry and expensive interface and conversion circuitry.

In the preceding 2 chapters "pulses" were action potentials emitted by biological neurons. But pulses are also used widely in electronics, where they have in general shapes that differ from those of action potentials. An engineer will generally think of pulses as being rectangular in time. But, as will be shown in this chapter and the subsequent chapters on electronic hardware, the timing of such pulses can be of similar use as the timing of action potentials in biological systems.

In the VLSI context, pulses represent an interesting and powerful hybrid computational style that can, if used carefully, bring together many of these advantages of analog techniques together with some of the robustness of a purely digital approach. It was this potential that attracted the author to pulses in the mid-1980's [Murray and Smith, 1987b] and still justifies an interest and significant ongoing programme of research. Of course, implementation of pulsed systems as software simulations on digital hardware is possible. The primary advantages of implementation as mixed signal (analog/digital) VLSI are massive parallelism and direct interface, without A/D and D/A conversion, to and from the analog world. To date, our experience of pulsed circuitry has been aimed at Multi-Layer Perceptron [Churcher et al., 1993] and latterly Radial Basis Function [Mayes et al., 1996] networks, where pulses are used as a electronic "trick" to implement a computational paradigm that has evolved independently. Their inherent computing power, that forms the subject of this book, has not been exploited directly. If and when true pulsed computational circuits are developed, the advantages will become much clearer, as the paradigm is developed to fit the computational medium.

3.2 Pulsed Coding: A VLSI Perspective

Like any other processing system, a neural network consists of circuit elements dealing with "computation" and "communication". The choice between analog and digital implementation of these individual elements can be made independently for the different subsystems, with the overall goal of optimisation in terms of silicon area, speed, accuracy, and power consumption etc. *for the whole network*. Furthermore, since it is now commonplace to mix analog and digital circuits on the same chip, hybrid integrated VLSI neural networks are a practical proposition.

Pulse encoding of electronic information is not a new idea. Communications systems have used Pulse Amplitude Modulation, Pulse Width Modulation and Pulse Code Modulation for data transmission for some time. In fact, a variant of Pulse Code Modulation (PCM) signalling was introduced in 1987, as the conversion principle behind *Bit-stream* D/A and A/D converters by Phillips, reducing binary samples (e.g. 16 bit) to a much faster single bit coded signal. This technique now underlies the converters in most superior Compact Disc players. It is not appropriate here to present a lengthy review of PCM techniques, as the only relevance to pulse-stream neural VLSI is that some of the merits of PCM - robustness, ease of regeneration, the ability to time-multiplex - carry through into the neural domain, as we will show. Horowitz and Hill [Horowitz, and Hill, 1989] present a condensed review of pulsed techniques in communications, while Stark and Tuteur (pp 134-183 [Stark, and Tuteur, 1979]) provide a more comprehensive treatment. The factors that are relevant here are drawn out in the following discussion.

Pulse stream encoding was first used and reported in the context of neural integration in 1987 [Murray and Smith, 1987a, Murray and Smith, 1987b]. The underlying rationale is simple:

- Analog computation is attractive in neural VLSI, for reasons of compactness, potential speed, asynchronousness and lack of quantisation effects.
- Analog signals are far from robust with respect to noise and interference, are susceptible to process variations between devices, and are not robust to the rigours of inter-chip communication.
- Digital silicon processing is more readily available than analog.
- Digital signals are robust, easily transmitted and regenerated and fast.
- Digital multiplication is area- and power-hungry.

These considerations all encourage a hybrid approach, blending the merits of both digital and analog technology. Such a hybrid scheme must be constructed carefully, however, as examples abound where the disadvantages of two techniques have been combined to produce a seriously non-optimal system. The pulse-stream technique uses *digital* signals to carry information and control *analog* circuitry, while storing further *analog* information on the time axis, as will be described below. A number of possible techniques exist, for coding a neural state $0 < v_i < 1$ on to a pulsed waveform v_i with frequency f_i, amplitude A_i and pulse width δ_i. A representative selection of these is illustrated in Figure 3.1, where a time-varying analog state signal v_i has been encoded in each of the following ways:

Pulse Amplitude Modulation

Pulse Width Modulation

Pulse Frequency Modulation (average repetition rate of pulses)

Pulse Phase Modulation (delay between two pulses on different lines)

In addition, further variants exist - *Pulse Code Modulation* (weighted bits) and *Pulse Density Modulation* (delay between a pulse pair on the same line). These are not particularly useful in this context, and furthermore we have no direct experience in their use.

Pulse Width, Pulse Frequency, Pulse Phase, and Pulse Density Modulation all encode information *in the time domain*, and can be viewed as variants of

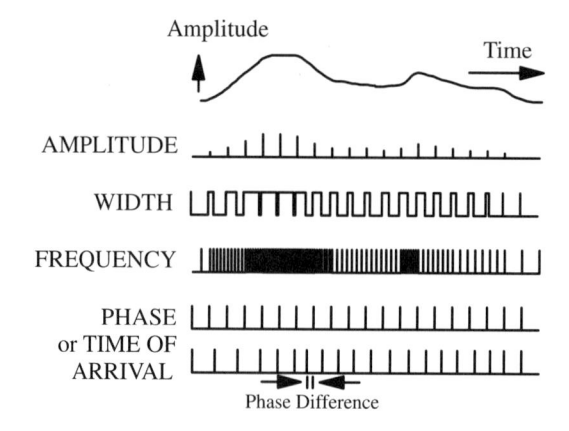

Figure 3.1. Modulation schemes that encode analog values as a pulsed waveform.

pulse rate. In other words, Pulse Density and Pulse Phase Modulation are essentially equivalent to Pulse Frequency Modulation with no averaging over pulse intervals. Such non-averaged pulse modulation techniques are used in various natural systems, particularly where spatial or temporal information is derived from the time of arrival of individual pulses or pulse pairs [Simmons, 1989]. This theme will be developed in other chapters of this book.

3.2.1 Pulse Amplitude Modulation

Here the pulsed waveform amplitude A_i ($v_i = A_i \times$ *constant frequency pulsed signal*) is modulated in time, reflecting the variation in v_i. This technique, useful when signals are to be multiplexed on to a single line, and can be interleaved, is not particularly satisfactory as a long-range signalling scheme in neural nets. It incurs the disadvantages in robustness and susceptibility to processing variations inherent in analog VLSI, as information is transmitted as analog voltage levels.

3.2.2 Pulse Width Modulation

This technique is similarly straightforward, representing the instantaneous value of the state v_i as the *width* of individual digital pulses in v_i. The advantages of a hybrid scheme now become apparent, as no analog voltage is present in the signal, and information is coded as described along the time axis. This signal is therefore robust, and furthermore can be decoded to yield an analog value by integration. The constant frequency of signalling means that either the leading or trailing edges of neural state signals all occur simultaneously unless steps are taken to prevent this. In massively parallel neural VLSI, this synchronism represents a drawback, as current will be drawn on the supply lines by all the neurons (and synapses) simultaneously, with no averaging effect. Power supply lines must therefore be oversized to cope with the high instantaneous currents involved. Alternatively, individual neural signals can be staggered in time, to keep edges out of phase. This latter approach does, however, incur a disadvantage in complexity, and in the imposition of an artificial synchronism.

It is interesting to note that Pulse Width Modulation is equivalent to the "time-to-first-spike-code" or "(absolute) delay code" discussed in Chapter 1, where the rising edge of the (synchronous) pulses defines time = 0 and the falling edge is analogous to the first spike time.

3.2.3 Pulse Frequency Modulation

Pulse frequency modulation is essentially the same as the rate code technique referred to in Chapters 1 and 2. Here, the instantaneous value of the state v_i is represented as the instantaneous frequency of digital pulses in v_i whose widths are equal. Again, the hybrid scheme shows its value, for the same reasons as described above for Pulse Width Modulation. The variable signalling frequency skews both the leading and trailing edges of neural state signals, and avoids the massive transient demand on supply lines. The power requirement is therefore averaged in time. On the negative side, however, using frequency as a coding medium implies that several pulses must occur before the associated frequency can be inferred. This apparent drawback is, however, not fundamental, as the neural state information is captured (albeit crudely) in the time domain as the inverse of the inter-pulse time. We will return to this observation.

3.2.4 Phase or Delay Modulation

In this final example, two signals are used to represent each neural state, and the instantaneous value of v_i is represented as the *phase difference* between the two waveforms - in other words by modulating the delay between the occurrence of two pulses on one or two wires[2]. The significant difference between pulse phase modulation and rate coding is that rate is viewed as the intensity of a Poisson process. Pulse phase codes cannot be viewed usefully as variants of pulse rate coding, as the intervals between pulses have high variance. The technique enjoys many of the advantages of the Pulse Width Modulation and Pulse Code Modulation variants described above, but it does imply the use of two wires for signalling, unless one of the signals is a globally-distributed reference pulse waveform. If this choice is made, however, signal skew becomes a problem, distorting the phase information across a large device, and between devices. In a massively parallel analog VLSI device, signal skew is a fact of life.

In summary, pulsed techniques can code information across several pulses or within a single pulse. The former enjoys an advantage in terms of accuracy, while the second sacrifices accuracy for increased bandwidth.

---
[2]In biological neural systems, decisions are often made on a timescale comparable with the inter-pulse time, thus implying that a time-domain, rather than frequency-domain process is at work [Simmons, 1989]. While this does not of itself provide justification for any technique, it is an interesting parallel.

3.2.5 Noise, Robustness, Accuracy and Speed

The four techniques described above share some attributes, but differ in several respects from each other and in most respects from other techniques. All the techniques except Pulse Amplitude Modulation are only really susceptible to FM (or edge-jitter) noise, which will be less significant in a conventionally noisy environment. Edge jitter is equivalent to a non-zero variance in the pulse edge times. For instance, a small degradation in the voltage representing a logical 1 will only have a small effect on a system using time as the information coding axis for analog state, and such signals can survive transfer between devices in a multi-chip network much better than analog (or Pulse Amplitude Modulation) signals. Furthermore, signals which are purely digital (albeit asynchronous) are easily regenerated or "firmed up" by a digital buffer, which restores solid logic levels without altering pulse widths or frequencies. In contrast, Pulse Amplitude modulation is neither better nor worse than straightforward Amplitude Modulation with respect to robustness.

Accuracy is, as in all analog systems, limited by noise, rather than by the choice of word length, as it is in a digital system. We have been designing systems with 1% accuracy in synapse weights, for instance, but there is no *a priori* reason why higher or lower accuracy cannot be achieved, at the expense of more or less area. It is possible to envisage systems where a feedback, on-chip learning scheme may in part compensate for circuit inaccuracies (e.g. spread of transistor threshold). On the other hand, networks with off-line learning must rely on the precision of weights programmed into the silicon memories, or perform an elaborate pre- processing of the weights before applying them to the silicon. As we shall see later in this chapter, the issue of analog noise in the arithmetic of an analog VLSI device is not a simple one. Simply equating 1% noise to 6-7 bit digital (in)accuracy will not do. Digital inaccuracy imposes a quantisation error on weights and states that implies that certain values are explicitly forbidden. Analog inaccuracy, on the other hand, allows any weight/state value within the range of allowable values, but imposes a scatter of "actual" values around that "desired" value. The implications of this apparently subtle distinction are significant [Murray, 1991], [Murray and Edwards, 1994] and will be discussed briefly later in this chapter.

Speed of operation is perhaps the most difficult and contentious "figure of merit" to quantify in all essentially analog, asynchronous systems. We can clarify the issues involved by looking at a Pulse Frequency Modulation system. The most crucial parameter is the minimum pulse width. This defines the minimum time in which anything at all can happen, and hence the maximum pulse frequency. The minimum pulse frequency is then *chosen* to give the desired dynamic range in the multiplication process. This then defines the overall speed at which "calculations" are made. The final factor is the number of pulses over which averaging is performed, to arrive at an individual product $w_{ij}v_j$, and thus at the accumulated activity $\sum w_{ij}v_j$. Clearly, the technique used for multiplication, the dynamic range of the weights, and the level of activity in the network can all affect a speed calculation. We present below the results only of an attempt to estimate the speed of computation in one of the networks developed in Edinburgh, where we have been working to date on systems which require 100 pulses to drive a silicon neuron fully "on" or "off". We do not present [3] this as a serious figure of merit for our networks, but only as a guide to the sort of speed that can be achieved, basing the calculation around a modest process speed. As an example - consider a pulse-frequency system, with a *maximum* pulse frequency conservatively set at 20MHz, and assume that on average, the neurons are switching from an activity level of 50% to 100% of the full-scale value. For a two-layer multilayer perceptron with an average level of activity (a mean neural activity of 10MHz), and a typical distribution of synaptic weights (mean value, 50% of the full-scale synaptic weight value) the settling time is of the order of 25µs, *regardless of the number of synapses on the chip*. The average computational speed may therefore be estimated as $\frac{N_s}{25 \times 10^{-6}}$ operations/sec, where N_s is the number of synapses. For a typical 3600 synapse network, this equates to over 108 operations (multiply/adds) per second - a respectable number for a self-contained single chip. We treat this sort of calculation with the greatest skepticism, however, masking as it does the data dependence of the result, and the asynchronousness it implies. This is purely an averaged result, and individual calculations may take longer or shorter times.

This is but one simple example, however, and if a fast pulse-stream system is required, a move to a pulse - width technique, where the state information is encapsulated in the width of each neural pulse, will increase the speed by orders of magnitude. The price paid, however, will be a loss of accuracy, as the inaccuracies in pulse edge times will no longer be integrated over several pulses, as in a Pulse Frequency Modulated system. The resultant state value will therefore have a faster response time, but will be noisier there is always a trade off [Hamilton et al., 1994].

3.3 A MOSFET Introduction

The Metal Oxide Silicon Field Effect Transistor (MOSFET) is the commonest semiconductor device in use, in neural and other VLSI chips. MOSFETs come in two basic types - n-type and p-type (n for Negative, p for Positive). Current in n-types is carried by negative electrons, while current in p-types is carried by positive "holes". An n-type device is formed in and on top of a p-type substrate, and *vice versa*. The MOSFET is a four terminal device - the terminals are the Gate, Source, Drain and Substrate. In the interests of simplicity and without loss of integrity, we will disregard the Substrate as its influence is complex and of smaller magnitude than the Gate, Source and Drain. It has a characteristic voltage associated with it, the *threshold* V_t that represents the crossover point between different operating modes. The analogy with a neural threshold is useful conceptually, but should not be stretched to infer a closer relationship. For our purposes, it will be enough to describe its functionality qualitatively, and follow this with a few equations that encapsulate the important aspects of MOSFET behaviour.

---

[3] In this chapter, a "neuron" is defined as the circuit that aggregates all synaptic inputs, applies an activation function and threshold to the result and outputs a pulse or pulses.

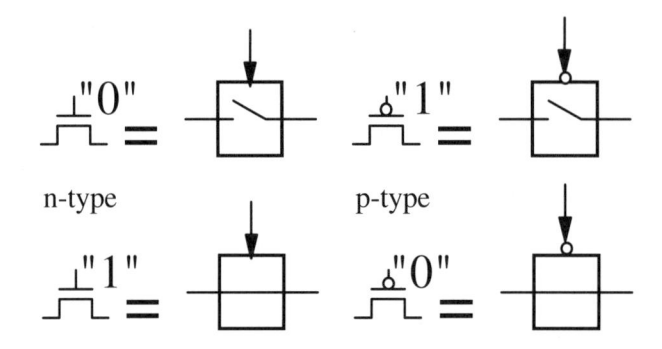

94   3. Pulse-Based Computation in VLSI Neural Networks

Figure 3.2. *n*- and *p*-type MOSFETs, used as binary switches

Figure 3.2 shows the simplest possible abstracted view of a MOSFET's functionality. The MOSFET can be used as a simple binary switch - passing a logic value between its source and drain terminals, under control of a third gate terminal (shown as an arrow in Figure 3.2). *n*-types pass data when the gate signal is logically high, and *p*-types when the gate is logically low. A MOSFET in this mode can pass either digital or analog signals coded as currents or voltages.

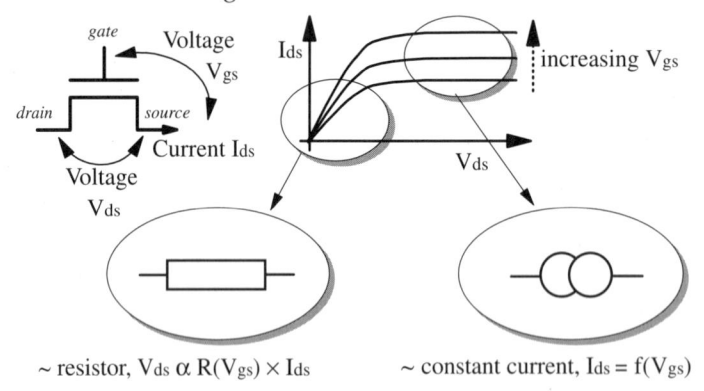

Figure 3.3. *n*-type MOSFET, with its drain-source current→voltage characteristic.

Viewed as a more overtly analog device, the MOSFET has three distinct operating modes and it is necessary to deal with these separately. Taking the *n*-type MOSFET first as an example (Figure 3.3) - current flows from drain to source if a voltage is applied across the drain-source. No DC current flows into the gate, and only very small currents flow into the substrate.

1) Weak Inversion or "OFF" Mode If the voltage between the gate and the source is below a value called the transistor *threshold*, the current flowing from source to drain is also very small (although not zero). In this mode, the transistor is said to be OFF.

2) Linear Mode If the gate-source voltage is above the threshold, the drain-source current is a function of that voltage - getting bigger as the gate-source voltage gets bigger. This behaviour depends critically on the positive gate-source voltage attracting negative carriers from the p-type substrate to the surface, where they can act as the carriers of the drain-source current. A p-type device is therefore a mirror-image, with respect to its operational characteristics.

For a p-type device, the source is the more positive and the drain the more negative terminal. The gate must be more than a transistor threshold below the source for the MOSFET to be on (conducting, source-drain). We can thus more or less alternate between thinking about n- and p-type devices by changing polarities everywhere, and calling the terminals the appropriate names.

The all-important threshold voltage is determined by a large number of process-determined factors. Typically, transistor thresholds are around 1V, in a process designed for 5V operation. Unfortunately, even turned-ON MOSFETs do not obey a single equation with respect to drain-source current. When the gate-source voltage is large, and the drain-source voltage relatively small, the MOSFET is said to be in its linear region, and obeys the equation:

$$I_{ds} = \frac{\mu C_{ox} W}{L} \left[(V_{gs} - V_t) V_{ds} - \frac{V_{ds}^2}{2} \right] \qquad (3.1)$$

3) Saturated Mode When the drain-source voltage is raised (or the gate-source voltage lowered) such that $V_{ds} > V_{gs} - V_t$, the transistor becomes *saturated*, and is governed by:

$$I_{ds}(sat) = \frac{\mu C_{ox} W}{2L} (V_{gs} - V_t)^2 , \qquad (3.2)$$

where

C_{ox} = oxide capacitance/area - determined by the fabrication process

μ = carrier mobility - determined by the fabrication process

W = Transistor gate Width - determined by the MOS designer

L = Transistor gate Length (Source to Drain) - determined by the MOS designer

Both equations, (3.1) and (3.2) become invalid if the transistor is OFF ($V_{gs} < V_t$). We will return to this mode of operation in the next section. Both equations contain a term that can be adjusted by changing the transistor length or width. This is the VLSI designer's primary influence on what goes on. To see what the two equations mean, it is worth looking at graphs showing the drain-source current for different drain-source and gate-source voltages, as shown in Figure 3.3. For a MOSFET that is ON, the current rises initially, as V_{ds} is increased from 0V, almost linearly. This is the term $(V_{gs} - V_t) V_{ds}$ at work, giving the "linear" region its name. In this region, the MOSFET is behaving essentially as a resistor, with a resistance value given by $\left[\frac{\mu C_{ox} W}{L} \times (V_{gs} - V_t) \right]^{-1}$. As V_{ds} increases further and the MOSFET enters the saturation regime, equation (3.2) suggests that the curve should flatten. It is almost flat above $V_{ds} > V_{gs} - V_t$ - the slight slope is a second-order effect, albeit an important one. We do not need to understand it here, but we must be aware of it, as it determines how well MOSFETs behave, particularly when used as current sinks, sources, or mirrors. In the MOSFET equations, it is taken account of by multiplying both (3.1) and (3.2) by $(1 + \lambda V_{ds})$, where λ is a small, empirically-determined parameter.

Modelling transistor behaviour is fraught with this sort of difficulty. There are many other second order effects, whose physical explanations are not all well established. Much of the time, they can be ignored. In designing precision analog circuits, they must be accounted for via simulation, and the designer needs to make himself aware of the models underlying his simulations - they will be baroque versions of (3.1) and (3.2), in the case of MOSFETs.

3.3.1 Subthreshold Circuits for Neural Networks

The first foray into neural silicon by Carver Mead's group at Caltech developed a Hopfield memory in which each w_{ij} weight could be set to one of 3 values $(+1, 0$ or $-1)$ at the cost of 41 transistors per synapse. Since this early work, Mead has evolved what amounts to a complete subculture of analog neural CMOS design methods, circuits and devices based on subthreshold (weak inversion) MOSFET operation [Mead, 1988], although it should be remembered that subthreshold circuits are far from new [Vittoz, 1985]. It is impossible in a review of this nature to do more than give a flavour of the type of work done. As discussed in the section on MOSFET equations, digital designers tend to view a MOSFET as a device whose drain-source current I_{ds} is zero for $V_{gs} \leq V_t$. Analog designers (and DRAM designers) have long known this to be far from true. A "turned off" MOSFET continues to pass current from drain to source, albeit of the order of nA ($Amps \times 10^{-9}$). To the creative analog designer, this is a fascinating feature to be utilised - while to the DRAM designer, who wishes to use the MOSFET as a switch with zero ON resistance and infinite OFF resistance, it is a serious problem. In fact, in this operating regime, drain-source current depends *exponentially* on gate-source voltage:

$$I_{ds} \, \alpha \, e^{KV_{gs}}, \tag{3.3}$$

where K depends on the detailed theory of weak inversion operation (we employ the notation $A\alpha B$ to indicate that A is proportional to B). This relationship allows circuits developed for bipolar transistors (see below), whose input-output relationship is similar, to be adapted directly for MOS usage, and the extremely small currents involved reduce the power consumption in subthreshold devices to very low levels. This fact has been used for some time [Vittoz, 1985] to design circuits with low power consumption. A price is paid, however, in terms of noise immunity. Concerns regarding the noise immunity of such circuits may be answered, in principle at least, by the robustness implied by the massive parallelism in a neural network. Certainly, the biological nervous system copes with noise.

Some attempts have been made to analyse the effects of noise in neural networks [Bishop, 1990, Holmstrom, and Koistinen, 1992, Murray, 1991], and some studies indicate that noise may indeed be at least tolerable, and perhaps helpful [Murray and Edwards, 1994] in neural computation. Mead takes the neurobiological analog one step further, and points out that the dependence of nerve membrane conductance on the potential across the membrane is also exponential [Mead, 1988]. Mead's philosophy is that MOSFET non- linearities are a feature to be celebrated and utilised, rather than lamented.

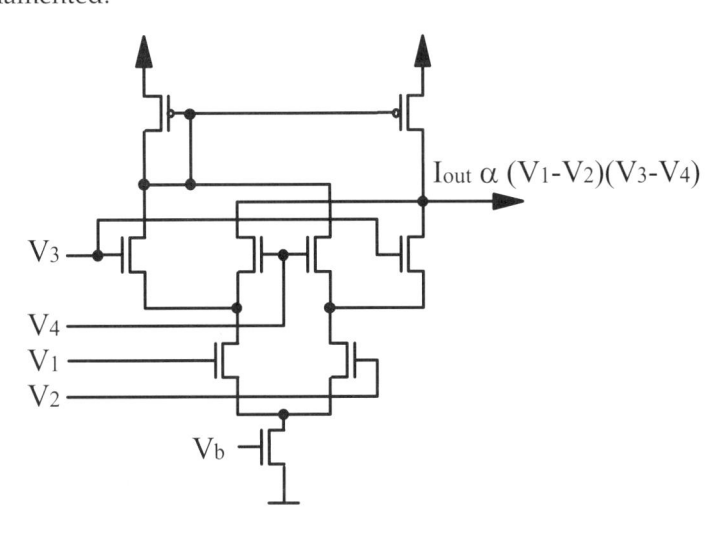

Figure 3.4. MOS Gilbert Multiplier [Gilbert, 1968]

Mead's book [Mead, 1988] is full of clever circuits. It would be foolish even to attempt to capture any more than the flavour of its contents. Purely as an example of a circuit using sub-threshold MOSFETs Figure 3.4 shows the *Gilbert Multiplier* [Gilbert, 1968], well-known in bipolar design as an efficient, four-quadrant multiplier that produces an output current, I_{out}, that is proportional to $(V_1 - V_2) \times (V_3 - V_4)$ over a limited operating regime. Furthermore, the product saturates elegantly (via a *tanh* function) as it tries to exceed the bias current I_b. Mead's group has designed many special purpose chips using this and similar circuits and techniques building on biological exemplars - even to the extent of designing a silicon slug [Ryckebusch et al., 1988]. The contrast between Mead's approach and that of (say) Bell Labs [Le Cun et al., 1990] illustrates the diversity of opinion that exists in the neural research community over the importance (or otherwise) of the biological exemplar. For some, it is merely the inspiration behind the neural paradigm, and sometimes embarrassing, while others regard it as a splendid working example, that should be adhered to in detail, as well as in general terms.

3.4 Pulse Generation in VLSI

One of the primary motivations for our early pulse work was the ease with which pulses can be generated on silicon. Oscillatory circuits often happen by accident! Figure 3.5 shows the simplest possible form of pulsed "neuron".

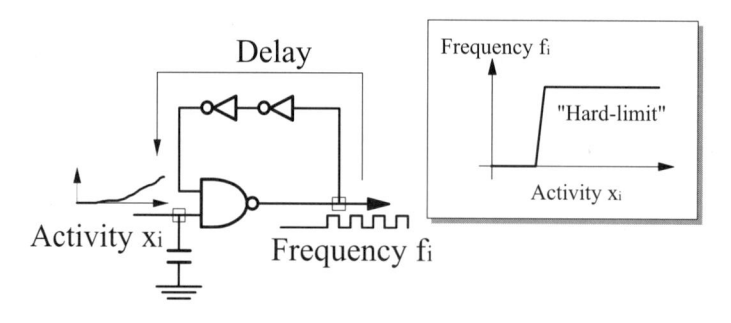

Figure 3.5. Pulsed neuron (simple "ring oscillator")

When the activity voltage is 0, the NAND gate output is fixed at a logic 1 and the ring is broken - no oscillation. When the activity voltage rises above a threshold determined by the MOSFETs that make up the NAND gate, the ring is completed and contains an odd number of inversions (two from the inverters and one from the NAND gate). The output will then oscillate at a frequency determined by the delays around the ring. This output pulse train will have a pulse width and frequency determined by the rise and fall times in the gates that form the loop - so it can be configured to produce a sequence of short spikes. While this form of "pulsed neuron" is extremely simple, its performance is not elegant. It forms a "hard limit" neuron, where the output pulse frequency switches very suddenly from $0 \rightarrow$ maximum and is not tunable.

Figure 3.6 shows a more complex design with a more flexible and elegant switch-on characteristic.

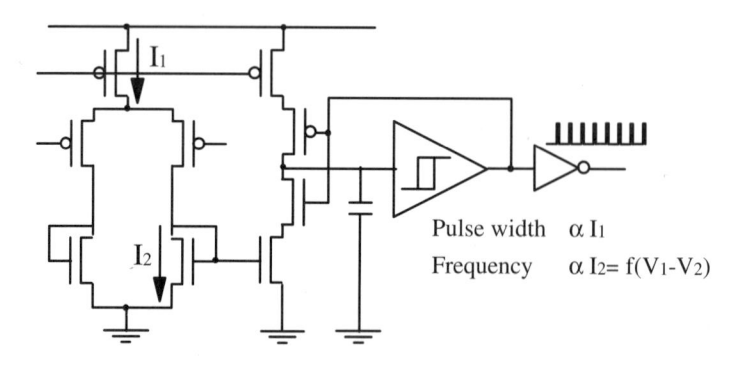

Figure 3.6. Differential pulsed neuron with a smooth switching characteristic [Hamilton, 1993]

This circuit uses a hysteretic loop and allows adjustment of both pulse width and frequency electronically via a bias current and a voltage difference respectively. It is by no means unique and other circuits have been developed with more biologically-oriented aims - for example [Linares-Barranco et al., 1992].

3.4.1 Pulse Intercommunication

This topic is the subject of Chapters 6 and 7 - but it is worth noting at this stage that pulses offer a great deal in terms of intra- and inter-chip communication in VLSI. Pulses encode information in the time domain (unless Pulse Amplitude Modulation is used) and most interference from external sources affects signal amplitudes. Pulsed signals are therefore robust when transmitted over long distances on a chip or a board. Furthermore, pulses can be "regenerated" - a pulsed signal can be passed through a buffer circuit to restore its drive capability or allow it to fan out to a large number of destinations. Precision buffering in the amplitude domain is not necessary.

Finally, pulses allow communication bottlenecks to be eased. Two distinct approaches have been studied to allow multiple pulsed signals to share a single-wire communication channel. The STICCUP system imposed a self-timed time-sequence of channel access [Murray et al., 1992] to allow neurons on separate chips to communicate without explicit address information. In the system that is described later in chapters 6 and 7, pulses are labelled as "events" and each event has an address associated with it. This increases flexibility (any two neurons can exchange signals) at the expense of extra signal generation and distribution (the address information). In addition, the system is not lossless - indeed any system that compresses multiple, dynamic signals on to a single channel loses some information.

3.5 Pulsed Arithmetic in VLSI

There are two functions essential to the evaluation of $\sum w_{ij} v_j$ in an artificial neural network - multiplication and addition. In digital systems, these are well-defined functions, although they may be implemented in detail in several ways. In analog and pulse stream systems, there is more than one generic approach to each operation. These are discussed below, in the context of the hybrid analog/digital pulse stream systems that are the subject of this chapter.

3.5.1 Addition of Pulse Stream Signals

Figure 3.7 illustrates two generic approaches to addition of pulsed (and weighted) neural states, using a frequency modulated state signal v_i as an example. The two approaches are (i) voltage pulse addition and (ii) curent pulse addition. Figure 3.7 shows how loss-free and lossy aggregation can be achieved in both techniques.

Voltage Pulse Addition (Add = Logical OR) This technique is based on the assertion that, if the frequency of a series of fixed-width pulses (or rather their density in time - more correctly the pulsed signal's *duty cycle*) is the representational medium, performing a logical OR between two

3. Pulse-Based Computation in VLSI Neural Networks

Voltage pulses - small circuit, lossy aggregation, fully digital

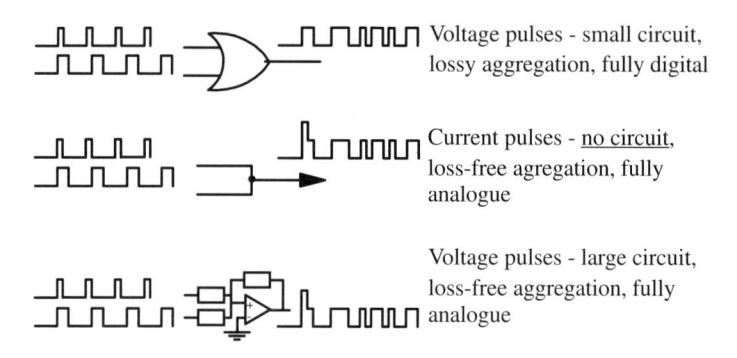

Current pulses - <u>no circuit</u>, loss-free agregation, fully analogue

Voltage pulses - large circuit, loss-free aggregation, fully analogue

Figure 3.7. Techniques for pulse addition.

uncorrelated pulse streams is equivalent to addition of the signals they represent. In other words, if the *probability that a pulsed signal is a logical 1* is taken to represent the "analog" value of that signal, then ORing it with another such signal will add the probabilities, and thus, effectively, the analog values. The underlying assumption is that pulses are by no means mutually exclusive - i.e. they can and do overlap. They are, however, *statistically independent* and their overlap is thus a stochastic occurrence, and is amenable to standard statistical analysis. This OR-based add function is thus distorted by pulse overlap, which can be estimated very simply for a neural OR-based accumulator with N inputs.

OR'ing pulsed signals together to form the add function assumes that the probability p_{out} that the output of the OR gate is logically high is given by the sum of the probabilities that the individual pulsed inputs are each high,

$$p_{out}(ideal) = \sum_{0}^{N_1} p_n \qquad (3.4)$$

It is interesting to note that this immediately produces a potential nonsense, in that p_{out} can exceed 8. This observation alone should act as a warning that the OR-based technique is relying on unsound assumptions.

The technique of OR'ing signals together, can be shown to work in small networks [Murray and Smith, 1987b] but it does not scale at all well, and is not usable in most circumstances [Murray and Tarrassenko, 1994]. Clearly, in our own early development of the pulse-stream method [Murray and Smith, 1987a, Murray and Smith, 1987b, Murray and Smith, 1988] we only succeeded in making this technique work because the level of integration in the test device ($\approx$ 10 neurons) and maximum ratio between pulse period and width ($\approx$ 100 : 1) placed the level of accuracy at 97%. The use of these efficient but approximate arithmetic techniques is explored further in Chapter 13.

Current Pulse Addition It is clearly possible to add pulsed voltages in the more conventional analog way, but current pulse addition requires simpler circuitry. The same considerations relating to the rate of occurrence of pulse overlap apply here. It is their *consequences* that are different. Whereas in a voltage OR-based system, coinciding pulses register as a single pulse, in a current-based network, current pulses add, as indicated in Figure 3.7, producing a current pulse twice the size of the individual pulses. Provided the pulses are subsequently integrated in a way that preserves the integrity of this current, this does not incur any loss of activity information.

Current may be accumulated either as charge on a capacitor ($V = \frac{Q}{C} = \frac{\int I dt}{C}$), or via an active integrator, based on an operational amplifier circuit, if the voltage shift in the node to which current is summed cannot be tolerated. In either case, it is clear that current summation is infinitely preferable to the voltage OR'ing technique alluded to above, and should be adopted for all serious pulse stream implementations. Output from current summation is no longer a pure Pulse Rate Modulated signal; it usually is averaged, and feeds a Voltage Controlled Oscillator thereby regenerating a Pulse Rate Modulated pulse stream.

3.5.2 Multiplication of Pulse Stream Signals

This is altogether a more serious issue, about which no such straightforward and clear-cut conclusions can be drawn. As far as our experience goes, there are two generic approaches - pulse *width* modulation, and pulse *height* modulation. We will therefore discuss the surrounding issues within this framework. The earliest pulse stream work used a simple technique that worked in the small networks in which it was tried. We do not, however, believe that these early attempts [Murray and Smith, 1988] represent good use of the power of pulse stream signalling.

Synaptic gating was achieved by dividing time artificially into periods representing $\frac{1}{2}, \frac{1}{4} \ldots$ of the time, by means of "chopping clocks", synchronous to one another, but asynchronous to neural activities. In other words, clocks are introduced with the ratios between pulse width and period equal to 1:1, 1:2, 1:4, etc., to define time intervals during which input pulses may be passed or blocked. These chopping clocks therefore represent binary weighted bursts of pulses. They are then "enabled" by the appropriate bits of the synapse weights stored in digital RAM local to the synapse, to gate the appropriate *proportion* (i.e. $\frac{1}{2}, \frac{1}{4}, \frac{3}{4}, \ldots$) of pulses v_j to either an excitatory or inhibitory accumulator column. Multiplication takes place when the presynaptic pulse stream v_j is logically AND'ed with each of the chopping clocks enabled by the bits of w_{ij}, and the resultant pulse bursts (which will not overlap one another for a single synapse) OR'ed together. The result is an irregular succession of aggregated pulses at the foot of each column.

The introduction of pseudo-clock signals to subdivide time in segments is inelegant. Furthermore, OR'ing voltage pulses together to implement the accumulation function incurs a penalty in lost pulses due to overlap. We have therefore abandoned this technique, in favour of techniques using pulse width modulation and transconductance multiplier-based circuits. The small network introduced via this method [Murray and Smith, 1988], while not of intrinsic value, nevertheless served to prove that the pulse stream technique was viable, and could be used to implement networks that behaved similarly to their simulated counterparts.

Pulse Width Multiplication When pulse frequency f_i is used to encode presynaptic neural state $f_i \alpha v_i$, individual pulses can be stretched or compressed in time to represent multiplication. For example, if the presynaptic pulse width is D, the postsynaptic pulse width, after passing through a synapse of weight $w_{ij} \leq 1$ is $w_{ij} \times D$. Pulses generated in this way represent the multiplication as postsynaptic pulses of a *width in time proportional to the synaptic weight*, and at a *frequency controlled by the presynaptic neural state*. They can therefore be accumulated in time by either of the methods described above (although we recommend current summation, for the reasons given).

Pulse Amplitude Multiplication This is the most obvious technique, whereby presynaptic pulse widths and frequencies D and f_i are left unchanged, and modulation of pulse magnitude is used to perform multiplication. The resultant postsynaptic signal consists of pulses of a constant width, at a *frequency controlled by the presynaptic neural state*, and of an *amplitude proportional to the synaptic weight*. Such pulses can also be accumulated in time by either of the methods described above.

3.5.3 MOS Transconductance Multiplier

The MOS transconductance multiplier was the basic building block for transversal filters [Mavor et al., 1983] before it became possible to implement digital filters on Digital Signal Processing (DSP) chips with their on-chip digital multipliers. In the neural context, the use of a transconductance multiplier means that *both* the weights w_{ij} and the neural state v_j are represented by analog voltages. Analog multipliers are classified as one-, two-, or four-quadrant multipliers. With most neural networks, the neural state v_j can be restricted to a range between 0 and 1, and two-quadrant multiplication is therefore sufficient. The synaptic weights are usually stored *dynamically* using similar principles to dynamic RAMs. Permanent storage of analog weights is much more difficult to achieve in VLSI and specialised techniques are required here.

3.5.4 MOSFET Analog Multiplier

The expression for the drain-source current, I_{ds}, for a MOSFET in the linear or triode region has already been given earlier in this chapter:

$$I_{ds} = \beta \left[(V_{gs} - V_t) V_{ds} - \frac{V_{ds}^2}{2} \right] \text{ where } \beta = \frac{\mu C_{ox} W}{L} \ . \quad (3.5)$$

This equation can be re-written as follows:

$$I_{ds} = \beta \times V_{gs} \times V_{ds} - \beta \times V_t \times V_{ds} - \beta \times V_{ds}^2 \ . \quad (3.6)$$

The first term in the above equation is the product of two analog voltages and a constant - in a form that could, for example, be used to multiply v_j by w_{ij}. The other two terms are, in effect, error terms which can be removed by a second MOSFET, as shown in Figure 3.8. For this circuit, I_1 and I_0 are given by:

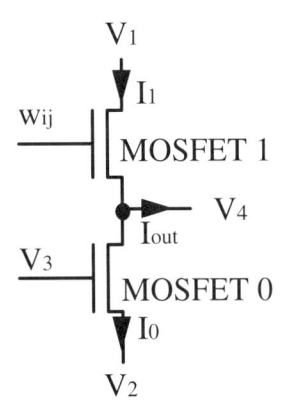

Figure 3.8. Transconductance multiplier - the output current is the voltage product $(w_{ij} - V_3)(V_1 - V_4)$.

$$I_1 = \beta_1 \left[(V_{gs1} - V_t)V_{ds1} - \frac{V_{ds1}^2}{2} \right] \tag{3.7}$$

$$I_0 = \beta_0 \left[(V_{gs0} - V_t)V_{ds0} - \frac{V_{ds0}^2}{2} \right] \tag{3.8}$$

If $\frac{W_1}{L_1} = \frac{W_0}{L_0}$ (i.e., $\beta = \beta_1 = \beta_0$) and $V_{ds1} = V_{ds0}$ then:

$$I_{out} = I_1 - I_0 = \beta(V_{gs1} - V_{gs0})V_{ds} \tag{3.9}$$

Hence $I_{out} = \beta V_X V_Y$ and we could assign $V_X = V_{gs1} - V_{gs0} = w_{ij}$ and $V_Y = V_{ds} = v_j$, to perform a synaptic multiplication function.

The resultant product I_{out} is a current, proportional to the product of two voltages; the currents from different $w_{ij}V_j$ multiplications can be summed together at the input of an op-amp which then gives an output voltage proportional to $\sum w_{ij}V_j$. Figure 3.9 shows how this circuit can be used to form the basis of an efficient pulsed (two-quadrant) multiplier. In the pulsed form, voltages $V_1 \to V_4$ are fixed reference voltages and the transconductance multiplier formed by the two MOSFETs simply produces an output current I_{out} that is linearly proportional to the synaptic weight w_{ij}. It can be positive (excitatory synapse) or negative (inhibitory synapse). Multiplication is achieved by pulsing this current through a third MOSFET operating as a binary switch with the presynaptic signal v_j as its gate signal. The circuit thus produces pulses of current with a magnitude proportional to w_{ij} and a frequency or width proportional to v_j. When integrated, these current pulses form $\sum w_{ij}v_j$.

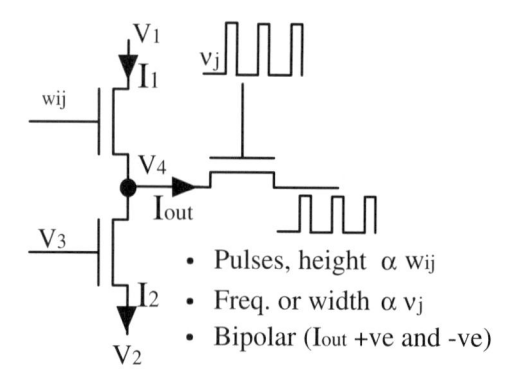

104   3. Pulse-Based Computation in VLSI Neural Networks

Figure 3.9. Pulsed neural multiplier

3.6 Learning in Pulsed Systems

Training algorithms based on back-propagation have been studied [Jabri, and Flower, 1992, Murray, 1992] and have been applied to pulsed systems [Cairns, 1995, Murray et al., 1994]. The results are not encouraging as there is always a requirement for either high accuracy in error-propagation back through multiple layers [Murray et al., 1994] or for measurement of extremely small variations in output signal during weight perturbation [Cairns, 1995]. In both contexts, analog and pulsed systems are found wanting.

Ideally, training algorithms for VLSI should be:

- Local - requiring only locally-available signals such as v_i, v_j and w_{ij} to update w_{ij}.
- Simple - requiring as few operations as possible
- Robust - demanding only moderate accuracy

Hebb's rule [Hebb, 1949] and its derivatives meet these criteria. For example - the simplest imaginable rule is that the synaptic weight w_{ij} increases with correlations between the presynaptic and postsynaptic states v_j and v_i represented by the pulsed signals ν_{pre} and ν_{post} in Figure 3.10 respectively.

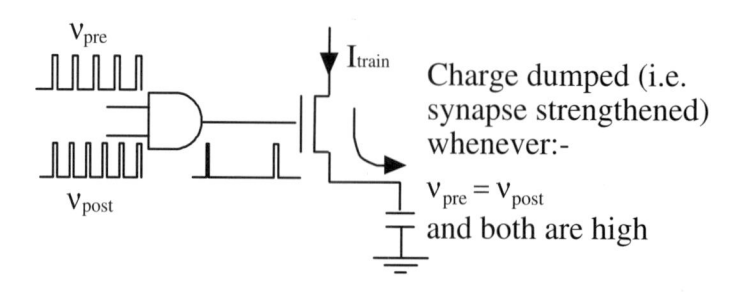

Figure 3.10. A simple pulsed circuit for Hebb's Rule.

If v_j and v_i are both pulsed signals and w_{ij} is stored on a capacitor, the circuit shown in Figure 3.10 implements this rule. Whenever pre- and postsynaptic pulses occur together, the single MOSFET gate is pulsed and a small current carries a small packet of charge on to the capacitor. This learning rule is, however, of limited value. In particular, the value of w_{ij} will eventually saturate unless some weight-decay (or decrement) ability is included. In fact, the demerits of capacitors as weight storage devices bring about an automatic weight decay (albeit an uncontrollable and not very useful form). Figure 3.11 shows the three mechanisms that cause a capacitively-stored weight to decay. These mechanisms, coupled with the lack of robustness to interference from other (particularly digital) signals renders capacitive storage largely unusable in real applications and has led to a strong drive towards non-volatile memory technologies [Buchan et al., 1997, Holler et al., 1989, Holmes et al., 1995, Sage et al., 1989]. A discussion of these techniques is beyond the scope of this chapter and will form the basis of a subsequent paper.

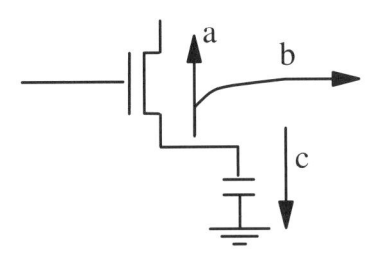

Figure 3.11. Leakage mechanisms associated with capacitive weight storage. **a** is sub-threshold conduction, **b** is leakage into the substrate through reverse-biased diodes and **c** is leakage through the capacitor itself (generally negligible).

3.7 Summary and Issues Raised

It should be clear from this chapter that analog VLSI circuits based on pulses offer significant potential advantages over purely analog forms, in the context of "neural" computation. The major issues are:

1) Coding method: Pulse-width (or pulse-timing) modulation offers fast computation, while pulse-frequency coding offers a time-averaging ability that improves accuracy. In general, accuracy and speed are traded off against one another

2) Complexity: Pulsed MOSFET circuits can implement multiplication, addition and simple correlation functions in small areas. Most success with pulsed VLSI is likely to result from architectures and algorithms that use the natural nonlinear behaviour of MOS (and other) VLSI devices. Algorithms that require extremely high accuracy or linearity, for example, are poor candidates for VLSI.

3) Intercommunication: Often, communication, not computation, is the most significant bottleneck and problems of intra- and inter-chip communication can be eased (but not removed) by pulse-coding

4) Memory: Analog memory is problematic. It can be simple, capacitive and volatile, or difficult, technology-based, non-volatile and expensive. Capacitive storage is suitable for short-term memory but special-technology is required for for long-term memory and products.

5) Accuracy : Any analog technique, including pulse-coding, is susceptible to noise and can never, therefor, offer 100% accuracy. It should be remembered, however, that analog noise and digital (quantisation-limited) inaccuracy are not equivalent, as illustrated schematically in Figure 3.12. Quantisation imposes a fixed set of allowable values on a neural state or weight, while analog noise simply "smears" the parameter. It has been shown that analog noise has effects that are

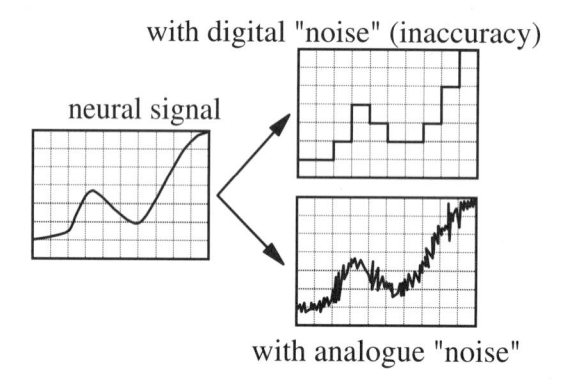

Figure 3.12. A neural signal subjected to digital quantisation and analog noise.

subtle, quite different from digital quantisation and often beneficial [Murray and Edwards, 1994].

6) Training: Algorithms for training VLSI systems should be simple, robust and useful. The optimal location for a VLSI neural network would seem to be at the real-world interface, where analog sensors and transducers present analog signals. Algorithms aimed at simple adaptive signal conditioning algorithms are likely to be most successful.

Of course, these arguments all relate to pulsed implementations of existing artificial neural networks. It is the express intention of this book to take a more fundamental look at the computational power of pulses per se. It is entirely feasible that pulses offer opportunities for totally new forms of neurally-inspired computation and that pulse-based computers could be fundamentally superior to other forms in some applications. Time will tell.

References

[Bishop, 1990] Bishop, C. (1990). Curvature-Driven Smoothing in Back-propagation Neural Networks. *Proc. Int. Neural Networks Conference*, 2:749–752.

[Buchan et al., 1997] Buchan, L. W., Murray, A. F., and Reekie, H. M. (1997). Floating gate memories for pulse-stream neural networks. *Electronics Letters*, 33(5):397–399.

[Cairns, 1995] Cairns, G. (1995). Learning with Analog VLSI Multi-Layer Perceptrons. *D. Phil. Thesis, (University of Oxford)*.

[Churcher et al., 1993] Churcher, S., Baxter D. J., Hamilton, A. , Murray, A. F., and Reekie, H. M. (1993). Generic analog neural computation - The EPSILON chip. *Advances in Neural Information Processing Systems, vol. 5*, Morgan Kaufmann, 773–780.

[Gilbert, 1968] Gilbert, B. A. (1968). Precise four-quadrant multiplier with sub- nanosecond response. *IEEE Journal of Solid-State Circuits*, SC-3:365–373.

[Hamilton, 1993] Hamilton, A. (1993). Pulse Stream VLSI Circuits and Techniques for the Implementation of Neural Networks. *Ph. D. Thesis (University of Edinburgh)*.

[Hamilton et al., 1994] Hamilton, A., Churcher, S., Murray, A. F., Jackson, G. B., Edwards, P. J., and Reekie, H. M. (1994). Pulse stream VLSI circuits and systems: The EPSILON neural network chipset. *International Journal of Neural Systems*, 4(4):395-406.

[Hebb, 1949] Hebb, D. O. (1949). *The Organisation of Behavior*. Wiley, New York.

[Holler et al., 1989] Holler, M., Tam, S., Castro, H., and Benson, R. (1989). An electrically trainable artificial neural network (ETANN) with 10240 "Floating Gate" synapses. *Int. Joint Conference on Neural Networks - IJCNN89*, Washington, IEEE, 191–196.

[Holmes et al., 1995] Holmes, A. J., Churcher, S., Hajto, J., Murray, A. F. and Rose, M. J. (1995). Pulsestream synapses with non-volatile analogue amorphous- silicon memories. *Advances in Neural Information Processing Systems, vol. 7*, MIT Press, 763–769.

[Holmstrom, and Koistinen, 1992] Holmstrom, L., and Koistinen, P. (1992). Using additive noise in back-propagation training. *IEEE Transactions Neural Networks*, 3(1):24–38.

[Horowitz, and Hill, 1989] Horowitz, P., and Hill, W. (1989). *The Art of Electronics*. Cambridge University Press.

[Jabri, and Flower, 1992] Jabri, M. A., and Flower, B. (1992). Weight perturbation: An optimal architecture for analog VLSI feedforward and recurrent multi- layer networks. *IEEE Trans. Neural Networks*, 3(1):154–157.

[Le Cun et al., 1990] Le Cun, Y., Jackel, L. D., Graf, H. P., Boser, B., Denker, J. S., Guyon, I., Henderson, D., Howard, R. E., Hubbard, W. E., and Solla, S. A. (1990). Optical character recognition and neural-net chips. *Proc. Int. Neural Network Conference (INNC-90)*, IEEE, Paris, 651–655.

[Linares-Barranco et al., 1992] Linares-Barranco, B., Rodriguez-Vazquez, A., Huertas, J. L., and Sanchez-Sinencio, E. (1992). CMOS Analog Neural Network Systems Based on Oscillatory Neurons. *International Conference on Circuits and Systems*, IEEE, San Diego, 2236–2239.

[Mavor et al., 1983] Mavor, J., Jack, M., and Denyer, P. (1983). *Introduction to MOS LSI Design*. Addison Wesley, 1983.

[Mayes et al., 1996] Mayes, D. J., Hamilton, A., Murray, A. F., and Reekie, H. M. (1996). A pulsed VLSI radial basis function chip. *Int. Symposium on Circuits and Systems*, IEEE, Atlanta, 3:297–300.

[Mead, 1988] Mead, C. (1988). *Analog VLSI and Neural Systems*, Addison-Wesley.

[Murray, 1991] Murray, A. F. (1991). Analogue noise-enhanced learning in neural network circuits. *Electronics Letters*, 2(17):1546–1548.

[Murray, 1992] Murray, A. F. (1992). Multi-layer perceptron learning optimised for on-chip implementation - a noise-robust system. *Neural Computation*, 4(3):366–381.

[Murray and Smith, 1987a] Murray, A. F. and Smith, A. V. W. (1987). A novel computational and signalling method for VLSI neural networks. *European Solid State Circuits Conference*. VDE-Verlag, Berlin, 19-22.

[Murray and Smith, 1987b] Murray, A. F. and Smith, A. V. W. (1987). Asynchronous arithmetic for VLSI neural systems. *Electronics Letters*, 23(12):642–643.

[Murray and Smith, 1988] Murray, A. F., and Smith, A. V. W. (1988). Asynchronous VLSI neural networks using pulse stream arithmetic. *IEEE Journal of Solid-State Circuits and Systems*, 23(3):688–697.

[Murray et al., 1992] Murray, A. F., Hamilton, A., Baxter, D. J., Churcher, S., Reekie, H. M., and Tarassenko, L. (1992). Integrated pulse-stream neural networks – results, issues and pointers. *IEEE Trans. Neural Networks*, IEEE, 385–393.

[Murray and Edwards, 1994] Murray, A. F. and Edwards, P. J. (1994). Synaptic weight noise during MLP training: Enhanced MLP performance and fault tolerance resulting from synaptic weight noise during Training. *IEEE Trans. Neural Networks*, 5(5):792–802.

[Murray and Tarrassenko, 1994] Murray, A. F. and Tarassenko, L. (1994). *Neural Computing: An Analogue VLSI Approach*. Chapman Hall.

[Murray et al., 1994] Woodburn, R. J., Murray, A. F., and Reekie, H. M. (1994). Pulse-stream circuits for on-chip learning in analogue VLSI neural networks. *Int. Symposium on Circuits and Systems*, London, 103–110.

[Ryckebusch et al., 1988] Ryckebusch, S., Mead, C., and Bower, J. (1988). Modelling small oscillating biological networks in analog VLSI. *Advances in Neural Information Processing Systems, vol. 1*, Morgan Kaufmann, 384-393.

[Sage et al., 1989] Sage, J. P., Withers, R. S., and Thompson, K. (1989). MNOS/CCD circuits for neural network implementations. *IEEE Proc. Int. Symposium on Circuits and Systems*, 1207–1209.

[Simmons, 1989] Simmons, J. A. (1989). Acoustic-imaging computations by echolocating bats: Unification of diversely-represented stimulus features into whole images. *Advances in Neural Information Processing Systems, vol. 2*, Morgan Kaufmann, 2-9.

[Stark, and Tuteur, 1979] Stark, H., and Tuteur, F. B. (1979). In *Electrical Communication - Theory and Systems*, Prentice-Hall.

[Vittoz, 1985] Vittoz, E. (1985). Micropower techniques. In *Design of MOS VLSI Circuits for Telecommunications*, Y. Tsividis and Angonetti, ed., Prentice Hall.

4 Encoding Information in Neuronal Activity

Michael Recce

4.1 Introduction

Neurons communicate by producing sequences of fixed size electrical impulses called action potentials or spikes. Perceptions, decisions, and ideas are all encoded into trains of action potentials, but the basis of this coding scheme is still not well understood. Deciphering this code is one of the primary goals in experimental neuroscience. This chapter presents some of the data on the firing properties of neurons, along with clues on the coding schemes that have emerged from this data.

As described in Chapter 1, it is widely believed that neurons use firing rate to signal the strength or significance of a response. This hypothesis was first proposed by [Adrian, 1926] from the study of the relationship between the activity pattern of a stretch receptor in frog muscle and the amount of weight applied to the muscle. Figure 4.1 shows some of the data that Adrian used to develop the firing rate code hypothesis. This nerve fiber has what is now considered a classic response function. The firing rate monotonically increases with an increase in the strength of the stimulus. The initial part of the response function is approximately linear and it saturates at the maximum firing rate of the neuron, which generally ranges from 100 to 500 spikes per second.

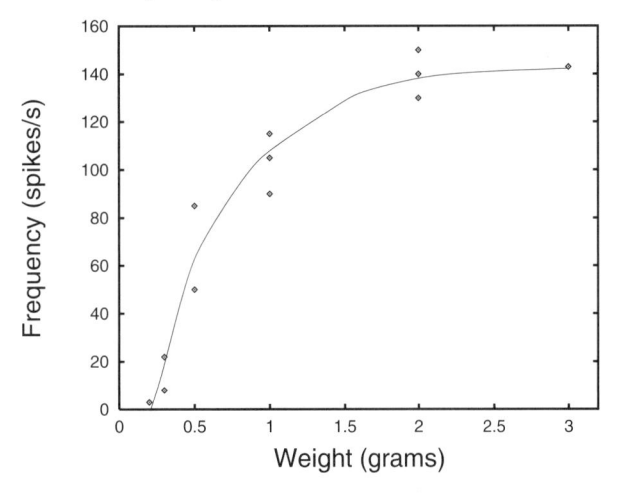

Figure 4.1. Relationship between the weight on a frog muscle and the firing rate of the muscle stretch receptor. Redrawn from Adrian, 1928.

112   4. Encoding Information in Neuronal Activity

Adrian also discovered that neurons only transiently sustain a high firing rate. In the presence of a persistent stimulus the firing rate gradually decreases [Adrian, 1926, Adrian, 1928].

This transient elevated firing is found in the majority of cells in the visual cortices [Hubel and Wiesel, 1962, Maunsell and Gibson, 1992], somatosensory cortex [Mountcastle, 1957], auditory cortex [Brugge and Merzenich, 1973] and many other brain regions. Adrian interpreted this decrease as an adaptation to the stimulus and his hypothesis was that the animal's perceived level of sensation was directly reflected by the instantaneous firing rate, as shown in Figure 4.2.

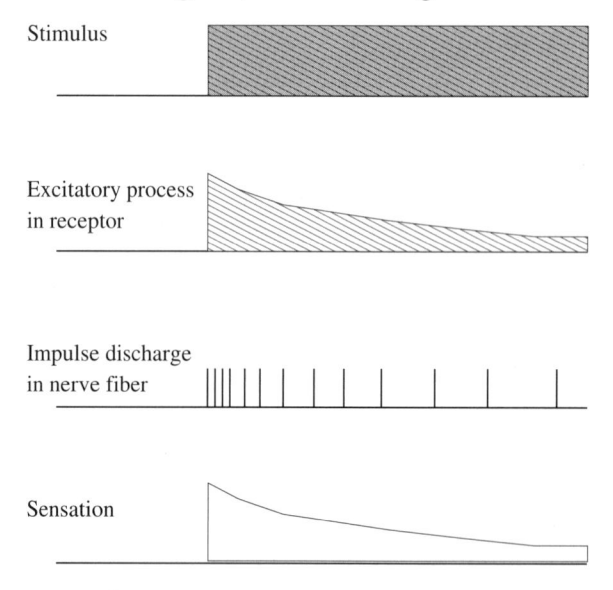

Figure 4.2. Relationship between firing rate and sensation proposed by Adrian (1928). If both the receptor and the organism habituate to a persistent stimulus with the same time scale then the post transient decrease in firing rate might exactly reflect the degree of sensation of the stimulus. Redrawn from Adrian, 1928.

The instantaneous firing rate of a neuron is considered to be a direct measure of the extent to which a recent stimulus matches the neuron's ideal stimulus.

Numerous studies in sensory and motor systems of a wide range of species have supported the validity of the firing rate code hypothesis. For example, pressure receptor cells in the skin appear to use a frequency code to signal the intensity of the stimulus. The contraction of a muscle is roughly proportional to the firing rate of the motor neuron that enervates the muscle. A subset of the output cells from the retina fire at a maximum rate when there is a bright circle of light surround by a dark angular ring illuminating a specific spot on the retina. The ideal stimulus pattern is also called the receptive field of the cell.

The success of the firing rate code hypothesis has led to a method in neuroscience in which the role of neurons is established by searching for the stimulus that elicits the largest firing rate from a cell [Lettvin et al., 1959].

In fact the firing rate code hypothesis has led to the discovery of the role of neurons that are further from sensory receptors or muscles. Hubel and Wiesel used the firing rate hypothesis to discover that some of the neurons in the primary visual cortex are edge detectors [Hubel and Wiesel, 1959, Hubel and Wiesel, 1962].

Place cells in a brain region called the hippocampus, which is anatomically far from the sensory and motor systems, were given this name because they fire maximally when an animal is in a particular place in a particular environment [O'Keefe and Dostrovsky, 1971]. Neurons in the temporal lobes of primates have also been found fire maximally in response to particular objects or for faces.

The properties of these and many other types of neurons in the central nervous system were discovered by applying the firing rate hypothesis.

Strong physiological support for the firing rate hypothesis is also found in the model of a neuron as a temporal integrator. As a temporal integrator, a neuron will lose the precise time of arrival of individual spikes. The amount of postsynaptic depolarization will depend only on the number of spikes arriving at the neuron and the process of synaptic transmission of these spikes. Further, if the firing rate is a direct function of the level of depolarization of the cell then the firing rate is a direct indication of the internal state (or the degree to which the cell is excited).

Neurons act as temporal integrators if the time constant of integration is long in comparison with the average time between spikes. In contrast if the integration time constant is short, the neuron could also act as a coincidence detector [Abeles, 1982, Konig et al., 1996], and therefore be sensitive to the precise arrival time of the spikes for presynaptic neurons.

The hypothesis that the firing rate is proportional to the level of depolarization in cortical cells has been tested explicitly by injecting fixed amplitude current pulses into the soma (e.g. [Mainen and Sejnowski, 1995]). While the firing rate is shown to be a function of the level of depolarization in these experiments, this fixed amplitude current results in a spike train in which the intervals between spikes varies between stimulus presentations. This type of variation in neuronal response to repeated identical stimuli is sometimes interpreted as noise [Shadlen and Newsome, 1994]. The nature of this apparent noise or jitter in neuronal activity is discussed in detail in Section 4.6.

Rate coding also makes it easier to model the function of the neurons, since the rate can be modeled by a single continuous variable. Essentially this removes the need to describe explicitly the behavior of the individual neurons in the system in the time domain. This simplification has been used in the majority of current models of networks of neurons.

However, in recent years evidence has been accumulating that suggests that firing rate alone cannot account for all of the encoding of information in spike trains. Some of this data supports encoding schemes that are in addition to firing rate, while other data describes changes in firing patterns that code for stimuli in the absence of changes in firing rate. Also, experimental evidence exists that places limits on what can be achieved by a firing rate coding alone.

All of these factors also involve the notion that populations of neurons or cell assemblies [Hebb, 1949] may be involved in alternative coding schemes or in overcoming the limitations of firing rate coding.

In this chapter, examples are presented in which the firing rate code does not appear to be sufficient to understand the data. Alternatives to firing rate coding are discussed, along with some of the possible coding problems that might limit the usefulness of a firing rate code. These coding problems include limitations on the dynamic range that can be achieved using a firing rate code, and measured properties of the apparent temporal noise or jitter. Another key issue is the effect of changes in the firing rate on the transmission of a signal to a postsynaptic cell. The impact of new data on the nature of some types of synapses is also important in considering firing rate coding. However all schemes that extend the ways in which neurons are thought to code information must build on, rather than replace firing rate coding, as this scheme has been demonstrated to be highly effective in explaining a wide range of experimental data.

4.2 Synchronization and Oscillations

One of the more strongly supported alternatives or additions to firing rate coding is synchronization and oscillations in populations of neurons. Neurons in numerous cortical and subcortical areas fire in a synchronized or highly correlated manner during specific periods that have been shown to correlate with particular mental or behavioral states. In this section several examples of this phenomenon are described. In some cases the synchronization coincides with an oscillation, but the synchronization does not depend on the presence of oscillations. Also in some cases the synchrony is present in addition to a firing rate change, while in other cases the synchrony is present without any change in the firing rate of the neurons.

Vaadia and coworkers described striking evidence for correlated firing in simultaneously recorded neurons in the frontal cortex of a rhesus monkey [Vaadia et al., 1995]. The neurons were recorded while the animal performed a task in which it had to delay its response to a visually presented spatial stimulus, and the interaction between the neurons were evaluated using a joint peri-stimulus time histogram (JPSTH) [Aertsen et al., 1989]. At the start of each trial one of two possible lights (or cues) was presented for 200 ms, followed by a 3-6 second delay and a trigger signal. The cues indicated if the trial was a GO or a NO-GO trial. In a GO trial the monkey received a reward if it released a center key and selected a correct key, and in a NO-GO trial it was rewarded if it held its hand in position on the center key. The JPSTH showed changes of the normalized correlation in the firing of pairs of neurons as a function of time from a fixed temporal event, such as the onset of a stimulus or a movement. Evidence was presented to show that even though the firing rate of the neurons appeared to be the same in the interspersed GO and NO-GO versions of the task, there was a significant difference in the correlated temporal structure of the activity of pairs of neurons.

In one example the correlated firing between two neurons during the GO tasks was highest during the first second after the onset of the stimulus and lower during the next second. During the NO-GO tasks the pattern of correlated firing was reversed. The correlation was low in the first second and high in the following second. There was no difference in the firing rates between the two paradigms and no difference in the cross-correlation. These rapid changes in the correlation of activity were found in 32% of 947 pairs of recorded neurons.

Most neurons in the auditory cortex have a transient response to the onset of a stimulus [Brugge and Merzenich, 1973]. In a recent experiment multiple isolated singe neurons from several sites in the auditory cortex of anesthetized marmoset monkeys were recorded from simultaneously, while the animal was presented with a pure tone stimulus (4 kHz) that is known to drive these neurons [deCharms and Merzenich, 1996].

The firing pattern, and the correlations between simultaneously recorded neurons in two separated recording sites, were examined in a number of different conditions, two of which are illustrated in Figure 4.3. In one of these conditions there is a persistent tone, and in the other there is a short (50 ms) tone. Cross correlations calculated during a 3 s period, 500 ms after stimulus onset, in each of these two conditions were compared. In both cases there was a transient change in the firing rate, but only during the persistent tone signal there was a zero phase shift synchronization between the firing of the neurons. The significance of this effect was higher when action potentials from several neurons recorded from the same site were combined and correlated with several neurons in a second recording site, suggesting that the correlated activity is a population phenomenon. This data suggests that the temporal structure of the population activity, rather than the firing rate of individual neurons, is used to encode the presence of the tone.

In a recent study sets of neurons in the primary motor cortex (M1) of the macaque monkey were found to synchronize when the animal was preparing to respond to a stimulus [Riehle et al., 1997]. In each trial the animal waited for one of four different delay periods (600, 900, 1200 and 1500 milliseconds), prior to making a motor response. The ordering of the trials was random so that the animal could not predict the length of a particular delay period. In the data from the longest delay trials there was a significant increase in the synchronized activity of pairs and triplets of neurons at points in time corresponding to the shorter delays. This synchronized activity was present without a change in the firing rate of the neurons. In contrast, the motor and sensory components of the task were correlated with changes in the firing rate of the neurons.

The synchronized firing of sets of neurons, which is suggested to be more correlated with internal, rather than external events can not be subsumed within a model or description of neuronal function that only includes firing rate. In all three examples discussed in this section firing rate did not indicate a state change that was only apparent by examining the synchronized activity of simultaneously recorded cells. The first example the synchronization supported the idea that there was a perceptual grouping of stimu-

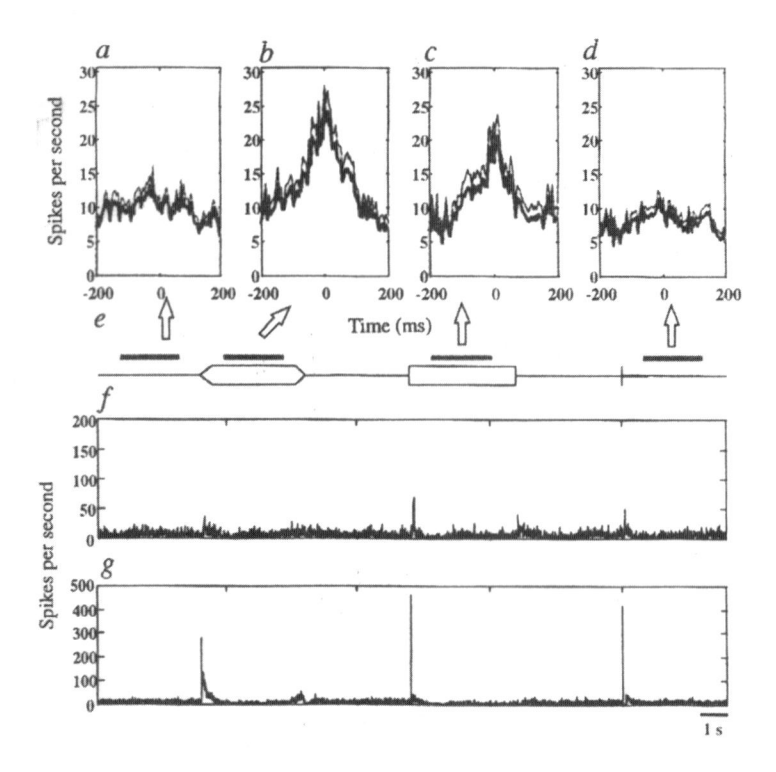

116   4. Encoding Information in Neuronal Activity

Figure 4.3. Mean firing rate and temporal correlation of neurons recorded by [deCharms and Merzenich, 1996] from the primary auditory cortex of a marmoset monkey. Part e of the figure shows the envelope of a 4kHz pure tone stimulus, f and g contain the mean firing rates of neurons simultaneously recorded from two cortical locations, and parts a-d contain average cross-correlations computed from 100 stimulus presentations. In parts a-d the mean is shown with a thick line and the mean plus standard error is shown with a thin line. Part a contains the cross correlation during a silent period before the stimulus; b is the correlation during a 3 second constant phase of a ramped onset pure tone; c is the 3 second period after a sharp onset pure tone; and d is the correlation during a silent period after a short 50 ms pure tone. Reprinted with permission from [deCharms and Merzenich, 1996.]

lus features [Milner, 1974, von der Malsburg, 1981]. In the second example the synchronization coded for the presence of a basic auditory feature, and in the third example the synchronization signaled the presence of an internal state that would otherwise not be observed (see also section 1.1.3.3).

4.3 Temporal Binding

Synchronized activity in populations of neurons in cortical and subcortical regions, and in species as diverse as turtles [Prechtl et al., 1997], pigeons [Neuenschwander et al., 1996], rats [Bragin et al., 1995], cats [Gray and Singer, 1989] and monkeys [Livingstone, 1996, Kreiter and Singer, 1996] is often found to coincide with oscillations in the gamma frequency range (20-70 Hertz). This synchronization can occur with zero phase delay across multiple visual association areas, between visual and motor areas, and between cortical and subcortical regions. The presence of the zero phase shift synchronized firing has been shown to exist between particular subsets of neurons within an area and to occur in relation to specific behavioral events. In the cat visual system synchronized activity was found in cells in separate cerebral hemispheres [Engel et al., 1991]. The evidence for synchronized activity and the significance of this phenomenon has been recently thoroughly reviewed [Singer and Gray, 1995, Engel et al., 1997].

It has been suggested that this synchrony provides a means to bind together in time the features that represent a particular stimulus [Milner, 1974, von der Malsburg, 1981, von der Malsburg, 1995]. There is substantial evidence to suggest that the individual features of a perceived object are encoded in distributed brain regions and fire collectively as a cell assembly [Hebb, 1949].

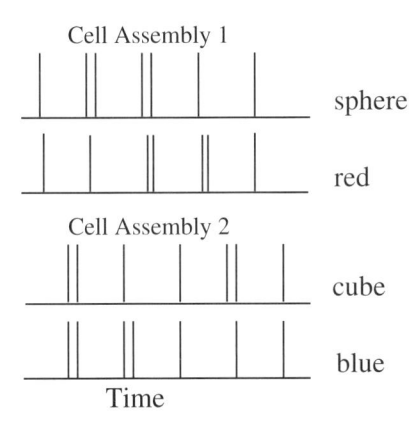

Figure 4.4. Temporal binding of features in cell assemblies. In this example both a red sphere and a blue cube are present in a scene. If sets of neurons code for the colors red and blue, and the for the shapes sphere and cube, then the correct association of color and shape might be represented in the brain by synchronizing the activity of the the neurons within each of the two cell assemblies. In this way neurons coding for red and sphere are active at a different time from those coding for blue and cube, and the two objects can be processed simultaneously.

The central idea is that there is some temporal process during which information about an object or group of objects is processed. In order to keep the attributes of these objects from interfering, they are separated in time, as illustrated in Figure 4.4. In this figure there are two cell assemblies, one that codes for the features of a red sphere and one that codes for the features of a blue cube. Within a cell assembly the neurons fire in a synchronized pattern with zero phase shift. There is a time shift between the two assemblies so that each remains coherent, and the scene is not confused with one containing a blue sphere and a red cube. With firing rate coding it is not possible to construct this type of neuronal system in which multiple, simultaneous use is made of a set of feature encoding neurons.

4.4 Phase Coding

During locomotion, the firing patterns of neurons in the rat hippocampus are modulated by a large 7-12 Hz sinusoidal oscillation called the theta rhythm. The theta rhythm is generated in the hippocampus [Green et al., 1960] from a pacemaker input located in the medial septum [Petsche et al., 1962] . It is highly coherent, with no phase shift over a large region of the hippocampus called CA1 [Bullock et al., 1990]. Many neurons in the CA1 and neighboring CA3 region of the hippocampus have a characteristic burst firing pattern pattern [Ranck, 1973, Fox and Ranck, 1975], and the activity pattern of the majority of these neurons, called place cells, is highly correlated with the animals location in an environment [O'Keefe and Dostrovsky, 1971].

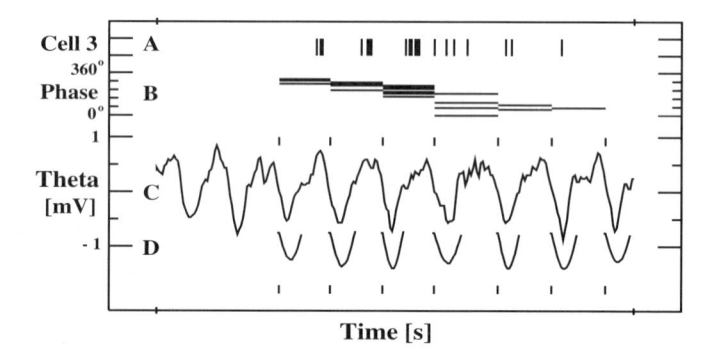

Figure 4.5. Extraction of the firing phase for each spike during a single run through the place field of a place cell on the linear runway. (A) Each action potential from cell 3 during the one second of data shown in the figure is marked with a vertical line. (B) The phase of each spike relative to the hippocampal theta rhythm. (C) Hippocampal theta activity recorded at the same time as the hippocampal unit. (D) Half sine wave fit to the theta rhythm which was used to find the beginning of each theta cycle (shown with vertical ticks above and below the theta rhythm). Reprinted from [O'Keefe and Recce, 1993].

The firing rate of a place cell, within its preferred spatial location, called its place field, has been modeled as a two dimensional Gaussian function [O'Keefe and Burgess, 1996]. Place cells have been recorded on a linear runway, as the animal runs from end to end for a food reward. In this paradigm the time at which an animal arrives at a location varies with running speed, but the activity pattern of the cell continues to be driven by its the spatial location.

As the animal runs through the place field the phase relationship between the spikes and the theta rhythm systematically changes [O'Keefe and Recce, 1993, Skaggs et al., 1996], as shown in the example in Figure 4.5. Each time the animal runs through the place field the firing of the place cell starts at the same phase and systematically precesses through the same phase change. The total amount of phase shift that occurred as the animal ran through the place field was always less than 360 degrees.

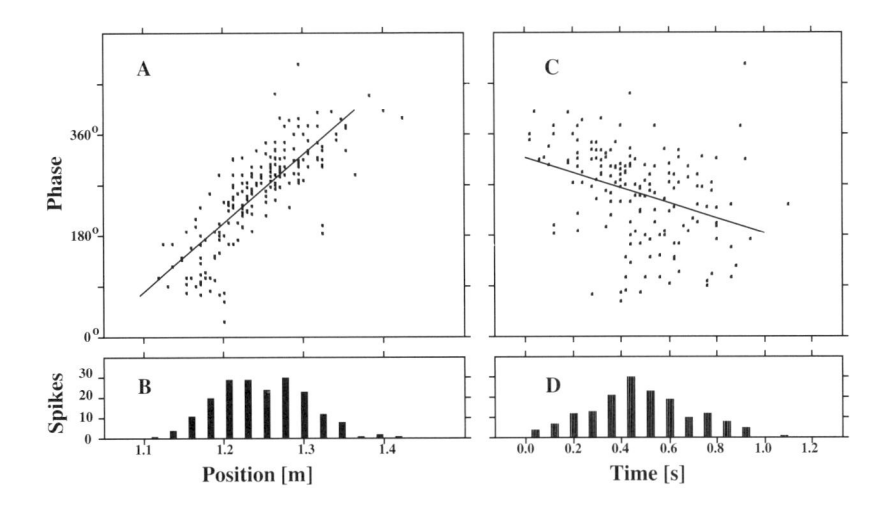

Figure 4.6. Phase of EEG at which a hippocampal place cell fired, (A) plotted against the position of the rat and (C) against the time after the rat crossed the nearest boundary of the place field. (B) and (D) show the distribution of the firing rate recorded in the 41 runs along the runway that were used to construct the figure. Reprinted from [O'Keefe and Recce, 1993].

In addition the phase relationship between the place cell activity and the theta rhythm was found to have a higher level of correlation with the animals spatial location than with the time that the animal has spent in the place field [O'Keefe and Recce, 1993]. Figure 4.6 illustrates this phenomena. In panel A, the phase of each spike from a place cell is plotted against the position of the animal, recorded on multiple runs along the runway. Panel B shows that the firing rate of the place cell is highest in the center of the place field. In panel C and panel D the same data are plotted as a function of the time that has passed since the animal entered the place field. The phase of the firing of this cell and 14 other place cells had a higher correlation to the spatial location, and the phase of firing was a better indication of the animal's location than the firing rate of the cell.

The phase of place cell firing provides additional information on the animal's spatial location which is independent of and more informative than a firing rate code. One possibility is that these different types of information are intended for different target regions in the brain. Also phase coding, like temporal binding, provides a way for the information on neighboring spatial locations to be processed simultaneously without interference (see also Section 1.1.3.2).

4.5 Dynamic Range and Firing Rate Codes

For over forty years it has been known that a firing rate code is not the most efficient way for a neuron to transmit information with action potentials

[MacKay and McCulloch, 1952]. As a simplified illustration consider the the output signal from a neuron that has a firing rate scale that ranges from zero to 200 spikes per second. With the further assumptions that: (1) the critical time interval for integrating the signal or measuring the firing rate is 100 ms, and (2) that there is uncertainty in the generation of spikes, the hypothetical neuron has approximately 20 distinct states.

In contrast if information is coded in the length of inter-spike intervals with five millisecond precision then there are over a million possible output states (2^{20}), although not all of these states would be equally probable. There are a wide range of possible codes that have more than 20 and less than a million different states in a 100 millisecond interval. In particular the coding scheme might look largely like a firing rate, but contain additional information that is only extracted by a subset of the neurons that receive inputs from a particular neuron.

One hundred milliseconds might also be an overestimate of the length of the time interval used to transmit the coded signal. A housefly can change its flight path in reaction to a change in visual input in just 30 milliseconds [Land and Collett, 1974]. In a recent study Thorpe and coworkers showed that the total time required for human subjects to perform a pattern recognition task was 150 milliseconds [Thorpe et al., 1996]. Since this task is thought to require many synaptic steps and substantial signal propagation delays, it appears that the information sampling interval taken by each neuron must be much less than 100 milliseconds.

Some of the most convincing evidence that precise timing of spikes provides additional information, not present in firing rate alone has come from experiments carried out by van Steveninch, Bialek and coworkers. The timing sequence of action potentials in the H1 neuron of the fly have been shown to contain the information needed to reconstruct the stimulus pattern. This reconstruction implies that there is a precision on the order of a millisecond in the firing of each spike. Furthermore they have shown that the H1 neuron only produces one or two spikes in the 30 milliseconds that a fly samples before it can make a response, suggesting that the information encoded in the interspike intervals must be used by the downstream neurons. These data and analysis are presented in great detail in a recent book [Rieke et al., 1997].

4.6 Interspike Interval Variability

All of the proceeding discussion in this chapter has neglected the presence of temporal noise or jitter in the firing patterns of neurons. Temporal noise obviously reduces the number of distinguishable states of an individual neuron, independent of the coding scheme that is being used. Softky and Koch examined the variability in the interspike intervals recorded from cortical cells [Softky and Koch, 1993], that were firing at an average constant rate and found that the intervals between spikes were randomly distributed. They considered this irregularity as evidence that the neurons were acting as coincidence detectors, and that the variability was part of the signal rather than noise. However, it has been argued [Shadlen and Newsome, 1994] that this data supported the hypothesis that neurons were undergoing an internal random walk that results from a roughly equal amount of inhibitory and excitatory input.

An explanation has been found for some of the measured firing irregularity in cortical neurons. Variability found in the interspike intervals of neurons in the visual cortex in anesthetized animals is in part due to the influence of intra-cortical and thalamocortical oscillations that are a direct result of the anesthesia [Arieli et al., 1996]. This noise can be reduced by using awake animals and by controlling for the noise introduced by small eye movements [Gur et al., 1997].

Some of the hypothesized noise in individual neurons might be removed by combining firing rate information accumulated from a population of neurons. Georgopoulos and coworkers have shown that in the motor cortex a population of neurons provides a better correlation to the motor activity than individual cells [Georgopoulos et al., 1986]. [Wilson and McNaughton, 1993] have shown one way in which the firing rate of a population of hippocampal place cells could be combined to provide a better estimate of a rat's location.

In general there are two ways in which a population of neurons can improve the accuracy of the encoding of a stimulus or motor output. Each neuron could have a coarse coding of the stimulus, which is made finer by the activity of a number of neurons. Alternatively each neuron could have independent noise, and this noise is removed by combining input from several neurons. In the two examples discussed here the combined population activity is more precise or informative because each neuron is providing additional information, rather than independent noise (see also Section 1.1.2.3).

If the interspike interval irregularity is noise it can only be removed if this noise is independent in the set of neurons whose activity is averaged. In a recent experiment Shoham and coworkers used voltage sensitive dyes to measure the extent to which neighboring neurons in the visual cortex have independent uncorrelated activity patterns [Shoham et al., 1997]. The activity patterns of neighboring regions of cortex were highly correlated, suggesting that a downstream neuron receives multiple projections with similar interspike intervals, and does not average out the variations. Prectle and coworkers found similar results is the visual cortex of the turtle [Prechtl et al., 1997]. A wave pattern is generated as a result of the presentation of a stimulus, which changes with each presentation of the stimulus but is correlated between neighboring regions of the cortex, within the presentation of the stimulus.

In one recent study, the amount of information and noise in spike trains was quantified. The results from this experiment show that the amount of variation in the interspike interval depends on the properties of the stimulus presented to an animal [de Ruyter van Steveninck et al., 1997]. The response properties of the neurons to static stimuli were highly variable between stimulus presentations. The variance in interspike intervals between stimulus presentations was essentially proportional to the mean firing rate, suggesting that the variation was Poisson distributed. In contrast, when the stimuli were more dynamic and "natural" the response of the H1

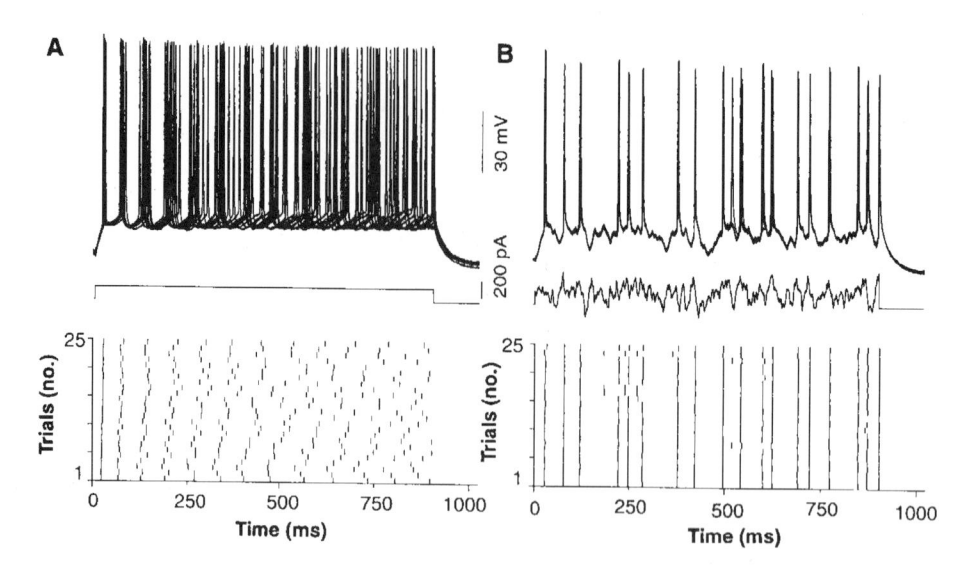

Figure 4.7. Variability of interspike intervals in a cortical neuron with constant or fluctuating current. (A) Superimposed recordings of a regular-firing layer 5 neuron, from 10 consecutive trials with a superthreshold d.c. current pulse (middle), also shown as a raster plot with 25 consecutive trials (lower). (B) The same as in (A) but the stimulus was a repeated signal fluctuating with Gaussian distributed white noise. From [Mainen and Sejnowski, 1995].

neuron to a particular signal was highly reproducible. An analysis of the information carried in the spike train showed that approximately half of the variation was signal and the other half was noise. The information rate was approximately 2.5 bits in 30 milliseconds (see also Section 1.1.3.4).

[Mainen and Sejnowski, 1995] have shown in an in vitro study that neurons in the visual cortex are capable of remarkably precise action potential timing. Their results suggest that the variability found in vivo is a result of variation in the incoming synaptic barrages from one stimulus presentation to the next. The neurons fired with a much higher temporal consistency in response to a repeated randomly fluctuating signal than to a fixed d.c. current pulse. The fluctuating signal was constructed by adding filtered white noise generated by a computer to a constant depolarizing pulse. An example of the data from this experiment is shown in Figure 4.7. The spike trains produced by the fluctuating input were reproducible to less than one millisecond.

In a recent experiment, Nowak and coworkers took this analysis a step further [Nowak et al., 1997]. They recorded from three different types of cells in the visual cortex of a ferret (in vitro). When presented with a fixed level current offset these cells are have different characteristic firing patterns, including: regular spiking, fast spiking and bursting. In contrast when presented with activity recorded from previously described "chattering cells" [Gray and McCormick, 1996], all of the cell types had similar firing pat-

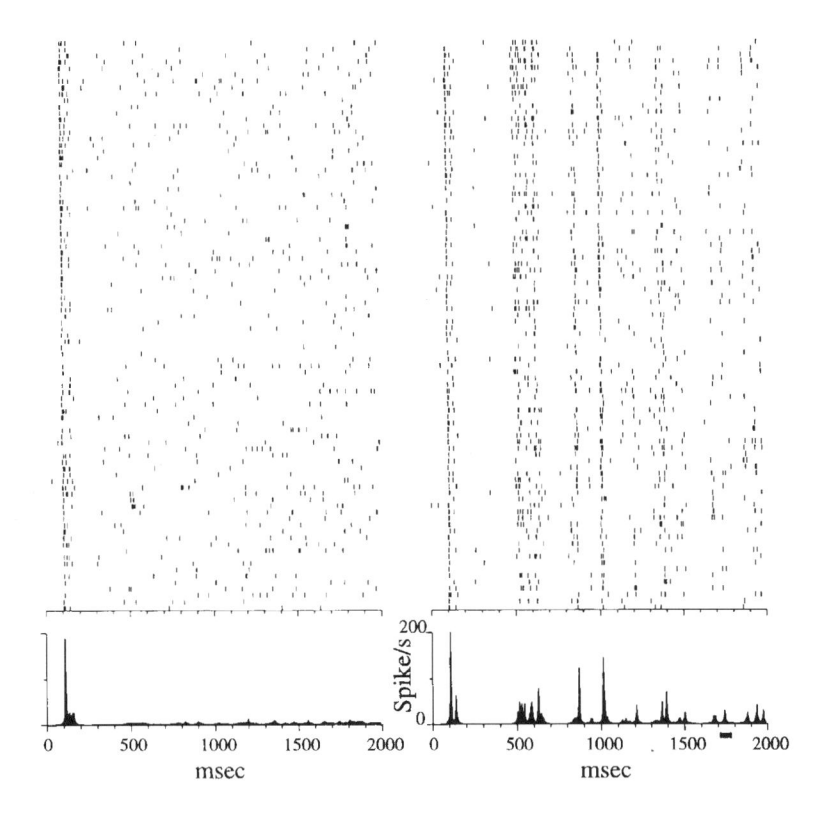

Figure 4.8. Response of one cell in area MT in a behaving macaque monkey to the two second presentation of a random dot pattern. Each raster pattern in the panel on the left shows the response of the cell to a different random dot pattern. The panel on the right shows the response to multiple presentations of the same random dot pattern, which were interleaved with other stimuli. While the response patterns in the left hand panel appear to capture only the onset of the stimulus. It is clear from the right hand pattern that other features of the stimulus pattern are reliably captured. The lower part of each panel contains a poststimulus time histogram (see Section 1.1.2.2). Reprinted from [Bair and Koch, 1996].

terns. They also presented the cells with a range of different noise signals with different spectral characteristics. When presented with real input the cells had a more variable firing pattern, but the firing was more consistent between stimulus presentations. The consistency was present in a much higher reliability and in less temporal jitter.

A similar result was also found in cells in the medial temporal area (V5 or MT) of the awake behaving macaque monkey [Bair and Koch, 1996]. Evidence suggests that this area is involved in visual motion processing [Dubner and Zeki, 1971]. Bair and Koch examined the activity patterns of neurons in response to different random stimuli. As shown in Figure 4.8, when data from different random stimuli were compared the response could be characterized by a transient followed spikes separated by a Poisson random set of interspike intervals. This data alone could be interpreted as evidence for errors or noise in neuronal activity

[Shadlen and Newsome, 1994]. However when presented multiple times with the same random stimulus (right panel of Figure 4.8) there was a high degree of consistency in the firing pattern of the neuron and very little jitter.

Most recently Buracas and coworkers [Buracas et al., 1997] used a Gabor function pattern moved in two or eight directions to study firing patterns of neurons in area MT of behaving macaque monkeys. They measured the information provided by the spike train n response to a stimulus that moved uniformly to one which randomly reversed direction every 30 to 300 ms. The primary finding in this study was that the neurons produced approximately 1 bit of information per second with a constant speed stimulus, and as many as 29 bits per second in response to dynamically changing stimulus.

The results were consistent with the findings of Bair and Koch in that the neurons fired with a reliable sequence in response pattern to a repeated random stimulus, but with highly variable spike trains in response to different random stimuli. They suggest that a neuron codes for the stimulus that results in the highest information rate, rather than the stimulus that produces the highest firing rate.

Buracas and coworkers also measured the information rate as a function of the time after the start of the constant stimulus pattern. Consistent with prior findings of in primate inferior temporal cortex [Optican and Richmond, 1987, Tovee et al., 1993] most of the information is in the first few hundred milliseconds after the onset of the stimulus pattern.

Recent experimental evidence suggests that more realistic stimuli and dynamic stimuli that place more demands on the processing of information within a system of neurons result in reliable and more variable firing patterns of the neurons.

4.7 Synapses and Rate Coding

Some of the strongest evidence against a simple rate code has come from recent studies of the nature of synaptic transmission between pyramidal cells in layer 5 of the rat visual cortex [Markram, 1997]. Paired activation in these synapses, as in other brain regions, has been shown to increase the influence of the presynaptic cell on the activity of the postsynaptic cell in a manner initially suggested by [Hebb, 1949]. However the properties of the synapses both before and after this change are not ideal for the use of rate coding.

As illustrated in Figure 4.8, [Markram and Tsodyks, 1996] demonstrated that modification of the synapse does not result in an increase in synaptic efficacy at all frequencies. With the frequency of input spikes shown in the figure, the response to the initial presynaptic action potential is potentiated, but the response to the subsequent action potentials is attenuated. The top trace contains the average excitatory post-synaptic potential (EPSP) before (solid line) and after (dashed line) pairing activity in the two pyramidal cells, measured as a result of the stimulation sequence shown in

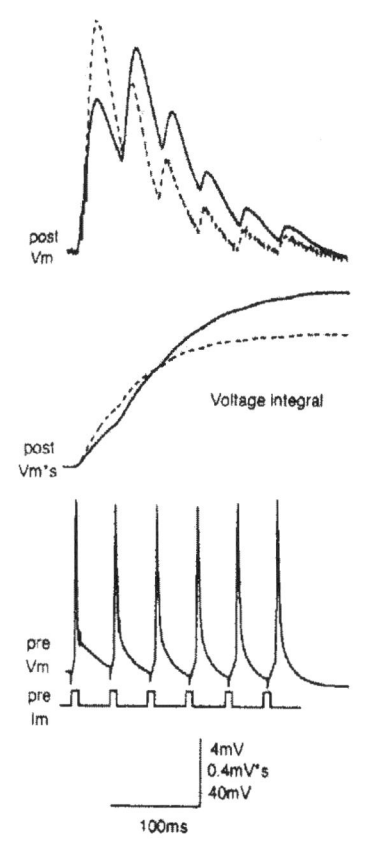

Figure 4.9. Effect of paired activation of synaptically connected layer V tufted cortical cells. The top panel shows the average EPSP before (solid line) and after (dashed line) paired activation. The center panel shows the integral of the normalized EPSPs, and the lower panel shows the presynaptic stimulation. Modified from [Markram, 1997].

the bottom trace. The center part of the figure contains the integral of the EPSP data shown in the top part of the figure. Note that one effect of the potentiation of the initial input and depression of later inputs is to increase the synchrony in the activity of the pre and post synaptic cells.

In later studies [Tsodyks and Markram, 1997, Abbott et al., 1997] it was shown that the post-transient effective synaptic strength is inversely proportional to the firing rate of the presynaptic neuron. This effectively cancels the persistent firing rate signal in the postsynaptic neuron, but leaves a strong response to a transient change in firing rate. These new insights into the synaptic modification rules suggest that some synapses do not effectively transmit persistent rate code information. This issue will be discussed in more detail in Chapter 12.

4.8 Summary and Implications

In this chapter, a small number of selected examples have been presented to illustrate the ways in which the rate coding hypothesis is being changed.

Recent data on the temporal structure of the activity of neurons and the properties of synaptic transmission have highlighted a need to use more realistic computational models to study the properties of systems of neurons. Highlighted differences in the reliability of neuronal firing that result when comparing stimulation with artificial and with more realistic inputs. In particular fixed firing rates and fixed synaptic weights will most likely be insufficient to model the properties of real neurons. The spiking neuron models described in the other chapters of this book capture some of the essential structure needed to construct useful models of systems of neurons. The importance of explicitly modeling the temporal structure of neuronal activity has been made elsewhere [Gerstner et al., 1993], and they have demonstrated that an associative memory can be constructed with spiking neurons.

It is clear that firing rate coding is used by neurons to signal information. However the temporal structure of this firing rate code is likely to contain additional information, which may only be used by a subset of the downstream neurons that receive the message. These examples also highlight the importance in simultaneously measuring the activity patterns in large numbers of neurons and the temporal interactions between these neurons.

References

[Abbott et al., 1997] Abbott, L. F., Varela, J. A., Sen K., and Nelson, S. B. (1997). Synaptic depression and cortical gain control. *Science*, 275:220–224.

[Abeles, 1982] Abeles, M. (1982). Role of cortical neuron: integrator or coincidence detector? *Isr. J. Med. Sci.*, 18:83–92.

[Adrian, 1926] Adrian, A. D. (1926). The impulses produced by sensory nerve endings: Part i. *J. Physiol. (Lond.)*, 61:49–72.

[Adrian, 1928] Adrian, E. D. (1928). *The Basis of Sensation: The Action of the Sense Organs*. W. W. Norton, New York.

[Aertsen et al., 1989] Aertsen, A. M., Gerstein G. L., Habib M. K., and Palm, G. J. (1989). Dynamics of neuronal firing correlation-modulation of effective connectivity. *J. Neurophysiol.*, 61:900–917.

[Arieli et al., 1996] Arieli, A., Sterin A., Grinvald, A., and Aertsen, A. (1996). Dynamics of ongoing activity: explanation of the large variability in evoked cortical responses. *Science*, 273:1868–1871.

[Bair and Koch, 1996] Bair, W. and Koch, C. (1996). Temporal precision of spike trains in extrastriate cortex of the behaving macaque monkey. *Neural Computation*, 6:1184–1202.

[Bragin et al., 1995] Bragin, A., Jandó, G., Nádasdy, Z., Hetke, J. K., Wise K., and Buzsáki, G. (1995). Gamma (40-100 hz) oscillation in the hippocampus of the behaving rat. *J. Neurosci.*, 15:47–60.

[Brugge and Merzenich, 1973] Brugge, J. F. and Merzenich M. M. (1973). Responses of neurons in auditory cortex of the macaque monkey to monaural and binaural stimulation. *J. Neurophysiol.*, 36:1138–1158.

[Bullock et al., 1990] Bullock, T. H., Buzsaki, G. and McClune, M. C. (1990). Coherence of compound field potentials reveals discontinuities in the ca1-subiculum of the hippocampus in freely-moving rats. *Neuroscience*, 38:609–619.

[Buracas et al., 1997] Buracas, G.T., Zador, A., DeWeese, M., and Albright, T.D. (1997). Efficient discrimination of temporal patterns by motion-sensitive neurons in primate visual cortex *Neuron*, in press.

[de Ruyter van Steveninck et al., 1997] de Ruyter van Steveninck, R., Lewen, G. D., Strong, S. P., Koberle, R., and Bialek, W. (1997). Reproducibility and variability in neural spike trains. *Nature*, 375:1805–1808.

[deCharms and Merzenich, 1996] deCharms, R. C. and Merzenich, M. M. (1996). Primary cortical representation of sounds by the coordination of action-potential timing. *Nature*, 381:610–613.

[Dubner and Zeki, 1971] Dubner, R. and Zeki, S. M. (1971). Response properties and receptive fields of cells ina an anatomically defined region of the superior temporal sulcus in the monkey. *Brain Research*, 35:528–532.

[Engel et al., 1991] Engel, A. K., Konig, P., Kreiter, A., and Singer, W. (1991). Interhemispheric synchronization of oscillatory neuronal responses in cat visual cortex. *Science*, 252:1177–1179.

[Engel et al., 1997] Engel, A. K., Roelfsema, P. R., Fries, P., Brecht, M., and Singer, W. (1997). Role of the temporal domains for response selection and perceptual binding. *Cerebral Cortex*, 7:571–582.

[Fox and Ranck, 1975] Fox, S. E. and Ranck, J. B. (1975). Localization and anatomical identification of theta and complex spike cells in dorsal hippocampal formation of rats. *Exp. Neurol.*, 49:299–313.

[Georgopoulos et al., 1986] Georgopoulos, A. P., Schwartz, A., and Kettner, R. E. (1986). Neuronal populations coding of movement direction. *Science*, 233:1416–1419.

[Gerstner et al., 1993] Gerstner, W., Ritz R., and vanHemmen J. L. (1993). Why spikes? Hebbian learning and retrieval of time-resolved excitation patterns. *Biol. Cybern.*, 69:503–515.

[Gray and McCormick, 1996] Gray, C. M. and McCormick, D. A. (1996). Chattering cells: superficial pyramidal neurons contributing to the generation of synchronous oscillations in the visual cortex. *Science*, 274:109–113.

[Gray and Singer, 1989] Gray, C. M. and Singer W. (1989). Stimulus-specific neuronal oscillations in orientation columns of cat visual cortex. *Proc. Nat. Acad. Sci.*, 86:1698–1702.

[Green et al., 1960] Green, J. D., Maxwell, D. S., Schindler, W. J., and Stumpf, C. (1960). Rabbit eeg "theta" rhythm: its anatomical source and relation to activity in single neurons. *J. Neurophysiol.*, 23:403–420.

[Gur et al., 1997] Gur, M., A. Beylin, and Snodderly, D. M. (1997). Response variability of neurons in primary visual cortex (v1) of alert monkeys. *J. Neurosci.*, 17:2914–2920.

[Hebb, 1949] Hebb, D. O. (1949). *The Organization of Behavior*. Wiley, New York.

[Hubel and Wiesel, 1959] Hubel, D. H. and Wiesel T. N. (1959). Receptive fields of single neurons in the cat's striate cortex. *J. Physiol.*, 148:574–591.

[Hubel and Wiesel, 1962] Hubel, D. H. and Wiesel, T. N. (1962). Receptive fields, binocular interaction and functional architecture in the cat's visual cortex. *J. Physiol.*, 160:106–154.

[Konig et al., 1996] Konig, P., Engel, A. K., and Singer, W. (1996). Integrator or coincidence detector? the role of the cortical neuron revisited. *Trends in Neurosci.*, 19:130–137.

[Kreiter and Singer, 1996] Kreiter, A. K. and Singer, W. (1996). Stimulus-dependent synchronization of neuronal responses in the visual cortex of awake macaque monkey. *J. Neurosci.*, 16:2381–2396.

[Land and Collett, 1974] Land, M. F. and Collett, T. S. (1974). Chasing behavior of houseflies (fannia canicuclaris): A descritpion and analysis. *J. Comp. Physiol.*, 89:331–357.

[Lettvin et al., 1959] Lettvin, J. P., Maturana, H. R., McCulloch, W. S., and Pitts, W. (1959). What the frog's eye tells the frog's brain. *Proc. Inst. Rad. Eng.*, 47:1950–1961.

[Livingstone, 1996] Livingstone, M. S. (1996). Oscillatory firing and interneuronal correlations in squirrel monkey striate cortex. *J. Neurophysiol.*, 75:2467–2485.

[MacKay and McCulloch, 1952] MacKay, D. and McCulloch, W. S. (1952). The limiting information capacity of a neuronal link. *Bull. Math. Biophys.*, 14:127–135.

[Mainen and Sejnowski, 1995] Mainen, Z. F. and Sejnowski, T. J. (1995). Reliability of spike timing in neocortical neurons. *Science*, 268:1503–1506.

[Markram, 1997] Markram, H. (1997). A network of tufted layer 5 pyramidal neurons. *Cerebral Cortex*, 7:523–533.

[Markram and Tsodyks, 1996] Markram, H. and Tsodyks M. (1996). Redistribution of synaptic efficacy between neocortical pyramidal neurons. *Nature*, 382:807–810.

[Maunsell and Gibson, 1992] Maunsell, J. H. and Gibson, J. R. (1992). Visual response latencies in striate cortex of the macaque monkey. *J. Neurophysiol.*, 68:1332–1344.

[Milner, 1974] Milner, P. M. (1974) A model for visual shape recognition. *Psychol. Rev.*, 81:521–535.

[Mountcastle, 1957] Mountcastle, V. (1957). *J. Neurophysiol.*, 20:408–434.

[Neuenschwander et al., 1996] Neuenschwander, S., Engel, A. K., Konig, P., Singer, W., and Varela, F. J. (1996). Synchronization of neuronal responses in the optic tectum of awake pigeons. *Vis. Neurosci.*, 13:575–584.

[Nowak et al., 1997] Nowak, L. G., Sanchez-Vives, M. V., and McCormick, D. A. (1997). Influence of low and high frequency inputs on spike timing in visual cortical neurons. *Cerebral Cortex*, 7:487–501.

[O'Keefe and Burgess, 1996] O'Keefe, J. and Burgess, N. (1996). Geometric determinants of the place fields of hippocampal neurons. *Nature*, 381:425–428.

[O'Keefe and Dostrovsky, 1971] O'Keefe, J. and Dostrovsky, J. (1971). The hippocampus as a spatial map. preliminary evidence from unit activity in the freely-moving rat. *Brain Research*, 34:171–175.

[O'Keefe and Recce, 1993] O'Keefe, J. and Recce, M. L. (1993). Phase relationship between hippocampal place units and the eeg theta rhythm. *Hippocampus*, 3:317–330.

[Optican and Richmond, 1987] Optican, L. M. and Richmond, B. J. (1987). Temporal encoding of two-dimensional patterns by single units in primate inferior temporal cortex. iii. information theoretic analysis. *J. Neurophysiol.*, 57:162–178.

[Petsche et al., 1962] Petsche, H., Stumpf, C., and Gogolak, G. (1962). The significance of the rabbit's septum as a relay station between the midbrain and the hippocampus. i. the control of hippocampal arousal activity by the septum cells. *Electroencephalogr. Clin. Neurophysiol.*, 14:202–211.

[Prechtl et al., 1997] Prechtl, J., Cohen, L. B., Pesaran, B., Mitra, P. P., and Kleinfield, D. (1997). Visual stimuli induce waves of electrical activity in turtle cortex. *Proc. Nat. Acad. Sci.*, 94:7621–7626.

[Ranck, 1973] Ranck, J. B. (1973). Studies on signle neurons in dorsal hippocampal formation and septum in unrestrained rats. *Exper. Brain Research*, 41:461–555.

[Riehle et al., 1997] Riehle, A., Grun, S., Diesmann, M., and Aertsen, A. (1997). Spike synchronization and rate modulation differentially involved in motor cortical function. *Science*, 278:1950–1953.

[Rieke et al., 1997] Rieke, F., Warland, D., de Ruyter van Steveninck, R., and Bialek, W. (1997). *Spikes-Exploring the Neural Code*. MIT Press, Cambridge, MA.

[Shadlen and Newsome, 1994] Shadlen, M. N. and Newsome, W. T. (1994). Noise, neural codes and cortical organization. *Curr. Opin. Neurobiol.*, 4:569–579.

[Shoham et al., 1997] Shoham, D., Hebener, M., Schulze, S., Grinvald, A., and Bonhoeffer, T. (1997). Spatio-temporal frequency domains and their relation to cytochrome oxidase staining in cat visual cortex. *Nature*, 385:529–533.

[Singer and Gray, 1995] Singer, W. and Gray, C. M. (1995). Visual feature integration and the temporal correlation hypothesis. *Ann. Rev. Neurosci.*, 18:555–586.

[Skaggs et al., 1996] Skaggs, W. E., McNaughton, B. L., Wilson, M. A., and Barnes, C. A. (1996). Theta-phase precession in hippocampal neuronal populations and the compression of temporal sequences. *Hippocampus*, 6:149–172.

[Softky and Koch, 1993] Softky, W. R. and Koch, C. (1993). The highly irregular firing of cortical cells is inconsistent with temporal integration of random epsps. *J. Neurosci.*, 13:334–350.

[Thorpe et al., 1996] Thorpe, S., Fize, D., and Marlot, C. (1996). Speed of processing in the human visual system. *Nature*, 381:520–522.

[Tovee et al., 1993] Tovee, M. J., Rolls E. T., Treves, A., and Bellis, R. P. (1993). Information encoding and responses of single neurons in the primate visual cortex. *J. Neurophysiol.*, 70:640–654.

[Tsodyks and Markram, 1997] Tsodyks, M. and Markram, H. (1997). The neural code between neocortical pyramidal neurons depends on the transmitter release probability. *Proc. Nat. Acad. Sci.*, 94:719–723.

[Vaadia et al., 1995] Vaadia, E., Haalman, I., Abeles, M., Bergman, H., Prut, Y., Slovin, H., and Aertsen, A. (1995). Dynamics of neuronal interactions in monkey cortex in relation to behavioural events. *Nature*, 373:515–518.

[von der Malsburg, 1981] von der Malsburg, C. (1981). The correlation theory of brain function. *Internal Report 81-2. Gottingen: Max-Plank Institute for Biophysical Chemistry.*.

[von der Malsburg, 1995] von der Malsburg, C. (1995). Binding in models of perception and brain function. *Curr. Opin. Neurobio.*, 5:520–526.

[Wilson and McNaughton, 1993] Wilson, M. A. and McNaughton, B. L. (1993). Dynamics of the hippocampal ensemble code for space. *Science*, 265:1055–1058.

Part II
Implementations

5 Building Silicon Nervous Systems with Dendritic Tree Neuromorphs

John G. Elias and David P. M. Northmore

5.1 Introduction

Essential to an understanding of a brain is an understanding of the signaling taking place within it [Koch, 1997]. Questions as to the nature of neural codes are being tackled by collecting electrophysiological data and analyzing trains of action potentials or spikes for the information that they convey about sensory stimulation [Optican, and Richmond, 1987; Geisler et al., 1991]. As a result of these efforts, we can now see that spike trains encode information not just in their average frequency but also in their temporal patterning [Cariani, 1994; Rieke et al., 1997] (See Chapter 4, this volume).

The question as to how neurons, individually and in networks make use of and interpret such patterns is largely unanswered. Because the requisite experiments to trace information processing in living neural tissue are so difficult, simulation can be very helpful in bridging the gaps in our knowledge and developing insights. Realistic models of neurons connected as networks, can be simulated in computer software (e.g. Chapter 10) and studied for their ability to process spike-borne information. The justification for simulating networks of realistic neurons in VLSI or other special purpose hardware is that significant speed advantages can be gained, but at considerable cost, primarily that of sacrificing flexibility. However, in the hardware developments to be described, we have intentionally restrained processing speed to physiological rates. The reason is that our efforts are directed by the behavior-based or animat approach [Maes, 1993]. The idea is that by building working systems that behave in the real world in real time one acquires an understanding of what nervous systems achieve using fallible and variable components in noisy and messy environments. To be informative about nervous system design, the artificial system controlling behavior should be a reasonably faithful imitation of its biological prototype. It is our view that life-like behavior is likely to be generated by life-like components. Therefore one important requirement of the neuron-like elements, or neuromorphs, composing the artificial nervous system should be that they process information in the form of spike trains.

5.1.1 Why Spikes?

Signaling over long distances in nervous systems has to be carried out by the energy expensive process of propagated action potentials. Given the cost, it would be surprising if evolution had not done more with action potentials than simply encode analog variables like pressure on skin, or the wavelength of visible light into spike frequency for transmission. Sensory stimulation typically has important temporal qualities in addition to intensitive qualities (e.g. the modulations of speech sounds and the roughness of surface texture to the touch), and there would be advantages to capturing this information rather directly in the form of correspondingly patterned spike trains. The physical processes underlying sensory transduction also impose temporal structure on the signals generated (e.g. the rise time of photoreceptor signals depend on the rate of quantal capture), as may the subsequent neural processing. Even the inherently slow visual system deals in spike trains that convey substantially more information in their temporal patterning than in their average frequency [Optican and Richmond, 1987; McClurkin et al., 1991]. Moreover, spike trains can multiplex information [Gawne et al., 1991; Victor and Purpura, 1996]. In neurons of the auditory system, for example, spike frequency can carry information about sound intensity, while the phasing of its spikes indicates sound location [Geisler et al., 1991]. The relative timing of spikes from widely separated neurons in the brain may also carry meaning: if there is synchronization between them, the neurons could be dealing with the same stimulus object [Singer, 1995]. Thus, an emulated nervous system *should* traffic in spikes, not only to be realistic, but also to be efficient.

Fortunately, spike communication is well suited to VLSI implementations. As pulses of short duration, spikes can be sent rapidly to numerous, arbitrary destinations through conventional digital circuitry [Mahowald, 1992; Elias, 1992].

5.1.2 Dendritic Processing of Spikes

The means for interpreting trains of spikes, and their temporal patterning lies in the rich variety of mechanisms available to biological neurons. The structure that must play a critical role is the dendritic tree, so prominent and elaborate in neurons like the pyramidal cells of cerebral cortex and the Purkinje cells of the cerebellum. The classical conception of a neuron held that dendrites are passive, inexcitable, extensions of the neuronal cell body [Eccles, 1957]. Dendrites expand a neuron's surface area for multiple synaptic connections and extend its reach, creating a receptive field. At the same time, dendrites could also provide a mechanism for differentially weighting and delaying synaptic inputs. A line of theoretical work, pioneered by Rall, has investigated the kinds of spatial and temporal processing that could be performed by passive dendritic trees. Neurons vary enormously in the complexity of their dendrites, ranging from elaborately branched trees with numerous synaptic spines to cells with no dendrites at all. In some instances one can point to these differences as reflecting the kinds of temporal processing involved [Rose and Call, 1993]. Dendrites, modelled as passive cables though excessively simplified, could perform nontrivial functions like responding preferentially to direction of movement [Rall, 1964; Northmore and Elias, 1993].

It is clear from a growing body of physiological work on neurons in many areas of the brain that dendritic membranes contain ionic channels that are voltage-dependent or influenced by intracellular second messenger systems [Hille, 1992]. Such mechanisms open up the possibility for non-linear operations, such as the amplification of postsynaptic potentials and the generation of action potentials on the dendrites. Synaptic inputs would sum their effects linearly, but only until a local action potential is fired. In this way the results of local processing in the distal reaches of a dendritic tree could have noticeable effects on the spike firing of the cell's output axon. Non-linearities of this kind could greatly increase dendritic processing power [Mel, 1993]. While spiking events in dendrites have been known for some time, new electrophysiological experiments show that dendrites respond to axonal firings by conducting antidromic spikes back up the dendritic tree, causing changes in the efficacy of recently activated synapses [Markram et al., 1997]. Since our existing passive silicon dendrites are skeletons waiting to be fleshed out with active membrane channels, an important future step would be to emulate these active processes in neuromorphs. Until then, we prefer to mimic active processes by software and creative use of the spike distribution system that we describe below [Westerman et al., 1998].

5.1.3 Tunability

One objective is to produce a set of neuromorphs that are general purpose building blocks for networks of up to a few thousand units. To make the neuromorphs sufficiently flexible for use in specific applications, their operating characteristics should be tunable. Because neurons are capable of operating in different modes at different times (e.g. thalamic neurons [McCormick et al., 1992]), they should by tunable by means of their own activity, or by that of others in a network.

In describing the hardware implementation of our neuromorphs, we discuss the design of the various components: dendrites, synapses, spike generators, and the spike distribution system. The design choices are necessarily compromises between physiological verisimilitude on the one hand, and factors such as simplicity and compactness of implementation, low power consumption, and temperature insensitivity, on the other. If we seem to prefer expedience to physiological correctness, it is that we are eager to build networks large enough to perform capably in the real world. The deficiencies in performance due to the simplifications will show up soon enough, teaching us the important features to incorporate, and something of the design principles of nervous systems.

In the next Section, we introduce each of the main components with discussion of what they are intended to accomplish, and the factors that influenced the design. We briefly describe the electronic circuitry and give references to papers for details. The subsequent Section shows examples of neuromorphs in action, both singly and in small networks.

5.2 Implementation in VLSI

5.2.1 Artificial Dendrites

Like most computational models of neurons [Rall, 1964], our VLSI dendrites are composed of a series of identical compartments, each containing a membrane capacitance (C_m), and two resistors, R_a and R_m, representing the axial cytoplasmic and membrane resistances (see Figure 5.1). Each branch, typically 16 compartments long is connected to form a tree-like structure. In the examples, we use trees with 3 - 8 primary branches connected to a "soma", but higher order branching structures more complex than that of Figure 5.1 are possible. In order to make the dendrites

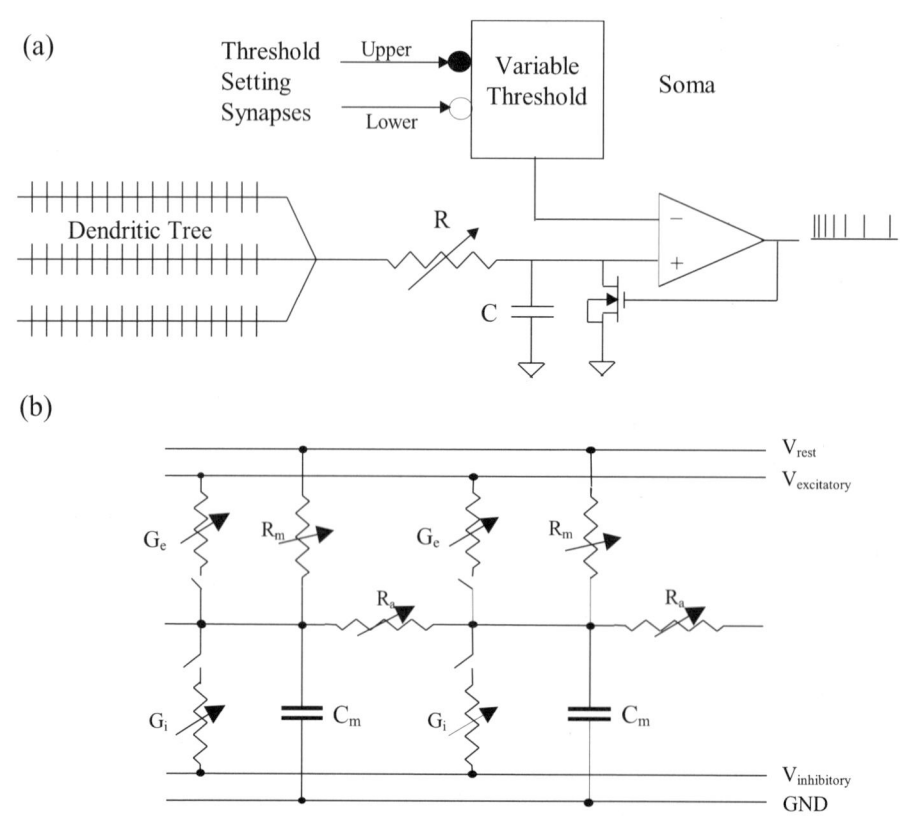

Figure 5.1. (a) Silicon neuron with dendritic tree. Synapses are located at the cross points and at the soma. Activating soma synapses sets the spike firing threshold for the integrate-and-fire spike generator. The integration time constant is determined by a programmable resistor, R, and a fixed capacitor, C. The integration capacitor is discharged whenever a spike is generated by the soma. (b) A two-compartment section of dendrite. Each compartment contains a storage capacitor (C_m) representing the membrane capacitance of an isopotential length of dendrite and a set of conductance paths from the capacitor to various potentials. The switched capacitor membrane (R_m) and axial (R_a) resistors connect the compartment to a resting potential and adjacent compartments. The excitatory (G_e) and inhibitory (G_i) synaptic conductances, which turn on momentarily when a synapse is activated, pull the compartment capacitor voltage towards their respective synapse supply potentials.

reasonably compact, the membrane capacitors, C_m, should be physically small, which means their capacitance will be less than 1 pF. To obtain time constants of physiologically realistic values (e.g. 50 msec), relatively large values are required for R_a and R_m. A problem in VLSI is making high-valued resistors that are linear over wide ranges of voltage at the resistor terminals. A solution which is well behaved in this sense is the switched capacitor circuit [Elias and Northmore, 1995] (see also Chapter 8, this volume). It consists of two switches in series, with a charge storage capacitor, C_h, at the junction of the two switches (see Figure 5.2). The switches are minimum-size transistors that are driven by continuous trains of gate pulses ϕ_1, ϕ_2 that do not overlap, ensuring that only one switch is on at a time. In operation, the first switch to close charges C_h to the potential of terminal A, the second switch transfers a packet of charge from C_h to terminal B. Because charge transferred is proportional to the potential difference between A and B, the device works like a resistor whose value is inversely proportional to the rate of switching. In order to achieve smooth compartment voltages, C_m must be considerably larger than C_h. This condition is satisfied by using parasitic capacitances for C_h, making the device very compact, and achieving effective resistances of 500 K Ohms to 1000 G Ohms.

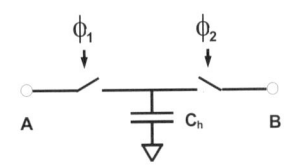

Figure 5.2. Switched capacitor circuit emulating a resistor between terminals A and B. C_h is a charge-holding capacitor formed by parasitic capacitances. ϕ_1, ϕ_2 are non-overlapping switching signals whose frequency determines the effective resistance.

Control of the switching signal frequencies makes it possible to change the values of R_a and R_m very easily, thereby changing the length constant, and the membrane time constant. We are also developing a system of controlling the values of R_a and R_m by spiking activity originating anywhere from the network, thereby exerting "modulatory control" over neuromorph parameters. In neurons, large changes in membrane time constant are predicted to be an effect of changes in the amount of background synaptic activity [Bernander et al., 1991].

5.2.2 Synapses

A spike that is afferent to the dendritic tree of a neuromorph activates either an excitatory or an inhibitory synapse, one of each type being provided in every dendritic compartment. In the early neuromorphs, synapses were emulated by transistors that acted as large, fixed conductances that briefly (50 ns) connected the compartmental capacitor to $+5v$ in the case of excitatory synapses, or to $0v$ in the case of inhibitory synapses

(Figure 5.1). When one of these synapses is activated, the compartment voltage almost immediately moves to its respective supply voltage and then decays as the charge diffuses in both directions along the dendrite. The postsynaptic potential (PSP) as it appears at the soma resembles an alpha function [Jack et al., 1975] with an amplitude that decreases exponentially with the distance of synaptic activation from the soma (Figure 5.3). At the same time the latency of the peak of the PSP increases, roughly in proportion to the distance from the soma [Jack et al., 1975]. Thus, one of the basic functions that could be performed by the artificial dendrite is to weight and delay an input signal by an amount depending upon the location of the activated synapse.

In order to control the amplitude and the delay of PSPs independently, we have fabricated neuromorphs with variable efficacy synapses [Westerman et al., 1997]. Although it is easy to make variable current sources in CMOS technology, fast chemical synapses in the nervous system should be emulated with variable conductances. Because the amount of charge a conductance carries depends upon the potential difference between the membrane potential and the synaptic driving potential, (the channel reversal potential), the efficacy of a single synaptic activation will depend upon recent events that have influenced the membrane potential. This effect is important to mimic in neuromorphs because it leads to sublinear summation of synaptic activations [Rall, 1964; Koch and Poggio, 1987; Shepherd and Koch, 1990; Northmore and Elias, 1996].

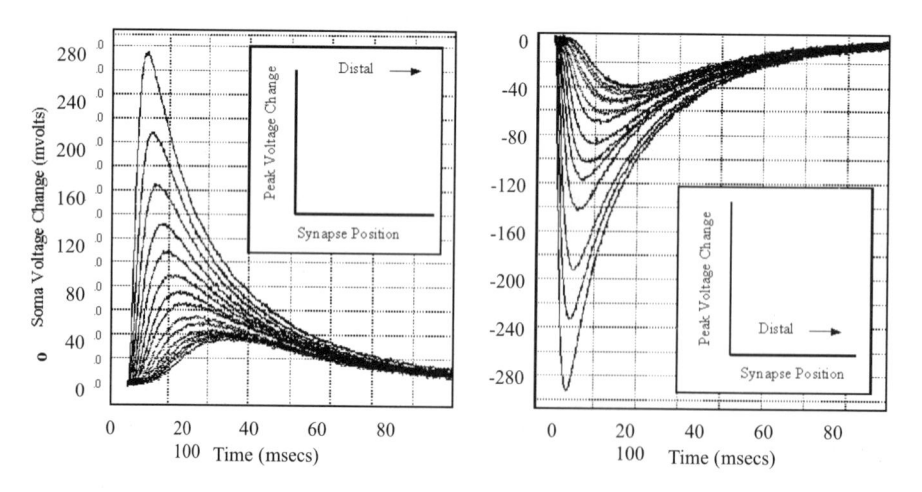

Figure 5.3. Measured impulse responses at the soma due to activating a single synapse at different locations for 100 nsec. Note that the responses last over 1,000,000 times longer than the signals that caused them. Activating progressively more distal compartments evokes responses with progressively lower amplitudes and longer peak latencies.

Rather than making a variable conductance for each synaptic site on all the dendrites, one of the hardware solutions tested involved arrays of switchable conductances that could be shared by many synapses on a chip. For the excitatory synapses, one array of 15 conductances was connected to +5v (the excitatory "reversal potential") and the conductance steps were arranged to produced equally spaced depolarizations of the compartment. Inhibitory synapses were similarly supplied by another array of 15 conductances connected to $0v$ (the inhibitory "reversal potential"). Because each synapse activation is brief (50 ns), the address of the conductance selected (i.e. the weight) can be time multiplexed with the synapse address. This allows spikes coming from different sources to activate one synaptic site with different efficacies. For details of the design see [Westerman et al.,1997].

5.2.3 Dendritic Non-Linearities

Because the artificial dendrite tree is a passive structure composed of linear components, a basic function that we should expect it to perform is summation. The classic modes of temporal and spatial summation of postsynaptic potentials are illustrated in Figure 5.4 a-d by the activation of maximum strength synapses at different times on different branches and observing complete summation of the individual PSPs at the soma. However, the utility of the dendritic tree as a spike processor mainly derives from the fundamental non-linearity alluded to in the last Section. Because synaptic activation opens a conductance to a voltage source, the charge flowing into the compartment is proportional to the difference between the present compartment potential and the driving potential. This means that if the compartment potential is already polarized by recent activations, a subsequent activation of the compartment by the same sign synapse will deliver a lesser amount of charge than if it had occurred to the compartment in a quiescent state. Since charge diffuses along the dendritic branches to the spike generator at the soma, the more recent activation will have a lesser effect on the output spike firing. This dendritic saturation effect results in sublinear summation of the two PSPs, and is therefore most severe when two activations of the same type, either both inhibitory or both excitatory, occur close together in time, and in compartments that are close together (Figure 5.4 e,f). As Figure 5.4 e-f shows, simultaneous activation of maximum strength excitatory synapses results in a PSP that is only as big as the PSP produced by one activation. As the time interval between the two activations increases, the summed PSP grows because saturation of the second impulse response diminishes. Still further increases in the interval result in less temporal summation of the individual PSPs and the summed response shrinks, the overall effect being to tune the response for activation interval. If spike threshold is set appropriately, firing of output spikes will only occur for a range of synapse activation intervals (Fig 5.4 h).

Conditions that retard the diffusion of charge from the activated compartment stretch the time period over which the sublinear summation occurs and lengthen the preferred time interval. One way of bringing about this retardation is by increasing the axial resistance, R_a; another is by contemporaneous activation of neighboring compartments with synapses of the same sign. The opposite effect, an acceleration of charge diffusion, can be brought about by activating neighboring compartments with synapses of opposite sign. Thus, the tuning characteristics of a segment of dendrite de-

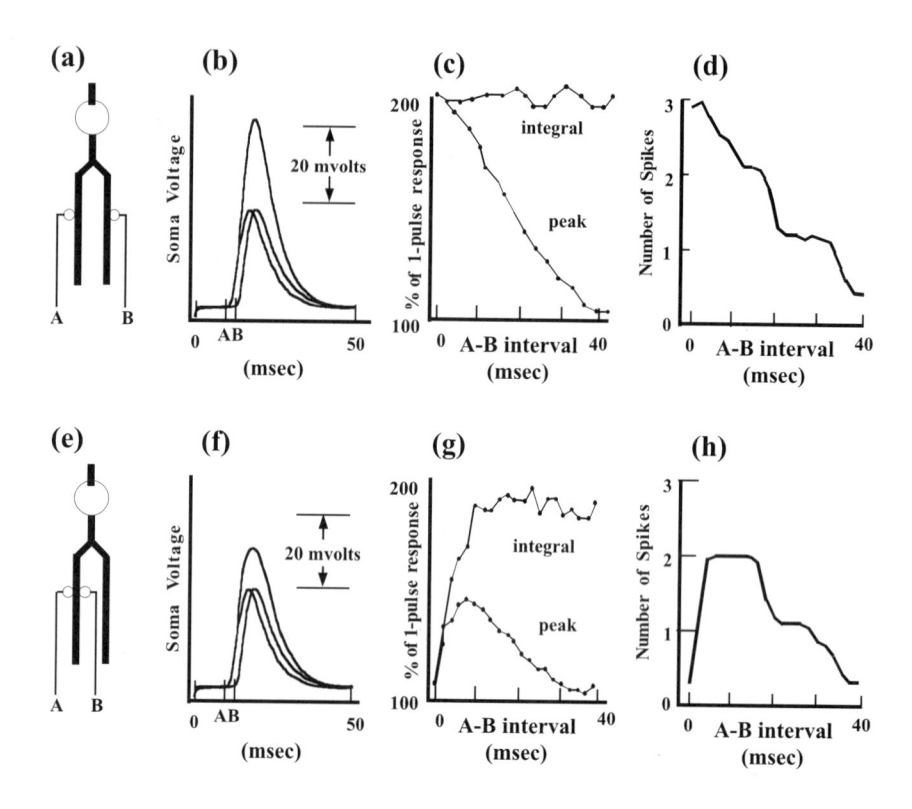

Figure 5.4. Temporal summation of two input pulses, A & B, delivered to excitatory synapses on different branches, of the dendritic tree. (a–d), or on the same branch (e–h). (b, f): Impulse responses measured at soma to input pulses A & B, individually (smaller curves), and together (larger curve). A-B interval = 2 msec. (c, g): Peak impulse response and interval as a function of AB interval. 100% denotes response peak or integral to a single input pass. (d, h): Mean number of spikes generated by the soma as a function of AB interval.

pends upon the configuration of synapses. Clusters of synapses on the same branch produce non-linearities and hence spike interval selectivities, whereas inputs distributed to distant synapses, especially on different branches of the dendritic tree will tend to be summed linearly [Northmore and Elias, 1996]. These effects may well occur in neurons, because there is good evidence that saturating non-linearities limit the response of pyramidal cells in visual cortex under normal conditions of visual stimulation [Ferster and Jagadeesh, 1992].

5.2.4 Spike-Generating Soma

In the classical neuron, spike generation does not occur in the dendrites, but only in the axon initial segment and soma. Accordingly, our current neuromorphs have a single spike generator in a "soma" (Figure 5.1). Rather than attempt to model the ionic channel mechanisms responsible for firing action potentials in neurons, we employ a leaky integrate-and-fire spike generator. This is simple and compact to implement electronically, its behavior is well understood [Knight, 1972], and is widely used in simulations of spiking neurons [e.g. Gerstner et al., 1996].

The potential, V_s, appearing at the soma end of the dendritic tree is applied via a source follower to an RC integrator (see Fig 5.1). When the voltage on C exceeds Vthr, the comparator fires a spike that also discharges C. The gain of the spike generator is determined by R, which is a switched capacitor controlled by a separate clocking signal. Output spike frequency is given by:

$$F_{\text{out}} = -\left(RC \cdot \log\left(1 - \frac{V_{th}}{V_s}\right)\right)^{-1} \qquad (5.1)$$

Note that while spike frequency is not limited by a refractory period, as it is in neurons, refractoriness could be implemented easily by having the comparator trigger a one-shot to switch on the discharge transistor for the requisite period. Although we have explored this and other methods of producing refractoriness, we have not felt compelled to introduce refractoriness for our experimental models, other forms of non-linearity, particularly at the synapses, seem to offer more immediate computational advantages [Northmore and Elias, 1996].

5.2.5 Excitability Control

In addition to the fast synaptic inputs that we have considered so far, neurons are subject to slower modulatory influences that alter their excitability [Hille, 1992]. Because such mechanisms play an important part in the feedback loops that regulate neural activity, an essential feature of a neuromorph should be a capability to adjust certain parameters using the neuromorph's own activity, or the activity originating in a network of neuromorphs. Our solution was to bring these parameters under the control of spiking activity by exploiting the flexibility of the spike distribution system (see next Section). The first implementation of such a capability was the control of V_{thr}. The mechanism we used to control it, the "flux capacitor", turned out to have other applications, including a short-term, analog memory [Elias et al., 1997].

The flux capacitor (see Figure 5.5) uses a conventional MOS capacitor, C_h, to hold charge. The voltage upon C_h, used for V_{thr} in this case, is set by two opposing pairs of switches (labeled Upper & Lower synapses in Figs 5.1a and 5.5). Each switch pair is independently operated by incoming spikes, addressed in the same fashion as synapses. On every activation of the "upper synapse" by a spike, the switch closest to the supply voltage source, V_U, turns on briefly, charging C_U. Then the other switch of the pair turns on briefly, transferring a small packet of charge to C_h, raising its voltage. Similarly, activation of the "lower synapse" removes charge from C_h, lowering its voltage. The device can be made very compact because only two transistors are used for each synapse and the capacitors C_U and C_L are formed by the parasitic diffusion capacitances between the transistors. The voltage stored on C_h depends upon the ratio of spike frequencies delivered to upper and lower synapses. Because the decay time constant is relatively long (ca. 700 secs with C_h = 0.5 pF), low frequency spike trains are sufficient to maintain V_{thr} or any other control voltage used to set neuromorph parameters.

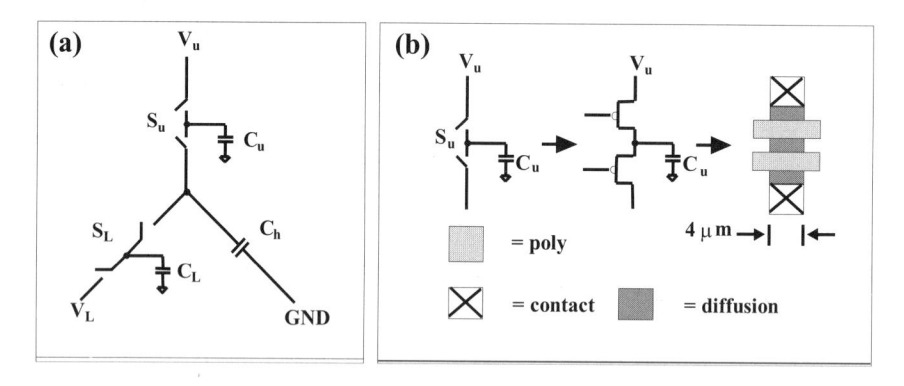

Figure 5.5. (a) Circuit for flux capacitor analog memory. S_u and S_L are the upper and lower synapses, respectively, V_u and V_L are the corresponding synaptic supply potentials. State is held on C_h. The effective synaptic weights are determined by C_u and C_L relative to C_h. (b) Synapse circuit schematic and VLSI layout. Each synapse is made up of two MOS transistors in series. The physical layout is minimum size and C_u and C_L are formed by the parasitic diffusion capacitance between the transistors.

5.2.6 Spike Distribution - Virtual Wires

Building networks of neuromorphs places a heavy responsibility on the system used for interconnecting the units. Like an axonal pathway, it should distribute spikes generated by one neuron to a potentially large number of recipient synapses. Inevitably, axons incur delays proportional to their length, but differential conduction delays, together with synaptic and dendritic delays can be useful in neural information processing. Therefore, a prime requirement of the system should be an ability to fan out spikes from a neuromorph source, delivering them with delays specific to each destination. A practical system should also allow synaptic connections and network architecture to be set up and altered with speed and flexibility. This is especially important when searching for connection patterns by simulated learning, development or evolution. The Virtual Wire system (Figure 5.6) is a solution that satisfies these requirements.

A number of neuromorphs, say up to 1000, residing on some 16 chips, can be accommodated on one circuit board that we call a domain. Within a domain, neuromorphs may be densely interconnected rather as in a cortical region where most of the interneuronal connections are short. The Scanning Machine (see Figure 5.6) continuously polls all potential sources of spikes within its domain. When a spike occurs, the Connection Machine uses the spike source to look up the addresses of the destination

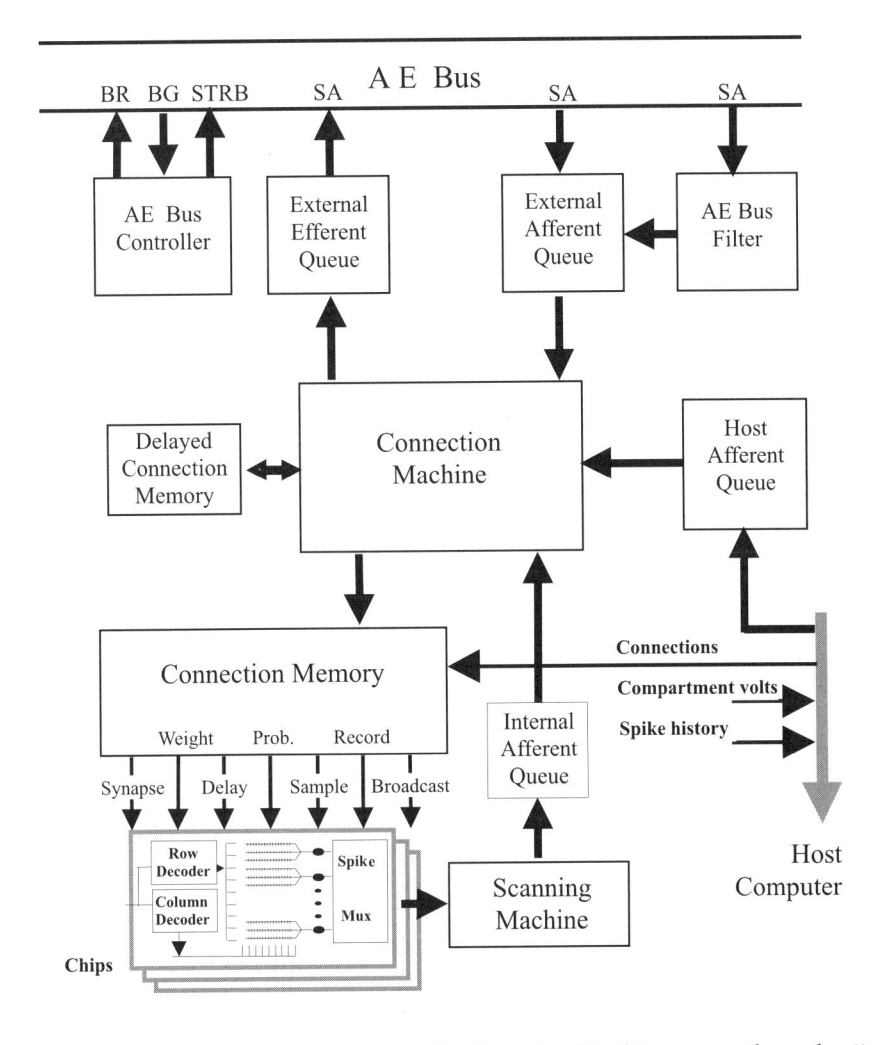

Figure 5.6. Virtual Wires System. The Scanning Machine scans through all on-board neuromorphs (currently set at 1000) in 100 μsec, storing the addresses of spiking neuromorphs in the Internal Afferent Queue. Spike Addresses of neuromorphs from other Domains travel on the Address Event Bus ane are stored in the External Afferent Queue. Spike Addresses generated by the host computer are stored in the Host Afferent Queue. The Connection Machine interrogates the various queues for addresses of spike sources. When it finds one, it activates all the target synapses of that source, either immediately, or after a delay specified in the Delayed Connection Memory.

synapses in the Connection Memory. It then activates those synapses that are due to be activated by sending address information to the neuromorph chips where row and column decoders direct a pulse to the appropriate synaptic destination. The Connection Memory also stores, together with the synapse address, a delay for activation, the synaptic weight, a synaptic activation probability, and several other bits used for sampling compartmental voltages. If an activation is to be delayed, the address and weight of its synaptic destination are stored temporarily in the Delayed Connection Memory. During its polling, the Connection Machine also checks this memory executing any pending activations that are due.

A feature of this scheme is that a single dendritic compartment can be synaptically activated from any number of sources with different delays, weights and probabilities. In this way a dendritic compartment with its excitatory and inhibitory synapse circuits can do the duty of a segment of dendrite with multiple synapses. The scanning machine runs fast enough to introduce, at most, 0.1 msec asynchrony between activations that are supposed to be simultaneous. Longer range connections between domains are made via an Address-Event bus [Mahowald, 1992].

5.3 Neuromorphs in Action

The following experimental results were obtained from neuromorphs with dendritic trees composed of 4 primary branches of 16 compartments. Chips, with 2-4 neuromorphs, were fabricated with a 2 μm CMOS double-poly n-well process on a 2 x 2 mm MOSIS Tiny Chip format.

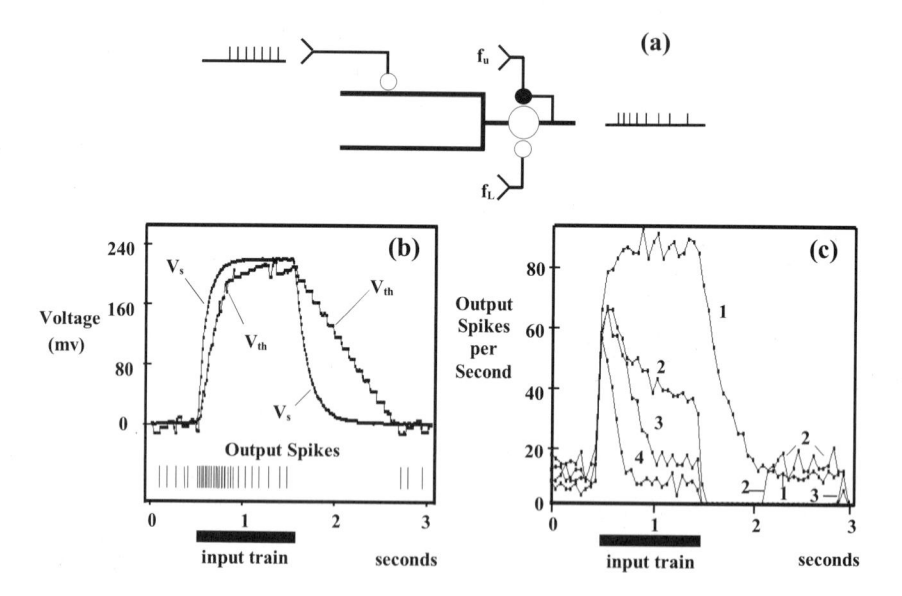

Figure 5.7. (a) Feedback connections on a dendritic tree neuromorph. A spike train of one second duration is input to an excitatory synapse on one branch of the dendritic tree. Tonic spike trains of frequency f_u and f_L are delivered to the upper and lower threshold-setting synapses plus various amounts of feedback to the upper synapse from the output. (b) Soma voltage (V_s), and threshold voltage (V_{th}) as a function of time, together with output spikes. Horizontal bar shows 100 spikes/sec input train applied to the excitatory synapse while f_u = 0/sec and f_L =10/sec. When the input train stops, the threshold slowly returns to the previous level due to tonic activation of the lower threshold synapse. (c) Spike output frequency for 4 different combinations of f_u and f_L and feedback. Curve 1: $f_u = 12.5$, $f_L = 20$, no feedback; Curve 2: $f_u = 42$, $f_L = 111$, feedback = 1 upper activation/output spike; Curve 3: $f_u = 0$, $f_L = 12.5$, feedback = 1 upper activation/output spike; Curve 4: $f_u = 0$, $f_L = 12.5$, feedback = 2 upper activations/output spike.

5.3.1 Feedback to Threshold-Setting Synapses

Figure 5.7 shows connections allowing a neuromorph to regulate its own excitability by use of the upper and lower threshold-setting synapses on the soma,. A continuous train of spikes is supplied to the lower synapse, while the neuromorph's output spikes are fed back with zero delay to the upper synapse. The neuromorph then generates spikes spontaneously at a rate, F_{out}, that balances the train to the lower synapse. The application of a train of spikes activating an excitatory synapse on the dendritic tree, raises V_s well above V_{thr} and the neuromorph starts to fire at a high rate, which, by the feedback connection, raises V_{thr}. Output firing then drops, eventually to a rate slightly above its spontaneous rate. When the excitatory input train ceases, V_{thr} now exceeds V_s, and firing stops. Only when V_{thr} has fallen to its original level does spontaneous firing resume.

One useful effect of this arrangement is to generate spike trains with onset and offset transients, very much like those generated by neurons in sensory pathways, for example. These temporal filtering characteristics which accentuate onsets and offsets can easily be changed. By making more than one feedback connection from the output to the upper synapse gives a still more sharply transient response (Fig 5.7c), and other combinations are easily arranged to tailor a particular response [Elias et al., 1997]. The output firing frequency, F_{out}, is given by

$$F_{\text{out}} = -\left(RC \cdot \log\left(-\frac{\left(\sum_{i=0}^{N} \Delta V_U + \sum_{t=0}^{M} \Delta V_L\right)}{V_s}\right)\right)^{-1} \quad (5.2)$$

where again, V_s is the "membrane potential" and RC is the time constant of the integrate-and-fire soma. V_{th} of Equation (1) is replaced with the change in flux capacitor voltage due to N feedback connections to the upper synapse, and $M = F_L/F_{\text{out}}$, where F_L is the frequency of activation of the lower synapse. Since Fout appears as an argument in the log function Equation (5.2) is most easily solved numerically.

Operating neuromorphs with such negative feedback connections brings other benefits. One is that it minimizes the effects of threshold variation between individual neuromorphs, which is especially noticeable between different chips. It also allows neuromorphs to translate increments in the soma potential, V_s, into increments of output spike frequency in a linear fashion; decrements in V_s, unless small, will cut off spike firing, thereby providing a thresholding non-linearity. These are typical neuronal response characteristics.

5.3.2 Discrimination of Complex Spatio-Temporal Patterns

To demonstrate the power of the dendritic tree as a processor of spike-encoded information, we built a small, feed-forward network of two layers of neuromorphs, to discriminate spatio-temporal patterns that could, for example, represent the waveforms of spoken vowel sounds. The first layer consisted of five J-units and the second of three K-units. The aim was to have each of three input vowels fire a different output (K) neuromorph. Each vowel waveform was digitized into three concurrent spike trains as follows. A spike in a given train was generated at the moment that the waveform crossed a fixed threshold level designated for that train. It turned out to be easy to train the network to discriminate the three vowel sounds \a\, \i\ and \u\, probably because they were encoded by trains of different average spike frequencies. To pose a more challenging problem, therefore, we set the network to discriminate the input patterns of Figure 5.8, each of which were composed of three, 250 msec spike trains of the same frequency, differing only in their phase relationships. The trains of each input pattern were distributed with delays to excitatory and inhibitory synapses on the dendrites of a first layer of neuromorphs, the J-layer. The J-unit thresholds were feedback regulated so that they fired spontaneously and operated in the "linear mode", whereas the K-units of the output layer operated with fixed thresholds that were high enough to ensure that they were normally silent.

The synaptic connections to the J-units and their associated delays were found by a random search procedure so as to provide a partial discrimination of the input patterns. The selection of connections onto the J-units was done by searching through random combinations of synapse type (excitatory/inhibitory), synapse site, and transmission delay, evaluating each combination for its ability to discriminate between the three input patterns. (Only fixed weight synapses were available for these experiments.) Rejected were combinations that, during the 250 msec input, yielded less than 12 spikes to at least one pattern, or nearly equal numbers of spikes to each pattern. Saved for possible use were combinations that yielded at least a 75% difference in spike number between the most and the least effective input patterns. Screening of combinations was done in parallel by presenting each pattern simultaneously to five neuromorphs via different connections, allowing two combinations to be screened per second. About 2% of the combinations were useful.

Having picked the input-J connections to form "basis units", the patterns were fully discriminated by training connections to the K units, which functioned as a layer of linear threshold units. Each J unit made a single synaptic connection to the dendritic tree of each K unit. The synaptic inputs of the different J units were summed linearly by locating them on separate branches of the K dendritic trees. The J-K connections were readily trained by a Perceptron-type learning rule to make the designated K unit fire at least 10 spikes, and the others as few spikes as possible. An error function, based on the total number of spikes fired during the 250 msec input period, was designed to change the effective J-K synaptic weights after each trial. The sign of a weight was set by selecting an excitatory or inhibitory synapse, and its efficacy was increased by moving it along the dendritic branch toward the soma.

As Figure 5.8 shows, the J-units, which fired spontaneously, responded to input trains with complex, temporally structured firing that depended upon the specific input pattern. It is noteworthy that much of the differentiation of the responses was due to latency differences. Because the K-layer works like a Perceptron, summing input spikes, it has to wait for several J-units to fire before it produces its output. Consequently, the processing by this layer did not take advantage of the temporal structure of its inputs. If it were to do so, as in the following example, the speed of classification could be greatly increased.

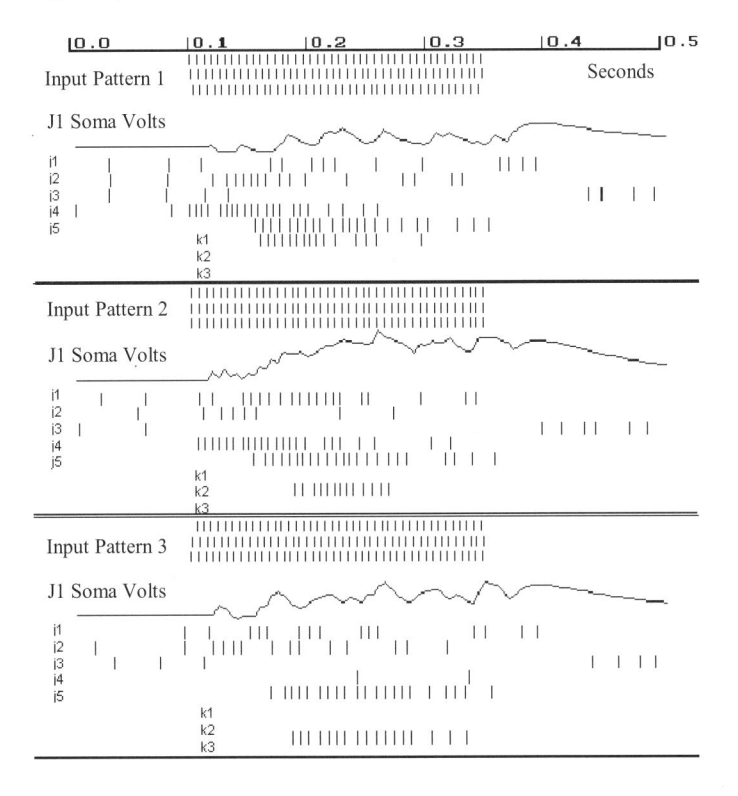

Figure 5.8. Temporal pattern discrimination. The three parts of this figure show the responses of all the neuromorphs in the network to different input patterns, each of which consists of three spike trains of the same frequency, differing only in their phase relations. "J1 Soma volts" shows an example of the potential waveforms generated at the soma. Spike trains labeled J1-J5 show the responses of all the J-units. Note the spontaneous activity before the stimulus onset. Spike trains labeled K1-K3 show the responses of the output units after training. Note that a different K unit fires to each input pattern.

5.3.3 Processing of Temporally Encoded Information

Cerebral cortex performs complex discriminations very rapidly, making decisions based on only one or two spikes in about a 30 msec time window [Thorpe and Imbert, 1989; Rolls and Tovee, 1994]. For such high speed performance a recognition network needs to exploit the timing of individual spikes, and [Maass, 1997] (see also Chapter 2) has shown that neurons could do this by integrating the initial phases of post synaptic potentials to generate temporally coded output spikes. Here we demonstrate a neuromorph used in just this fashion.

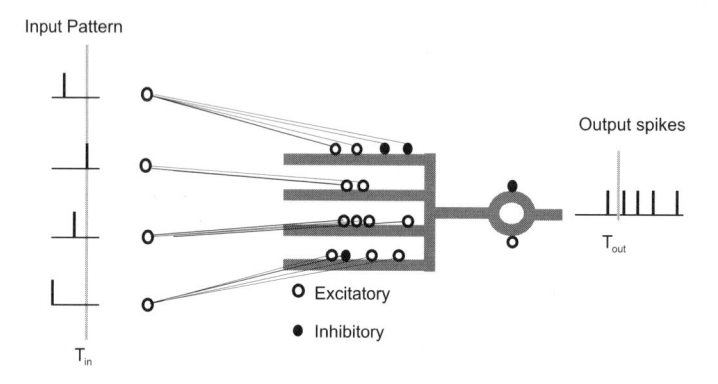

Figure 5.9. Processing spike-time coded inputs. An input pattern is represented by the time advance of four spikes relative to the reference time T_{in}. The input spikes are sent to excitatory and inhibitory synapses on separate branches of a 4-branch dendritic tree. The output value is encoded by the relative time advance of the first output spike generated by the soma relative to the reference time T_{out}.

Figure 5.9 shows four input units each sending a spike with zero delay to a set of synapses on one branch of a neuromorph, an arrangement that ensures that the PSPs generated on each branch are summed linearly at the soma. As in Maass's formulation, the input pattern vectors, with components x_j, are the relative time advances of the constituent spikes. Figure 5.10 shows three different input patterns coded by the time advances of their spikes relative to the reference time, T_{in}. Each input spike alone would generate a PSP at the soma with a rate of rise depending upon the net efficacy of all the synapses that that spike activates. For example, the synapses on the top branch of Figure 5.9 would be net inhibitory because the inhibitory synapses are closer to the soma; those on the third branch would be strongly excitatory. Each input spike, representing x_j by its timing, was accorded an effective weight, w_j, by looking-up in a table of synapse combinations - only full-strength synapses were available. The table of synapse combinations was ordered in terms of the maximum rate of rise of the PSPs that they generated at the soma when they were all activated simultaneously on one dendritic branch. Presenting a 4-spike input pattern generated a PSP at the soma (V_s in Figure 5.10) representing the summation of each branch's PSP. The average rate of rise of the potential, and therefore the time at which the neuromorph's firing threshold was reached, depended upon the temporal ordering of the input spikes, and upon the weight accorded each spike. A supervised, Perceptron-type learning rule was used to adjust synaptic connections so as to generate a first output spike close to target latencies arbitrarily chosen for each input pattern. In the result shown in Figure 5.10, we used the target times of 0, 2 and 1 msec, measured as time-advances relative to a reference time, T_{out}. Training was performed by presenting all three input patterns and obtain-

ing an error for each pattern p, $E_p = T_p - y_p$, where T_p is the target time and yp is the first spike time, both measured as a time advance relative to T_{out}. As a practical matter, it was necessary to truncate Ep to +1.5 msecs before use in the following formula for the change in weight for input spike j,
$$\Delta w_j = \varepsilon \sum_p E_p x_{jp}.$$

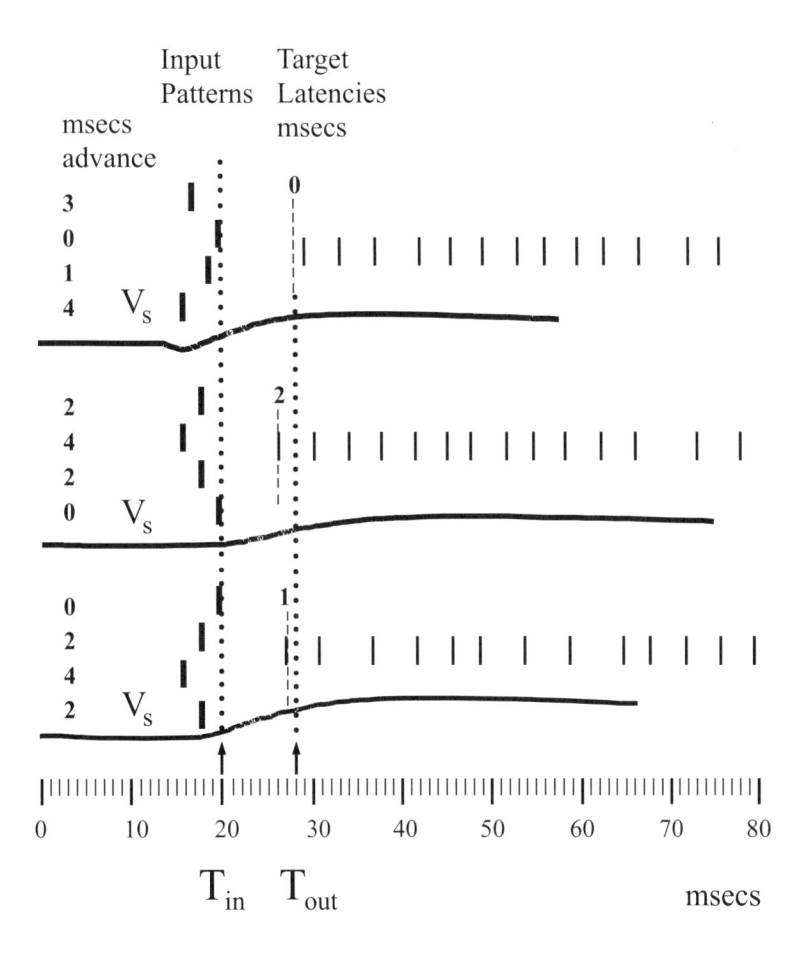

Figure 5.10. Processing three spike time-coded input patterns. Each input pattern is represented by the time advance of four spikes relative to $T_{\text{in}} = 20$ msecs. The network of Figure 5.9 was trained to generate a first output spike with a time advance relative to $T_{\text{out}} = 28$ msecs shown by the dashed lines labelled "Target latencies". V_s is the potential appearing at the soma in response to the input spikes.

As Figure 5.10 shows, each input pattern generated a train of output spikes, the first of which occurred close to the target latencies. Achieving this performance was not easy because the timing of spikes produced by the soma is subject to some jitter, apparently caused by noise at the inputs to the spike generator. There was also the problem of selecting synapses so that their PSPs summed to the requisite rise time at the soma, given that a synapse's PSP peak latency is inversely related to its peak amplitude. The use of neuromorphs with variable efficacy synapses will provide additional control over rise time. Nevertheless, this demonstration shows that a dendritic tree neuromorph can interpret information contained in a purely temporal code of minimal spike number. However, as we have seen in Section 5.3.2, discrimination was more robust when input patterns were spike trains in which the information to be decoded lay in the time differences between multiple spikes.

Cerebral cortex performs complex discriminations very rapidly, making decisions based on only one or two spikes in about a 30 msec time window [Thorpe and Imbert, 1989; Rolls and Tovee, 1994]. For such high speed performance a recognition network needs to exploit the timing of individual spikes, and [Maass, 1997] (see also Chapter 2) has shown how this can be done by neurons that integrate the initial phases of post synaptic potentials. Here we show a neuromorph used in just this fashion.

Figure 5.9 shows four input units each sending a spike with zero delay to a set of synapses on one branch of a neuromorph, an arrangement that ensures that the PSPs generated by each branch are summed linearly at the soma. As is Maass's formulation, the input patterns are represented by the relative time advance of the constituent spikes. Figure 5.10 shows three different input patterns coded by the time advances of their spikes relative to the reference time, T_{in}. Each input spike alone would generate a postsynaptic potential at the soma with a rate of rise depending upon the net efficacy of all the synapses that that spike activates. For example, the synapses on the top branch of Figure 5.9 would be net inhibitory because the inhibitory synapses are closer to the soma; those on the third branch would be strongly excitatory. The weight accorded an input spike was set by using calibrated combinations of full-strength synapses together on one branch. The presentation of a 4-spike input pattern generated an excitatory PSP at the soma (V_s) due to summation of individual PSPs. The average rate of rise of the potential, and therefore the time at which the neuromorph's firing threshold was reached, depended upon the temporal ordering of the input spikes. A supervised, Perceptron-type learning rule was used to adjust net synapse efficacies so as to generate output spikes with latencies at the target times, relative to the reference time, T_{out}. As can be seen, each input pattern generated a train of output spikes, the first of which occurred close to the target latencies.

Achieving this performance was not easy because the timing of spikes produced by the soma is subject to some jitter, apparently caused by noise at the inputs to the spike generator. There was also the problem of selecting synapse locations giving different rise times and peak amplitudes, so as to sum to the requisite rise time at the soma. The use of neuromorphs with the variable efficacy synapses should give an additional degree of control over rise time. Nevertheless, this demonstration shows that a dendritic tree neuromorph can interpret information contained in a purely temporal code of minimal spike number. However, as we have seen in Section 5.3.2, discrimination was more robust when input patterns were spike trains in which the information to be decoded lay in the time differences between multiple spikes.

5.4 Conclusions

Modelled as classical neurons with passive dendrites, our silicon neuromorphs have the dynamical properties to process spike trains much as the nervous system does. The artificial dendrites are able to sum PSPs linearly, or to exhibit a saturating non-linearity, depending on the timing and location of synaptic activations. The integrate-and-fire soma issues spikes in temporally patterned bursts and trains that not only look biologically realistic but are able to convey discriminative information for subsequent stages of neuromorphic processing [Northmore and Elias, 1997]. Real neurons elaborate upon the classical theme with a variety of voltage- and chemical-sensitive ion channels in their cell membranes, which expand their processing capabilities in ways that we have barely begun to appreciate. However, the process of building, even along classical lines, is beginning to teach us something about neural styles of computation.

The incorporation of active channels into the artificial dendrite is a current aim, but it is feasible to emulate only a few of the known channel mechanisms if the dendrites are not to be burdened with circuit complexity. A first priority would be a channel that confers a "superlinearity" to the summation of synaptic inputs, such as the NMDA channel [Mel, 1993]. This channel is also implicated in long-term potentiation of synaptic efficacy, a mechanism for learning [Bliss and Collingridge, 1993].

Learning, in its various forms looms as a challenge to neuromorphic endeavors. A goal to strive for is activity-dependent modification with long-term setting of synaptic efficacy at multiple sites on a dendritic tree. We now know how to make dendritic trees; distributing long term storage over dendrites is more of a problem, but one that could be solved by existing technologies such as floating gates [Diori et al., 1995] or flux capacitors. At present, our approach to adding channel complexity and learning capability to artificial dendrites is one of circumspection. The understanding of how channel mechanisms contribute to the overall function of dendrites is at a primitive stage, while new experimental techniques are still yielding important discoveries (e.g. Markram et al., 1997]. To explore how channel mechanisms in artificial dendrites might implement rules of learning we are currently taking a hardware-software hybrid approach before committing to silicon. Neuromorphs, with passive dendrites and integrate and fire somata, accept and generate spikes in real time, while a host computer samples compartment potentials and spiking activity. On the basis of these data software executes learning rules by changing synaptic weights, connection patterns, or global neuromorph parameters. In this fashion, the Virtual Wire system is being used to explore Hebbian association between real incoming spikes and simulated spikes back-propagated over the dendritic tree [Westerman et al.,1998].

Acknowledgments
Supported by NSF Grants BCS-9315879, and BEF-9511674.

References

[Allen and Sanchez-Sinencio, 1984] Allen, P.E. and Sanchez-Sinencio, E. (1984) *Switched Capacitor Circuits*. Van Nostrand Reinhold Company, New York.

[Bernander et al., 1991] Bernander, O., Douglas, R. J., Martin, K. A. C. and Koch, C. (1991). Synaptic background activity influences spatiotemporal integration in single pyramidal cells. *Proc. Natl. Acad. Sci. USA*, 88:11569–11573.

[Bliss and Collingridge, 1993] Bliss, T.V.P. and Collingridge G. L. (1993). A synaptic model of memory: long-term potentiation in the hippocampus. *Nature*, 361:31–39.

[Cariani, 1994] Cariani, P. (1994). As if time really mattered: Temporal strategies for neural coding of sensory information. In *Origins: Brain and Self-organization*, K. Pribram, ed., Lawrence Erlbaum, Hillsdale, NJ., 208–252.

[Diori et al., 1995] Diori, C., Hasler, P., Minch, B., and Mead, C. (1995). A high-resolution non-volatile analog memory cell. *Advances in Neural Information Processing Systems, vol. 7*, MIT Press, 817-824.

[Eccles, 1957] Eccles, J. C. (1957). *The Physiology of Nerve Cells*. Johns Hopkins Univ. Press, Baltimore, Maryland.

[Elias, 1992] Elias, J. G. (1992). Target Tracking using Impulsive Analog Circuits. *Applications of Artificial Neural Networks III, Proc. SPIE 1992*, Steven K. Rogers, ed., vol. 1709, 338–350.

[Elias, 1993] Elias, J. G. (1993). Artificial dendritic trees. *Neural Computation*, 5:648–663.

[Elias and Northmore, 1995] Elias, J. G. and Northmore, D. P. M. (1995). Switched-capacitor neuromorphs with wide-range variable dynamics. *IEEE Trans. Neural Networks*, 6:1542–1548.

[Elias et al., 1997] Elias, J. G. and Northmore, D. P. M. and Westerman, W. (1997). An analog memory device for spiking silicon neurons. *Neural Computation*, 9:419-440.

[Ferster and Jagadeesh, 1992] Ferster, D. and Jagadeesh, B. (1992). EPSP-IPSP interactions in cat visual cortex studied with in vivo whole-cell patch recording. *J. Neuroscience*, 12:1262-1274.

[Gawne et al., 1991] Gawne, T. J., McClurkin, J. W., Richmond, B. J. and Optican, L. M. (1991). Lateral geniculate neurons in behaving primates, III. response predictions of a channel model with multiple spatial filters. *J. Neurophysiol.*, 66:809–823.

[Geisler et al. 1991] Geisler, W. S., Albrecht, D. G., Salvi, R. J. and Saunders, S. S. (1991). Discrimination performance of single neurons: Rate and temporal-pattern information. *J. Neurophysiol.*, 66:334–362.

[Gerstner et al., 1996] Gerstner, W., Kempter, R., van Hemmen, J. L. and Wagner, H. (1996). A neuronal learning rule for sub-millisecond temporal coding. *Nature*, 383:76–78.

[Hille, 1992] Hille, B. (1992). *Ionic Channels of Excitable Membranes*. Sinauer, Sunderland, Massachusetts.

[Jack et al., 1975] Jack, J. J. B., Noble, D., and Tsien, R. W. (1975). *Electric Current Flow in Excitable Cells*. Oxford University Press, London.

[Knight, 1972] Knight, B. (1972). Dynamics of encoding in a population of neurons. *J. General Physiology*, 59:734-766.

[Koch, 1997] Koch, C. (1997). Computation and the single neuron. *Nature*, 385:207–210.

[Koch and Poggio, 1987] Koch, C. and Poggio, T. (1987). Biophysics of computation: neurons, synapses, and membranes. *Synaptic Function*, G. Edelman, W. Gall, and W. Cowan, eds.,Wiley-Liss, New York, 637–697.

[Maass, 1997] Maass, W. (1997). Fast sigmoidal networks via spiking neurons. *Neural Computation*, 9:279–304.

[Maes, 1993] Maes, P. (1993). Behavior-based artificial intelligence. *From Animals to Animats 2*. Meyer, J., Roitblat, H., and Wilson, S., eds., MIT Press, Cambridge, Massachusetts.

[Mahowald, 1992] Mahowald, M. A. (1992). Evolving analog VLSI neurons. *Single Neuron Computation*, T. McKenna, J. Davis, S. Zornetzer, eds., Academic Press, San Diego, California, 413–435.

[Markram et al., 1997] Markram, H., Lübke, J., Frotscher, M. and Sakman, B. (1997). Regulation of synaptic efficacy by coincidence of postsynaptic APs and EPSPs. *Science*, 275:213–215.

[McClurkin et al., 1991] McClurkin, J. W., Gawne, T. J., Optican, L. M., and Richmond, B. J. (1991). Lateral geniculate neurons in behaving primates. II. Encoding of visual information in the temporal shape of the response. *J. Neurophysiol.*, 66:794–808.

[McCormick et al., 1992] McCormick, D. A., Huguenard, J., and Strowbridge, B. W. (1992). Determination of state-dependent processing thalamus by single neuron properties and neuromodulators. *Single Neuron Computation*, T. McKenna, J. Davis, S. Zornetzer, eds., Academic Press, San Diego, California.

[Mel, 1993] Mel, B. W. (1993). Synaptic integration in an excitable dendritic tree. *J. Neurophysiol.*, 70:1086–1101.

[Mel, 1994] Mel, B. W. (1994). Information processing in dendritic trees. *Neural Computation*, 6:1031–1085.

[Northmore and Elias, 1993] Northmore, D. P. M. and Elias, J. G. (1993). Directionally selective artificial dendritic trees. In *Proc. of World Congress on Neural Networks*, Lawrence Earlbaum Associates, Hillsdale, NJ, 4:503–508.

[Northmore and Elias, 1996] Northmore, D. P. M. and Elias, J. G. (1996). Spike train processing by a silicon neuromorph: The role of sublinear summation in dendrites. *Neural Computation*, 8:1245–1265.

[Northmore and Elias, 1997] Northmore, D. P. M. and Elias, J. G. (1997). Discrimination of phase-coded spike trains by silicon neurons with artificial dendritic trees. *Computational Neuroscience: Trends in Research 1997*, J. M. Bower, ed., Plenum Press, New York, 153–157.

[Optican and Richmond, 1987] Optican, L. M. and Richmond, B. J. (1987). Temporal encoding of two-dimensional patterns by single units in primate inferior temporal cortex. III. Information theoretic analysis. *J. Neurophysiol.*, 57:162–178.

[Rall, 1964] Rall, W. (1964). Theoretical significance of dendritic trees for neuronal input-output relations. *Neural Theory and Modeling*. R. F. Reiss, ed., Stanford University Press, 73–79.

[Rieke et al., 1997] Rieke, F., Warland, D., de Ruyter van Steveninck, R., and Bialek, W. (1997) *Spikes: Exploring the Neural Code*. MIT Press, Cambridge, Massachusetts.

[Rolls and Tovee, 1994] Rolls, E. T. and Tovee, M. J. (1994). Processing speed in the cerebral cortex and the neurophysiology of visual masking. *Proc. Roy. Soc. (Lond.) B.*, 257:9–15.

[Roseand Call, 1993] Rose, G. J. and Call, S. J. (1993). Temporal filtering properties of midbrain neurons in an electric fish: implications for the function of dendritic spines. *J. Neurosci.*, 13:1178-1189.

[Singer, 1995] Singer, W. (1995). Synchronization of neuronal responses as a putative binding mechansim. *The Handbook of Brain Theory and Neural Networks*, M. A. Arbib, ed., MIT Press, Cambridge, Massachusetts, 960–964.

[Thorpe and Imbert, 1989] Thorpe, S. J. and Imbert, M. (1989). Biological constraints on connectionist models. *Connectionism in Perspective*, R. Pfeifer, Z. Schrete, and F. Fogelman-Soulie, eds., Elsevier, Amsterdam, 63–92.

[Victor and Purpura, 1996] Victor, J. D. and Purpura, K. P. (1996). Nature and precision of temporal coding in visual cortex: A metric-space analysis. *J. Neurophysiol.*, 76:1310–1326.

[Westerman et al., 1997] Westerman, W., Northmore, D. P. M., and Elias, J. G. (1997). Neuromorphic synapses for artificial dendrites. *Analog integrated circuits and signal processing*, 13:167–184.

[Westerman et al., 1998] Westerman, W., Northmore, D. P. M., and Elias, J. G. (1998). Antidromic spikes drive Hebbian learning in an artificial dendritic tree. *Analog integrated circuits and signal processing*. In press.

6 A Pulse-Coded Communications Infrastructure for Neuromorphic Systems

Stephen R. Deiss, Rodney J. Douglas and Adrian M. Whatley

6.1 Introduction

Neuromorphic engineering [Mead, 1989, Mead, 1990, Douglas et al., 1995] applies the computational principles used by biological nervous systems to those tasks that biological systems perform easily, but which have proved difficult to do using traditional engineering techniques. These problems include visual and auditory perceptive processing, navigation, and locomotion. Typically, current neuromorphic systems are hybrid analog-digital electronic systems fabricated using CMOS VLSI technology [Mead, 1989, Douglas and Mahowald, 1995]. Research has focused on the sub-threshold analog operation of these circuits, because in this regime it is possible to construct compact analog circuits that compute various biologically relevant operations such as logarithms, exponents and hyperbolic tangents.

The greatest successes of neuromorphic analog VLSI (aVLSI) to date have been in the emulation of peripheral sensory transduction and processing of the kind performed by biological retinas and cochleas. The sensory periphery is a logical place to begin an analog neuromorphic system, since the light impinging onto a retina or sound waves entering the cochlea are all continuous analog signals. Furthermore, these structures are easily accessible to neurobiologists and their purpose is obvious, at least in the general sense, so a great deal is known about their biology. These structures also have a relatively simple organization, consisting of arrays of similar processing elements that interact only with nearest neighbours. Such circuits have a repeating two-dimensional, 'crystalline', structure that can be tiled across the surface of a single chip, and the output of the computation can be sampled by raster scan.

Finally, however, the amount of computation that can be performed on a single chip is limited by silicon area, and the utility of the computations is limited by access to the number of inputs and outputs to and from the computation. For example, silicon retinae have a few thousand pixels, but only about 100 contacts can be made by macroscopic wires onto the circuitry on the surface of the retina chip. The goal of neuromorphic engineers is to incorporate many such chips, performing a variety of computations, into behaving systems. To build such systems, a number of methods for performing general communication between analog chips have been developed [Lazzaro et al., 1993, Mahowald, 1994, Boahen, 1996], thus overcoming the limitations of chip inputs and outputs, and now the first simple multi-chip neuromorphic systems are being constructed. Typically, these systems use modifications of previously designed sensory chips as input devices to multi-chip processing systems.

In this chapter we will describe a multi-sender multi-receiver communication framework for neuromorphic systems, and provide some examples of its operation in the context of networks of simple aVLSI neurons.

6.2 Neuromorphic Computational Nodes

One of the major advantages of analog systems is that the physical processes that contribute to a particular computation can be constructed very compactly in comparison to digital circuits. Of course, this efficiency is only possible if the functions that can be composed using just a few aVLSI components match those required by the computation [Hopfield, 1990], and if the computation is not very sensitive to noise.

A further advantage is that analog systems typically store their state very densely, as voltages on capacitors for example, and so the state variables can be co-localised in space with the computations that affect them. These properties lead naturally to very localised, fine-grained, parallelism. This architecture is unlike that of conventional digital processors, whose large amount of computational state is usually stored at some distance from the relatively few processors that affect them.

The dense and co-localised nature of analog computation lends itself to processes which are widely distributed and which depend on many regional factors. Examples of such processes are adaptation, learning, and decorrelation of adjacent signals. Unfortunately, technical limitations restrict the spatial extent over which fine-grained parallel analog processing circuits can be built. For example, the two and a half dimensional structure of present day silicon circuits, and the computational hardness of routing algorithms, restrict the number of physical point-to-point wires that can be routed between circuit devices. Consequently, the computational nodes of neuromorphic systems take on the hybrid organisation shown in Figure 6.1. Each computational process is composed of a region of analog circuitry, the output(s) of which are converted into an event code. The region accepts one or more event inputs which are processed by the analog circuitry. Networks of silicon neurons prove an example of this architecture.

6.3 Neuromorphic aVLSI Neurons

Neuromorphic silicon neurons emulate the electrophysiological behaviour of biological neurons. The emulation uses the same organisational technique as traditional numerical simulations of biological neurons. The continuous neuronal membrane of the dendrites and soma is divided into a series of homogeneous, isopotential compartments [Koch and Segev, 1989, Traub and Miles, 1991]. The connectivity of the compartments expresses the spatial morphology of the modelled cell. In general, more compartments imply a more accurate simulation. The resolution of the segmentation is a compromise between the questions that must be addressed by the

6.3 Neuromorphic aVLSI Neurons

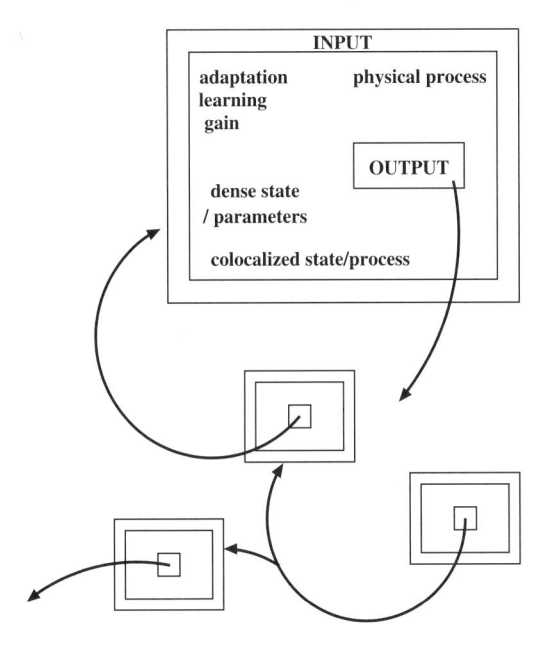

Figure 6.1. Abstract computational node in a neuromorphic system. Each node is represented by a rectangle, one of which is enlarged to show more detail. Each node consists of an input region that receives pulse events from other source nodes. The central region consists of analog circuitry that processes the inputs and generates an output. The processing is performed by analog VLSI circuits that implement physical processes analogous to those used by real neurons for their computation. The state variables and parameters that control the computation are (ideally) stored locally (e.g. as voltages on capacitors) to minimise the power inefficiencies that result from having memory and processing separated as in conventional digital computers. Arrows indicate paths of event transmission.

model, the resources required by each compartment, and error tolerance. For example, neurons with between 5–30 compartments are a common compromise for digital simulations of cortical and hippocampal circuits [Douglas and Martin, 1992, Traub and Miles, 1991].

Elias [Elias, 1993, Northmore and Elias, 1998] has constructed neuromorphic VLSI neurons with 112 passive compartments which model the leakiness of the cellular membrane and the axial resistance of the intracellular medium using space-efficient switched-capacitors to implement resistances. However, in recent years it has become clear that neuronal dendrites are not simply passive cables [Johnston and Wu, 1995, Koch, 1998], but that voltage and ion-sensitive conductances play a major role in active spatio-temporal filtering of signals transmitted through the dendrites. This means that neuromorphs too should provide for active dendritic processing.

The active conductances of biological neuronal membranes control the flow of ionic current between the various ionic reversal potentials and the membrane voltage on the membrane capacitance (Figure 6.2). These active conductances are usually sensitive to either the transmembrane potential, or the concentration of a specific ion. In our silicon neurons [Mahowald and Douglas, 1991, Douglas and Mahowald, 1995], the dendritic and somatic compartments that comprise the model neuron are populated by modular aVLSI sub-circuits, each of which emulates the physics of a particular ionic conductance. Each module is a variant of a prototypical ion conductance circuit (Figure 6.3) that obeys Hodgkin-Huxley principles [Mahowald and Douglas, 1991, Rasche et al., 1998]. The voltage dependence of the ion channel is achieved by a transconductance amplifier that has a sigmoidal steady-state current voltage relation similar to that observed in biological active membrane channel conductances. The temporal dynamics of the conductances are emulated by a leaky follower integrator. The various voltage-sensitive conductances are simple modifications of this general theme. The ion or ligand sensitive modules are a little more sophisticated. For example, conductances that are sensitive to calcium concentration rather than membrane voltage require a separate voltage variable representing free calcium concentration, and synaptic conductances that are sensitive to ligand concentrations require a voltage variable representing neurotransmitter concentration. The dynamics of the neurotransmitter concentration in the cleft is governed by additional time constant circuits.

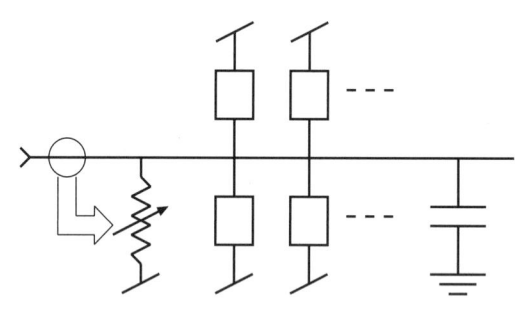

Figure 6.2. Simplified model of neuronal elecrophysiology. The membrane capacitance at right carries a charge which appears as a transmembrane potential difference. For convenience, the potential of the exterior of the cell is set to ground. The interior of the cell is represented by the long horizontal wire, which is attached to the inner terminal of the capacitance. Charge flows on and off the capacitor via the vertical wires, each of which consists of a conductance mechanism (box) and a power supply (inclined line). Power supplies above the horizontal line are positive (e.g. sodium or calcium reversal potentials), while power supplies below the horizontal line are negative (e.g. potassium reversal potential). Typically, a box contains a voltage dependent conductance for some ion. The features of such a conductance mechanism are shown at left. A variable conductance controls the flow of current off the membrane capacitor (e.g. a potassium current). The current is the product of the conductance and the voltage drop across the conductance (or driving potential). The conductance is voltage sensitive. The circle on left senses the membrane potential, and uses this information to modify the conductance appropriately (arrow), with some time constant. The electrophysiology of neurons is essentially the result of chargings and dischargings of the membrane capacitance by a population of conductances to various ions.

So far, we have used these general principles to design modules that emulate the sodium and potassium spike currents, persistent sodium current,

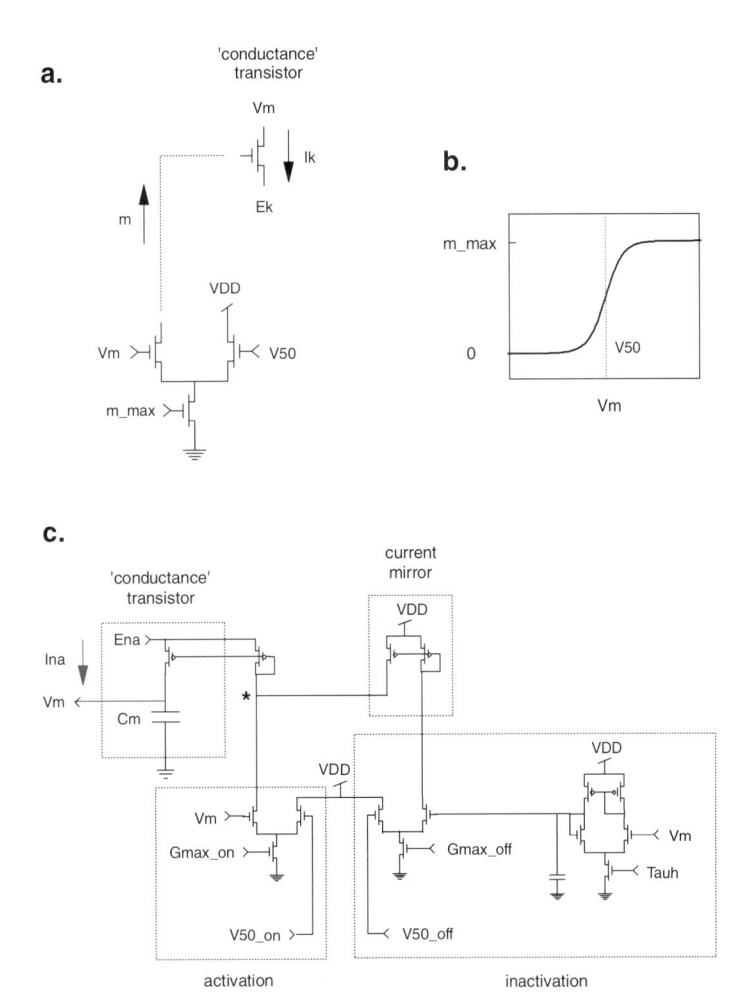

Figure 6.3. Example of a neuromorphic CMOS aVLSI circuit. (a. & b.) Basic circuit that emulates transmembrane ion currents in the silicon neuron (Mahowald & Douglas 1991). (a.) A differential pair of transistors that have their sources linked to a single bias transistor (bottom). The voltage, m_max, applied to the gate of the bias transistor sets the bias current, which is the sum of the currents flowing through the two limbs of the differential pair. The relative values of the voltages, Vm and V50, applied to the gates of the differential pair determine how the current will be shared between the two limbs. The relationship between Vm and the output current, m, in the left limb is shown in (b.). The current, m, is the activation variable that controls the potassium (in this example) current, Ik, that flows through the 'conductance' transistor interposed between the ionic reversal potential, Ek, and the membrane potential Vm. (c.) The circuit that generates the sodium current of the action potential is composed of activation and inactivation sub-circuits that are similar to (a.). The activation and inactivation circuits compete for control of the sodium 'conductance' transistor by summing their output currents at the node marked by the asterisk. The current mirror is a technical requirement that permits a copy of the inactivation current to interact with the activation current. In this example, sodium current, Ina, flows from the sodium reversal potential, Ena, onto the membrane capacitance, Cm. The transconductance amplifier and capacitor on the right of the inactivation circuit act as a low pass filter, causing the inactivation circuit to respond to changes in membrane voltage with a time constant set by the voltage, Tauh. Parts a. and c.: Reprinted with permission from *Nature*, [Mahowald and Douglas, 1991]. Copyright (1991) Macmillan Magazines Limited.

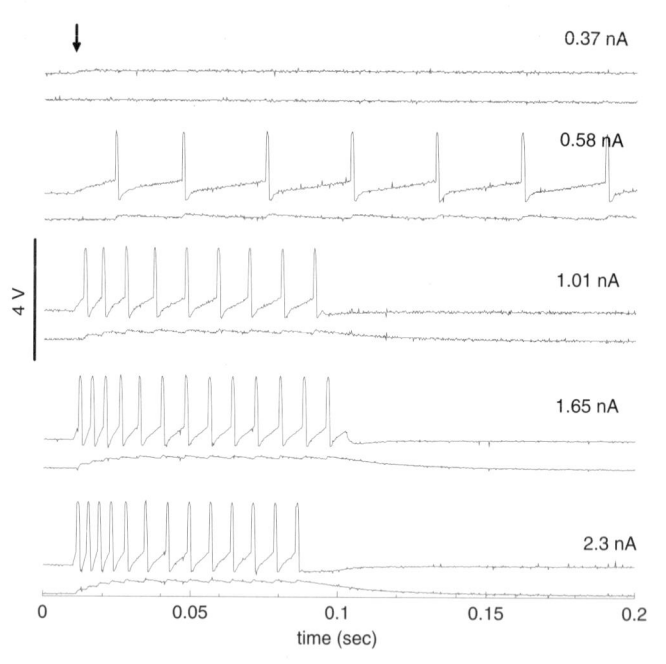

Figure 6.4. Responses of a silicon neuron to intra-somatic injections of current steps applied at time of arrow above. Membrane voltage and calcium concentration are shown in response to 5 increasing current stimuli. Current offset occurs at various times (not indicated). In the upper two traces the current is sustained to the end of the observation period. In the three lower cases offset occurs a little after the last spike. The noise in these recordings arises mainly from quantisation effects in the digitising oscilloscope.

various calcium currents, calcium-dependent potassium current, potassium A-current, non-specific leak current, exogenous (electrode) current source, excitatory synapse, potassium mediated inhibitory synapse, and chloride mediated (shunting) inhibitory synapse.

When these modules are incorporated into the compartmental morphology of typical silicon neurons, they give rise to state-dependent dynamics that strongly resemble those observed in real neurons (Figure 6.4). But the importance of the silicon neuron in the present context, is as an example of a neuromorphic analog circuit that receives event inputs at its synapses, computes a result via multiple local interacting analog circuits, and encodes this result as a temporal train of events at its output in the style of Figure 6.4. The routing of the events between the outputs and inputs of the computational nodes, which may be distributed across the multiple chips of the neuromorphic system, is the task of the address-event communication system.

6.4 Address Event Representation (AER)

We have developed an interchip-communication protocol that is an asynchronous digital multiplexing technique using *address-event representation* (AER). It has the characteristics of event-driven multiplexed pulse-frequency modulation in which the address of the node which is the source of an event is broadcast during the pulse, to all computational nodes within a defined region. The nodes decode the broadcast neuronal addresses.

Like neuronal action potentials, events in this system are stereotyped digital events, and the interval between events is analog. Each digital event is a digital word representing the identity of the neuron that is generating an action potential. It is placed on the common communications bus (which is effectively a universal, multiplexed axon) at the time the action potential is generated. Thus, information is encoded in the temporal pattern of events.

The savings in the number of wires required for communication between neurons is due to the replacement of N axonal fibres, with one active at a time, by $(1 + \log_2 N)$ wires, which are simultaneously active. However, in a real nerve bundle, several axons may be simultaneously active. We can accommodate this condition by making the event duration very short (approximately 1 microsecond) compared with the width of neural action potentials (approximately one millisecond). These short-duration events are less likely to overlap. Since, as in a real neuron, the maximum firing rate of a node is limited, even if events from several nodes did occur synchronously, they could be arranged such that they occurred in close succession with little loss of information in a rate coding scheme. The degree of loss depends on the requirement for exact timing of events in the neural process. Much cortical spike processing has a temporal resolution in the order of a millisecond [Singer, 1994, Abeles, 1994] or longer [Shadlen and Newsome, 1994], whereas the maximum time-skew introduced by queuing of address events is much shorter — of the order of 0.1 milliseconds. However, some processing, such as occurs in special purpose auditory processing neurons like those found in the brain-stems of barn owls [Moiseff and Konishi, 1981] require higher temporal resolution (≈ 0.1 milliseconds). Neurons with such high resolution may still be manageable within the context of AER systems. However, analogs of such special purpose non-cortical neuronal circuits with higher temporal resolution requirements are probably best implemented using hardwired connections on single chips, and only their results reported via AER. Alternatively, a different coding scheme may be required, such as described in Section 6.8.

The address-event representation is illustrated in Figure 6.5. The neurons in the sender array generate a temporal sequence of digital address events to encode their output. This representation is conceptually equivalent to a train of action potentials generated by a real (or a silicon) neuron. However, in the AER case, the output of each computational node (for example, a silicon neuron) is associated with a digital address that uniquely identifies it.

Whenever a neuron signals an event, the encoding circuitry broadcasts that neuron's address on the inter-chip data bus. The outputs have a refractory time that limits the frequency at which they can issue events and, like their biological counterparts, only a small fraction of the silicon neurons embedded in a network are generating action potentials at any time. The inter-event interval at a neuron is much longer than is the time required to broadcast the neuron's address. Therefore, events from many neurons can be multiplexed on the same bus. The receiver interprets the broadcast of

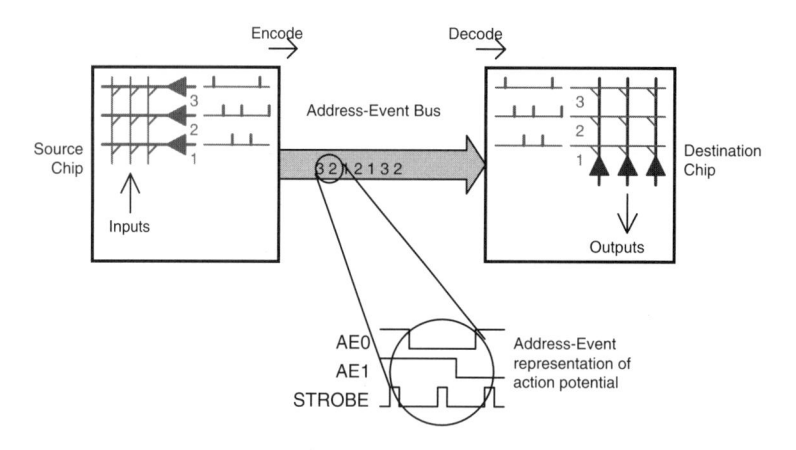

164   6. A Pulse-Coded Communications Infrastructure

Figure 6.5. The address-event representation. Self-timed neurons on the sending chip generate trains of action potentials. The neurons request control of the bus when they generate action potentials and are selected to have their addresses encoded and transmitted by the multiplexing circuitry. A temporal stream of addresses passes between the sender chip and the receiver chip. This temporal stream is decoded by the receiver into trains of action potentials that reach their proper postsynaptic targets. Relative timing of events is preserved over the Address-Event bus to the destination as long as the source neurons do not generate action potentials that are too close together in time.

the address as an event that corresponds to the occurrence of an action potential from the neuron identified by that address. The receiving nodes or synapses that are 'connected' to the source neuron detect that their source neuron has generated an action potential, and they initiate a synaptic input on the dendrite to which they are attached.

If neuronal events were broadcast and removed from the data bus at frequencies of about 1 megahertz, about one thousand address-events (AE) could be transmitted in the time it takes one neuron to complete a single 1 millisecond action potential. If say 10% of the neurons discharge at 100 spikes per second, one single such bus could support a population of up to 10^5 rate encoded neurons, at which point the bus would be saturated.

Debates continue over the question of whether biological neurons signal the intensity of their inputs in their rate of discharge, or whether their discharge encodes the coincidence of input events on their dendritic trees [Singer, 1994, Abeles, 1994, Shadlen and Newsome, 1994, Fujii et al., 1996]. The experimental neurophysiological literature remains divided on the nature of the coding. One view is that information is encoded in the exact times and coincidence of spike occurrence, but the resolution of this timing is not known. Psychophysical studies of visual and auditory processing suggest that sub-millisecond precision may be required. (Although there is at present no experimental evidence for such precision at the level of single spike processing in *cortical* neurons, so the psychophysical observations may depend on a population mechanism.) Coincidence detection implies high time resolution, and would place a much greater burden on the AE timing. The alternative view is that neuronal information is encoded in the discharge rate of neurons, and that the rate is measured on a time scale of about ten milliseconds. Fortunately, much of early sensory processing is dominated by rate-coding [Orban, 1984], and so is well within the capability of present AER technology.

Because very few neurons within a network are active at any one time, AER is more efficient at transmitting this sparse representation of data across the neural population than the non-event driven multiplexing methods, such as scanning, that have been used in earlier neuromorphic work [Mead, and Delbruck, 1991].

6.5 Implementations of AER

Initially inter-chip communication networks provided only simple unidirectional, point-to-point connectivity between arrays of neuromorphs on two neuromorphic chips [Mahowald, 1994, Boahen, 1996]. These communication schemes map spikes from output nodes in the sending chip to any appropriate input nodes in the receiving chip. The mapping occurs asynchronously, and provides random-access to the receiver nodes. The spikes are actually represented as addresses. An address-encoder at the output node generates a unique binary address that identifies that node (neuron).

The output addresses are transmitted over a shared bus to the receiving chip, where an address decoder selects the appropriate receiver node (input) and activates it. Two versions of this random-access scheme have been proposed, a hard-wired version, and an arbitered version.

In the hardwired version [Mortara et al., 1995], output nodes (neurons) always have direct access to the input lines of the address-encoder, and each spike activates the encoder as soon as it occurs. This scheme has the virtue of simplicity, and permits high-speed operation. But when the spikes of two or more neurons collide and activate the encoder simultaneously, the encoder generates an invalid address. For random (Poisson) firing times, these collisions increase exponentially as the spiking activity increases, and the collision rates are even more prohibitive when neurons fire in synchrony. The invalid addresses generated by collisions can be detected, but this costs material and address space.

In the arbitered version of the random-access scheme, an arbiter is interposed between the output nodes and the address-encoder. The arbiter detects potential collisions and ensures that only one of the contending output nodes gains access to the encoder at any time. The output of the rejected nodes can be ignored and discarded (partially arbitered), or queued until they are selected by the arbiter (fully arbitered). Intermediate queuing strategies, which queue a limited number of events, or discard ageing events, have also been investigated [Marienborg et al., 1996].

Arbitration preserves the integrity of the addresses that are transmitted, but the statistics and temporal structure of events may be distorted by the discarding or queuing. For random (Poisson) firing rates of events of finite duration, the queuing time is inversely proportional to the rate at which empty event slots occur. Thus, the queuing time decreases as technological improvements reduce the cycle time even when channel utilization remains the same. For synchronous bursts, the delay is proportional to the activity level.

The selection of an arbitration method depends on the task that must be solved by the neuromorphic system. When spike timing is random and high error rates can be tolerated, the hard-wired version provides the highest throughput. On the other hand, when spikes occur in synchrony and low error rates are desired, the arbitered version provides the highest throughput but will introduce some timing uncertainty.

6.6 Silicon Cortex

'Silicon Cortex' (SCX) is a particular instantiation of a fully arbitered address-event communication infrastructure that can be used to test inter-chip communication in simple neuromorphic systems. The SCX framework is designed to be a flexible prototyping system, providing reprogrammable connectivity among on the order of 10^4 computational nodes spread across multiple chips on a single board, or more across multiple boards. The present version of SCX is implemented on a VME board design called SCX-1 [1] [Sheu and Choi, 1995]. Each SCX-1 board can support up to six chips or other AE sources, and multiple boards can be linked together to form larger systems.

The SCX was devised to test and refine several fundamental problems encountered in building systems of analog chips that use the address-event representation:

- Co-ordinating the activity of multiple sender/receiver chips on a common bus
- Providing a method of building a distributed network of local busses sufficient to build an indefinitely large system
- Providing a software-programmable facility for translating address-events that enables the user to configure arbitrary connections between neurons
- Providing extensive digital interfacing opportunities via VME bus
- Providing 'life-support' for custom analog chips by maintaining volatile analog parameters or programming analog non-volatile storage

Of course, VME cards and VME crates are extremely bulky, and inconsistent with the final aims of neuromorphic systems, which lie in the direction of compact autonomous low-power systems. However, SCX was designed to provide an experimental environment for exploring AER communication issues under well controlled conditions. The principles learned can

---

[1] designed and fabricated by Applied Neurodynamics, Inc. of Encinitas, California, USA. +1 760 944 8859

then be implemented in future on a smaller scale, in more specific, neuromorphic systems.

One immediate application of SCX-1 is as a real-time neuronal network emulator, in which the computational nodes are silicon neurons, and the output address-events are generated by the occurrence of neuronal action potentials. We have designed a number of multi-neuron chips (MNC) that are compatible with the SCX-1. Each chip comprises 36 neuromorphic neurons. One class of MNC chip has neurons with six dendritic compartments and over two hundred parameters that control the behaviour of the active conductance modules, synapse modules, and electrotonic properties similar to those described in Section 6.3. A second class of MNC chips is composed of very simple integrate-and-fire type neurons, which are optimised for testing SCX communication rather than for exploring neuronal network behaviour *per se*.

When an analog action potential occurs in a neuron, it triggers the transmission of that neuron's address on the Local Address Event Bus (LAEB), which is local to the SCX-1 board on which the source neuron is located. That address is detected by a digital signal processor (DSP) that translates the source address into a train of afferent synaptic addresses which then activate the appropriate synapses on target neurons. In this way the DSP source-destination lookup table defines the stable connectivity (axonal structure) of the neurons. The efficacy of particular synapses is set at neuron level.

Since a number of neurons must share an AEB with limited bandwidth, the number of neurons that can be supported by the AEB is limited (at present) to about 10^4. However, the number of neurons in an entire system can be much larger, because most of the connectivity of neurons in cortex is local, and so different AEBs can support adjacent populations of neurons in a manner analogous to the columnar structure of cortex. The DSP that effects the local connectivity is also able to transmit source addresses to more distant populations via domain AEBs, so emulating long-range connections.

Once configured, the Silicon Cortex system runs completely autonomously, and in real-time. However, there are two levels of standard digital software that control its operation. Low level software controls the operation of the DSP. This software enables the DSP to maintain the parameters of the various neurons that control their biophysical 'personality'. The second level of software (still under development) runs on a host computer, and enables the user to configure the neurons and the network, and to monitor their performance.

In addition to providing a neuronal network emulation environment for neurophysiological investigation, the SCX framework can be used to develop more specific neuromorphic systems that include sensors such as retinas and cochleas, and motor effectors.

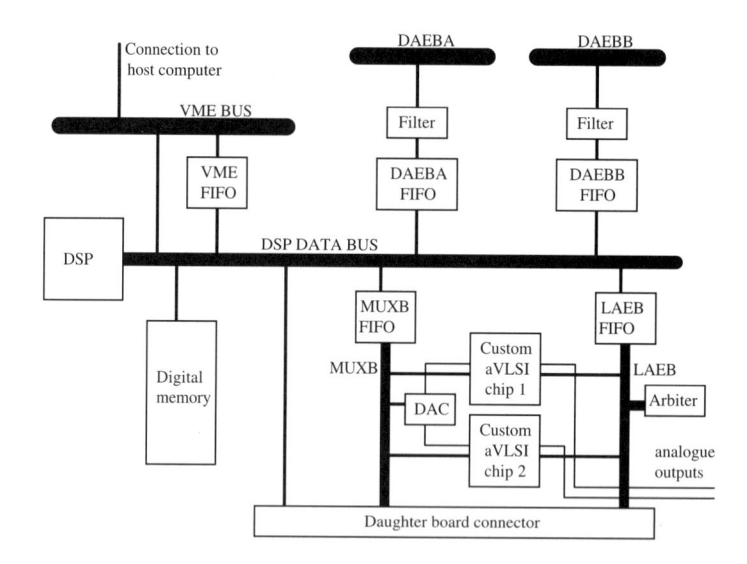

168   6. A Pulse-Coded Communications Infrastructure

Figure 6.6. The SCX-1 board has sockets for two custom aVLSI chips and a daughter-board may hold up to four more. Communication between these chips takes place on the local address event bus (LAEB). The LAEB arbiter arbitrates among the event outputs of all of the custom chips. The custom chips may exchange local information directly in this manner. Programmable interconnection is effected by a DSP, which stores translation tables in its digital memory. The DSP system is configured initially by a host computer. The DSP receives input events and generates output events through a number of bi-directional FIFOs. Translated presynaptic events pass through the MUXB to the local custom chips; events to and from other devices connected to the domain busses pass through the DEABA and DEABB FIFOs, and events to and from the VME bus pass through the VME FIFO. The AE traffic on the domain busses, to which a number of other SCX-1 boards may be attached, is filtered before being loaded into the domain FIFOs, so that events that are not required on this board are not passed on to it. These filters are essential for limiting the work of the DSP. An additional task of the DSP is to provide configuration services for the custom chips. Analog parameters on the custom chips are loaded by the DSP via the DAC and MUXB FIFO. The analog outputs of the custom chips can be monitored directly with an oscilloscope.

6.6.1 Basic Layout

The design of SCX-1 is a compromise between providing the AE infrastructure described above, the need to test some particular technical ideas about the AER communication, a convenient physical implementation, forward compatibility with future AER systems, and cost.

The SCX-1 board layout is illustrated schematically in Figure 6.6. There are two 84-pin pin-grid-array (PGA) sockets to accommodate custom neuron chips. A daughter-board connector is also provided. Daughterboards can be fabricated by users. Daughterboards can contain up to four elements that need to talk on the LAEB. For example, the board could carry four additional custom neuron chips, or receiver chips that transform patterns of address events into images for display on a video monitor. Daughterboards (or the daughter board connector) can be used to interface to peripheral sensory devices, such as retinae, or motor drivers that use address-events.

Communication among all of the chips in this system takes place on three address-event busses (AEBs). The control of the AEBs is mediated by an asynchronous protocol on the local AEB (LAEB) used for intra-board communication, and a synchronous protocol on the domain AEBs (DAEBs) used for inter-board communication. Both the asynchronous LAEB and the synchronous DAEB protocols are broadcasts, and so there is no handshake between the transmitter and receivers. Details of the LAEB protocol are described elsewhere (http://www.ini.unizh.ch).

Communication between the chips on the SCX board takes place via the LAEB. The occurrence of an event on any chip is arbitrated within that chip, and leads to a request from the chip to the bus arbiter. The bus arbiter determines which chip will have control of the LAEB at each cycle, and that chip will broadcast an AE on the bus. These events can be read by all chips attached to the bus. In particular, the bus is monitored by a DSP chip, which can route the AEs to a number of different destinations. For example, the DSP chip can use a lookup table to translate a source AE into many destination AEs. Or it can translate events from the LAEB onto two domain busses (DEABA and DEABB) that make connections between boards.

Although the neuromorphic chips running on the SCX are finally expected to read and write their own data directly to the LAEB without the assistance of additional external circuitry, in this experimental system we have provided an alternative means of writing data to the neuromorphic chips. (Figure 6.7.) The alternative route for data is a private route between the DSP chip and the custom chips, called the multiplexor bus (MUXB). The DSP can transmit destination-encoded events to the custom chips via the MUXB. In addition, the MUXB bus allows the DSP to supply analog parameters on the custom chips via a DAC. These parameters can be refreshed periodically if stored on capacitors. Alternatively, a high-voltage input line and digital control lines are provided for analog chips that use floating-gate parameter storage.

Also, in this experimental system, the DSP is buffered from the busses it reads and writes by FIFOs (first-in first-out buffer). To off-load DSP processing, digital circuitry filters the events that occur on the DEABs and recognises events that are relevant to the neurons on its board or which need to be transferred through this board to the other DAEB. The filters place the domain events in FIFOs so that they too can be serviced by the DSP chip. The DSP chip can feed events back to the LAEB again via a FIFO, or to the DAEBs via their FIFOs, as appropriate.

The parameters and connections of a neuronal network implemented on the SCX-1 are programmable. The DSP's digital memory stores a list of connections for the neurons that the DSP must service. Loading a new list reconfigures the neuronal network. To do this, or to amend an existing connection list, a host computer communicates with the SCX-1 via

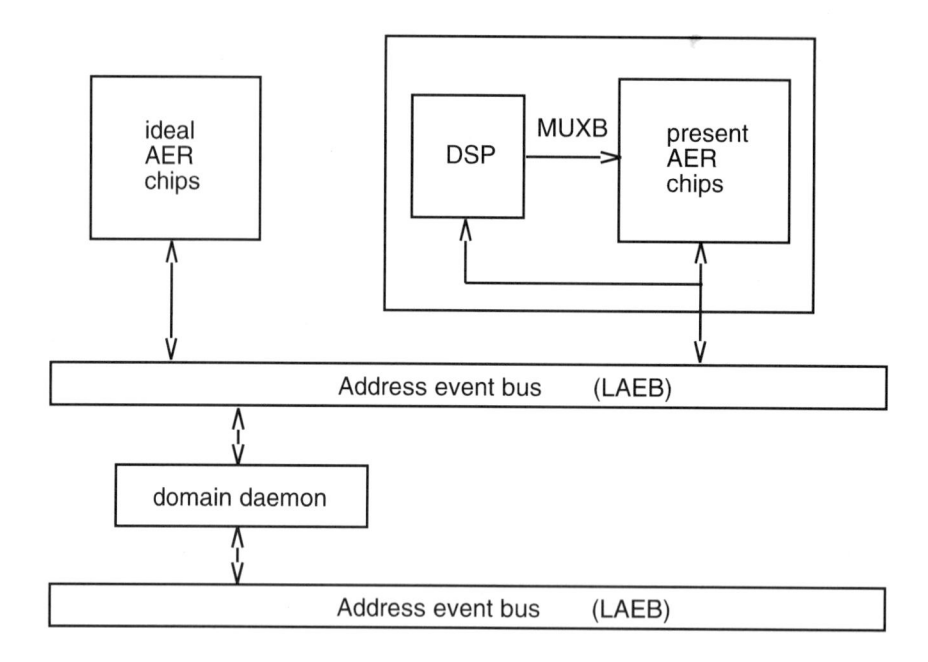

Figure 6.7. Ideal address-event chips (top left) have a simple bi-directional communication with the local AE bus. Individual AEs are broadcast via the local AE bus, and may evoke a response at many target nodes. Ideally, each node should recognise its relevant source events, but our present multi-neuron chips use a DSP chip and a lookup table to implement the fan-out from source address to the individual target synaptic addresses. The DSP accesses an on-chip demultiplexor via the multiplexor bus (MUXB). In this case the DSP and chip form a functional unit (top right, delineated by a broken line) equivalent to the ideal case. One local AE bus and its associated AER chips that together constitute a domain, may be bridged to another domain by means of a 'domain daemon' that filters and optionally re-maps AEs between the busses.

the VME bus. Once loaded, connection lists and parameter values can be stored along with the DSP software code in non-volatile memory on the SCX-1 board.

6.7 Functional Tests of Silicon Cortex

6.7.1 An Example Neuronal Network

Amongst the first tests of the ability of the SCX-1 system to support neural computation using the AE protocol, was a test of communication between neurons in a simple network. We configured this neuronal network (Figure 6.8) using the multi-neuron chips containing simple integrate-and-fire neurons referred to above. In this network, there are two main populations of twelve 'excitatory' neurons each. All the neurons in both of these populations are driven by a constant current input via current injection circuitry included on the chips. Each neuron has an excitatory connection to each of the other neurons in its population, and an inhibitory connection to each

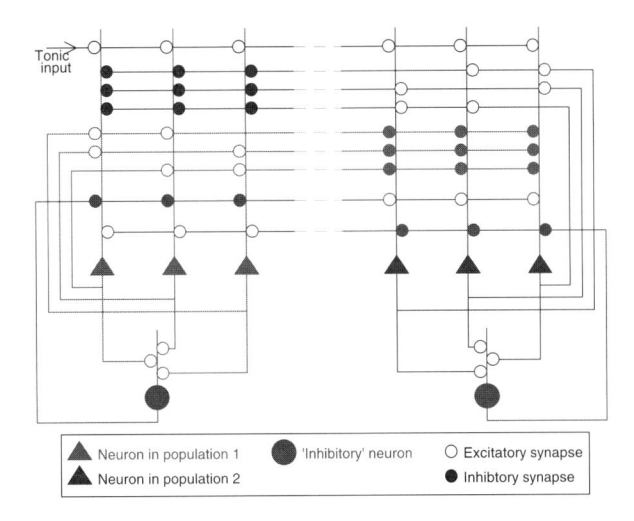

Figure 6.8. Partial schematic representation of the example two population neuronal network described in the text. Filled triangles represent identical 'excitatory' neurons. Large filled circles represent identical 'inhibitory' neurons. Small open circles represent excitatory inputs, small filled circles represent inhibitory inputs. For simplicity, only three neurons are shown in each population of 'excitatory' neurons, whereas the network was implemented with twelve neurons in each population.

of the neurons in the other population. Associated with each of the two 'excitatory' populations, is an 'inhibitory' neuron that receives excitatory input from each of the neurons in that population. The output of these 'inhibitory' neurons are connected back to inhibit all of the neurons in the associated 'excitatory' population and excite all of the neurons in the other population.

With suitably adjusted connection strengths, the network settles into an oscillatory firing pattern. The neurons in one 'excitatory' population fire for a period whilst neurons in the other population are silent, then the pattern of activity swaps over between the two populations. When one population is firing, each output contributes to the inhibition that prevents neurons in the other population from firing, and also produces an EPSC in the associated 'inhibitory' neuron. After integrating a certain number of such inputs, this neuron will reach its threshold and fire. When it does so, it produces a large inhibitory effect on the neurons in the population that was firing, thus bringing their activity to a halt. Neurons in the previously silent population thus no longer receive inhibitory input and can now begin to fire, and continue to do so until their associated 'inhibitory' neuron fires. The cycle then repeats (Figure 6.9). Overall, the network acts as nothing more than a flip-flop, but in doing so it tests the communication performance of SCX.

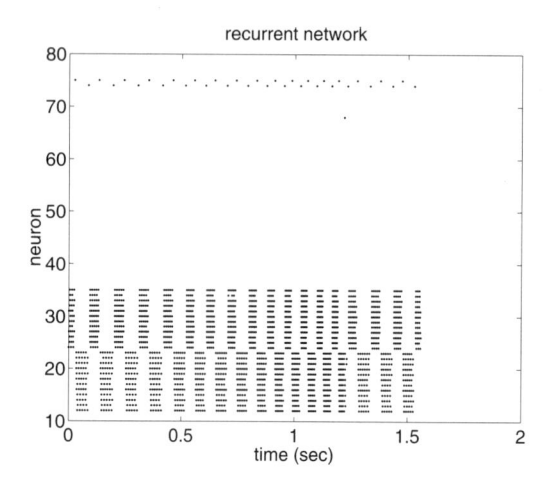

172   6. A Pulse-Coded Communications Infrastructure

Figure 6.9. A raster plot of address-event activity over the course of several oscillatory cycles of the network described in the text. The vertical axis gives the addresses of the neurons in the network. Each plotted point represents the occurrence of an address-event on the LAEB, and hence the firing of a neuron. The lower twelve traces (of neurons numbered 12 to 23 inclusive) represent the activity of one of the populations of 'excitatory' neurons. The next twelve traces (of neurons numbered 24 to 35 inclusive) represent the activity of the other population of 'excitatory' neurons. The populations' associated 'inhibitory' neurons are at addresses 74 and 75 respectively.

In all cases, the communication between neurons is takes place through the conversion of the firing of a neuron on a MNC into an AE, the transmission of that AE from the MNC over the LAEB to the DSP, the fan-out to a list of destinations by the DSP, and the onward transmission of those destination addresses over the MUXB back to neurons on the MNC. Since the DSP software is always involved in the routing and fan-out of connections from source to target neurons, it is possible to re-configure the network essentially instantaneously. For instance, when two MNCs are fitted, rather than using twenty-six neurons on the same chip to implement the circuit just described, it is possible to redistribute the use of neurons across the two chips, for example to have one 'excitatory' population and its associated 'inhibitory' neuron on one chip, and the other neurons on the second chip. This is done by down-loading a new configuration from the host computer via the VME bus.

6.7.2   An Example of Sensory Input to SCX

The most promising path for the development of analog neural networks is interfacing them to sensors and effectors that can interact dynamically with the real world [Etienne-Cummings et al., 1994]. Linking the SCX neural network to sensors requires building sensors that use the same AE-based communications protocol. The AER has been used to interface a silicon cochlea to a SUN SparcStation, with the goal of using the cochlea as input for a backpropagation-based speech recognition algorithm [Lazzaro et al., 1993]. Primitive silicon retinae using the AER have been used to provide input to a chip for computing stereo disparity [Mahowald, 1994], and are now being evolved for use with AER systems [Boahen, 1996].

We have now interfaced a retina chip to SCX-1 as an example of sensor to analog neural network communication. The retina chip we have used is a development of that described by [Liu and Boahen, 1995] that produces AER output. It has 1024 pixels arranged in a square array. Each pixel can produce both an 'ON' AE and an 'OFF' AE distinguished by one of the AE bits. The retina was connected to an SCX-1 daughterboard of the kind referred to in Section 6.6.1. This daughterboard simply buffers the output signals onto the LAEB. Thus AEs from the retina are received by the DSP in the same way as AEs from MNCs on the SCX-1 board itself.

The retina chip was stimulated by a drifting square-wave luminosity grating. During stimulation, the average event rate generated by the all the pixels of the retina was about 10KHz, with peak rates of about 100KHz. Of all these pixel outputs, the AEs generated by a 3×3 patch of retinal ON pixels was mapped by the DSP chip onto a group of neurons located in the MNCs. A histogram of the AEs received from the 'ON' outputs of the patch of pixels on the retina as a single ON bar in the grating pattern drifts past them is shown in Figure 6.10a. The SCX-1 was configured such that these nine pixels formed the receptive field of one of the integrate-and-fire neurons on a MNC. The synaptic strength of these inputs was adjusted so that many inputs from the nine retinal cells must summate to reach the threshold for action potential generation in the MNC neuron. The output of one MNC neuron is also shown in a histogram in Figure 6.10b. This simple experiment demonstrates the integrity of the SCX communication infrastructure, and shows how external sensory (or motor) chips can be used in conjunction with SCX. Of course, the MNC chips in their present form do not provide very interesting sensory processing, they merely demonstrate the communication. However, work is in progress to transform more abstract processing chips (such as those that detect focus of expansion [Indiveri et al., 1996]) for operation using AER protocol. The aim is to allow multiple visual processing chips to operate simultaneously on a single stream of retinal AEs.

At present, with the DSP software as yet un-optimised, neuronal events can be broadcast and removed from the LAEB at frequencies of ~ 0.1 megahertz. Therefore, about 100 address-events can be transmitted in the time it takes one neuron to complete a single 1 millisecond action potential. And if, say, 10% of neurons discharge at 100 spikes per second, a single bus can support a population of about 10^4 neurons before saturating. Of course, many more neurons than this will be required to emulate even one cortical area. Fortunately, the limitation imposed by the bandwidth of the AER bus is not as bad as it may seem. The brain has a similar problem in space. If every axon from every neuron were as long as the dimensions of the brain, the brain would increase exponentially in size as the number of neurons increased. The brain avoids this fate by adopting a mostly local wiring strategy in which the average number of axons ema-

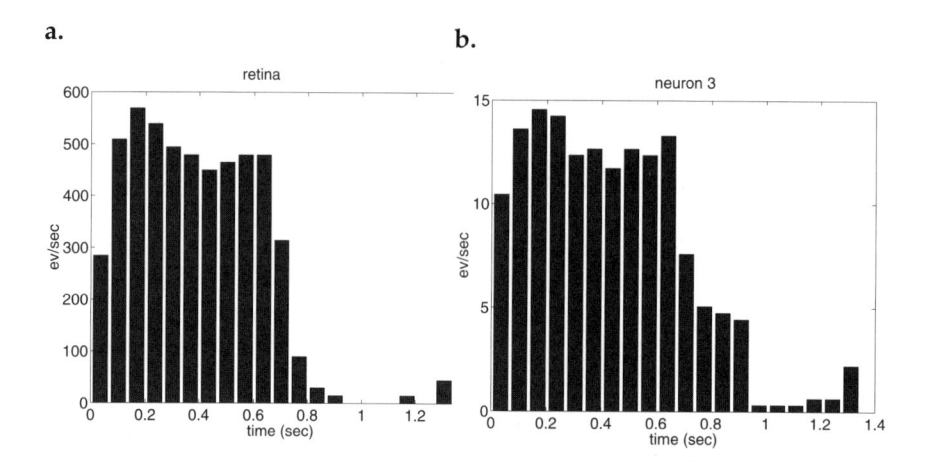

Figure 6.10. A simple test of silicon retinal input to the silicon cortex. A 3 × 3 receptive field of neurons in the silicon retina projected to a group of neurons in the silicon cortex. The retina was stimulated by a drifting square-wave luminosity grating. **a.** Histogram showing address events arriving on the local event address bus from the retina. The active region of the histogram (0–0.7s) corresponds to the time when the ON phase of the grating activates the retinal cells, whereas the inactive region corresponds to the OFF phase of the grating. **b.** Histogram of the output address event activity of one of the MNC neurons. Similar ON and OFF responses. The discharge rate of the MNC neuron is less than the input event rate because many excitatory events summate in the MNC neurons to produce an output event from that cell.

nating from a small region decreases at least as the inverse square of their length [Mead, 1990, Mitchison, 1992, Stevens, 1989]. If the action potential traffic on the AER bus were similarly confined to a local population of neurons, the same bus could repeat in space, and so serve a huge number of neurons. The SCX domain busses, which permit the construction of repeating populations of neurons, are a small first step toward exploring these issues.

6.8 Future Research on AER Neuromorphic Systems

AER and Silicon Cortex have provided a practical means for communication between aVLSI neuromorphic chips. For the immediate future, research efforts will be focused on transforming existing aVLSI sensory processing chips into a form suitable for incorporation in AER systems. There are many technical problems to be solved here, particularly in relation to the construction of hybrid circuits that must mix small signal analog processing with digital inter-node communication.

As we move toward the implementation of neuronal networks that perform useful sensory and motor processing, we must confront the open question of how much accuracy or consistency is required in the time of delivery of AER signals over the network of local and domain busses. The answers to this question are closely tied into the use of timing in the neural code itself, which also remains an open research question in neurobiology [Shadlen and Newsome, 1994, Abeles, 1991, Rieke et al., 1997, Mainen and Sejnowski, 1995].

Deiss has proposed a Space-Time-Attribute (STA) coding scheme for event messages that is partially motivated by the need to route, schedule and deliver events in a timely fashion in a large broadcast or other network system [Deiss, 1994a, Deiss, 1994b]. The arrival time over a global shared bus or network is no longer necessarily prompt nor consistent. If event coincidence is part of the neural code, then the system must maintain the representation of these coincidences. The STA code requires the ability to represent the simulated 3 space location (S) of an event source as well as the time of the event (T) along with optional attributes (A) of the event. One implementation of STA would involve transmission and filtering of packets containing these code subfields. Events could be filtered by daemons sensitive to time and or location of the source event or a destination attribute field. Resources did not permit developing a filter daemon of this sophistication for SCX-1 domain busses. Instead, the SCX-1 domains filter single word events with no subfield processing. While it would be possible to allow all events to pass through unfiltered and then have software decode packet boundaries and sort and filter the events, the peak event rate on the domains is sufficiently high that the DSP would not keep up unless event rates were restricted. Each domain bus has more than an order of magnitude more bandwidth than the LAEB for single word events in order to provide for more prompt delivery of messages and delay-based scheduling. Filtering algorithms that can be implemented in hardware have since been developed by Deiss, but they would require extensive changes to SCX.

In practice, the existing AER technology already provides a suitable environment for practical applications. For example, the behaviour of large networks of spiking neurons can be emulated in real time. We expect that the much slower digital simulations of spiking networks, of the kind reported in this volume, could be replaced by hardware emulation on SCX type systems. Furthermore, we expect to see small special-purpose AER systems appearing in neuromorphic applications, such as the use of multiple aVLSI sensors to provide primitive sensorimotor reflexes for simple robots.

Acknowledgements

We remember the late Misha Mahowald's seminal contribution to neuromorphic engineering in general, and to the SCX project in particular. We thank Shih-Chii Liu and Jörg Kramer for providing the AER retina chip. The SCX project has been supported by the Gatsby Charitable Foundation, the US Office of Naval Research, and Research Machines plc. Chips were fabricated by MOSIS.

References

[Abeles, 1991] Abeles, M. (1991). *Corticonics – Neural Circuits of the Cerebral Cortex*. Cambridge University Press.

[Abeles, 1994] Abeles, M. (1994). Firing rates and well-timed events in the cerebral cortex. *Models of Neural Networks II*, E. Domany, J. L. van Hemmen, and K. Schulten, eds., Springer-Verlag, New York, chapter 3, 121–140.

[Boahen, 1996] Boahen, K. (1996). A retinomorphic visual system. *IEEE Micro*, 16:30–39.

[Deiss, 1994a] Deiss, S. R. (1994). Temporal binding in analog VLSI. *World Congress on Neural Networks - San Diego*, INNS Press, Lawrence Earlbaum Associates, 2:601–606.

[Deiss, 1994b] Deiss, S. R. (1994) Connectionism without the connections. *Proc. of the International Conference on Neural Networks, vol. 2*, Orlando, Florida, June 28–July 2 1994, IEEE Press, 1217–1221.

[Douglas and Mahowald, 1995] Douglas, R. and Mahowald, M. (1995). Silicon neurons. *The Handbook of Brain Theory and Neural Networks*, M. Arbib, ed., MIT Press, Boston, Massachusetts, 282–289.

[Douglas et al., 1995] Douglas, R., Mahowald, M., and Mead, C. (1995). Neuromorphic analog VLSI. *Ann. Rev. Neurosci.*, 18:255–281.

[Douglas and Martin, 1992] Douglas, R. J. and Martin, K. A. C. (1992). Exploring cortical microcircuits: a combined anatomical, physiological, and computational approach. *Single Neuron Computation*, J. Davis T. McKenna and S. Zornetzer, eds., Academic Press, Orlando, Florida, 381–412.

[Elias, 1993] Elias, J. G. (1993). Artificial dendritic trees. *Neural Computation*, 5:648–664.

[Etienne-Cummings et al., 1994] Etienne-Cummings, R., Donham, C., Van der Spiegel, J., and Mueller, P. (1994). Spatiotemporal computation with a general purpose analog neural computer: Real-time visual motion estimation. *Proc. of the International Conference on Neural Networks, vol. 3*, Orlando, Florida, June28-July2 1994, IEEE Press, 1836–1841.

[Fujii et al., 1996] Fujii, H., Ito, H., Aihara, K., Ichinose, N., and Tsukada, M. (1996). Dynamical Cell Assembly Hypothesis — Theoretical Possibility of Spatio-temporal Coding in the Cortex. *Neural Networks*, 9:1303–1350.

[Hopfield, 1990] Hopfield, J. J. (1990). The effectiveness of analogue 'neural network' hardware. *Network*, 1:27–40.

[Horiuchi et al., 1994] Horiuchi, T., Bishofberger, B., and Koch, C. (1994). An analog VLSI saccadic eye movement system. *Advances in Neural Information Processing Systems, vol. 6*, Morgan Kaufmann, San Mateo, California, 582–589.

[Indiveri et al., 1996] Indiveri, G., Kramer, J., and Koch, C. (1996). System implementations of analog VLSI velocity sensors. *IEEE Micro*, October 1996, 16(5):40–49.

[Johnston and Wu, 1995] Johnston, D. and Wu, S. (1995). *Foundations of Cellular Neurophysiology*. MIT Press, Cambridge, Massachusetts.

[Koch, 1998] Koch, C. (1998). *Computational Biophysics of Neurons*. MIT Press, Cambridge, Massachusetts, in press.

[Koch and Segev, 1989] Koch, C. and Segev, I. (1989). *Methods in Neuronal Modelling: From Synapses to Networks*. MIT Press, Cambridge, Massachusetts.

[Kramer et al., 1997] Kramer, J., Sarpeshkar, R., and Koch, C. (1997). Pulse-based analog VLSI velocity sensors. *IEEE Trans. Circuits and Systems II: Analog and Digital Signal Proc.*, 44:86–101.

[Lazzaro et al., 1993] Lazzaro, J., Wawrzynek, J., Mahowald, M., Sivilotti, M., and Gillespie, D. (1993). Silicon auditory processors as computer peripherals. *IEEE Trans. Neural Networks*, 4:523–528.

[Liu and Boahen, 1995] Liu, S-C. and Boahen, K. (1995). Adaptive retina with center-surround receptive field. *Advances in Neural Information Processing Systems, vol. 8*, MIT Press, Massachusetts, 678–684.

[Mahowald, 1992] Mahowald, M. (1992). *VLSI Analogs of Neuronal Visual Processing: A Synthesis of Form and Function*. PhD thesis, Department of Computation and Neural Systems, California Institute of Technology, Pasadena, California.

[Mahowald, 1994] Mahowald, M. (1994). *An Analog VLSI System for Stereoscopic Vision*. Kluwer, Boston.

[Mahowald and Douglas, 1991] Mahowald, M. and Douglas, R. (1991). A silicon neuron. *Nature*, 354:515–518.

[Mainen and Sejnowski, 1995] Mainen, Z. F., and Sejnowski, T. J. (1995). Reliability of spike timing in neocortical neurons. *Science*, 268:1503–1506.

[Marienborg et al., 1996] Marienborg, J-T., Lande, T. S., Abusland, A., and Høvin, M. (1996). An analog approach to "neuromorphic" communication. *Proc. IEEE Intl. Symposium on Circuits and Systems, vol. 3 (ISCAS'96)*, IEEE Operations Center, Piscataway, NJ, 397–400.

[Mead, and Delbruck, 1991] Mead, C. and Delbrück, T. (1991). Scanners for visualizing activity of analog VLSI circuitry. *Analog Integrated Circuits and Signal Processing*, 1:93–106.

[Mead, 1989] Mead, C. A. (1989). *Analog VLSI and Neural Systems*. Addison-Wesley, Reading, Massachusetts.

[Mead, 1990] Mead, C. (1990). Neuromorphic electronic systems. *Proc. IEEE, vol. 78*, IEEE, New York, 1629–1636.

[Mitchison, 1992] Mitchison, G. (1992). Axonal trees and cortical architecture. *Trends in Neuroscience*, 15:122–126.

[Moiseff and Konishi, 1981] Moiseff, A. and Konishi, M. (1981). Neuronal and behavioral sensitivity to binaural time differences in the owl. *J. Neurosci.*, 1:40–48.

[Mortara et al., 1995] Mortara, A., Vittoz, E., and Venier, P. (1995). A communication scheme for analog VLSI perceptive systems. *IEEE J. Solid-State Circuits*, 30:660–669.

References

[Northmore and Elias, 1998] Northmore, D. P. M and Elias, J. G. (1998). Building silicon nervous systems with dendritic tree neuromorphs. In *Pulsed Neural Networks*, W. Maass and C. Bishop, eds., The MIT Press, MA.

[Orban, 1984] Orban, G. A. (1984). *Neural Operations in the Visual Cortex*. Springer-Verlag, Berlin.

[Rasche et al., 1998] Rasche, C., Douglas, R., and Mahowald, M. (1998). Characterization of a pyramidal silicon neuron. *Neuromorphic Systems: Engineering Silicon from Neurobiology*, L. S. Smith and A. Hamilton, eds., World Scientific, 1st edition, in press.

[Rieke et al., 1997] Rieke, F., Warland, D., de Ruyter van Steveninck, R., and Bialek, B. (1997). *Spikes: Exploring the Neural Code*. MIT Press, MA.

[Shadlen and Newsome, 1994] Shadlen, M. and Newsome, W. T. (1994). Noise, neural codes and cortical organization. *Current Opinion in Neurobiology*, 4:569–579.

[Sheu and Choi, 1995] Sheu, B. J. and Choi, J. (1995). *Neural Information Processing and VLSI*. The Kluwer International Series in Engineering and Computer Science. Kluwer Academic Publishers, chapter 15, 486–488.

[Singer, 1994] Singer, W. (1994). Putative functions of temporal correlations in neocortical processing. *Large-Scale Neuronal Theories of the Brain*, C. Koch and J. Davis, eds., Bradford Books, Cambridge, Massachusetts, 201–237.

[Stevens, 1989] Stevens, C. F. (1989). How cortical connectedness varies with network size. *Neural Computation*, 1:473–479.

[Traub and Miles, 1991] Traub, R. D. and Miles, R. (1991). *Neuronal Networks of the Hippocampus*. Cambridge University Press, Cambridge, UK.

7 Analog VLSI Pulsed Networks for Perceptive Processing

Alessandro Mortara and Philippe Venier

7.1 Introduction

Chapter 3 has provided the reader with a basic understanding of MOS transistor operation and of the application of VLSI (very large scale integration) technology to pulsed neural networks hardware. Chapters 5 and 6 have specialized this approach to particular areas of neural networks and this chapter provides a third handle into the domain of pulsed neural hardware for perception tasks.

Analog VLSI perceptive systems go beyond simply restoring a scene: they extract relevant information in real time from a continuously changing environment. To be unambiguous, extraction results from collective processing performed by several layers each sensitive to different modalities such as shape, color or motion in vision. The need for a perceptive system to combine several modalities encourages a multi-chip structure where each chip is specialized for a particular task [Arreguit and Vittoz, 1994].

The work presented in this chapter started with the goal to obtain biological-like connectivity among subsystems capable of processing sensory data through several hierarchical layers. As a consequence of the thin sheet organization of their biological counterparts, the realized layers consist almost invariably of several one- or two-dimensional arrays of neurons. The output of every neuron, its *activity*, is relevant to further processing and should be available for communication to the next layer.

To ease communication requirements, the possibility exists of taking at least some advantage of the particular way data are processed by neural systems. It is known, for example, that the biological retina responds faster to the variation of an intense excitation than to the change of a dark area into an even darker one [Dowling, 1987], thus an adapted communication system will tolerate a worse performance in the communication of weak activities.

As it has been pointed out [Lazzaro et al., 1993], the long distance biological communication strategy reduces power consumption because no energy is allocated to transmit "useless" data. Is it possible to mimick this behaviour with silicon hardware? If on the one hand a purely sequential conditioning (such as Analog-Digital conversion or buffering in the case of analog transmission) and scanning of the analog activities in a large neural network would mean energy waste, the fully parallel communication architecture of some parts of the nervous system is not realizable in VLSI because of on- and off-chip wiring and pin limitations. One way out of this apparent dead end is to trade the speed of silicon for the connectivity intrinsic to the nervous system. This approach has led at first to a communication architecture, described and theoretically evaluated in [Mortara and Vittoz, 1994] and [Mortara, 1995], then to a small-scale realization [Mortara et al., 1995] containing all the essential hardware building blocks. This scheme is somewhat related to the AER protocol discussed in Chapter 6. The scheme is now evolving from a way to set up point-to-point connections between single elements located on different chips to a more general system where other types of connections can be envisaged such as diverging connections by projective field generation.

This chapter focuses on the principles, recent developments, possible applications and on the experimental verification of the theoretical basis of the method. The theory used to design pulsed communication/computation hardware is presented. The proposed method is then applied to interface a silicon retina and a cortical chip. The realized circuits are described in detail and the advantage of the pulsed representation of the neuronal activity will hopefully be apparent to the reader.

7.2 Analog Perceptive Nets Communication Requirements

7.2.1 Coding Information with Pulses

Analog VLSI has been acknowledged as an attractive fast and compact medium to carry out computation in perceptive tasks. However, as system functions place a large bonus over multichip organizations, the communication bottleneck must be faced and resolved. The direct use of voltage and current values as information carrying quantities is prone to several serious drawbacks. The effect of noise is irreversible and results in a cumulative signal degradation along the communication chain. Even assuming that the effect of noise is negligible, analog quantities have different "meanings" on different chips as a consequence of mismatches in technological parameters. Although very interesting biasing schemes have been proposed to overcome this problem [Heim, 1993], they can only be applied at acceptable complexity increase to systems with at most a few tens of neurons.

As already pointed out in Chapter 3, the classic solution to the problems encountered with direct transmission of analog quantities is to translate them into a time interval delimited by transitions between two highly discernible levels. Signals representing information by the time between transitions can be regenerated after exposure to noise with minimal information loss. In addition, noise added to the signal must be large to cause ambiguity. These properties warrant for the robustness of this mode of communication. Two of the basic schemes routinely used to implement it are PWM (pulse width modulation) and PFM (pulse frequency modulation). In PWM (Figure 7.1.b) the transitions delimiting the time interval are the rising and falling edge of a pulse, in PFM, (Figure 7.1.c), two subsequent rising edges. No clear-cut advantage speaks for one or the other technique since the only disadvantage of PWM - the synchrony of either

7.2 Analog Perceptive Nets Communication Requirements

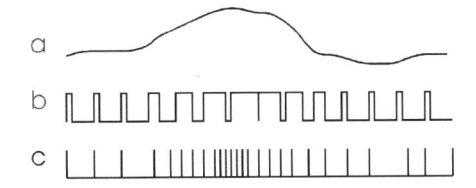

Figure 7.1. a: original signal, b: PWM representation, c: PFM representation

the leading or the trailing edge of the pulses emitted by the neurons can be overcome, as shown in Chapter 3 of this book. The real problem lies in the multiplexing of the signals issued by each neuron.

7.2.2 Multiplexing of the Signals Issued by Each Neuron

Several solutions have been proposed and studied to tackle the multiplexing. An overview of the alternatives is given in Figure 7.2.

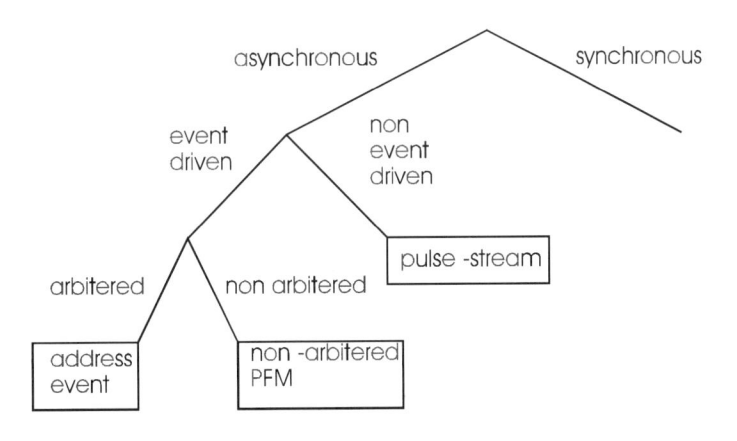

Figure 7.2. Multiplexing alternatives.

Three of the possibilities (the leaves of the tree in Figure 7.2) considered to be representative in the context of neural communication, are described in this book. The names are somewhat misleading: in fact the three systems are "pulse stream" (they use PFM as modulation format) and both event-driven schemes use address-event representation. The names have nevertheless been conserved because address-event and pulse-stream have almost become trade marks of the groups that first proposed them [Mahowald, 1992], [Murray et al., 1991].

The three systems share the concern of avoiding a blind allocation of the communication channel but the proposed solutions are significantly different. This chapter deals with the non-arbitered PFM scheme (shortly NAPFM), both from the theoretical evaluation and its practical implementation aspects.

7.2.3 Non-Arbitered PFM Communication

The structure of this communication/computation system [Mortara and Vittoz, 1994] is shown in Figure 7.3.

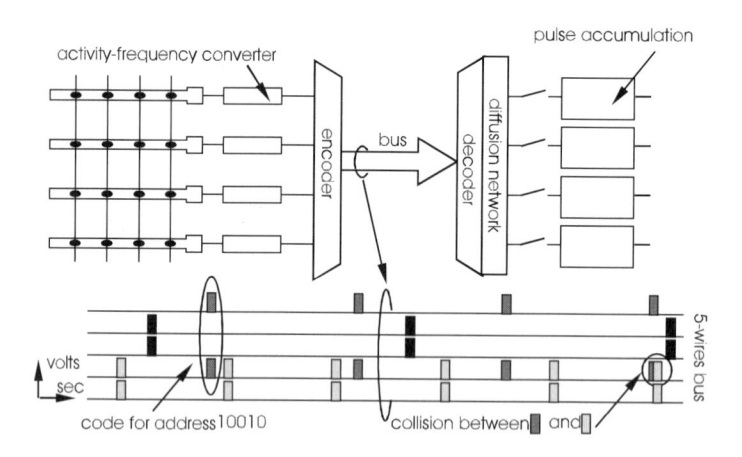

Figure 7.3. The Non-Arbitered PFM Communication Scheme.

All output units have access to one parallel bus (possibly split into a row bus and column bus) on which the code identifying each neuron is wired. When activity in a neuron (with no particular neuron model implied) determines a pulse emission, and if no other pulses are simultaneously emitted, the bus configuration carries the identity of the emitting neuron for the duration of a pulse (in this respect the scheme is related to the address-event representation discussed in the previous chapter). Pulses are decoded and accumulated by the units on the target chip over a time window dictated by the application. The encoding circuitry must compensate for the most notable difference with the biological communication channel: the possibility of collisions whenever 2 or more neurons attempt to access the channel at the same time. In the non-arbitered scheme, if two neurons simultaneously fire, the coding ensures that the resulting bus configuration is non valid and automatically ignored by the decoder. The bus content is constantly monitored by the decoder and, every time its configuration corresponds to a valid code, a line and a column are selected and the pulse reaches the target neuron at the receiver core. The received pulses form the input of the target layer's neurons and are locally accumulated. This scheme features thus:

- asynchronous access to the channel

- no management of priority: collisions produce non-valid codes and result in the loss of the participating events

- event-driven behaviour

7.3 Analysis of the NAPFM Communication Systems

7.3.1 Statistical Assumptions

In this section, the intrinsic properties of the non arbitered PFM communication system are discussed. The model presented is based on the two assumptions of complete asynchronicity of the pulses generated by any two neurons in the network and of activity variations occurring at a time scale much larger than the pulse duration. As opposed to a clocked system, where transitions occur at predictable instants, here it is assumed that the neurons emit pulses in such a way that *coherent phenomena between pulses* do not take place. This is a way of taking advantage of the intrinsic limitations of an analog VLSI system: if mismatches between components are large enough and if the system's time resolution is of the order of or smaller than the RMS value of the unavoidable phase jitter of the activity-to-frequency converter, the possibility of two neurons emitting synchronously and colliding systematically is ruled out. A scheme to force co-occurring pulses to split in time is presently under study and simulation at the circuit level shows a significant performance enhancement (reduction of about a factor 4 of the collision probability).

In biological perceptive systems like cochleas or retinas, which respond vigorously and immediately to changes, many events (begin of an action potential emission) co-occur within, perhaps, a few milliseconds. In the VLSI systems considered here, simultaneity means events separated by a time of the order of ten to a hundred nanoseconds. The latter being a very conservative figure for the minimum event duration needed to elicit a valid logic pulse in the receiver (time resolution). In other words, events that are indistinguishable by biological structures on the basis of their time separation are sufficiently separated in the VLSI context. Note also that this mode of operation does not prevent the use of simultaneity as a particular encoding modality: further implementation work is warranted on this point.

Consider a network containing N neurons. Let δ be the minimum time necessary to generate a suitable pulse at the receiver and $\nu_i f_0$ the neuron's pulse rate, where ν_i is the activity of neuron $i (0 < \nu_i < 1)$ and f_0 is the frequency corresponding to maximum activity. If the average activity a is defined as:

$$\alpha = \frac{1}{N} \sum_{i=1}^{N} \nu_i \tag{7.1}$$

and the point process of the beginning of a pulse emission anywhere in the network is modeled by a Poisson process with rate $\lambda = N\alpha f_0$ the probability that a neuron trying to put a pulse through the channel succeeds without undergoing collision can be calculated. If the neuron starts firing at time t, there will be a collision if any other neuron fires any time between $t - \delta$ and $t + \delta$. This will result in correct bus configurations, corresponding to the firing neurons' codes, for a time shorter than Δ: not enough to properly drive the receiver. The probability of this event is given by the probability of one or more events in a time interval 2Δ for a set of Poisson points:

$$q = \sum_{k=1}^{\infty} \frac{(2\lambda\Delta)^k}{k!} = 1 - e^{-2\lambda\Delta} \quad (7.2)$$

thus the probability of safe emission is

$$p = e^{-2\lambda\alpha} \quad (7.3)$$

For a single neuron the probability that the interpulse time at the corresponding receiver is k, expressed in units of $1/\nu_i f_0$ is:

$$prob(k) = pq^{k-1} \quad (7.4)$$

derived by noting that $k - 1$ consecutive pulses must undergo collision, which happens with probability q^{k-1}, while the last one must pass, which happens with probability p. This distribution is shown in Figure 7.4 for

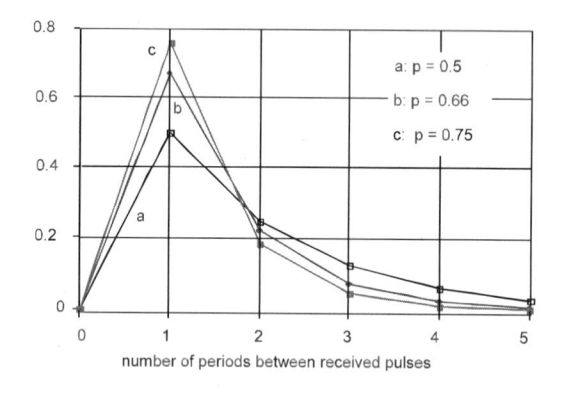

Figure 7.4. Interpulse time probability distribution due to the effect of collisions for different values of p. Curve a: p=0.5, curve b: p=0.66, curve c: p= 0.75

several values of p.

7.3.2 Detection

7.3.2.1 Detection by Time-Windowing

The receiver observes the pulses coming from neuron i and retrieves the information contained in the number k_i of pulses coming from neuron i in the observation time T (short enough to follow the time scale of variation of ν_i): it estimates the observed activity by $k_i/T f_0$. Collisions are responsible of the loss of part of the emitted pulses, thus k_i is a random variable. Its probability distribution is now derived.

Dropping the index i, in a time window T, the number of times the neuron fires is also a random variable V with 2 possible values: $n = \lfloor \nu T f_0 \rfloor$, the bar denoting the largest integer smaller than $\nu T f_0$, and $n + 1$. These values

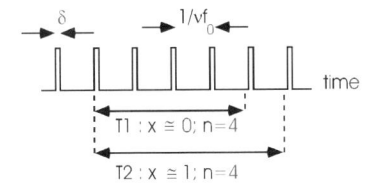

7.3 Analysis of the NAPFM Communication Systems 185

Figure 7.5. Illustrating the derivation of (7.5). If the receiver observation time is $T1$ and the frequency observed is νf_0, there is a very small probability x of observing five pulses [corresponding to $n+1$ in (7.5)]. If the observation time is T2, this probability is close to 1. The pulse duration is δ.

occur with respective probability $(1-x)$ and x where $x = \nu T f_0 - n$. These definitions are illustrated in Figure 7.5.

Using the total probability theorem: $pr(k) = pr(k|V = n)pr(V = n) + pr(k|V = n+1)pr(V = n+1)$, the probability of k can be written as a combination of binomial distributions:

$$prob(k) = x\binom{n+1}{k}p^k q^{n+1-k} + (1-x)\binom{n}{k}p^k q^{n-k} \qquad (7.5)$$

Using mean value and second moment of the binomial distribution with parameters μ (number of trials) and π (probability of favorable event), given respectively by $\mu\pi$ and $\mu^2\pi^2 + \mu\pi(1-\pi)$, the mean m, second moment m_2 and variance $\sigma^2 = m_2 - m^2$ of the distribution (7.5) are calculated:

$$m = x(n+1)p + (1-x)np = p(n+x) \qquad (7.6)$$

$$\sigma^2 = pq(n+x) + p^2 x(1-x) \qquad (7.7)$$

The relative error $\varepsilon^2 = \sigma^2/m^2$ is thus:

$$\varepsilon^2 = \frac{q/p}{n+x} + \frac{x(1-x)}{(n+x)^2} \qquad (7.8)$$

$1/\varepsilon^2$ can be interpreted as the signal-to-noise ratio of the received pulse stream.

7.3.2.2 Direct Interpulse Time Measurement

To estimate activity, we can also resort to a direct measurement of the interpulse time. The effect of collisions is to attribute to this measurement a confidence level: the measurement of an interspike interval can yield as result, with different probabilities, any integer multiple of the underlying periodic process. If instead of one we measure two subsequent intervals and take the smaller of them as the right result, the probability of error is considerably decreased. If, in general, we decide to measure I subsequent intervals, and then select the smallest as our estimate then:

$$\text{probability of error} = \sum_{N1=1}^{\infty}\sum_{N2=1}^{\infty}\cdots\sum_{Ni=1}^{\infty} pq^{N1-1}pq^{N2-1}\ldots pq^{Ni-1} \qquad (7.9)$$

$$= \left(\sum_{N=2}^{\infty} pq^{n-1}\right)^i = \left(\frac{pq}{1-q}\right)^i = q^i$$

186   7. Analog VLSI Pulsed Networks for Perceptive Processing

The trade-off is reflected in the number of intervals considered in the measurement: few intervals yield low confidence level but fast estimate.

7.3.3 Performance

7.3.3.1 Detection by Time-Windowing

According to (7.6), a measurement of activity for $\varepsilon \ll 1$ yields pulse counts narrowly distributed around $p(n+x)$. Thus every neuron seen from the outside seems to have an activity approximately reduced to a fraction p of its real activity. This, for instance in an image, corresponds only to a general darkening but not to contrast reduction or noise addition. Noise is described by the spreading around $p(n+x)$ of the pulse count coming from the observed neuron or equivalently by (7.8). ε^2 consists of 2 terms:

- $x(1-x)/(n+x)^2$ dominates at low pulse counts and describes the blurring of the frequency measurement when the observation time is just a few periods of the observed frequency.
- $(q/p)/(n+x)$ more specifically reflects the uncertainty introduced by collisions, even when the observation time is long compared to the interpulse spacing.

Using (7.2), (7.3) and the expression of λ in (7.8) we can write:

$$\varepsilon^2 = \frac{\exp(2N\alpha f_0 \Delta) - 1}{\nu f_0 T} + \frac{x(1-x)}{(\nu f_0 T)^2} \qquad (7.10)$$

introducing $K = (\nu/\alpha)(T/2N\Delta)$ and $\xi = 2N\alpha f_0 \Delta$ and rewriting $x = \xi K - \lfloor \xi K \rfloor$ we get:

$$\varepsilon^2 = \frac{\exp(\xi) - 1}{\xi K} + \frac{(\xi K - \lfloor \xi K \rfloor)(1 - \xi K + \lfloor \xi K \rfloor)}{(\xi K)^2} \qquad (7.11)$$

K is *the neuron's activity normalized to the average activity and multiplied by the scale factor* $(T/2N\Delta)$. The scale factor is the ratio of the observation time, determined by the application, to the characteristic time $2N\Delta$ (twice the time needed to scan the network spending a time Δ in each neuron). Assuming for T the maximum value allowed by the application, a system based on pure scanning will simply not work (i.e. will exhibit aliasing) unless the scale factor is $> 1/2$. The system we are examining, conversely, shows graceful degradation of performance as the scale factor diminishes: there will not be aliasing but just a noisier reproduction of the transmitted data as K decreases.

ξ is the *average frequency* αf_0 *normalized to the inverse of the characteristic time*. The first term in the right-hand side of (7.11) can be termed a collision noise and rewritten $(1/K)f(\xi)$ where the function $f(\xi) = [\exp(\xi) - 1]/\xi$ converges to 1 for $\xi \to 0$. Hence performance is ultimately limited by $1/K$ that sets the absolute minimum relative error. The second term contributes a spiky structure whose envelope decreases as $1/(\xi K)^2$ (granularity noise).

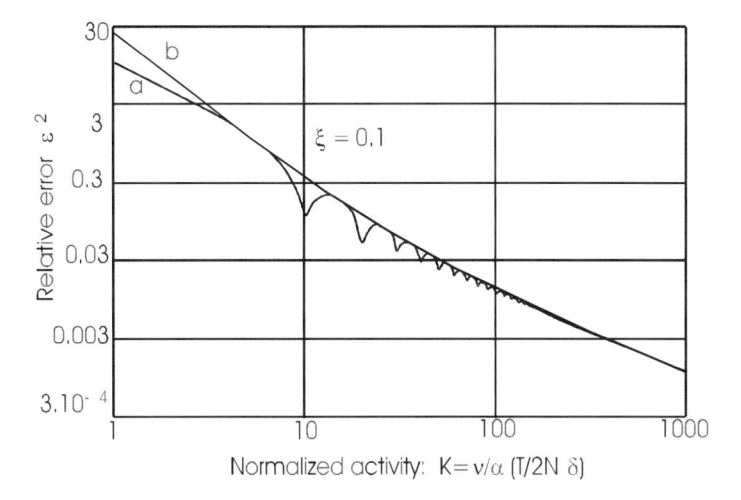

7.3 Analysis of the NAPFM Communication Systems

Figure 7.6. Error-activity relationship. Curve a: exact value, curve b: expression (7.12). For a given maximum-activity frequency, the curve provides the receiver error as a function of transmitted local activity. Larger activities are estimated with a smaller error.

Degradation relative to collision noise occurs at the onset of the jagged behavior of error, as shown in Figure 7.6 which plots ε^2 as a function of the normalized activity K for a particular value $\xi = 0.1$. Note, looking back to (7.11), that for n sufficiently larger than 1 the maxima of the lobes are about $1/4/(\xi K)^2$ since the maximum of $x(1-x)$ is $1/4$ for $0 < x < 1$. Using this fact, the envelope of the relative error, also plotted in Figure 7.6, can be rewritten:

$$\varepsilon^2 = \frac{1/4}{\xi^2}\left(\frac{2N\alpha\Delta}{\nu T}\right)^2 + f(\xi)\left(\frac{2N\alpha\Delta}{\nu T}\right) \tag{7.12}$$

and solved for ν to yield:

$$\nu = \frac{N\alpha\Delta}{T}\left(\frac{f(\xi) + \sqrt{(f(\xi))^2 + \varepsilon^2/\xi^2}}{\varepsilon^2}\right) \tag{7.13}$$

Equation (7.13) provides the relationship between the minimum activity ν that can be observed with a given error ε^2 and the normalized maximum-activity frequency ξ. It is illustrated in Figure 7.7 for several values of ε^2. The minimum activity is expressed in terms of the minimum attainable K : K_{min} and the maximum-activity frequency is expressed by ξ. Figure 7.7 shows that a best ξ exists which optimizes the dynamic range $1/nu_{min}$ for a given tolerable error level, the minimum is achieved at slightly different values of the optimal ξ for different values of ε^2. However, since none of the minima corresponding to different ξ's is sharp, setting ξ to about 0.1, thus the f_0 value to about $0.1(1/2N\alpha\Delta)$, guarantees operation to be very close to the optimum for every practical error range. The order of magnitude of the minimum activity measured at a given error level is $N\alpha\Delta/T\varepsilon^2$. In order to be around the optimal operating frequency, the value of f_0 will be controlled by the average activity according, in a non-critical manner, to

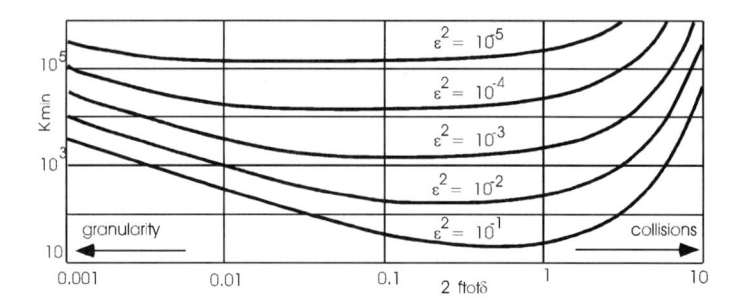

188   7. Analog VLSI Pulsed Networks for Perceptive Processing

Figure 7.7. Dynamic range-maximum activity frequency relationship. Each curve shows how to choose the best ξ to attain the largest dynamic range (i.e. the smallest minimum activity detectable with a given tolerable error) The optimum (minimum of the curves) occurs at slightly different values of normalized frequency but satisfactory behavior, although suboptimal, is obtained in all cases for $\xi \approx 0.1$.

the relationship

$$\alpha f_0 \approx 0.1/2N\Delta \tag{7.14}$$

This will be the case, unless otherwise specified, in most of the following discussion.

7.3.3.2 Direct Interpulse Time Measurement

Consider again the second detection method proposed in 7.3.2.1. We need to calculate one more quantity of interest: the average update time of the measurement. This is just the mean value of the distribution (7.4), which can be computed as follows: the event "wait k periods before the next pulse is received" occurs with probability:

$$prob.(k) = pq^{k-1} \tag{7.15}$$

The mean value of this distribution is:

$$m = \sum_{k=1}^{\infty} kpq^{k-1} = p\frac{d}{dq}\left(\sum_{k=1}^{\infty} q^k\right) = p\frac{d}{dq}\left(\frac{1}{1-q}\right) = \frac{p}{(1-q)^2} = \tag{7.16}$$

$$\frac{p}{p^2} = e^{\xi}$$

Note also that, for a dynamic situation where activity varies, this measurement procedure is only able to quickly follow increasing activities for large number of measured subsequent interpulse times I. Indeed, a decrease of activity, resulting in a longer interspike time, will in general be interpreted as collision and ignored until the $I - 1$ values of the previous measurement have all been replaced by values corresponding to the new activity. In order to follow at comparable speeds increases and decreases of activity, it seems thus reasonable to choose $I = 2$, i.e. to compare two subsequent interval values and take the smaller one as an estimate for interpulse time. This choice is of course interesting for circuit simplicity but sets the limit of the confidence level we can attribute to each measurement. If this option is retained, an increasing [respectively decreasing] activity's measurement can be updated every $\exp(\xi)$ [respectively $2\exp(\xi)$] periods with $[1-\exp(-\xi)]^2$ error probability. This mode thus features natural adaptation of the sampling rate to the activity value: larger activity levels are sampled more often than lower values.

Bearing in mind that ξ is proportional to the maximum-activity frequency, which is under designer's control, all periods of the emitting neurons' pulse trains are proportional to $1/\xi$ and the mean update time, for an activity ν, is given by $(2N\alpha\Delta/\nu\xi)\exp(\xi)$ where the first parenthesis is the interpulse time corresponding to activity ν and $\exp(\xi)$ is the average number periods to wait for an update. The relationship between error probability and average update time, normalized to $(2N\alpha\Delta/\nu)$ is shown in Figure 7.8 for different ξ values. Figure 7.8 demonstrates once again the basic trade-

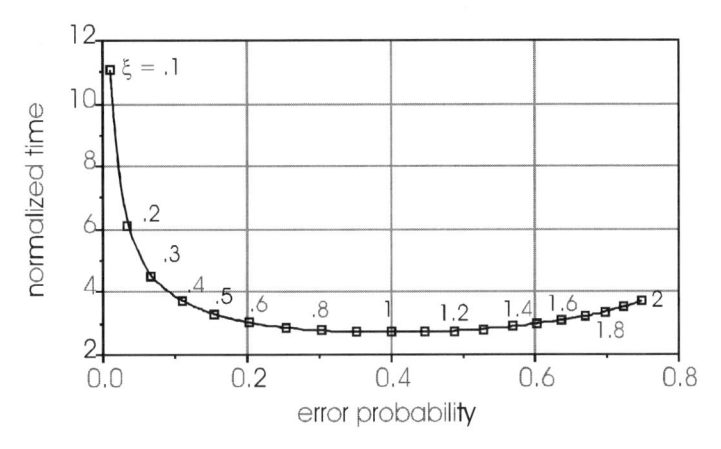

Figure 7.8. Relationship between error probability and normalized mean update time for the direct interpulse time measurement detection method for $I=2$.

off between speed and precision. Increasing ξ to more than 1 increases both mean update time (an update is only available on the average much less often than every period) and error probability (the measurement will be wrong) because of collisions. This ξ range must therefore be avoided. For $\xi < 1$, a reduction of the maximum-activity frequency increases the update time (periods become longer) but reduces the error probability (collisions are less probable). The curve also shows that there is not much value in staying around $\xi = 1$: normalized waiting time is barely increased by moving from $\xi = 1$ to $\xi = 0.5$ while the error probability is considerably reduced.

7.3.4 Data Dependency of System Performance

We have until now examined the behaviour of the system from the standpoint of a neuron with activity ν. We observed that it seems adapted in several respects to the communication of neural activities but that performance can be data-dependent: the average activity α is an essential parameter in the attainable dynamic range for the time-window detection

190   7. Analog VLSI Pulsed Networks for Perceptive Processing

method, for instance. The purpose of this section is to investigate further this data-dependency and to provide a quantitative indication of the system's behaviour at the global level. For the direct interpulse time measurement detection method, there is no meaningful way of defining a signal-to-noise ratio: the measurement outcome is, in principle, either the exact value or an integer multiple thereof. As already pointed out, the confidence level of the result is only a function of the collision probability and not of ν and does not therefore depend on the details of the distribution, at least as long as the Poisson assumption holds (a large enough pool of neurons is simultaneously active.) Is there an influence of the detailed shape of activity distribution over the communication performance in the time-window detection method? Let us recall the expression of the relative error associated to an activity ν:

$$\varepsilon^2 = \frac{1/4}{\xi^2}\left(\frac{2N\alpha\Delta}{\nu T}\right)^2 + f(\xi)\left(\frac{2N\alpha\Delta}{\nu T}\right) \tag{7.12}$$

This expression contains the data-dependent parameter α, a simple characteristic of the activity distribution. The resulting number of bits of precision to which ν can be communicated is:

$$L = -\frac{1}{2}\log_2\left[\left(\frac{N\alpha\Delta}{\xi\nu T}\right)^2 + \frac{2N\alpha\Delta(e^\xi - 1)}{\xi\nu T}\right] \tag{7.17}$$

Hence, if $Np(\nu)d\nu$ (where $p(\nu)$ is the probability density function of activities) is the number of neurons with activity between ν and $\nu + d\nu$, we can write the following expression for the total bit rate on the bus:

$$BR = \frac{N}{T}\int_0^1 -\frac{1}{2}\log_2\left[\left(\frac{N\alpha\Delta}{\xi\nu T}\right)^2 + \frac{2N\alpha\Delta(e^\xi - 1)}{\xi\nu T}\right]p(\nu)d\nu \tag{7.18}$$

To a first approximation, the data distribution can be characterized by its mean value and its standard deviation. As a model for this distribution the simple two-parameters expression (a truncated Gaussian for $0 < n < 1$) was chosen:

$$p(\Theta) = \frac{\exp(-\frac{\nu-\gamma}{\sqrt{2}\lambda})^2}{\int_0^1 \exp(-\frac{\nu-\gamma}{\sqrt{2}\lambda})^2 d\nu} \tag{7.19}$$

which is a smooth function with mean and variance mainly determined by γ and λ respectively. To compute the bit rate carried by the bus consider the following two contributions: the final result of the communication act is *a set of values*, known with an average precision calculated from (7.17), (7.18) and (7.19), *associated to a set of addresses*. The latter information can be estimated as $\log 2(N)$ bits every T seconds.

The sum of these two contributions, normalized to N/T, is plotted in Figure 7.9 as a function of γ for several values of λ. The normalized bit rate is the *average number of bits allocated to each neuron in an observation time T*. In the curves, T/Δ, the ratio of the silicon bandwidth to the process bandwidth, was set to 10^5 (this is the case, for example, if T=10 ms and

$\Delta = 100$ ns). ξ, following the analysis of Section 7.3.3.1, was set to 0.1 and the number of neurons to 1000. The main effect is the reduction of the normalized bit rate following an increase of the average activity. This reduction is smoother for wider distributions as can be seen by comparing the three curves. The variation of the normalized bit rate with the number of neurons N is plotted in Figure 7.10.

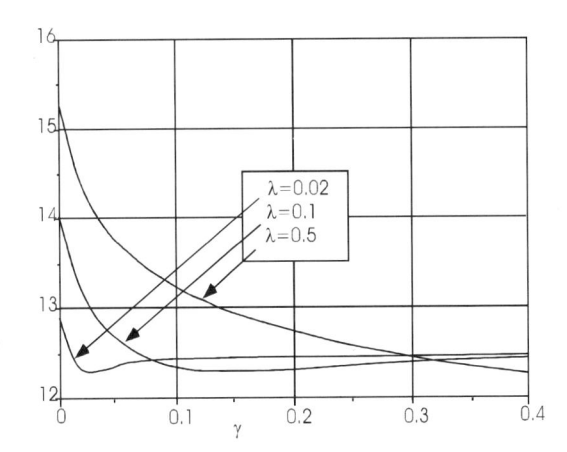

Figure 7.9. Normalized bit rate carried by the bus as a function of the average activity parameter γ for different distribution widths. $T/\Delta = 10^5, \xi = 0.1$ and $N = 1000$.

7.3.5 Discussion

7.3.5.1 Detection by Time-Windowing

Consider first the dependency of the relative error on average activity, for a neuron whose activity is fixed. If the condition for maximum dynamic range ($2N\alpha f_0\Delta = 0.1$) is fulfilled, an increase of α corresponds to a decrease in f_0. Referring to (7.11), this reduction in the maximum-activity frequency reduces both denominators in the right-hand side. Thus the system performs better for activity distributions concentrated on few neurons, likely to be found in neural computation networks. On the local scale, again referring to (7.11), for a fixed average activity α, the relative error increases with decreasing local activity ν. Precision is better for larger activities in conformity to the principle of allowing those neurons which have "something to say" to communicate it quickly and precisely.

In some cases it may be interesting to trade dynamic range for speed and the condition $2N\alpha f_0\Delta = 0.1$ can be relaxed. If, for instance, it is desired to detect a bright spot on a grid of detectors or to quickly report the output of an edge detecting system a rough distinction between active and inactive regions is sufficient. The inactive background's activity can be known with a large *relative* error since its absolute value is small ((7.12) with small ν values.) Thus f_0 can be increased and accordingly T, the observation time,

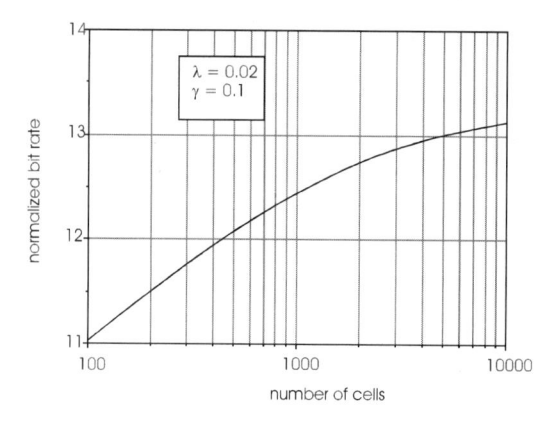

192   7. Analog VLSI Pulsed Networks for Perceptive Processing

Figure 7.10. the variation of normalized bit rate with the network's size. In this curve, $\gamma = 0.1, \lambda = 0.5, \xi = 0.1$ and $T/\Delta = 10^5$.

can be reduced and it is enough to observe for a very short time to draw a significant conclusion on where the spot or the edges are located.

We are interested in comparing the expected system performance with that of a scanned communication. The philosophies of the two approaches, however, are so different that only a gross comparison, in term of average bit rates, is possible.

We start by some further comment on the global curves of Figure 7.9 and Figure 7.10. Looking at Figure 7.9, consider a 1000-neurons system with average activity of 0.1, a spread of 0.1 about it, a process bandwidth of 100 Hz and silicon bandwidth of 10 MHz. The corresponding normalized bit rate can be read off Figure 3.7 for $\gamma = 0.1$ and amounts to 12.7. Then, for $N/T = 10^5 s^{-1}$, the throughput of the channel is then approximately 1.25 Mbits/s. A scanned system with the same channel bandwidth and a parallel bus with W wires could send a bit of information on each bus wire every $2\Delta = 200$ ns. With, say, $W = 5$, to fully exploit the channel bandwidth requires either an on-chip multiplexed 5-bit A/D converter working at 5 Msamples/s or a converter per neuron, working 1000 times slower. The second solution is clearly unpractical and the first would certainly be hardware- (a flash converter would probably be necessary for this kind of speed) and power-hungry. The bus throughput would be 2.5 Mbit/s and update rate would be limited to 200 μs/frame. The identity information can be an essential component in specific processing tasks and is totally missing in scanned, aliasing-prone systems.

7.3.5.2 Detection by Direct Interpulse Time Measurement

By renouncing to a clocked structure, and to the possibility of orderly and tightly aligning the pulses on the bus, we must be prepared to tolerate an average pulse separation larger than the minimum set by the bus bandwidth so that the average pulse separation on the bus becomes $1/N\alpha f_0 = 2\Delta/\xi$ instead of 2Δ for the clocked system. To simplify the comparison with a clocked system, assume that the network has only N_{act}

active neurons with identical activities. Each neuron will thus emit pulses separated by $N_{act}2\Delta/\xi$. With reasonable collision probability, this is also the order of magnitude of the measurement's update time thus information over all activities is obtained after $N_{act}2\Delta/\xi$ seconds. For a clocked system, conversely, the same information is on the average available after $(N/2)2\Delta$ seconds. The non clocked system is better if $N_{act}2\Delta/\xi N\Delta <=> N_{act}/N < \xi/2$. Again the property of better performance for networks where activity is distributed among few neurons appears. Figure 7.7 gives an indication on the ξ value to select for an acceptable error probability. The selection of this last parameter is an additional degree of freedom and can be very different for different applications.

7.4 Address Coding

The results of the preceding section hold if the only effect of collisions is the loss of all colliding pulses, but during a collision, the code present on the bus may correspond to a false address. In our implementations, the bus performs the bitwise wired OR operation on the colliding codes. This property suggests a straightforward code: all addresses are coded with the same number k of "ones"; the bitwise OR of the codes of two colliding neurons results in a code with at least $k+1$ "ones" which is automatically ignored by the decoder. If m wires are used in the bus, the largest number C of code words is obtained by taking for k the integer part of $m/2$. This code will be called "optimal" from now on. It turns out that redundancy is limited to less than 2 wires up to values of m of 20: an acceptable overhead. The asymptotic relationship between the number of bus wires and number of codewords is determined applying Stirling's formula:

$$m! \approx \sqrt{2\pi m} \cdot \left(\frac{m}{e}\right)^m \tag{7.20}$$

to the number of code words:

$$C = \frac{m!}{(m/2!)^2} \approx 2^m \sqrt{\frac{2}{\pi m}} \tag{7.21}$$

which shows a mildly less-than-exponential growth of number of code words with bus width. We now turn to additional practical properties of the code.

Neurons are addressed by monitoring and decoding the configuration of bits on the NAPFM bus. An example of the decoding logic is given in Figure 7.11 for the code 11000. Note that the AND (or NOR, depending on the chosen configuration) gate needs only 4 inputs: because of the way the code is constructed and because no additional zero can be produced by a collision, a codeword is completely caracterized by the position of its "zeros". A check for a "one" in any remaining wire is enough to determine the presence of an event. Thus, for this family of codes, the decoder logic needs only one more input as there are "zeros" in the code. Suppose hardware has been realized to decode an m-wires optimal code.

Is it possible to use the same hardware to decode activities from transmitters with $m-1$ or less wires? The following procedure can be used to build

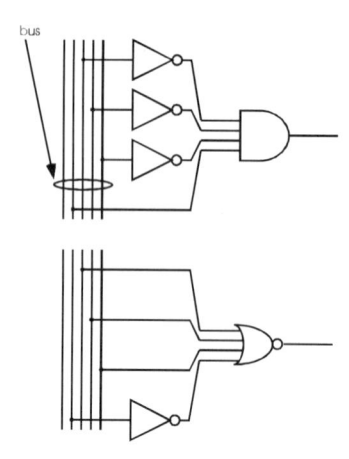

Figure 7.11. Logic to decode address 11000, in a 5-wire bus example. The top and bottom gates are equivalent but the bottom one is simpler and the NOR gate can be implemented with just a p-type transistor in the pull-up branch.

recursively an m-wires code starting from an $m-1$ wires code: i) If m is even, start from the "m-1-wires with (m+2)/2 ones" code and concatenate it with an additional bit (the MSB) set to 0. Then juxtapose the result with the "$m-1$-wires with $(m-2)/2$ ones" code with the MSB set to 1. This operation results in the optimal "m-wires with $m/2$ ones " code. The optimal "$m-1$-wires with $(m+2)/2$ ones" code is thus by construction a subset of the larger code and a decoder designed for the latter, with the MSB clamped to 0 will be sensitive to the smaller code. ii) If m is odd, start from the "$m-1$-wires with $(m-1)/2$ ones" code and concatenate it with an additional bit (the MSB) set to 0. Then juxtapose the result with the "$m-1$-wires with $(m-1)/2-1$ ones" code with the MSB set to 1. Application of the well-known identity: $n!/(k!(n-k)!) = (n,k) = (n-1,k)+(n-1,k-1)$ shows that the resulting code is the optimal "m-wires with $(m+1)/2$ ones" code and, again, the optimal "$m-1$-wires with $(m-1)/2$ ones" code is by construction a subset of the larger code.

Extension of m-wires decoding hardware to decode $m+1$-wires (or more) codes is the inverse problem. It can be carried out by using a ROM.

We now turn to examples of hardware implementations of he ideas presented up to now.

7.5 Silicon Retina Equipped with the NAPFM Communication System

7.5.1 Circuit Description

As an application of the NAPFM communication architecture, this section presents a silicon retina that can be used as the first layer of a biomimetic vision system. The silicon retina has been successfully interfaced with another analog chip, also equipped with NAPFM communication, implementing a cortical layer for orientation enhancement. The silicon retina is basically an array of hexagonally arranged neurons interconnected in such a way that the spatial high-pass filtering of the image projected on the chip surface can be carried out and the results of the computation passed over to the next layer using the NAPFM technique. Every neuron contains part of a normalizer and a pulse generator connected to a parallel bus in exactly the same way as described in [Mortara et al., 1995] and [Arreguit et al., 1993]. This section's main interest is to present conclusive measurements concerning the validity of the assumptions in [Mortara and Vittoz, 1994] and a larger-scale realization than in [Mortara et al., 1995].

Edge enhancement can be obtained by subtracting from the image its spatially low-pass filtered version. This operation results in a center-surround receptive field. A low-pass spatial filter can be realized by using a resistance-conductance diffusive network implemented with an array of resistors, difficult to integrate in CMOS technology if large enough resistances must be used for low consumption. A solution to this problem is to use a transistor with a particular gate bias and to operate it in its conduction mode. A clever gate biasing scheme has been proposed [Mahowald, 1991] to implement with MOSFETs a resistor-like connection between two nodes. However, the range of linearity of this element's conductance is limited and depends on its source/drain potentials in a saturating fashion (the saturating non linearity, however, turns out to be useful in segmentation tasks).

It has been shown that linear networks can be efficiently implemented using CMOS transistors instead of resistors. Reference [Vittoz and Arreguit, 1993] gives full details about the underlying principle which can be so stated: *the current distribution in the branches of a current-driven resistive network is the same as that of a current driven MOS network (all transistors having the same gate voltage) where resistor terminals are replaced by sources and drains and conductance ratios are replaced by W/L ratios. Grounded resistor terminals must be replaced by MOS terminals at a potential larger than their pinch-off potential V_P (pseudo-ground)* which permits easy extraction of the current entering a pseudo-ground node by means of a complementary current mirror. In particular, if transistors are restricted to operate in the weak inversion domain, the analog of conductance in the resisitve network, the pseudo conductance can be also tuned by adjusting the gate voltage [Vittoz and Arreguit, 1993]. Pseudo-conductance becomes then a linear function of W/L and an exponential function of the gate voltage V_G.

The schematic diagram of one pixel is shown in Figure 7.12. The photodiode is a n-well/substrate junction. The photogenerated current enters the pixel's share $T_{N1} - T_{N2} - T_{N3}$ of a chip-wide normalizer integrated using MOS transistors in weak inversion. Although a "real" translinear network should be made using bipolar or compatible lateral bipolar transistors [Gilbert, 1984],[Vittoz, 1983] the MOS solution was chosen for its smaller area even with rather large transistors in the translinear loop and because exact normalization does not seem critical in this application. The normalization current is directly related to the network's total activity and can be used to tune bus occupation to the best value according to Equation (7.14). The normalizer has two outputs T_{N2} and T_{N3}. The current delivered by T_{N2} is injected in the pseudo-conductance network. The contribution to

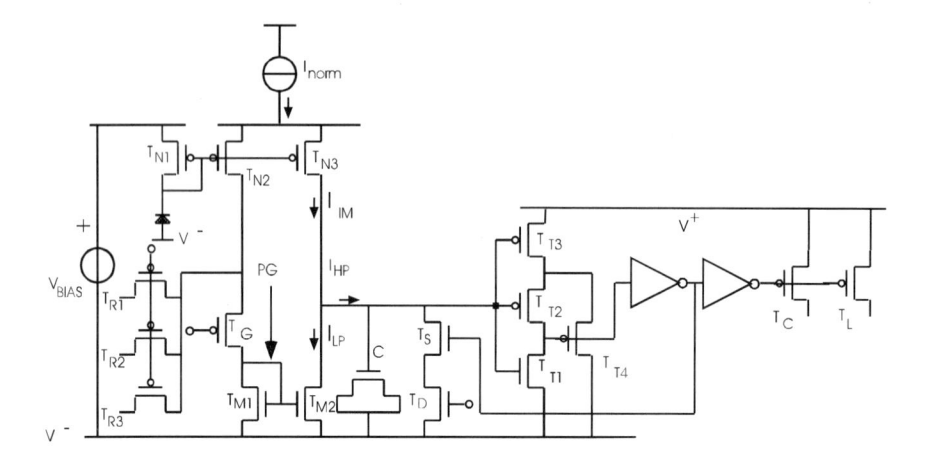

196   7. Analog VLSI Pulsed Networks for Perceptive Processing

Figure 7.12. Schematic diagram of a pixel.

the network of each neuron is a conductance T_G to the pseudo-ground node PG and three "outgoing" pseudo-resistances to nearest neighbors T_{R1}, T_{R2} and T_{R3}. The three other pseudo-resistive connections are provided by remaining neighbors. The current injected in the pseudo-resistive grid is spatially low-pass filtered and the result of this operation, I_{LP}, flows through T_G, is collected by the current mirror $T_{M1} - T_{M2}$, and subtracted from the current I_{IM} (a normalized version of the original image) flowing through the second normalizer's output T_{N3}. The difference I_{HP}, represents the local value of the spatially high-pass filtered version of the image. It drives the pulse generator composed by a Schmitt trigger (transistors T_{T1}, T_{T2}, T_{T3} and T_{T4}) and transistors T_D and T_S. The input node of the Schmitt trigger (transistors T_{T1}, T_{T2}, T_{T3} and T_{T4}) is alternatively charged by I_{HP} and discharged by I_{dis} (imposed by discharge transistor T_D when switch T_S is ON) between its upper threshold V_H^+ and its lower threshold V_H^-. Introducing $\Delta V = V_H^+ - V_H^-$, the pulse frequency f depends only on the normalized activity current I_{HP} : $f = I_{HP}/C\Delta V$ and its duration Δ is controlled by I_{dis} assumed much larger than I_{HP} : $\delta \approx C\Delta V/I_{dis}$. The network's total activity is:

$$f_{tot} = I_{norm}/C\Delta V \qquad (7.22)$$

therefore controlling the normalization current is enough to realize condition (7.14). The neuron encodes of course only positive values of the high-pass filtered image. Similarly to what has been described in [Mortara et al., 1995], current pulses generated by T_C and T_L reach a 7-wires column and a 7-wires row internal bus. The row and column codes are 7-bits with 3 "ones" (35 possibilities). The internal bus current configuration is converted into voltage pulses by the same circuitry as in [Mortara et al., 1995].

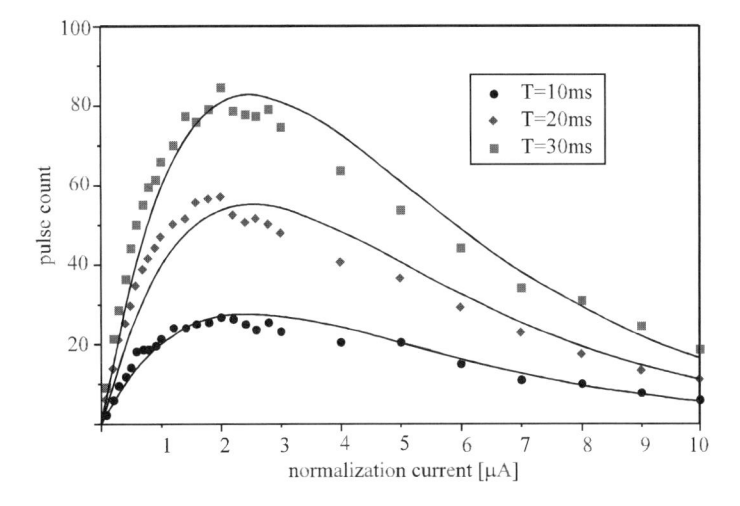

7.5 Silicon Retina Equipped with the NAPFM Communication System 197

Figure 7.13. Pulse count coming from one neuron as a function of the normalization current. Solid line: theoretical fit with an $KI_{norm} \cdot \exp(-KI_{norm})$ -like behaviour as predicted from Equation (7.3): a number of pulses of the form KI_{norm} is emitted with a probability of safe arrival of the form $\exp(-KI_{norm})$ resulting in an average number of arriving pulsed of the form shown.

7.5.2 Noise Measurement Results

The most important theoretical result to test from the communication's point of view is the dependence of relative error ε^2 as a function of bus occupation for a given chip activity. Bus occupation depends only on chip total pulse rate and is proportional to the normalization current. To perform this measurement, pulses coming from a particular neuron have been accumulated by the timer of a microcontroller which also provided ways of storing the readings in a file. The chip was illuminated with a uniform spot and transistor T_G had its gate at V^+ to exclude filtering action. Measurements have been done for different values of the normalization current. For each current, 35 readings of the pulse counts over different time windows have been recorded. The average and standard deviation of the counts have then been computed with a spreadsheet. Average pulse counts for observation times of 10, 20 and 30 ms are shown in Figure 7.13 as a function of normalization current, directly related to the probability of collision, Equation (7.3). Note the good agreement of the measurements with the expected behaviour in $I_{norm} \cdot e^{-I_{norm}}$ (intuitively, the number of received pulses is the product of the number of emitted pulses, proportional to I_{norm}, times the probability of safe reception, which goes exponentially with $-I_{norm}$). This is a first solid confirmation of the validity of the Poisson assumption.

The measured relative error ε^2 is shown in Figure 7.1 (only points for T = 10 and 30 ms are shown for clarity). To obtain an analytical fit, we used

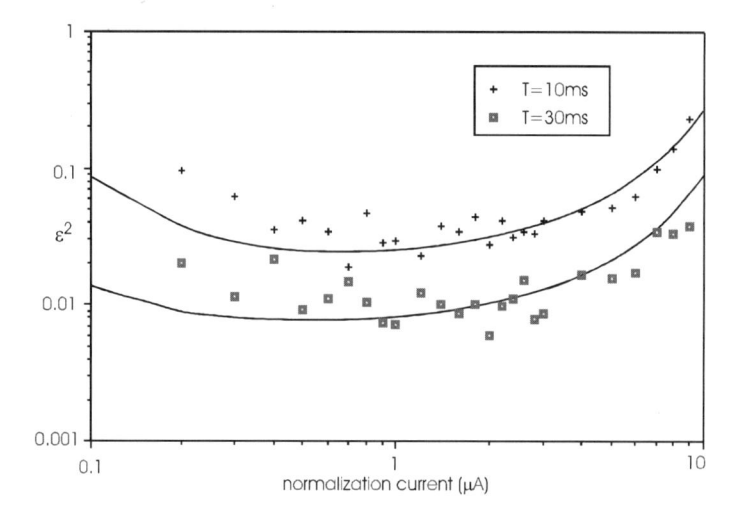

198   7. Analog VLSI Pulsed Networks for Perceptive Processing

Figure 7.14. Variation of ε^2 as a function of normalization current. Squares: measured values, solid line: theoretical prediction based on Equation (7.12).

Equation (7.12):

$$\varepsilon^2 = \frac{2N\alpha f_0 \Delta - 1}{\nu f_0 T} + \frac{1/4}{(\nu f_0 T)^2} \tag{7.12}$$

In our measurements, $T = 10$, 20 and 30 ms. With uniform illumination, $\Theta f_0 T = 1/N f_{tot} T$, with $N = 35 \times 35 = 1225$ and f_{tot} given by (7.22). To determine Δ, the system's time resolution in our set-up, we increased the discharge current of the pulse generators until a sharp decrease of the pulse count was observed for a discharge current between 3 and 4 μA. In this case the pulse duration is too small for the receiver logic to operate properly and a conservative estimate for the largest allowable discharge current is 3 μA (corresponding to $\delta \approx 300$ ns, which is not surprisingly large since the measuring set-up included a cascade of 2 gate-array-logic chips as decoders, one AND gate and a rather adventurous connection to the controller mounted on a printed circuit). Dedicated receiver hardware can push system bandwidth much higher: an array of analog pulse demodulators [Mortara and Vittoz, 1995] has demonstrated 40 ns operation and a digital receiver chip, described in Section 7.8, has also been designed to that purpose. All the parameters have thus been estimated to fit the measurements with (7.12). The result of the fitting is shown in Figure 7.14. A good order-of-magnitude estimate of the relative error is provided by the theory despite the many sources of uncertainty (for instance over the determination of the number of active neurons, over the real value of Δ, the real value of ΔV used to determine the chip pulse rate f_{tot} and especially real value of ν).

The same set-up was used to produce images with the chip. In this case the neurons were sequentially observed and pulses coming from each address accumulated over 20 ms. Figure 7.15 shows the result obtained by projecting a light bar on the chip. Two acquisitions were done to obtain a visual impression of the fixed-pattern noise and of the noise contributed

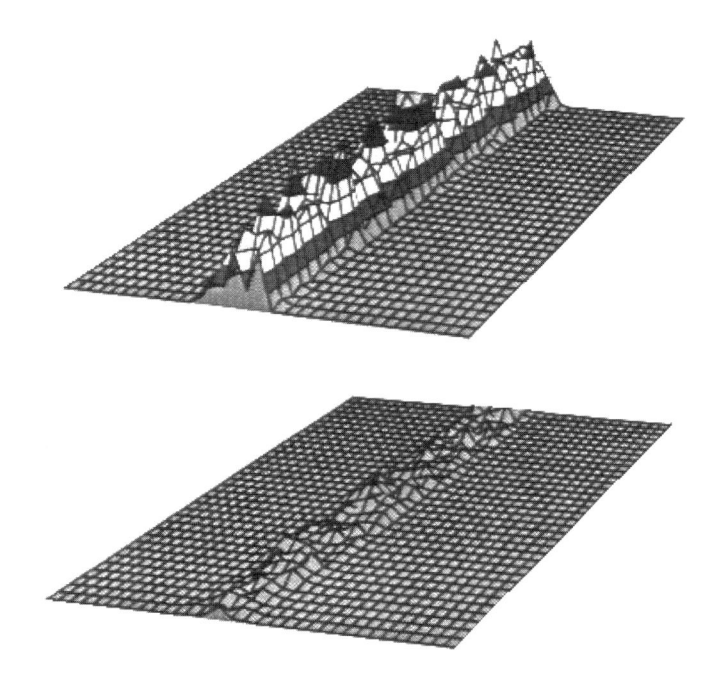

Figure 7.15. Signal recorded while illuminating the chip with a light bar. Top: average of 2 recordings, observation time 20 ms; bottom: difference of the two same recordings (visualizes transmission noise).

by the communication system. The average value of the two acquisitions is displayed on the top of the figure (and can be interpreted as a representation of the light signal plus fixed-pattern noise) while the absolute value of their difference, originating only from transmission noise, is displayed on the bottom of the figure. As can be observed, fixed pattern noise definitely dominates over transmission noise and contributes high-frequency spatial components difficult to separate from actual edges in the signal by a linear spatial filtering operation without other cues. It is likely that an adaptation method like the one proposed in [Mahowald, 1991] is necessary to auto-zero the system and reduce mismatch effects. As far as communication is concerned, though, the results obtained with this chip are satisfactory.

7.6 Projective Field Generation

7.6.1 Overview

In this section an extension of the NAPFM communication scheme is proposed. Instead of a one-to-one mapping between layers, pulses from an emitting neuron are received by several target neurons, distributed into a 'projective field'. These fields, in biology, result from direct connections between collaterals of previous layers' axons and synapses of the receptive neurons. Their shape and size determine the neuron's functionality [Hubel, 1987],[Dowling, 1992]. For example, in the primary visual cor-

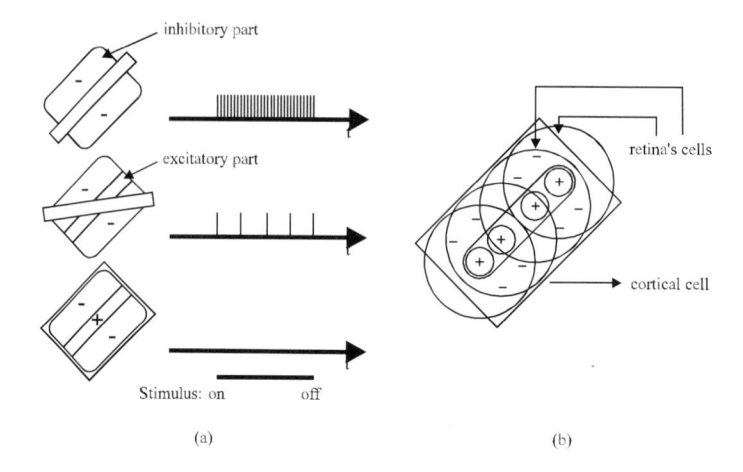

Figure 7.16. (a) Typical responses of a 'simple neuron' sensitive to oriented light bar. (b) Combination of several center-surround receptive fields to obtain an elongated oriented receptive field [Hubel, 1987].

tex, the behavior of different kinds of neurons, involved in spatial visual processing and sensitive to oriented edges or line terminations can be explained by the shape of the receptive field. Consider a cortical neuron with an elongated receptive field, as in Figure 7.16(a). When a light bar, correctly oriented, matches the middle excitatory part of the receptive field, the response of the neuron is maximal. With a different orientation, the excitatory part is only partially recovered and the neuron gives a weaker response. The inhibitory part of the field prevents the neuron from responding when the illumination is uniform. Figure 7.16(b) shows how, by integrating the activity of several aligned retina neurons, a cortical neuron can obtain the appropriate receptive field for an orientation detection [Hubel, 1987].

In VLSI, direct connections by wire between neurons to spread activities are possible, but when connections with neurons other than the nearest neighbors are needed, the area taken by connections on the layout becomes too large. Moreover the shape and size of the projective field cannot be changed since it is defined by physical wires on the circuit. Another possibility is to compute orientations when information is transmitted out of the silicon retina. With an on-chip sample-and-hold chain, a three-valued orientation image is computed during the scanning [Allen et al., 1988]. Orientations are no longer computed continuously and in parallel everywhere on the silicon retina; they are determined sequentially and discretely. Our solution also uses the transmission out of the silicon retina to compute orientations but with a pulsed communication scheme instead of the scanning scheme. In this way, the processing stays continuous and parallel and avoids drawbacks related to scanning [Mortara and Vittoz, 1994].

We combine the pulse frequency representation of transmitted activities and a property of the communication scheme 'only one neuron is addressed at a given time' to spread the neuron activity on the receptive layer around the addressed neuron, through a nonlinear network. The shape and size of the projective field are the same for each emitter neuron but are not predefined by physical connections. By modifying network biases, shape and size of the projective field can be changed. It is an example of opportunistic use of pulse coding to carry out such an eminently linear computation as the convolution with a kernel with intrinsically non linear circuitry. Amplitude information is carried by frequency of events (pulses), but the nonlinear circuitry is always excited by the same stimulus (the pulse itself) so that nonlinear behavior (distortion with changing stimulus amplitude) cannot appear.

7.6.2 Anisotropic Current Pulse Spreading in a Nonlinear Network

The communication scheme transmits the activity of each emitter layer neuron to the corresponding receptive neuron. All received pulses are propagated into the nonlinear network around the receptive neuron and generate the desired projective field by temporarily creating an activation bubble. The neuron element of the network is shown in Figure 7.17 for an

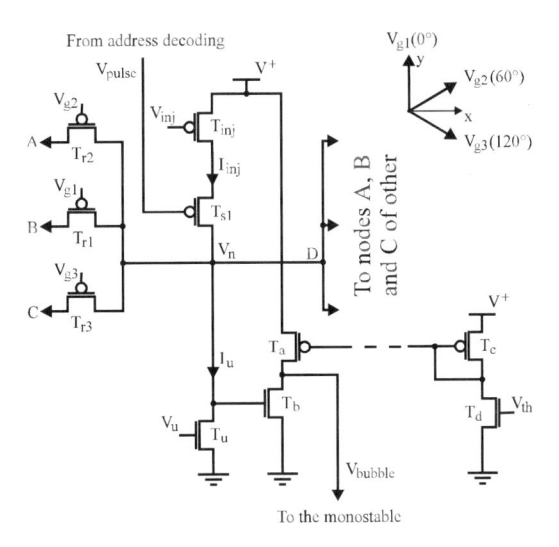

Figure 7.17. Schematic of a nonlinear network element included in each neuron. V_{inj} and V_u are external bias voltages. Transistors T_c and T_d are shared by all neurons and set the threshold voltage of the level detector (T_a, T_b) at V_{th}.

hexagonal scheme of connections. Each time a pulse is received by a neuron from the upstream circuit, it closes the switch T_{s1} and allows a current I_{inj} to be injected into the nonlinear network formed by T_{r1}, T_{r2}, T_{r3} and T_u. A linear resistance-conductance (RG) network, originally proposed by [Mead, 1989], could also be used to propagate current pulses. However the rapidly decreasing exponential voltage characteristic of the RG network is not suited to define a large bubble because most of the injected current I_{inj} is sunk near the injection node and has very little effect at long distance.

We use a variation of this network [Heim et al., 1991] that exploits nonlinearities to get a distribution of the node voltages V_n with a more constant slope and to generate a well-controlled variable size bubble. The lateral resistances R of [Mead, 1989] are replaced by a nonlinear element which provides a decreasing resistance with increasing channel voltage. This element is realized with equal-sized transistors, T_{r1}, T_{r2} and T_{r3}. The vertical conductances G of [Mead, 1989] are replaced by current limiting devices T_u which are the outputs of a current mirror of unit value I_u. Since the outputs of the mirror, one per neuron, can not sink more than I_u, the injected current I_{inj} must spread within an area roughly equal to I_{inj}/I_u units. At the boundary of the bubble, the remaining currents absorbed by the nearest neurons are smaller than I_u, so outside the bubble, all N-MOS mirror outputs are in their conduction mode. The voltage difference between mirror outputs inside and outside the bubble is larger than the difference of the pinch-off voltages of transistors T_{r1}, T_{r2} or T_{r3} and T_u (one volt or more) and allows an easy binary determination of neurons inside the bubble. These neurons define an activation bubble for the duration of the pulse. Output V_{bubble} of the activated neurons is set to ground by a voltage level detector composed of T_a and T_b. Transistors T_c and T_d are shared by all neurons and set the threshold voltage of the detector at V_{th}. Different gate voltages V_{g1}, V_{g2} and V_{g3} determine different conductances in the three directions of the hexagonal network. This anisotropy favors pulse propagation in the more conducting direction and allows to define an elongated bubble in this direction.

7.6.3 Analysis of the Spatial Response of the Nonlinear Network

Depending on the problem at hand, the gate voltages V_{g1}, V_{g2} and V_{g3}, always referred in this report to the local substrate potential V^+, will be set to different values to generate a projective field of a specific orientation and elongation. Unfortunately it is not possible to give an analytical solution for the spatial response of the two-dimensional network as a function of V_{g1}, V_{g2} and V_{g3}. However some information about this response is necessary to properly design the network, especially concerning the node voltage V_n where the current I_{inj} is injected into the network and the voltage drop between enabled neurons and the others. Thus we consider two extreme cases of the network configuration which bound all other possible responses of the network, whatever the combination of V_{g1}, V_{g2} and V_{g3}:

(a) one-dimensional network for which all gate voltages $V_{gi}(i = 1, 2, 3)$ are zero except one. The activation bubble is a segment oriented in the direction of the nonzero conductances and includes I_{inj}/I_u activated neurons.

(b) isotropic two-dimensional network where all gate voltages V_{gi} are equal, i.e. $V_{g1} = V_{g2} = V_{g3}$. The activation bubble is a circle containing of I_{inj}/I_u activated neurons.

The case (b) has been extensively studied and used in [Heim, 1993] to generate learning neighborhood, therefore the calculation of the spatial response is limited to the case (a). The drain current of a MOS transistor in the conduction mode is [Enz et al., 1995]:

$$I_D = \beta \cdot (V_D - V_S) \cdot (V_G - V_{TO} - \frac{n}{2}(V_D + V_S)) \tag{7.23}$$

$$\text{for } V_D, V_S < V_P = (V_G - V_{TO})/n$$

where $\beta = \mu \cdot C_{ox} \cdot W/L = \beta_0 \cdot W/L$ is the transconductance parameter, V_{TO} the threshold voltage, V_P the pinch-off voltage and n the slope factor. In this equation potentials are referred to the local substrate. The resistance of a lateral transistor T_{ri} is defined by the ratio of the differential voltage $\Delta V = (V_D - V_S)$ centered around a common mode voltage $V_{CM} = (V_D + V_S)/2$ to the drain current I_D, i.e. $R(V_{CM}) = 1/(\beta \cdot n \cdot (V_P - V_{CM}))$. By referring V_n and V_{off} to the global substrate, $V_{off} = V^+ - V_P, V_n = V^+ - V_{CM}$, we have:

$$R(V_n) = \frac{1}{\beta \cdot n \cdot (V_n - V_{off})} \tag{7.24}$$

The network is converted into a continuous model, the unit current source is replaced by an ideal constant current density $J_u \neq 0$ for $V_n > 0$, otherwise $J_u = 0$. The horizontal discrete resistors are replaced, in (7.25), by continuous elements of resistance $dR(x)$ of width W and length dx where x is the distance from the injection point:

$$dR(x) = \frac{dx}{\beta_0 \cdot W \cdot n \cdot (V_n - V_{off})} \tag{7.25}$$

Furthermore the current flowing along the x-axis is the difference between the current injected and the current already absorbed to ground:

$$I(x) = I_{inj} - 2 \cdot J_u \cdot W \cdot x \tag{7.26}$$

and the decreasing potential from the injected node can be expressed as

$$dV_n(x) = -dR(x) \cdot I(x) \tag{7.27}$$

This differential equations can be solved with the boundary condition $V_n(x_{max}) = V_{off}$, x_{max} is calculated from Equations (7.26) with the condition $I(x_{max}) = 0$ and correspond to the half-length of the bubble. This leads to:

$$V_{n(a)}(x) = \sqrt{\frac{I_{inj} \cdot x_{max(a)}}{2 \cdot \beta_0 \cdot W \cdot n}} \left(1 - \frac{x}{x_{max(a)}}\right) + V_{off}, \text{ for } x \leq x_{max(a)} \tag{7.28}$$

$$\text{otherwise } V_{n(a)}(x) = 0$$

An index (a) is added to distinguish this spatial response from the one of the case (b) available in [Heim, 1993], where equal gate voltages V_{gi} bias isotropically the network:

$$V_{n(b)}(x) = \sqrt{\frac{I_{inj}}{2 \cdot \pi \cdot n\beta_0}} \cdot \sqrt{\left(\frac{x}{x_{max(b)}}\right)^2 - 1 - 2 \cdot \ln\left(\frac{x}{x_{max(b)}}\right)} \tag{7.29}$$

$$+V_{off}, \text{ for } x \leq x_{max(b)} \text{ otherwise } V_{n(b)}(x) = 0$$

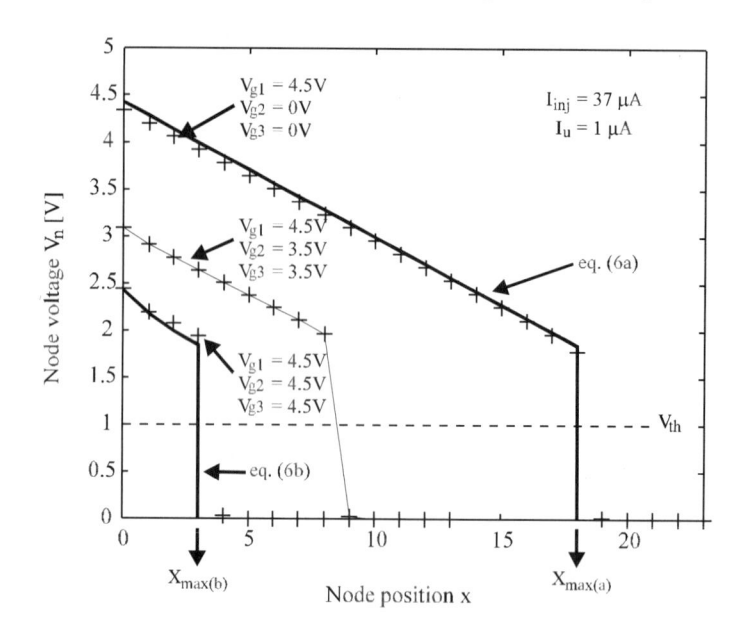

204   7. Analog VLSI Pulsed Networks for Perceptive Processing

Figure 7.18. Spatial responses of the nonlinear network for different gate voltages V_{g1}, V_{g2} and V_{g3} referred to V^+. Equations (7.28) in solid line are compared to three results of simulation. Currents I_{inj} and I_u are the same for all curves.

Figure 7.18 plots these two equations with three results of simulation. Note that (7.28) and (7.29) are good approximations of the spatial response and that they bound all possible responses of the network, whatever the gate voltages V_{gi} are, for I_{inj} and I_u given. Case (a) is the most constraining from the point of view of the design of the network because the range of the voltage V_n is the largest.

7.6.4   Analysis of the Size and Shape of the Bubbles Generable by the Nonlinear Network

By setting differently the gate voltages V_{gi} of the nonlinear network, we generate a bubble elongated in the direction the most conductive and therefore we favor the spreading of the activity of the emitting neuron in this direction. Cases (a) and (b) are two extreme situations where, respectively, the spreading is done in only one direction and where no direction is favored. What happens between these two extremes? Figure 7.19 shows four measurements of a generated bubble with the same currents I_{inj} and I_u but with different gate voltages. To study systematically all bubble shapes which can be generated by the network, it is necessary to define mathematically what 'orientation' and 'elongation' of a bubble mean. Firstly we assume that the set of neurons belonging to a bubble defines a geometrical area and secondly we calculate the position and both axes of the inertia ellipse of this area. The orientation of the bubble is then defined as the angle of the axis of least inertia and its elongation as the length ratio of the two ellipse axes. In more concrete terms elongation determines with which

7.6 Projective Field Generation   205

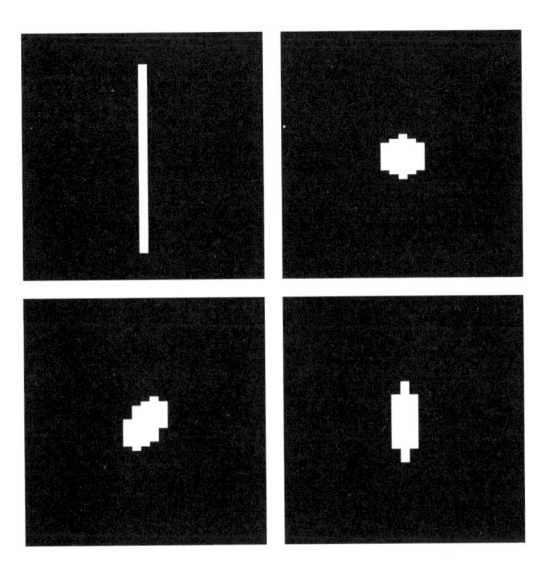

Figure 7.19. Four measurements of a generated bubble with $I_u = 1\mu A$ and $I_{inj} = 20\mu A$, injected at the center of the network. The different gate voltages are respectively (a) $V_{g1} = 4.5$ V, $V_{g2} = 0$ V, $V_{g3} = 0$ V, (b) $V_{g1} = 4.5$ V, $V_{g2} = 4.5$ V, $V_{g3} = 4.5$ V, (c) $V_{g1} = 4.5$ V, $V_{g2} = 4.5$ V, $V_{g3} = 0$ V, (d) $V_{g1} = 4.5$ V, $V_{g2} = 4$ V, $V_{g3} = 4$ V.

angular selectivity the orientation enhancement is applied. A very narrow bubble enhances only precisely well-oriented edges, whereas a wider bubble reinforces activity of all approximately well-oriented edges. If a rectangular tiling is considered, each neuron has four nearest neighbors and two gate voltages V_{g1}, V_{g2} biasing respectively the vertical and horizontal conductance. All inertia ellipses of the possible bubbles can be described by:

$$(x/a)^2 + (y/b)^2 = 1 \qquad (7.30)$$

a is the length of the x-half axis and b that of the y-half axis of the ellipse. Clearly, the bubbles will be oriented vertically if V_{g1} is larger than V_{g2} and horizontally if V_{g1} is smaller. The situation changes for a network with more than two main directions, e.g. an hexagonal or octagonal network. It is then possible to obtain bubbles with an orientation different from those of the wired axes of the network. Consider an hexagonal nonlinear network with V_{g3} set to zero. The set of orientations and elongations possible for any combination of V_{g1} and V_{g2} can be deduced from Equation (7.30) by applying a linear transformation of coordinates:

$$\begin{aligned} x' &= \cos(\alpha) \cdot x \\ y' &= \sin(\alpha) \cdot x + y \end{aligned} \qquad (7.31)$$

This transformation corresponds to the modification of the elementary mesh between a rectangular network and the hexagonal one. a is defined on Figure 7.20 and for an hexagonal network $\alpha = 30°$. Replacing (7.31) into

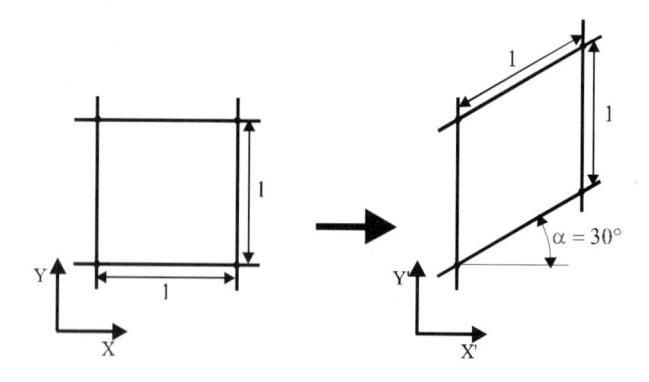

Figure 7.20. Transformation of a rectangular mesh into an hexagonal one.

(7.30) leads to the general equation:

$$\left(\frac{1}{\cos^2(\alpha) \cdot a^2} + \frac{\tan^2(\alpha)}{b^2}\right) \cdot x'^2 - \frac{2 \cdot \tan^2(\alpha)}{b^2} \cdot x' \cdot y' + \frac{1}{b^2} \cdot y'^2 - 1 = 0 \quad (7.32)$$

which describes the inertia ellipse of all bubbles possible with only two voltages V_{gi} different from zero.

Calculating the orientation and the elongation of this set of ellipses for all values a and b and plotting the results as elongation versus orientation, we obtain, for an hexagonal network, the curve shown in Figure 7.21. It is assumed that V_{g1} corresponds to 0° and V_{g2} to 60°. This means that for a certain pair (V_{g1}, V_{g2}), the bubble points in a certain direction (this direction can be determined by an electrical simulation) and its elongation is given by the curve in Figure 7.21. Now if the third voltage V_{g3} which corresponds to 120° is increased, the orientation of the bubble will change and the elongation will decrease. The same reasoning can be applied to all other pairs of successive gate voltages, i.e. (V_{g2}, V_{g3}) and (V_{g3}, V_{g1}): the curves are the same as that in Figure 7.21, simply shifted on the x-axis by 60° and 120°. The area under the solid line covers therefore the set of bubbles that an hexagonal nonlinear network can generate by choosing the right values V_{g1}, V_{g2} and V_{g3}. On Figure 7, the calculated curve in solid line is compared to a measurement done on the integrated network of 27 x 27 neurons. It is shown that all orientations are available but for certain orientations, e.g. 30°, 90° and 150°, the elongation is limited to 1.73. As mentioned previously, elongation determines angular selectivity of the orientation enhancement. Depending on the applications, this angular selectivity can be insufficient. It is then possible to increase the number of wired directions. With an octagonal network, $\alpha = 45°$ and four gate voltages V_{g1} V_{g2} V_{g3} V_{g4}, bubble elongation for angles bisecting the wired orientations is increased to 2.41. To obtain more elongated bubbles, more complicated networks including first and second nearest neighboring neurons can be considered. Equation (7.32) is general and can be applied to these other types of networks, simply by adapting the network mesh angle α.

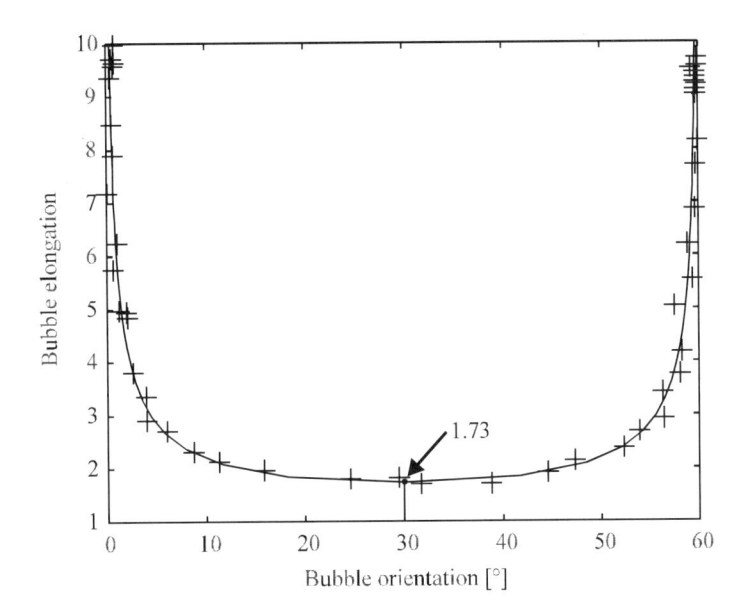

Figure 7.21. Calculated and measured curves of the bubble elongation for V_{g1} and V_{g2} different from zero and $V_{g3} = 0$.

7.7 Description of the Integrated Circuit for Orientation Enhancement

7.7.1 Overview

The nonlinear network described in the preceding chapter has been used on an integrated circuit which enhances oriented edges. The circuit (ED088) contains 27 x 27 neurons and is integrated in a 2 mm, double metal CMOS technology (ALP2LV). The neurons contain no photosensitive device but receive their inputs from a previously integrated silicon retina which performs edge enhancement. The detection of the oriented edge is simple and follows the biological principle explained in Figure 7.16: activities of center-surround retinal neurons roughly aligned are summed and the angular selectivity is determined by the direction and the elongation of the projective field.

7.7.2 Circuit Description

The complete block diagram of the orientation detection system is shown in Figure 7.22. It is composed of standard optics which project an image on a silicon retina located on the focal-plane. We use the one described in Chapter 7.5, it contains a matrix of photosensitive neurons intended for edge enhancement. The activity of each neuron is converted in pulse trains sent on the common bus by encoding the neuron address. Pulses are received by the cortical circuit, decoded and sent to the neuron placed at the same location in the matrix of cortical neurons.

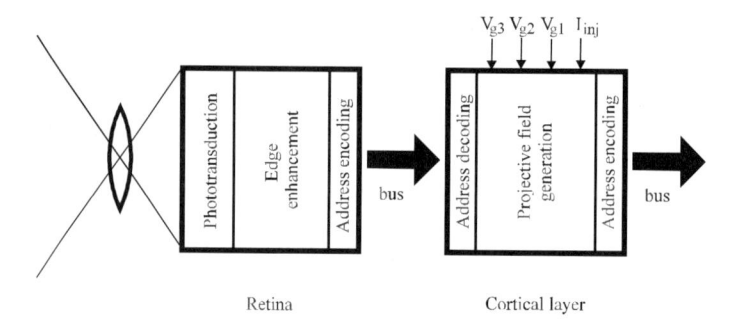

208   7. Analog VLSI Pulsed Networks for Perceptive Processing

Figure 7.22. Schematic of the orientation detection system.

The cortical layer contains a matrix of 27 x 27 neurons which processes pulses by spreading them to their neighbors through the nonlinear network and accumulating them. Activity of the cortical neurons is proportional to the results of accumulation over a temporal window. V_{g1}, V_{g2} and V_{g3} of the nonlinear network are tuned to define an elongated bubble corresponding to the preferred orientation enhancement. To read out the results, the same address-event communication system is used. In this way, the circuit can be connected to additional higher level cortical circuits. Furthermore it is possible to use several cortical circuits connected in parallel on the same bus with different biases to detect simultaneously edges and lines in several orientations. Implementation details of the cortical circuit are given in [Venier et al., 1997].

7.7.3 System Measurement Results

Figure 7.23 and Figure 7.24 give results of measurements done with the complete system of Figure 7.22. All images of these figures are acquired by computer from the output bus of the cortical circuit. The computer counts successively for each neuron the number of emitted pulses during a typical time of 100 ms and displays the result using a gray scale, the most active neurons are white. Figure 7.23(a) and (b) show respectively, the photodiode response and the edge enhancement done by the silicon retina measured from the output bus of the cortical chip, i.e. $V_{g1} = V_{g2} = V_{g3} = 0$. Figure 7.23(c) and (d) give two orientation enhancements for respectively 0° and 60°. In both cases, the projective field is an oriented line about 8 neurons long. The region of the well-oriented edge has a strong activity whereas the other has a weaker and more diffuse response. The high activity of certain cortical neurons not belonging to a well-oriented edge, especially on Figure 7.23(d) for the vertical part, does not arise from the orientation enhancement process but from the noisy response of the silicon retina. Image noise results mainly from mismatch of the silicon retina's transistors working in weak inversion and also from light source inhomogeneities. For 30°, 90° and 150°, the elongation obtained by an hexagonal network are the weakest. Figure 7.24(b) gives the result of enhancement for one of these directions. Notwithstanding a weak elongation of the projective field of 1.73, the well-oriented part of the stimulus is clearly enhanced.

7.7 Description of the Integrated Circuit for Orientation Enhancement

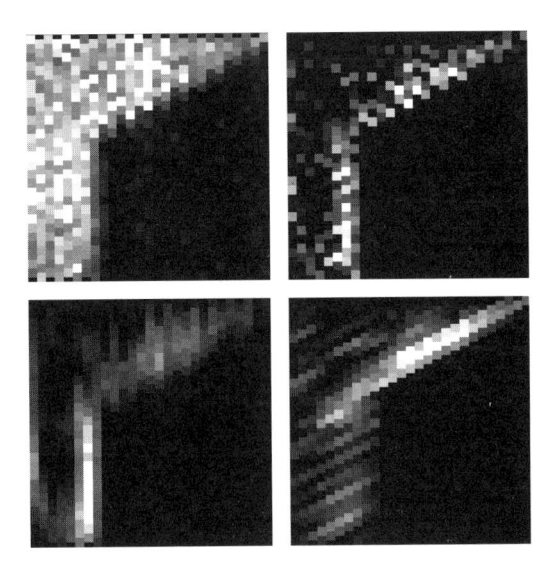

Figure 7.23. Measurements results on a same stimulus: (a) photodiode response, (b) edge enhancement, (c) and (d) orientation enhancement for 0° and 60°.

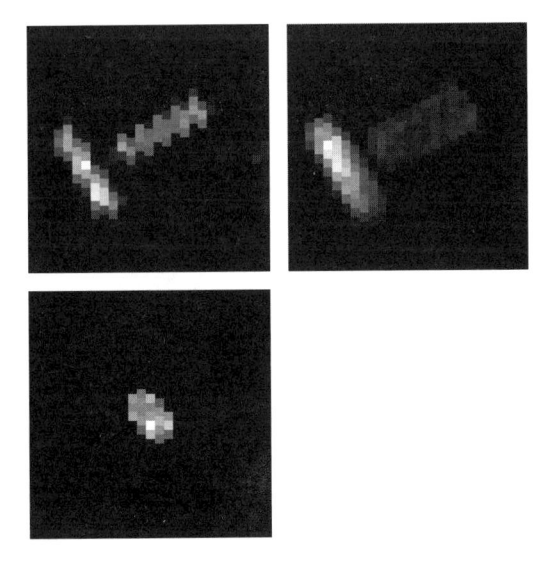

Figure 7.24. Measurements results: (a) edge enhancement with (b) 150° orientation enhancement. (c) is the impulse response of the cortical chip, applied in (b). The total power consumption of both chips is 9 mA at $V^+ = 5V$, independently of the visual stimulus and of the illumination level. More than 90 % of the power is dissipated by output bus drivers.

7.7.4 Other Applications

7.7.4.1 Weighted Projective Field Generation

Up to now in this report, only projective fields with a time-constant current I_{inj} have been studied: at each received pulse, always the same number of

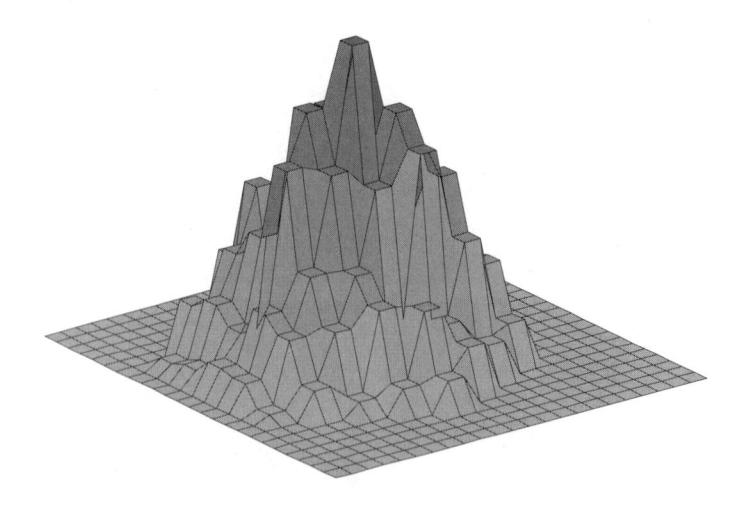

Figure 7.25. A weighted projective field measured from the cortical chip. Only activity of 10 x 10 neurons are displayed. See text for other details.

neurons is activated. Another possibility is to generate projective fields from a periodic time-varying current I_{inj}. Depending on the time when a pulse is received by a neuron, the value of I_{inj} will be low or high and therefore the generated projective field will include a few or many neurons. Therefore emitting neuron activity is transmitted with a higher weighting at neurons at the center of the field than at those at the periphery.

Figure 7.25 shows an example of a measured weighted projective field obtained from the cortical chip. The current I_{inj} is generated by a K220 programmable source current and takes on a period of 50 ms five different values: 3 μA, 21 μA, 70 μA 120 μA and 220 μA. Only the neuron at the center of the layer is excited by a train of pulses at 20 kHz and the activity of the whole layer is acquired by computer from the output bus, as before for Figure 7.23 and Figure 7.24. The acquisition time is equal to the period of the current I_{inj}. The resulting projective field is a stack of several centered cylinders approximating a conical shape. The size of the cylinders is determined by the different values of I_{inj} and their height by the application time of these values of I_{inj}. By choosing the right distribution of current I_{inj}, it is possible to roughly approximate any linear, gaussian or other profiles of centered and decreasing projective fields.

Compared to the expected projective field on Figure 7.26, the measured field is quite noisy. This is explained by the bad matching of the pulse frequency-to-pulse frequency converters and by the high rate of collision on the output bus. This high rate of collision is not natural but induced by the measurement itself: only one neuron receives pulses and pulses are generated periodically by a pulse generator. Therefore the emission of pulses by converters tends to be not independent but more synchronous, increasing the probability of collisions on the output bus.

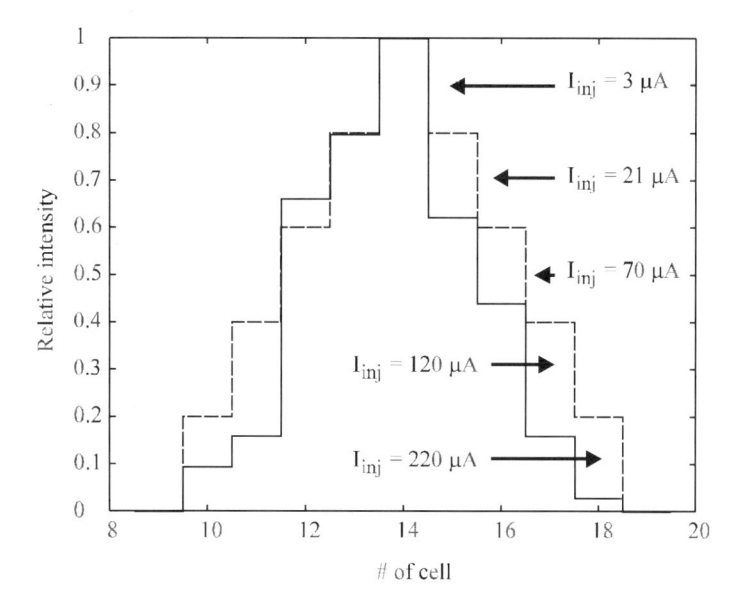

Figure 7.26. Cross-section of the projective field shown on Figure 7.25 and cross-section (dahed line) of the expected projective field for these values of I_{inj}.

7.7.4.2 Complex Projective Field Generation

Orientation enhancement based on only one projective field is only a demonstrative application of the projective field generation. More interesting processings as orientation detection or corner detection need more complex projective fields such as those of the simple neurons, complex neurons or end-stopped neurons [Hubel, 1987]. A possibility to create these fields is to combine the elementary projective fields of several nonlinear networks integrated on a same chip.

Figure 7.27 shows a system which combines two elementary projective fields to create a more complex excitatory/inhibitory projective field. Four unidimensional nonlinear networks, described in Figure 7.28, are also used to generate an offset (x, y) between the initial received address and the center of the two elementary projective fields.

An alternative is to replace these four unidimensional nonlinear networks by a ROM or a EEPROM and to directly read the elementary projective field center positions, according to the neuron address presently on the input.

7.8 Display Interface

To observe the NAPFM bus and display the results of a computation a digital integrated circuit has been designed. Its core is a 20 x 20 matrix of asynchronous 5-bit ripple counters interfaced by 3-state buffers to a common output bus as shown in Figure 7.29. Each counter is accessed asynchronously through the same kind of decoding circuitry used in the cortical chip. The circuit operation divides into an accumulation, or

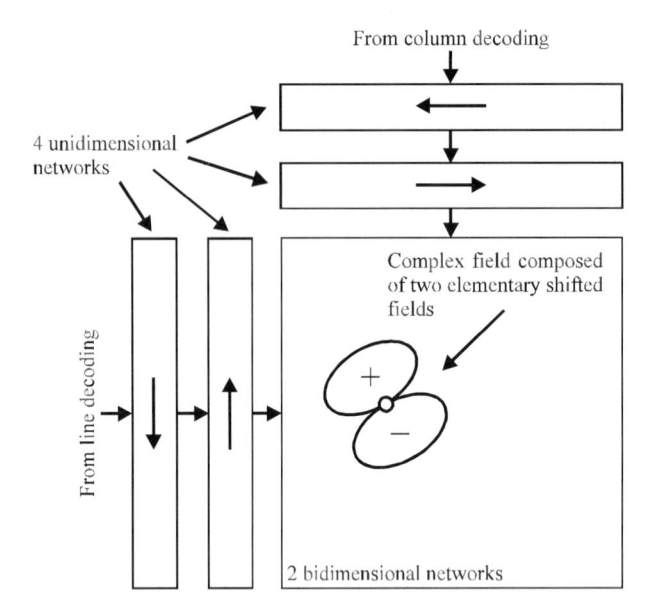

212   7. Analog VLSI Pulsed Networks for Perceptive Processing

Figure 7.27. Schematic of a complete system able to create complex projective fields.

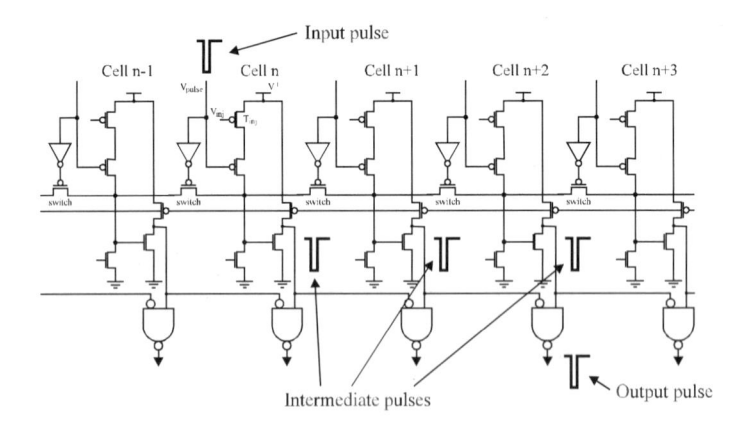

Figure 7.28. Schematic of the unidimensional nonlinear network used to create a programmable offset. With this unidimensional nonlinear network and its supplementary switches, pulses diffuse only to the right. The NAND gate set allows to activate only the last neuron of the generated bubble. For example with a I_{inj} and I_u current ratio equal to 2, the generated bubble covers three neurons and the generated offset is $3 - 1 = 2$.

counting phase and a readout phase. In the counting phase, a counter can be incremented asynchronously by the simultaneous assertion of signals PULSELIN and PULSECOL issued by the decoders. Once counting attains the maximum value (32 in our case), further counter increment is inhibited through signal SATBAR. In the readout phase, when the neuron must connect to the output bus, the signals READLIN nad READCOL are asserted and the counter's value is connected via a 3-state buffer (enabled by signal NOE) to the output bus.

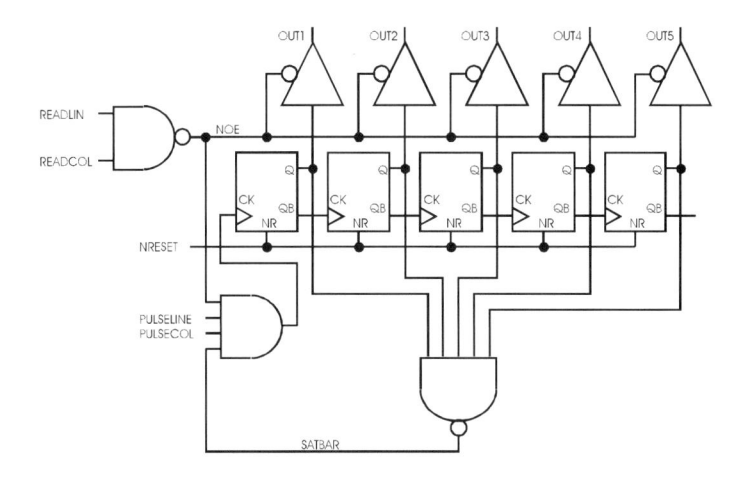

Figure 7.29. Schematic diagram of the interface circuit neuron.

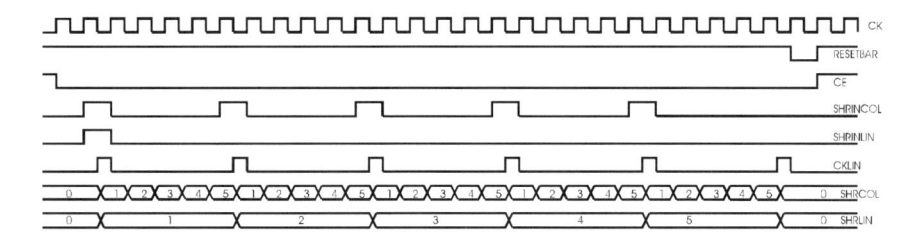

Figure 7.30. Chronogram for the interface circuit.

The circuit can be used as shown in the chronogram in Figure 7.30 depicting the observation of a 5 x 5 array (this figure can be increased to any value if the appropriate number of bus observation circuits is used.). A new sequence starts with the end of an observation period (falling edge of CE). When CE is low, asynchronous pulses do not reach the core of the receiver and the counting is frozen. Next, the scanning row and column shift registers are initialized by the signals SHRINLIN and SHRINCOL, and the result of the counting in the neuron of the first line and first column appears on the output bus. The token in the shift registers is then clocked over by the falling edges of the clock signal CK for the column register and by the falling edge of CKLIN for the row register. New tokens for the column register are generated with SHRINCOL which, ANDed with CKBAR, generates CKLIN. Once all neurons have been read, the registers and the counters are reset by RESETBAR and a new observation cycle begins. In the chronogram, the status of the scanning shift registers is shown as the token position within the register (signals SHRCOL and SHRLIN).

Four of these circuits have been assembled on an acquisition board and used to set up a 40 x 40 receiver matrix for display purposes. An example is given in Figure 7.31, showing the output of a silicon retina on which the image of a face has been focused.

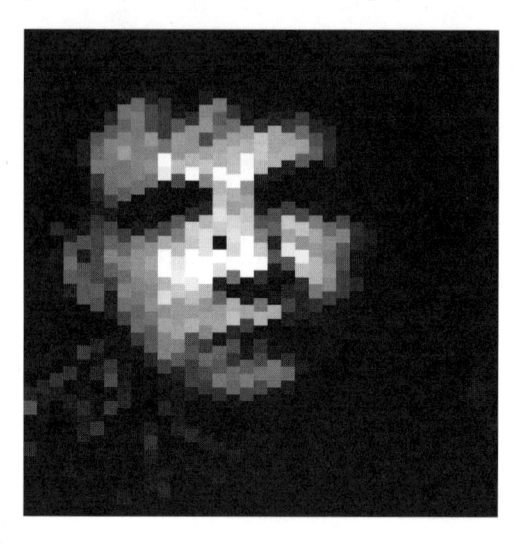

Figure 7.31. The retinal output as obtained through the NAPFM bus from the acquisition board

7.9 Conclusion

This chapter has presented a particular view of the possibilities offered by the pulsed representation of activities in a parallel processing network, as perceived by workers with an electrical engineering background.

The theory used to design pulsed communication/computation hardware has been outlined to provide the interested reader with quantitative criteria and design relationships. The proposed method has been applied to efficiently interface a silicon retina and a cortical chip, taking advantage of the pulsed representation of the neuronal activity to perform processing. Additional circuitry to visualize bus activity has also been presented.

The main message from the results provided in this chapter is that fully asynchronous, analog VLSI systems performing useful tasks are feasible with current technology. They offer several advantages over more traditional, clocked sequential systems in terms of hardware compactness and power consumption, at least for selected applications. Pulses are also practical for driving actuators. For example, the pulsed output of a perceptive system can be used to operate a motor at a much lower stimulus level than would a continuous signal, unable, below a certain threshold, to overcome friction i the actuator It is another instance where the effect of a nonlinearity (the "dead zone" in the actuator caracteristic at low driving levels) is easily overcome by pulsed representation of signals.

Some tantalizing possibilities appear in the biological and computer-theoretical literature involving such subtle encoding modalities as synchronous or coherent firing (their main caracteristics are discussed in Chapters 1 and 3 of this book, for instance). They are the reflection of delicate interactions between nervous cells which we hope, in the future, to understand in engineering terms so that circuits can be built, which are based on a more mature interaction between theoretical and applied disciplines.

References

[Allen et al., 1988] Allen T., Mead C., Faggin F., Gribble G. (1988). Orientation-selective VLSI retina. *SPIE Visual Communications and Image Processing*, 1001:1040–1046.

[Arreguit et al., 1993] Arreguit X., Vittoz E. A., Van Schaik F. A., Mortara A. (1993). Analog Implementation of Low-Level Vision Systems. *ECCTD '93*, H. Dedieu, editor, Elsevier Science Publishers B.V.: 275–280.

[Arreguit and Vittoz, 1994] Arreguit X. and Vittoz E. A. (1994). Perception systems implemented in analog VLSI for real-time applications. *Proceedings of the PerAc'94 Conference*, EPFL, Lausanne Switzerland, IEEE Computer Society Press.

[Dowling, 1987] Dowling J. E. (1987). *The Retina: An Approachable Part of the Brain*. Belknap Harvard.

[Dowling, 1992] Dowling J. E. (1992). *Neurons and Networks: an Introduction to Neuroscience*. The Belknap Press of Havard University Press, Cambridge.

[Enz et al., 1995] Enz C. C., Krummenacher F., Vittoz E. A. (1995). An analytical MOS transistor model valid in all regions of operation and dedicated to low-voltage and low-current applications. *Analog Integrated Circuits and Signal Processing*, 8:83–114.

[Gilbert, 1984] Gilbert B. (1984). A monolithic 16-channel analog array normalizer. *IEEE Journal of Solid State Circuits*, 19(6):956–963.

[Heim, 1993] Heim P. (1993). CMOS Analogue VLSI Implementation of a Kohonen Map. *Ph.D. Thesis n 1174*, EPFL, Lausanne.

[Heim et al., 1991] Heim P., Hochet B., Vittoz E. A. (1991). Generation of learning neighbourhood in Kohonen feature Maps by means of simple nonlinear network. *Electronics Letters*, 27(3):275–277.

[Hubel, 1987] Hubel D. (1987). *Eye, Brain and Vision*. Scientific American Library.

[Lazzaro et al., 1993] Lazzaro J., Wawrzynek J., Mahowald M., Sivilotti M., and Gillespie D. (1993). Silicon auditory processors as computer peripherals. *IEEE Transactions on Neural Networks*, 4(3):523–528.

[Mahowald, 1991] Mahowald M. (1991). Silicon retina with adaptive photoreceptors. *SPIE's International Symposium on Optical Engineering and Photonics in Aerospace Sensing*, Orlando, FL, Society of Optical Engineers.

[Mahowald, 1992] Mahowald M. (1992). VLSI Analogs of Neuronal Visual Processing: A Synthesis of Form and Function. *Ph. D Thesis, Computation and Neural Systems*, California Institute of Technology.

[Mead, 1989] Mead C. (1989). *Analog VLSI and Neural Systems*. Addison-Wesley, Reading: 107–116, 339–351.

[Mortara, 1995] Mortara A. (1995). Communication techniques for analog VLSI perceptive systems. *Ph.D. Thesis n 1329*, EPFL, Lausanne.

[Mortara et al., 1995] Mortara A. and Vittoz E. A., and Venier P. (1995). A communication scheme for analog VLSI perceptive systems. *IEEE Journal of Solid State Circuits*, 30(6):660–669.

[Mortara and Vittoz, 1994] Mortara A. and Vittoz E. A. (1994). A communication architecture tailored for analog VLSI artificial neural networks: Intrinsic performance and limitations. *IEEE Trans. Neural Networks*, 5(3):459–466.

[Mortara and Vittoz, 1995] Mortara A., Vittoz E. A. (1995). A 12-transistor PFM demodulator for analog neural networks communication. *IEEE Transactions on Neural Networks*, 6(5):1280-1283.

[Murray et al., 1991] Murray A. F., Del Corso D. and Tarassenko L. (1991). Pulse stream VLSI neural networks mixing analog and digital techniques. *IEEE Transactions on Neural Networks*, 2(2):193–204.

[Venier et al., 1997] Venier P., Mortara A., Arreguit X. and Vittoz E. A. (1997). An integrated cortical layer for orientation enhancement. *IEEE Journal of Solid State Circuits*, 32(2):177–186.

[Vittoz, 1983] Vittoz E. A. (1983). MOS transistors operated in the lateral bipolar mode and their application in CMOS technology. *IEEE Journal of Solid State Circuits*, 18(3):273–279.

[Vittoz and Arreguit, 1993] Vittoz E. A. and Arreguit X. (1993). Linear networks based on transistors. *Electronics Letters*, 29(3):297–299.

8 Preprocessing for Pulsed Neural VLSI Systems

Alister Hamilton and Kostas A. Papathanasiou

8.1 Introduction

This chapter presents ongoing research into a new approach to programmable signal processing in analog and mixed-signal VLSI [Papathanasiou and Hamilton, 1996a, Papathanasiou and Hamilton, 1996b, [Papathanasiou and Hamilton, 1996c, Papathanasiou and Hamilton, 1997]. The origins of this work may be found in the implementation of pulsed neural networks [Hamilton et al., 1992, Hamilton et al., 1993] and the realisation that the preprocessing of data for presentation to neural VLSI was an important function that had received insufficient attention. The results of this work have significance beyond the realms of neural network VLSI. The technique reported here is ideally suited to the implementation of Field Programmable Analog Arrays (FPAA's) [Bratt and Macbeth, 1996, Grundy, 1994, Gulak, 1996] and Field Programmable Mixed-Signal Arrays (FPMA's) which are now beginning to emerge in the market place.

This chapter illustrates the need for preprocessing in pulsed neural systems, reviews the dominant strategies for analog signal processing and introduces the *Palmo*[1] technique - a new pulse based methodology for implementing programmable analog VLSI. The operation of an analog Palmo cell is described implemented in Complimentary Metal-Oxide-Semiconductor (CMOS) technology. We show how the Palmo cell may be used to implement an analog filter and illustrate its flexibility in implementing mixed-signal functions. Finally we allude to circuit performance and our new Palmo cells, implemented in Bipolar Complimentary Metal-Oxide-Semiconductor (BiCMOS) technology, that will improve these performance figures.

At the time of writing we are in the midst of developing our Palmo techniques - we have got this far, but we believe there is much yet to be done.

8.2 A Sound Segmentation System

In order to illustrate the requirement for signal pre-processing, consider the sound segmentation system based on the early mammalian auditory system and implemented in software by Dr Leslie Smith [Smith, 1996] (Figure 8.1). This system uses onsets and offsets in the coding of sound as a stage

---
[1] The name *Palmo* is derived from the Hellenic word ΠΑΛΜΟΣ which means pulsebeat, pulse palpitation or series of pulses.

218   8. Preprocessing for Pulsed Neural VLSI Systems

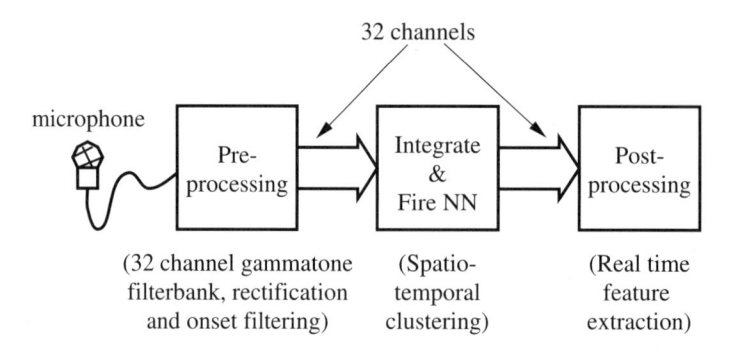

Figure 8.1. Sound Segmentation System.

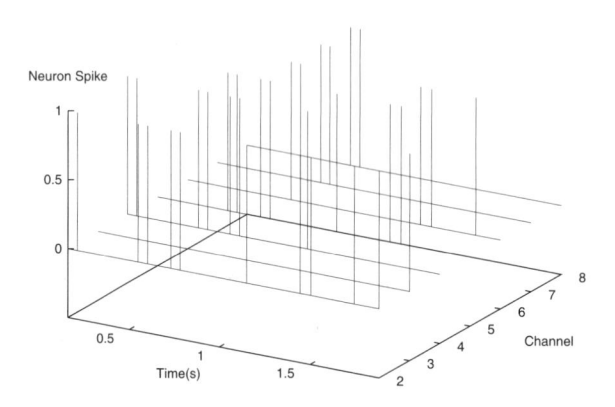

Figure 8.2. Clusters in onset signals from a female speaker produced by analog VLSI implementation of an integrate and fire neural network chip. Clusters are formed around onsets from channel 17. Channels 17-23 are shown.

in its interpretation or processing. An onset is defined as the start point and an offset the end point of an element of sound.

Naturally occurring sound signals are pre-processed in order to expand the signal into streams of onset (or offset) signals. A bank of recursive auditory filters (the 32 channel gammatone filter) is followed by rectification, compression and onset (or offset) enhancement in each channel to provide continuous streams of onset (or offset) signals to the integrate and fire neural network.

The integrate and fire neural network is composed of neurons of the type described in Section 1.2.3.2 of Chapter 1 (with an absolute refractory period) and performs spatio-temporal clustering of the pre-processed sound signals clustering onsets (or offsets) in the sound in time and across frequency channels. The integrate and fire neural network for this system has been implemented in analog VLSI [Glover et al., ress] and is shown performing spatio-temporal clustering of onset signals from a female speaker in Figure 8.2. In order to implement the complete sound segmentation system in analog VLSI we have to consider the implementation of the pre-processing functions as well as the integrate and fire neural network. The question then arises - how do we implement pre-processing functions for neural network VLSI?

In considering this question for a specific problem like the sound segmentation system, we can design circuits to implement the appropriate signal processing functions. However, if we want to find a solution to a broad range of application domains including those we have not yet thought of, we should make our solution to the pre-processing problem as flexible as possible. To satisfy this requirement the circuits we design should be programmable, so that we can change their parameters, and we should be able to interconnect them in different ways to perform different signal processing functions. In doing this, we hope to develop a technique that is applicable to signal processing problems in general and not specifically to those relating to neural networks. With these considerations in mind, we shall review the dominant analog techniques for signal processing in a search for a suitable circuit strategy.

8.3 Signal Processing in Analog VLSI

The most common signal processing function that is required in practical analog systems is the analog filter. In order to synthesise an analog filter, networks of passive components may be connected together; for example ladder circuits based upon inductors (L) and capacitors (C). Simple transformations may be used to change a low pass prototype into a high pass, bandpass or bandstop filter. These filters are sensitive to component variation and suffer from power loss between the signal source and load. This has led to the use of active circuits to emulate the function (differential integration) performed by L and C [Kuo, 1966, Williams and Taylor, 1995]. (An active circuit is one which incorporates an active device, for example a transistor or amplifier circuit, in its schematic.) Analog filters may therefore be constructed from a collection of differential integrators.

Active filters fall into two broad implementation categories - those that operate with continuous time analog quantities and those that operate with sampled analog quantities. Let us consider the principle strategies for implementing integrators in each of these categories and evaluate their suitability for our purposes.

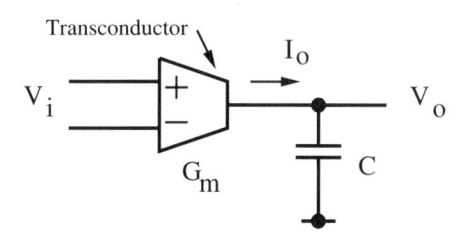

Figure 8.3. Active Gm/C filter.

8.3.1 Continuous Time Active Filters

High quality continuous time active filters may be realised over a wide frequency range $(50Hz \leq f100MHz)$ and may be implemented in a wide range of technologies. For the reasons alluded to above, the circuit design problem becomes one of how to design and interconnect integrator circuits. The principle continuous time active filter implementation strategies uses either active Resistor Capacitor (RC) integrators or the active G_m/C integrator. The integrator in Figure 8.3 contains a differential input voltage-to-current converter defined by a single parameter, G_m, its transconductance. The transconductance of this integrator is the ratio of the output current and the input voltage difference. RC integrators are still in use today, although special processing options or external resistors are needed. These circuits suffer from drift and uncertainty in the absolute capacitance and resistance values in VLSI. G_m/C integrators require no special processing or external components. The G_m and C values in the filter network are used to set the poles and zeros and hence the response of the filter. Since errors in the values of G_m and C due to fabrication tolerances will be uncorrelated, on-chip tuning is required to achieve precision. Such tuning is only possible over a limited range. Usually G_m/C circuits are tailored for a specific application in the high frequency range.

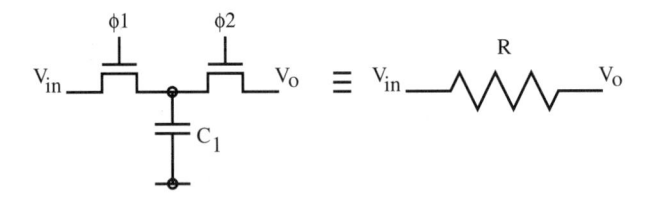

Figure 8.4. Switched capacitor resistor equivalent.

8.3.2 Sampled Data Active Switched Capacitor (SC) Filters

Active switched capacitor circuits are the principle sampled data technique used in VLSI systems and emerged in MOS technologies in 1972 [Fried, 1972].

The fundamental innovation that makes this technique ideally suited to MOS technology is the replacement of a resistor with a switched capacitor. This principle is illustrated in Figure 8.4. Two analog switches are controlled by non-overlapping clock signals $\phi 1$ and $\phi 2$ whose frequency is f_s. The amount of charge, Q, transferred between the terminals during one cycle of the non-overlapping clock signals is $(V_{in} - V_o)C_1$. If the V_{in} and V_o are slowly varying in relation to the clock frequency, f_s, the charge flow defines a current, $I(t) = C_1 f_s (V_{in} - V_o)$. Thus from Ohms law,

$$R = \frac{1}{f_s C_1} \qquad (8.1)$$

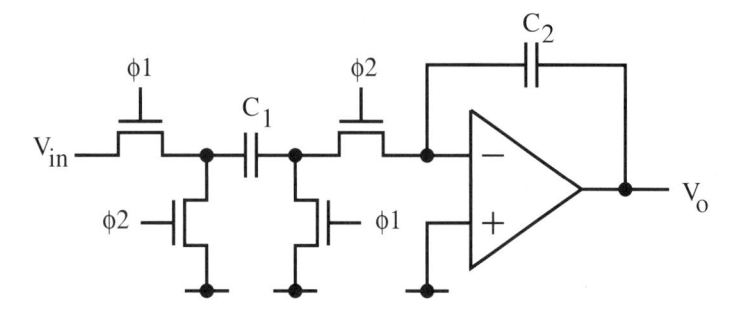

Figure 8.5. Parasitic insensitive SC integrator.

This equivalent resistance may be altered by modifying f_s or C_1 or a combination of both.

An RC network may be created by simply adding a capacitor, C_2, at the output of the network. RC networks may be used to define the position of the poles of the filter response, where

$$\omega_p = \frac{1}{R_1 C_2} = f_s \frac{C_1}{C_2} \qquad (8.2)$$

Thus ω_p can be varied over a wide range for typical sampling frequencies of $8kHz \leq f_s 10MHz$. The poles and zeros of SC circuits depend on a highly accurate crystal controlled f_s and the ratio of capacitors. While absolute values of capacitors are difficult to achieve due to variations in the materials from which they are made, ratios of capacitors can be achieved to accuracies of less than 0.1 percent by using careful layout in VLSI. If using capacitors to define the frequency response of a filter, one must be aware of the parasitic capacitances that naturally exist in the materials that circuits are made from. The circuit of Figure 8.4 is sensitive to these parasitic capacitances which will affect the frequency response of the circuit. The SC integrator circuit of Figure 8.5 is a design which is insensitive to these parasitic effects. In this typical SC circuit an operational amplifier is used as the active circuit, C_2 is the integrating capacitor and C_1 and its associated switches form the "resistor".

8.3.3 Sampled Data Active Switched Current (SI) Filters

The downward trend in power supply voltages for standard digital VLSI and the trend for technologies to be optimised for digital circuits rather than analog ones has led to the development of an alternative technique to SC. SC circuits represent signals as voltages, therefore any drop in power supply voltage effects dynamic range. Standard digital VLSI processes do not require high quality floating capacitors therefore the implementation of SC circuits in these processes is impractical.

An alternative, proposed in 1989 [Hughes et al., 1989], was to use currents rather than voltages to convey analog information. Of course, any circuit which handles signal currents must generate internal voltages, but the

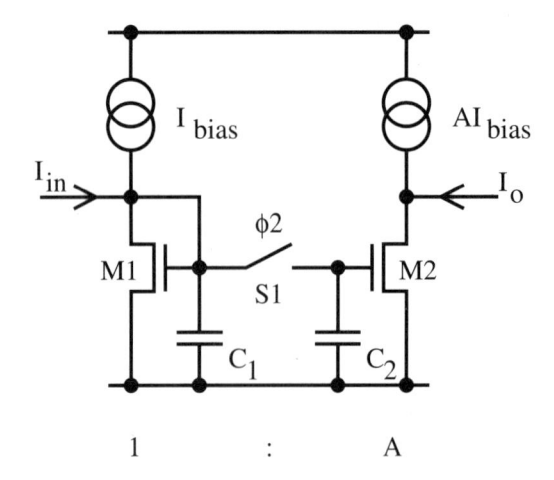

Figure 8.6. SI N-type memory cell.

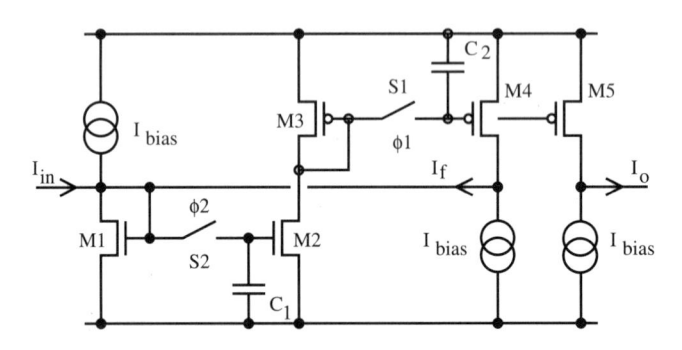

Figure 8.7. SI non-inverting integrator cell.

voltages in SI circuits are incidental to the signal processing and are not used to represent the signals. The basic building bock of SI circuits is the current memory (Figure 8.6). In this circuit the input current, I_{in}, is added to a bias current, I_{bias}, and flows through transistor M1. This current flow generates a proportional voltage on C_1. When the switch is closed, the voltage on C_1 is transferred to C_2. The voltage on C_2 now induces a current in M2. The size of the current that flows in M2 is $A \times (I_{in} + I_{bias})$, where

$$A = \frac{Width_{M2}}{Length_{M2}} \times \frac{Length_{M1}}{Width_{M1}} \quad (8.3)$$

If the bias current for M2 is AI_{bias}, then the output current is AI_{in}. The capacitors in this circuit are grounded at one end and need not be linear to achieve a linear transfer characteristic. They are therefore implementable in standard digital technology.

An SI integrator (Figure 8.7) combines the N-type memory with a P-type memory with the output of the P-type memory being fed back to the input. When the switch S2 is closed, the current flowing through M1 is

$$I_{M1}(n) = I_{in}(n) + I_{bias} + I_f(n-1). \quad (8.4)$$

This current induces a voltage which is stored on C_1 when $\phi 2$ is removed. When the switch S1 is closed, the current $I_{M1}(n)$ also flows through M2, M3 and M4. The new feedback current value is

$$I_f(n) = I_{in}(n) + I_f(n-1) \tag{8.5}$$

which gets fed back to the integrator input for the next integration clock cycle. Thus the circuit integrates the incoming signal. The integrator output is a current, I_o, and therefore a separate output circuit (M5) is required for each load to be driven.

8.3.4 Discussion

Having described the dominant techniques for signal processing in analog VLSI, let us evaluate their suitability for implementing pre-processing functions for neural network applications. The main requirement we have is programmability - can we program each analog cell and can we interconnect the cell to others in a flexible manner?

Technique	Programmable Cell?	Programmable Interconnect?
G_m/C	On chip tuning required	Yes - but only local
SC	Yes	Yes - but only local
SI	Yes - but clumsy	Yes

Table 8.1. Comparison of the programmability of different analog VLSI signal processing techniques.

Connecting SI cells together using programmable switches is easily done. The principle disadvantage is that each analog cell output requires a separate circuit so that a high fan out is not possible. Programming the gain of an SI integrator is performed by controlling the ratio of transistor sizes within the integrator. Making this electronically programmable is clumsy. Voltage mode cells (G_m/C and SC) may be connected together using programmable switches. The principle restriction here is that interconnection may only be local to a cell. Driving long interconnect wires requires operational amplifiers with high drive capabilities and attention to layout to minimise noise pickup on the signal. Buffering the signal to give additional drive capability requires additional operational amplifier circuits. However, the SC technique is excellent for the design of programmable cells whose parameters may be set using precise capacitor ratios and clock frequencies. G_m/C techniques on the other hand are not best suited to the implementation of programmable cells due to the tuning problems mentioned earlier.

Summarising these points in Table 8.1, it is clear that none of the techniques we have reviewed are ideal for programmable analog processing - the best technique is SC. We now turn our attention to a new technique being developed at the University of Edinburgh that answers an unqualified "Yes" to the questions asked in Table 8.1.

224   8. Preprocessing for Pulsed Neural VLSI Systems

8.4 Palmo - Pulse Based Signal Processing

The Palmo signal processing technique combines the best attributes of the digital and analog domains. In contrast to other implementations Palmo signals are digital pulses that carry suitably encoded analog signal information. These digital signals are robust and easy to transmit - even over long distances. They are easy to route using simple digital logic gates. They may be processed by Palmo cells or conventional digital logic.

The Palmo cell is an analog integrator circuit whose gain is electronically programmable. analog circuit techniques are used to give a small and potentially low power circuit. The Palmo cell receives and transmits analog signal information via digitally encoded Palmo signals.

A Palmo signal processing system combines analog Palmo cells with programmable digital logic which defines interconnect and may also perform signal processing.

8.4.1 Basic Palmo Concepts

8.4.1.1 The Palmo Signal Representation

The Palmo signal processing technique transforms incoming analog voltage (or current) signals into a sampled data form where analog information is encoded in a digital pulse. In the system reported here, the width of a single pulse is used to encode the magnitude of the analog signal, while the sign of the signal is determined by whether the pulse occurred in the positive or negative cycle of a global *sign* clock (Figure 8.8). Other encoding strategies are possible (see Chapter 3). All signal information is transmitted between processing blocks in this form, and processing blocks may be digital or analog. This new analog sampled data signal processing strategy allows an entirely novel class of circuits and techniques to be developed.

8.4.1.2 The Analog Palmo Cell

The functions performed by the analog Palmo cell are scaling and integration, since it is possible to perform most linear signal processing functions by the use of these operators. A typical block diagram of an analog Palmo cell is shown in Figure 8.9. Input pulses are integrated over time by the use

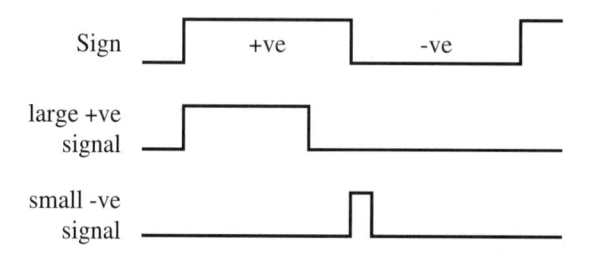

Figure 8.8. Palmo signal representation.

8.4 Palmo - Pulse Based Signal Processing

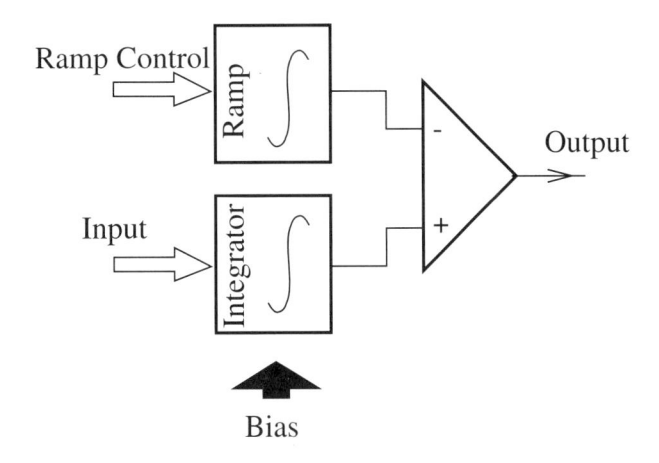

Figure 8.9. Typical analog Palmo cell.

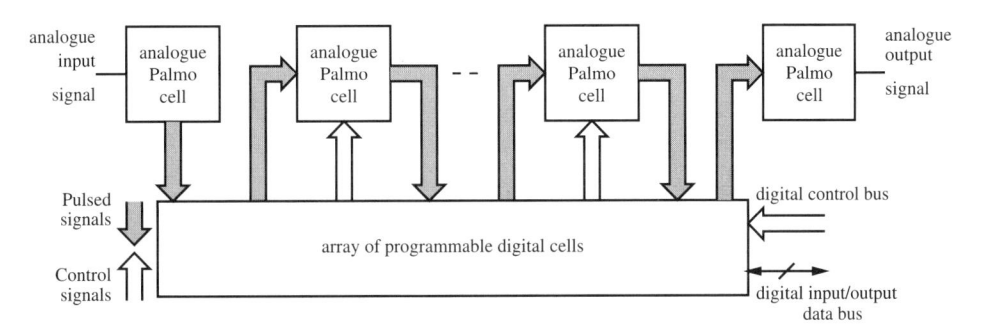

Figure 8.10. Typical Palmo signal processing system.

of an analog intergator. This is usually done by charging or discharging a capacitor with a constant current. This integrated value is then compared to a ramp using an analog comparator circuit in order to generate the pulsed output. The ramp is generated from a step signal by the use of an identical integrator. The overall gain of the analog Palmo cell is controlled by the ratio of the gains of the two integrators which may be set by a digital control word.

8.4.1.3 A Palmo Signal Processing System

A Palmo signal processing system is comprised of a number of analog Palmo cells and programmable digital logic (Figure 8.10). The analog Palmo cell may be used for analog to pulse width conversion, a number of primitive signal processing functions and pulse width to analog conversion. The programmable logic is used to interface to a controller, define the interconnection between analog Palmo cells, provide the appropriate timing and control signals to the analog Palmo cell and may be used to perform digital processing of Palmo signals.

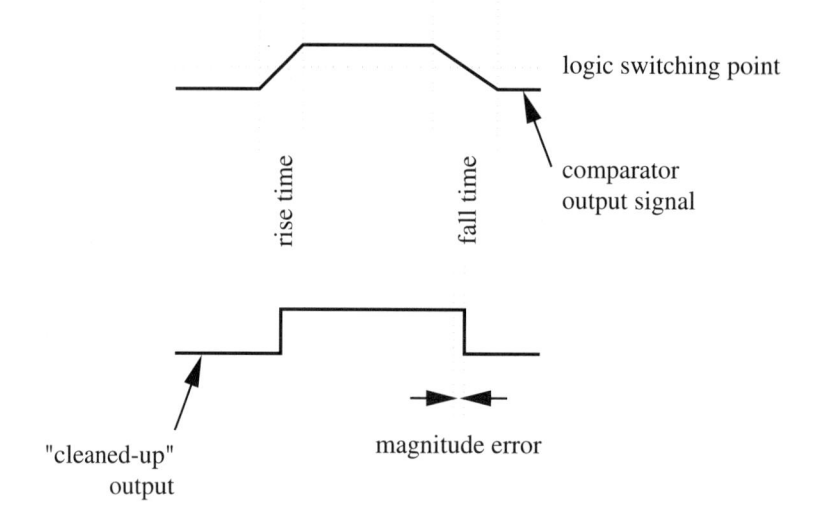

Figure 8.11. Magnitude error introduced by comparator output rise and fall time differences.

8.4.1.4 Sources of Harmonic Distortion in a Palmo System

The comparator circuit used in the analog Palmo cell will introduce harmonic distortion to the signal due to the different rise and fall times of the comparator output [Papathanasiou and Hamilton, 1996b]. The comparator output in Figure 8.11 has a short rise time and a longer fall time. The magnitude of the analog quantity represented by the width of the comparator output pulse will thus be distorted by an amount equal to the difference in the rise and fall times. For this reason, the comparator design is of critical importance.

The other principle source of harmonic distortion is inaccuracies introduced by the current sources used in the integrator and ramp circuits of Figure 8.9. In addition noise in these current sources will add jitter to the signal.

Distortion due to mismatches will tend to dominate at low frequencies where small integrating and ramp currents will be used. At high frequencies, distortion introduced by the comparator will be dominant where comparator delays become comparable to the sampling rate.

8.4.2 A CMOS Analog Palmo Cell Implementation

The analog Palmo cell is an integrator which accepts input pulses, integrates them in time, and generates a pulsed output. Here we describe how these functions may be implemented in CMOS technology.

8.4 Palmo - Pulse Based Signal Processing   227

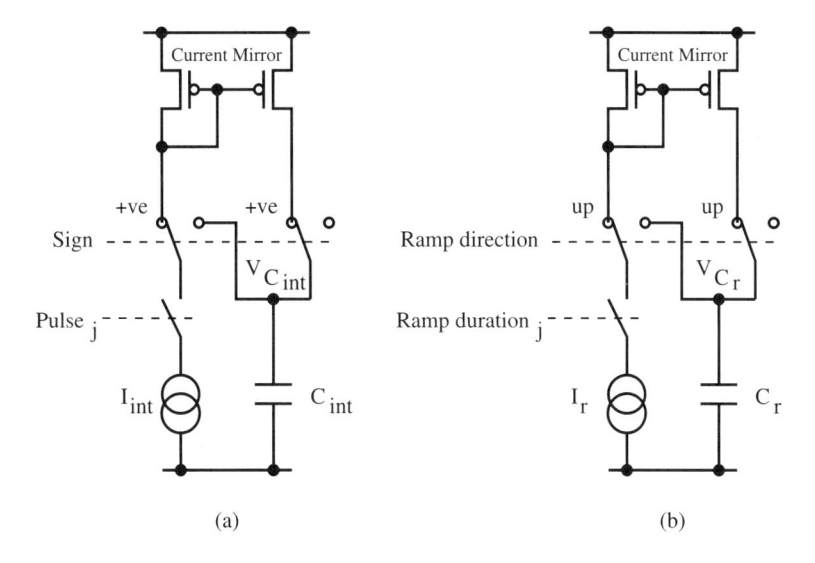

Figure 8.12. (a) Palmo basic pulsed integrator. (b) Ramp generator circuit.

8.4.2.1 The Analog Palmo Cell: Details of Circuit Operation

Pulses arriving at the integrator input ($Pulse_j$ in Figure 8.12(a)) cause an integrating current, I_{int}, to charge or discharge a capacitor, C_{int}. Any pulse arriving when the sign bit is high is positive and the current I_{int} charges C_{int} via the current mirror. Any pulse arriving when the sign bit is low is negative and the current I_{int} discharges C_{int} directly. Once a pulse or se-

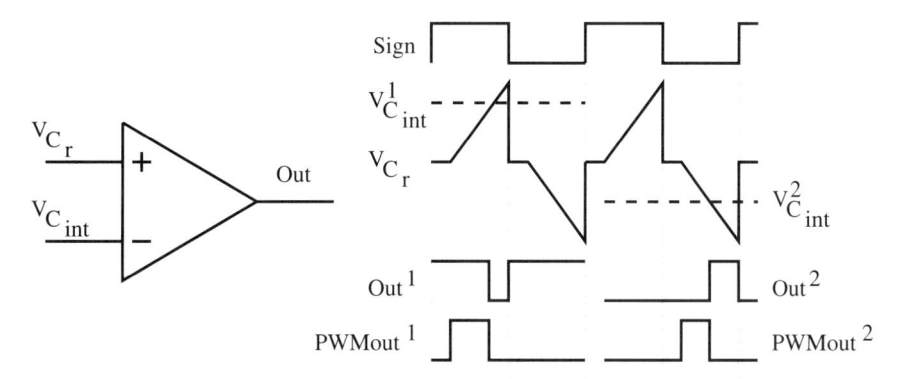

Figure 8.13. Analog Palmo cell output pulse generator.

ries of pulses has been integrated, an output pulse must be generated from the cell. This is achieved by comparing the integrated voltage, $V_{C_{int}}$, to a ramp voltage waveform, V_{C_r}. The ramp waveform, shown in Figure 8.13, is generated by the circuit of Figure 8.12 (b) which uses a current, I_r, to charge and discharge a capacitor, C_r in a similar manner to that described for Figure 8.12(a). To illustrate the operation principles of this circuit a positive integrated voltage, $V^1_{C_{int}}$, and a negative integrated voltage, $V^2_{C_{int}}$, are compared to the ramp waveform (Figure 8.13) and the output pulses Out^1

and Out^2 are produced. These comparator output signals are combined with the control signals $RampDur$ and $RampDir$ that define the duration and direction (Up when $RampDir = 1$, down when $RampDir = 0$) of the ramp signal respectively, to produce the output of the Palmo cell, PWMout (Equation 8.6).

$$PWMout = RampDur \cdot RampDir \cdot Out + RampDur \cdot \overline{RampDir} \cdot \overline{Out} \quad (8.6)$$

Using these simple circuits, we have an analog integrator that accepts pulsed inputs and generates pulsed outputs using the Palmo signal representation. In this implementation example a two stage clamped comparator with positive feedback has been used to minimise rise and fall time differences at the comparator output and thus reduce harmonic distortion.

$$K = \frac{C_r}{C_{int}} \cdot \frac{I_{int}}{I_r} \quad (8.7)$$

The gain of this analog Palmo cell is defined by Equation 8.7. In this implementation, the gain of the cell may be made electronically programmable by controlling the ratios of capacitors and currents. As mentioned earlier accurate capacitor ratios may be made using appropriate circuit layout techniques. In the final circuit (Figure 8.14) a 9 element capacitor array laid out using the common centroid layout technique is used to make capacitors with values C, 2C, 2C and 4C which may be assigned to either C_{int} or C_r by setting appropriate switches. This arrangement gives a 3 bit programmable capacitor ratio. Accurate current ratios may be made by using a number of techniques - we have chosen to multiplex a single 6 bit programmable current digital to analog converter (I_{DAC}) in time to generate I_{int} and I_r. Thus the gain of the analog Palmo cell has 9 bits of resolution. Since this 9 bit resolution is a product of a 6 bit current ratio and a 3 bit capacitor ratio, the chip area occupied by the cell is much less than the equivalent resolution in a SC implementation where 512 capacitors would be required.

8.4.3 Interconnecting Analog Palmo Cells

In order to be able to use the analog Palmo cell we shall now consider how the circuit of Figure 8.14 may be used to convert an analog signal to the Palmo signal representation, how it may be used to implement integrators of subtly different types, and how analog Palmo cells may be interconnected.

Converting an analog signal into the Palmo signal representation may be achieved by connecting the incoming analog voltage to $V_{C_{int}}$, generating ramp waveforms on V_{C_r} (Figure 8.14), and using the appropriate logic (Equation 6) to condition Out_j. An analog signal output may be obtained from an analog Palmo cell by buffering the voltage $V_{C_{int}}$ and taking it off chip.

The Palmo cell may be used to implement a differential integrator in a number of ways. The simplest technique is to use a single Palmo cell and

8.4 Palmo - Pulse Based Signal Processing

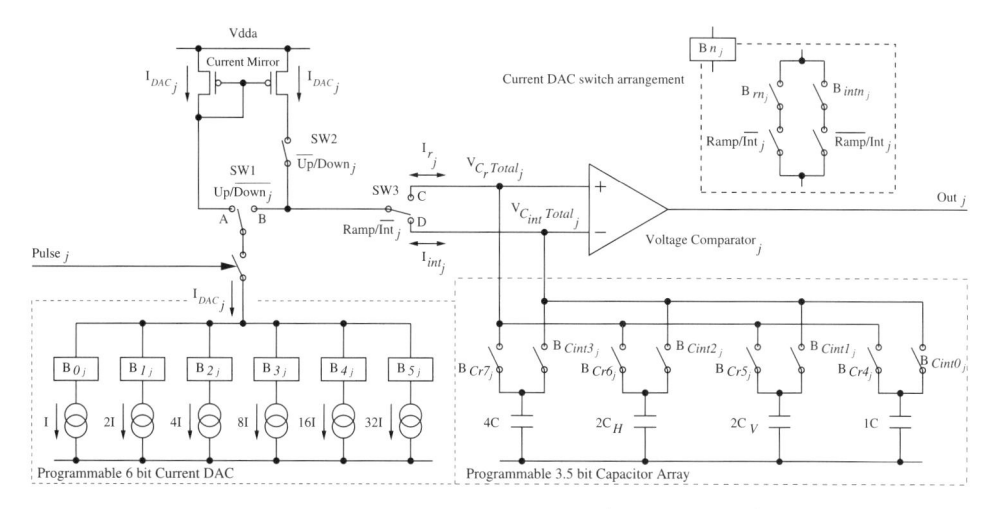

Figure 8.14. Palmo cell circuit diagram. Switches B_{rn_j} set the ramp current, I_{r_j}. Switches B_{intn_j} set the integrating current, I_{int_j}. Switches $B_{C_{int0_j}}$ to $B_{C_{int3_j}}$ set C_{int_j}. Switches $B_{C_{r4_j}}$ to $B_{C_{r7_j}}$ set C_{r_j}.

alternate the integration and output pulse generation functions on successive cycles of the sign clock. In this configuration the cell may not integrate and generate output pulses at the same time.

Simultaneous integration and pulse generation may be achieved by connecting two Palmo cells in parallel. The integrating capacitors, C_{int}, of the two cells are connected together and one cell is operated as an integrator while the other acts as an output pulse generator. Thus the "cell" may integrate and generate an output pulse on each sign clock cycle. This configuration operates at twice the speed of that of the single cell and has a larger programmable capacitor range.

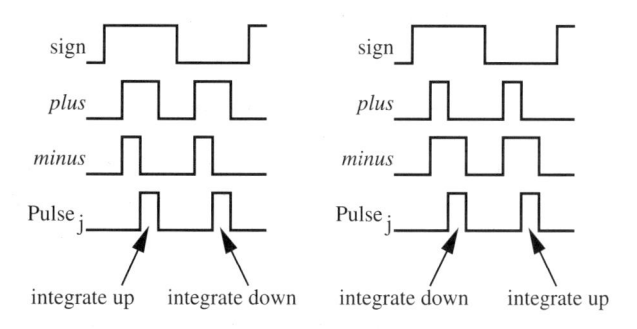

Figure 8.15. Typical Palmo Signals at the input to the Differential Integrator.

A slightly more complicated strategy for increasing performance involves using a Palmo cell to determine whether a signal is positive or negative and modifying a local sign clock to reflect the signal polarity. Thus while the signal is positive, for example, no negative cycle of the sign clock is required doubling the operating speed of the circuit.

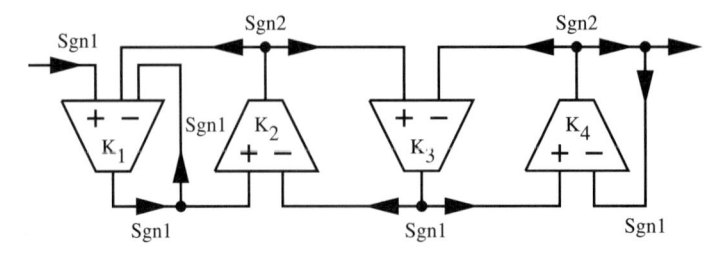

230   8. Preprocessing for Pulsed Neural VLSI Systems

Figure 8.16. 4th Order Filter Implementation using Differential Integrators.

A differential integrator has two inputs *plus* (+) and *minus* (-). Due to the differential nature of the integrator and the Palmo signal representation, pulses arriving at the *plus* and *minus* inputs will cancel where they coincide (Figure 8.15); otherwise they combine with the sign clock to define $Pulse_j$ and $Up/\overline{Down}_j$ (Table 8.2). When the cell is used as an output pulse generator $Pulse_j$ is controlled by $RampDur$ and $Up/\overline{Down}_j$ by $RampDir$ (Table 8.2) defined earlier. Thus in order to implement a differential integrator, the Boolean expressions for $Pulse_j$ and $Up/\overline{Down}_j$ are :

$$Pulse_j = (plus \oplus minus) \cdot \overline{Ramp/\overline{Int}_j} + RampDur \cdot Ramp/\overline{Int}_j \quad (8.8)$$

$$Up/\overline{Down}_j = (sign \cdot plus + \overline{sign} \cdot \overline{plus}) \cdot \overline{Ramp/\overline{Int}_j} + RampDir \cdot Ramp/\overline{Int}_j \quad (8.9)$$

Cell Function	$Pulse_j$	$Up/\overline{Down}_j$	$Ramp/\overline{Int}_j$
Differential Integrator	$plus \oplus minus$	$\overline{Ramp/\overline{Int}_j}$	0
Output Pulse Generator	RampDur	RampDir	1

Table 8.2. Palmo Cell Function and control signal settings.

Let us consider how Palmo cells may be interconnected using these techniques to implement the 4th order filter of Figure 8.16 which has been designed using standard filter theory derived from L-C ladder circuits mentioned earlier. Since the first and last integrators have their outputs fed back to their inputs they must be able to integrate the outputs they produce. Therefore we require to use two Palmo cells in parallel for each of these integrators. The first integrator of Figure 8.16 is implemented using analog Palmo Cells 1 (integration) and 2 (output pulse generation) in Figure 8.17 and the last integrator of Figure 8.16 is implemented using analog Palmo Cells 5 (integration) and 6 (output pulse generation) in Figure 8.17. The other two integrators (analog Palmo Cells 3 and 4) may each be implemented using a single Palmo cell operating in two sign clock cycles, $Sgn1$ and $Sgn2$. Let us assume that on $Sgn1$ analog Palmo Cell 3 integrates and analog Palmo Cell 4 outputs a pulse. Therefore on $Sgn2$ analog Palmo Cell 3 outputs a pulse and analog Palmo Cell 4 integrates. The input to the filter arrives on $Sgn1$ and may coincide with a pulse arriving at the *minus* input.

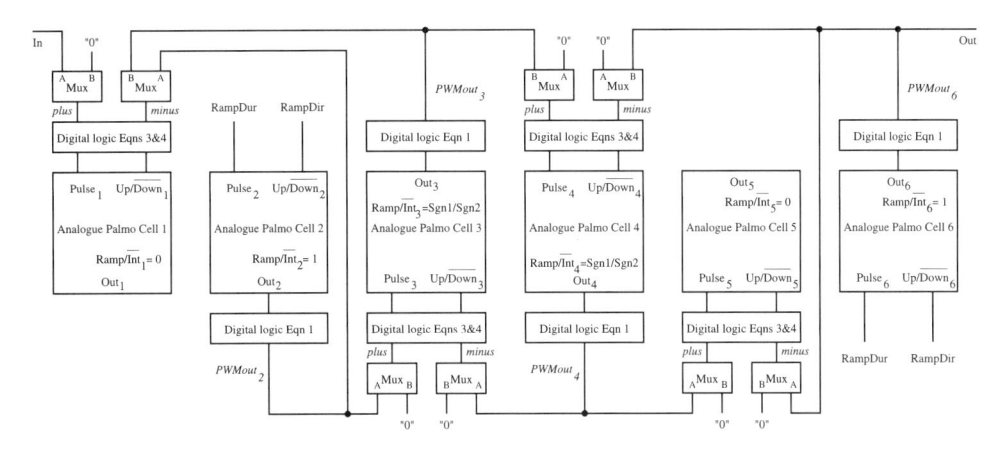

Figure 8.17. Palmo implementation of the 4th order filter of Figure 8.16. Multiplexors (Mux) are controlled by the Sgn1/Sgn2 clock. Nodes $V_{C_{int}}$ on Cells 1 and 2 and 5 and 6 are connected together.

8.4.4 Results from a Palmo VLSI Device

1st, 2nd and 3rd order filters has been designed using the standard established filter synthesis techniques mentioned earlier that define the interconnection and gain factors of individual differential integrators. Digital logic is used to connect individual analog Palmo integrators together in an identical manner to the circuit in Figure 8.17. The results in Figure 8.18 are from the first Palmo device (not described here) and show both theoretical characteristics and measured VLSI results for low pass filters at cut-off frequencies of 1kHz and 2kHz.

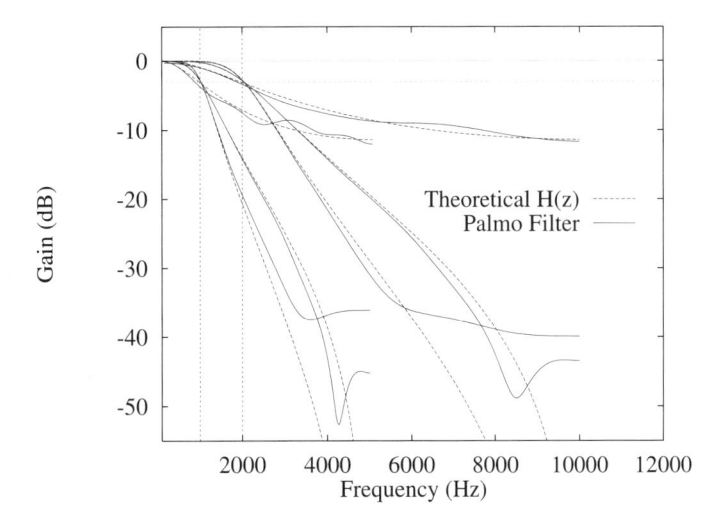

Figure 8.18. Palmo analog low-pass filter implementation results.

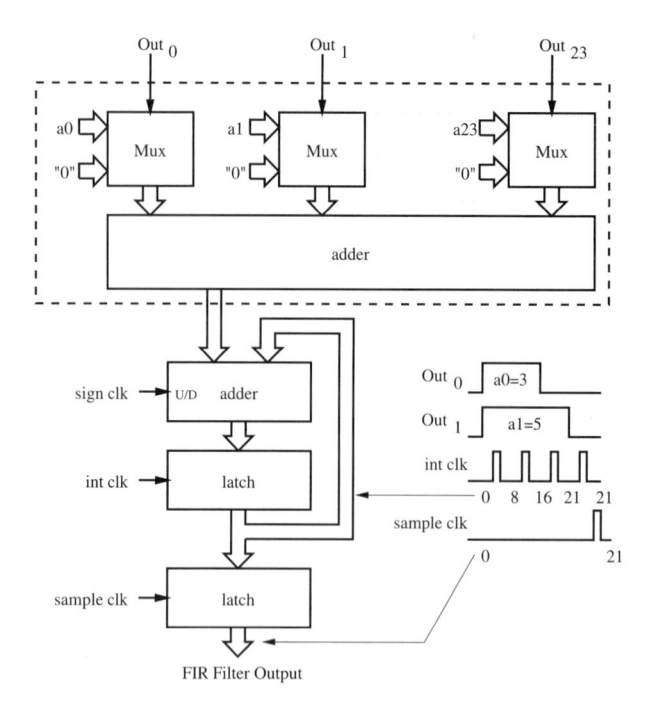

232   8. Preprocessing for Pulsed Neural VLSI Systems

Figure 8.19. Digital Processing of Palmo signals for a 24 tap FIR filter implementation.

8.4.5 Digital Processing of Palmo Signals

Since the Palmo technique encodes analog quantities in time, performing arithmetic functions on pulsed signals in the digital domain is straightforward. Pulses allow the efficient transmission and processing of signals both in the analog and digital domains. Signal processing may occur using only analog Palmo cells, or by using a combination of analog and digital cells where appropriate. Figure 8.19 shows the digital circuit used for performing the multiplication and addition of the digital finite impulse response (FIR) algorithm. The pulsed outputs of the analog cells, $Out_0 - Out_{23}$, gate the coefficients $a0 - a23$ and the sum of those outputs is integrated in time. The waveform diagram in Figure 8.19 demonstrates the operation of this circuit for two pulsed inputs, Out_0 and Out_1. The coefficients associated with these inputs are $a0 = 3$ and $a1 = 5$. At each integrating clock epoch, the sum of coefficients of active inputs is added to the previous accumulated value. Thus for the first two epochs $3 + 5 = 8$ is added, for the third epoch 5 is added. At the end of the sample period the result appears on the filter output - in this example the value 21.

The results from VLSI of a 24 tap FIR filter implemented using these techniques is shown in Figure 8.20. The results show an excellent match to the theoretical filter characteristic. Note that the output of the filter in this example is a digital word - so the analog to digital conversion and the filter function are performed using the Palmo technique.

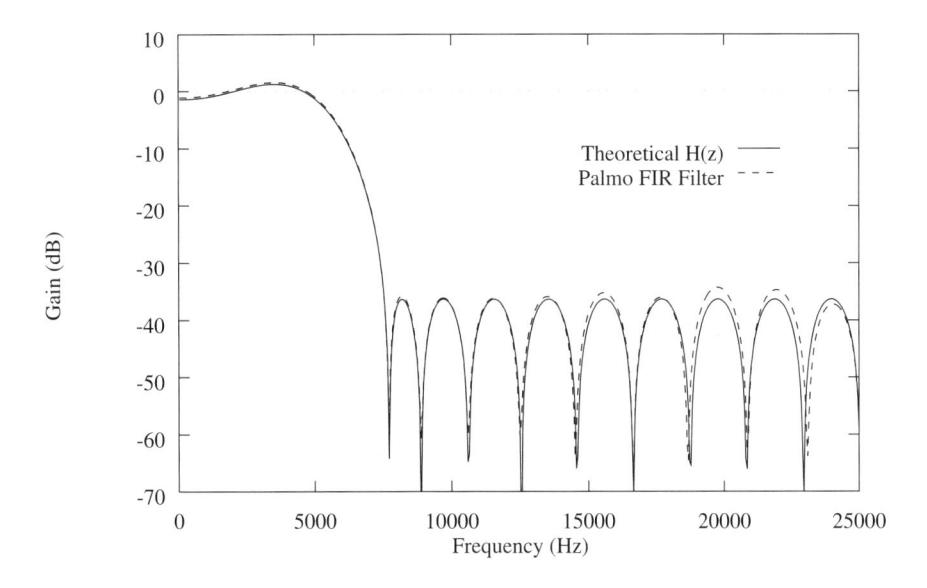

Figure 8.20. Palmo mixed signal 24 tap FIR filter implementation results.

8.4.6 CMOS Analog Palmo Cell: Performance

The dynamic range of the CMOS analog Palmo cell is largely determined by the resolving capability of the comparator within the cell. This is typically around 10 bits giving a dynamic range of approximately $60dB$. The sampling frequency of the CMOS analog Palmo cell is also determined by the switching time of the comparator. Currently the maximum sampling frequency is below 1MHz.

8.5 Conclusions

The Palmo technique is an entirely new mixed-signal signal processing strategy that uses pulses to communicate analog information between processing cells. analog Palmo cells are fully programmable and their interconnection may be defined by programmable logic. The Palmo technique may be applied to a wide range of signal processing applications.

Here we have shown the Palmo technique implementing analog filtering functions, and a FIR filter that might have otherwise been implemented with a Digital Signal Processor (DSP). The technique is capable of implementing many more functions. The Palmo cell may be used to implement an adder, a scaler, a short term analog memory, an integrator and a differential integrator. The combination of Palmo cells and programmable digital logic allows the implementation of analog filters, sigma delta analog to digital converters and adaptive signal processing algorithms to name but a few. It is the rich mix of analog and digital circuit techniques and the ease with which Palmo signals may be transferred between analog and digital domains that gives the range of application.

The Palmo strategy is ideal for preprocessing data for pulsed neural network VLSI. For example, the gammatone filterbank, rectification and onset filtering used in the sound segmentation system (Figure 8.1) may all be implemented using Palmo techniques.

This strategy, proposed here for pulsed neural networks, is also of interest to the wider electronics and signal processing community. We see the application of the Palmo techniques in the emerging area of Field Programmable Analog Arrays and Field Programmable Mixed-Signal Arrays.

8.6 Further Work

At the time of writing, we are developing new Palmo cells to be implemented with log domain BiCMOS circuits [Punzenberger and Enz, 1996] and current-mode comparators [Tang and Toumazou, 1994].

They operate in much the same way as the CMOS Palmo cells except signals within the cell are represented using currents rather than voltages. These new circuits are capable of operating at much higher sampling frequencies (around 5MHz) and at much reduced power supply voltages (5V or 3.3V).

8.7 Acknowledgements

The authors acknowledge the support of the U.K. Engineering and Physical Sciences Research Council (EPSRC) and the work of Mark Glover and Thomas Brandtner.

References

[Bratt and Macbeth, 1996] Bratt, A. and Macbeth, I. (1996). Design and implementation of a field programmable analogue array. *Fourth International Symposium on Field Programmable Gate Arrays (FPGA'96)*, Monterey, California, ACM/SIGDA.

[Fried, 1972] Fried, D. L. (1972). Analog sample-data filters. *IEEE Journal Solid State Circuits*, SC-7:302–304.

[Glover et al., ress] Glover, M. A., Hamilton, A., and Smith, L. S. (press). Analogue VLSI integrate and fire neural network for clustering onset and offset signals in a sound segmentation system. *Neuromorphic Systems: Engineering Silicon from Neurobiology*, Smith, L. S. and Hamilton, A., eds., World Scientific.

[Grundy, 1994] Grundy, D. L. (1994). A computational approach to VLSI analog design. *Journal of VLSI Signal Processing*, 8:53–60.

[Gulak, 1996] Gulak, P. G. (1996). Field-programmable analog arrays: A status report. *The Fourth Canadian Workshop on Field-Programmable Devices, Toronto, CA*, pages 138–141.

[Hamilton et al., 1993] Hamilton, A., Churcher, S., Edwards, P. J., Jackson, G. B., Murray, A., and Reekie, H. M. (1993). Pulse stream VLSI circuits and systems: The EPSILON neural network chipset. *International Journal of Neural Systems*, 4(4):395–406.

[Hamilton et al., 1992] Hamilton, A., Murray, A., Baxter, D., Churcher, S., Reekie, H., and Tarassenko, L. (1992). Integrated pulse-stream neural networks - results, issues and pointers. *IEEE Trans. Neural Networks*, 3(3):385–393.

[Hughes et al., 1989] Hughes, J. B., Bird, N. C., and Macbeth, I. C. (1989). Switching currents - a new technique for analogue sampled-data signal processing. *IEEE International Symposium on Circuits and Systems*, pages 1584–1587.

[Kuo, 1966] Kuo, F. F. (1966). *Network Analysis and Synthesis*. John Wiley, Toppan.

[Papathanasiou and Hamilton, 1996a] Papathanasiou, K. A. and Hamilton, A. (1996a). Novel Palmo analogue signal processing IC design techniques. *IEE Colloquium on Analog Signal Processing, November 1996, Oxford, England*, Institute of Electrical Engineers, 5/1–5/6.

[Papathanasiou and Hamilton, 1996b] Papathanasiou, K. A. and Hamilton, A. (1996b). Palmo signal processing : VLSI results from an integrated filter. *International Conference on Electronics, Circuits and Systems 1996, Rhodes, Greece*, IEEE Computer Society Press.

[Papathanasiou and Hamilton, 1996c] Papathanasiou, K. A. and Hamilton, A. (1996c). Pulse based signal processing : VLSI implementation of a Palmo filter. *International Symposium on Circuits and Systems, Atlanta, USA*, IEEE Computer Society Press, 1:270–273.

[Papathanasiou and Hamilton, 1997] Papathanasiou, K. A. and Hamilton, A. (1997). Advances in programmable pulse based mixed-signal processing VLSI. *2nd IEEE-CAS Region 8 Workshop on Analog and Mixed IC Design, Baverno, Italy*, IEEE Computer Society Press, 106–110.

[Punzenberger and Enz, 1996] Punzenberger, M. and Enz, C. (1996). A new 1.2v BiCMOS log-domain integrator for companding current-mode filters. In *1996 IEEE International Symposium on Circuits and Systems-Circuits (ISCAS) 1996*, IEEE Service Center, Atlanta, 125–128.

[Smith, 1996] Smith, L. S. (1996). Onset-based sound segmentation. In *Advances in Neural Information Processing Systems, vol. 8*, MIT Press, 729–735.

[Tang and Toumazou, 1994] Tang, A. T. K. and Toumazou, C. (1994). High performance CMOS current comparator. *Electronics Letters*, 30(1):5–6.

[Williams and Taylor, 1995] Williams, B. and Taylor, F. J. (1995). *Electronic Filter Design Handbook*. McGraw-Hill.

9 Digital Simulation of Spiking Neural Networks

Axel Jahnke, Ulrich Roth and Tim Schönauer

9.1 Introduction

The motivation of digital simulation of artificial neural networks is as diverse as the background of the researchers. Biologists, mathematicians, physicists, psychologists, computer scientists or engineers, all contribute to the field of neural networks. In one case, a very complex model of a single neuron has to be simulated. In another case, a large network of usually simpler neurons must be taken care of. Due to programmability, digital hardware offers a high degree of flexibility and provides a platform for simulations on neuron level as well as on network level. In opposite to signals in nature, digital signals are discrete in value and in time. Therefore, for digital simulations a suitable neuron model needs to be derived. Hence, at first we examine the digital representations of spiking neuron models in subsection 9.2. Then, subsection 9.3 gives an overview of programming environments. The subsequent subsections 9.5-9.7 address the speed-up of pulse-coded neural network simulations by algorithmic improvements and by taking advantage of high-performance hardware.

If simulation time is critical, the first step is to increase the efficiency of the simulation algorithm. Several concepts to reduce simulation time are introduced in subsection 9.4. Especially large networks, very complex models and/or real-time requirements necessitate high-performance hardware. A fair amount of dedicated digital and analog hardware for neural networks has been developed in the past years [Ienne, 1997]. Analog hardware profits from many analogies of neurobiology and the physics of semiconductors and allows the building of very compact, low-power sensor-integrated systems. Analog VLSI neural networks are discussed in Chapter 3. The strength of digital hardware is based on reprogrammability and uncomplicated data memories as well as a continuously increasing speed and density of logical circuits. Supercomputers represent high-performance general-purpose capabilities, but are constrained by costs and programming complexity. Dedicated digital hardware exploits the characteristics of types or classes of neural networks and thereby allows an implementation with a better ratio of performance to costs. An essential approach of high-performance digital hardware is to parallelize. Hence, Section 9.5 describes how networks can be mapped on a parallel computer. Section 9.6 finally evaluates the performance of some digital hardware platforms for the simulation of spiking neural networks.

9.2 Implementation Issues of Pulse-Coded Neural Networks

A detailed overview of neuron models was given in Chapter 1 and Chapter 2 with models ranging from simple integrate-and-fire models to very complex compartmental models such as the Hodgkin-Huxley model. In Section 1.2, a generic Spike Response Model was defined, which represents an intermediate description level. In the current chapter we focus on such types of models. The mathematical description, as already given in Section 1.2.1, is summarized here for convenience:

$$u_i(t) = \sum_{t_i^{(f)} \in \mathcal{F}_i} \eta_i\left(t - t_i^{(f)}\right) + \sum_{j \in \Gamma_i} \sum_{t_j^{(f)} \in \mathcal{F}_j} w_{ij} \varepsilon_{ij}\left(t - t_j^{(f)}\right) \qquad (9.1)$$

$$\mathcal{F}_i = \{t_i^{(f)}; 1 \leq f \leq n\} = \{t \mid u_i(t) = \vartheta\}. \qquad (9.2)$$

$$\Gamma_i = \{j \mid j \text{ presynaptic to } i\}. \qquad (9.3)$$

where $u_i(t)$: state variable (membrane potential) of neuron i.
$t_i^{(f)}, t_j^{(f)}$: firing time of neuron i and neuron j, respectively.
$\mathcal{F}_i$: set of all firing times of neuron i.
ϑ: if threshold ϑ is reached by $u_i(t)$, neuron i emits a spike.
Γ_i: set of neurons j presynaptic to i.
$\eta_i(\cdot)$: kernel to model the refractory period.
w_{ij}: synaptical strength.
$\epsilon_{ij}(\cdot)$: kernel to model the postsynaptic normalized potential of neuron i induced by a spike of neuron j.

For the sake of a better illustration, we now choose simple filters for the kernels η_i and ϵ_{ij} to construct an example model neuron. We assume that the refractoriness of the neuron is modeled by the kernel definition

$$\eta_i(s) = -\eta_0 \exp(-\frac{s}{\tau})\mathcal{H}(s) \qquad (9.4)$$

where $s = (t - t_i^{(f)})$, τ is the decay time constant, $\mathcal{H}$ represents the Heavyside step function and the constant η_0 resembles the amplitude of the relative refractoriness. The response to presynaptic spikes we model with the kernel

$$\epsilon_{ij}(s) = \exp\left(-\frac{s}{\tau_{ij}}\right)\mathcal{H}(s) \qquad (9.5)$$

where τ_{ij} is another decay time constant. Now, the expression

$$\sum_{t_j^{(f)} \in \mathcal{F}_j} \exp(-\frac{s}{\tau_{ij}})\mathcal{H}(s) \qquad (9.6)$$

can be interpreted as a leaky integrator, which accumulates incoming spikes from the neuron j and decreases them in time according to their time of arrival and the decay constant τ_{ij}. Correspondingly, in the expression

$$-\eta_0 \sum_{t_i^{(f)} \in \mathcal{F}_i} \exp(-\frac{s}{\tau_i})\mathcal{H}(s) \qquad (9.7)$$

9.2 Implementation Issues of Pulse-Coded Neural Networks

the sum can also be represented by a leaky integrator, which accumulates spikes fed back from the neuron i and decays them in time with the time constant τ_i. The example neuron is illustrated graphically in Figure 9.1. At

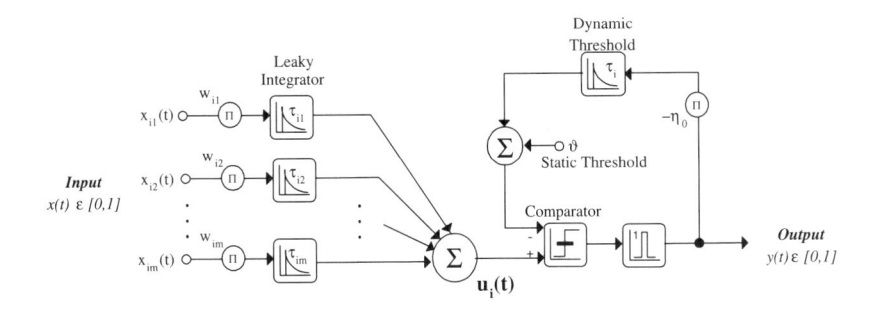

Figure 9.1. Example model neuron with leaky-integrators

any time, a spike might arrive at the input or might be generated at the output: the model is time-continuous. For digital signals on the other hand, both time and amplitude are discrete. Therefore a discrete-time model needs to be derived and its values need to be digitized with a certain resolution.

9.2.1 Discrete-Time Simulation

To compute a network in discrete-time, a continuous-time period is divided in intervals of a constant duration T. The period T is commonly referred to as time slice, time slot, bin or time step. Within a time slice the new state of the network is calculated. That means all neurons are computed based on the inputs they receive (e.g. spikes generated during the previous time slice) and their internal state variables. The result of this computation is a new state of the network including output spikes generated within this time slice. They become input to postsynaptic neurons during the following time slice. Figure 9.2 shows a discrete-time representation of the example neuron model. Compared to Figure 9.1, the leaky integrators are now substituted by first-order recursive digital filters with a relaxation factor relating to the time constant τ

$$r = \exp(-\frac{T}{\tau}) \qquad (9.8)$$

yielding a discrete-time recursive relation for the membrane potential $u_i(n)$

$$u_i(n) = -\{\eta_0 y(n) + r_i u_{ti}(n-1) + \vartheta\} + \sum_{j \in \Gamma_i} \{w_{ij} x_{ij}(n) + r_{ij} u_{fij}(n-1)\} \qquad (9.9)$$

where u_{fij} denotes the output of each filter element in the input branches of the model neuron and u_{ti} represents the output of the filter in the threshold loop (see Figure 9.2).

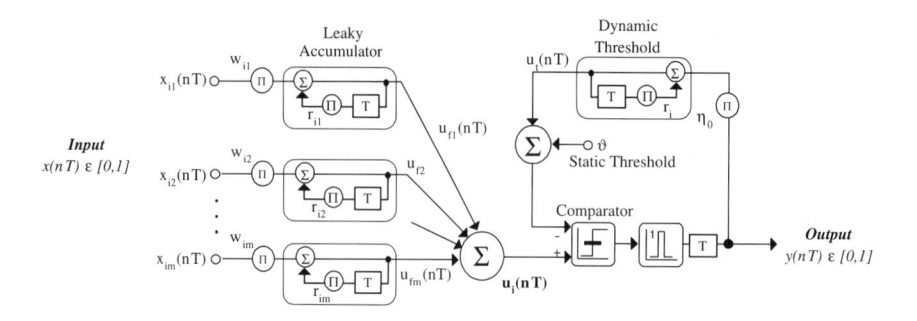

240   9. Digital Simulation of Spiking Neural Networks

Figure 9.2. Example model neuron in discrete-time with first-order recursive digital filters

A period T needs to be chosen in such a way, that the behavior of the neural networks is resolved sufficiently in time while not wasting computational resources by computing steps which are too fine. A commonly chosen value for a time slice is 1ms. This interval represents approximately the duration of an action potential. Therefore, a simulation is regarded a real-time simulation, if a time-slice is computed within 1ms or less.

In order to reduce the computational requirements, the model neuron in Figure 9.2 can be simplified as already mentioned in Section 1.2.3.1. The simplification is to assume that several input branches x_{ij} decay with the same time constant τ_{ij}. In this case the summing of these input branches can be performed before the leaky integration. Thereby several synapses represented by the input branches x_{ij} share one filter. This simplified example model neuron will be considered in the following sections.

9.2.2 Requisite Arithmetic Precision

For simulations on workstations, floating-point representation is a natural choice. Such computers are equipped with fast floating-point units, and so the computation with values in integer or fixed-point representation does not yield an advantage. The situation is quite different for neurocomputers and dedicated digital neuro chips. These systems almost never provide a floating point unit, because it would require significant design effort and a large chip area. So the question arises what the requisite precision for computation with spiking neurons is [Roth et al., 1995]. Regarding the representation with fixed-point numbers, we have to know the requisite precision $k.f$, where k represents the bit length of the integer part and f the bit length of the fraction part. The representation using fixed-point numbers compared to integer numbers has the major advantage that we can change the scaling by shifting the decimal point without changing the total word length $k+f$. The maximum representable value $v_{lim} = 2^k - 2^{-f}$ will be called limitation value. A quantity exceeding this value will be set to the limitation value. The minimum representable number $q = 2^{-f}$ is called quantization step. Quantities smaller than the quantization step will be truncated. In order to determine the requisite arithmetic precision, we need a lower bound for the limitation value and an upper bound for the quantization step. We will focus our discussion on the values of the filter functions. The requisite resolution of other values like membrane potentials or synaptic strength can be derived from the results.

A criterion for the lower bound of the limitation value is easily established. Proper network function demands that the limitation value for the output value of a filter element is larger than the maximum quantity u_{max} this output value may reach:

$$v_{lim} > 2^n \text{ and } n = \text{ceil}\left(ld(u_{max})\right) \tag{9.10}$$

where ceil() yields the next greater integer number. For a stationary input sequence u_{max} can be computed for our kernel function as the limit value of the sum over a geometric series:

$$u_{max} = \frac{w}{1 - r^k} \tag{9.11}$$

where k denotes the mean time interval between two spikes, and w the mean synaptic strength averaged over time and the various inputs of a filter element.

Computation with truncation has two effects: weights with smaller magnitude are added (weight quantization) and the values of the potentials are lowered after each multiplication with the relaxation factor (arithmetic error). Thus, output values of the filter elements are decaying at a faster rate and arrive at zero, when their value falls below q. As a criterion for the upper bound of the quantization step q we demand, that a received spike should at least be able to have an influence over a distinct time. We will call this time interval k_{inf}, measured in discrete time steps T. Regarding for example a network with a background oscillation as described in Section 1.1.3.2, k_{inf} would be the period of this oscillation.

In the following we will show how the upper bound can be computed for our kernel function ε_{ij}. Our criterion for the upper bound of the quantization step q demands that a weighted and k_{inf}-times relaxed spike is still larger than q:

$$q < \text{trunc}(w_{min} r^{k_{inf}}) \tag{9.12}$$

where trunc() denotes computation with truncation, and w_{min} the minimum weight value.

At the arrival time of a spike, the synaptic strength is lowered by a quantization error e_0.

$$n = 0 \: : \: \text{trunc}(w) = w - e_0 \tag{9.13}$$

The next time step lowers the output value of the filter function by arithmetic error e_1

$$n = 1 \: : \: \text{trunc}(wr) = r\left(w - e_0\right) - e_1) \tag{9.14}$$

and so on. Now we will assume that the maximum possible error q occurs at each time step and compute the accumulated error as the limit value of the sum over a geometric series:

$$\text{trunc}\left(w_{min} r^{k_{inf}}\right) = r^{k_{inf}} w_{min} - q\left(\frac{1 - r^{k_{inf}+1}}{1-r}\right) \quad (9.15)$$

Substituting the right-hand term in equation 9.12 yields the upper bound for the quantization step q:

$$q < w_{min}\left(\frac{r^{k_{inf}} - r^{k_{inf}+1}}{2 - r - r^{k_{inf}+1}}\right) \quad (9.16)$$

For other kernel functions the upper and lower bound can be derived in a similar fashion.

9.2.3 Basic Procedures of Network Computation

During each time slice the new state of the network is computed. One way of dividing the computation of a time slice into phases is:

1. **Input-Phase** ▷ execute $InputFunction$ for all neurons:
   $pi_{ij}(n) = w_{ij} \cdot x_{ij}(n), po_i(n) = \eta_0 \cdot y(n)$
2. **Filter-Phase** ▷ execute $FilterFunction$ for all neurons:
   $fi_{ij}(n) = pi_{ij}(n) + r_{ij} \cdot u_{fij}(n-1)\}$
   $fo_i = po_i(n) + r_i \cdot u_{ti}(n-1)$
3. **Output-Phase** ▷ execute $OutputFunction$ for all neurons:
   ○ compute membrane potential $u_i(n)$:
   $u_i(n) = -\{fo_i + \vartheta\} + \sum_{j \epsilon \Gamma_i} fi_{ij}$
   ○ emit spike, if $u_i(n)$ exceeds threshold
4. **Learning-Phase** ▷ adjust weights according to learning rule

These phases represent a way of structuring the computation of a new state of the network. They will be of importance in the following sections when examining simulation strategies. Since the implementation of learning depends on the specific learning algorithm, for most of the following general considerations, we omit the Learning Phase.

9.3 Programming Environment

Once a model suitable for a digital simulation has been derived, a software environment and a hardware platform needs to be chosen. The programming of neural networks might be done with programming languages like *C, C++* or *Fortran*, mathematic software tools such as *MATLAB* [MATLAB, 1995] or *mathematica* [Freeman, 1994], or even with neural network simulators such as *GENESIS, PDP++* or *SNNS*. These different programming environments are now discussed in turn.

The use of a programming language is the most flexible approach. Usually it leads to the most efficient implementation in terms of computation speed, too. A graphical user interface and visualization tools can be incorporated with *X11* library functions or tool kits like *Tcl/Tk*. Tool kits ease significantly the development of graphical extensions. Some of them e.g. *Tcl/Tk* even allow implementations which are portable to different hardware platforms and operating systems. Separating the implementation into computational expensive tasks, still coded in a programming language like *C*, and graphical tasks ensures the benefit of a fast implementation. With *Java*, an unified implementation is possible avoiding interface issues, which are sometimes difficult to tackle. However, until a compiler for *Java* is available, performance degradation compared to compiled implementation has to be accepted. All these approaches have in common that they require significant programming skills and programming effort. One usually has to start from scratch and code reusability is only possible to a certain extent. Up to now there are no class libraries available for spiking neurons, only for standard model neurons (e.g. [Blum, 1992]).

Standard mathematic software tools also offer a great amount of flexibility while supplying many built-in mathematical functions and visualization features. They allow thereby convenient programming and simulation of neural networks. However, up to now *MATLAB* or *mathematica* provide a tool-box only for simulations of standard model neurons. Spiking neurons have to be assembled with blocks for kernel functions and so on. Regarding execution times, mathematic software tools are only useful for the simulation of small scale networks or the evaluation of prototype implementations.

Neural network simulators can help to reduce the effort of programming a network to an even greater extent. They are often equipped with a graphical user interface and visualization tools tailored for neural networks. Usually they allow the entering of a network structure graphically or on a high-level, abstract syntax consisting of e.g. objects (neurons, connection-types) and topology (layer, connections) definitions. The abstract, modular syntax allows not only faster programming but also a better comprehensibility and transparency of the code simplifying debugging and changes in the code. Unfortunately, available neural network simulators are not well suited for the simulation of spiking neurons. The underlying model neurons either do not contain temporal behavior (e.g. *SNNS* or *PDP++*) or the model is too detailed regarding spiking neurons (e.g. *GENESIS*). So the simulation of spiking neurons is not possible with neural simulators for standard model neurons. Incorporating model neurons with temporal behavior into these simulators usually requires significant programming efforts and might lead to an inefficient implementation.

Simulators for compartmental models like *GENESIS* are useful for the detailed simulation of single neurons or small ensembles of neurons. *PGENESIS*, a parallel version of *GENESIS* allows simulation of a few up to thousand neurons on cluster of workstations or supercomputers. In the field of spiking neurons *GENESIS* is mostly used for the comparison of the behavior of detailed bio-physical models and the simplified spiking neurons. The simulation of large-scale networks of spiking neurons requires a significant amount of unnecessary modeling effort and is also not efficient regarding computation times.

In the following we consider different implementations of spiking neurons abstractly. The study of different algorithms will be done with pseudo-code.

9.4 Concepts of Efficient Simulation

Implementing large networks of spiking neurons a huge number of operations and/or memory accesses has to be executed on a digital computer. TS timesteps of a network with N neurons, each with F filters with S synapses each, should be simulated. $F \cdot S$ is the number of connections C per neuron. A straight-forward approach A_1 is shown in the following algorithm:

```
1 foreach timestep in TS do
2    foreach neuron in N do
3       foreach filter in F do
4          foreach synapse in S do
5             InputFunction()
6       FilterFunction()
7 OutputFunction()
```

The number of operations N_{OP} -assuming one operation per $Function()$- and the number of memory accesses N_{MA} could be estimated as follows:

$$N_{OP} \approx TS \cdot N \cdot F \cdot S$$

$$N_{MA} \approx 2 \cdot TS \cdot N \cdot F \cdot S$$

It should be noted that $N_{OP} \leq N_{MA}$ is due to read/write operations of the filter value and indicates the I/O-boundness of our algorithm. This point is crucial for the implementation of spiking neurons on digital signal processors which are optimized for the computation of compute-bounded problems ($N_{OP} \gg N_{MA}$).

The network activity a (average number AN of spikes per TS / N) is usually quite low in spiking networks. A very efficient communication scheme for such networks is the event-list protocol [Lazarro et al., 1993]. Only the addresses of those neurons which fire in the present time slice –in the following called active neurons– are registered in a spike event-list. This information is distributed by spikes via the connections C for inputs to all connected neurons in algorithm A_2:

```
1 foreach timestep in TS do
2    foreach active_neuron in AN do
3       foreach connection in C do
4          InputFunction()
5       foreach neuron in N do
6          foreach filter in F do
7             FilterFunction()
8          OutputFunction()
```

The number of operations and memory accesses for A_2 could be estimated as follows:

$$N_{OP} \approx TS \cdot N \cdot (F + a \cdot C)$$
$$N_{MA} \approx 2 \cdot TS \cdot N \cdot (F + a \cdot C)$$

A high percentage of filters will be negligible due to the low network activity which means they could be neglected for the computation of a time slice without any change in the results. Concerning a filter state f, we can define a certain threshold Δf. Filters with an absolute value less than Δf should be *negligible* filters while the other filters are *non-negligible*. This is implemented in algorithm A_3:

```
1  foreach timestep in TS do
2      foreach active_neuron in AN do
3          foreach connection in C do
4              InputFunction()
5      foreach neuron in N do
6          foreach filter in F_nn do
7              FilterFunction()
8              | f |≤ Δf ⇒ filter is neligible
9          OutputFunction()
```

F_{nn} is the number of non-negligible filters. The dependency of F_{nn} from the network activity is denoted by a function $f_{nn}(a)$. We observed in our simulations $f_{nn}(x) \approx 10 \cdot x$, but this might change for different network structures and parameters. The number of operations and memory accesses for A_3 could be estimated as follows:

$$N_{OP} \approx TS \cdot (f_{nn}(a) \cdot N \cdot F + a \cdot C)$$
$$N_{MA} \approx 2 \cdot TS \cdot (f_{nn}(a) \cdot N \cdot F + a \cdot C)$$

Until now we did not take into account the memory structure required to store the network connectivity. Typically, the connectivity of a neural network would be stored as a weight matrix W. This is well suited for fully-connected networks where $C = N$. Hence, the required memory size is N^2. However, spiking neural networks are more sparse than fully connected ($C \ll N$) and the weight matrix will mostly be filled with zeros. Besides the waste of memory space the zeros slow down the simulation, because the following loop over N (and not over C!) has to be excuted for the Input Phase instead of the lines 2-4 in A_3:

```
foreach active_neuron in AN do
foreach connection in N do
if connection ≠ 0 then
InputFunction()
```

So, using A_2 or A_3 together with a weight matrix is not efficient for sparse networks where $C \ll N$. A more efficient method for the representation of sparse connectivity is the use of lists, one for each neuron n_i

246   9. Digital Simulation of Spiking Neural Networks

[Hartmann et al., 1997]. Each list is accessed by the neuron's base address

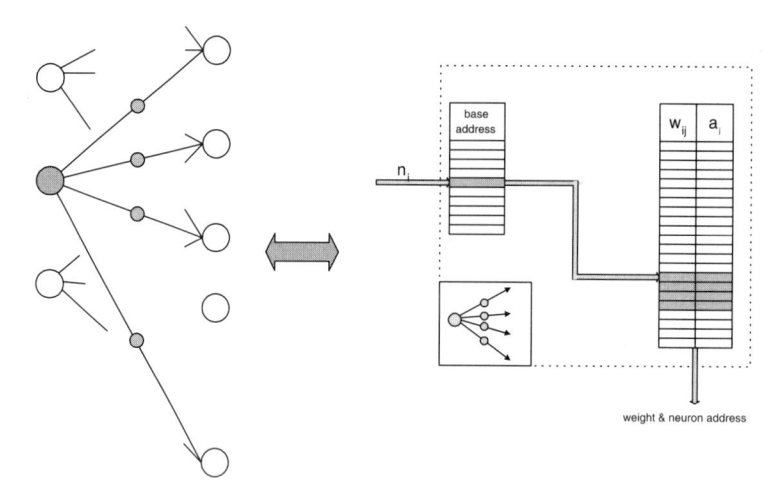

Figure 9.3. Connectivity List

n_i : address of sending neuron i
a_i, w_{ij} : address/weight of receiving neuron j

(see Figure 9.4). The items in the lists are datasets consisting of weights and addresses. The addresses a_j in the list may denote the neuron n_j, to which n_i sends a spike or from which n_i receives a spike. Obviously, the sender-oriented connectivity will be preferred for an algorithm like A_2 or A_3 where we have to know the neurons to which a sending neuron will send a spike. However, for a learning mechanism of the Hebbian type also the reverse direction is required. Hence, a second receiver-oriented list - which will be sender-oriented for the learning phase - is needed. This is equivalent to the need for the transposed weight matrix using weight matrices to store the connectivity.

Connectivity as in Figure 9.4 follows some simple deterministic rules and is quite regular for neurons of one layer. It will be called *regular connectivity* (RC). So all neurons in a layer are connected according to the same simple rules. Hence, we can compute the regular connections using these rules instead of storing them. On-line computation of the connections reduces the required amount of storage for connection lists drastically [Roth et al., 1997]. Furthermore, in some cases the weight vectors for all neurons in a layer are similiar (weight sharing). We only need to store one *regular weight vector* per layer for the whole network. Unfortunately the on-line computation itself requires several operations per connection depending on the hardware platform. Therefore, this approach is only useful for computers with limited I/O-bandwidth and on-chip memory, e.g. the CNAPS described in Section 9.6.2.

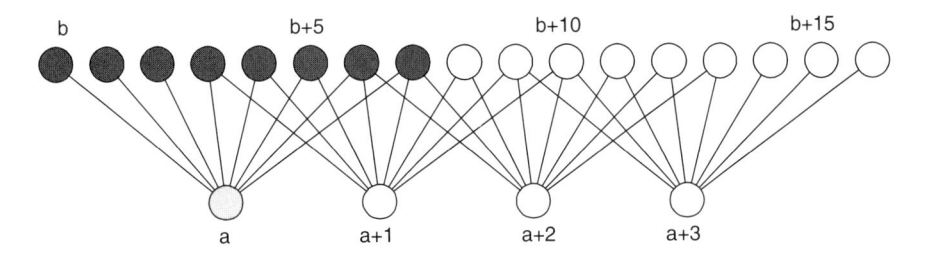

Figure 9.4. Regular Connections

9.5 Mapping Neural Networks on Parallel Computers

In the next section we will examine the performance of different hardware platforms like workstations, DSPs, neurocomputer and supercomputer for the simulation of spiking neural networks. Neurocomputers, supercomputers, and sometimes DSPs are parallel computers. They consist of a few up to thousand and more processing elements (PEs) that can communicate and cooporate to solve large problems quickly.

But how can we map a specific network of spiking neurons on a parallel computer in order to achieve the maximum performance? The key concepts of an efficient mapping in order to maximize the performance will be load balancing, minimizing inter-PE communciation and minimizing synchronization between the PEs. Furthermore, the mapping should be scalable both for different network sizes, and for different numbers of processing elements.

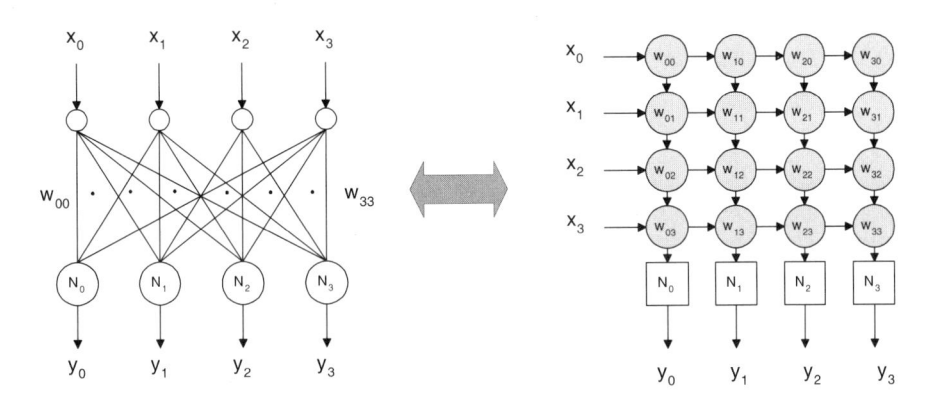

Figure 9.5. Presentation of the Neural Network

Some basic concepts for an efficient mapping will be discussed in the next subsections. A more detailed discussion concerning the mapping of conventional neural networks can be found e.g. in [Ienne, 1997]. The weight matrix presentation of a simple neural network (four neurons with four synapses each) used in the following is shown in the right of Figure 9.5, while the left side shows the conventional presentation of the same network. In the case of the Spike Response model with only one unique response function, the rectangle N denotes the computation of the response function. The circle w_{ij} stands for the computation of the synapse: $y_i = w_{ij} \cdot u_j + y_{i-1}$ where y_{i-1} is the result from the preceeding synapse.

9.5.1 Neuron-Parallelism

Let us assume we would like to simulate a network with N spiking neurons on a parallel computer with N_{PE} PEs. We will illustrate the mapping with $N = 4$ and $N_{PE} = 4$ in the following sections. A common approach for this configuration is shown in Figure 9.6. The synapses of one neuron and the output function are mapped to the same PE and N_{PE} neurons are computed in parallel. We will call it *neuron-parallel* or simply *n-parallel*.

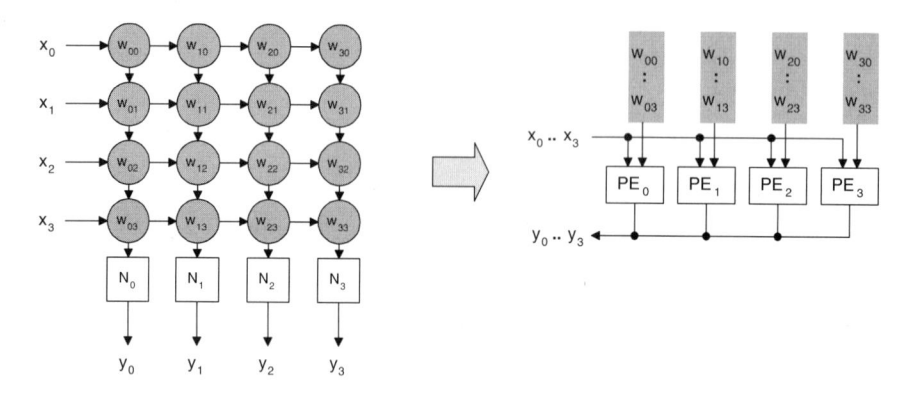

Figure 9.6. N-Parallelism

9.5.2 Synapse-Parallelism

Instead of mapping the synapses of one neuron to the same PE they can be mapped to different PEs. So, N_{PE} synapses -not necessarily from the same neuron- will be computed in parallel. The output functions of a neuron can be processed either on a seperate PE serially (mid part of Figure 9.7) or can be distributed over the PEs (right part of Figure 9.7). Hence, we will call the first kind of mapping *s(ynapse)-parallel* and the latter *sn-parallel*.

Small circles in Figure 9.7 denote registers which are only enabled every fourth cycle. So, PE_0 receives only input signal x_0, PE_0 only x_1 .... It should be noted that for the Output Phase the actual weight values have to be collected from several other PEs. This could be done either by distributed accumulation like in mid/right part of Figure 9.7 or by local accumulation on the PE computing the neuron. The latter would require a high communication bandwidth.

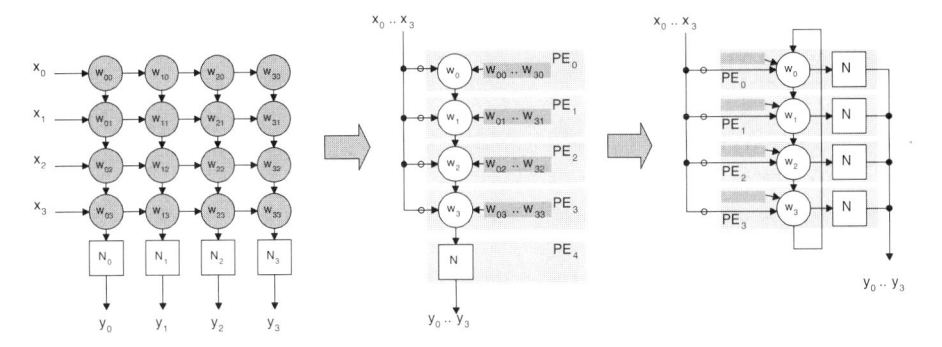

Figure 9.7. S- and SN-Parallelism

9.5.3 Pattern-Parallelism

In order to reduce the required communication bandwidth *p(attern)-parallelism* has been used for conventional networks such as MLPs with backpropagation learning. Each PE of the parallel processor simulates the response of the network for a different input pattern. Unfortunately, different patterns will be presented to the spiking neural network at different times nT and the state of the network for time $(n+1)T$ is not independent of the state for time nT. Therefore, we have to simulate pattern after pattern and can not use *p-parallelism*!

9.5.4 Partitioning of the Network

An important aspect of mapping is which synapse (in the case of *s-/sn-parallel*) or which neuron (in the case of *n-/sn-parallel*) exactly is mapped to which processing element for a specific hardware architecture in order to achieve a balanced workload of all processing elements.

Discussing this scenario, the degree of parallelism -the ratio N_{PE}/N- is important. A commonly used distinction exists between fine-grain and coarse-grain parallelism. In the case of spiking neural networks we will define it as follows:

fine-grain parallelism: $\quad N_{PE} \approx N$
coarse-grain parallelism: $\quad N_{PE} \ll N$

Furthermore, the synchronization of the parallel computer has to be taken into account: SIMD (Single Instruction Multiple Data) or MIMD (Multiple Instruction Multiple Data). At any given time all processors of a SIMD computer execute the same operation (single instruction) on different data (multiple data). Hence, all PEs of a SIMD computer are synchronized. On a MIMD computer, all PEs could execute different operations (multiple instruction) on different data (multiple data). There is a need for synchronisation between PEs only in the case of data exchange.

Concerning a SIMD computer we have to remember that for any given network state neither all synapses/neurons (A_2/A_3) nor all IPs (A_3) have to be computed. Assuming spatial and temporal correlated activity, the active neurons of one time step nT are forming one or more local activity clusters. Furthermore, a high percentage of neurons receiving spikes in $(n+1)T$ also belong to these activity clusters. In the worst case, the only activity cluster is mapped to one PE which has to compute all the active synapses/IPs/neurons while the other PEs are idle. In order to avoid this worst case scenario we could use *sender-oriented s- or sn-parallel mapping*. All synapses w_{ij} receiving spikes from neuron n_j will be equally distributed to PEs. Hence, all PEs have to update their synaptic values during the Input Phase. So the workload for the Input Phase will be balanced.

In the case of n-parallelism, we could use the following *block-based* mapping scheme for n-parallelism (see Figure 9.8). The network layers l_i will

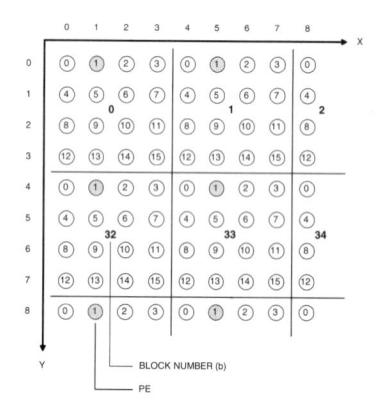

Figure 9.8. Network Mapping Sheme

be divided in blocks of n_b adjacent neurons with $n_b \leq N_{PE}$. Each neuron of a block bn is mapped to a different PE, while neurons of different blocks but the same x/y position relative to their block are mapped to the same PE. The neurons on a PE are distinguished by their block and layer number (see Figure 9.8). Thus, the coordinates $C_0 = (x, y, l)$ can be transformed into to the coordinates $C_1 = (np, bn, l)$, where np denotes also the PE to which the neuron will be mapped.

- np is the one-dimensional neuron position relative to the block
- bn is the block number
- l is the layer number

Now, neurons of an active cluster will be mapped to different PEs and the workload is more likely to be balanced for the Filter and Output Phase. Even the balancing of the workload for the Input Phase will be enhanced in the case of local connectivity.

Concerning the implementation on a coarse-grain MIMD parallel computer a huge network can be decomposed into smaller parts which will be computed on different PEs. Due to the MIMD architecture there is no need for synchronization. However, the communication bandwidth will now become the main bottleneck. Therefore, only n-parallel mapping is suitable. Furthermore, in order to minimize the communication the interconnectivity of the neurons can be used as the main criterion for the decomposition of the neural network. Hence, neurons with high interconnectivity with each other, regardless to which layer they belong, will be mapped to the same PE. An example for this decomposition can be found in [PGENESIS], which describes an implementation for PGENESIS.

9.6 Performance Study

After the explanations of some basic concepts for the simulation of spiking neural networks on digital computers, we want to take a look at the performance of real computers. As a model network for our performance evaluation we chose the neural network presented by Reitboeck, Stoecker et al. [Reitböck et al., 1993]. The network performs a basic segmentation task. It consists of a two-dimensional layer of neurons which receive an input spike from a corresponding pixel of the input image. Each neuron is a Spike-Response Neuron with 3 filters each and is connected to its 90 nearest neighbors and recurrently to a inhibitory neuron. For our comparative studies we used different network sizes varying from 8kN up to 512kN. Further distinctions will be made between RC and NRC networks. This is of particular interest regarding hardware with limited on-chip memory capacity where the connectivity has to be stored locally.

9.6.1 Single PE Workstations

We used algorithm A_3 for the implementation of the model network on single PE workstations. For an integer implementation, different fixed point number representations are necessary. Hence, a large number of shift operations is required for the computation of the network. This may be the reason why we noticed a similar performance for both the integer and the floating point implementation. Therefore, we used a floating implementation for further investigations. Our results in Figure 9.9 and the execution profiles indicate that the Filter Phase accounts for the major workload on single PE workstations [Jahnke et al., 1995]. Furthermore, the results for SUN Ultra-1 (166 MHz) show that available single PE computer do not have enough performance for real-time simulation of spike-processing neural networks where simulation times of less than 1 millisecond are required (see Chapter 9.2.1).

9.6.2 Neurocomputer

The **CNAPS/256** (Adaptive Solutions) is a SIMD parallel computer consisting of 256 16b PEs (50 MHz) with 4KB local memory each, communicating via two 8b buses (see Figure 9.10). The implementable network size is limited to $nmax_{rc} \approx 32\text{kN}$ for RC networks and to $nmax_{nrc} \approx 500N$ for NRC networks. For the latter, the whole connectivity has to be stored in local memory. Overcoming these limits with extensive use of external memory leads to an unacceptable decrease of performance and a speedup $\ll 1$ over

252   9. Digital Simulation of Spiking Neural Networks

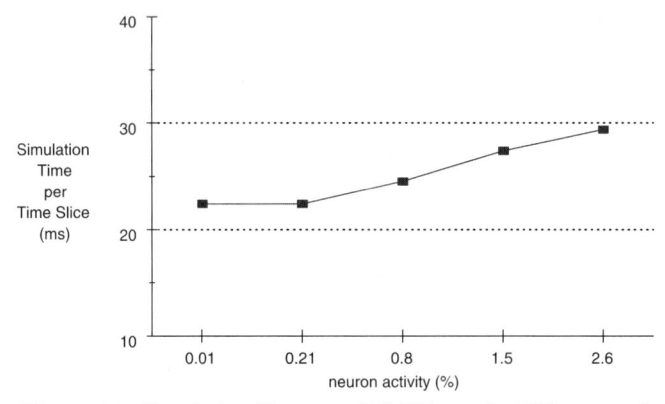

Figure 9.9. Simulation Times on SUN Ultra of a 128k network

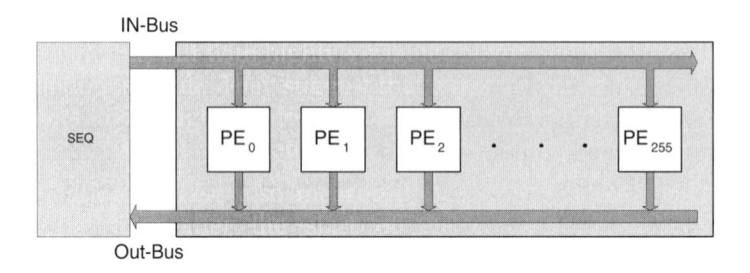

Figure 9.10. Neurocomputer CNAPS/256

a single PE, since 256 PEs would need to communicate with the external memory via two 16b buses only. Furthermore, the bottle-neck of inter-PE-communication requires that the connectivity of all neurons mapped to one PE must be either stored or computed directly on this PE. Therefore, a sender-oriented connectivity is not useful, since the whole network topology would need to be stored on each PE leading to an early exploitation of the limited on-chip memory resources.

However, using the block-based mapping scheme described above for only regular connectivity, we could avoid purely receiver-oriented connections. In a block-based mapping scheme each neuron is unambiguously defined by its coordinates (np, bn, l). Broadcasting this identification code of a spike-emitting neuron to the PEs, each PE could detect in a sender-oriented fashion, which local neuron receives a spike. This could be done with low effort by using the np values -taking into account the block borders- for the computation of local neurons connected to the sending neuron.

```
1  foreach time step in TS do
2     foreach proc_element in K do
3        foreach active_neuron in AN(proc_element) do
4           SentToBus(active_neuron)
5           begin  ParallelCode
6              ComputeConnectedNeuron(active_neuron)
7           end  ParallelCode
```

```
7    foreach neuron in N do
3        ParallelCode ...
```

In order to evaluate the speedup through parallelization of this algorithm, we measured computation times while varying N and/or N_{PE}. Our results indicate, that the speedup is approximately linear to N_{PE} as long as inter-PE-communication is not a dominating factor. This is true for network activity $< 1\%$. Staying within these limits, a speedup of up to 15 over single PE computers has been measured (see Figure 9.12). The performance could be further increased by using microcoding. Thereby, real-time requirements could be fulfilled for RC networks with up to 16kN. However, the use of CNAPS/256 for real-time applications is limited by the low network complexity as indicated by the values of $nmax_{rc}$ and $nmax_{nrc}$.

The **SYNAPSE** (Siemens AG) is a systolic array processor optimized for matrix-matrix operations. SYNAPSE achieves a very high performance for computing highly connected, conventional neural networks using s- and p-parallel mapping [Ramacher et al., 1991]. The simulation of conventional, static neural networks in general constitute a compute-bounded problem. However, our algorithms are I/O-bounded. So, with barely any on-chip memory and no sufficient bandwidth to communicate with external memory, systolic array processors like SYNAPSE are inadequate for the simulation of spiking neural networks.

9.6.3 Parallel Computers

The **TMS320C80** (Texas Instruments) is a digital signal processor including 4 MIMD 32b PEs with 12kB local memory each and one 32b PE for vector processing. All PEs are communicating via a crossbar structure (see Figure 9.11). All network parameter of RC networks up to 20kN could be stored in

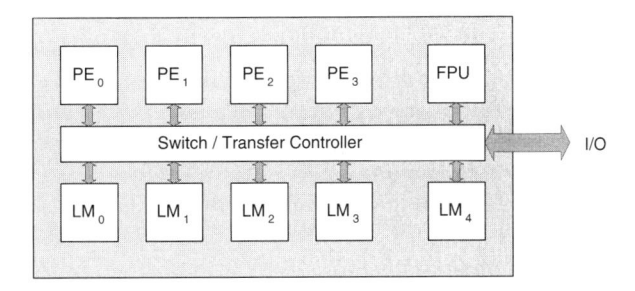

Figure 9.11. Digital Signal Processor TMS320C80

local memory. Using algorithm A_3 and n-parallel mapping, a performance similar to the CNAPS could be achieved (see Figure 9.12). On one hand, CNAPS can profit from a higher number of PEs. On the other hand, the MIMD architecture of the TMS320C80 allows a high workload for input and decay and output phases without using a specific mapping scheme. Also compared to CNAPS, the crossbar structure allows better inter-PE-communication which is also diminished due to the larger on-chip memory per PE of the TMS320C80. Simulating larger RC networks or NRC networks > 1 kN requires extensive use of external memory. Even the high memory bandwidth (400 MB/s) of the TMS320C80 is not sufficient and the simulation times approach those of single PE computers.

The **4xP90** is a MIMD parallel computer with four Pentium P90 and shared memory architecture. Neither the on-chip cache is sufficient to store all network parameters nor are the cache algorithms appropriate to achieve a good hit-rate. Hence, concerning the simulation of spiking neural networks the problem arises that more than one PE needs access to the shared memory at a given time period. Therefore we noticed a poor speed-up of less than 1.3 over a single P90 implementation and a performance similiar to the performance of a single-PE SUN Ultra.

The **SP2** is a MIMD parallel computer with up to 256 R6000 PEs, local memory architecture and high speed 16-to-16 switches for inter-PE communication. N-parallel mapping and sender-oriented connectivity has been used for the implementation [Mohraz, 1997]. On the one hand, a single PE exhibited significantly less performance than e.g. a P90 which must be a result of very unsatisfactory compiler settings and requires further investigations. On the other hand, we noticed a speedup of only 1.12/1.23/1.25 using 2/4/8 PEs over a single PE implementation. Hence, the performance is mainly limited by inter PE communication (computation and communication could not be done in parallel on SP2) which results in the observed poor PE-scaling behavior.

The Connection Machine **CM-2** is a SIMD parallel computer with 16k 1b PEs and hypercube architecture. It has been shown by E.Niebur et.al. that networks with up to 4M simple Spike Response neurons with one filter function can be simulated efficiently on the CM-2 [Niebur and Brettle, 1993]. While n-parallelism and sender-oriented connectivity is most efficient for Filter/Output Phase, only a few neurons are active at a given time step of Input Phase and most of the PEs are idle. Niebur et al. showed that sn-parallelism is more efficient for the CM-2. We already mentioned the inefficieny of sn-parallelism for Filter/Output Phase but this does not matter for the CM-2 with its powerful communication network. On the basis of the results of [Niebur and Brettle, 1993] we estimated the simulation times in Figure 9.12 for our model network. Even for large networks the real-time requirements are met.

9.6.4 Results of the Performance Study

As Figure 9.12 shows, only supercomputers like the CM-2 exhibit enough performance for real-time simulation of large-scale spiking neural networks. The simulation times indicate that the main reason for the poor performance of other parallel computers is the limited I/O-bandwidth which is a result of the I/O-bounded character of computing spiking networks. This was a motivation to develop dedicated hardware for the simulation of spike-processing neural networks which has been presented recently [Jahnke et al., 1996].

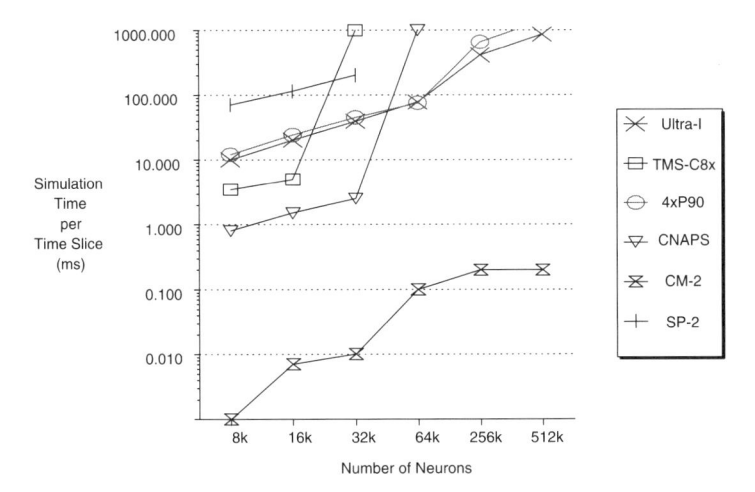

Figure 9.12. Evaluation Results

9.6.5 Conclusions

We have discussed implementation issues concerning the digital simulation of spiking neural networks.

A method has been presented to calculate requisite fixed point precision. Fixed point representation becomes crucial for simulation on neurocomputers, neurochips and digital signal processors.

Three general algorithms for the simulation of spiking neural networks have been shown: a straight-forward approach, an algorithm using spike-event list and a more sophisticated approach by computing only the non-negligible parts of each neuron. Furthermore, on-line computation of the network connectivity could be useful in order to implement algorithms.

We investigated the performance of our algorithms on available computers such as CNAPS, SYNAPSE, TMS320C80 and CM-2. Our results indicate that only a supercomputer exhibits enough performance to compute spike-processing neural networks in real-time.

Therefore, we see two directions for future work. On the one hand, an efficient simulation enviroment for spiking neural networks should be available for a broad class of parallel computers and heterogeneous workstation cluster. This could be a distributed and event-driven simulator that will provide fast but also detailed analysis of larger spiking neural networks [Grassmann, 1997]. On the other hand, there is still the need for dedicated hardware which is currently under developement [Jahnke et al., 1996]. Such hardware could be used either as a low-cost simulator or for real-world applications where both real-time behavior, low power consumption and small size would be needed.

References

[neuro simulators] A list of available neural network simulators. http://www.neuronet.ph.kcl.ac.uk/neuronet/software/software.html.

[PGENESIS] Examples for PGENESIS. http://www.psc.edu/Packages/PGENESIS/examples.html.

[MATLAB, 1995] MATLAB - User's Guide (1995), Prentice Hall, Englewood Cliffs.

[Blum, 1992] Blum A. (1992) *Neural Networks in C++*. Wiley, New York.

[Grassmann, 1997] Grassmann, C., (1997). Private Communication, Institut für Informatik II, Universität Bonn.

[Hartmann et al., 1997] Hartmann, G., Frank, G., Schaefer, M., and Wolff, C. (1995). SPIKE 128K - An accelerator for dymamic simulation of large puls-coded networks. *Proc. MicroNeuro'97*, H. Klar, A. König, U. Ramacher, eds., University of Technology Dresden, 130–139.

[Hammerstrom, 1990] Hammerstrom, D. (1990). A VLSI architecture for high-performance, low-cost, on-chip learning, *Proc. Int. Joint Conf. on Neural Networks 1990 (IJCNN'90)*, Lawrence Erlbaum Associates Publishers, 537–543.

[Ienne, 1997] Ienne, P. (1997). Digital connectionist hardware: Current problems and future challenges. *Proc. Int. Work-Conf. on Artificial and Natural Neural Networks 1997 (IWANN'97)*, J. Mira, R. Moreno-Diaz, J. Cabestany, eds., Springer-Verlag, 688–713.

[Jahnke et al., 1995] Jahnke, A., Roth, U., and Klar H. (1995). Towards Efficient Hardware for Spike-Processing Neural Networks. *Proc. World Congress on Neural Networks 1995*, 460–463.

[Jahnke et al., 1996] Jahnke, A., Roth, U., and Klar H. (1996). A SIMD/dataflow architecture for a neurocomputer for spike-processing neural networks (NESPINN). *Proc. MicroNeuro'96*, IEEE Computer Society Press, 232–237.

[Lazarro et al., 1993] Lazarro, J. and Wawrzynek, J. (1993). Silicon auditory processors as computer peripherals. *Advances in Neural Information Processing Systems, vol. 5*, Morgan Kaufmann Publishers, 820–827.

[McClelland and Rummelhardt, 1988] McClelland, J. L. and Rummelhardt, D. E. (1988). *Explorations in Prallel Distributed Processing*. MIT Press.

[Freeman, 1994] Freeman, J. A. (1994). *Simulating Neural Networks with Mathematica*. Addison-Wesley.

[Niebur and Brettle, 1993] Niebur, E. and Brettle, D. (1993). Efficient simulation of biological neural networks on massively parallel supercomputers with hypercube architecture. *Advances in Neural Information Processing Systems, vol. 6*, Morgan Kaufmann Publishers, 904–910.

[Mohraz, 1997] Mohraz, K. (1997). Parallel simulation of pulse-coded neural networks. *Proc. Int. Association for Mathematics and Computers in Simulation (IMACS) World Congress 1997 on Scientific Computation, Modeling and Applied Mathematics*.

[Ramacher et al., 1991] Ramacher, U. Beichter, L., and Brüls, N. (1991). Architecture of a general purpose neural signal processor. *Proc. Int. Joint Conf. on Neural Networks 1991 (IJCNN'91)*, IEEE Service Center, I:443–446.

[Reitböck et al., 1993] Reitböck, H. J., Stöcker, M., and Hahn, C. (1993). Object separation in dynamic neural networks. *Proc. Int. Conf. on Neural Networks 1993 (ICNN'93)*, IEEE Service Center, II: 638–641.

[Roth et al., 1995] Roth, U., Jahnke, A., and Klar, H. (1995). Hardware requirements for spike-processing neural networks. *Proc. Int. Work-Conf. on Artificial and Natural Neural Networks 1995 (IWANN'95)*, J. Mira, F. Sandoval, eds., Springer-Verlag, 720–727.

[Roth et al., 1997] Roth, U., Eckardt, F., Jahnke, A., and Klar, H. (1997). Efficient on-line computation of connectivity: Architecture of the connection unit of NESPINN. *Proc. MicroNeuro'97*, H. Klar, A. König, U. Ramacher, eds., University of Technology Dresden, 31–39.

[Zell et al., 1993] Zell, A., Huebner, R. et al. (1993). SNNS: An efficient simulator for neural nets. *Proc. Int. Workshop on Modeling, Analysis and Simulation of Computer and Telecommunication Systems 1993 (MASCOTS'93)*, H. Schwetmann, ed., Society for Computer Simulation, 17–20.

Part III

Design and Analysis of Pulsed Neural Systems

10 Populations of Spiking Neurons

Wulfram Gerstner

10.1 Introduction

In standard neural network theory, neurons are described in terms of mean firing rates. The analog input variable I is mapped via a nonlinear gain function g to an analog output variable $\nu = g(I)$ which may be interpreted as the mean firing rate. If the input consists of output rates ν_j of other neurons weighted by a factor w_{ij}, we arrive at the standard formula

$$\nu_i = g(\sum_j w_{ij}\, \nu_j) \qquad (10.1)$$

which is the starting point of most neural network theories.

As we have seen in Chapter 1, the firing rate defined by a temporal average over many spikes of a single neuron is a concept which works well if the input is constant or changes on a time scale which is slow with respect to the size of the temporal averaging window. Sensory input in a real-world scenario, however, is never constant. Moreover reaction times are often short which indicates that neurons do not have the time for temporal averaging.

There is, however, another interpretation of 'rate' which may be used even for fast changing input. Instead of an average over time, rate may be defined as an average over a population of neurons with identical (or at least similar) properties. To distinguish this concept clearly from the temporally averaged mean firing rate, we refer to the population averaged rate as the population activity $A(t)$; cf. Chapter 1.

In this chapter we will focus on the properties of such a population of neurons. All neurons are identical, receive the same input $I(t)$ and are mutually coupled by synapses of uniform strength; cf. Figure 10.1.

Can we write down a dynamic equation in continuous time that describes the evolution of the population activity? This problem comes up in various models and has been studied by several researchers [Wilson and Cowan, 1972, 1973; Amari, 1974; Gerstner and van Hemmen, 1992, 1993, 1994; Bauer and Pawelzik, 1993; Gerstner, 1995; Pinto et al., 1996; Senn et al., 1996; Eggert and van Hemmen, 1997]. A frequently adopted solution is to replace (10.1) by a differential equation

$$\tau \frac{dA_i(t)}{dt} = -A_i(t) + g\left(\sum_j \int_0^\infty \epsilon_{ij}(s)\, A_j(t-s)\, ds\right) \qquad (10.2)$$

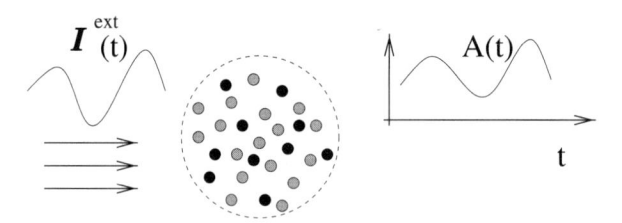

Figure 10.1. Population of neurons (schematic). All neurons receive the same input $I^{\text{ext}}(t)$ (left) which results in a time dependent population activity $A(t)$ (right).

where we have supposed that there are different populations A_i which are coupled to each other with a delay-kernel ϵ_{ij}; e.g., [Wilson and Cowan, 1972, Cohen and Grossberg, 1983, Hopfield, 1984, Pinto et al., 1996]. For stationary problems, the left-hand side of (10.2) vanishes and, with the replacement $A_i \longrightarrow \nu_i$; $\int \epsilon_{ij}(s)ds \longrightarrow w_{ij}$ we are back to (10.1).

The problem with (10.2) is that it introduces a time constant τ which is basically *ad hoc*. If we perform simulations of (10.2), what value should we take for τ?. It has been argued that τ is the membrane time constant of the neurons, an assertion which is correct in the limit of slowly changing activities only. The activity is, however, not always slowly changing. It has been shown previously that the population activity can react quasi instantaneously to abrupt changes in the input [Tsodyks and Sejnowski, 1995, van Vreeswijk and Sompolinsky, 1996]. Transients in networks of non-leaky integrate-and-fire neurons can be very short [Hopfield and Herz, 1995]. Moreover, homogeneous networks may be in an oscillatory state where all neurons fire exactly at the same time; e.g., [Mirollo and Stogatz, 1990; Gerstner and van Hemmen, 1993; Gerstner et al., 1996; Somers and Kopell, 1993; van Vreeswijk et al., 1994; Hansel, 1995; Terman and Wang, 1995]. In this case, the population activity changes rapidly between zero and a very high activity. These phenomena are inconsistent with a differential equation of the form (10.2).

In this chapter, we will analyze the population dynamics and derive a dynamic equation which is exact in the limit of a large number of neurons. The relevant equation is an integral equation with interesting properties. We focus on three special cases and discuss them in turn.

(i) How does a population of neurons react to a fast change in the input? We show that, during the initial phase of the transient, the population activity reacts instantaneously [Tsodyks and Sejnowski, 1995]. The end of the transient is, on the other hand, rather slow and indeed characterized by the membrane constant τ.

(ii) What are the conditions for exact synchrony in the firing of all neurons? We show that neurons are 'locked' together, if firing occurs while the postsynaptic potential is rising [Gerstner et al., 1996].

(iii) What are the conditions to make the neurons fire in an optimally asynchronous manner? We discuss why, without noise, asynchronous firing is almost always unstable [Abbott and van Vreeswijk, 1993; Gerstner and van Hemmen, 1993; Gerstner, 1995]. We show that with a proper choice of the delays and a sufficient amount of noise the state of asynchronous firing can be stabilized [Gerstner and van Hemmen, 1994; Gerstner, 1998].

The integral equation of the dynamics allows us to discuss all of the above three phenomena from a unified point of view.

Studies of population activity have a fairly long history. Wilson and Cowan [Wilson and Cowan, 1972] described the population activity by an integral equation which they subsequently approximated by a differential equation similar to (10.2). Other researchers have developed population equations which are formulated as maps for homogeneous [Gerstner and van Hemmen, 1992; Bauer and Pawelzik, 1993] or inhomogeneous populations [Senn et al., 1996]. In this chapter we review the population equations in *continuous* time developed in detail in [Gerstner and van Hemmen, 1992, 1994; Gerstner, 1995]. Some of the arguments follow closely the text of [Gerstner, 1998].

10.2 Model

Our discussion starts from the spike response model, our generic neuron model introduced in Chapter 1. We consider the variant of a neuron with short-term memory, Section 1.2.1., Equation (1.16), and allow for noise in the reset; cf. Section 1.2.3.3. Equation (1.55). For the sake of convenience, we recall the neuronal equation. A neuron i fires if its membrane potential ("state variable") u_i hits the threshold ϑ. The membrane potential is of the form

$$u_i(t) = \eta(t - \hat{t}_i) + h(t) \tag{10.3}$$

where $\hat{t}_i$ is the most recent firing time of neuron i, the kernel $\eta(s)$ is a (negative) contribution due to refractoriness and

$$h(t) = \sum_{j \in \Gamma_i} \sum_{t_j^{(f)} \in \mathcal{F}_j} w_{ij} \epsilon(t - t_j^{(f)}) + J^{\text{ext}} \int_0^\infty \tilde{\epsilon}(s) I^{\text{ext}}(t-s) ds \tag{10.4}$$

is the postsynaptic potential caused by firings $t_j^{(f)}$ of presynaptic neurons $j \in \Gamma_i$ or by external input $I^{\text{ext}}(t)$.

Since we are interested in a homogeneous population of neurons, the kernels η, ϵ, and $\tilde{\epsilon}$ have no indices i, j and all neurons receive the same input $I^{\text{ext}}(t)$. Moreover, the interaction strength between the neurons is uniform

$$w_{ij} = \frac{J_0}{N} \tag{10.5}$$

where J_0 is a parameter. The interaction strength scales with one over the number N of neurons so that the total input remains finite in the limit of $N \to \infty$.

The theory we are going to discuss is valid for arbitrary response kernels ϵ. For simulations of the model, we usually take a simple response kernel with a small number of parameters

$$\epsilon(s) = \begin{cases} 0 & \text{for } s < \Delta^{\text{ax}} \\ \frac{s - \Delta^{\text{ax}}}{\tau^2} \exp\left(-\frac{s - \Delta^{\text{ax}}}{\tau}\right) & \text{for } s \geq \Delta^{\text{ax}} \end{cases} \tag{10.6}$$

Here Δ^{ax} is the axonal delay and τ is a membrane time constant. The normalization is $\int \epsilon(s)ds = 1$ as desired. For the external input we take in the simulations

$$\tilde{\epsilon}(s) = \frac{1}{\tau} \exp\left(-\frac{s}{\tau}\right) \mathcal{H}(s) \qquad (10.7)$$

with the same time constant τ as in (10.6). As always, $\mathcal{H}(s)$ is the Heaviside step function with $\mathcal{H}(s) = 0$ for $s \leq 0$ and $\mathcal{H}(s) = 1$ for $s > 0$.

We mentioned already that we allow for noise in the reset. Specifically, we consider a refractory kernel

$$\eta(s) = \begin{cases} 0 & \text{for } s \leq 0 \\ -\eta_0 \exp(r/\tau) \exp(-s/\tau) & \text{for } s > 0 \end{cases} \qquad (10.8)$$

where r is a random variable with zero mean. After each spike, a new value of r is drawn randomly from a Gaussian distribution $\mathcal{G}_\sigma(r)$ with variance $\sigma \ll \tau$. In the language of the integrate-and-fire neuron, we can describe the effect of r as a stochastic component in the value of the reset potential; cf. Chapter 1, Section 1.2.3. In the language of the Spike Response Model, we may say that a value of $r \neq 0$ shifts the response kernel horizontally along the time axis.

This is seen most easily in the following scenario. Let us consider a single neuron with constant external input I_0 and $\vartheta > 0$. There is no input from other neurons ($J_0 = 0$). After some transient the postsynaptic potential is $h_0 = J^{\text{ext}} I_0$ where, as always, we have assumed a normalization $\int \tilde{\epsilon}(s)ds = 1$. Given a constant input potential $h_0 > \vartheta$, the neuron fires regularly with some period T_0. For neurons with short memory, we calculate the period from (10.3) and the threshold condition $u(t) = \vartheta$. This yields

$$\eta(T_0) = \vartheta - h_0 \qquad (10.9)$$

and with (10.8)

$$T_0 = \tau \ln \frac{\eta_0}{h_0 - \vartheta} \qquad \text{for } h_0 > \vartheta . \qquad (10.10)$$

What happens in the presence of noise? The period T_r for a given value of r is again found from the threshold condition $\eta(T_r) = \vartheta - h_0$. We use (10.8) and find

$$T_r = T_0 + r . \qquad (10.11)$$

Thus the Gaussian distribution $\mathcal{G}_\sigma(r)$ of the noise variable r maps directly to a Gaussian distribution of the intervals around the mean T_0.

In order to formalize this idea, we use the notation introduced in Chapter 1, Section 1.2.3. We want to calculate the probability density $P_{h_0}(t|\hat{t})$ that the next spike occurs at time t given that the last spike was at $\hat{t}$ and the external input potential is h_0. From (10.11) we get the answer

$$P_{h_0}(t|\hat{t}) = \mathcal{G}_\sigma(t - \hat{t} - T_0) \qquad (10.12)$$

where T_0 is the interval in the noiseless case. In particular, for noiseless neurons ($\sigma \to 0$), the right-hand side of (10.12) reduces to a Dirac δ-function,

$$\lim_{\sigma \to 0} P_{h_0}(t \,|\, \hat{t}) = \delta(t - \hat{t} - T_0) \tag{10.13}$$

as it should be. We will make repeated use of (10.12) and (10.13) throughout this chapter.

As noted in chapter 1, the Spike Response Model with the specific kernels (10.8) and (10.6), is closely related to the integrate-and-fire model. Specifically, the response kernel (10.6) corresponds to a synaptic time constant $\tau_s = \tau_m = \tau$ (where τ_m is the membrane time constant) and an additional axonal transmission delay Δ^{ax}. To make the models fully equivalent, we should consider a sum over the η's in order to include effects of earlier spikes, but here we restrict ourselves to the short-term memory approximation. For the numerical analysis later on, we have adjusted the threshold ϑ so that the interval T_0 is exactly $T_0 = 2\tau$. In this case, $e^{-T/\tau} \ll 1$ and therefore $\eta(nT_0) \ll \eta(T_0)$, so that the effect of the earlier spikes can indeed be neglected.

10.3 Population Activity Equation

We consider a homogeneous and fully connected network of spiking neurons in the limit of $N \to \infty$. We aim for a dynamic equation which describes the evolution of the population activity over time. Let us recall the definition of the population activity from chapter 1, Section 1.1.2.3. In any short interval Δt, we count the total number of spikes n_{act} emitted by all neurons in the population

$$n_{\mathrm{act}}(t) = \sum_{i=1}^{N} \sum_{t_i^{(f)} \in \mathcal{F}_i} \int_{t-\Delta t}^{t} \delta(t' - t_i^{(f)}) \, dt' . \tag{10.14}$$

The population activity may formally be defined as

$$A(t) = \lim_{N \to \infty} \lim_{\Delta t \to 0} \frac{1}{\Delta t} \left[\frac{n_{\mathrm{act}}(t)}{N} \right] . \tag{10.15}$$

A different way of writing this is

$$A(t) \, dt = \lim_{N \to \infty} \frac{1}{N} \sum_{i=1}^{N} \delta(t - t_i^{(f)}) \, dt . \tag{10.16}$$

10.3.1 Integral Equation for the Dynamics

The dynamics of the population activity is given by the integral equation

$$A(t) = \int_{-\infty}^{t} P_h(t \,|\, \hat{t}) \, A(\hat{t}) \, d\hat{t} . \tag{10.17}$$

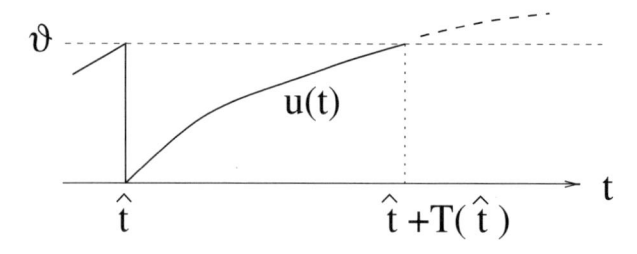

Figure 10.2. Threshold condition and definition of the inter-spike interval.

A detailed derivation is given in [Gerstner and van Hemmen, 1992, 1994; Gerstner, 1993, 1995]. Intuitively, (10.17) is easy to understand. The kernel $P_h(t\,|\,\hat{t})$ is the probability density that the next spike of a neuron which is under the influence of a potential $h(t)$ occurs at time t given that its last spike was at $\hat{t}$. The number of neurons which have fired at $\hat{t}$ is proportional to $A(\hat{t})$ and the integral runs over all times in the past.

To get a better understanding of (10.17), let us consider the noise-free case. The probability density reduces to a Dirac δ-function,

$$P_h(t\,|\,\hat{t}) = \delta[t - \hat{t} - T(\hat{t})] \qquad (10.18)$$

where $T(\hat{t})$ is the interspike interval given by the threshold condition

$$T(\hat{t}) = \min\{(t - \hat{t})\,|\,u(t) = \vartheta;\, t > \hat{t}\}\,. \qquad (10.19)$$

In words, the interval T is given by the first threshold crossing after the spike at $\hat{t}$; cf. Figure 10.2.

We recall that $u(t) = \eta(t - \hat{t}) + h(t)$ is the membrane potential defined in (10.3) with h defined in (10.4). Making use of Dirac's δ-function notation, we can rewrite (10.4) in the form

$$h(t) = J_0 \int_0^\infty \epsilon(s) \left[\frac{1}{N} \sum_{j=1}^N \sum_{t_j^{(f)} \in \mathcal{F}_j} \delta(t - t_j^{(f)} - s) \right] ds + \qquad (10.20)$$

$$J^{\text{ext}} \int_0^\infty \tilde{\epsilon}(s) I^{\text{ext}}(t - s)\, ds$$

where we have used $w_{ij} = J_0/N$. In the limit of $N \to \infty$, the term in the square brackets reduces to the population activity A defined in (10.16). Thus, in the limit $N \to \infty$, (10.20) becomes

$$h(t) = J_0 \int_0^\infty \epsilon(s)\, A(t - s)\, ds + J^{\text{ext}} \int_0^\infty \tilde{\epsilon}(s)\, I^{\text{ext}}(t - s)\, ds\,. \qquad (10.21)$$

The equation (10.17) with the kernel $P_h(t\,|\,\hat{t})$ calculated for the potential h given by (10.21) defines the dynamics in a homogeneous network of spiking neurons with short-term memory. We remark that even though (10.17) looks linear, it is in fact a highly non-linear equation because the kernel $P_h(t\,|\,\hat{t})$ depends on h and h in turn depends again on the activity via (10.21).

A generalization of (10.17) and (10.21) to several populations is possible. As a short detour, let us consider a network which is subdivided into several pools. Within each pool, neurons are homogeneous. The activity of a pool m is $A_m(t)$. Neurons within each pool are connected with strength $w_{mm} = J_{mm}/N_m$ where N_m is the number of neurons in pool m. A neuron in pool m receives input from all neuron in pool n with strength $w_{mn} = J_{mn}/N_n$. The total input potential to pool m is then given by a straightforward generalization of (10.21) [Gerstner, 1995]

$$h_m(t) = \sum_n J_{mn} \int_0^\infty \epsilon(s) A_n(t-s) \, ds \,. \tag{10.22}$$

For the sake of simplicity we have suppressed the term accounting for external input. The dynamic equation (10.17) remains unchanged but has to be applied to each pool separately.

In the following sections we concentrate on the dynamics of a single pool with homogeneous internal and external coupling J_0 and J^{ext}, respectively.

10.3.2 Normalization

A final remark concerns the proper normalization of the activity. It is clear that (10.17) is invariant under a rescaling of the activity $A \longrightarrow cA$ with some constant c. Thus the variable A in (10.17) is not necessarily the activity defined in (10.15).

In order to find the correct normalization we use the following consideration [Gerstner, 1995]. We have defined $P_h(t\,|\,\hat{t})$ as the probability density that a neuron which has fired at $\hat{t}$ and is under the influence of an input h fires again at t. The integral $\int_{\hat{t}}^t P_h(s\,|\,\hat{t})\,ds$ gives therefore the probability that it fires its next spike sometime between $\hat{t}$ and t. Consequently, we can define a survival probability

$$S_h(t\,|\,\hat{t}) = 1 - \int_{\hat{t}}^t P_h(s\,|\,\hat{t})\,ds\,, \tag{10.23}$$

i.e., the probability that a neuron which is under the influence of h and has fired its last spike at $\hat{t}$ 'survives' without firing up to time t.

Let us now return to our homogeneous network and consider the state at time t. The portion of neurons which have fired their *last* spike between t_0 and t is

$$\int_{t_0}^t S_h(t\,|\,\hat{t})\,A(\hat{t})\,d\hat{t}\,. \tag{10.24}$$

In a network which is not completely noise free, all neurons have fired at *some* point in the past, thus

$$\int_{-\infty}^t S_h(t\,|\,\hat{t})\,A(\hat{t})\,d\hat{t} = 1\,, \tag{10.25}$$

which must hold at any arbitrary time t. (10.25) is the desired normalization condition [Gerstner, 1995]. It is sufficient to impose (10.25) at one instant $\tilde{t}$. The dynamics (10.17) automatically assures that the normalization remains correct for all times $t > \tilde{t}$. In fact, taking the derivative of (10.25) yields the activity dynamics (10.17).

In the following sections the population equations (10.17) and (10.25) are analyzed for various scenarios.

10.4 Noise-Free Population Dynamics

We study (10.17) in the noiseless case. As mentioned above, the integration kernel $P_h(t \,|\, \hat{t})$ reduces for noiseless neurons to a δ-function,

$$A(t) = \int_{-\infty}^{t} \delta(t - \hat{t} - T(\hat{t})) \, A(\hat{t}) \, d\hat{t}. \tag{10.26}$$

Here $T(\hat{t})$ is the interval given implicitly by the threshold condition (10.19). When performing the integration we have to take the dependence of T upon $\hat{t}$ into account. If we do so, we find

$$A(t) = k(t) \, A(t - T) \tag{10.27}$$

where T is the interval calculated from (10.19). The scaling factor k on the right-hand side of (10.27) is given by [Gerstner, 1998]

$$k(t) = \left[1 + \frac{dT}{d\hat{t}}\right]^{-1} = 1 + \frac{h'(t)}{\eta'(T)}. \tag{10.28}$$

As usual, the primes on h and η denote a temporal derivative.

The meaning of the factor k is illustrated in Figure 10.3. A neuron which has fired at $\hat{t}$ will fire again at $t = \hat{t} + T(\hat{t})$. Another neuron which has fired slightly later at $\hat{t} + \delta t'$ fires its next spike at $t + \delta t$. If the input potential is constant between t and $t + \delta t$, then $\delta t = \delta t'$. If, however, h increases between t and $t + \delta t$ as is the case in Figure 10.3, then the firing time difference is reduced.

The compression of firing time differences is directly related to an increase in the activity A. To see this, we note that all neurons which fire between $\hat{t}$ and $\hat{t} + \delta t'$, must fire again between t and $t + \delta t$. This is due to the fact that the network is homogeneous and the mapping $\hat{t} \to t = \hat{t} + T(\hat{t})$ is monotonous. If firing time differences are compressed, the population activity increases.

Let us now return to Equation (10.28). For a standard integrate-and-fire type neuron, the kernel η has slope $\eta'(s) > 0$ for all $s > 0$; cf. Equation (10.8). An input with $h' > 0$ implies then, because of (10.27), an increase of the activity: $k > 1 \implies A(t) > A(t - T)$. Similarly, $h' < 0$ causes a decrease of the activity ($k < 1$). This is a rather general property of the noise-free equations which will be exploited in the following two sections.

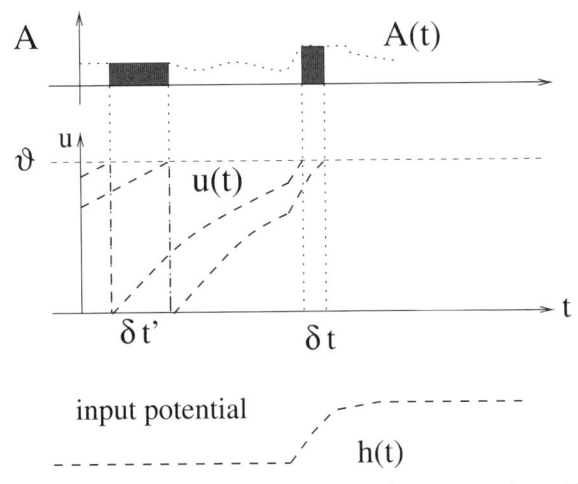

Figure 10.3. A change in the input potential h with positive slope $h' > 0$ (bottom trace) shifts neuronal firing times closer together (middle trace). As a result, the activity $A(t)$ is higher at $t = \hat{t} + T(\hat{t})$ than it was at time $\hat{t}$. Taken from [Gerstner, 1998].

10.5 Locking

As a first application of the population equations (10.17), let us reconsider, from the point of view of population dynamics, the 'locking theorem' developed in Gerstner et al. [Gerstner et al., 1996].

The question we are going to study is the following. We consider a homogeneous network with constant external input I_0. What are typical states? If we perform simulations of the neuron model, we find two extreme situations. The first one is that, after some time, the neurons all fire exactly in synchrony. This is called an oscillatory state and the phenomenon of firing together is called locking. The activity in this case exhibits a large-amplitude oscillation; cf. Figure 10.4.

The other extreme situation is that of a network where neuronal firing is maximally asynchronous so that the population activity is, apart from minor fluctuations, constant. We call this a state of asynchronous firing; see Section 10.7.

The question now is the following. If we know the parameters of the neurons and the neuronal couplings, can we predict whether the system will end up in a synchronous 'locked' state or whether it will end up in an asynchronous state? More precisely, what are the conditions on the parameters for existence and stability for a locked state? This is the question which we will address in this section. The analysis of the asynchronous state which is slightly more complicated is delayed to Section 10.7.

Before we start we note that the situation with constant external input is equivalent to a network without input but slightly different threshold. After some initial transient the external input gives a constant contribution $h^{\text{ext}} = J^{\text{ext}} I_0$ to the membrane potential. We can include this part in the threshold by the replacement $\vartheta - h^{\text{ext}} \longrightarrow \vartheta$ and treat the network as having no external input.

270   10. Populations of Spiking Neurons

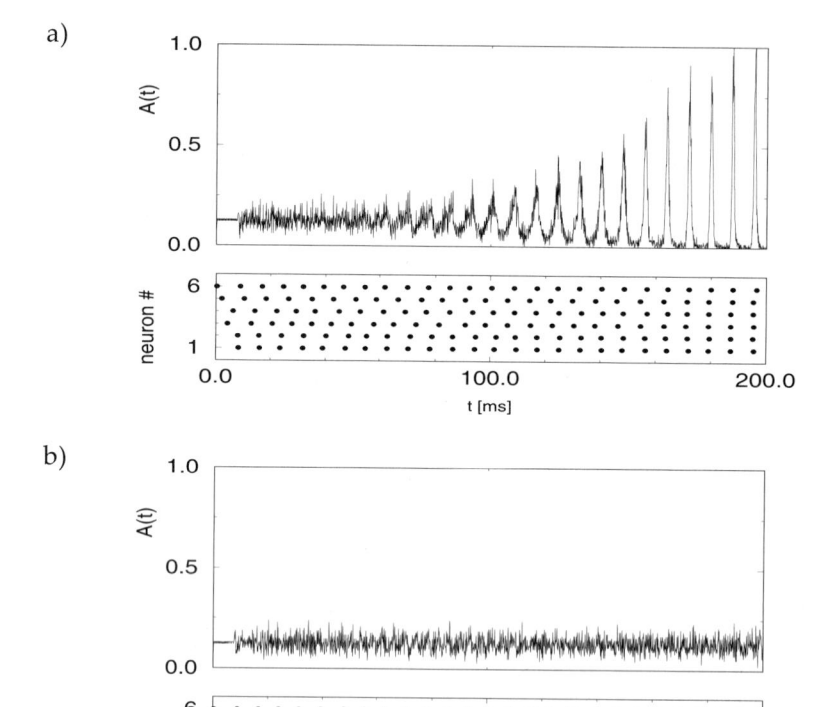

Figure 10.4. Two typical networks states: Oscillations (a) or asynchronous firing (b). In both cases the upper graph shows the networks activity $A(t)$ and the lower graph the spike trains of 6 neurons in the network. Each spike is denoted by a black dot. The initialization of the network occurs during the first 8 ms; afterwards the system runs freely without external input. Simulation parameters: network of 1000 neurons with $\tau = 4$ ms, $\vartheta = -0.01$, $J_0 = 1$ ms, $\sigma = 0.5$ ms. Delay $\Delta^{\text{ax}} = 7$ ms in (a) and 3 ms in (b).

10.5.1 Locking Condition

Our considerations will focus on locking in populations of noiseless neurons. In order to analyze the stability of oscillatory states as in Figure 10.4a, we start from the noise-free dynamic equations (10.27). We assume that the network is already very close to perfect synchronization and fires nearly regularly with period T. In order to keep the arguments transparent, let us assume that the population activity for times $t < T/2$ can be approximated by a sequence of square pulses

$$A(t) = \sum_{n=-m}^{0} \frac{1}{2\delta^n} \mathcal{H}(t - nT + \delta^n) \, \mathcal{H}(nT + \delta^n - t), \quad (10.29)$$

where m is some small integer, say $m = 3$, and $\mathcal{H}(.)$ denotes the Heaviside step function with $\mathcal{H}(s) = 1$ for $s > 0$ and $\mathcal{H}(s) = 0$ for $s \leq 0$. The

10.5 Locking

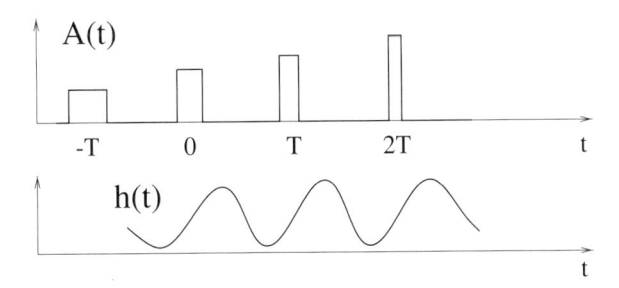

Figure 10.5. A sequence of square activity pulses contracts to δ-pulses, if firing occurs always when the input potential h is rising (schematic).

parameters δ^n with index n are assumed to be small, i.e., $\delta^n \ll T$ where T is the period.

Equation (10.29) is an 'Ansatz' which is ad hoc. We now have to check whether (10.29) is consistent with the noise-free population dynamics (10.27). More precisely, we ask the following question; cf. Figure 10.5. Is there some period T and some sequence δ^n for $n = -m, -m + 1, \ldots, 0, 1, 2, \ldots$ so that the sequence of square pulses described by (10.29) continues for $t > T/2$? We are going to determine T and the sequence δ^n self-consistently. If we find $\delta^n \to 0$ for $n \to \infty$, then the square pulses contract to δ-functions and we say that a synchronous T-periodic oscillation is a stable solution.

To proceed we have to determine the potential $h(t)$. From the derivative of h we can calculate the factor k given by (10.28). The period T is found from the threshold condition $\vartheta = \eta(T) + h(t)$. Let us see how this works.

To get h, we put (10.29) in (10.21). Under the condition that $\delta^n \ll T$, we can easily perform the integration. To first order in δ^n we find

$$h(t) = \sum_{n=0}^{n_{\max}} J_0\, \epsilon(t + nT) + \mathcal{O}\left[(\delta^n)^2\right] \qquad (10.30)$$

The sum runs over all pulses back in the past. Since $\epsilon(s)$ decays off quickly for $s \gg T$, it is usually sufficient to keep only a finite number of terms, e.g., $n_{\max} = 1$ or 2.

As the next step we determine the period T. To do so, we consider a neuron in the *center* of the square pulse which has fired its last spike at $\hat{t} = 0$. Since we consider noiseless neurons the relative order of firing the neurons can not change. To make the Ansatz (10.29) consistent, the next spike of this neuron must therefore occur at $t = T$, viz. in the center of the next square pulse. We use $\hat{t} = 0$ in the threshold condition (10.19) which yields

$$T = \min\left\{ t \mid \eta(t) + J_0 \sum_{n=0}^{n_{\max}} \epsilon(t + nT) = \vartheta \right\}. \qquad (10.31)$$

If a synchronized solution exists, (10.31) defines the period.

We now return to Equations (10.27) and (10.28). On the right-hand side of

272   10. Populations of Spiking Neurons

(10.28), we need the derivative

$$h'(t) = J_0 \sum_{n=0}^{n_{\max}} \epsilon'(t + nT). \quad (10.32)$$

We are interested to find out whether the amplitude of the square pulse increases or decreases over time. According to (10.27), the new value of the activity at time $t = T$ is the old value multiplied by k. Thus for $k > 1$ we have an increase, for $k < 1$ a decrease. With the kernel η given by (10.8), we have $\eta'(T) > 0$ whatever T. We therefore see immediately from (10.29) that for $h'(T) > 0$, we have $k > 1$ and the amplitude of the square pulse increases. From (10.32) and (10.27) we have the result

$$h'(T) = J_0 \sum_{n=1}^{n_{\max}+1} \epsilon'(nT) > 0 \quad \Longrightarrow \quad A(T) > A(0) \quad (10.33)$$

which is the essence of the locking theorem [Gerstner et al., 1996].

An increase in the amplitude should correspond to a compression of the width of the pulse. To check that this is indeed the case, let us consider one of the 'corner neurons' which has fired at $t = \pm\delta^0$. Its input potential is given by (10.30). The next spike occurs at $t = T \pm \delta^1$ where T is the period and δ^1 is determined now. We recall the threshold condition for the neuron in the center of the pulse

$$\eta(T) + h(T) = \vartheta. \quad (10.34)$$

For the corner neuron we have

$$\eta\left(T \pm (\delta^1 - \delta^0)\right) + h(T \pm \delta^1) = \vartheta. \quad (10.35)$$

An expansion to first oder in δ^1 yields

$$\delta^1 = \left[1 + \frac{h'(T)}{\eta'(T)}\right]^{-1} \delta^0. \quad (10.36)$$

Thus, for $h'(T) > 0$ the width of the square pulse contracts as expected. Moreover the pulse remains normalized since

$$\delta^1 = \frac{1}{k(T)} \delta^0$$
$$A(T) = k(T) A(0) \quad (10.37)$$

with $k(T) = 1 + h'(T)/\eta'(T)$. By iteration of the argument for $t = nT$ with $n = 2, 3, 4, \ldots$ we see that the sequence δ^n converges to zero and the square pulses approach a Dirac δ-pulse under the condition that $h'(T) = \sum_n \epsilon'(nT) > 0$. In words, the T-periodic synchronized solution with T given by (10.31) is stable, if the postsynaptic potential at the moment of firing is rising [Gerstner et al., 1996]. Equation (10.36) is exactly the locking equation for neurons with short memory. Generalizations to neurons with long memory (where we have to sum over several η-kernels) are straightforward but involve some more indices [Gerstner et al., 1996]. With an additional amount of effort an extension from homogeneous to weakly inhomogeneous networks is also possible [Gerstner et al., 1993, Chow, 1998]. In the following subsection we give a graphical interpretation of the locking theorem.

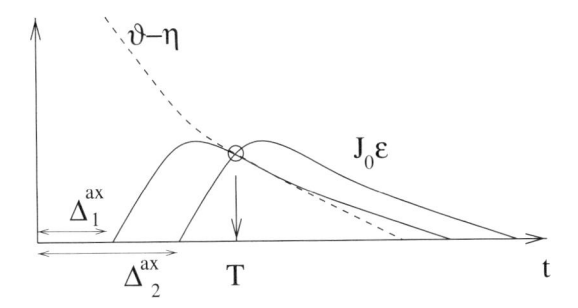

Figure 10.6. The period T of a synchronous oscillation is found from the first intersection between the total postsynaptic potential $J_0 \epsilon(t)$ and the dynamic threshold $\vartheta - \eta(t)$. All neurons have fired synchronously at $t = 0$ and fire again $t = T$. Two different cases are shown: case 1 with short axonal delays Δ_1^{ax} and case 2 with a longer transmission delay Δ_2^{ax}. The synchronous solution is stable if the intersection occurs where ϵ' is positive as in case 2 and is unstable in case 1. Adapted from [Gerstner et al., 1996].

10.5.2 Graphical Interpretation

In order to get a better intuitive understanding of the locking principle, let us consider a simplified scenario. We assume that all neurons have fired synchronously at $t = 0$. Let us suppose that the postsynaptic potential is rather short so that only one term in the sum on the right-hand side of (10.30) contributes, viz.,

$$h(t) = J_0 \, \epsilon(t) \tag{10.38}$$

In this case the threshold condition (10.31) may be written as

$$T = \min \{ t \, | \, J_0 \, \epsilon(t) = \vartheta - \eta(t) \} \,. \tag{10.39}$$

Equation (10.39) has a simple interpretation. The next spike occurs when the total postsynaptic potential caused by the spikes emitted at $t = 0$ surpasses the dynamic threshold $\vartheta - \eta$. Since all neurons have identical parameters and have fired synchronously at $t = 0$, the threshold condition (10.39) is the same for all neurons and they will therefore continue to fire synchronously. Therefore, we may say that a synchronous network state exists whenever (10.39) has a solution. The locking theorem furthermore tells us that this solution is stable if the firing occurs on the rising slope of the postsynaptic potential. In Figure 10.6 we see that, in case of excitatory interaction, this is possible when the axonal transmission delay is rather long. For shorter delay values, the intersection point is on the downward slope of $J_0 \epsilon$ and the synchronous solution is therefore unstable.

Since the derivation of the locking condition was rather general, we can apply our results not only to excitatory but also to inhibitory interaction. Obviously, to make the inhibitory neurons fire we need some external input I_0 which we take to be constant. It gives a contribution $h^{ext} = J^{ext} I_0$ to the membrane potential which we can either subtract from the threshold or else add to the postsynaptic potential. In Figure 10.7 we have chosen the latter possibility. We see that for inhibition with short or medium

274   10. Populations of Spiking Neurons

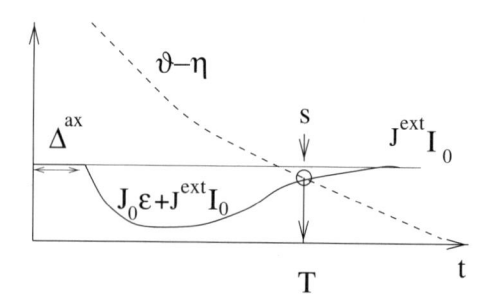

Figure 10.7. The locking argument applied to neurons with inhibitory interaction. The synchronized solution is stable since the intersection $J_0 \epsilon(t) + J^{ext} I_0 = \vartheta - \eta(t)$ occurs at a moment t when $\epsilon'(t) > 0$ (arrow marked 's'); taken from [Gerstner et al., 1996].

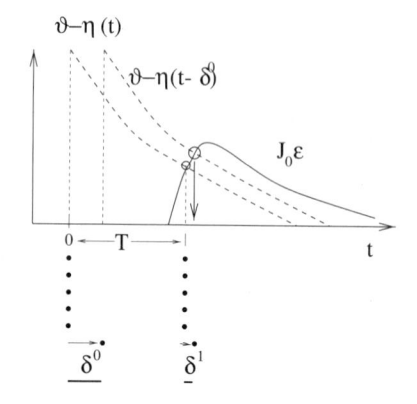

Figure 10.8. In the lower half of the figure we show schematically the spikes (marked by dots) of 6 neurons. All neurons have fired at $t = 0$ except the neuron in the bottom trace which is late by an amount δ^0. The synchonous neurons fire their next spike at time T; the late neuron becomes active at $T + \delta^1$. Note that $\delta^1 < \delta^0$ which shows that the synchronous oscillation is stable.

delays the intersection point occurs on the *rising* part of the postsynaptic potential (decreasing inhibition = increasing postsynaptic potential). The synchronous solution with period T is therefore stable.

Can we understand the condition on the slopes graphically? Let us focus on Figure 10.8. All neurons have fired synchronously at $t = 0$ except for one neuron which has fired late by an amount δ^0. The bulk of the neurons fires again at $t = T$ given by $J_0 \epsilon(T) = \vartheta - \eta(T)$. The threshold of the neuron which has fired late, however, comes down with a delay δ^0 with respect to the others. Graphically this is equivalent to shifting the curve $\vartheta - \eta$ by an amount δ^0 to the right. The intersection point between $\vartheta - \eta(t - \delta^0)$ and the potential $J_0 \epsilon(t)$ caused by the spikes of the other neurons gives the next firing time of the 'late' neuron. We see directly from Figure 10.8 that the shift δ^1 is reduced with respect to δ^0. Thus the neuron is pulled back into the collective oscillation. For $\epsilon' = 0$ we would have $\delta^1 \approx \delta^0$ and for $\epsilon' < 0$ the shift is even increased.

So far, we have always assumed that there was a finite transmission delay δ^{ax}. In the case of a fast rising postsynaptic potential with zero delay, the graphical construction is slightly more complicated. As soon as the neurons fire the spikes are felt by the other neurons. Apart from the spikes of the preceding cycle, we therefore have also to include the immediate effect of the spikes of the *same* cycle. The results are graphically shown in Figure 10.9. We consider the time course of the postsynaptic potential $h(t)$ and the dynamic threshold $\vartheta - \eta$ over several periods. Firings at $t = 0$, $t = T$, $t = 2T$ increase the dynamic threshold and at the same time the postsynaptic potential; cf. 10.9a. As in the preceding figure, we now assume that one of the neurons fires slightly out of tune with a time shift δ^0 which may be either positive or negative; cf. Figure 10.9b. If it fires early, we have to shift the curve $\vartheta - \eta$ to the left; if it fires late, we have to shift it to the right. We see from Figure 10.9b that for a neuron which has fired early, the next crossing is on the downward slope of the postsynaptic potential and the time shift is *increased*. For a neuron which fires late with respect to the others, the time shift is *decreased*. Thus, the synchronous solution is *locally unstable* for negative time shifts.

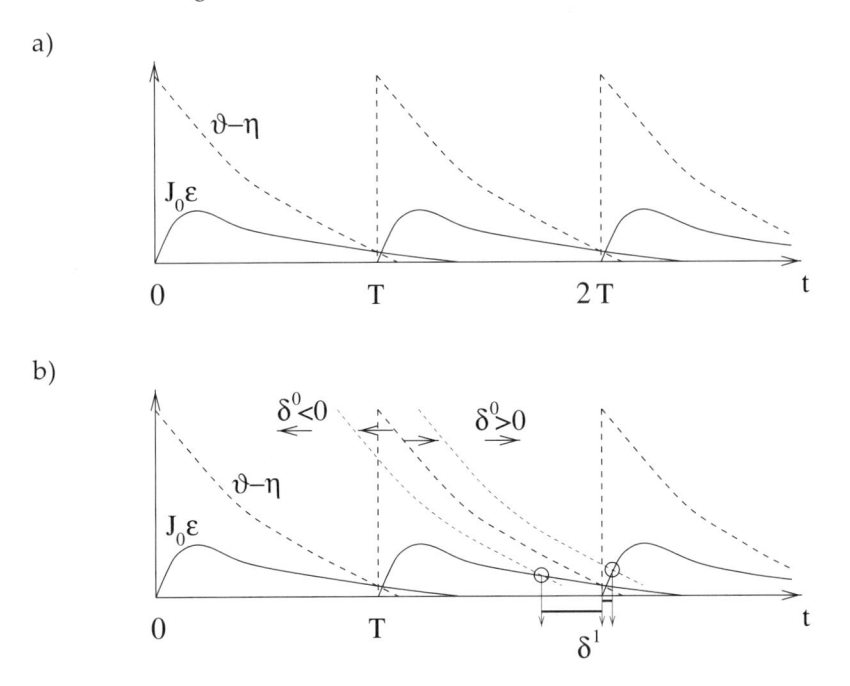

Figure 10.9. Excitatory interaction with zero delay. a) The neurons fire where the total postsynaptic potential $J_0\epsilon$ crosses the dynamic threshold $\vartheta - \eta$. The pattern repeats periodically with period T. b) For a neuron which has fired at time $t = T + \delta^0$ instead of $t = T$ the dynamic threshold is shifted by an amount δ^0 to the left (for $\delta^0 < 0$) or right (for $\delta^0 > 0$). For $\delta^0 < 0$ the time shift with respect to the synchronous firing of the other neurons increases from one cycle to the next ($|\delta^1| > |\delta^0|$). For a neuron which has fired late ($\delta^0 > 0$), the time shift is decreased ($|\delta^1| < |\delta^0|$) and it is therefore pulled back into the collective oscillation; taken from [Gerstner et al., 1996].

As shown by Mirollo and Strogatz [Mirollo and Strogatz, 1990], synchronized firing in a network with zero-delay coupling may nevertheless be *globally* stable. The reason is, that a neuron which has fired early, will fire even more early the next time and so on. After several firings, it has drifted away by nearly a full period and it now appears to be *late* with respect to the previous synchronous firing of the other neurons. As we have seen above, a neuron which fires late is then pulled back into the collective firing. The Mirollo-Strogatz model is reviewed in Chapter 11.

10.6 Transients

As a second application of the noise-free population dynamics, let us study the response of the population activity to a rapid change in the input. To keep the arguments as simple as possible, we consider an input which has a constant value I_0 for $t < t_0$ and changes then abruptly to a new value $I_0 + \Delta I$. Thus

$$I(t) = \begin{cases} I_0 & \text{for } t \leq t_0 \\ I_0 + \Delta I & \text{for } t > t_0 \end{cases}$$

How does a homogeneous population of neurons react to such a step current input? In this section we try to find an answer to the above question. The arguments follow directly those developped in [Gerstner, 1998].

In order to analyze the situation, let us suppose that for $t < t_0$ the network is in a state of *incoherent* firing. In other words, all neurons fire at the same mean firing rate, but their spikes are not synchronized. Rather the firing times are maximally spread out over time. Such a state has been called the 'splay phase' [Chow, 1998]. In the limit of $N \to \infty$, the population activity is then a constant $A(t) = A_0$. In Section 7 we will study the conditions under which a state of incoherent firing can be a stable state of the system. Here we just assume the we can set the parameters so that the network fires indeed asynchronously and with constant activity.

In order to keep the arguments simple, we assume that the neurons are not coupled to each other. For $t \leq t_0$ all neurons receive a constant input potential $h_0 = J^{\text{ext}} I_0$ since $\int \tilde{\epsilon}(s) ds = 1$. For $t > t_0$, the input potential changes due to the additional current ΔI. Thus

$$h(t) = \begin{cases} h_0 & \text{for } t \leq t_0 \\ h_0 + J^{\text{ext}} \Delta I \int_0^{t-t_0} \tilde{\epsilon}(s) ds & \text{for } t > t_0 \end{cases}$$

In the noiseless case, neurons which receive a constant input potential h_0 fire regularly with a period T_0 given by

$$\eta(T_0) = \vartheta - h_0. \tag{10.40}$$

The mean activity A_0 for $t < t_0$ is simply $A_0 = 1/T_0$. The reason is that, for a constant activity, averaging over time and averaging over the population must be the same. To see this consider a long measurement interval Δta. For $\Delta t \gg T_0$ the populations of $N \gg 1$ neurons will emit $n_{\text{act}} = N \Delta t / T_0$ spikes in the time Δt. Taking the limits $N \to \infty$ and $\Delta \to 0$ yields the activity $A_0 = 1/T_0$; cf. (10.15).

10.6 Transients

Let us now return to the population dynamics. We recall the formulas (10.27) and (10.28) for the noiseless case

$$A(t) = \left[1 + \frac{h'(t)}{\eta'(T)}\right] A(t - T) \qquad (10.41)$$

where T is implicitly given by the threshold condition (10.19). For $t < t_0$, the input potential is constant $h(t) = h_0$, thus $h' = 0$ and $T = T_0$. Equation (10.41) then yields $A(t) = A(t - T_0)$ as it should be for a constant activity A_0.

What happens for $t > t_0$? In order to use (10.41), we have to calculate the derivative $h'(t)$. We find from (10.40)

$$h'(t) = J^{\text{ext}} \Delta I \, \tilde{\epsilon}(t - t_0). \qquad (10.42)$$

If the change ΔI in the input current is small, we expect that the interspike interval T changes only slightly. In order to keep the arguments transparent, we make a zero order approximation and set $A(t - T) \approx A(t - T_0)$ and $\eta'(T) \approx \eta'(T_0)$. The population equation (10.41) then yields

$$A(t) = [1 + a \, \tilde{\epsilon}(t - t_0)] \, A(t - T_0) \qquad (10.43)$$

with a constant $a = J^{\text{ext}} \Delta I / \eta'(T_0)$.

Let us now concentrate on the initial phase of the transient $t_0 < t < t_0 + T_0$. For a t taken from that interval, we have $A(t - T_0) = A_0$ which simplifies the right-hand side of (10.43):

$$A(t) = A_0 + \Delta A \, \tilde{\epsilon}(t - t_0) \quad \text{for } t_0 < t < t_0 + T_0 \qquad (10.44)$$

with $\Delta A = a \, A_0$. Thus the shape of the initial transient reflects the time course $\tilde{\epsilon}$ of the postsynaptic potential caused by external input.

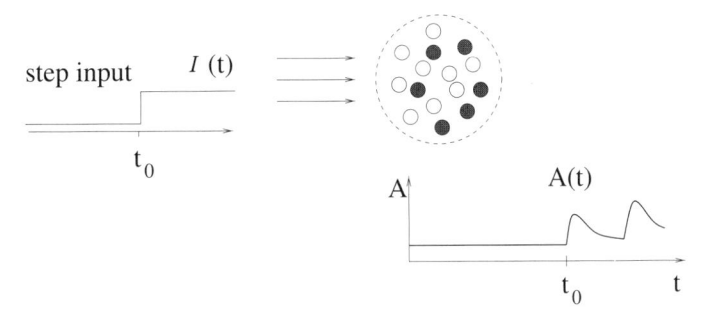

Figure 10.10. Response of a population of neurons to a step input (schematic).

To appreciate the consequences, let us consider the kernel (10.7). The response of the input *potential* to the step current (10.40) is given by (10.40) and has the typical low-pass filter characteristic $h(t) = h_0 + J^{\text{ext}} \Delta I \left[1 - \exp[-(t - t_0)/\tau]\right]$ for $t > t_0$. The population activity, however, reacts *instantaneously* to the step current. In our little example, the initial transient is

$$A(t) = A_0 + \Delta A \, \frac{1}{\tau} \exp\left(-\frac{t - t_0}{\tau}\right) \mathcal{H}(t - t_0) \quad \text{for } t_0 < t < t_0 + T_0 \quad (10.45)$$

278   10. Populations of Spiking Neurons

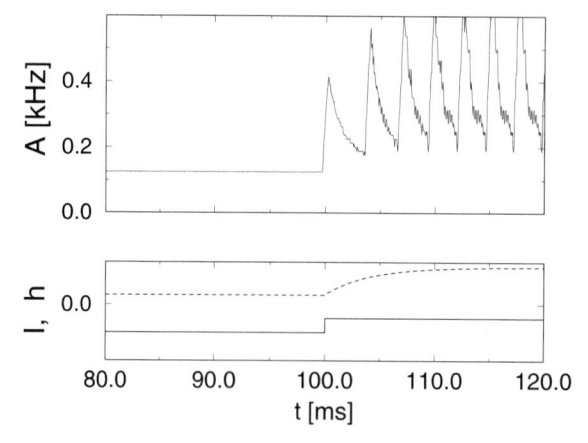

Figure 10.11. Simulation result. The population activity (top) in response to a step input current (bottom, solid line). The population activity reacts instantaneously to the step input, even though the input potential h (dashed line) caused by the step current responds only slowly. Simulation parameters: 100 neurons withoug interaction ($J_0 = 0$) in the limit of no noise $\sigma = 0$. In order to smooth out numerical artefacts the activity has been plotted after taking a running averag over 1 ms. Taken from [Gerstner, 1998].

where $\mathcal{H}(.)$ is the Heaviside step function. This implies in particular that the dynamic rate model (10.2) defined by a differential equation with time constant τ can not describe the initial phase of the transient. This is the precise meaning of the claim made in the introduction. A simulation in Figure 10.11 confirms the rapid initial response of the population.

Equation (10.45) is valid only during the initial phase of the transient. As soon as every neuron has fired once, the activity on the right-hand-side of (10.43) can no longer be considered constant. For $t > t_0 + T_0$ we must therefore include the first order correction $\Delta A \, \tilde{\epsilon}(t - t_0)$, for $t > t_0 + 2T_0$ a second order correction and so forth. The consequences are shown schematically in Figure 10.10. A simulation result is shown in Figure 10.11. The peaks in the activity repeat and slowly build up towards a periodic state. The peaks occur at times t_0, t_1, t_2 with $t_k \approx t_0 + kT$. We can estimate the sequence of peak values from the iteration

$$A(t_{k+1}) = A(t_k) \left[1 + \frac{h'(t_{k+1})}{\eta'(T_0)} \right]. \tag{10.46}$$

In our little example discussed above, we have $h' \propto \exp[-(t-t_0)/\tau]$, and the solution of (10.46) is therefore of the form

$$A(t_k) = A_{\text{fin}} \left[1 - \exp\left(-\frac{t_k - t_0}{\tau} \right) \right]. \tag{10.47}$$

Equation (10.47) shows that the sequence of peaks follows the same exponential time course as the input potential h. Similarly, the temporally *averaged* activity would follow an exponential time course. Taking a temporal averages does, of course, lead back to rate models. Our detailed approach outlined above shows, however, that the initial transient of the activity is much faster than that predicted from an exponential activity dependence.

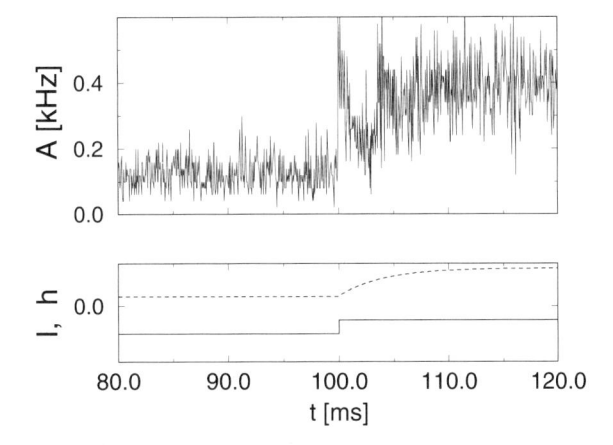

Figure 10.12. Simulation result. Same as in the previous figure but at a noise level of $\sigma = 1$. Taken from [Gerstner, 1998].

So far, we have considered noiseless neurons. In the presence of noise, subsequent pulses get smaller and broader and the network approaches a new incoherent state; cf. Fig 10.12. If, in addition, there is also some interaction $J_0 \neq 0$ between the neurons, then the value of the new stationary state is shifted. A particularly interesting state is inhibitory interaction $J = -1$. In this case the new value of the stationary activity for $t > t_0$ is only slightly higher than that for $t < t_0$. The fast transient with a sharp first peak is clearly visible and marks the moment of input switching. Fast switching has previously been seen in heterogeneous networks with balanced excitation and inhibition [Tsodyks and Sejnowski, 1997, van Vreeswijk and Sompolinsky, 1996]. Here it is demonstrated and analyzed for homogeneous networks.

Finally we may wonder whether we can understand fast switching intuitively. Before the abrupt change the input was stationary. For the theoretical analysis, we have assumed that the population was in a state of *incoherent* firing. For the simulations, parameters where chosen so that neurons fire asynchronously. Incoherent firing was defined as a state where neuronal firing times are spread out maximally. Thus some of the neurons fire, others are in the refractory period, again others approach the threshold. There is always a group of neuron whose potential is just below threshold. An increase in the input causes those neurons to fire immediately - and this accounts for the strong population response during the initial phase of the transient.

10.7 Incoherent Firing

We have seen in the preceding section that a population of neurons reacts instantaneously to a change in the input – given that the network is in a state of *incoherent* firing. What are the conditions for incoherent firing be a stable state of the network dynamics? This is the question we study in this subsection.

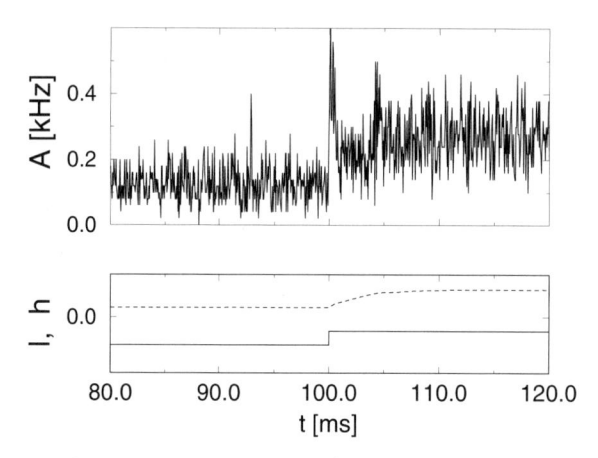

Figure 10.13. Simulation result. Same as in the previous figure but with inhibitory interaction ($J_0 = -1$); noise parameter $\sigma = 1$. Taken from [Gerstner, 1998].

We will proceed in three steps. First we want to show the *existence* of states of incoherent firing and calculate the value of the activity A_0. Second, we study the *stability* of incoherent firing. The stability analysis involves some lengthy calculations which can be found in subsection 2.7.2.1. and may be omitted by those readers who are not interested in the details. Finally, we apply the stability results to a specific model system and discuss the results. The text follows the arguments developed in [Gerstner, 1993, 1995, 1998].

10.7.1 Determination of the Activity

Incoherent firing may be defined as a macroscopic firing state with constant activity $A(t) = A_0$. In this subsection we want to calculate the value of A_0.

Before we start we note that in the case of constant activity A_0 and constant external input I_0, the total postsynaptic potential is also constant

$$h(t) = h_0 = J_0 A_0 + J^{\text{ext}} I_0, \tag{10.48}$$

where we have used the normalization $\int \epsilon(s) ds = 1 = \int \tilde{\epsilon}(s) ds$.

Let us focus on the noise-free situation first. Given a constant input potential h_0, the neurons in the population fire with a period T_0 given by

$$\eta(T_0) = \vartheta - h_0. \tag{10.49}$$

Intuitively we expect that, if all neurons fire incoherently and with the same period T_0, then the population activity should be

$$A_0 = \frac{1}{T_0}. \tag{10.50}$$

(10.50) relies on the general ideal that, in a situation where everything is constant, averaging over time (for a single neuron) should be the same as

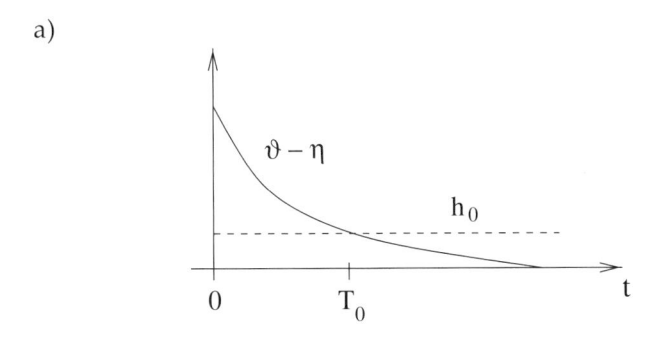

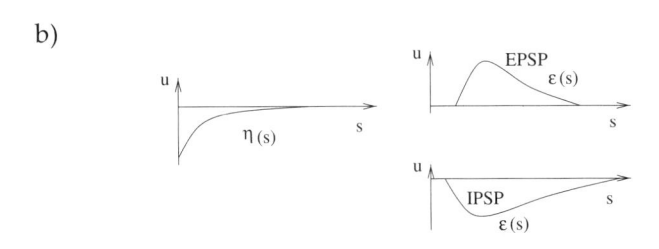

Figure 10.14. a) Determination of the interspike interval T_0 in case of incoherent firing. b) A plot of $1/T_0$ as a function of h_0 gives the gain function of the neuron (schematically).

averaging over a population of identical neurons. We will show in the following that, with the proper normalization defined in (10.25) our intuition and hence (10.50) are correct.

Moreover, the same consideration also holds in the noisy case. The population activity A_0 in an incoherent state must equal the mean firing rate ν,

$$A_0 = \nu = \frac{1}{\langle T \rangle} \quad (10.51)$$

where $\langle T \rangle$ is the mean interval length.

In order to show that (10.50) and (10.51) are correct, we start from the normalization (10.25). For constant input potential h_0, the survivor function $S_h(t\,|\,\hat{t})$ and the interval distribution $P_h(t\,|\,\hat{t})$ can not depend explicitly upon the absolute time, but only on the time difference $t - \hat{t}$. We set

$$\begin{aligned} S_0(s) &= S_{h_0}(\hat{t} + s\,|\,\hat{t}) \\ P_0(s) &= P_{h_0}(\hat{t} + s\,|\,\hat{t}) \end{aligned} \quad (10.52)$$

and from the definition of $S_h(t\,|\,\hat{t})$ in (10.23) we find

$$\frac{d}{ds} S_0(s) = -P_0(s). \quad (10.53)$$

The normalization (10.25) reduces to

$$1 = A_0 \int_0^\infty S_0(s)\,ds. \quad (10.54)$$

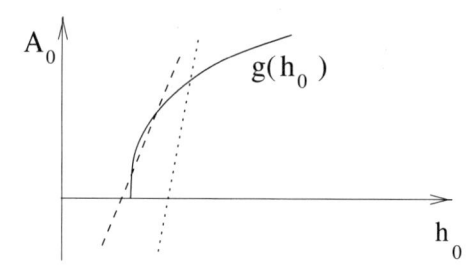

Figure 10.15. The intersection of the gain function $g(h_0)$ with the straight line $A_0 = [h_0 - J^{\text{ext}} I_0]/J_0$ gives the values of the activity A_0. Note that several solutions may coexist (dashed line).

Integrating (10.54) by parts yields

$$\frac{1}{A_0} = \int_0^\infty 1\, S_0(s)\, ds$$
$$= \int_0^\infty s\, P_0(s)\, ds \tag{10.55}$$

since $s S_0(s)$ vanishes for $s = 0$ and $s \to \infty$. The term on the right-hand side of (10.55) is the first moment of the interval distribution, hence the *mean interval*

$$\langle T \rangle = \int_0^\infty s\, P_0(s)\, ds\,. \tag{10.56}$$

Thus, as promised above, for a given input potential h_0 the population activity is $A_0 = 1/\langle T \rangle$.

We recall that $P_0(s) = P_{h_0}(\hat{t} + s \mid \hat{t})$ is the interval distribution for constant input potential h_0. For our specific noise model, $P_0(s)$ is a Gaussian centered at the noise-free interval T_0

$$P_0(s) = \mathcal{G}_\sigma(s - T_0) \tag{10.57}$$

where σ is the width of the distribution. Thus, for this noise model,

$$A_0 = \frac{1}{\langle T \rangle} = \frac{1}{T_0} \tag{10.58}$$

as in the noise-free case. Equation (10.58) shows one of the advantages of the noise in the reset. For other noise models, the mean interval, and hence A_0, change with the level of noise. The expression (10.58) will prove rather useful for analysis of stability as a function of the noise-level.

We remark that the mean interval $\langle T \rangle$ depends on the input potential h_0. The relation is most easily understood in the noiseless case; cf. (10.49) and Figure 10.14. For each value of h_0 we have a solution T_0. If we plot the rate $1/T_0$ as a function of h_0, we get the gain function $g(h_0)$ of the neuron. Similarly, for the noisy case, we have

$$\nu = \frac{1}{\langle T \rangle} = g(h_0) \tag{10.59}$$

and with (10.51)

$$A_0 = g(h_0). \qquad (10.60)$$

As shown in (10.48), h_0 depends itself upon A_0. Thus, (10.60) is an implicit equation for A_0. A solution may be constructed graphically. It is convenient to transform (10.48) to

$$A_0 = \frac{1}{J_0}(h_0 - J^{\text{ext}} I_0). \qquad (10.61)$$

In Figure 10.15 we have plotted (10.60) and (10.61) as a function of h_0. The intersection points between the gain function (10.60) and the straight line defined by (10.61) gives potential solutions for A_0. This is just the same construction as for the Curie-Weiss theory of ferromagnetism which can be found in any physics textbook. More generally, the structure of the equations corresponds to a mean-field solution of a system with feedback.

As shown in Figure 10.15, several solutions may coexist, but it may also occur that *all* solutions are unstable. In the latter case, the network must leave the state of asynchronous firing and may evolve towards an oscillatory state. The stability analysis of the asynchronous state is the topic of the next subsection.

10.7.2 Stability of Asynchronous Firing

In this subsection we will analyze the stability of incoherent firing or 'splay state' [Chow, 1998]. The basic ideas is sketched in Figure 10.16. During asynchronous firing, the neuronal firing times are spread out over the full period T_0 which can be calculated from $h_0 = \vartheta - \eta(T_0)$. The characteristics of this state are clearly seen, if we order the neurons according their firing times. Due to the nice pattern, such a state has also been called a 'rotating wave' or a 'merry-go-round' state.

Let us now assume that the activity is subject to a small perturbation

$$A(t) = A_0 + A_1 e^{i\omega t} \qquad (10.62)$$

with $A_1 \ll A_0$. We have adopted a complex notation; the physical solution is, as usually, found by taking the real part. The perturbation in the activity induces a perturbation in the postsynaptic potential

$$\begin{aligned} h(t) &= J_0 A_0 \int_0^\infty \epsilon(s) ds + J_0 A_1 \left[\int_0^\infty \epsilon(s) e^{-i\omega s} ds \right] e^{i\omega t} \\ &= h_0 \quad\quad\quad + \quad h_1 e^{-i\alpha(\omega)} e^{i\omega t} \end{aligned} \qquad (10.63)$$

with

$$\begin{aligned} h_0 &= J_0 \hat{\epsilon}(0) A_0 \\ h_1 e^{-i\alpha(\omega)} &= J_0 \hat{\epsilon}(\omega) A_1 \end{aligned} \qquad (10.64)$$

284   10. Populations of Spiking Neurons

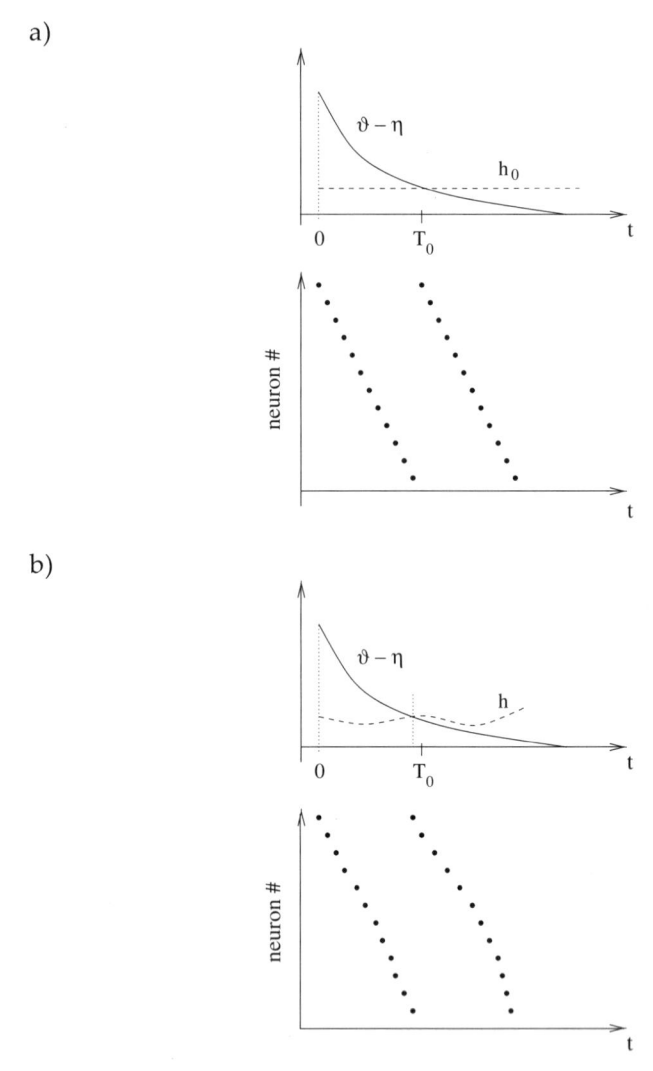

Figure 10.16. a) In an asynchronous state neuronal firing times are spread out maximally over the period T. The neurons have been ordered so that it is easy to see that they fire one after the other. b) In case of a small perturbation, neuronal firing times are no longer maximally spread out, but cluster slightly. This induces a perturbation in the field $h = h_0 + h_1 \cos\omega t$. As a result the neuronal firing times are shifted even more (vertical dashed line). This may lead to a build-up of a periodic perturbation.

where

$$\hat{\epsilon}(\omega) = |\hat{\epsilon}(\omega)| e^{-i\alpha(\omega)} = \int_0^\infty \epsilon(s) e^{-i\omega s} ds \qquad (10.65)$$

is the Fourier transform of ϵ. (The lower bound of the integral can be extended to $-\infty$, since $\epsilon(s)$ vanishes for $s \leq 0$.)

The argument runs now as follows; cf. Figure 10.16. The periodic change in the potential causes some of the neurons to fire earlier (when the change in h is positive) others to fire later (whenever the change is negative). This

10.7 Incoherent Firing

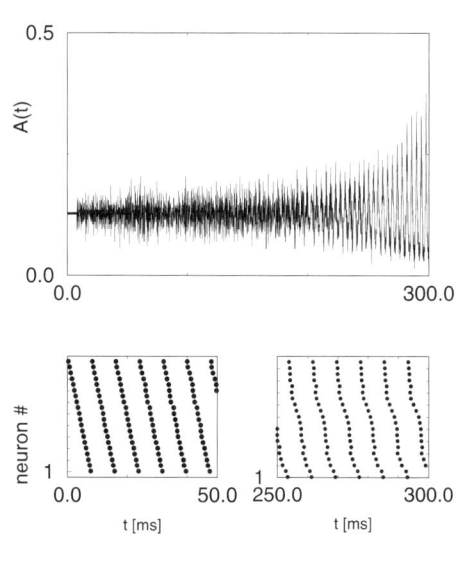

Figure 10.17. Simulation result. During the first 50 ms of the simulations, neuronal firing times are equally spread out (lower left). 250 ms later, there is a clear tendency that the firings cluster together which also shows up in an oscillation of the population activity. Parameters: excitatory coupling $J = 1$, delay $\Delta^{\mathrm{ax}} = 3\,\mathrm{ms}$, noise $\sigma = 0.05\,\mathrm{ms}$.

may disturb the activity $A(t)$ even further and drive it away from the asynchronous state with constant A_0; cf. Figure 10.17. Whether this happens depends on the frequency ω of the perturbation and the phase shift α between the activity $A(t)$ and the potential $h(t)$. The exact conditions are derived in the following paragraphs. We apologize for the fact that the derivation is rather lengthy. Those readers who are not interested in the details of a mathematical argument may jump immediately to the paragraph labeled *results* further down below.

Mathematical steps We start from the general dynamic equation (10.17) for the population activity. On both sides of the equation, we put in our periodic Ansatz (10.62). Note that the interval distribution $P_h(t\,|\,\hat{t})$ depends on the potential h which changes due to the perturbation. We carefully expand to first order in h_1 or A_1 and find

$$\begin{aligned}
A_0 + A_1 \, e^{i\omega t} &= \int_{-\infty}^{t} \left[P_{h_0}(t\,|\,\hat{t}) + \frac{dP_h}{dh_1}(t\,|\,\hat{t})|_{h_1=0}\, h_1 \right] \left(A_0 + A_1\, e^{i\omega \hat{t}} \right) d\hat{t} \\
&= A_0 \int_{-\infty}^{t} P_0(t-\hat{t})\, d\hat{t} + A_1 \int_{-\infty}^{t} P_0(t-\hat{t})\, e^{i\omega \hat{t}}\, d\hat{t} \\
&\quad + h_1\, A_0 \int_{-\infty}^{t} \frac{dP_h}{dh_1}(t\,|\,\hat{t})|_{h_1=0}\, d\hat{t} + \mathcal{O}(h_1\, A_1). \quad (10.66)
\end{aligned}$$

After the second equality sign we have used (10.52) and omitted the second order term $\propto h_1 A_1$. As it should be, the zero-order terms cancel since $\int_{-\infty}^{t} P_0(t-\hat{t})d\hat{t} = \int_0^{\infty} P_0(s)ds = 1$. The second integral on the right-hand side of (10.66) has a simple interpretation since it is the Fourier transform

286   10. Populations of Spiking Neurons

of the interval distribution

$$\int_{-\infty}^{t} P_0(t-\hat{t})\,e^{i\omega\hat{t}}d\hat{t} = e^{i\omega t}\int_0^{\infty} P_0(s)\,e^{-i\omega s}\,ds$$
$$= e^{i\omega t}\,\hat{P}(\omega). \tag{10.67}$$

This leaves us with

$$A_1\,e^{i\omega t}\left[1-\hat{P}(\omega)\right] = A_0\,h_1\int_{-\infty}^{t}\frac{dP_h}{dh_1}(t\,|\,\hat{t})|_{h_1=0}\,d\hat{t}. \tag{10.68}$$

Equation (10.68) is our first general result.

To treat the integral on the right-hand side of (10.68), we make the assumption of low noise. To understand the basic idea, let us consider the limit of no noise, first. A neuron which has fired at $\hat{t}$, fires again at $\hat{t}+T(\hat{t})$ given by the threshold condition

$$h[\hat{t}+T(\hat{t})] = \vartheta - \eta[T(\hat{t})]. \tag{10.69}$$

For a constant potential h_0, (10.69) yields the interval T_0. A change in the potential by $\delta h = h_1 e^{i\alpha}\,e^{i\omega t}$ shifts the firing time and hence the interval length. To first order in δh, the new interval is

$$T(\hat{t}) = T_0 - \frac{\delta h(\hat{t}+T_0)}{\eta'(T_0)}$$
$$= T_0 - \frac{h_1}{\eta'(T_0)}\,e^{i\alpha}\,e^{i\omega(\hat{t}+T_0)}. \tag{10.70}$$

Note that for $\delta h > 0$ the interval gets shorter and for $\delta h > 0$ it gets longer, as expected from the sketch in Figure 10.16b.

In the case of a small amount of noise, the interval is not precisely determined, but has some distribution around the value $T(\hat{t})$ calculated in (10.70). We *assume* that, for a small amount of noise, the main effect of the perturbation is to shift the center of the interval distribution from the reference value T_0 to the perturbed value $T(\hat{t})$ calculated in (10.70). The approximation to the exact solution is expected to be good, if the width of the distribution is small compared to the period of the perturbation ($\omega\sigma \ll 1$). Thus we write

$$P_h(t\,|\,\hat{t}) = P_0\!\left(t-\hat{t}+\frac{h_1}{\eta'}e^{-i\alpha}\,e^{i\omega(\hat{t}+T_0)}\right). \tag{10.71}$$

With (10.71) the integral on the right-hand side of (10.68) can be solved using integration by parts. To do so, we note that because of (10.71)

$$\frac{d}{dh_1}P_h(t\,|\,\hat{t})|_{h_1=0} = \frac{d}{dh_1}P_0\!\left(t-\hat{t}+\frac{h_1}{\eta'}e^{-i\alpha}\,e^{i\omega(\hat{t}+T_0)}\right)\Big|_{h_1=0}$$
$$= -\frac{d}{d\hat{t}}P_0(t-\hat{t})\,\frac{1}{\eta'}e^{-i\alpha}\,e^{i\omega(\hat{t}+T_0)}. \tag{10.72}$$

With view to (10.68), we integrate (10.72)

$$\int_{-\infty}^{t}\frac{d}{dh_1}P_h(t\,|\,\hat{t})|_{h_1=0}\,d\hat{t} = \frac{i\omega}{\eta'}e^{-i\alpha}\,e^{i\omega T_0}\,\hat{P}(\omega)\,e^{i\omega t}. \tag{10.73}$$

After all these transformations, we may now use (10.73) on the right-hand side of (10.68) and arrive at our final result

$$1 - \hat{P}(\omega) = \frac{i\omega}{\eta'} J_0 A_0 e^{i\omega T_0} \hat{\epsilon}(\omega) \hat{P}(\omega) \tag{10.74}$$

where we have used $h_1 e^{-i\alpha} = J_0 A_1 \hat{\epsilon}(\omega)$ and cancelled the common factor $A_1 e^{i\omega t}$ on both sides of the equation.

Equation (10.74) is an approximative result which was derived on the assumption that the perturbation only shifts the center of the distribution, but does not change its form. In [Gerstner, 1998] a different approach is taken which does not rely on this assumption. The resulting equation is somewhat different from (10.74). The regions of stability and the qualitative structure of the solutions are, however, unchanged and we will therefore use (10.74) for the following discussion.

Application The result (10.74) is quite general. We now want to apply it to our specific model.

With Gaussian noise in the reset, the interval distribution is a Gaussian centered at T_0,

$$P_0(s) = \mathcal{G}_\sigma(s - T_0) = \frac{1}{\sqrt{2\pi}} \frac{1}{\sigma} \exp\left[-\frac{(s - T_0)^2}{2\sigma^2}\right]. \tag{10.75}$$

We need the Fourier transform

$$\hat{P}(\omega) = \exp\left[-\frac{1}{2}\sigma^2 \omega^2\right] e^{-i\omega T_0}. \tag{10.76}$$

The maximum of $|\hat{P}|$ is at $\omega = 0$ and has the value $|\hat{P}(0)| = 1$ independent of σ. In the limit of no noise ($\sigma \to 0$) the interval distribution is $P_0(s) = \delta(s - T_0)$ and $|\hat{P}(\omega)| \equiv 1$.

We also need to specify the response kernel ϵ. The Fourier transform of (10.6) is

$$\hat{\epsilon}(\omega) = |\hat{\epsilon}(\omega)| e^{-i\alpha(\omega)} \tag{10.77}$$

with amplitude and phase

$$\begin{aligned} |\hat{\epsilon}(\omega)| &= \frac{1}{(1 + \omega^2 \tau^2)} \\ \alpha(\omega) &= \omega \Delta^{\text{ax}} + 2 \arctan(\omega \tau). \end{aligned} \tag{10.78}$$

We note that a change in the delay Δ^{ax} only affects the *phase* of the Fourier transform and not the amplitude. This is a convenient property which we will exploit later.

Furthermore, we need the derivative of the response kernel η. We take the kernel (10.8) and therefore

$$\eta'(T_0) = \frac{\eta_0}{T_0} \exp\left(-\frac{T}{\tau}\right). \tag{10.79}$$

288   10. Populations of Spiking Neurons

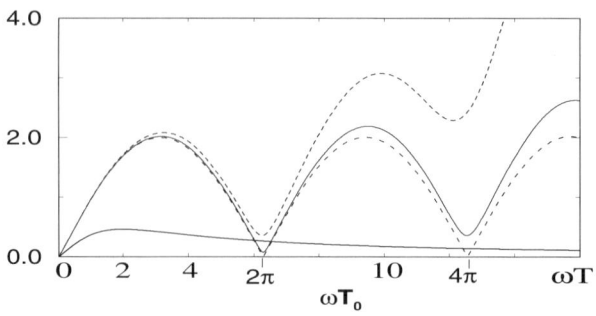

Figure 10.18. Graphical solution of the amplitude condition for bifurcation of an oscillatory solution. The crossing points lie at frequencies $\omega \approx \omega_n = n \, 2\pi/T_0$. For the plot we have set $T_0 = 2\tau$, $J_0 = \eta_0 = 1$ which yields a factor of $C = 0.92$. Three values of noise are shown. For $\sigma = 1.0$ ms (long dashed curve, top), no crossing point except the one at $\omega = 0$ exists. For $\sigma = 0.5$ ms (thin solid line), two solutions of the amplitude condition with $\omega\tau = 2\pi \pm \delta$ with $\delta \ll 1$ exist. For $\sigma = 0.1$ ms (dotted line), crossing points at $\omega T_0 \approx 2\pi$ and 4π are shown. The thick solid line is $C\, \hat{f}(x)$ with $\hat{f}(x) = x/(1+x^2)$ and $C = 0.92$; adapted from [Gerstner and van Hemmen, 1994].

Let us now collect the various terms from (10.8), (10.76), (10.78), and (10.79) and put them into (10.74). The result is

$$\exp\left[-\frac{1}{2}\sigma^2 \omega^2\right] - e^{-i\omega T_0} = C\, e^{-i(\alpha - \frac{\pi}{2})} \frac{\omega\tau}{1+\omega^2 \tau^2} \qquad (10.80)$$

with a factor

$$C = \frac{J_0}{\eta_0\, \tau} \exp\left(\frac{T_0}{\tau}\right). \qquad (10.81)$$

Are there frequencies ω so that (10.80) has a solution? To check this, we take the absolute value on both sides of (10.80)

$$\left[1 + \exp\left(\sigma^2 \omega^2\right) - 2\cos(\omega\, T_0) \exp\left(\frac{\sigma^2 \omega^2}{2}\right)\right]^{1/2} = C\, \frac{\omega\tau}{1+\omega^2 \tau^2} \qquad (10.82)$$

and plot both the left-hand side and the right-hand side as a function of ω; cf. Figure 10.18. For $\sigma \to 0$ the left-hand side is $2|\sin(\omega T_0/2)|$ and solutions are possible only for frequencies $\omega \approx \omega_n = n\, 2\pi/T_0$ with integer n. A solution with ω_1 implies that the period of the population activity is identical to the period of individual neurons. The other solutions correspond to higher harmonics. We see from Figure 10.18 that higher harmonic solutions disappear at some finite noise level. At high noise level, even the solution $\omega \approx \omega_1$ disappears.

Equation (10.82) only gives an *amplitude* condition for solution of (10.80). In order to derive the phase equations, we have to work a little bit harder. Since we now know that solutions are possible only for $\omega \approx \omega_n$, we set

$$\omega = \omega_n + \nu_n\,. \qquad (10.83)$$

Furthermore, for $n \geq 1$ and $T = 2\tau$, we have $\omega_n \tau = n\pi > 3$ and we can approximate the arctan in (10.78) by $\arctan(x) \approx (\pi/2) - (1/x)$. The phase factor in (10.80) is therefore

$$\alpha - \frac{\pi}{2} = \omega \Delta^{\text{ax}} - \frac{2}{\omega \tau} + \frac{\pi}{2}. \tag{10.84}$$

The aim is now to write down conditions for the real and the imaginary part of (10.80). In order to simplify the notation, we set

$$\hat{f}(\omega) = \frac{\omega \tau}{1 + \omega^2 \tau^2}$$
$$\hat{g}(\omega) = \exp\left(\frac{1}{2}\sigma^2 \omega^2\right) \tag{10.85}$$

Furthermore we note that, because of (10.83), the phases simplify $i\omega T_0 = i\nu_n T_0$. Grouping the real and the imaginary part of (10.80) in two equations yields

$$\hat{g}(\omega) - \cos(\nu_n T_0) = C \hat{f}(\omega) \sin \psi$$
$$\sin(\nu_n T_0) = -C \hat{f}(\omega) \cos \psi \tag{10.86}$$

with $\psi = (2/\omega\tau) - \omega\Delta^{\text{ax}}$. We have solved (10.86) numerically for different values of the delay δ^{ax} and different levels of the noise σ. The results are shown in Figure 10.19 and discussed in the next paragraph.

Results We have studied a population of neurons with ϵ given by (10.6) and η by (10.8). Neurons interact with strength $J_0 = 1$ and The value of the threshold ϑ was adjusted so that $T = 2\tau$. In our simulations we have taken $\tau = 4$ ms and a total number of $N = 1000$ neurons.

The results of our analytical stability analysis are shown in the phase diagram in the center of Figure 10.19. The y-axis is the level of noise, the x-axis the value of the axonal transmission delay devided by the interspike interval T_0. Let us study a network with interaction delay $\Delta^{\text{ax}} = 2$ ms. This corresonds to a x-value of $\Delta^{\text{ax}}/T_0 = 0.25$ in Fig, 10.19. The phase diagram predicts that, at a noise level of $\sigma = 0.5$ ms, the network is in a state of asynchronous firing. The activity during a simulation run is shown in the inset in the upper right-hand corner. It confirms that the activity fluctuates around a constant value of $A_0 = 1/T_0 = 0.125$ kHz.

We imagine now that we reduce the noise level of the network. At some point we cross the short-dashed line. The line is the boundary at which the constant activity state becomes unstable with respect to an oscillation with $\omega \approx 3\,(2\pi/T_0)$. A simulation result for a network at a noise level of $\sigma = 0.1$, but otherwise the same parameters as before confirms that the population activity exhibits an oscillation with period $T^{osc} \approx T_0/3 \approx 2.6$ ms.

Let us return to our original parameters of $\sigma = 0.5$ ms and $\Delta^{\text{ax}} = 2$ ms. We now keep the noise level fixed and reduce the axonal transmission delay. In this case we move horizontally across the phase diagram in Figure 10.19. At some point, we cross the solid line which marks the transition to an instability with frequency $\omega_1 = 2\pi/T_0$. Again this is confirmed by the simulation results shown in the inset in the upper left corner. If we now decrease the noise level, the oscillation becomes more pronounced (bottom right).

290   10. Populations of Spiking Neurons

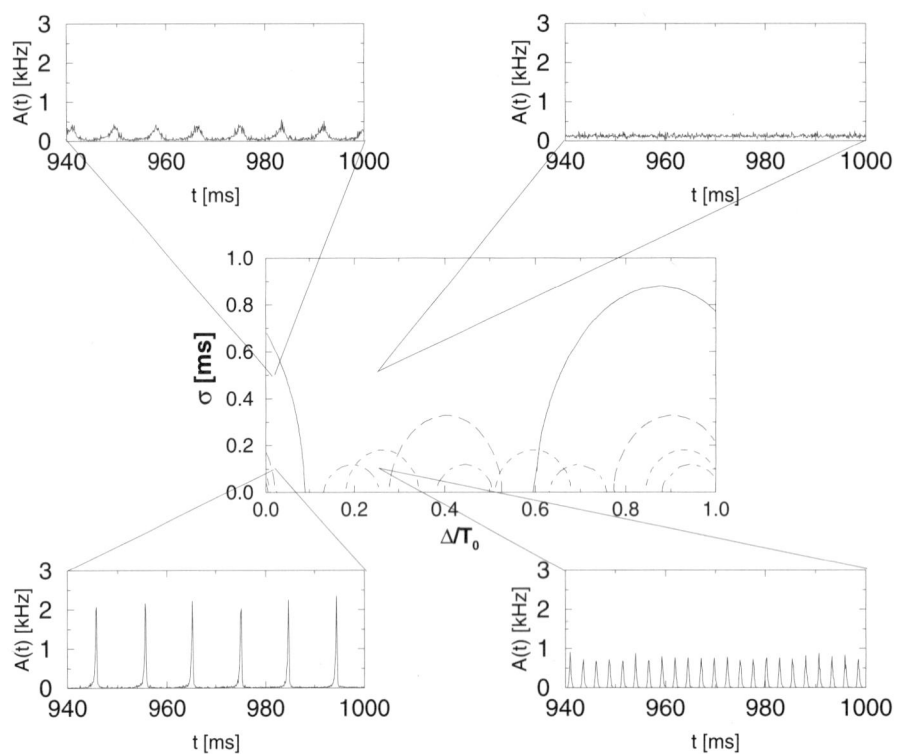

Figure 10.19. Stability diagram (center) as a function of noise σ (y-axis) and delay Δ^{ax} (x-axis). The diagram shows the borders of the stability region with respect to $\omega_1, \ldots, \omega_4$. For high values of the noise, the asynchronous firing state is always stable. If the noise is reduced, the asynchronous state becomes unstable with respect to an oscillation either with frequency ω_1 (solid border lines), or ω_2 (long-dashed border lines), or ω_3 (short-dashed border lines), or ω_4 (long-short dashed border lines). Four insets shows typical patterns of the activity as a function of time taken from a simulation with 1000 neurons. Parameters $\sigma = 0.5$ ms and $\Delta^{\mathrm{ax}} = 0.2$ ms (top left); $\sigma = 0.5$ ms and $\Delta^{\mathrm{ax}} = 2.0$ ms (top right); $\sigma = 0.1$ ms and $\Delta^{\mathrm{ax}} = 0.2$ ms (bottom left); $\sigma = 0.1$ ms and $\Delta^{\mathrm{ax}} = 2.0$ ms (bottom right); Since the pattern repeats along the x-axis with period T_0, we have plotted a normalized delay Δ^{ax}/T_0. Adapted from [Gerstner, 1998].

For practically all values of the delay, the incoherent network state is unstable in the limit of no noise ($\sigma \to 0$). This is exemplified in Figure 10.20 where we have explored different values of the delay for a constant noise level $\sigma = 0.04$ ms. For a very short delay, the network oscillates with frequency of about ω_1, increasing the delay it passes through oscillations with ω_6, ω_5, ω_4, ω_3, and ω_2.

We emphasize that the specific location of the stability borders depends on the form of the postsynaptic response function ϵ. The qualitative features of the phase diagram in Figure 10.19 are generic and hold for all kinds of response kernels.

Finally, what happens if the excitatory interaction is replaced by inhibitory coupling? Not much. For each harmonic, the region along the delay axis where the incoherent state is *unstable* for excitatory coupling (cf. Fig-

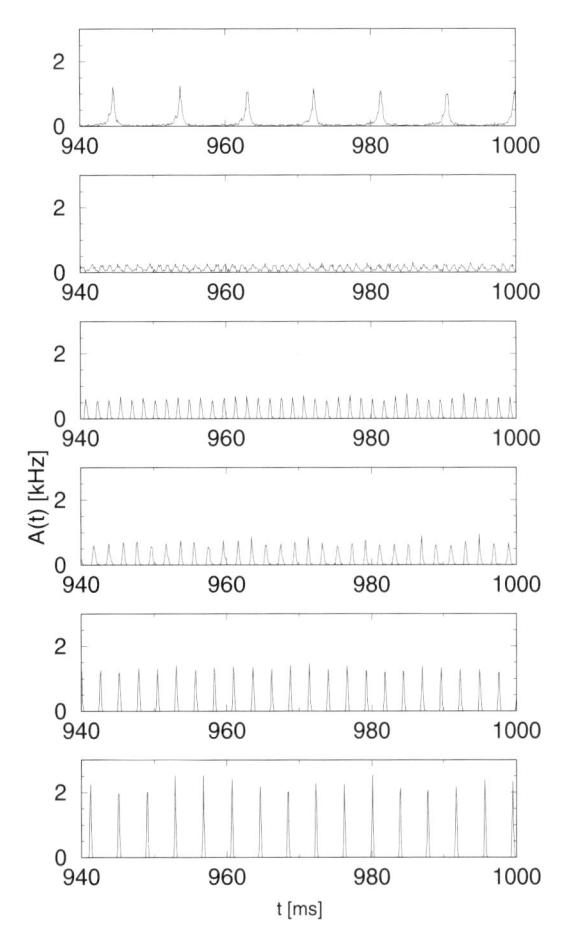

Figure 10.20. Activity for different values of the delay at a low noise level ($\sigma = 0.04$ ms). From top to botton: $\Delta^{\mathrm{ax}} = 0.4$ms; 1.0 ms; 1.2 ms; 1.4 ms; 2.0 ms; 3.0 ms. Taken from [Gerstner, 1998].

ure 10.19) becomes *stable* for inhibition and vice versa. In other words, we simply have to shift the instability tongues for each frequency ω_n horizontally by an amount $\Delta/T_0 = 1/(2n)$. Otherwise the pattern remains the same.

10.8 Conclusions

We have seen that the population activity in a homogeneous population of neurons can be described by an integral equation. A description by differential equations of the form (10.2) is, in general, not possible. A systematic reduction of the integral equation to a single differential equation of the form (10.2) always supposes that the activity changes only *slowly* compared to the typical interval length [Wilson and Cowan, 1972, Gerstner, 1995, Pinto et al., 1996]. The existence of perfectly synchronized oscillations and the fast initital transients discussed in this contribution, clearly show that an assumption of slow changes is, in general, not justified. It seems therefore preferable to work directly on the level of the integral equation. A useful approximation might be to describe the activity of a single population by a set of several coupled differential equations [Gerstner, 1993; Eggert and van Hemmen, 1997].

The population equation (10.17) is valid for neurons with short memory, i.e., only the most recent spike matters. More generally, the condition of short memory leads to the class of renewal models [Perkel et al., 1967, Stein, 1967, Cox, 1962] and this is where the integral equation applies; cf. [Gerstner, 1995]. A generalization to neuron models with longer memory, in particular adaptation, does not seem straightforward.

One of the solution of the integral equation is that of neurons firing in perfect synchrony. The synchronous solution is stable, if the input potential h is increasing in the moment of firing. This is the essence of the locking theorem [Gerstner et al., 1996]. The locking theorem is a special case of a more general property of the integral equation: firing times are compressed and, hence, the activity increases, whenever firing occurs while the input potential is rising ($h' > 0$).

Another solution of the integral equation is the state of incoherent firing. If the network is firing incoherently, then the population acitivity responds immediately to an abrupt change in the input [Tsodyks and Sejnowski, 1995, van Vreeswijk and Sompolinsky, 1996]. There is no integration delay. In the case of incoherent firing, there are always *some* neurons close to threshold – and this is why the system as a whole can respond immediately. This property suggests that a population of neurons may transmit information fast and reliably. Fast information processing seems to be a necessary requirement for biological nervous systems, if the reaction time experiments are to be accounted for [Thorpe et al., 1996].

It follows that the state of incoherent firing may be particularly interesting for information transmission. Incoherent firing can be stabilized by a suitable choice of time constants, transmission delay, and noise. [Abbott and van Vreeswijk, 1993; Gerstner and van Hemmen, 1993, 1994; Gerstner, 1995]. For low noise, incoherent states are *unstable* for nearly all choices of parameters. Instabilities lead towards oscillations, either with a period comparable to the typical interval of the neuronal spike trains, or much faster (higher harmonics) [Golomb et al., 1992, Gerstner and van Hemmen, 1993, Ernst et al., 1994, Golomb and Rinzel, 1994]. The harmonics have also been called cluster states since neurons spontaneously split into groups of neurons which fire approximately together. The higher harmonics can be easily suppressed by noise.

Finally, we would like to emphasize that there are no completely homogeneous populations in biology. The population equations discussed in this chapter may nevertheless be a useful starting point for a theory of heterogeneous populations [Senn et al., 1996, Chow, 1998]. We expect that most of the results discussed in the present chapter also hold for non-homogeneous networks.

References

[Abbott and van Vreeswijk, 1993] Abbott, L. F. and van Vreeswijk, C. (1993). Asynchronous states in a network of pulse-coupled oscillators. *Phys. Rev. E*, 48:1483–1490.

[Amari, 1974] Amari, S. (1974). A method of statistical neurodynamics. *Kybernetik*, 14:201–215.

[Bauer and Pawelzik, 1993] Bauer, H. U. and Pawelzik, K. (1993). Alternating oscillatory and stochastic dynamics in a model for a neuronal assembly. *Physica D*, 69:380–393.

[Chow, 1998] Chow, C. C. (1998) Phase-locking in weakly heterogeneous neuronal networks. *preprint*.

[Cohen and Grossberg, 1983] Cohen, M. A. and Grossberg, S. (1983). Absolute stability of global pattern formation and parallel memory storage by competitive neural networks. *IEEE trans. on systems, man, and cybernetics*, 13:815–823.

[Cox, 1962] Cox, D. R. (1962). *Renewal Theory*. Mathuen, London.

[Eggert, 1997] Eggert, J. (1997). Derivation of pool dynamics from microscopic neuronal models. *Artificial Neural Networks - ICANN'97*, W. Gerstner, A. Germond, M. Hasler, and J.-D. Nicoud, eds., Springer-Verlag, 109–114.

[Ernst et al., 1994] Ernst, U., Pawelzik, K., and Geisel, T. (1994). Multiple phase clustering of globally coupled neurons with delay. *Proc. of the ICANN'94*, M. Marinaro and P. G. Morasso, eds., Springer-Verlag, Berlin Heidelberg New York, 1063–1065.

[Gerstner, 1993] Gerstner, W. (1993). *Kodierung und Signalübertragung in Neuronalen Systemen: Assoziative Netzwerke mit stochastisch feuernden Neuronen*, volume 15 of *Reihe Physik*. Harri–Deutsch Verlag, Frankfurt/Main, 1993. Dissertation Nov. 1992, TU München.

[Gerstner, 1995] Gerstner, W. (1995). Time structure of the activity in neural network models. *Phys. Rev. E*, 51(1):738–758.

[Gerstner, 1998] Gerstner, W. (1998) Population dynamics for spiking neurons: fast transients, asynchronous states and locking. *preprint*, 1997.

[Gerstner et al., 1993] Gerstner, W., Ritz, R., and van Hemmen, J. L. (1993). A biologically motivated and analytically soluble model of collective oscillations in the cortex: I. theory of weak locking. *Biol. Cybern.*, 68:363–374.

[Gerstner and van Hemmen, 1992] Gerstner, W. and van Hemmen, J. L. (1992). Associative memory in a network of 'spiking' neurons. *Network*, 3:139–164.

[Gerstner and van Hemmen, 1993] Gerstner, W. and van Hemmen, J. L. (1993). Coherence and incoherence in a globally coupled ensemble of pulse emitting units. *Phys. Rev. Lett.*, 71(3):312–315.

[Gerstner and van Hemmen, 1994] Gerstner, W. and van Hemmen, J. L. (1994). Coding and information processing in neural networks. In *Models of neural networks II*, E. Domany, J. L. van Hemmen, and K. Schulten, eds., Springer-Verlag, New York, 1–93.

[Gerstner et al., 1996] Gerstner, W., van Hemmen, J. L., and Cowan, J. D. (1996). What matters in neuronal locking. *Neural Computation*, 8:1689–1712.

[Golomb et al., 1992] Golomb, D., Hansel, D., Shraiman, B., and Sompolinsky, H. (1992). Clustering in globally coupled phase oscillators. *Phys. Rev. A*, 45:3516–3530.

[Golomb and Rinzel, 1994] Golomb, D. and Rinzel, J. (1994). Clustering in globally coupled inhibitory neurons. *Physica D*, 72:259–282, 1994.

[Hansel et al., 1995] Hansel, D., Mato, G., and Meunier, C. (1995). Synchrony in excitatory neural networks. *Neural Computation*, 7:307–337.

[Hopfield, 1984] Hopfield, J. J. (1984). Neurons with graded response have computational properties like those of two–state neurons. *Proc. Natl. Acad. Sci. USA*, 81:3088–3092.

[Hopfield and Herz, 1995] Hopfield J. J. and Herz, A. V. M. (1995). Rapid local synchronization of action potentials: towards computation with coupled integrate-and-fire networks. *Proc. Natl. Acad. Sci. USA*, 92:6655.

[Mirollo and Strogatz, 1990] Mirollo, R. E. and Strogatz, S. H. (1990). Synchronization of pulse coupled biological oscillators. *SIAM J. Appl. Math.*, 50:1645–1662.

[Perkel et al., 1967] Perkel, D. H., Gerstein, G. L., and Moore, G. P. (1967). Neuronal spike trains and stochastic point processes. (i) the single spike train. *Biophys. J.*, 7:391–418.

[Pinto et al., 1996] Pinto, D. J., Brumberg, J. C., Simons, D. J., and Ermentrout, G. B. (1996). A quantitative population model of whiskers barrels: re-examining the Wilson-Cowan equations. *J. Comput. Neurosci.*, 3:247–264.

[Senn et al., 1996] Senn, W., Wyler, K., Streit, J., Larkum, M., Lüscher, H.-R., Mey H., Müller, L., Steinhauser, D., Vogt, K., and Wannier, T. (1996). Dynamics of random neural network with synaptic depression. *Neural Networks*, 9:575–588.

[Somers and Kopell, 1993] Somers, D. and Kopell, N. (1993). Rapid synchronization through fast threshold modulation. *Biol. Cybern.*, 68:393–407.

[Stein, 1967] Stein, R. B. (1967). Some models of neuronal variability. *Biophys. J.*, 7:37–68.

[Terman and Wang, 1995] Terman, D. and Wang, D. (1995). Global competition and local cooperation in a network of neural oscillators. *Physica D*, 81:148–176.

[Thorpe et al., 1996] Thorpe, S., Fize, D., and Marlot, C. (1996). Speed of processing in the human visual system. *Nature*, 381:520–522.

[Tsodyks and Sejnowski, 1995] Tsodyks, M. V. and Sejnowski, T. (1995). Rapid state switching in balanced cortical networks. *Network*, 6:111–124.

[van Vreeswijk and Sompolinsky, 1996] van Vreeswijk, C. and Sompolinsky, H. (1996). Chaos in neuronal networks with balanced excitatory and inhibitory activity. *Science*, 274:1724–1726.

[van Vreeswijk et al., 1994] van Vreeswijk, C., Abbott, L. F., and Ermentrout, G. B. (1994). When inhibition not excitation synchronizes neural firing. *Journal of Computational Neuroscience*, 1:313–321.

[Wilson and Cowan, 1972] Wilson, H. R. and Cowan, J. D. (1972). Excitatory and inhibitory interactions in localized populations of model neurons. *Biophysical J.*, 12:1–24.

[Wilson and Cowan, 1973] Wilson, H. R. and Cowan, J. D. (1973). A mathematical theory of the functional dynamics of cortical and thalamic nervous tissue. *Kybernetik*, 13:55–80.

11 Collective Excitation Phenomena and Their Applications

David Horn and Irit Opher

11.1 Introduction

Spiking neurons are highly non-linear oscillators. As such they display collective behavior that may have important calculational manifestations. Synchronization between the firing of different neurons is the first topic to which we devote our attention. This behavior can be brought about in our integrate-and-fire model through excitatory synaptic couplings without delays, or inhibitory couplings with delays. Once the mechanism of synchronization is established, this phenomenon can be used for defining data clustering. The clusters correspond to neurons that fire synchronously, with different clusters firing at different times. This behavior can also be described as temporal segmentation, separating data through phase lags between excitations of different aggregates. This separation is characteristically limited to a small number of segments, a limitation that is inherent to the behavior of coupled non-linear oscillators.

The importance of synchrony as signifying binding, i.e. the belonging of neural events to one another and their joint formation of a consistent picture or concept, was emphasized by von der Malsburg [von der Malsburg, 1981]. Experiments in the late 80's [Eckhorn et al., 1988, Gray et al., 1989] showed the correlation of synchrony in the visual cortex with binding in the input scene. Taking it one step further, one may ask for the co-occurrence of several synchronized neuronal assemblies. This could explain distributed attention [von der Malsburg and Schneider, 1986]. It was studied in various neural models [Wang et al., 1990, Horn and Usher, 1991, Horn et al., 1991] but has no experimental verification.

Employing quasi-local excitatory connections one can use these principles for image analysis. After covering cluster formations we turn to the use of an image as an external input to a two dimensional array of spiking neurons, and demonstrate how we can perform edge detection as well as scene segmentation. Finally, we study spatio-temporal coherent phenomena that homogeneous neural systems may develop by themselves. We show how solitary waves of spiking activity arise on neuronal surfaces, and characterize their structures.

In order to demonstrate the various concepts and phenomena we use our continuous version [Horn and Opher, 1997a] of integrate-and-fire (IAF) neurons, that were discussed in Section 1.2.3.4 of Chapter 1. We employ a coupled set of differential equations of two variables, as described in the next subsection.

11.1.1 Two Variable Formulation of IAF Neurons

The two variables that we use to describe an IAF neuron are v, a subthreshold potential, and m which distinguishes between two different modes in the dynamics of the single neuron, the active depolarization mode and the inactive refractory period. They obey

$$\dot{v} = -kv + \alpha + cmv + mI \qquad (11.1)$$

$$\dot{m} = -m + \mathcal{H}(m - v) \qquad (11.2)$$

$\mathcal{H}(x)$ is the Heaviside step function. The neuron is influenced by an external input I, which is quenched in the absolute refractory period, when $m = 0$. Starting out with $m = 1$, the total time derivative of v is positive, and v follows the dynamics of a charging capacitor. Hence this represents the depolarization period of v. During all this time, since $v < m$, m stays unchanged. The dynamics change when v reaches the threshold (that is arbitrarily set to 1). Then m decreases rapidly to zero, causing the time derivative of v to be negative, and v follows the dynamics of a discharging capacitor. Parameters are chosen so that the time constants of the charging and discharging periods are different.

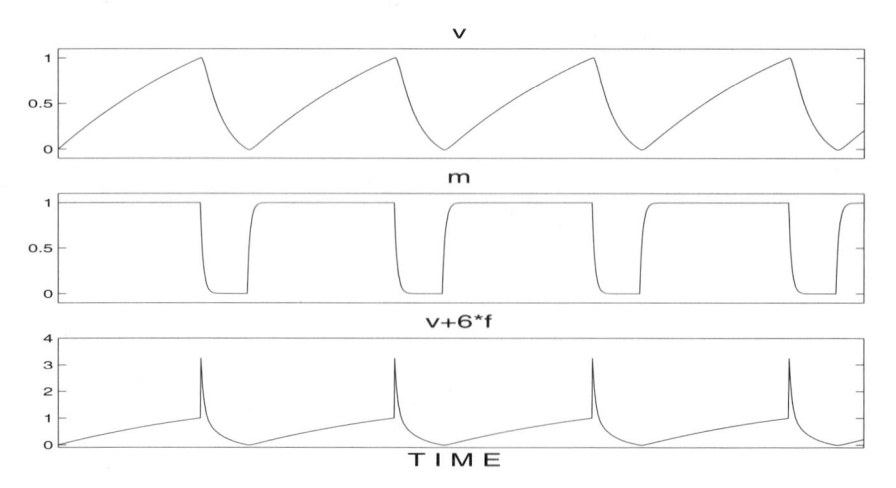

Figure 11.1. Dynamics of the single IAF neuron. The upper frame displays v, the subthreshold membrane potential, as a function of time. The second frame shows m, the variable that distinguishes between the depolarization state, $m = 1$, and refractoriness, $m = 0$. In the third frame we plot $v + 6f$, where f is our spike profile, to give a schematic presentation of the total cell potential. Parameters for this figure are: $k = 0.45$, $\alpha = -0.09$, $c = 0.35$, $I = 0.29$.

To complete this description of an IAF neuron we need a quantity that represents the firing of the neuron. We introduce for this purpose

$$f \propto -\frac{dm}{dt}\mathcal{H}(-\frac{dm}{dt}) \qquad (11.3)$$

that vanishes at all times except when v arrives at the threshold and m changes rapidly from 1 to 0. This can serve therefore as a description of the action potential. An example of the dynamics of v and m is shown in Figure 11.1. In a third frame we plot $v + af$, with $a = 6$, representing the total soma potential. The value of a is of no consequence in our work. It is used here for illustration purposes only.

This description can be readily extended to an array of pulse coupled neurons by replacing Equation (11.1) with

$$\dot{v}_i = -kv_i + \alpha + cm_i v_i + m_i(I + \Sigma_j w_{ij} f_j) \tag{11.4}$$

where $i = 1, \cdots, N$ denotes the number of the neuron. Note that in this formulation the interactions are instantaneous, and are quenched during the refractory period, when $m_i = 0$. It is straightforward to introduce neuritic time delays, e.g. by switching $f_j = f_j(t)$ to $\bar{f}_j = f_j(t-\Delta)$ on the right hand side of this equation. One should note that the spike, represented here by f, has some width of its own, so a small effect of temporal extension is embedded automatically in the definition of our model.

11.2 Synchronization of Pulse Coupled Oscillators

Synchrony of events is an intriguing physical phenomenon. The fact that most living organisms depend upon it for their survival makes it even more interesting. Synchronization plays an important role in many physiological activities including breathing, motor control and information processing in the central nervous system. It can also occur in biological environments that include many organisms such as groups of fireflies that flash in synchrony or groups of criquets chirping in unison [Strogatz and Stewart, 1993].

Most biological systems that exhibit synchronization can be described as coupled oscillators, where the fully synchronized state is only one of many possible dynamic attractors. One can divide models of coupled oscillators into two kinds: phase coupled [Golomb et al., 1992, Grannan et al., 1993, Terman and Wang, 1995] and pulse coupled ones [Mirollo and Strogatz, 1990, Hopfield and Herz, 1995, Johnson, 1994]. The latter reduces to the former in the limit in which every oscillator couples to a large number of others [Abbott and van Vreeswijk, 1993, Kuramoto, 1990, Gerstner et al., 1993, Usher et al., 1993]. We will devote our attention to pulse coupled systems, analyzing cases of both small and large numbers of neurons.

In this chapter we address collective activity in neuronal populations with various types of coupling. In this section, we concentrate on all-to-all couplings. This will serve as the basis for understanding cases in which the synaptic couplings reflect structure in data or the geometry of a manifold to which neurons are attached. A thorough analysis of the large N limit of such systems is given in Chapter 10. Let us start with all-to-all excitatory couplings, a case studied by [Mirollo and Strogatz, 1990]. They considered a population of N identical pulse coupled oscillators, fully connected by excitatory connections, without transmission delays and with no refractory period. The state of the single oscillator is described by a monotonic increasing function of its phase, representing the integration that the membrane potential performs over its inputs. Once an oscillator reaches its threshold it emits a spike and is automatically reset to zero. Under the simple assumption that the monotonic function is concave, the authors prove that for almost all initial conditions the neuronal population will reach a stable synchronized state after a finite number of time steps, for any value of N. In the case of inhibitory connections they show that for a system of 2 neurons, the asynchronous solution is stable. Although they do not prove it for a larger system, this result is supported by numerical simulations and by other models, as will be shown below.

The situation is quite different when transmission delays are added to such a model. Nischwitz and Glünder [Nischwitz and Glünder, 1995] report that, for a wide range of parameters, transmission delays cause desynchronization. However, if excitatory connections are replaced by inhibitory ones, transmission delays induce synchronization. Following a numerical study, they conclude that delayed local inhibition is the best scheme for spike synchronization. This conclusion agrees with [van Vreeswijk and Abbott, 1994], who studied a system of two integrate and fire units interacting through a dynamic synapse described by an α function. They showed that while the synchronous state is not stable for an excitatory synapse, it is stable when the synapse is inhibitory. In fact, the synchronous state is always stable when the synapse is inhibitory, although its domain of attraction shrinks as the interaction becomes faster. In the excitatory case, the stable synchronous state is reached only when the interaction is instantaneous.

Whereas in our model synaptic response is instantaneous, and neuritic delays are introduced at will, realistic models cope with both synaptic and neuritic temporal structures, leading to various effects. As an example let us mention [Hansel et al., 1995], who study realistic neural models using both analytic calculations (after reduction to a phase model) and numerical simulations. They differentiate between two types of responses to excitatory postsynaptic potentials (EPSP). In the first case, the EPSP advances the next firing of the excited neuron. In the second case, it can either delay the spike or advance it, depending on the arrival time of the EPSP relative to the refractory period. A synchronized state is not stable in the first scenario[1], while it can be stable in the second one, provided the synaptic interactions are fast enough.

The importance of the timing of a spike is further emphasized in the locking theorem of [Gerstner et al., 1996] (see Section 10.2.5.2). It states the conditions for stability of the fully synchronous solution in a more complex case (the spike response model introduced in section 1.2.3.1 of Chapter 1) that incorporates the form of the postsynaptic potential as well as axonal delays and refractoriness. Collective firing is shown to be stable if the firing occurs while the postsynaptic potential is rising.

In the more simplistic models, including ours, the general conclusion is that both instantaneous excitation and delayed inhibition can lead to synchrony. Instantaneous excitation has the advantage that synchrony follows

---
[1]It may, however, be stable for instantaneous synapses.

quickly once the interaction is strong enough. In the case of delayed inhibition one has to find the correct window of parameters and wait longer for synchrony to set in, but once it is obtained it is very stable. Recent studies [Crook et al., 1997, van Vreeswijk and Hansel, 1997] have shown that synaptic adaptation has an interesting effect: it leads to synchrony of spiking neural systems in the presence of excitatory synaptic interactions with realistic temporal structures. Thus, once we allow for more elaborate interactions, there exist many ways of inducing synchrony.

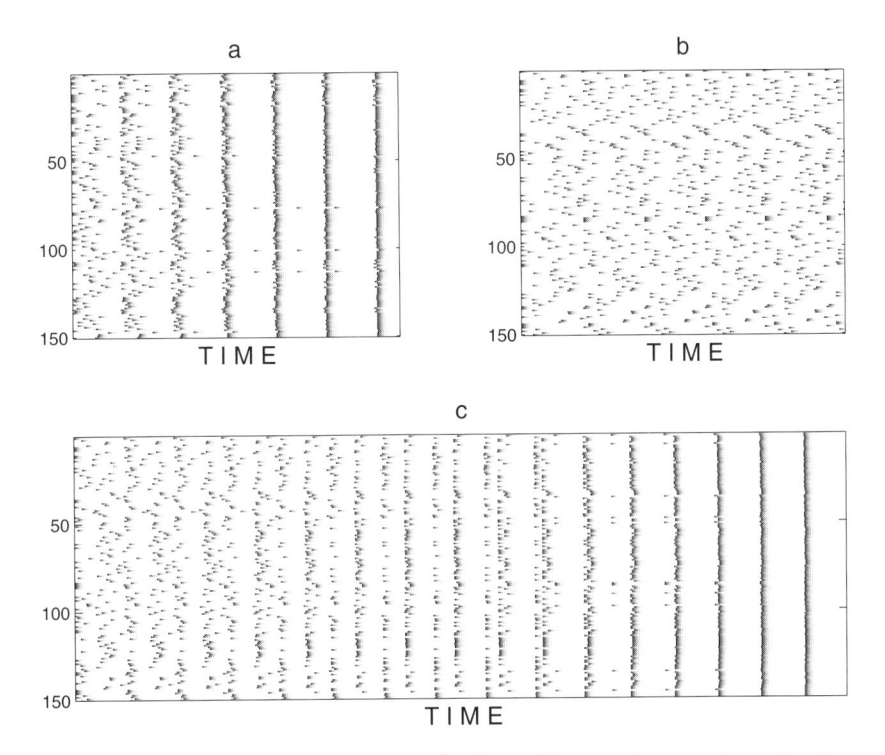

Figure 11.2. Firing of 150 IAF neurons with all-to-all interactions vs. time. Starting from random initial conditions, the global behavior depends on the connections: (a) Excitatory connections without delay lead quickly to almost perfect synchronization. (b) In the presence of inhibitory connections without delay, the system converges to non-synchronized periodic behavior. (c) Delayed inhibition inducing perfect synchronization after a long time.

We illustrate in Figure 11.2 the build-up of synchrony in our system of IAF neurons [Horn and Opher, 1997a] for different types of interactions. For all-to-all excitatory instantaneous couplings we display a system of neurons that starts out with random initial conditions and turns, after four periods, into a synchronous system. When the interactions are inhibitory, the system is periodic but asynchronous. Finally, inhibition with fixed transmission delays leads to the build-up of synchrony through merger of synchronous clusters.

In discrete temporal simulations, there exists a subtlety regarding the exact updating scheme. One can either reset the IAF neuron to its rest state, no matter how much current it received before firing, or to a higher value, if the input it received before firing exceeded the amount it needed to reach threshold. When refractoriness is present, as is the case in our model, the situation is similar to the first updating scenario. It becomes the only possible one, since current that arrives during and immediately after the spike cannot drive the neuron to fire.

Throughout this chapter we discuss systems of IAF neurons whose interactions depend on some underlying geometrical structure. Once we allow for deviations from all-to-all couplings, new interesting phenomena develop. Hopfield and Herz [Hopfield and Herz, 1995] have investigated several types of models in which each neuron is excitatorily connected to four nearest neighbors on a two dimensional grid. They find that all models exhibit rapid convergence to cyclic solutions, although not all solutions are globally synchronous. Their two models of leaky IAF neurons reach either global synchrony or a state of phased locked oscillations, i.e. a number of synchronized clusters of neurons, where the different clusters are phase shifted with respect to each other. Each cluster contains at least one triggering neuron and its nearest neighbors. The authors show that the type of cyclic attractor depends on the updating scheme chosen for the model. They conclude that spatially connected networks exhibit richer collective phenomena than globally connected networks. A discussion of spatiotemporal patterns that evolve in spatially connected networks will be presented in the last section. It is important to note that most of the systems discussed in this chapter are composed of neurons with the same internal period. Models of random intrinsic frequencies [Strogatz and Mirollo, 1988] that exhibit other interesting dynamic behavior are beyond the scope of this chapter.

11.3 Clustering via Temporal Segmentation

Clustering is an important concept in data analysis [Duda and Hart, 1973]. When data are presented in some given space one may follow any one of a set of parametric approaches that exist in the literature. But if the space is very large, it is advantageous to concentrate not on the location of the data points but on the distances between them. In that case an analogy with a neural system may suggest itself, associating the data points with neurons and the distances with synaptic interactions between them. Such an approach was recently suggested in [Blatt et al., 1997], where the authors have applied methods of statistical mechanics to such a system, using the analogy of ferromagnetic interactions among spins. This leads to impressive results for a host of problems where, as a function of one parameter, the temperature, one can follow a tree of bifurcations into different clusters.

In the present Section we demonstrate how a system of IAF neurons can be used to perform such a task, relying on the fact that coupled IAF neural systems can exhibit staggered oscillations of neuronal cell assemblies. These assemblies are defined through the synchrony of their neurons, and we use them to represent clusters. Typically we will be able to segregate data into sets of a few clusters in this fashion. The limit on the possible number of clusters will be discussed in the next section.

Suppose we are given an $N \times N$ symmetric distance matrix, defined for N

11.3 Clustering via Temporal Segmentation

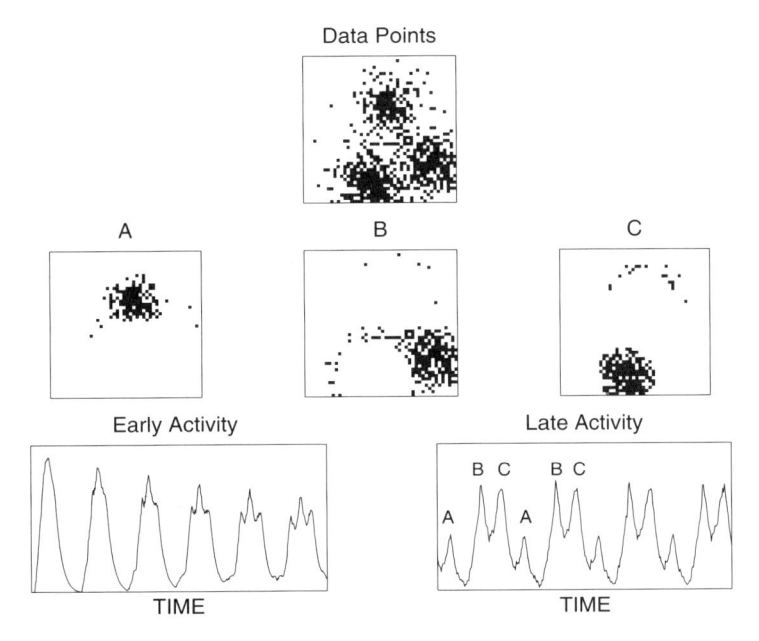

Figure 11.3. Clustering of 547 data points with a spiking system. The data points are shown in the upper frame. Each point is associated with an oscillatory neuron (same constant input). Initial conditions are all zero, and the interactions are defined according to the relative distances between the points. To induce synchrony we use delayed inhibition between all neuron pairs whose distance is below 6, with the delay time being roughly a third of the neuron's oscillation period. Competition is induced by global instantaneous inhibition. The two bottom frames show the total activity of the system, that starts out as a single synchronized state which later separates into three different peaks. Each peak corresponds to one of the clusters displayed in the middle frames.

data points. For the solution of the clustering problem we have in mind, in which clusters are composed of groups of points, we define a set of symmetric synaptic connections among N IAF neurons, that are negatively correlated with distance. Thus short distances will imply strong excitatory interactions, and long distances may lead to inhibition. The neurons are assumed to be under the influence of some common input, so that, in the absence of interactions, they will behave like free non-linear spiking oscillators. When the interactions are turned on we obtain, in general, staggered oscillations of groups of neurons. These groups will be associated with the required clusters. To make sure that global synchronization will not be reached, competition between the different clusters can be induced by global instantaneous inhibition that is proportional to the total spiking activity. This turns Equation 11.4 into

$$\dot{v}_i = -kv_i + \alpha + cm_i v_i + m_i(I + \Sigma_j w_{ij} \bar{f}_j - \gamma \Sigma_j f_j). \tag{11.5}$$

In the presence of such global inhibition, classification into clusters of roughly the same size is favored by this method. In the example of Figure 11.3 we see clustering of 547 data points formed by slightly overlapping three gaussian distributions. We have used here inhibitory connections with delays (that lead to synchronization, as shown in Section 11.2) with an additional instantaneous global inhibition. The system converges onto a periodic solution of staggered oscillations. Each peak in the total activity (lower right frame) corresponds to one of the clusters, shown in the middle frames. Approximately 90% of the data points are classified correctly.

Clustering problems are often ill defined. Usually there are many partitions of the data that can qualify as clusters. Moreover, within a given method there may exist many solutions to a given problem. This is also the case in our method when the distance matrix is not as clearly structured as in the example given above. When faced with such a situation one may impose a constraint based on the assumption of simply connected topology of clusters, and require that the average distance within a cluster be smaller than the average distance to points in different clusters. This would of course fail for non-trivial topologies where the distance condition does not hold. Examples of such problems were given in [Blatt et al., 1997].

Clustering becomes a complex problem when the number of data points is large. An exhaustive search for solutions, e.g. seeking groups of points that obey the distance condition, becomes computationally time consuming. Therefore one looks for heuristic methods to solve such problems. The advantages of our pulse-coupled system is that it relies only on distances between the points, it can be applied to problems of arbitrary size, and it does not require preprocessing that is problem specific. Its disadvantages are that it naturally leads to a small number of clusters, e.g. 3 or 4, independent of the size of the problem, and it is biased toward clusters of the same average size.

11.4 Limits on Temporal Segmentation

Clustering was achieved in the previous section via temporal segmentation. The fact that this method leads to a small number of clusters is characteristic of non-linear oscillators that perform staggered oscillations (e.g. [Hansel et al., 1995, Golomb et al., 1992]). This is readily observed in associative memory systems that are based on continuous oscillatory neurons [Wang et al., 1990, Horn and Usher, 1991]. These models provide temporal segmentation into 3 to 6 components only. It is tempting to speculate that this feature could provide an explanation [Horn and Usher, 1992] for the known limits on short term memory such as Miller's 7 ± 2 rule [Miller, 1956].

To understand why one obtains the limit on segmentation we have studied a dynamical system composed of n continuous excitatory neurons interacting with one inhibitory neuron [Horn and Opher, 1996a]. Here each neuron, or oscillatory unit, can be thought of as representing a cell assembly of spiking neurons.

$$dU_i/dt = -U_i + M_i - aM^I - b\theta_i + I_i \qquad (11.6)$$

$$d\theta_i/dt = M_i - c\theta_i \qquad (11.7)$$

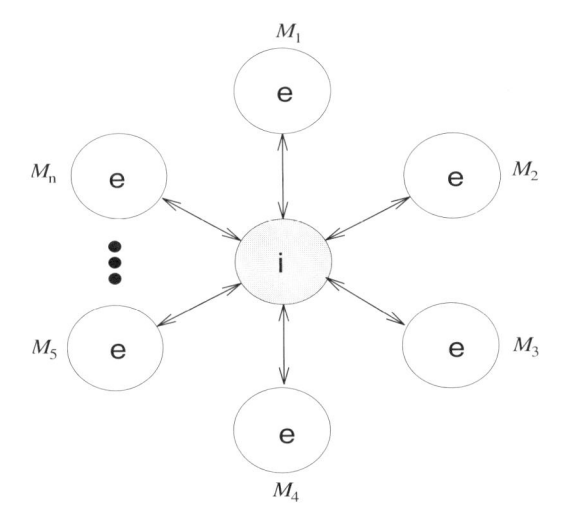

Figure 11.4. A schematic representation of a model of identical excitatory oscillators coupled to an overall inhibitory unit.

$$dU^I/dt = -gU^I - eM^I + f\sum_i M_i \tag{11.8}$$

U_i, for $i = 1, \cdots, n$ denote postsynaptic currents of excitatory neurons, whose average firing rates are

$$M_i = (1 + e^{-\beta U_i})^{-1} \tag{11.9}$$

while U^I and M^I are analogous quantities for an inhibitory neuron that induces competition between all excitatory ones. θ_i are dynamical thresholds that rise when their corresponding neurons i fire. They quench the active neurons and lead to oscillatory behavior. $a, \cdots, g$ and β are fixed parameters. To study segmentation we choose $I_i = I$ as a common external input, in which case the system becomes fully symmetric under the interchange of any two neurons $i \leftrightarrow j$. A schematic representation of the model is displayed in Figure 11.4.

For a wide range of parameters this system can be shown to converge into limit cycles that include segmentation. However, full segmentation is obtained only up to $n = 5$. Above that, only partial segmentation can be obtained. An example of the latter is shown in Figure 11.5. To understand why full segmentation cannot be obtained in this model for $n > 5$ we note that the overall period of the repeating pattern, τ, stays roughly the same, for all n. On the other hand a single oscillatory beat cannot be too narrow. Technically the limit follows from an analysis of the subharmonic oscillations of an excitatory unit in response to the input it receives from the inhibitory unit, which oscillates at a higher frequency due to the influence of all other oscillatory excitatory units. Narrow subharmonic oscillations are restricted to $n \leq 5$, thus providing the reason for the limit on full segmentation. Moreover, subharmonic oscillations of $n = 3$ are the most stable ones, which explains their dominance in partial segmentation patterns such as the one shown in Figure 11.5.

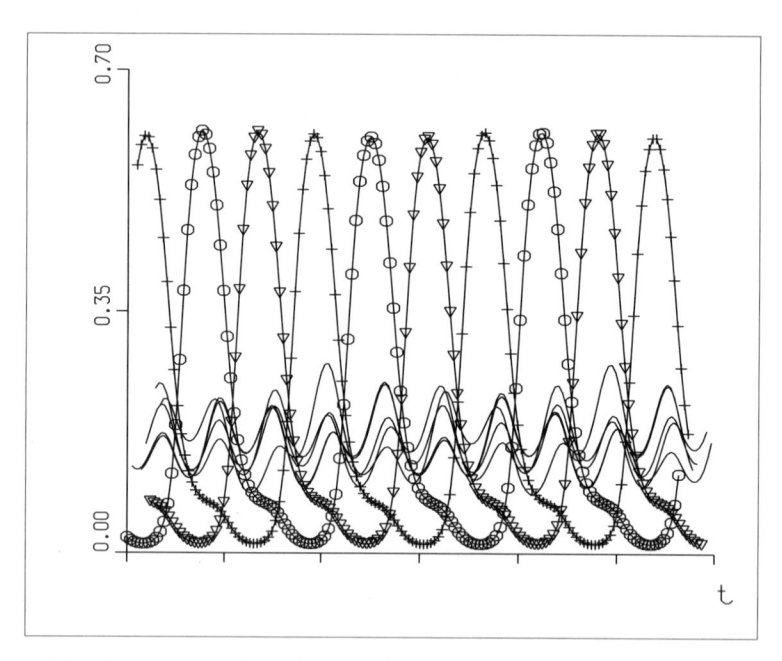

Figure 11.5. A quasiperiodic solution of the $n = 8$ problem that displays partial segmentation. The eight M values of the different oscillators are shown. The three large amplitudes form a segmented pattern, while the low amplitudes display very different periodicities.

This limitation can be overcome if one allows appropriate noisy inputs [Horn and Opher, 1996b]. We have worked with inputs of the type $I_i = 0.4 + 0.1\xi_i$, where ξ_i is a random variable between 0 and 1, that changes rapidly. For $n = 3$ this leads to a regular structure of full segmentation. The symmetry is obtained in spite of the random component in the input. The interesting effect of noise in this system is to select full segmentation as the only surviving limit cycle. Increasing n to 4 and more, we find that all symmetrical structures are broken. The general pattern is one of approximate segmentation. For large n values ($n > 5$) simple noise does not induce full segmentation. There exists either large overlap between different oscillators (degenerate segmentation) or partial segmentation in a very disordered fashion. In order to obtain full segmentation one has to make sure that the (random) input affects no more than five oscillators at a time. We have therefore employed two random components. One assigns to each oscillator a random input, and the other selects the five oscillators that are allowed to have their input active at a given time. The two independent random sequences are chosen to have rapid variations, i.e. time scales less than 0.1τ. This type of input has a random Fourier decomposition. The results are displayed in Figure 11.6. Segmentation is quite evident. The order of the dominant oscillators is random, yet, on the average, all oscillators are being excited. Our conclusion from this study is that for appropriate noise patterns, of the type described above, segmentation can be induced for any number of oscillators [Horn and Opher, 1996b].

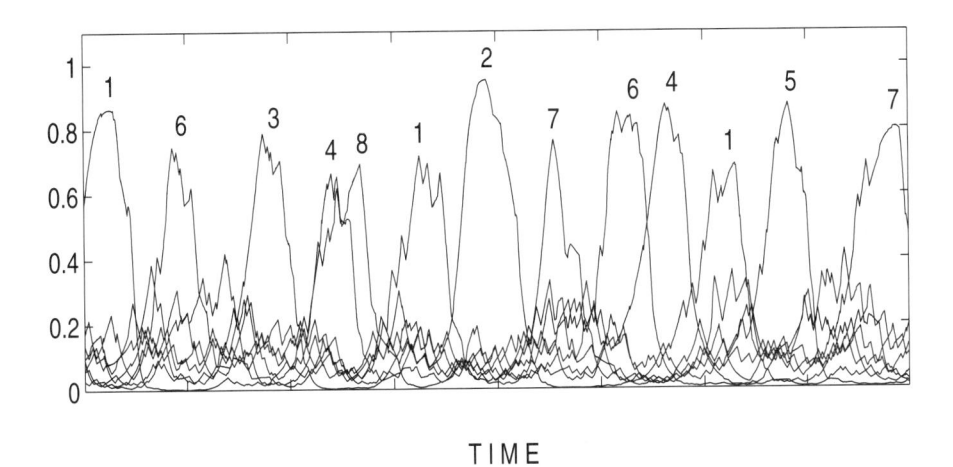

Figure 11.6. Staggered oscillation of the $n = 8$ problem is obtained for random inputs with rapid variation, affecting a few oscillators at a time. Activities of all oscillators are displayed as function of time.

11.5 Image Analysis

Analysis of a visual scene is one of the most difficult tasks performed by animal brains. It involves, among other sub-tasks, image segmentation, feature extraction and edge detection. Image analysis is also an important requirement of many artificial intelligence systems used in various fields from navigation to medicine. Great effort has been devoted towards inventing good algorithms for image analysis. However, an algorithm that does not require preprocessing (i.e. one that is not image specific) is hard to find. Therefore, as is the case in other AI implementations, it might prove useful to imitate biology, which is the best known performer of these tasks. This could be done via the temporal binding hypothesis suggested by von der Malsburg in 1981 [von der Malsburg, 1981, von der Malsburg and Schneider, 1986]. According to this idea, activities of neurons that correspond to the same feature are synchronized while representations of different features are temporally decorrelated. There exists evidence that such a strategy may be employed by the brain [Eckhorn et al., 1988, Gray et al., 1989].

Examples of the implementation of this idea in an oscillatory neural network for segmentation and binding exist in the literature [Wang et al., 1990, horn et al., 1991, von der Malsburg and Buhmann, 1992, Johnson, 1994, Ritz et al., 1994, Horn and Opher, 1996a, wang and Terman, 1997]. All these models share some interesting features. One of these is the necessity of competition between the different oscillators, usually in the form of global inhibition, allowing only a small number of oscillators to rise simultaneously. Another common feature is the limited segmentation ability. In most models, only a small number of objects can be segmented. This ties in with the limit on temporal segmentation that we discussed before.

11.5.1 Image Segmentation

The phenomenon of clustering, and the fact that we have a neural computational mechanism to achieve it, can be employed to perform image segmentation. For this purpose let us embed IAF neurons on a regular two dimensional surface with open boundary conditions. Each neuron is being fed an input whose amplitude corresponds to the grey scale of a pixel of a given image. The problem of segmentation is to define clusters that represent different objects in the image. The simplest way of clustering is to rely on similarity in the grey scale within some given radius. Hence it is natural to define an input dependent interaction that leads to mutual excitations between neurons that receive similar inputs, and to mutual inhibition between those that have very different inputs. This can be achieved through the following choice:

$$w_{ij} = F\left(\frac{1}{1+|I_i - I_j|}\right) \mathcal{H}(d_{max} - d_{ij}) \tag{11.10}$$

$$F(x) = \begin{cases} \frac{2}{\theta^2}(x^2 - x\theta) & x \leq \theta \\ \frac{1}{1-\sqrt{\theta}}\left(\sqrt{x} - \sqrt{\theta}\right) & x \geq \theta \end{cases} \tag{11.11}$$

where $\theta = \frac{1}{1+0.5(I_{max}-I_{min})}$, and $I_{max,(min)}$ are the maximal (minimal) pixel values of the image. The specific choice of $x(I_i, I_j)$ and of $F(x)$ is arbitrary [Wang and Terman, 1997] as long as F is kept negative for large values of $|I_i - I_j|$ and positive for similar values of I_i and I_j. Our choice was inspired by the BCM model [Bienenstock et al., 1982]. We find that using such a form of interactions contributes to the binding of neurons that belong to the same object, thus improving segmentation of different objects. An example is shown in Figure 11.7, where segmentation of 4 objects is obtained.

This form of interaction is quite similar to the one used by Wang and Terman [Wang and Terman, 1997], who work with phase-coupled nonlinear oscillators. They name their model LEGION, implying local excitation and global inhibition. Since a previous version of their model [Terman and Wang, 1995] leads to limited temporal segmentation, they have devised an algorithm that allows them to do much better. In their model they have introduced complex lateral interactions that may shunt the input to an oscillator. These interactions allow for the definition of leading oscillators, that are the elements prone to lateral excitation, which play key roles in forming clusters or segments. The algorithm builds on the general characteristics of nonlinear oscillatory dynamics, but does not follow the same temporal development. In particular, once a segment is activated it may be prevented from firing again until all other segments are activated. As a result, they are able to achieve high degrees of segmentation in images of natural scenes and of medical interest.

Johnson [Johnson, 1994] studied the use of pulse-coupled neural networks for image analysis. His model is inspired by the linking field neural network of [Eckhorn et al., 1990]. It is much more complex than the networks

11.5 Image Analysis

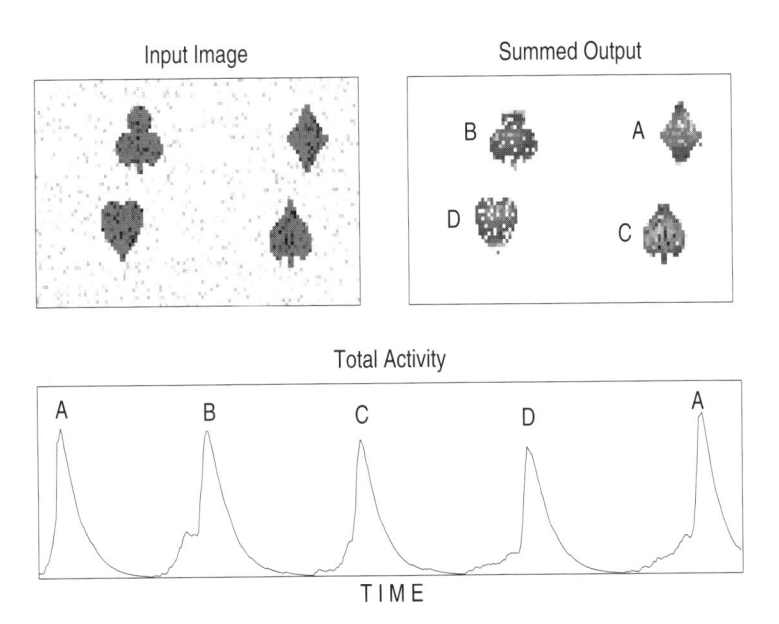

Figure 11.7. Segmentation of 4 non-spherical objects using input dependent connections restricted to a circle of radius 9 around each neuron. The peaks in total activity, shown in the bottom frame, correspond to separate activation of each one of the four objects that are displayed together in the upper right frame. Temporal segmentation is achieved through global inhibition.

that we use in this chapter. He shows that the frequency histogram of the total activity of his system is stimulus specific. With a certain parameter choice, this histogram can be insensitive to translation and scaling of an object. Implementation of the network as a hybrid optical system yields temporal image segmentation as a result of weak linking between neurons whose thresholds depend dynamically on their own outputs. A similar network is used by [Lindblad et al., 1997] to perform image analysis, where the interaction between two neurons is inversely proportional to their distance. Noise reduction is done by changing the input to a neuron that is not synchronized with its neighbors. The amount of change depends on the time lag between the firings of the neuron and those of its neighbors. This method produces segmentation whose character changes during the temporal development of the system. Moreover, it also leads to edge detection. The edges of a segment are activated in the iteration that follows the activation of the segment, due to the linking between the perimeter neurons and their neighbors that did not fire. Note that pulse-coupled networks are able to perform both segmentation and edge detection, whereas, so far, only segmentation was implemented by phase-coupled oscillators.

11.5.2 Edge Detection

The problem of edge detection is complementary to that of segmentation. Whereas segmentation implies finding areas that belong together,

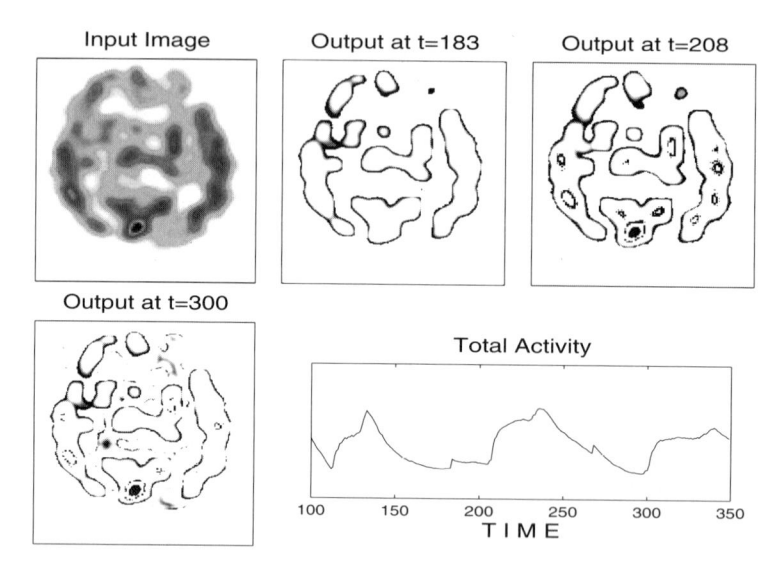

Figure 11.8. Edge detection in a SPECT brain image. The edges of most shaded areas appear at different local minima of the total activity. The behavior of the activity in time is rather complicated, due to the complexity of the input image. Therefore, different combinations of edges appear at time steps that correspond to different minima of the total activity of the system.

edge detection finds the borderlines between such areas. Edge detection is an important task of image analysis. In various applications, such as in medicine, defining the boundaries of elements in a picture is crucial.

To confront this problem we find it useful to start with synaptic couplings that are not structured by the data. A good candidate is the difference-of-gaussians (DOG) interaction

$$w_{ij} = C_E e^{-d_{ij}^2/d_E} - C_I e^{-d_{ij}^2/d_I}. \qquad (11.12)$$

Here d_{ij} is the distance between two points and we have four constants denoting the strength and radii of excitation and inhibition. Since the interactions are symmetric, it is only reasonable that the temporal evolvement of the spiking activity will reflect asymmetries that exist in the input. We find, indeed, that when an image is used as an input then, after the firing pattern settles into a periodic structure, edges can be read off at minima of the total activity.

An example of such behavior can be seen in Figure 11.8, where the edges of most shaded areas in a SPECT (single photon emission computed tomography) brain image[2] are detected, at time steps that correspond to minima of the total activity of the system. In this analysis we have not employed global inhibition and, therefore, we do not obtain temporal segmentation. At peaks of the total activity, many areas of the image will be active. Nonetheless, using the delineation of boundaries that is observed at minima, we obtain a highly segmented picture.

---
[2] Image provided by I. Prohovnik, private communication

11.6 Solitary Waves

Wilson and Cowan [Wilson and Cowan, 1973] have realized that if one builds aggregates of neurons one may naturally obtain the formation of unattenuated traveling waves as a result of a localized input. Studying two dimensional layers of interacting neurons, [Ermentrout and Cowan, 1979] have observed formations of moving stripes. They have pointed out that if their model is applied to V1, it can provide an explanation of drug-induced visual hallucinations, relying on the retinocortical map interpretation of V1. In a more recent work using spiking neurons, [Föhlmeister et al., 1995] have obtained, in addition to stripe formations, rotating spirals, expanding concentric rings and collective bursts. Most of these coherent excitations, whose structure is continuous in space and time, can be characterized as solitary waves [Meron, 1992]. They move in space with some well defined speed, or expand from, or rotate around, some focus. This holds until they meet some other wave-front of similar character, in which case they annihilate one another.

In the present section we provide some examples of this behavior and explain the topologic character of the resulting solitary waves. In our analysis we employ a constant input for the whole surface of neurons. In the absence of any interactions among the neurons, and starting from random initial conditions, this would lead to random periodic behavior of the type of Figure 11.2b. This changes once we introduce an interaction such as in Equation (11.12). For strong enough simultaneous excitations the system develops a coherent character, i.e. neighboring neurons become synchronized, thus leading to spatial order. The system turns then into a structured cyclic attractor. The details of the structure depend in a critical manner on the interaction parameters.

In Figure 11.9 we display results of propagating stripes, as well as formations of merging lines. When viewed at different time frames one observes a homogeneous motion of these structures. The two formations represent the same type of solution, namely propagating fronts. They were obtained with the same set of interaction parameters, but with different boundary and initial conditions. The parallel stripes of Figure 11.9a are the result of periodic boundaries and the merging lines of Figure 11.9b and c are the result of open boundaries. The latter cause the activity to start at boundary neurons, that receive less inhibition than others. The convergence onto a specific solution depends on initial conditions of the complex nonlinear system. The distinction between solutions belonging to periodic or open boundary conditions is always quite evident.

Rotating spirals and expanding rings are other types of solutions, that are well known examples of solitary wave formations [Meron, 1992]. Both formations are often encountered in 2-d arrays of IAF neurons [Jung and Mayer-Kress, 1995, Milton et al., 1993]. An example of colliding rings is displayed in Figure 11.10. This example is obtained by keeping only few nearby neighbors in the interaction. The number of expanding rings is inversely related to the span of the interactions. We note the spontaneous creation of two foci from which the expanding rings emerge. Spikes exists only at the boundary between $m = 0$ and $m = 1$ areas. This

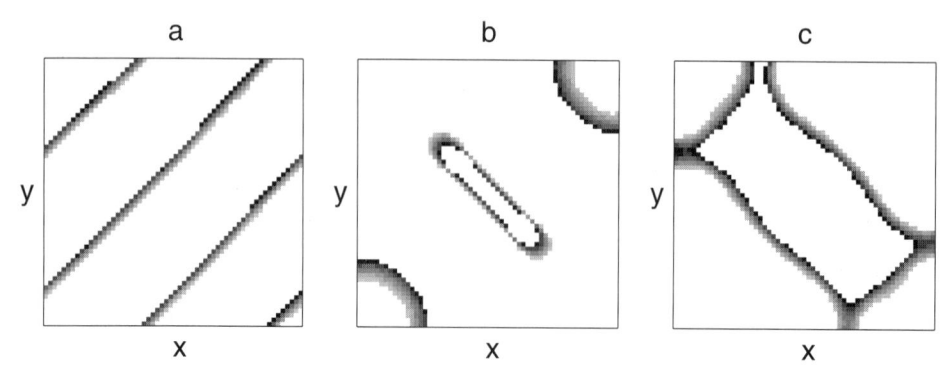

Figure 11.9. Two solutions with propagating spiking fronts (the grey scale is proportional to the strength of f_i) on a 60×60 grid using the same interaction parameters. (a) Periodic boundary conditions lead to parallel stripes. Frames (b) and (c) display two snapshots of a solution corresponding to open boundary conditions. In (b) we see two arcs propagating from opposite corners, merging in (c) with fronts that started in the other corners, to form a rectangle that eventually shrinks to the structure seen in the center of (b). Interaction parameters are $C_E = 0.2$, $C_I = 0.02$, $d_E = 15$, $d_I = 100$, restricted to an area of radius 20 around each neuron. Other parameters are the same as in Figure 11.1.

property reflects the fact that for each neuron a spike is followed by a refractory period. It is responsible for the vanishing of two firing fronts that collide, because, after collision, there remains only a single $m = 0$ area, formed by the merger of the two former $m = 0$ areas. All these simulations are carried out on some finite lattice, containing typically 60×60 IAF neurons. Once the system adapts to its coherent behavior, the structure of its underlying lattice becomes unimportant. In fact, it turns into a continuous problem of interacting neural fields. There is a topologic rule that we can deduce from this continuity. Once $m(\vec{x}, t)$ is continuous, it has the same dimensionality D (2 in the cases discussed here) as the manifold to which the neurons are attached. Since all firing formations occur at moving fronts of $m(\vec{x}, t) = 1$ patches, these solitary waves have to be of dimensionality $D - 1$. This is well exemplified in Figure 11.10. It holds for all the coherent solutions that we obtain, arcs, spirals, stripes and expanding rings.

We have obtained coherent solutions also when some forms of synaptic delays were introduced. Coherence can be broken by strong noise in the input or by randomness in the synaptic connections. What we would expect in this case is that the DOG interactions specify the resulting behavior of the system. This is, indeed, the case, as demonstrated in Figure 11.11 which shows an irregular, but patchy, behavior. These patches have a typical length scale that is of the order of the range of excitatory interactions. We believe that this is the explanation for the moving patches of activity reported by other authors [Hill and Villa, 1994, Usher et al., 1994]. These are incoherent phenomena, emerging in models with randomly distributed radial connections.

We learn therefore that our model embodies two competing factors. The DOG interactions tend to produce patchy firing patterns, but the coher-

11.6 Solitary Waves 313

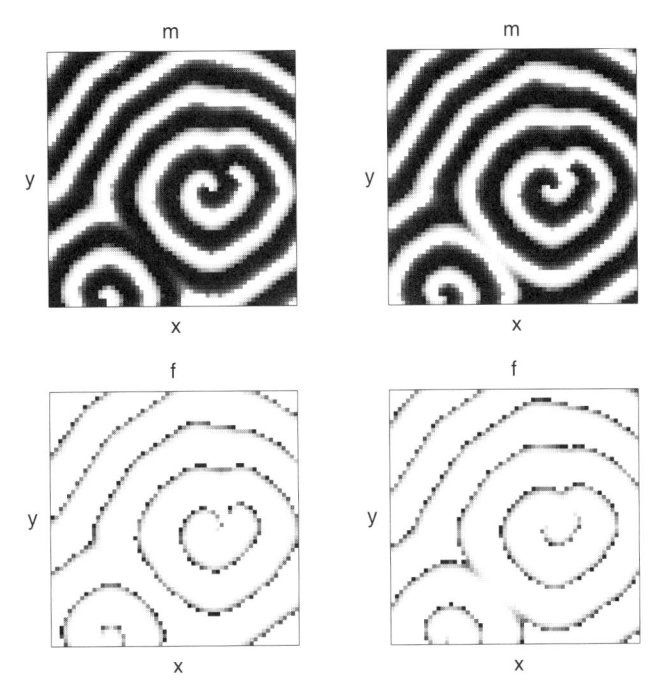

Figure 11.10. Collision of two expanding rings formed on a 60×60 grid. The top frames display m fields at two time steps, with $m = 0$ in white and $m = 1$ in black. The bottom frames exhibit the corresponding coherent firing patterns, that appear at boundaries between areas of $m = 0$ and $m = 1$. In this simulation we use excitatory interactions only, coupling each neuron to its 8 neighbors with an amplitude of 0.3.

ence, that is brought about by the excitatory connections, leads to the formation of one dimensional solitary waves on a two dimensional manifold. If, however, strong fluctuations exist, i.e. the neurons can no longer be described by homogeneous physiological and geometrical properties, the resulting patterns of firing activity are incoherent, and their spatial extension reflects the range of the underlying interactions.

Are there situations where coherent firing activity exists in neuronal tissue? If the explanation of hallucinatory phenomena [Ermentrout and Cowan, 1979] is correct, then this is expected to be the case. It could be proved experimentally through optical imaging of V1 under appropriate pharmacological conditions. Other abnormal brain activities, such as epileptic seizures, could also fall into the category of coherent firing patterns. Does coherence occur also under normal functioning conditions? The interesting spatiotemporal evoked activity, reported by [Arieli et al., 1996] in areas 17 and 18 in cat, may be due to underlying neurons that fire incoherently. But the thalamo-cortical spindle waves generated by the reticular thalamic nucleus [Golomb et al., 1994, Contreras and Steriade, 1996] may well be an example of coherent activity. Another example could be the synchronous bursts of activity that propagate as wave fronts in retinal ganglion cells of neonatal mammals [Meister et al., 1991, Wong, 1993]. It has been suggested that

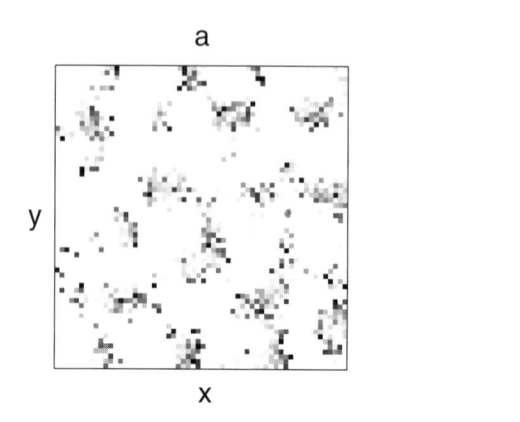

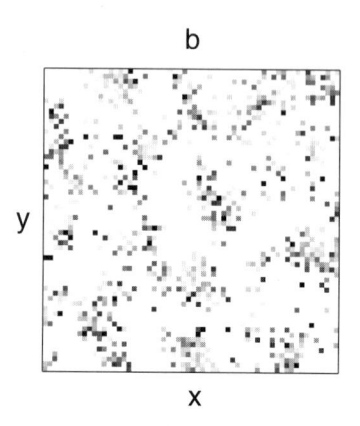

314   11. Collective Excitation Phenomena and Their Applications

Figure 11.11. Incoherent firing patterns for (a) high variability of synaptic connections, or (b) noisy input. In (a) we have multiplied 75% of all synapses by a random gaussian component (mean=1., s.d=3.) that stays constant in time. In (b) we have employed a noisy input that varies in space and time (mean=0.29, s.d.=0.25). In both frames the firing patterns are no longer coherent. We can see the formation of small clusters of spiking neurons. The typical length scale of these patches is of the order of the span of excitatory interactions. This is a manifestation of the dominance of interactions in determining the spatial behavior in the absence of continuity that imposes the topologic constraint.

these waves play an important role in the formation of ocular dominance layers in the LGN [Meister et al., 1991].

11.7 The Importance of Noise

The effects of noise, displayed in Figure 11.11, are deconstructive, in the sense that noise causes desynchronization and, therefore, eliminates the coherent behavior. However, desynchronization may also have useful aspects, as seen in section 11.4 and displayed in Figure 11.6, where noise helped us to overcome temporal segmentation constraints. This observation goes back to [Horn et al., 1991], where it was shown that noise can serve the binding process by forming a nucleation source for synchronization of one segment. As such it can serve also in image segmentation analysis [Wang and Terman, 1997].

It is interesting that, under certain conditions, noise can also be employed to allow for solitary wave formation, rather than destroy it. This is the case in a dissipative regime in which the IAF neurons do not have a constant input that keeps them oscillating, as already noted by [Jung and Mayer-Kress, 1995]. A one dimensional example [Horn and Opher, 1997b] of such a system is shown in Figure 11.12. Once a neuron fires, the spreading of activity depends on the situation of near-by neurons. If they happen to be in a refractory period, or under the influence of small, or even negative input, activation will not spread. However, once activation does spread, it behaves in the same way as in the oscillatory regime. In this one dimensional example we observe creation and annihilation of solitary waves. Note that this system can no longer have the global periodic structure that is characteristic of the oscillatory regime.

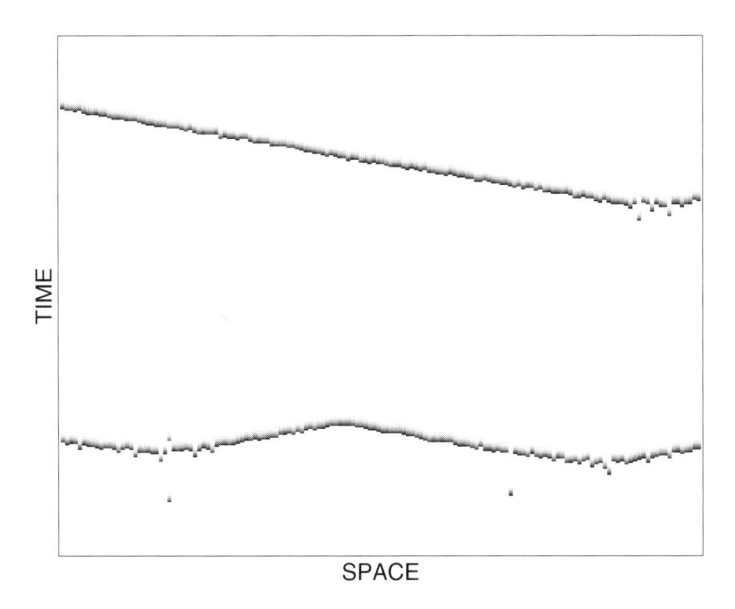

[Figure: space-time plot with TIME on vertical axis and SPACE on horizontal axis]

Figure 11.12. Space time description of coherent spiking activity on a one dimensional neural manifold in a dissipative regime. The coherent propagation of excitation, induced by random inputs, is similar to what is observed in the oscillatory regime, except that it is not periodic and less frequent. Parameters are: $w = 1.2$ for 10 neighbors on each side. I is normally distributed with mean and standard deviation of 0.02. Its values change at random time steps.

Note that in this example noise serves only as the source of energy for the system to excite itself, and it is not strong enough to break the underlying homogeneous structure. If we strengthen it considerably we will end up again with the type of behavior displayed in Figure 11.11.

11.8 Conclusions

Using synchrony of spiking neurons, we have analyzed different cases of coherent firing activity that lead to interesting spatiotemporal formations. These phenomena can be employed for clustering of data consisting of a few tens of elements and ranging up to ten thousand elements, as is the case for image segmentation.

Our analysis was carried out on a fairly simple system. It could, therefore, serve as a general framework within which we attack a wide scope of problems, covering clustering (section 11.3), image segmentation (section 11.5.1), edge detection (section 11.5.2) and formation of solitary waves (section 11.6). Emphasizing the generality of the method, we inevitably lose on its ability to lead in the technical application frontier over other specialized techniques.

One of the main features of temporal segmentation with non-linear oscillators is the inherent limit that we discussed in Section 11.4. This limit constrains our general analysis of clustering, and limits our ability to perform image segmentation. In order to have better designs for application purposes one has to find tricks to overcome this limit, using methods that are no longer motivated by biological intuition. It is satisfying to note that limited segmentation is characteristic of human ability to process simultaneously different streams of data.

If we try to define the type of computational tasks that our system performs, the appropriate classification would be feature extraction. Conventional neural computation techniques that are being used for such purposes are based on unsupervised competitive learning. Such learning was not performed in our model, although in principle it could be added to it. We have used throughout this chapter fixed synaptic weights. However competition was built into our system, often through explicit inhibitory actions. The winner-take-all feature of the conventional techniques of unsupervised learning, is replaced in our models by the dominance of a particular cluster during a specific time frame. In other words, temporal segmentation is a way of breaking a given problem (or data set) into several clusters such that each one becomes a winner sometimes. By performing computation along the time axis, we are able to carry out feature extraction without a training algorithm.

Finally let us emphasize that the coherent behavior described in this chapter is quite robust, as long as the underlying system of spiking neurons is homogeneous and its interactions are suitable for mutual synchronization. The interesting spatiotemporal properties of such systems may play an important role in pattern analysis and pattern formation in both biological and artificial neural systems.

Acknowledgment

This work was partly supported by the Israel Science Foundation.

References

[Abbott and van Vreeswijk, 1993] Abbott, L. F. and van Vreeswijk, C. (1993). Asynchronous states in networks of pulse-coupled oscillators. *Physical Rev. E*, 48:1483–1490.

[Arieli et al., 1996] Arieli, A., Sterkin A., Grinvlad A., and Aertsen A. (1996). Dynamics of ongoing activity: explanation of the large variability in evoked responses. *Science*, 273:1868–1871.

[Bienenstock et al., 1982] Bienenstock, E. L., Cooper, L. N., and Munro, P. W. (1982). Theory for the development of neuron selectivity: orientation specificity and binocular interaction in visual cortex. *The J. of Neurosci.*, 2:32–48.

[Blatt et al., 1997] Blatt, M., Wiseman, S., and Domany, E. (1997). Data clustering using a model granular magnet. *Neural Computation*, 9:1805–1842.

[Contreras and Steriade, 1996] Contreras, D. and Steriade, M. (1996). Spindle oscillation in cats: the role of corticothalamic feedback in a thalamically generated rhythm. *J. of Physiology*, 490:159–179.

[Crook et al., 1997] Crook, S. M., Ermentrout, G. B., and Bower, J. M. (1997). Spike frequency adaptation affects the synchronization properties of networks of cortical oscillators. *Comp. Neurosc. Meeting, CNS*97*, Big-Sky, MO.

[Duda and Hart, 1973] Duda, R. O. and Hart, P. E. (1973). *Pattern Classification and Scene Analysis*. Wiley-Interscience, New-York.

[Eckhorn et al., 1988] Eckhorn, R., Bauer, R., Jordan, W., Brosch, M., Kruse, W., Munk, M., and Reitboeck, H. J. (1988). Coherent oscillations: a mechanism of feature linking in the visual cortex? *Biol. Cybern.*, 60:121–130.

[Eckhorn et al., 1990] Eckhorn, R., Reitboeck, H. J., Arndt, M., and Dicke, P. (1990). Feature linking via synchronization among distributed assemblies: simulations of results from cat visual cortex. *Neural Computation*, 2:293–307.

[Ermentrout and Cowan, 1979] Ermentrout, G. B. and Cowan J. D. (1979). A mathematical theory of visual hallucination patterns. *Biol. Cybern.*, 34:136–150.

[Föhlmeister et al., 1995] Föhlmeister, C., Gerstner, W., Ritz, R., and van Hemmen, J. L. (1995). Spontaneous excitation in the visual cortex: stripes, spirals, rings and collective bursts. *Neural Computation*, 7:905–914.

[Gerstner et al., 1993] Gerstner, W. Ritz, R., and van Hemmen, J. L. (1993). A biologically motivated and analytically soluble model of collective oscillations in the cortex I. Theory of weak locking. *Biol. Cybern.*, 68:363–374.

[Gerstner et al., 1996] Gerstner, W., van Hemmen, J. L., and Cowan, J. D. (1996). What matters in neuronal locking. *Neural Computation*, 8:1653–1676.

References

[Golomb et al., 1992] Golomb, D., Hansel, D., Shraiman, S., and Sompolinsky, H. (1992). Clustering in globally coupled phase oscillators. *Physical Rev. A.*, 45:3516–3530.

[Golomb et al., 1994] Golomb, D., Wang, X. J., and Rinzel, J. (1994). Synchronization properties of Spindle oscillations in a thalamic reticular nucleus model. *J. of Neurophys.*, 72:1109–1126.

[Grannan et al., 1993] Grannan, E. R., Kleinfeld, D., and Sompolinsky, H. (1993). Stimulus-dependent synchronization of neuronal assemblies. *Neural Computation*, 5:550–569.

[Gray et al., 1989] Gray, C. M., König, P., Engel, A. K., and Singer, W. (1989). Oscillatory responses in cat visual cortex exhibit intercolumnar synchronization which reflects global stimulus properties. *Nature*, 338:334–337.

[Hansel et al., 1995] Hansel, D., Mato, M., and Meunier, C. (1995). Synchrony in excitatory neural network. *Neural Computation*, 7:307–337.

[Hill and Villa, 1994] Hill, S. L. and Villa, A. E. P. (1994). Global spatiotemporal activity influenced by local kinetics in a simulated "cortical" neural network. *Supercomputing in Brain Research: From Tomography to Neural Networks / Workshop on Supercomputing in Brain Research.* H .J. Herrmann, D. E. Wolf, and E. Poppel, eds., World Scientific.

[Horn and Usher, 1991] Horn, D. and Usher, M. (1991). Parallel activation of memories in an oscillatory neural network. *Neural Computation*, 3:31–43.

[Horn et al., 1991] Horn, D., Sagi, D., and Usher, M. (1991). Segmentation, binding and illusory conjunctions. *Neural Computation*, 3:510–525.

[Horn and Usher, 1992] Horn, D., and Usher, M. (1992). Oscillatory model of short term memory. *Advances in Neural Information and Processing Systems, vol. 4*, Morgan Kaufmann Publishers, 125-132.

[Horn and Opher, 1996a] Horn, D. and Opher, I. (1996). Temporal Segmentation in a Neural Dynamical System. *Neural Comp.*, 8:375–391.

[Horn and Opher, 1996b] Horn, D. and Opher, I. (1996). The importance of noise for segmentation and binding in dynamical neural systems. *Int. Journal of Neural Systems*, 7:529–535.

[Horn and Opher, 1997a] Horn, D. and Opher, I. (1997). Solitary waves of integrate and fire neural fields *Neural Comp.*, 9:1677–1690.

[Horn and Opher, 1997b] Horn, D. and Opher, I. (1997). Solitary waves on manifolds of integrate-and-fire neurons. To be published in *Phyl. Mag. B, Proc. of the Minerva workshop on Mesoscopics, Fractals and Neural Networks*, Taylor and Francis Group, London.

[Hopfield and Herz, 1995] Hopfield, J. J. and Herz, A. V. M. (1995). Rapid local synchronization of action potentials: toward computation with coupled integrate-and-fire neurons *Proc. Natl. Acad. Sci., USA*, 92:6655–6662.

[Johnson, 1994] Johnson, L. J. (1994). Pulse-coupled neural nets: translation, rotation, scale, distortion and intensity invariance for images. *App. Optics*, 33:6239–6253.

[Jung and Mayer-Kress, 1995] Jung, P. and Mayer-Kress, G. (1995). Noise controlled spiral growth in excitable media. *Chaos*, 5:458–462.

[Kuramoto, 1990] Kuramoto, Y. (1990). Collective synchronization of pulse-coupled oscillators and excitable units. *Physica D*, 50:15–30.

[Lindblad et al., 1997] Lindblad, Th., Becanovic V., Lindsey C. S., and Szekely, G. (1997). Intelligent detectors modelled from the cat's eye. *Nuclear Instruments and Methods in Physics Research* A, 389:245–250.

[von der Malsburg, 1981] von der Malsburg, C. (1981). The correlation theory of brain function. Internal Report 81-2, Max-Planck-Institute for Biophysical Chemistry. Reprinted in *Models of Neural Networks II*, Domany et al., eds., Springer, 1994, 95–119.

[von der Malsburg and Schneider, 1986] von der Malsburg, C. and Schneider, W. (1986). A neural cocktail party processor. *Biol. Cybern.*, 54:29–40.

[von der Malsburg and Buhman, 1992] von der Malsburg, C. and Buhman, J. (1992). Sensory segmentation with coupled neural oscillators. *Biol. Cybern.*, 67:233–242.

[Meister et al., 1991] Meister M., Wong R. O. L., Denis A. B., and Shatz C. J. (1991). Synchronous bursts of action potentials in ganglion cells of the developing mammalian retina. *Science*, 252:939–943.

[Meron, 1992] Meron, E. (1992). Pattern formation in excitable media. *Physics Reports*, 218:1–66.

[Miller, 1956] Miller, G. A. (1956). The magical number seven, plus or minus two: Some limits on our capacity of processing information. *Psychological Rev.*, 63:81–97.

[Milton et al., 1993] Milton, J. G., Chu, P. H., and Cowan, J. D. (1993). Spiral waves in integrate-and-fire neural networks. *Advances in Neural Information Processing Systems, vol. 5*, Morgan Kaufmann, 1001–1007.

[Mirollo and Strogatz, 1990] Mirollo, R. E. and Strogatz, S. H. (1990). Synchronization of pulse-coupled biological oscillators *SIAM J. Appl. Math.*, 50:1645–1662.

[Nischwitz and Glünder, 1995] Nischwitz, A. and Glünder, H. (1995). Local lateral inhibition: a key to spike synchronization? *Biol. Cybern.*, 73:389–400.

[Ritz et al., 1994] Ritz, R., Gerstner, W., Feuntes, U., and van Hemmen, J. L. (1994). A biologically motivated and analytically soluble model of collective oscillations in the cortex II. Application to binding and pattern segmentation. *Biol. Cybern.*, 71:349–358.

[Strogatz and Stewart, 1993] Strogatz, S. H. and Stewart, I. (1993). Coupled oscillators and biological synchronization *Scientific American*, Dec. 93, 68–75.

[Strogatz and Mirollo, 1988] Strogatz, S. H. and Mirollo R. E. (1988). Phase locking and critical phenomena in lattices of coupled nonlinear oscillators with random intrinsic frequencies. *Physica D.*, 31:143–168.

[Terman and Wang, 1995] Terman, D. and Wang, D. L. (1995). Global competition and local cooperation in a network of neural oscillators. *Physica D*, 81:148–176.

[Usher et al., 1993] Usher, M., Schuster, H. S., and Niebur, E. (1993). Dynamics of populations of integrate-and-fire neurons, partial synchronization and Memory. *Neural Computation*, 5:570–586.

[Usher et al., 1994] Usher, M., Stemmler, M., Koch, C., and Olami, Z. (1994). Network Amplification of local fluctuations causes high spike rate variability, fractal firing patterns and oscillatory local field potentials. *Neural Computation*, 6:795–836.

[van Vreeswijk and Abbott, 1994] van Vreeswijk, C. and Abbott, L. F. (1994). When inhibition not excitation synchronizes neural firing *J. of Comp. Neurosci.*, 1:313–321.

[van Vreeswijk and Hansel, 1997] van Vreeswijk, C. and Hansel, D. (1997). Rhythmic bursting in networks of adaptive spiking neurons. *Comp. Neurosc. Meeting, CNS*97*, Big-Sky, MO.

[Wang et al., 1990] Wang, D., Buhman, J., and von der Malsburg, C. (1990). Pattern segmentation in associative memory. *Neural Computation*, 2:94–106.

[Wang and Terman, 1997] Wang, D. and Terman, D. (1997). Image Segmentation Based on Oscillatory Correlation. *Neural Computation*, 9:805–836; Err: 9:1623–1626.

[Wilson and Cowan, 1973] Wilson, H. R. and Cowan, J. D. (1973). A mathematical theory of the functional dynamics of cortical and thalamic nervous tissue. *Kybernetik*, 13:55–80.

[Wong, 1993] Wong R. O. L. (1993). The role of spatio-temporal firing patterns in neuronal development of sensory systems. *Curr. Op. Neurobiology*, 3:595–601.

12 Computing and Learning with Dynamic Synapses

Wolfgang Maass and Anthony M. Zador

12.1 Introduction

The models in all other chapters in this book assume that synapses are *static*, i.e., that they change their "weight" only on the slow time scale of learning. We will discuss in this chapter experimental data which show that this assumption is not justified for biological neural systems. As a matter of fact, this assumption is also unjustified for all hardware implementations of artificial neural nets where the sizes of synaptic "weights" are stored by analog techniques (see chapter 3). The consequences of this are threefold:

i) It is not clear whether implementations of pulsed neural nets in wetware or silicon are able to carry out computations in a way that is predicted by currently existing theoretical models for pulsed neural nets with static synapses.

ii) The inherent temporal dynamics of synaptic weights may not just be a curse, but also a blessing: dynamic synapses provide novel computational units for neural computation in the time series domain, i.e., in an environment where the inputs (and possibly also the outputs) of the networks are functions of time.

iii) One has to revise the foundations of learning in neural nets. In fact, it is not even clear anymore which are the parameters of networks of spiking neurons in which their "program" is stored. In particular all classical learning algorithms for neural nets that provide rules for tuning synaptic "weights" become dubious in this context. Furthermore, in view of point ii) it is not even clear what the goal of a learning algorithm for pulsed neural nets should be: the goal to learn a *function* (from input-vectors to output-vectors of numbers) or a *functional* (from input-functions to output-functions)?

In this chapter we will review in Section 12.2 results about the dynamic behaviour of biological synapses, we will survey in section 12.3 the available quantitative models for the temporal dynamics of biological synapses, and we will discuss possible computational uses of that dynamics in Section 12.4. Some consequences of synaptic dynamics for learning in neural nets will be discussed in Section 12.5.

12.2 Biological Data on Dynamic Synapses

In most models for networks of spiking neurons one assumes that the weight (or "efficacy") of a synapse is a parameter that changes only on the slow time scale of learning. It has however been known for quite some time (see for example [Katz, 1966, Magleby, 1987, Zucker, 1989] that synaptic efficacy changes with activity.

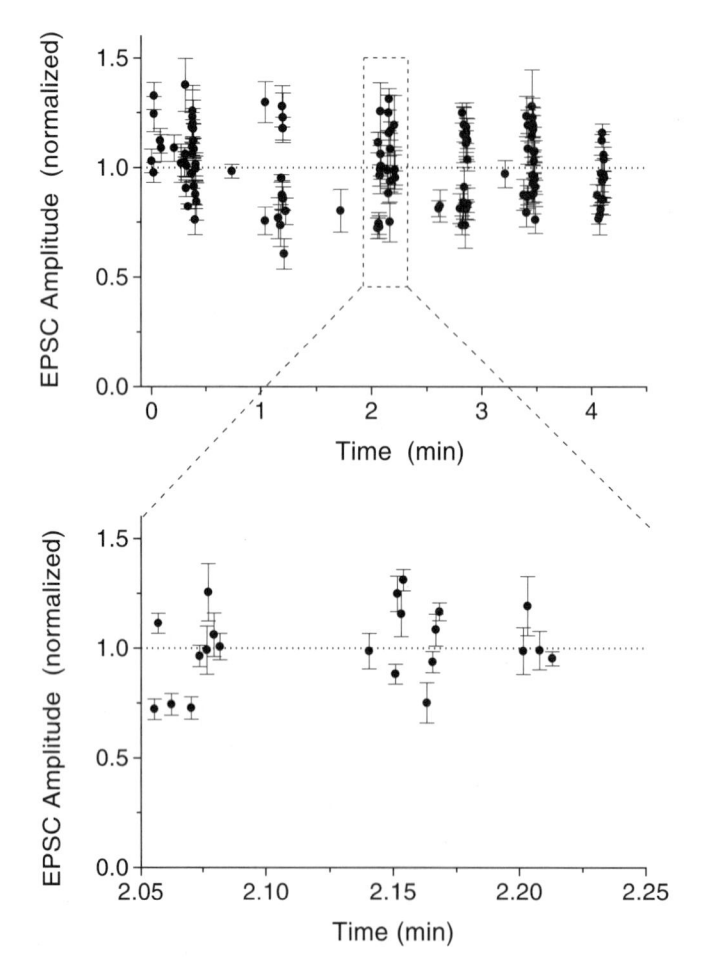

Figure 12.1. Synaptic response depends on the history of prior usage: Excitatory postsynaptic currents (EPSCs) recorded from a CA1 pyramidal neuron in a hippocampal slice in response to stimulation of the Schaffer collateral input. The stimulus is a spike train recorded *in vivo* from the hippocampus of an awake behaving rat, and "played-back" at a reduced speed *in vitro*. The presynaptic spikes have an average interspike interval of 1,950 msec that varies from a low at 35 msec to a maximum at 35 sec. The normalized strength of the EPSC varies in a deterministic manner depending on the prior usage of the synapse. For a constant synaptic weight, the normalized amplitudes should all fall on the dashed line. (A) EPSC as a function of time. The mean and standard deviation (4 repetitions) are shown. Note the response amplitude varies rapidly by more than two-fold. (B) AN excerpt is shown at a high temporal resolution. Unpublished data from L. E. Dobrunz and C. F. Stevens.

Phenomenon	Duration	Locus of Induction
Short-term Enhancement		
Paired-pulse facilitation (PPF)	$100\ msec$	Pre
Augmentation	$10\ sec$	Pre
Post-tetanic potentiation	$1\ min$	Pre
Long-term Enhancement		
Short-term potentiation (STP)	$15\ min$	Post
Long-term potentiation (LTP)	$> 30\ min$	Pre and post
Depression		
Paired-pulse depression (PPD)	$100\ msec$	Pre
Depletion	$10\ sec$	Pre
Long-term Depressions (LTD)	$> 30\ min$	Pre and post

Table 12.1. Different forms of synaptic plasticity
Synaptic plasticity occurs across many time scales. This table is a list of some of the better studied forms of plasticity. Included also are very approximate estimates of their associated decay constants, and whether the conditions required for induction depend on pre- or on postsynaptic activity, or on both. This distinction is crucial from a computational point of view, since Hebbian learning rules require a postsynaptic locus for the induction of plasticity. Note that for LTP and LTD, we are referring specifically to the form found at the Schaffer collateral input to neurons in the CA1 region of the rodent hippocampus; other forms have different requirements.

The responses shown in Figure 12.1 represent the complex interactions of many use-dependent forms of synaptic plasticity, many of which are listed in Table 12.2. Some involve an increase in synaptic efficacy (called "facilitation" or "enhancement"), while others involve a decrease ("depression"). They differ most strikingly in duration: some (e.g. facilitation) decay on the order of about 10 to 100 milliseconds, while others (e.g. long-term potentiation, or LTP) persist for hours, days or longer. The spectrum of time constants is in fact so broad that it covers essentially every time scale, from the fastest (that of synaptic transmission itself) to the slowest (developmental). The terms "paired-pulsed facilitation" and "paired-pulsed depression" in Table 12.2 refer to experiments where the stimulus consists of just two spikes, and the second spike causes a larger (smaller) postsynaptic response.

These forms of plasticity differ not only in time scale, but also in the conditions required for their induction. Some – particularly the shorter-lasting forms – depend only on the history of presynaptic stimulation, independent of the postsynaptic response. Thus facilitation, augmentation, and post-tetanic potentiation (PTP) occur after rapid presynaptic stimulation, with more vigorous stimulation leading to more persistent potentiation. Other forms of plasticity depend on some conjunction of pre- and postsynaptic activity: the most famous example is LTP, which obeys Hebb's rule in that its induction requires simultaneous pre- and postsynaptic activation.

In view of these data it becomes unclear which parameter should be referred to as the current weight or efficacy of a synapse, and what *learning* in a biological neural system means. For example [Markram and Tsodyks, 1996] have exhibited cases where pairing of pre- and postsynaptic firing (i.e., Hebbian learning) does not affect the average amplitudes of postsynaptic responses. Instead, it *redistributes* smaller and larger responses among the spikes of an incoming spike train (see Figure 12.2).

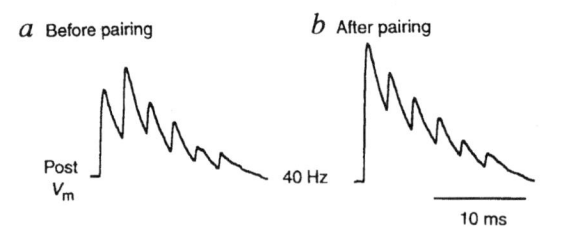

Figure 12.2. Postsynaptic responses to a regular 40 Hz spike train before and after Hebbian learning. From [Markram and Tsodyks, 1996].

In all of the abovementioned data the postsynaptic neuron was connected by several (typically about a half-dozen or more) synapses to the presynaptic neuron, and the recordings actually show the *superposition* of the responses of these multiple synapses for each spike of the presynaptic neuron. It is experimentally quite difficult to isolate the response of a *single* synapse, and data have become available just very recently [Dobrunz and Stevens, 1997]. The results are quite startling. Those single synapses (or more precisely: synaptic release sites) in the central nervous system that have been examined so far exhibit a *binary* response to each spike from the presynaptic neuron: either the synapse releases a single neurotransmitter-filled vesicle or it does not respond at all. In the case when a vesicle is released, its content enters the synaptic cleft and opens ion-channels in the postsynaptic membrane, thereby creating an electrical pulse in the postsynaptic neuron. It is shown in the lower panel of Figure 12.3 that the mean-size of this pulse in the postsynaptic neuron does not vary in a systematic manner for different spikes in a spike train from the presynaptic neuron. The *probability*, however, that a vesicle is released by a synapse varies in a systematic manner for different spikes in such spike train.

The stochastic nature of synaptic function is the basis of the *quantal hypothesis* [Katz, 1966], which states that vesicles of neurotransmitter are released in a probabilistic fashion following the invasion of the presynaptic terminal by an action potential. The basic quantal model, first developed to explain results at the neuromusular junction has been validated at many different synapses, including glutamatergic and gabaergic terminals in the mammalian cortex.

The history-dependence of synaptic release probability was first studied at the neuromuscular junction. Depending on experimental conditions, these synapses show some combination of facilitation (a use-dependent increase in release probability) and depression (a use-dependent decrease in release probability). Subsequent studies have revealed that use-dependent changes in presynaptic release probability underlie many forms of short-term plasticity, including some seen in the hippocampus and neocortex (reviewed in [Magleby, 1987, Zucker, 1989, Fisher et al., 1997, Zador and Dobrunz, 1997]). These changes occur on many different time scales, from seconds to hours or longer (reviewed in [Zador, 1998]).

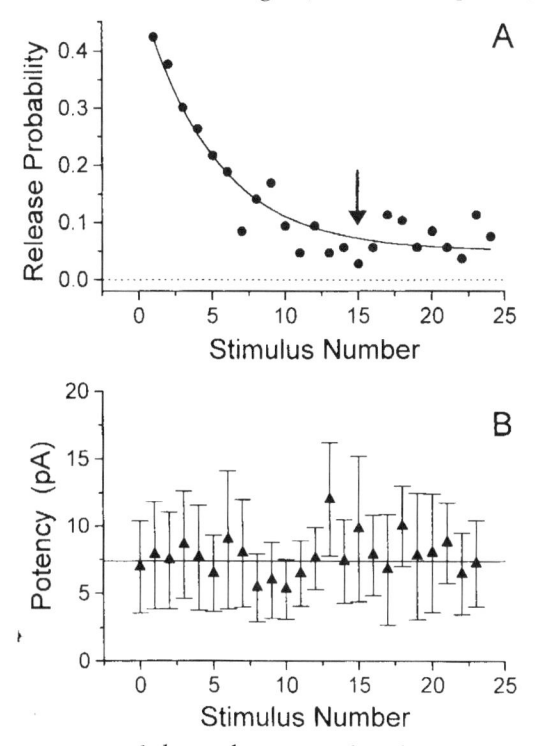

Figure 12.3. The upper panel shows the temporal evolution of release probabilities for a train of a 10 Hz spike train with regular interspike interval in a synapse from rat hippocampus. The lower panel shows the mean size and standard deviation of the amplitude of the postsynaptic pulses for the same spike train in those cases when a vesicles was released. From [Dobrunz and Stevens, 1997]

On first sight the binary response (release/failure of release) of a single synapse might appear to be inconsistent with the multitude of reproducible response sizes shown in Figure 12.1. However one should keep in mind that Figure 12.1 shows the superposition of responses from *many* synapses. Hence for each pulse the size of the postsynaptic response scales with the *number* of individual synapses that release a vesicle. For each spike the expected number of released vesicles equals the *sum of the release probabilities* at the individual synapses times the response at each synapse.

In this way a multi-synaptic connection between two neurons may be subject to an even richer dynamics and learning capability than the preceding models suggest, since there exists evidence that individual synapses have quite different temporal dynamics. While the heterogeneity of release properties at different release sites has long been suspected (e.g. [Atwood et al., 1978, Brown et al., 1976]), only recently has direct evidence for such heterogeneity become available at central synapses.

Three main lines of evidence support this heterogeneity. First, the activity-dependent synaptic channel blocker MK-801 blocks synapses at different rates, as would be expected from a population of synapses with many different release probabilities [Hessler et al., 1993, Rosenmund et al., 1993, Castro-Alamancos and Connors, 1997, Manabe and Nicoll, 1994] Second, minimal stimulation [Allen and Stevens, 1994, Dobrunz and Stevens, 1997, Stratford et al., 1996] and paired recordings [Stratford et al., 1996, Markram and Tsodyks, 1996, Bolshakov and Siegelbaum, 1995] indicate that different connections have different properties. Finally, visualization of the vesicular marker FM-143 [Ryan et al., 1996, Murthy et al., 1997] indicates that release at different terminals is different.

12.3 Quantitative Models

A rather simple but very successful quantitative model for the size of the postsynaptic response caused by *multiple* synapses was proposed in [Varela et al. 1997]. The amplitude $A(t_i)$ of the postsynaptic pulse for the ith spike arriving at time t_i is modeled as a product

$$A(t_i) = A_0 \cdot F(t_i) \cdot D_1(t_i) \cdot D_2(t_i)$$

of a constant A_0 and three functions F, D_1, and D_2. The function F models the effect of facilitation: a fixed amount Δ is added to F for each presynaptic spike. Between spikes the value of F decays exponentially back to its initial value. The functions D_1 and D_2 model synaptic depression in a dual fashion: for each presynaptic spike the current value of D_i is multiplied by a factor $d_i \in (0, 1)$, and the value of D_i recovers exponentially (with some time constant τ_i) back to the initial value of D_i; $i = 1, 2$. It turns out that two terms D_1 and D_2 with efficient constants d_i and τ_i provide a substantially better fit to experimental data than just a single one. Sometimes even three terms are used. Figure 12.4 shows that with suitable choice of parameters this model can predict quite well the amplitude of multi-synaptic responses to a 4 Hz Poisson train. A somewhat related but more complex quantitative model for the response of multiple synapses was proposed in [Tsodyks and Markram, 1997] for the case of depressing synapses and extended in [Markram and Tsodyks, 1997] to allow also facilitation effects.

We had indicated already at the end of the preceding section that the actual dynamics of a synapse in the central nervous system of a biological organism differs from the preceding models since it is stochastic, and the synaptic response to each spike apparently ranges over just two discrete values (release/failure of release). Based on earlier quantitative models for partial aspects of synaptic dynamics (see for example [Dobrunz and Stevens, 1997]), a computational model for individual dynamic stochastic synapses was proposed in [Maass and Zador, 1998]. In this model a spike train is represented as in Chapter 1 by a sequence $\underline{t}$ of firing times, i.e. as an increasing sequence of numbers $t_1 < t_2 < \ldots$ from $\mathbf{R}^+ := \{z \in \mathbf{R} : z \geq 0\}$. For each spike train $\underline{t}$ the output of synapse S consists of the sequence $S(\underline{t})$ of those $t_i \in \underline{t}$ on which vesicles are "released" by S, i.e. of those $t_i \in \underline{t}$ which cause an excitatory or inhibitory postsynaptic

A

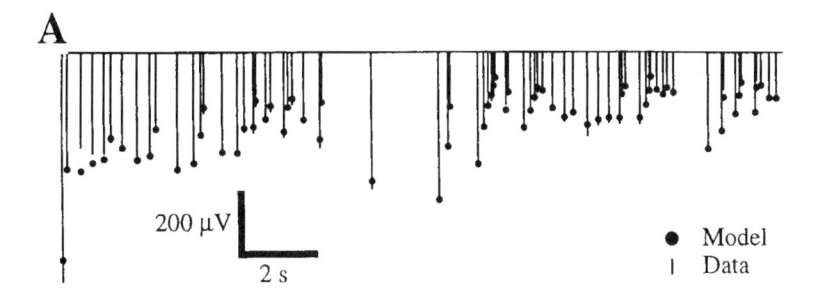

[figure: measured vs predicted EPSP amplitudes, 200 μV scale bar, 2 s scale bar, Model (•) and Data (|) legend]

Figure 12.4. Measured and predicted amplitude (field potentials) of the postsynaptic response to a 4 Hz Poisson spike train. Predictions result from fit of model with three terms F, D_1, D_2. From [Varela et al. 1997]

potential (EPSP or IPSP, respectively). The map $\underline{t} \to S(\underline{t})$ may be viewed as a stochastic function that is *computed* by synapse S. Alternatively one can characterize the output $S(\underline{t})$ of a synapse S through its *release pattern* $q = q_1 q_2 \ldots \in \{R, F\}^*$, where R stands for release and F for failure of release. For each $t_i \in \underline{t}$ one sets $q_i = R$ if $t_i \in S(\underline{t})$, and $q_i = F$ if $t_i \notin S(\underline{t})$. The central equation in this model gives the probability $p_S(t_i)$ that the ith spike in a presynaptic spike train $\underline{t} = (t_1, \ldots, t_k)$ triggers the release of a vesicle at time t_i at synapse S,

$$p_S(t_i) = 1 - e^{-C(t_i) \cdot V(t_i)}. \tag{12.1}$$

The release probability is assumed to be nonzero only for $t \in \underline{t}$, so that releases occur only when a spike invades the presynaptic terminal (*i.e.* the spontaneous release probability is assumed to be zero). The functions $C(t) \geq 0$ and $V(t) \geq 0$ describe, respectively, the states of facilitation and depletion at the synapse at time t.

The dynamics of facilitation are given by

$$C(t) = C_0 + \sum_{t_i < t} c(t - t_i), \tag{12.2}$$

where C_0 is some parameter ≥ 0 that can for example be related to the resting concentration of calcium in the synapse. The exponential response function $c(s)$ models the response of $C(t)$ to a presynaptic spike that had reached the synapse at time $t - s$: $c(s) = \alpha \cdot e^{-s/\tau_C}$, where the positive parameters τ_C and α give the decay constant and magnitude, respectively, of the response. The function C models in an abstract way internal synaptic processes underlying presynaptic facilitation, such as the concentration of calcium in the presynaptic terminal. The particular exponential form used for $c(s)$ could arise for example if presynaptic calcium dynamics were governed by a simple first order process.

The dynamics of depletion are given by

$$V(t) = \max(0, V_0 - \sum_{t_i: \, t_i < t \text{ and } t_i \in S(\underline{t})} v(t - t_i)), \tag{12.3}$$

for some parameter $V_0 > 0$. $V(t)$ depends on the subset of those $t_i \in \underline{t}$ with $t_i < t$ on which vesicles were actually released by the synapse, i.e. $t_i \in S(\underline{t})$. The function $v(s)$ models the response of $V(t)$ to a preceding release of the same synapse at time $t - s \leq t$. Analogously as for $c(s)$ one may choose for $v(s)$ a function with exponential decay where $\tau_V > 0$ is the decay constant. The function V models in an abstract way internal synaptic processes that support presynaptic depression, such as depletion of the pool of readily releasable vesicles. In a more specific synapse model one could interpret V_0 as the maximal number of vesicles that can be stored in the readily releasable pool, and $V(t)$ as the expected number of vesicles in the readily releasable pool at time t.

In summary, the model of synaptic dynamics presented here is described by five parameters: C_0, V_0, τ_C, τ_V and α. The dynamics of a synaptic computation and its internal variables $C(t)$ and $V(t)$ are indicated in Figure 12.5.

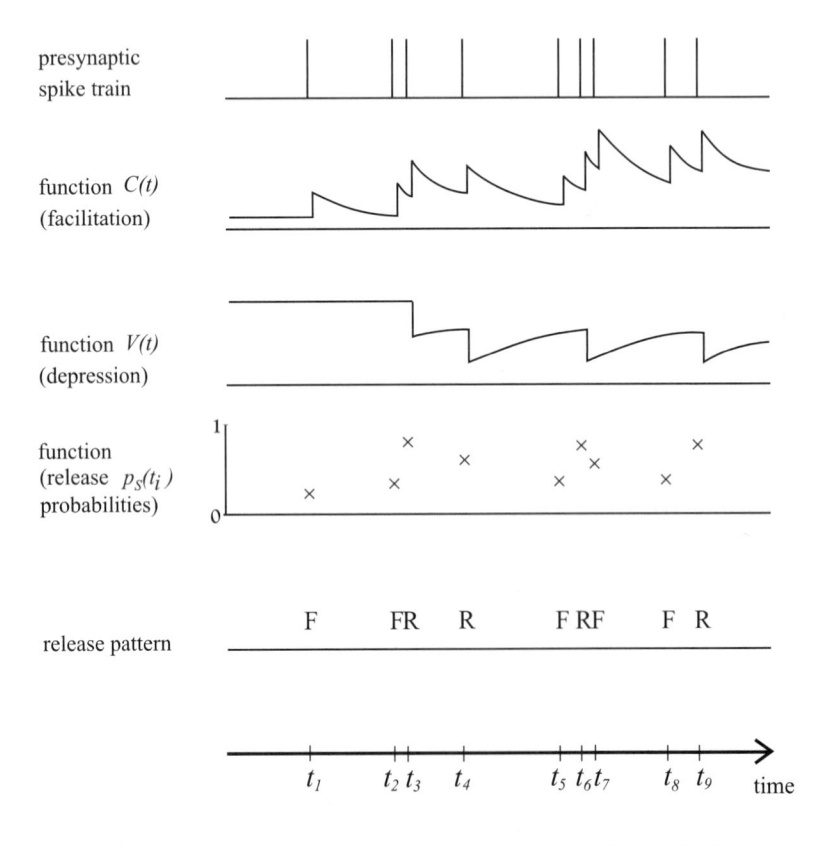

Figure 12.5. Synaptic computation on a spike train $\underline{t}$, together with the temporal dynamics of the internal variables C and V of our model. Note that $V(t)$ changes its value only when a presynaptic spike causes release.

This model for the dynamics of a single stochastic synapse is closely related to the previously discussed model for the combined response of multiple synapses by [Varela et al. 1997], since Eq. (12.1) can be expanded to first order around $r(t) := C(t) \cdot V(t) = 0$ to give

$$p_S(t_i) = C(t_i) \cdot V(t_i) + O([C(t_i) \cdot V(t_i)]^2). \quad (12.4)$$

According to Eq. (12.2) the dynamics of $C(t_i)$ is quite similar to that of the facilitation term $F(t_i)$ in [Varela et al. 1997], and according to Eq. (12.3) the term $V(t_i)$ is closely related to their depression terms $D_j(t_i)$. This correspondence becomes even closer in variations of the previously described most basic model for an individual synapse that are discussed in [Maass and Zador, 1998].

In order to investigate macroscopic effects caused by stochastic dynamic synapses one can expand the previously described model to a mean field version that describes the mean response of a population of dynamic synapses that connect populations of neurons. In this approach [Zador et al., 1998] the input to a population of "parallel" synapses can be described by a continuous function $r(t)$ which represents the current firing activity in the preceding pool of neurons. The impact that this firing activity has on the next pool of neurons is described by a term $w \cdot p(t) \cdot r(t)$, where $p(t) = 1 - e^{C(t) \cdot V(t)}$ is a continuous function with values in $[0, 1]$ that represents the current mean release probability in the population of synapses that connect both pools of neurons. The dynamics of the auxiliary functions $C(t)$ and $V(t)$ is defined as in equation (12.2) and (12.3), but with an integral over the preceding time window and the input $r(t)$ instead of a sum over spikes. The latter may be viewed as a special case of such integral by integrating over a sum of δ-functions, as described in Chapter 1.

12.4 On the Computational Role of Dynamic Synapses

Quantitative models for biological dynamic synapses are relatively new, and the exploration of their possible computational use has just started. We will survey in this section some of the ideas that have emerged so far.

[Abbott et al., 1997] and [Tsodyks and Markram, 1997] point out that depression in dynamic synapses provides a dynamic gain control mechanism: a neuron i can detect whether a presynaptic neuron j suddenly increases its firing rate by a certain percentage – independently of the current firing rate of that presynaptic neuron j. Assume that some of the predecessors of neuron i fire at a high rate and others at a low rate. Then with *static* synapses the neuron i is rather insensitive to changes in the firing rates of slowly firing presynaptic neurons, since its membrane potential is dominated by the large number of EPSP's from rapidly firing presynaptic neurons. However according to the model by [Varela et al. 1997] described at the beginning of Section 3, one can achieve with multiple dynamic synapses that the amplitude of the EPSP's caused by a presynaptic neuron j with a firing rate r_j (and regular interspike intervals) scales like $1/r_j$. This implies that an increase in that firing rate by a fraction $p \cdot r_j$ causes an increase of the postsynaptic response by $\frac{p \cdot r_j}{r_j} = p$, independently of the current value of r_j. In this way the neuron becomes equally sensitive to changes by a percentage p in the firing rate of slowly firing and rapidly firing presynaptic neurons.

For realistic values of the parameters in the synapse model of [Varela et al. 1997] (that result from fitting this model to data from multiple synapses in slices of rat primary visual cortex) the previously described effect, whereby the amplitude of EPSP's from presynaptic neuron j scales like $1/r_j$, sets in for firing rates r_j above 10 Hz. A startling consequence of this effect is that the neuron i becomes insensitive to changes in the sustained firing rates r_j of presynaptic neurons j if these rates lie above 10 Hz. This implies that the traditional "non-spiking" model for biological neural computation, where biological neurons are modeled by sigmoidal neurons with inputs and outputs encoded by firing rates, becomes inapplicable for input firing rates above 10 Hz. On the other hand the typical membrane time constants of a biological neuron lie well below 100 msec, so hat this traditional model also becomes questionable for input firing rates below 10 Hz.

[Markram and Tsodyks, 1997] emphasize that different synapses in a neural circuit tend to have different dynamic features. In this way a spike train from a neuron whose axon makes on the order of 1000 synaptic contacts may convey different messages to the large number of postsynaptic neurons, with the synapses acting as filters that extract different special features from the spike trains. They also point out that in a circuit with excitatory and inhibitory neurons, where the response of the inhibitory neurons is delayed in a frequency-dependent manner via facilitating synapses, a frequency-dependent time window ($\sim 1/r^2$) is created for excitation to spread before inhibition is recruited.

Other possible computational uses of dynamic synapses can be derived from the synapse model of [Maass and Zador, 1998] described at the end of Section 3. The following result shows that by changing just two of the synaptic parameters of this model, a synapse S can choose virtually independently the release probabilities $p_S(t_1)$ and $p_S(t_2)$ for the first two spikes in a spike train.

Theorem 12.1 *Let $\langle t_1, t_2 \rangle$ be some arbitrary spike train consisting of two spikes, and let $p_1, p_2 \in (0,1)$ be some arbitrary given numbers with $p_2 > p_1 \cdot (1 - p_1)$. Furthermore assume that arbitrary positive values are given for the parameters α, τ_C, τ_V of a synapse S. Then one can always find values for the two parameters C_0 and V_0 of the synapse S so that $p_S(t_1) = p_1$ and $p_S(t_2) = p_2$.*

Furthermore the condition $p_2 > p_1 \cdot (1 - p_1)$ is necessary in a strong sense. If $p_2 \leq p_1 \cdot (1 - p_1)$ then no synapse S can achieve $p_S(t_1) = p_1$ and $p_S(t_2) = p_2$ for any spike train $\langle t_1, t_2 \rangle$ and for any values of its parameters $C_0, V_0, \tau_C, \tau_V, \alpha$. ∎

One can use this result for a rigorous proof that a spiking neuron with dynamic synapses has more computational power than a spiking neuron with static synapses: Let T be a some given time window, and consider the computational task of detecting whether at least one of n presynaptic neurons $a_1, \ldots, a_n$ fire at least twice during T ("burst detection"). To make this task computationally feasible we assume that none of the neurons $a_1, \ldots, a_n$ fires outside of this time window.

12.4 On the Computational Role of Dynamic Synapses

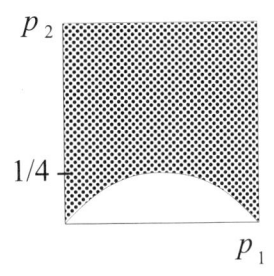

Figure 12.6. The dotted area indicates the range of pairs $\langle p_1, p_2 \rangle$ of release probabilities for the first and second spike through which a synapse can move (for any given interspike interval) by varying its parameters C_0 and V_0.

Theorem 12.2 *A single spiking neuron with dynamic stochastic synapses can solve this burst detection task (with arbitrarily high reliability). On the other hand no spiking neuron with static synapses can solve this task (for any assignment of "weights" to its synapses).* [1]

In order to show that a single spiking neuron with dynamic synapses can solve this burst detection task one just has to choose values for the parameters of its synapses S so that $p_S(t_1)$ is close to 1 and $p_S(t)$ is close to 0 for all $t \in [t_1, t_1 + T]$. We refer to [Maass and Zador, 1998] for a proof that a spiking neuron with static synapses cannot solve this burst detection task.

Another possible computational use of stochastic dynamic synapses is indicated by the following example. Two arbitrary Poisson spike trains A and B were chosen, that each consist of 10 spikes and hence represent the same firing rate.

Figure 12.7 compares the response of a synapse with fixed parameters to two spike trains A and B. The synaptic parameters were adjusted so that the average release probability (computed over the 10 spikes) was greater for A than for B. Figure 12.8 compares the response of a different synapse to the same two spike trains; in this case, the parameters were chosen so that the average response to B was greater than to A. These examples indicate that even in the context of rate coding, synaptic efficacy may not be well-described in terms of a single scalar parameter w. In the mean field version of this synapse model (described at the end of section 3) one can show that the internal synaptic parameters can be chosen in such a way that a population of synapses computes a function that either approximates an arbitrary given linear filter, or higher order terms in the Volterra-series expansion of a nonlinear filter.

Curiously enough the view of synapses as linear filters had already been explored before by [Back and Tsoi, 1991, Principe, 1994], and others in the context of artificial neural nets. They pointed to various potential computational uses of the resulting neural nets in the context of computations

---

[1] We assume here that neuronal transmission delays differ by less than $(n-1) \cdot T$, where by *transmission delay* we refer to the temporal delay between the firing of the presynaptic neuron and its effect on the postsynaptic target.

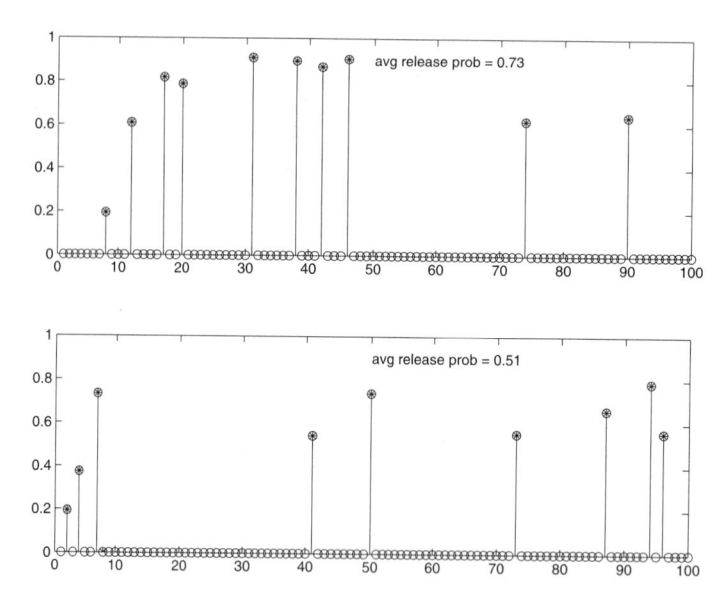

332   12. Computing and Learning with Dynamic Synapses

Figure 12.7. Example of a synapse whose average release probability is 22 % higher for spike train A, shown in the top panel. Release probabilities of the same synapse for spike train B are shown in the bottom panel. The fourth spike in spike train B has a release probability of nearly zero and so is not visible. The spike trains shown here are the same as in the next figure.

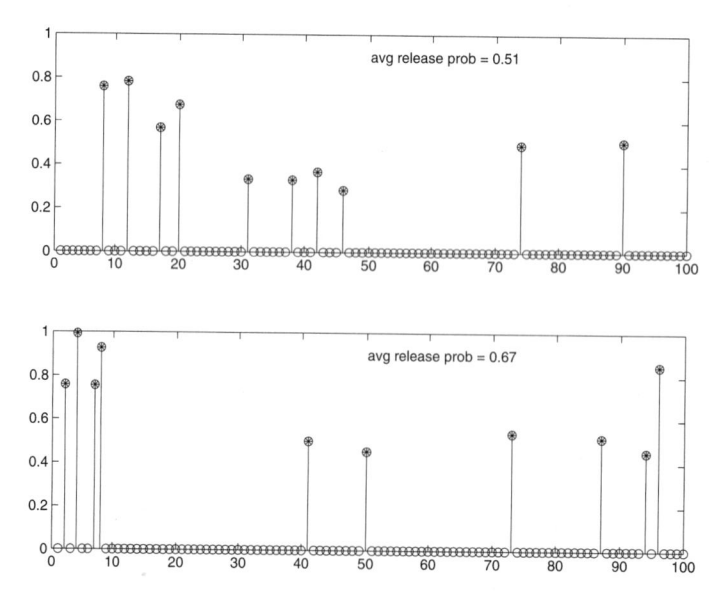

Figure 12.8. Example of a synapse whose average release probability is 16 % higher for spike train B, shown in bottom panel. Release probabilities of the same synapse for spike train A are shown again in the top panel. The spike trains shown here are the same as in the previous figure.

on time series without having at that time any indication that biological neural systems might be able to implement such sets.

12.5 Implications for Learning in Pulsed Neural Nets

The preceding experimental data and associated models show that it is quite problematic to view a biological synapse as a trivial computational unit that simply multiplies its input with a fixed scaler w, its synaptic "weight". Instead, a biological synapse should be viewed as a rather complex nonlinear dynamical system. It is known that the "hidden parameters" that regulate the dynamics of a biological synapse vary from synapse to synapse [Dobrunz and Stevens, 1997], and that at least some of these hidden parameters can be changed through LTP (i.e., through "learning"). This has drastic consequences for our view of learning in biological neural systems. Since synapses are history-dependent it does not suffice to consider training examples that consist of input- and output vectors of numbers. Instead a neural system learns to map certain input functions of time to given output functions of time. Hence a training example consists of a pair of *functions* or *time series*. Furthermore the learning algorithm itself has to specify not only rules for changing the scaling parameter w of a synapse, but also for changing the internal synaptic parameters that regulate the dynamic behavior of the synapse. Experimental evidence that Hebbian learning ("pairing") in biological neural system changes the *dynamic* behavior of a synapse, rather than just the average amplitude of its responses, was provided by [Markram and Tsodyks, 1996]. Their data (see Figure 12.2) suggest that learning may *redistribute* the strength of synaptic responses among the spikes in a train, rather than changing its average response. The particular change in synaptic dynamics that is shown in Figure 12.2 makes the postsynaptic neuron more sensitive to transients, i.e., to rapid changes in the firing rate of the presynaptic neuron. In this way synaptic plasticity may change the sensitivity of a neuron to different neural codes. In this examples it increases the sensitivity for temporal coding, while at the same time decreasing its limiting frequency above which it is unable to distinguish between different presynaptic firing rates. [Liaw and Berger, 1996] have shown that interesting changes of the dynamic properties of a neural circuit with dynamic synapses can already be achieved by just changing the scaling factors of excitatory and inhibitory connections, without changing the hidden parameters that control the dynamics of the synapses themselves.

Preliminary results from [Zador et al., 1998] show that by applying gradient descent learning also to the hidden parameters of a synapse, a neural circuit can in principle "learn" to realize quite general given operators that map input time series to given output time series. We employ here the mean field model for dynamic synapses (described at the end of section 12.3) in order to be able to consider arbitrary bounded time series as network-input and -output. This approach is related to the previous work by [Back and Tsoi, 1991], who have carried out gradient descent for the hidden parameters of linear filters that replace synapses in their model.

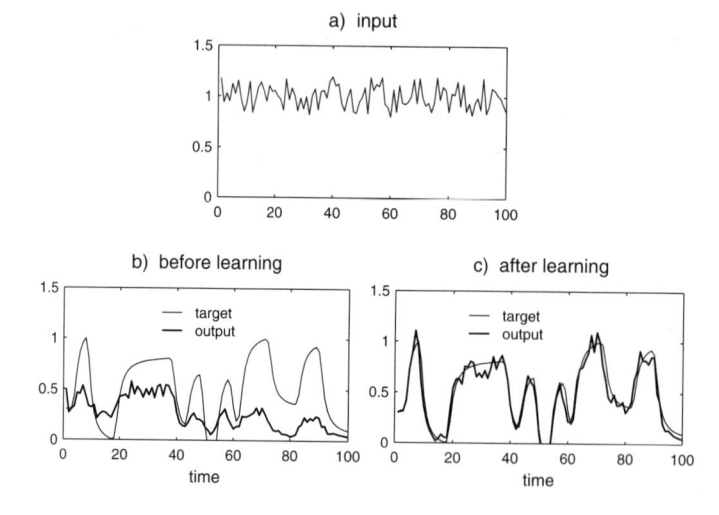

Figure 12.9. Result of gradient descent training for the hidden synaptic parameters in a feedforward neural net with one hidden layer consisting of 12 neurons. The common input time series to the synapses of these 12 neurons is shown in panel a). The target time series and the actual sum of the output time series of the 12 neurons before training are shown in panel b). Panel c) shows the same target time series together with the sum of the output time series of the 12 neurons after applying gradient descent to the 5 hidden parameters $C_0, V_0, \tau_C, \tau_V, \alpha$ of each synapse according to section 12.3. From [Zador et al., 1998].

12.6 Conclusions

We have shown that synapses in biological neural systems play a rather complex role in the context of computing on spike trains. This implies that one is likely to lose a substantial amount of computational power if one models biological networks of spiking neurons by artificial pulsed neural nets that employ the same type of static synapses that are familiar from traditional neural network models.

It has been shown that dynamic synapses of the type that we have described in this chapter can easily be simulated by electronic circuits [Fuchs, 1998], and hence can in principle be integrated into neural VLSI. In addition all analog techniques for storing a weight in neural VLSI automatically create "dynamic synapses", since the value of the stored weight tends to drift. An exciting challenge would be to find computational uses for such inherent synaptic dynamics, which so far has only been viewed as a defect. Finally we have indicated that the notion of learning and the nature of learning algorithms changes if one takes into account that synapses have to be modelled as history-dependent dynamical systems with several hidden parameters that control their dynamics, rather than as static scalar variables ("synaptic weights"). Hence if one wants to mimic adaptive mechanisms of biological neural systems in artificial pulsed neural nets, one is forced go beyond the traditional ideas from neural network theory and look for new types of learning algorithms.

References

[Abbott et al., 1997] Abbott, L., Varela, J., Sen, K., and S.B., N. (1997). Synaptic depression and cortical gain control. *Science*, 275:220–4.

[Allen and Stevens, 1994] Allen, C. and Stevens, C. (1994). An evaluation of causes for unreliability of synaptic transmission. *Proc. Natl. Acad. Sci.*, USA, 91:10380–3.

[Atwood et al., 1978] Atwood, H., Govind, C., and I., K. (1978). Non homogeneous excitatory synapses of a crab stomach muscle. *Journal of Neurobiology*, 9:17–28.

[Back and Tsoi, 1991] Back, A. D. and Tsoi, A. C. (1991). FIR and IIR synapses, a new neural network architecture for time series modeling. *Neural Computation*, 3:375–385.

[Bolshakov and Siegelbaum, 1995] Bolshakov, V. and Siegelbaum, S. A. (1995). Regulation of hippocampal transmitter release during development and long-term potentiation. *Science*, 269:1730–4.

[Brown et al., 1976] Brown, T., Perkel, D., and Feldman, M. (1976). Evoked neurotransmitter release: statistical effects of non uniformity and non stationarity. *Proc. Natl. Acad. Sci.*, USA, 73:2913–2917.

[Castro-Alamancos and Connors, 1997] Castro-Alamancos, M. and Connors, B. (1997). Distinct forms of short-term plasticity at excitatory synapses of hippocampus and neocortex. *Proc. Natl. Acad. Sci.*, USA, 94:4161–4166.

[Dobrunz and Stevens, 1997] Dobrunz, L. and Stevens, C. (1997). Heterogeneity of release probability, facilitation and depletion at central synapses. *Neuron*, 18:995–1008.

[Fisher et al., 1997] Fisher, S., Fischer, T., and Carew, T. (1997). Multiple overlapping processes underlying short-term synaptic enhancement. *Trends in Neuroscience*, 20:170–7.

[Fuchs, 1998] Fuchs, H. (1998). Neural networks with dynamic synapses in analog electronics. In preparation.

[Hessler et al., 1993] Hessler, N., Shirke, A., and R., M. (1993). The probability of transmitter release at a mammalian central synapse. *Nature*, 366:569–572.

[Katz, 1966] Katz, B. (1966). *Nerve, Muscle, and Synapse*. New York, McGraw-Hill.

[Liaw and Berger, 1996] Liaw, J.-S. and Berger, T. (1996). Dynamic synapse: A new concept of neural representation and computation. *Hippocampus*, 6:591–600.

[Maass and Zador, 1998] Maass, W. and Zador, A. (1998). Dynamic stochastic synapses as computational units, *Advances in Neural Information Processing Systems*, vol. 10, 194–200. Journal version appears in *Neural Computation*.

[Magleby, 1987] Magleby, K. (1987). Short term synaptic plasticity. In *Synaptic Function*, Edelman, G. M., Gall, W. E., and Cowan, W. M., editors, Wiley, New York.

[Markram and Tsodyks, 1996] Markram, H. and Tsodyks, M. (1996). Redistribution of synaptic efficacy between neocortical pyramidal neurons. *Nature*, 382:807–10.

[Markram and Tsodyks, 1997] Markram, H. and Tsodyks, M. (1997). The information content of action potential trains: a synaptic basis. *Proc. of ICANN 97*, 13–23.

[Manabe and Nicoll, 1994] Manabe, T. and Nicoll, R. (1994). Long-term potentiation: evidence against an increase in transmitter release probability in the ca1 region of the hippocampus. *Science*, 265:1888–92.

[Murthy et al., 1997] Murthy, V., Sejnowski, T., and Stevens, C. (1997). Heterogeneous release properties of visualized individual hippocampal synapses. *Neuron*, 18:599–612.

[Principe, 1994] Principe, J. C. (1994). An analysis of the gamma memory in dynamic neural networks. *IEEE Trans. on Neural Networks*, 5(2), 331–337.

[Rosenmund et al., 1993] Rosenmund, C., Clements, J., and Westbrook, G. (1993). Nonuniform probability of glutamate release at a hippocampal synapse. *Science*, 262:754–757.

[Ryan et al., 1996] Ryan, T., Ziv, N., and Smith, S. (1996). Potentiation of evoked vesicle turnover at individually resolved synaptic boutons. *Neuron*, 17:125–34.

[Stratford et al., 1996] Stratford, K. J., Tarczy-Hornoch, K., Martin, K. A. C., Bannister, N. J., and Jack J. J. B. (1996). Excitatory synaptic inputs to spiny stellate cells in cat visual cortex. *Nature*, 382:258–61.

[Tsodyks and Markram, 1997] Tsodyks, M. and Markram, H. (1997). The neural code between neocortical pyramidal neurons depends on neurotransmitter release probability. *Proc. Natl. Acad. Sci.*, USA, 94:719–23.

[Varela et al. 1997] Varela, J. A., Sen, K., Gibson, J., Fost, J., Abbott, L. F., and Nelson, S. B. (1997). A quantitative description of short-term plasticity at excitatory synapses in layer 2/3 of rat primary visual cortex. *J. Neurosci*, 17:7926–7940.

[Zador, 1998] Zador, A. M. (1998). Synaptic plasticity. In *Biophysics of Computation, in press*, Koch, C., editor, MIT Press, Boston.

[Zador and Dobrunz, 1997] Zador, A. and Dobrunz, L. (1997). Dynamic synapses in the cortex. *Neuron*, 19:1–4.

[Zador et al., 1998] Zador, A. M., Maass, W., and Natschläger, T. (1998) Learning in neural networks with dynamic synapses, in preparation.

[Zucker, 1989] Zucker, R. (1989). Short-term synaptic plasticity. *Annual Review of Neuroscience*, 12:13–31.

13 Stochastic Bit-Stream Neural Networks

Peter S. Burge, Max R. van Daalen, Barry J. P. Rising and John S. Shawe-Taylor

'Stochastic computing' studies computation performed by manipulating streams of random bits which represent real values via a frequency encoding. This contrasts with the approach adopted in Chapter 2 where the timing of the spikes plays a crucial role in the encoding. For stochastic computing it is the irregularity of the spike trains that is exploited in the computation and in this sense the two approaches are very different.

Stochastic computing also allows us the avoid using analog techniques as are for instance proposed in Chapter 3. In other respects the approach is much closer to that described in that chapter, since the encoding is via the weight of the spike train, the difference being that in stochastic computing all spikes have the same weight.

From this perspective the approach could be said to be the simplest of those described in this book – the spikes are represented by individual bits being set and the value of the train by the frequency with which they appear. The benefit of this simplicity is twofold. Firstly, networks can be implemented in very simple digital hardware, and secondly, analysis and simulation of their functionality are relatively straightforward.

This chapter will review results obtained in applying this approach to neural computation. The main advantage of using this encoding is that the silicon area needed to implement a neuron can be made very small, at the cost of slightly altering the functionality and reducing the accuracy of the result. In contrast to analog techniques the reduction of accuracy can be exactly determined and does not accumulate if the computation occurs in several layers. The reliance on digital implementation also avoids the use of analog devices.

The chapter is divided into subsections describing the results that have been obtained using this approach in different problem areas. We begin with an introduction setting the historical context for the ideas. In the second section the basic computational unit is described at a functional rather than a hardware level. The third section describes their use in feedforward networks and Section 4 provides some results on their generalization performance.

The neural design has also been used for combinatorial optimization in recurrent networks. This approach is described in Section 5 with an application to graph colouring in Section 6. Finally, a hardware implementation using FPGA's is outlined in Section 7.

A final section summarises the prospects for further analysis and applications of the approach to neural computation.

This chapter does not aim to present new results though some new perspectives are included. Its main contribution, however, is to form a coherent report of the potential of the bit-stream neural design from research reported in papers published in widely differing communities ranging from theoretical learning conferences to workshops on Field Programmable Gate Arrays (FPGAs).

13.1 Introduction

The study of artificial Neural Networks has on the whole been restricted to one or two classical models which were originally inspired by studying the behaviour of biological neurons. Reproducing this functionality in silicon is often not easy involving either large areas of digital processing or analog techniques that are less reliable and inevitably introduce unpredictable noise.

Stochastic computing was first considered in the 1960's [Gaines, 1969]. It uses a probabilistic representation of real values via a Bernouilli sequence whose probability is related to the value represented. The advantage of the approach is that certain operations can be performed in extremely compact hardware, at the cost of reduced accuracy in the output.

The observation that stochastic spike trains using a frequency encoding might be combined at a neuron to perform multiplication was made by Srinivasan and Bernard [Srinivasan and Bernard, 1976] in a biological context, an idea picked up again later by Koch and Poggio [Koch and Poggio, 1992]. Against this background the proposal of applying stochastic computing to implement neural functionality was first made by [Alspector et al., 1987]. Early designs involved a multiple input *or* gate at the heart of the neuron which though useful in some applications has a tendency to saturate and so has only limited functionality. The first design to overcome this problem was reported in [Shawe-Taylor et al., 1991] and it is this design which is the subject of this review. We hope to demonstrate that by adapting the neural design to the constraints of silicon rather than biological wetware, we can gain enormous simplification of the implementation at relatively little cost to the underlying functionality and problem solving capabilities.

13.2 Basic Neural Modelling

A *Bernouilli sequence* p is a stream of random bits generated independently with each bit having a probability p of being a 1. We will also refer to such sequences as *bit-streams*.

For a logical binary operation $\circ$, we denote by $p \circ q$ the Bernouilli sequence obtained by applying the operation to the two sequences bit wise. Hence, for example

$$p \text{ AND } q = pq,$$

and
$$p \text{ XNOR } q = pq + (1-p)(1-q).$$

A stochastic representation of real values is a mapping
$$S : [a, b] \longrightarrow [0, 1],$$

which maps a range of real values to a corresponding probability value for a Bernouilli representation. Hence, $x \in [a, b]$ is represented by a Bernouilli sequence with probability $S(x)$.

We will consider two stochastic representations.

- The *AND* repesentation is the identity mapping S_{And} on the interval $[0, 1]$. For this representation we can multiply two numbers using the fact that
$$S_{And}(x) \text{ AND } S_{And}(y) = S_{And}(xy).$$
Hence, a bit-wise *AND* creates a Bernouilli sequence representing the product of the two numbers.

- The second representation is the *XNOR* implementation for which the mapping S_{Xnor} maps the interval $[-1, 1]$ by
$$S_{Xnor}(x) = (x+1)/2.$$
For this representation we can multiply two numbers using the fact that
$$S_{Xnor}(x) \text{ XNOR } S_{Xnor}(y) = S_{Xnor}(xy).$$

Using either representation we can now implement the multiplication of weights and inputs using single logical gates operating on bit-streams representing the appropriate values. The key question in designing a neuron is how the values can be summed and passed through an activation function.

The solution we consider is to sum the bits in one time slice and compare the number obtained with a threshold value. If the sum is larger than the threshold a 1 is put on the output bit-stream, which is otherwise fed a 0. Hence, the neuron outputs one bit after using a bit from each of its input streams and each of its weight streams. It also must use one threshold value.

In the case when the *AND* representation is used the weight streams are augmented with a bit to indicate whether the weight is negative. The output of the neuron is the probability that the bit it generates is a 1. This probability depends on the input probabilities and the distribution used to generated the threshold values. Detailed analysis of the *AND* neuron is contained in [Shawe-Taylor et al., 1991], while the *XNOR* case is reported in [Zhao, 1995]. In both cases choosing the threshold values uniformly at random results in a linear activation function of the weighted sum of the inputs. As the threshold distribution concentrates more on a fixed value, the shape of the activation function becomes more sigmoid-like. It should, however, be noted that it is only in the linear case that the output can be expressed as a function of the weighted sum.

Most of the hardware designs that have been considered use time multiplexing of the input streams, which means that a neuron only receives a bit from one input stream and its corresponding weight at one time. As a result all that is required to implement the neuron is a digital counter preset to a value determined by the threshold. This will be discussed in more detail in the section on FPGA implementations.

The question of how to generate bit-streams with a particular probability has been studied in two papers [Jeavons, Cohen and Shawe-Taylor, 1994, van Daalen et al., 1993]. These demonstrate that linear feedback shift registers can be used to generate $p = 0.5$ sequences, and that k such sequences can be combined to produce any p sequence to k bit accuracy. This technique is exploited in the designs described in the hardware section.

We finish this section by discussing the efficiency and accuracy trade-off that is dictated by the stochastic computing paradigm. On the positive side, the fact that each neuron outputs one bit for each set of single bits it receives from its inputs means that the processing in multi-layer networks can be pipelined. As a result the bits emerging from the last layer do so with the required probabilities after the delay caused by the number of layers. In other words for an L layer network, from the $L+1$-st bit onwards the output bits form a Bernouilli sequence with probability $S(y)$, where y is the output value and S the stochastic representation function being used.

Since the distribution of the number of 1's output in the sequence y is binomial with probability $S(y)$, if the output probability needs to be determined with an error margin of ϵ, then we must sample the output for approximately

$$\frac{S(y)^2(1-S(y))^2}{\epsilon^2} \leq \frac{1}{16\epsilon^2}$$

bits. Even after sampling this many bits, the result is only accurate to within $\pm\epsilon$ with some confidence, since this number of bits means that ϵ is one standard deviation from the mean. In order to increase the confidence interval to two standard deviations the number of bits sampled should be multiplied by 4.

Clearly, the number of bits required will become prohibitive if the accuracy required is much tighter than $\epsilon = 2^{-8}$, unless the value output is close to 0 or 1. A very rough comparison with an implementation using binary multiplication can be made by noting that the area required for a binary k-bit multiplier is $O(k^2)$, while the time required for obtaining k-bit accuracy in a stochastic implementation grows exponentially in k. For small values of k the bit-stream implementation will be more efficient in hardware for a given speed, while for $k > 8$, the time delay of the stochastic implementation is greater than the saving in silicon area over a binary implementation. Hence, assuming a fixed silicon area and perfect parallelism in both implementations, we would expect a binary implementation to be preferable for $k > 8$.

In the light of the above discussion the application areas where we might expect stochastic neurons to outperform a classical implementation are classification problems which can be well separated by a threshold, that is positive outputs satisfy $S_{And}(y) \gg 0.5$, and negative outputs satisfy $S_{And}(y) \ll 0.5$.

13.3 Feedforward Networks and Learning

In this section we consider feedforward networks of stochastic neurons. The first question of interest is their computational power, in particular how does it compare with that of standard sigmoidal neurons. Before we can answer this question it is necessary to develop an algorithm for training a network of such neurons to perform a particular input/output mapping.

There are three techniques that have been proposed in previous publications on this topic. We will also mention a fourth approach which is worthy of further investigation. We first discuss those that rely on modelling the behaviour of the neuron by computing the probability values in a simulation, instead of using the stochastic representations.

13.3.1 Probability Level Learning

Two of the learning techniques mentioned above use a probability level representation, as does the novel approach. The original paper describing the basic neural functionality [Shawe-Taylor et al., 1991] proposed that such networks could be trained by simulating their behaviour at a probability level. This means that the output of the neurons is calculated as a real value in the range $[0, 1]$, being the value $S(x)$ for the output x of that neuron. By manipulating probability generating functions it was shown how this explicit probability value could be computed for the *AND* implementation. A similar computation was performed by Zhao [Zhao, 1995] for the *XNOR* implementation.

Once the function has been computed we also need to compute its derivative in order to implement a gradient descent style learning algorithm. There is a slight complication in that the functionality of a stochastic neuron cannot be descibed as an activation function applied to a weighted sum. Hence, the derivatives of the output with respect to each input cannot be obtained by a simple application of the chain rule. The details of the two computations are given in [Zhao, 1995, Shawe-Taylor et al., 1991]. This is the *first learning technique*. In [Zhao et al., 1996, Zhao, 1995] results of applying these learning algorithms to simple benchmark problems are described, showing that the networks can successfully realise standard mappings often with no more neurons than required by a sigmoid network.

As an example of a network obtained using this training method Figure 13.1 shows an encoder-decoder network of *XNOR* bit-stream neurons. The T values given inside each computational neuron are the (fixed) thresholds.

The extra complication in calculating the derivatives make the simulations quite slow. This prompted Zhao [Zhao et al., 1996, Zhao, 1995] to derive a

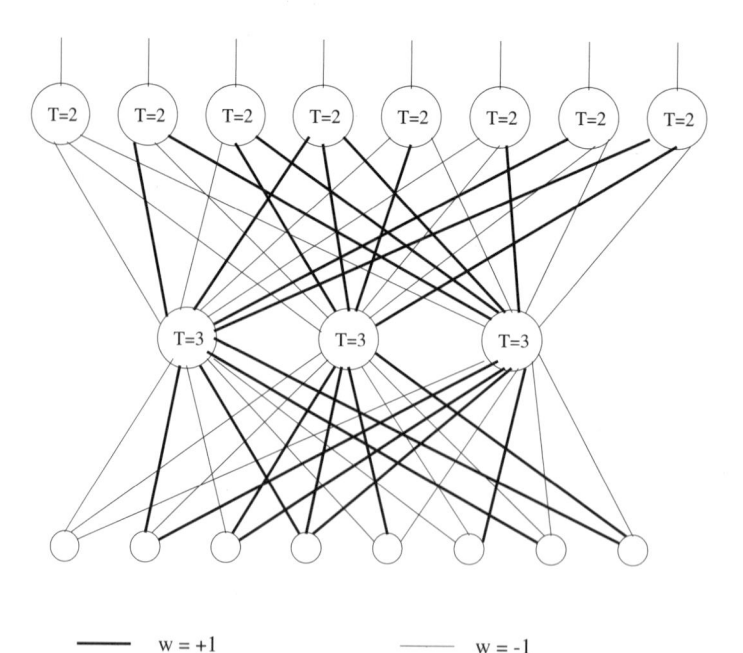

Figure 13.1. Encoder-decoder network of *XNOR* bit-stream neurons

more efficient technique by making a Gaussian approximation of the distribution of values assumed by the neuron's counter. This is the *second learning technique*. This approximation is sufficiently accurate for neurons with 10 or more inputs and meant that more substantial problems could be solved [Zhao et al., 1996] [Zhao, 1995].

An interesting alternative strategy that could be investigated would be to attempt to use the Support Vector Machine approach [Cortes and Vapnik, 1995]. This would require using the functionality of a bit-stream neuron as the kernel function. It is not clear that the function would satisfy Mercer's conditions, i.e. that the matrix of inner products would be guaranteed to be positive semi-definite. Assuming that this property could be proven, the resulting network would have a single hidden layer of bit-stream neurons feeding into a linear output neuron. This is the *novel approach* alluded to above. The nice feature of the SVM strategy in this connection is that maximising the margin corresponds to reducing the time required to obtain an accurate result at the output (see the discussion at the end of Section 13.2).

13.3.2 Bit-Stream Level Learning

The following observation is due to [van Daalen et al., 1994, Zhao, 1995] and opens up the possiblity of on-chip learning. This will be the *third learning technique*.

The probability of generating a '1' as the output bit on a given operational cycle of a bit-stream neuron, with weighted inputs i_1 to i_m, and preloaded threshold value t_n, may be written as shown in equation (13.1).

$$O_n = \Pr(i_1 + i_2 + i_3 + \cdots + i_m > t_n) \quad (13.1)$$

$$\begin{aligned}= &\Pr(i_1 + i_2 + i_3 + \cdots + i_{k-1} + i_{k+1} + \cdots + i_m > t_n) \\&+ \Pr(i_1 + i_2 + i_3 + \cdots + i_{k-1} + i_{k+1} + \cdots + i_m = t_n) \\&\cdot \Pr(i_k = 1) \quad (13.2)\end{aligned}$$

This function may be rewritten as equation (13.2), which is now easily differentiated with respect to the arbitary input i_k, giving equation (13.3),

$$\frac{\partial O_n}{\partial i_k} = \Pr(i_1 + i_2 + i_3 + \cdots + i_{k-1} + i_{k+1} + \cdots + i_m = t_n) \quad (13.3)$$

This implies that a bit-stream which contains a 1 each time the above equation holds will be a stochastic representation of the derivative in the *AND* representation. Since, this derivative calculation forms the core of the back-propagation algorithm, to complete a full implementation of on-chip learning we need only combine the streams from nodes receiving output from a given node. The combination is a weighted linear sum which can again be realised with the bit-stream technology.

This approach has yet to be tested for multi-neuron networks though the individual derivative calculations for a single neuron have been implemented and are described in more detail in the hardware section.

13.4 Generalization Analysis

Two papers have looked at the generalization of stochastic neural networks [Shawe-Taylor,1995, Shawe-Taylor and Zhao, 1995]. They adopt the PAC framework and bound the number of examples required to obtain a bound of ϵ on the generalization error with confidence $1 - \delta$. The bound obtained is as follows,

$$m \geq m_0(\epsilon, \delta) = \frac{1}{\epsilon(1 - \sqrt{\epsilon})} \left[2W \ln\left(\frac{4e\sqrt{s(d+W)}}{\epsilon}\right) + \ln\left(\frac{2W/(W-1)}{\delta}\right) \right],$$

for a network with W weights and input dimension d. This is the tightest known in the PAC framework for a real valued neural network and is similar to bounds for a network of threshold neurons.

The analysis relies on viewing the stochastic network as a boolean circuit fed with stochastic bit-streams. In this view a stochastic neuron is simply a threshold gate. In fact the analysis applies to any boolean circuit used in this fashion. The complexity only depends on the number of bit-streams that are fed into the network and not on the complexity of the network itself, a somewhat surprising result.

The generalization performance of stochastic networks has been compared with that of sigmoid networks on some standard benchmark problems. Initial results indicate that the improved generalization bound for stochastic networks is confirmed by experimental results [Shawe-Taylor and Zhao, 1995, Zhao et al., 1996].

13.5 Recurrent Networks

Recurrent neural networks have been studied with several different applications in mind, for example time series generation, content addressable memories, and applications to combinatorial optimization. Research in recurrent bit-stream neural networks has focussed on applications in combinatorial optimization. The motivation for choosing problems of this type is the difficulty reported in the literature with the time taken for networks to settle into optimal or near optimal solutions [Peterson and Anderson, 1987]. It was therefore of interest whether similar functionality could be obtained using the stochasticity of bit-stream neurons in place of the stochastic update of the Boltzmann machine. If this were possible, the prospect of massively parallel combinatorial optimization in relatively simple hardware could be realised.

The method proposed in [Zhao and Shawe-Taylor, 1995, Zhao, 1995] is to multiply all of the weights by a factor $T \leq 1$, a parameter which controls the amount of randomness. The functionality of the neuron is left unchanged except that the threshold is fixed at an intermediate value. If $T = 1$ and all the weights have integral values the network behaves like a parallel Hopfield network, but as the temperature is reduced individual connections are randomly excluded, introducing randomness into the update rule. Hence, at the bit level the network operates very much like a Boltzmann machine, while viewed at the bit-stream probability level it is performing a bit-stream implementation of Mean Field Annealing [Peterson and Anderson, 1987].

Experiments [Zhao, 1995, Zhao and Shawe-Taylor, 1995] applying the approach to graph partitioning showed that the performance was entirely comparable with that of a standard Boltzmann machine, with the quality of solution being improved in many cases, while the time to convergence remained very similar.

These results suggest that the approach holds out a realistic prospect of delivering impressive speeds of convergence when implemented in parallel. This has not been done for the graph partitioning problem, but hardware has been constructed for a more powerful network designed to solve graph colouring problems. This work will be described in the next section.

13.6 Applications to Graph Colouring

It is a fairly straightforward task to generalise the Boltzmann machine to operate over a finite alphabet [Shawe-Taylor and Zerovnik, 1992]. The graph colouring problem maps directly onto a Generalised Boltzmann Machine (GBM) by an appropriate setting of the connections. In this way a graph colouring algorithm due to Petford and Welsh [Petford and Welsh, 1989] is recovered.

Once again the question is whether stochastic neurons could be adapted to perform a comparable operation to neurons in a GBM. In this more general situation a neuron can be in one of a finite number of states. In the case of graph colouring the number of states is equal to the number

13.6 Applications to Graph Colouring

of available colours. A separate counter is used for each potential colour of a neuron and each accumulates counts of neighbours with the corresponding colour. This implements a simple gradient descent version of the GBM. By using a parameter T to multiply the connection weights we can introduce stochasticity into the update in a way that parallels the binary case described in the previous section. The hardware is somewhat complicated by the need to determine which counter has the least number, but this problem can be solved efficiently with very little overhead in silicon area [Burge and Shawe-Taylor, 1995]. This model has been termed the multi-state bit-stream neuron (MSBSN). Again at the individual bit level it can be viewed as behaving like a GBM, while at the bit-stream probability level it simulates the Mean Field Annealing algorithm for Potts-Glass neurons [Peterson and Anderson, 1987].

Figure 13.2 shows a section of a graph which requires colouring and the corresponding network of multi-state bit-stream neurons. Each pair of vertices which are not connected gives rise to an edge with weight 0 – i.e. no information is transmitted. For graph edges there is a corresponding network edge which has weight set to a fixed value T which controls the amount of randomness in the update rule as described above.

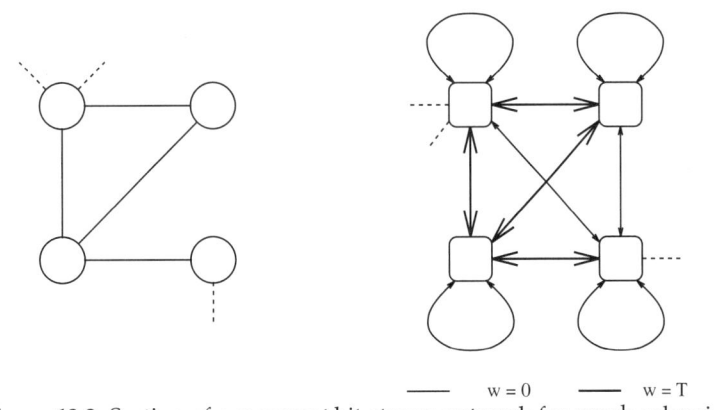

Figure 13.2. Section of a recurrent bit-stream network for graph colouring

Benchmark trials, using the MSBSN, performed on randomly generated 3-colourable graphs have shown comparable performance to other randomised algorithms [Burge and Shawe-Taylor, 1995]. Furthermore, in particular regions of the graph colouring problem space it was observed that the MSBSN algorithm outperformed standard Mean Field Annealing.

A prototype hardware implementation has been made with 8 neurons in the system. Rising *et al.* [Rising et al., 1997] have applied the approach to a set of graphs known as the Leighton graphs, which were specifically designed to be hard to colour [DIMACS]. The graphs have 450 vertices and are 5 colourable. The hardware was typically able to colour the graphs in under 100 attempts.

In order to assess how the implementation will scale we need to understand how performing the updates in parallel will affect the results. Extensive simulations on 450-node graphs have been carried out to find an ideal level of parallelism for the network [Rising, 1996]. These results (Figure 13.3) show that the best results are achieved when the network updates 30-40% of its nodes at the same time. Hence at least 30% of the full benefit of the parallelism can be obtained even when the graph is no larger than the number of neurons available.

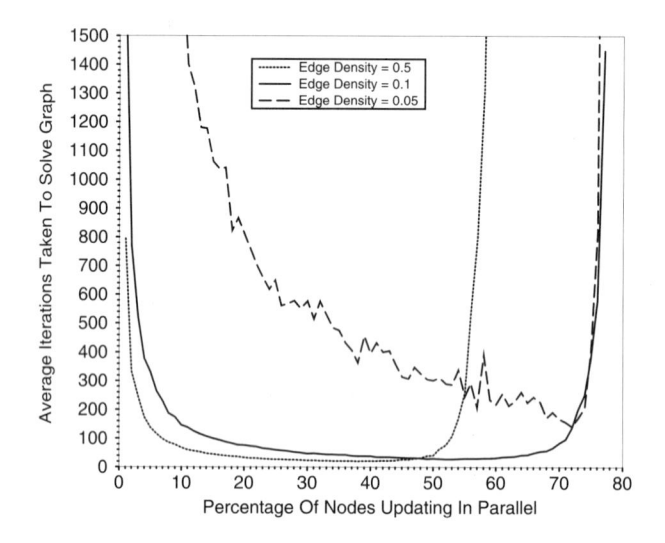

Figure 13.3. Efficiency of parallelism for graph colouring

The hardware is described in more detail in the following sections. Field Programmable Gate Arrays have been used which has aided rapid prototyping, but meant that the implementations have been quite small. In the case of graph colouring 8 neurons have been used through a multiplexing approach, but the experiments are sufficient to demonstrate the feasibility of the approach and we estimate that the Leighton graphs could be coloured in a few seconds by a 100MHz full custom implementation. This compares very favourably with the several minutes required on an Alpha workstation.

13.7 Hardware Implementation

13.7.1 The Stochastic Neuron

The circuitry required to construct a single stochastic neuron, is shown in Figure 13.4. The neuron has only one physical input and weight connection, but may have many logical input connections. This is achieved by time multiplexing the bits of each of these logical signals onto the physical connection.

Such neurons may be grouped to form individual layers, often sharing one physical input. Their outputs may be collected in parallel by a shift register, which when clocked provides a time multiplexed output in the same format as used for the logical inputs (assuming that there was one physical input). Thus layers may be cascaded, forming an efficient pipeline. For a more detailed description of how such neurons may be combined into large networks, and the required support circuitry, see [van Daalen et al., 1993].

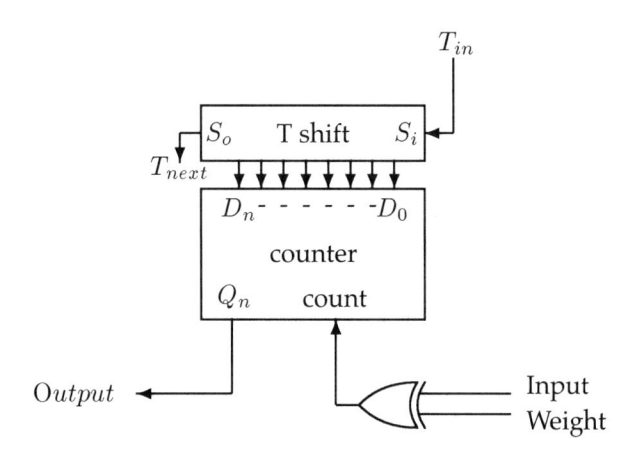

Figure 13.4. The elements of a single stochastic neuron

The core of the neuron is a k bit counter, which may be preloaded with a threshold value. The counter only increments when the *count* input is active, and this is directly controlled by the weighted input signals, as produced by the XOR gate. Each weighted input value therefore contributes 0 or 1 to the counter, on each operational cycle. Hence, the total net input contribution to the counter, after summing the contributions due to all of the inputs to the neuron, will be an integer between 0 and the number of inputs, n, and the probability distribution of this value will depend on the weighted input values represented by the input bit-streams.

Unique threshold values are supplied to the neurons by a long shift register, with each individual neuron tapping into its own local section. The threshold value is chosen such that it will cause an overflow into the top most counter bit, when a given input count, t, is achieved or exceeded. Thus the output of the neuron is taken from the most significant bit of the counter.

Varying the distribution of the threshold value alters the probability that this output bit will be set, and hence alters the effective activation function computed by the neuron. A fixed threshold distribution generates a sigmoidal like activation, and a uniformly distributed threshold generates a linear activation function. For a more detailed analysis of this activation function, and a description of an appropriate back-propagation learning algorithm see [Zhao, 1995, van Daalen et al., 1993], [Shawe-Taylor et al., 1991], [Shawe-Taylor et al., 1995].

13.7.2 Calculating Output Derivatives

If we wish to implement the derivative bit-stream described in Section 13.3.2, additional hardware will be required. This circuitry must prevent the input i_k from contributing to the internal counter, and also must detect the condition that the counter exactly matches the preloaded threshold value. This is easily arranged, as the preloaded threshold value is chosen such that it sets the most significant bit of the counter when achieved. So if i_k is '0' then the circuitry must detect the counter value '1000···00', or if i_k is '1', it must detect the value '1000···01'. This functionality can be achieved with a simple combinatorial circuit.

13.7.3 Generating Stochastic Bit-Streams

A stochastic bit-stream generator is constructed as a pipeline of k series connected single bit modulators, one for each bit of resolution in the required probability value. The input consists of a k bit binary value, representing a probability in the range 0_2 to $0.1111\ldots111_2$. The individual k binary bits of this value will be called "modulation bits", and they are each connected, in sequence, to one of the k bit modulators. Additionally, each bit modulator requires a unique "carrier stream". These randomly generated bit-streams are easily produced, and have an independent bit probability of $\frac{1}{2}$. Ultimately, a bit steam generator operates by appropriately combining these carrier streams within its constituent bit modulators.

The generation of the carrier streams makes use of a single maximal length Linear Feedback Shift Register (LFSR). The streams are simply obtained directly by tapping successive elements of the LFSR. These bit streams are highly overlapping, but almost perfectly uncorrelated [van Daalen et al., 1993], [Jeavons, Cohen and Shawe-Taylor, 1994].

Any realistic device will require a large number of carrier streams, such that typical shift register lengths will be of the order of 1000 bits (lengths of this order will also produce extremely long PRBS sequences). Such a shift register would be sectioned up, with each portion supplying carrier streams to the local stream generators. In this way a large LFSR can be conveniently and efficiently distributed across a chip.

In order to ensure that the carrier stream inputs to successive modulators in a bit-stream generator do not *coincide* we simply clock the LFSR and the stochastic bit-stream generators such that they produce their bit-streams in opposite directions relative to each other. In this way the elements of the LFSR sequence (s_i) which are used for the generation of the j-th bit from a bit-stream generator with k modulators are $s_j, s_{j+2}, \ldots, s_{j+2k-2}$. Provided $2k \leq n$, where n is the length of the LFSR, then all possible k-binary sequences will be generated equally often at these positions, as the LFSR is clocked, with the exception of the all zero sequence which will have a probability deficit of $1/(2^n - 1)$. Hence for large values of n, the inputs to the modulators will be effectively uncorrelated and will have almost exactly the correct frequencies of 0's and 1's.

13.7.4 Recurrent Networks

A prototype system for solving graph colouring problems using a Multi-State Bit Stream Neural Network (MSBSN) has been developed [Rising, 1996, Rising et al., 1997]. We give a brief overview of this design.

An individual MSBSN contains a number of up/down counters (or subneurons), one to represent each of the available colours. Whilst updating, a MSBSN looks at all of its adjacent nodes and increments the relevant counter according to the colour of the adjacent nodes and a stochastic weight value (a stochastic bit-stream encoded with a bit probability providing a fixed temperature).

At the start of a given MSBSN update cycle, all of its internal counter bits are set to '1' except for the top most bits which are set to '0' (i.e. 8 bit counters would be initialized to the value $7F_{16}$). If at some stage during this update cycle all of these internal counters get 1's in their top most bit positions (i.e. every counter has been incremented at least once), then the counters are all decremented by 1. The result of this procedure will be that the lowest valued counters always have 0's in their top bit positions.

The MSBSN's new colour is then chosen as the state represented by the lowest internal MSBSN counter value. In the event of a tie, the new colour is chosen randomly from the lowest values via an external look-up table.

13.8 Conclusions

This chapter has given an overview of the results obtained by following a particular design strategy for implementing neural networks using stochastic computing. The fact that the neural functionality had to be altered to ensure a simple hardware realisation made it necessary to confirm that the new neurons were capable of useful computation.

Adaptation of standard learning approaches and development of some novel techniques demonstrated that interesting mappings can be realised by networks of bit-stream neurons in many cases using a comparable number of neurons to that required by a network of sigmoidal units.

The neurons have also been used in recurrent networks for combinatorial optimization after suitable adaptation of the functionality. Again performance was very comparable with that of sigmoidal or Boltzmann machine networks.

The conclusion of our research in this area is that the novel neurons do appear to compare favourably with more standard sigmoidal neurons, whether we compare their computational power, their generalization ability or their performance as combinatorial optimisers. In some areas they have even been found to outperform sigmoidal neurons.

The motivation for the approach was to show that by adapting to the hardware constraints we could produce a neural design that was comparable in its overall functionality, while being far simpler to implement.

Prototype implementations have used FPGA's to realise a recurrent network to perform graph colouring as well as single feedforward neurons. In all cases they have confirmed the predictions of initial software simulations and mathematical analysis.

We believe that the research to date has given affirmative answers to the initial questions raised by the approach. We therefore feel that the models are now at a stage where a larger scale prototype could be justified both for feedforward and recurrent networks. Such a prototype will inevitably raise additional practical and theoretical questions which will require further analysis to clarify and solve.

References

[Aarts and Korst, 1989] Aarts, E. and Korst, J. (1989). *Simulated Annealing and Boltzmann Machines*. John Wiley & Sons.

[Alspector et al., 1987] Alspector, J., Allen, R., Hu, V., and Satyanarayana, S. (1987). Stochastic learning networks and their electronic implementation. *Proc. of the Workshop on Neural Information Processing Systems – Natural and Synthetic*. Morgan Kaufmann, Palo Alto, CA.

[Burge and Shawe-Taylor, 1995] Burge, P. and Shawe-Taylor, J. (1995). Bit-stream neurons for graph colouring. *Journal of Artificial Neural Networks*, 2(4): 443–448.

[Cortes and Vapnik, 1995] Cortes, C. and Vapnik, V. (1995). Support-vector networks. *Machine Learning*, 20:273–297.

[DIMACS] DIMACS colouring benchmarks, available via anonymous ftp at `dimacs.rutgers.edu` in the directory `pub/challenge/graph/benchmarks/color`.

[Gaines, 1969] Gaines, B. (1969). Stochastic computing systems. *Advances in Information Systems Science*, 2:37–172.

[Hall et al., 1995] Hall, T., Peiffer, W., Hands, M., Thienpont, H., Crossland, W., Shawe-Taylor, J., and van Daalen, M. (1995) Considerations of the optical and opto-electronic hardware requirements for implementation of stochastic bit-stream neural nets. *Optical Computing*, 95.

[Jeavons, Cohen and Shawe-Taylor, 1994] Jeavons, P., Cohen, D., and Shawe-Taylor, J. (1994). Generating binary sequences for stochastic computing. *IEEE Transactions on Information Theory*, 40:716–720.

[Koch and Poggio, 1992] Koch, C. and Poggio, T. (1992). Multiplying with Synapses and Neurons. In: *Single Neuron Computation*, T. McKenna, J. Davis, and S.F. Zornetzer, eds., Academic Press, Boston, 315–345.

[Peterson and Anderson, 1987] Peterson, C. and Anderson, J. (1987). A mean field theory learning algorithm for neural networks, *Complex Systems*, 1:995–1019.

[Petford and Welsh, 1989] Petford, A. and Welsh, D. (1989). A randomised 3-colouring algorithm. *Discrete Mathematics*, 74:253–261.

[Pignon et al., 1996] Pignon, D., Parmiter, P., Slack, J., Hands, M., Hall, T., van Daalen, M., and Shawe-Taylor, J. (1996). Sigmoid neural transfer function realised by percolation. *Optics Letters*, 21(3):222–224.

[Rising, 1996] Rising, B. (1996). Hardware design of multi-state bit-stream neurons for graph colouring. *Technical Report, Royal Holloway, University of London*, CSD-TR-96-12.

[Rising et al., 1997] Rising, B., van Daalen, M., Burge, P., and Shawe-Taylor, J. (1997). Parallel graph colouring using FPGAs. *Field Programmable Logic and Applications*, (FPL'97), Springer, 1304:121–130.

[Shawe-Taylor,1995] Shawe-Taylor, J. (1995). Generalisation analysis for classes of continuous neural networks. *Proc. of IEEE International Conference on Neural Networks*, Piscataway, NJ: IEEE., 2944–2948.

[Shawe-Taylor et al., 1991] Shawe-Taylor, J., Jeavons, P., and van Daalen, M. (1991). Probabilistic bit-stream neural chip: Theory. *Connection Science*, 3(3):317–328.

[Shawe-Taylor and Pisanski, 1993] Shawe-Taylor, J. and Pisanski, T. (1993) Analysis of the mean field annealing algorithm for graph bisection. *Department of Computer Science, Royal Holloway, University of London.*

[Shawe-Taylor et al., 1995] Shawe-Taylor, J., van Daalen, M., and Zhao, J. (1995). Learning in feedforward bit-stream neural networks. *Neural Networks*, 9:991–998.

[Shawe-Taylor and Zerovnik, 1992] Shawe-Taylor, J. and Zerovnik, J. (1992). Generalised Boltzmann machines. *Department of Computer Science, Royal Holloway, University of London.*

[Shawe-Taylor and Zhao, 1995] Shawe-Taylor, J. and Zhao, J. (1996). Generalisation of a class of continuous neural networks. *Advances in Neural Information Processing Systems, vol. 8*, MIT Press, 267–273.

[Srinivasan and Bernard, 1976] Srinivasan, M. V. and Bernard, G. D. (1976). A proposed mechanism for multiplication of neural signals. *Biol. Cybernetics*, 21:227–236.

[van Daalen et al., 1990] van Daalen, M., Jeavons, P., and Shawe-Taylor, J. (1990). Probabilistic bit-stream neural chip: Implementation. *Oxford Workshop on VLSI for Artificial Intelligence and Neural Networks*, 285–294.

[van Daalen et al., 1993] van Daalen, M., Jeavons, P., and Shawe-Taylor, J. (1993). A stochastic neural architecture that exploits dynamically reconfigurable FPGAs. *IEEE Workshop on FPGAs for custom computing machines*, Los Alamitos, CA: IEEE Computer Society Press, 202–211.

[van Daalen et al., 1993] van Daalen, M., Jeavons, P., Shawe-Taylor, J., and Cohen, D. (1993). A device for generating binary sequences for stochastic computing. *Electronic Letters*, 29:80–81.

[van Daalen et al., 1994a] van Daalen, M., Kosel, T., Jeavons, P., and Shawe-Taylor, J. (1994) Emergent activation functions from a stochastic bit-stream neuron. *Electronic Letters*, 30:331–333.

[van Daalen et al., 1994b] van Daalen, M., Shawe-Taylor, J., Hall, T., and Crossland, W. (1994). Optical implementation of a stochastic neural system. *Optical Computational Intelligence Conference*, 139:395–398.

[van Daalen et al., 1994] van Daalen, M., Zhao, J., and Shawe-Taylor, J. (1994). Real time output derivatives for on chip learning using digital stochastic bit-stream neurons. *Electronic Letters*, 30:1775–1777.

[Zhao, 1995] Zhao, J. (1995). Stochastic Neural Networks: Theory, Simulations and Applications. *Ph. D. thesis*, Royal Holloway, University of London.

[Zhao and Shawe-Taylor, 1995] Zhao, J. and Shawe-Taylor, J. (1995). Stochastic connection neural networks. *Proc. of the Fourth IEEE Conference on Artificial Neural Networks*, 409:35–39.

[Zhao et al., 1996] Zhao, J., Shawe-Taylor, J. and van Daalen, M. (1996). Learning in stochastic bit-stream neural networks. *Neural Networks*, 9(6):991–998.

14 Hebbian Learning of Pulse Timing in the *Barn Owl* Auditory System

Wulfram Gerstner, Richard Kempter, J. Leo van Hemmen, and Hermann Wagner

Hebbian learning refers to an unsupervised correlation-based adaptation mechanism and is usually formulated in terms of mean firing rates. In this Chapter we study learning at the spike level. The learning process is driven by the temporal correlations between presynaptic spike arrival and postsynaptic firing.

To explore the effect of learning on pulse coding, we consider the example of auditory processing. The auditory system of the barn owl operates with a temporal precision in the microsecond range. After delay tuning, obtained by applying the learning rule to an integrate-and fire model of an auditory neuron, the temporal precision of spike firing is in the range of 20-30 microseconds. This level of precision, typical for the early stages in auditory processing, is necessary for sound source localization.

14.1 Introduction

The relevance of precise temporal spike timing in the cortex – or neural systems in general – is a fundamental, yet unsolved question [Abeles, 1994; Bialek et al., 1991; Hopfield, 1995; O'Keefe and Recce, 1993; Mainen and Sejnowski, 1995; Shadlen and Newsome, 1994; Softky, 1995; Rieke et al., 1996]; see also Chapters 1 and 4 of this book. There are, however, a few specialized subsystems for which the relevance of temporal information has been clearly shown. Prominent examples are the electro-sensory system of electric fish and the auditory system of barn owls [Carr and Konishi, 1990; Carr, 1993; Heiligenberg, 1991; Konishi, 1986; Konishi, 1993]. Here we use the latter as an example to study the following question: How can the timing of spikes be learned during early development? Specifically, how can processes of pulse generation and signal transmission be fine-tuned so as to achieve the required temporal precision?

The problem of spike-based learning arises whenever a neural system uses a strategy of temporal coding by action potentials. The auditory system is only one of several potential examples. Since we think that learning is a fundamental concept, we start in Section 2 with the problem of Hebbian learning and formulate a learning rule which operates on the level of single spikes. In Section 3 we give a quick overview of spike timing in the localization pathway of the *barn owl* auditory system. One of the key processes in the auditory system is phase locking discussed in Section 4. Finally, in Section 5, we bring the two strands, viz. Hebbian learning and auditory

14.2 Hebbian Learning

14.2.1 Review of Standard Formulations

D. Hebb formulated in 1949 a fundamental principle of learning [Hebb, 1949]:

When an axon of cell A is near enough to excite a cell B and repeatedly or persistently takes part in firing it, some growth process or metabolic change takes place in one or both cells such that A's efficiency, as one of the cells firing B, is increased.

Hebb's description states that correlations between the firings of the pre- and postsynaptic neurons drive changes in the transmission efficiency. Even though the idea of learning through correlations dates further back in the past, correlation-based learning rules are now generally called Hebbian learning.

In standard neural network theory, the Hebb rule is condensed to a formula for the change of synaptic efficacy as a function of pre- and postsynaptic firing rates; see, e.g., [Hertz et al., 1991; Haykin, 1994]. Let us write ν_j for the presynaptic firing rate and ν_i for the rate of the postsynaptic neuron. Then the change Δw_{ij} of the efficacy of a connection from j to i after a learning experiment of duration $\mathcal{T}$ is

$$\Delta w_{ij} = c_{ij}\,\nu_i\nu_j + c_{ii}\,\nu_i^2 + c_{jj}\,\nu_j^2 + b_i\,\nu_i + b_j\nu_j + a\,. \tag{14.1}$$

The first term on the right-hand side of (14.1) picks up the correlations between pre- and postsynaptic activity. The next terms are useful to impose some specific requirements like a proper normalization. The diagonal terms $c_{ii}\,\nu_i^2$ and $c_{jj}\,\nu_j^2$ are usually omitted.

As an example of (14.1), let us consider the learning rule

$$\Delta w_{ij} = \eta\,(\nu_i - \bar{\nu})\,\nu_j \tag{14.2}$$

which is a special case of (14.1) with parameters $c_{ij} = \eta, b_i = 0, b_j = -\eta\bar{\nu}, c_{ii} = c_{jj} = a = 0$. With the rule (14.2) the direction of synaptic change (increase or decrease) reverses if the output rate ν_i crosses the reference rate $\bar{\nu}$. For $\eta < 0$, (14.2) has an interesting property. Learning tends to move the output rate ν_i towards the reference value $\bar{\nu}$. Let us consider the situation where $\nu_i < \bar{\nu}$ and $\eta < 0$. Then *all* synapses grow ($\Delta w_{ij} > 0$ for all j) with a rate proportional to ν_j. Thus the overall input strength $\propto \sum_j w_{ij}\nu_j$ increases. Stronger input raises the output rate which therefore moves in direction of $\bar{\nu}$. Inversely, if $\nu_i > \bar{\nu}$, all synaptic efficacies decrease and so does ν_i. Our spike-based learning rule, to be discussed below, will have the same property of output normalization.

The Hebb rule (14.1) may be viewed as a special case of a general learning rule [Sejnowski and Tesauro, 1989; Kohonen, 1984]

$$\Delta w_{ij} = F(w_{ij};\nu_i,\nu_j) \tag{14.3}$$

where F is some arbitrary function of three variables. This rule (14.3) is a *local* learning rule, since the information about pre- and postsynaptic firing rates and the present state w_{ij} of the synaptic efficacy could easily be available at the location of the synapse. (The firing rate of other neurons $k \neq i, j$, however, would be not). Expansion of (14.3) to second order in the rates ν_i, ν_j yields (14.1). As mentioned before, the diagonal terms $c_{ii}\nu_i^2$ and $c_{jj}\nu_j^2$ are often set to zero; see, e.g., [Hopfield, 1982; Linsker, 1986; Miller et al., 1989]. Hebbian learning can also be generalized to time-dependent problems, e.g., sequence learning [Sompolinsky and Kanter, 1986; Herz et al., 1988, 1989; Minai and Levy, 1993; Abbott and Blum, 1996; Blum and Abbott 1996; Wu et al., 1996; Wimbauer et al., 1994].

The expansion coefficients $a, b_i, b_j, c_{ij}, c_{ii}, c_{jj}$ may, in general, depend on w_{ij}. The functional dependence of the parameters upon w_{ij} is useful to impose weight normalization; see, for example, [Oja, 1982; Kohonen, 1984; Miller and MacKay, 1994] . To see why normalization is necessary, let us return to (14.1). The Hebb rule (14.1) gives the change of the synaptic efficacy after a single learning session of duration $\mathcal{T}$. If the experiment is repeated over a large number of trials, the weights w_{ij} can, in principle, grow without bounds. To avoid unlimited growth, we can either (i) use the w_{ij}-dependence of the coefficients to impose some weight normalization, or (ii) impose explicit upper and lower bounds for w_{ij} or (iii) renormalize the weights by hand after each trial. In the spike based learning rule discussed in the following section we have chosen the second possibility: a weight w_{ij} is not modified, if $w_{ij} + \Delta w_{ij} > w^{\max}$ or $w_{ij} + \Delta w_{ij} < 0$.

Hebbian learning is considered one of the main driving forces for neuronal organization during development. The first model studies of cortical organization development [Willshaw and von der Malsburg, 1976; Swindale 1982], have incited a long line of research, e.g., [Kohonen, 1984; Linsker, 1986abc; Miller et al., 1989; MacKay and Miller, 1990; Obermayer et al., 1992]. Most of these models use in some way or another a correlation-based unsupervised learning rule similar to (14.1) or (14.3); for a review see [Erwin et al., 1995]. Note, however, that (14.1) and (14.3) are based on a rate coding hypothesis. The exact spike timing plays no role in the learning rule. Since we want to explore pulse coding in this book, we need learning rules which take spike timing into account. Spike-based learning is the topic of the following subsection.

14.2.2 Spike-Based Learning

Hebbian learning is often vaguely described as an adaptation rule where a synapse is strengthened if pre- and postsynaptic neuron are 'simultaneously' active. In the context of pulse coding, the meaning of 'simultaneously' must be specified.

We consider a synapse from neuron j to neuron i with efficacy w_{ij}. Let us denote the presynaptic spike train by $S_j(t) = \sum_{t_j^{(f)} \in \mathcal{F}_j} \delta(t - t_j^{(f)})$ where $t_j^{(f)}$ denotes the *arrival* time at the synapse. The symbol $\mathcal{F}_j$ stands for the set of all spike arrival time at synapse j. The spike train at the output is

$S_i(t) = \sum_{t_i^{(f)} \in \mathcal{F}_i} \delta(t - t_i^{(f)})$ where $t_i^{(f)}$ are the firing times and $\mathcal{F}_i$ the set of all output spikes. A synaptic change occurs if presynaptic spike arrival and postsynaptic firing coincide within some time window; for recent experimental measurements, see [Markram et al., 1997].

A simple rectangular time window of duration $2\bar{s}$ could, for example, be described by the condition $|t_j^{(f)} - t_i^{(f)}| < \bar{s}$. More generally, we may assume in our model a learning window $W(s)$ with some arbitrary dependence upon the time difference $s = t_j^{(f)} - t_i^{(f)}$. The change of the synaptic efficacy after a learning experiment of duration $\mathcal{T}$ is then

$$\Delta w_{ij} = \int_0^{\mathcal{T}} \int_0^{\mathcal{T}} W(t' - t)\, S_i(t)\, S_j(t')\, dt\, dt' + $$
$$+ \tilde{b}_i \int_0^{\mathcal{T}} S_i(t)\, dt + \tilde{b}_j \int_0^{\mathcal{T}} S_j(t)\, dt + \mathcal{T}\tilde{a}. \quad (14.4)$$

The first term of the right-hand side contains the learning window $W(s)$ and imposes the simultaneity constraint between presynaptic and postsynaptic firing. An example of a learning window is shown in Figure 14.1. For an interpretation of the linear terms in (14.4), we may note that $\int_0^{\mathcal{T}} S_k(t)dt = n_k$ (for $k = i, j$) is just the number of pre- or postsynaptic spikes that occur in the time window of length $\mathcal{T}$. In analogy to equation (14.1), we could add to (14.4) some diagonal terms $\tilde{c}_{ii}(t' - t)S_i(t)S_i(t') + \tilde{c}_{jj}(t' - t)S_j(t)S_j(t')$ but we will not do so.

Equation (14.4) gives the change Δw_{ij} after a learning run of duration $\mathcal{T}$. It is convenient to divide (14.4) by $\mathcal{T}$ in order to get the average rate of change

$$\frac{\Delta w_{ij}}{\mathcal{T}} = \frac{1}{\mathcal{T}} \int_0^{\mathcal{T}} \int_{-t}^{\mathcal{T}-t} W(s)\, S_i(t)\, S_j(t + s)\, ds\, dt$$
$$+ \frac{\tilde{b}_i}{\mathcal{T}} \int_0^{\mathcal{T}} S_i(t)\, dt + \frac{\tilde{b}_j}{\mathcal{T}} \int_0^{\mathcal{T}} S_j(t)\, dt + \tilde{a}. \quad (14.5)$$

On the right-hand side of (14.5) we have used the substitution $s = t' - t$.

Let us suppose that the learning window $W(s)$ has some finite width $\bar{s}$. If $\mathcal{T} \gg \bar{s}$, we can extend the limits of the s-integration to $\pm\infty$ without introducing a large error. This little trick allows us to rewrite (14.5) in a nice form

$$\langle \frac{d}{dt} w_{ij} \rangle = \int_{-\infty}^{\infty} W(s)\, \langle S_i(t)\, S_j(t+s) \rangle\, ds$$
$$+ \tilde{b}_i \langle S_i(t) \rangle + \tilde{b}_j \langle S_j(t) \rangle + \tilde{a} \quad (14.6)$$

where $\langle . \rangle$ means a temporal average over a time $\mathcal{T}$. On the left-hand side of (14.6) we have used $\langle dw_{ij}/dt \rangle = \mathcal{T}^{-1} \int_0^{\mathcal{T}} (dw_{ij}/dt)dt = \Delta w_{ij}/\mathcal{T}$. Equation (14.6) shows explicitly that the learning process is driven by the correlations $\langle S_i(t)\, S_j(t+s) \rangle$ between pre- and postsynaptic firing.

Equation (14.6) is the natural generalization of (14.1) to spike coding. To see the relation more clearly, let us assume rate coding (in the sense of a temporal average; see Chapter 1). For example, we may consider a situation where input and output spikes are generated stochastically with, respectively, rates ν_j and ν_i. Rate coding implies that (i) the rate is constant (or varies only slowly) over the learning session of duration $\mathcal{T}$ and (ii) that there are no correlations between input and output pulses apart from the correlations between the rates. Due to (i) we may use the spike count to estimate the rate, viz., $\langle S_i(t) \rangle = \nu_i$ and $\langle S_j(t) \rangle = \nu_j$. Because of (ii) we can set $\langle S_i(t) S_j(t+s) \rangle = \nu_i \nu_j$, independent of s. Thus (14.6) reduces to

$$\frac{\Delta w_{ij}}{\mathcal{T}} = \left[\int_{\infty}^{\infty} W(s) \, ds \right] \nu_i \nu_j + \tilde{b}_i \nu_i + \tilde{b}_j \nu_j + \tilde{a}. \qquad (14.7)$$

Comparison with (14.1) yields $\int_{-\infty}^{\infty} W(s) ds = c_{ij}/\mathcal{T}$, $\tilde{b}_i = b_i/\mathcal{T}$, $\tilde{b}_j = b_j/\mathcal{T}$, $\tilde{a} = a/\mathcal{T}$, and $c_{ii} = c_{jj} = 0$.

Asymmetric learning windows have previously been used in *rate* models for hippocampal navigation [Abbott and Blum, 1996; Blum and Abbott, 1996]. Related considerations have also appeared in rate models of sequence learning [Herz et al., 1988, 1989; Minai and Levy, 1993; Wu et al., 1996]. The learning rule (14.4), however, works on the level of correlation between *pulses* in the ms range. A spike-based learning rule with short time window has also been applied to the learning of spatio-temporal pulse patterns [Gerstner et al., 1993].

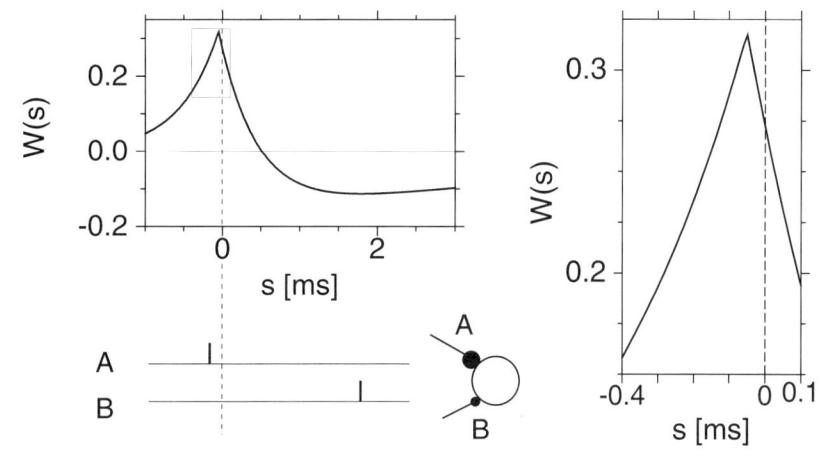

Figure 14.1. Learning Window W as a function of the delay s between postsynaptic firing and presynaptic spike arrival. The graph on the right-hand side shows the boxed region around the maximum on an expanded scale. If $W(s)$ is positive (negative) for some s, the synaptic efficacy is increased (decreased). The postsynaptic firing occurs at $s = 0$ (vertical dashed line). Learning is most efficient if presynaptic spikes arrive shortly before the postsynaptic neuron starts firing, as in synapse A. Another synapse B, which fires *after* the postsynaptic spike, is decreased. Taken from [Gerstner et al., 1996].

14.2.3 Example

In Section 5 we will use a special instance of the learning rule (14.4). We set [Gerstner et al., 1996]

$$\Delta w_{ij} = \int_0^T \int_0^T W(t' - t)\, S_i(t)\, S_j(t')\, dt\, dt' + \tilde{b}_j \int_0^T S_j(t)\, dt \qquad (14.8)$$

with $\tilde{b}_j > 0$ and a learning window

$$W(s) = \begin{cases} [A_+ - A_-]\exp[-(s^* - s)/\tau^{\mathrm{syn}}] & \text{for } s < s^* \\ A_+ \exp[-(s - s^*)/\tau_+] - A_- \exp[-(s - s^*)/\tau_-] & \text{for } s > s^* \end{cases} \qquad (14.9)$$

where $s = t_j^{(f)} - t_i^{(f)}$ is the delay between presynaptic spike arrival and postsynaptic firing. The parameters are $A_+ = 0.5$, $A_- = 0.2$, $\tau^{\mathrm{syn}} = 0.5\,\mathrm{ms}$, $\tau_+ = 0.5\,\mathrm{ms}$, $\tau_- = 5\,\mathrm{ms}$, and $s^* = -0.05\,\mathrm{ms}$. The linear term is $\tilde{b}_j = 0.1$. The learning window is plotted in Figure 14.1 and describes the following effects. If a presynaptic spike arrives slightly *before* the postsynaptic firing, the synaptic efficacy is increased ($W(s) > 0$ for $s < 0$). If a presynaptic spike arrives a few ms *after* the output spike, the synapse is weakened ($W(s) < 0$). Qualitatively, the form of the learning window (14.9) seems to be in accordance with experimental results on cortical neurons [Markram et al., 1997]. Time constants in the cortex are, however, much longer than those chosen in Figure 14.1 which is intended for neurons in the auditory pathway. In the cortex or the hippocampus, the learning window probably has a width of 50–200 ms [Bliss and Collingridge, 1993; Debanne et al., 1994].

Note that the maximum of the learning window $W(s)$ occurs for a value $s = s^* < 0$. Thus the synaptic increase is maximal if the input spike precedes the output spike by an amount $|s^*|$; see Figure 14.1. Stable learning requires that s^* be negative and of the order of the rise time of an excitatory postsynaptic potential [Gerstner et al., 1996; Kempter, 1997]. In accordance with Hebb's statement cited at the beginning of the Section, the stability requirement ensures that those synapses which are already strong and contribute most to triggering a spike receive the maximum reinforcement. The output spike occurs slightly delayed with respect to presynaptic spike arrival, and hence $s^* < 0$ must hold.

So far we have discussed the correlation term on the right-hand side of (14.8). Due to the linear term $\tilde{b}_j > 0$ each presynaptic spike has a weak positive influence on the synaptic efficacy, even if there is no output spike.

Let us now return to the rate interpretation (14.7). With the parameter settings given above we have $\int_{-\infty}^{\infty} W(s)\,ds < 0$ and $\tilde{b}_j > 0$. The other terms on the right-hand side of (14.7) vanish. Thus, the rate equivalent of the spike-based learning rule (14.8) is of the form (14.2) with a factor $\eta = \int W(s)\,ds < 0$. It follows from the discussion after (14.2) that the output rate will be automatically adjusted during learning to a mean level $\bar{\nu} = -\tilde{b}_j / \int W(s)\,ds$. Thus the total input $\sum_j w_{ij} \nu_j$ to neuron i remains normalized as well.

Nevertheless, individual weights could grow to very high values. To limit the growth, we have imposed upper and lower bounds, that is $\Delta w_{ij} = 0$, if $w_{ij} \geq w^{\max}$ or $w_{ij} < 0$.

14.2.4 Learning Window

In this Section we want to give a more detailed explanation for our choice of the learning window (14.9). In order to make the arguments more transparent we will consider instead of (14.9) the simple window

$$W(s) = \begin{cases} A \exp[-(s^* - s)/\tau^{\text{syn}}] & \text{for} \quad s < s^* \\ A \exp[-(s - s^*)/\tau] & \text{for} \quad s > s^* \end{cases} \quad (14.10)$$

The full window (14.9) can be constructed by linear superposition of two elementary windows of the form (14.10).

On a microscopic basis, Hebbian learning is thought to involve (at least) two components. We do not wish to speculate on the chemical nature of the components, but simply call them a and b. We assume that the first component is generated by a chemical reaction chain triggered by the arrival of a spike at the synapse. As a result of the processing chain the concentration $[a]$ of component a is, after a delay Δ, increased. In the absence of further input, the concentration decays with a time constant τ_a back to its resting level $[a] = 0$. A simple way to describe this process is

$$\frac{d}{dt}[a] = -\frac{[a]}{\tau_a} + \sum_{t_j^{(f)} \in \mathcal{F}_j} \delta(t - t_j^{(f)} - \Delta). \quad (14.11)$$

A high level of $[a]$ sets the synapse in a state 'ready to learn'. To generate the synaptic change and perform learning, another substance b is needed as well. The production of b is generated by a second process triggered by a *postsynaptic* spike

$$\frac{d}{dt}[b] = -\frac{[b]}{\tau_b} + \sum_{t_i^{(f)} \in \mathcal{F}_i} \delta(t - t_i^{(f)}) \quad (14.12)$$

where τ_b is another time constant. In analogy to (14.11), we could allow for a delay Δ_b in the dynamics of (14.12), but we will not do so.

Hebbian learning needs both substances to be present at the same time, thus

$$\frac{d}{dt} w_{ij}^{\text{corr}} = \gamma \, [a(t)] \, [b(t)] \quad (14.13)$$

with some learning rate γ. The upper index *corr* is intended to remind the reader that we are concerned with the Hebbian correlation term only and neglect for the moment the linear terms that appear on the right-hand side of (14.4).

Let us now consider the synaptic change caused by a single presynaptic spike at $t_j^{(f)}$ and a postsynaptic spike a $t_i^{(f)} = t_j^{(f)} - s$. Integration of (14.11) and (14.12) yields

$$[a] = \exp[-(t - t_j^{(f)} - \Delta)/\tau_a]\mathcal{H}(t - t_j^{(f)} - \Delta)$$
$$[b] = \exp[-(t - t_i^{(f)})/\tau_b]\mathcal{H}(t - t_i^{(f)}) \qquad (14.14)$$

where $\mathcal{H}(.)$ denotes as usual the Heaviside step function. The change caused by the pair of pulses $(t_i^{(f)}, t_j^{(f)})$ and measured after a time $\mathcal{T}$ is

$$\Delta w_{ij}^{\text{corr}}(t_i^{(f)}, t_j^{(f)}) = \int_0^{\mathcal{T}} \left(\frac{d}{dt} w_{ij}^{\text{corr}}\right) dt$$
$$= \gamma \int_{t_0}^{\mathcal{T}} \exp\left[-\frac{t - t_j^{(f)} - \Delta}{\tau_a} - \frac{t - t_j^{(f)} + s}{\tau_b}\right] dt \quad (14.15)$$

where $t_0 = \max\{t_j^{(f)} + \Delta, t_j^{(f)} - s\}$ and $s = t_j^{(f)} - t_i^{(f)}$. The integral in (14.15) can be performed. We introduce $s^* = -\Delta$ and find for $\mathcal{T} \gg \tau_a, \tau_b, \Delta$

$$\Delta w_{ij}^{\text{corr}}(t_i^{(f)}, t_j^{(f)}) = \begin{cases} A \exp[-(s^* - s)/\tau_a] & \text{for} \quad s < s^* \\ A \exp[-(s - s^*)/\tau_b] & \text{for} \quad s > s^* \end{cases} \qquad (14.16)$$

with $A = \gamma(\tau_a\tau_b/\tau_a + \tau_b)$. Equation (14.16) shows that the change of the synaptic efficacy $\Delta w_{ij}^{\text{corr}}$ caused by a pair of pulses $(t_i^{(f)}, t_j^{(f)})$ depends only on the time difference $s = t_j^{(f)} - t_i^{(f)}$. We write

$$\Delta w_{ij}^{\text{corr}}(t_i^{(f)}, t_j^{(f)}) = W(t_j^{(f)} - t_i^{(f)}). \qquad (14.17)$$

Equation (14.17) gives the change caused by a single pair of spikes. Given a train of presynaptic input spikes and a set of postsynaptic output spikes, many combinations of firing times $(t_i^{(f)}, t_j^{(f)})$ exist. Due to the linearity of the learning equation (14.13), the total change is

$$\Delta w_{ij}^{\text{corr}} = \sum_{t_i^{(f)} \in \mathcal{F}_i} \sum_{t_j^{(f)} \in \mathcal{F}_j} W(t_j^{(f)} - t_i^{(f)}) = \int_0^{\mathcal{T}} \int_0^{\mathcal{T}} W(t' - t) S_i(t) S_j(t') \, dt \, dt'.$$
(14.18)

Thus the microscopic two-component model developed in this subsection generates the correlation term on the right-hand side of the learning equation (14.4).

As mentioned before, the learning window (14.9) is slightly more complicated, since it has two phases: a positive phase of synaptic potentiation for s negative or around zero and a negative phase of synaptic depression for large s. The arguments presented in (14.11) - (14.18) would explain the positive phase only. To get both phases we must assume that the output spike triggers *two* components b_+ and b_-; the first one contributes to potentiation with intensity A_+ and the second to depression with intensity A_-. Repetition of the above steps then leads to the full learning window (14.9).

Even with this extra component, the above 'microscopic' model is still extremely simplified. In particular, it does not take into account other dynamic effects of synapses [Abbott et al., 1997; Nelson et al., 1997; Tsodyks and Markram, 1997; Markram and Tsodyks, 1996]. A fairly detailed model of these effects can be found in [Senn et al., 1997]; see also Chapter 12 in this book.

14.3 Barn Owl Auditory System

Owls hunt at night. From behavioral experiments it is known that owls can locate sound sources even in complete darkness with a remarkable precision. To do so, the signal processing in the auditory pathway must achieve a temporal precision in the microsecond range with elements that are noisy, unreliable and rather slow. In this Section we discuss the general problem of sound source localization and give a rough sketch of the auditory pathway. Sections 4 and 5 will focus on two specific aspects, viz., phase locking and delay tuning by Hebbian learning.

14.3.1 The Localization Task

Barn owls use interaural time differences (ITD) for sound source localization [Jeffress, 1948; Moiseff and Konishi, 1981; Carr and Konishi, 1990]. Behavioral experiments show that barn owls can locate a sound source in the horizontal plane with a precision of about 1-2 degrees of angle [Knudsen et al., 1979]. A simple calculation shows that this corresponds to a temporal difference of a few microseconds ($< 5\,\mu$s) between the sound waves at the left and right ear. Those small temporal differences must be detected and evaluated by the owl's auditory system; see Figure 14.2.

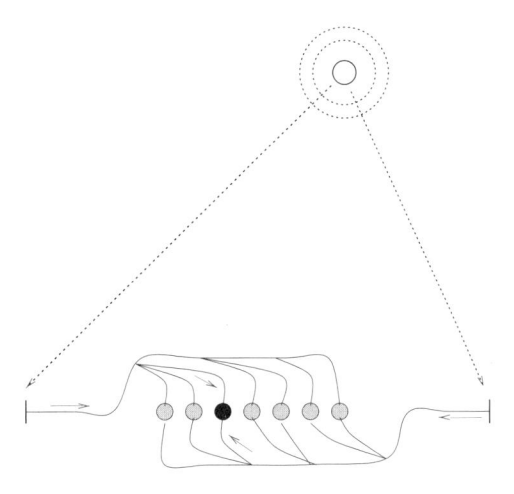

Figure 14.2. Jeffress Model. Sound waves from a source located to the right of the owl's head arrive at the two ears where they excite neuronal activity. Neuronal signals travel along transmission lines to an array of coincidence detectors. The coincidence-detecting neurons respond, if signals from both sides arrive simultaneously. Due to transmission delays, the position of the coincidence detector activated by the signals depends on the location of the external sound source.

The basic principle of how such a time-difference detector could be set up was discussed by Jeffress about 50 years ago [Jeffress, 1948]. It consists of delay lines and an array of coincidence detectors. If the sound source is on the right-hand side of the auditory space, the sound wave arrives first at the right ear and then at the left ear. The signals propagate from both ears along transmission lines towards the set of coincidence detectors. A signal originating from a source located to the right of the owl's head, stimulates a coincidence detector on the left-hand side of the array. If the location of the signal source is shifted, a different coincidence detector responds. The 'place' of responding coincidence detectors is therefore a signature for the location of the external sound source (Figure 14.2). Such a representation has been called 'place' coding [Konishi, 1986; Carr, 1993].

Remarkably enough, such a coincidence detector circuit was found four decades later by C.E. Carr and M. Konishi [Carr and Konishi, 1990] in the nucleus laminaris of the *barn owl*. The existence of the circuit confirms the general idea of temporal difference detection by delayed coincidence measurement. It gives, however, no indication of how the precision of a few microseconds is finally achieved.

In order to better understand how precise spike timing arises, we have to look at the first few processing steps in the auditory pathway. Three aspects are important: frequency separation, phase locking, and phase-correct averaging.

14.3.2 Auditory Localization Pathway

The first few processing steps along the auditory localization pathway are sketched in Figure 14.3. The figure represents, of course, a simplified picture of auditory information processing, but it captures some essential ingredients. At both ears the sound wave is separated into its frequency components. Signals then pass an intermediate processing area called nucleus magnocellularis (NM) and meet at the nucleus laminaris (NL). Neurons there are found to be sensitive to the interaural time difference (ITD). Due to the periodicity of a sinusoidal wave, the ITD of a single frequency channel is really a *phase* difference and leaves some ambiguities. In the next processing steps further up in the auditory pathway, information on phase differences from different frequency channels is combined to retrieve the temporal difference and hence the location of the sound source in the horizontal plane. Nice reviews of the basic principles of auditory processing in the owl can be found in [Konishi, 1986, 1993; Carr, 1993].

Let us now follow the first few processing steps in more detail. After cochlear filtering, different frequencies are processed by different neurons and stay separated up to the nucleus laminaris. In the following we may therefore focus on a single frequency channel and consider a neuron which responds best to a frequency of, say, 5 kHz.

If the ear is stimulated with a 5 kHz tone, neurons in the 5 kHz channel are activated and fire action potentials. At first sight, the spike train looks noisy. A closer look, however, reveals that the pulses are phase locked

14.3 Barn Owl Auditory System

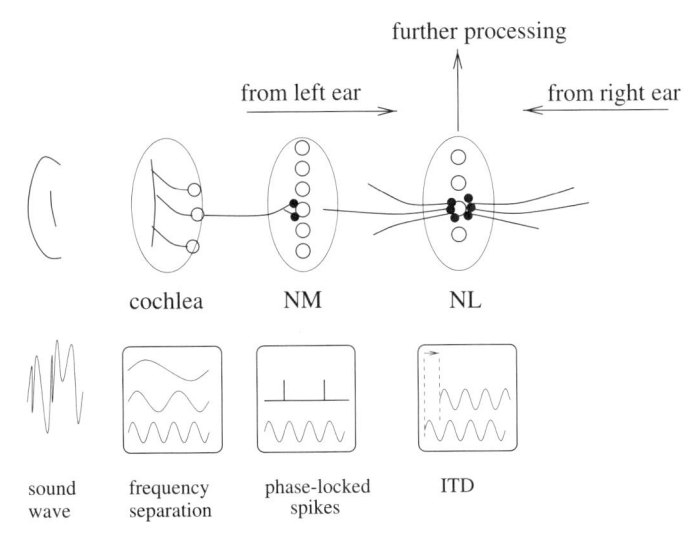

Figure 14.3. Auditory Pathway (schematic). At the cochlea a sound wave is separated into its frequency components. Phase locked spikes are transmitted along the auditory nerve to the nucleus magnocellularis (NM), an intermediate processing step. Action potentials at the output of the NM are phase locked as well. The signals from both ears meet in the nucleus laminaris (NL). Neurons in the NL are sensitive to the interaural time difference (ITD). In further processing steps, the output of neurons with different frequencies is combined to resolve remaining ambiguities.

to the stimulating tone: Spikes occur preferentially around some phase φ_0 with respect to the periodic stimulus. Phase locking is, of course, not perfect, but subject to two types of noise (Figure 14.4). First, spikes do not occur at every cycle of the 5 kHz tone. Often the neuron misses several cycles before it fires again. Second, spikes occur with a temporal jitter of about $\sigma = 40\,\mu\text{s}$ around the preferred phase [Sullivan and Konishi, 1984] [Sullivan and Konishi, 1984].

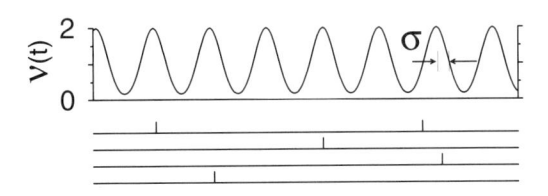

Figure 14.4. Spike trains in the auditory pathway show phase locking and can be described by a time dependent firing rate $\nu(t)$ which is modulated by the signal. Four samples of spike trains are shown at the bottom of the Figure.

To a fair approximation, we can describe the spike train by a Poisson process with a periodically modulated rate

$$\nu_j(t) = p \sum_{m=-\infty}^{\infty} \mathcal{G}_\sigma(t - mT - \Delta_j) \tag{14.19}$$

where T is the period of the tone (e.g., $T = 0.2\,\text{ms}$ for our 5 kHz signal), $\mathcal{G}_\sigma$ is a Gaussian with variance σ, and $\Delta_j = \varphi_j(T/2\pi)$ is a delay associated with the preferred phase φ_j of spikes of a given presynaptic neuron j. The amplitude p with $0 < p < 1$ is the probability of firing in one period. The temporally averaged mean firing rate is $\langle \nu_j \rangle = p/T$. The rate formula (14.19) does not take into account refractoriness of the spike trains; two spikes can be generated in arbitrary short intervals. For $p \ll 1$ short intervals are, however, unlikely and (14.19) is a useful approximation of real spike trains. In the simulations discussed in Section 5 we have imposed absolute refractoriness by requiring a minimum interspike interval of 0.5 ms. Examples of spike trains generated from (14.19) are shown in Figure 14.4.

Phase locking is seen along the auditory nerve connecting the cochlea and the nucleus magnocellularis, at the output of the nucleus magnocellularis, and also at the output of the nucleus laminaris. The phase jitter σ even decreases from one processing step to the next so that the temporal precision of phase locking increases from around 40 μs at the output of the nucleus magnocellularis to about 25 μs at the output of the nucleus laminaris. The precision of phase locking is the topic of the following subsection.

14.4 Phase Locking

14.4.1 Neuron Model

We focus on a single neuron i in the nucleus laminaris (NL). The neuron receives input from neurons in the nucleus magnocellularis (NM) through about 150 synapses. All input lines belong to the same frequency channel. The probability of spike arrival at one of the synapses is given by (14.19) where j labels the synapses and $T = 0.2\,\text{ms}$ is the period of the signal.

As a neuron model for i we take an integrate-and-fire unit (see Chapter 1.2.3) with time constant τ_m and input resistance R,

$$\tau_m \frac{du}{dt} = -u + R\mathcal{I}(t) \tag{14.20}$$

where the input current $\mathcal{I}(t)$ is generated by the synaptic spike input

$$\mathcal{I}(t) = \sum_j \frac{w_{ij}}{(R/\tau_m)} \sum_{t_j^{(f)} \in \mathcal{F}_j} \frac{1}{\tau_s} \exp\left(-\frac{t - t_j^{(f)}}{\tau_s}\right) \mathcal{H}(t - t_j^{(f)}) \tag{14.21}$$

where $t_j^{(f)}$ is the time of spike *arrival* at synapse j, w_{ij} is the synaptic efficacy of a connection from j to i, τ_s is a synaptic time constant, τ_m is the membrane time constant of neuron i, and $\mathcal{H}(.)$ is the Heaviside step function.

From (14.20) and (14.21) we may calculate the form of an excitatory postsynaptic potential (EPSP). The response of the membrane potential to a spike input at $s = 0$ is

$$\epsilon(s) = \frac{1}{1 - (\tau_s/\tau_m)} \left[\exp\left(-\frac{s}{\tau_m}\right) - \exp\left(-\frac{s}{\tau_s}\right)\right] \mathcal{H}(s). \tag{14.22}$$

If there is repeated spike input, then the resulting EPSPs (14.22) are added until the membrane potential reaches the threshold ϑ. The moment of threshold crossing defines the firing time $t_i^{(f)}$ of an output spike. After firing, the membrane potential is reset and the summation process starts again (see Chapter 1.2.3).

From experiments on chickens it is known that the duration of an EPSP in the NL is remarkably short (< 1 ms) [Reyes et al., 1994, 1996]. Neurons of an auditory specialist like the barn owl may be even faster. In our model equations, we have set $\tau_m = \tau_s = 0.1$ ms. These values correspond to an EPSP with a duration of about 0.25 ms.

The short duration of EPSPs in neurons in the NL and NM is due to an outward rectifying current which sets in when the membrane potential exceeds the resting potential [Manis and Marx, 1991; Oertel, 1983]. The purely *passive* membrane time constant is in the range of 2 ms [Reyes et al., 1994], but the outward rectifying current reduces the effective membrane resistance whenever the voltage is above the resting potential. In a conductance-based neuron model (see Chapter 1.2.4.), all membrane currents would be described explicitly. In our integrate-and-fire model, the main effect of the outward rectifying current is taken into account by working with a short *effective* membrane time constant $\tau_m = 0.1$ ms.

A membrane constant of 0.1 ms is much shorter than that found in cortical neurons where $\tau_m \approx 10 - 50$ ms seem to be typical values; see, e.g., [Bernander et al., 1991]. Note, however, that for temporal coding in the barn owl auditory system, $\tau_m = 0.1$ ms is quite long compared to the precision of phase locking of 25 μs found in auditory neurons and necessary for successful sound source localization. How the precision of phase locking arises is the topic of the next two paragraphs.

14.4.2 Phase Locking – Schematic

To get an intuitive understanding of how phase locking arises, let us study an idealized situation and take perfectly coherent spikes as input to our model neuron (Figure 14.5).

Specifically, let us consider a situation where 100 input lines converge on the model neuron. On each line, spike arrival is given by (14.19) with $\sigma \to 0$ and $p = 0.2$. The delays Δ_j are the same for all transmission lines ($\Delta_j = \Delta_0$). Then in each cycle a volley of 20 ± 5 synchronized spikes arrive. The EPSPs evoked by those spikes are added as shown schematically in Figure 14.5. The output spike occurs when the membrane potential crosses the threshold ϑ. Note that the threshold must be reached from below. It follows that the output spike must always occur during the *rise* time of the EPSPs generated by the last bunch of spikes before firing.

Since the input spikes are phase-locked to the stimulus, the output spike will also be phase-locked to the acoustic waveform. The preferred phase of the output spike φ_i will, of course be slightly delayed with respect to the input phase $\varphi_0 = \Delta_0(2\pi/T)$. The typical delay will be less than the rise

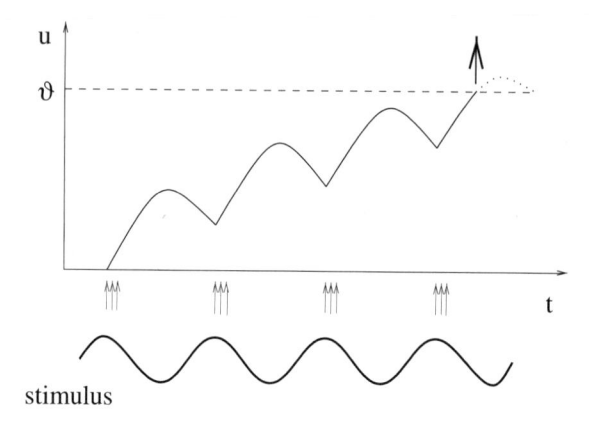

Figure 14.5. Phase Locking (schematic). Action potentials arrive periodically and are phase-locked to the stimulus in bundles of spikes (bottom). The postsynaptic potentials evoked by presynaptic spike arrival are summed and yield the total postsynaptic potential $u(t)$ which shows a pronounced oscillatory structure. Firing occurs when $u(t)$ crosses the threshold. The output spike is phase locked to the external signal, since the threshold crossing is bound to occur during a *rising* phase of u.

time τ_{rise} of an EPSP. Thus, $\varphi_i = (\Delta_0 + 0.5\,\tau_{\text{rise}})\,(2\pi/T)$ will be a reasonable estimate of the preferred output phase.

14.4.3 Simulation Results

Can we transfer the above qualitative arguments to a more realistic scenario? We have simulated a neuron with 154 input lines. At each synapse spikes arrive with rate (14.19). The temporal jitter has been set to $\sigma = 40\,\mu\text{s}$. The delays Δ_j (and hence the preferred phases) have a jitter of $35\,\mu\text{s}$ around some mean value Δ_0. As before, $p = 0.2$ for all inputs.

A short interval taken from a longer simulation run with these input parameters is shown in Figure 14.6. Part a shows the membrane potential $u(t)$ as a function of time; Figures 14.6b and c show the distribution of spike arrival times. Even though spike arrival is rather noisy, the trajectory of the membrane potential exhibits characteristic periodic modulations. From the qualitative arguments of the preceding paragraphs, we therefore expect the output spike to be phase-locked. Figure 14.7a confirms our expectations: the distribution of output phases exhibits a pronounced peak. The width of the distribution corresponds to a temporal precision of $\sigma_{\text{out}} = 25\,\mu\text{s}$, a significant increase in precision compared to the input jitter $\sigma = 40\,\mu\text{s}$.

So far we have assumed that the delays Δ_j have a small variation of $35\,\mu\text{s}$ only. Hence the preferred phases $\varphi_j = \Delta_j\,(2\pi/T)$ are nearly identical for all input lines. If the preferred phases are drawn stochastically from a uniform distribution over $[0, 2\pi]$, then spike arrival at the neuron is effectively *incoherent*, even though the spikes on each input line exhibit phase-locking. If input spikes arrive incoherently, the temporal precision is lost and the output spikes have a flat phase distribution; see Figure 14.7b.

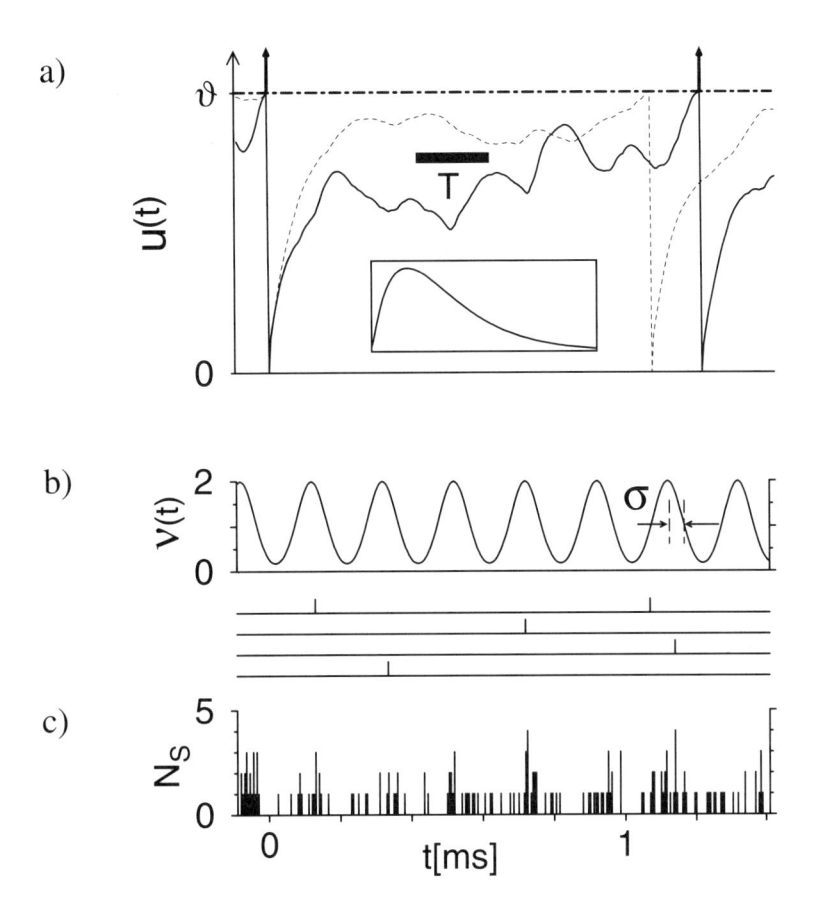

Figure 14.6. a) Membrane potential $u(t)$ of an integrate-and-fire neuron as a function of time. b) Rate $\nu_j(t)$ of presynaptic firing during 5 kHz stimulation and four samples of input spike trains (vertical bars). The model neuron receives input from 154 presynaptic neurons in volleys of phase-locked spikes with a jitter of $\sigma = 40\,\mu$s driven by a 5 kHz tone. Input spikes are generated by a stochastic process with periodically modulated rate (solid line in b)). A histogram of spike arrival times (number of spikes N_s in bins of 5 μs) summed over all 154 synapses is shown in c). Each input spike evokes an excitatory postsynaptic potential (EPSP) shown on an enlarged voltage scale (same time scale) in the inset of a). Each input spike evokes an excitatory postsynaptic potential (EPSP) shown on an enlarged voltage scale (same time scale) in the inset of a). The EPSPs from all neurons are added linearly and yield the membrane voltage u (a), main figure). With the spike input shown in c) the membrane voltage exhibits oscillations (solid line). The model neuron fires (arrow) if u reaches a threshold ϑ. Firing must always occur during the time when u increases so that, in the case of coherent input, output spikes are phase-locked as well (see also Figure 14.7a)). If input spikes arrive incoherently, $u(t)$ follows a trajectory with stochastic fluctuations but no systematic oscillations (dashed line in a)); see Figure 14.7b). Voltage in a): arbitrary units; the threshold ϑ is 36 times the amplitude of a single EPSP. Rate in b) in kHz. Taken from [Gerstner et al., 1996].

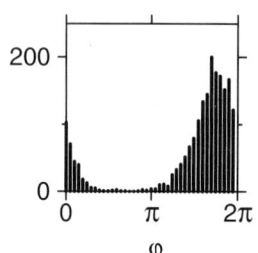

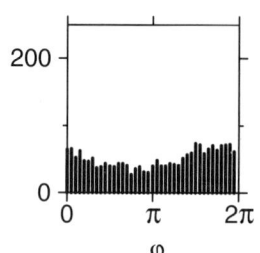

Figure 14.7. Phase histograms of output spikes. In *a* the input spikes from the 154 presynaptic neurons arrive *coherently* with the spiking statistics as shown in Figs. 6*b* and 6*c*. In this case, the distribution of output spikes exhibits a pronounced maximum indicating a high degree of phase locking. The width of the peak corresponds to a temporal precision of 25 μs. *b* If input spikes arrive incoherently, the histogram of output phases has no significant structure. Taken from [Gerstner et al., 1996].

We conclude that integrate-and-fire neurons are capable of transmitting phase information. Output spikes are generated with high temporal precision, if input spikes arrive with a high degree of coherence. If input spikes arrive incoherently, the temporal information is lost. The consequences of these observations are discussed in the following Section.

14.5 Delay Tuning by Hebbian Learning

14.5.1 Motivation

Each neuron in the nucleus laminaris (NL) of the barn owl receives input from about 150 presynaptic neurons [Carr and Konishi, 1990; Carr, 1993]. The high degree of convergence enables the neuron to increase the signal-to-noise ratio by averaging over many (noisy) transmission lines. As we have seen in the preceding Section, the temporal precision of phase locking is indeed increased from 40 μs in the input lines to 25 μs in the output of our model neuron in the NL.

Such an averaging scheme, however, can work only, if the preferred phases φ_j of all input lines are (nearly) the same. Otherwise the temporal precision is decreased or even lost completely as shown in Figure 14.7*b*. To improve the signal-to-noise ratio, 'phase-correct' averaging is needed. The question arises of how a neuron in the NL can perform correct averaging.

The total delay from the ear to the NL has been estimated to be in the range of 2–3 ms [Carr and Konishi, 1990]. Even if the transmission delays vary by only 0.1–0.2 ms between one transmission line and the next, the phase information of a 5 kHz signal is completely lost when the signals arrive at the NL. Therefore the delays must be precisely tuned so as to allow the neurons to perform phase-correct averaging. Tuning of delays may be achieved by an unsupervised Hebbian mechanism discussed in the following subsection.

14.5.2 Selection of Delays

Precise wiring of the auditory connections could be set up genetically. This is, however, rather unlikely since the owl's head grows considerably during development. Moreover, while neurons in the nucleus laminaris of the adult owl are sensitive to the interaural phase difference, no such sensitivity was found for young owls [Carr, 1995; see also Chuhma and Ohmori, 1998]. This indicates that delay tuning arises only later during development. It is clear that there can be no external supervisor or controller that selects the appropriate delays. What the owl needs is an adaptive mechanism which can be implemented locally and which achieves a tuning of appropriate delays.

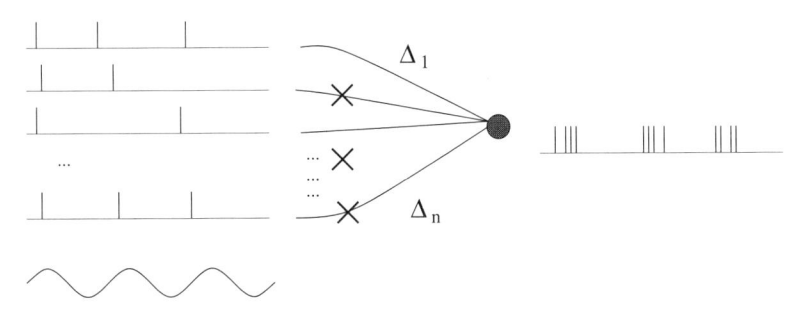

Figure 14.8. Unsupervised Learning mechanism (schematic). Several transmission lines converge on a single coincidence detector neuron in the nucleus laminaris. When pulses are generated at the ear, they are phase locked to the external sound wave (left part of figure). In order to achieve a high temporal resolution, pulses should *arrive* synchronously at the coincidence detector neuron which is possible only if the delays of the transmission lines are finely tuned. An unsupervised adaptive mechanism selects and reinforces some of the transmission lines and suppresses other (black crosses). After learning, pulses arrive with a high degree of coherence (right).

The basic idea of the learning model is sketched in Figure 14.8. Immediately after birth a large number of connections are formed. During an early period of post-natal development a tuning process takes place which selectively reinforces transmission lines with similar preferred phase and eliminates others.

To achieve this selection process, we have used the spike based Hebbian learning rule discussed in Section 2. The time window $W(s)$ is given by (14.9) and shown in Figure 14.1. The maximum of $W(s)$ is located at $s^* = -0.05$ ms. The choice $s^* = -\tau_{\text{rise}}/2$ guarantees stable learning [Gerstner et al., 1996; Kempter, 1997].

The results of a simulation run are shown in Figure 14.9. Before learning the neuron receives input over about 600 synapses from presynaptic neurons. Half of the input lines originate from the left, the other half from the right ear. The total transmission delays Δ_j are different between one line and the next and vary between 2 and 3 ms. At the beginning of learning all synaptic efficacies have the same strength $w_{ij} = 1$.

370   14. Hebbian Learning of Pulse Timing in the *Barn Owl* Auditory System

Both ears are stimulated by a pure 5 kHz tone with interaural time difference ITD = 0. The effect of stimulation is that spikes arrive at the synapses with periodically modulated rate $\nu_j(t)$ given by (14.19). During learning, synaptic weights are modified according to the Hebbian learning rule (14.8). The homogeneous distribution ($w_{ij} = 1$ for all j) becomes unstable during learning (Figure 14.9, Middle). The instability has also been confirmed analytically [Kempter, 1997].

After learning the synaptic efficacies have approached either the upper bound $w_{\max} = 3$ or they have decayed to zero. The transmission lines which remain after learning have either very similar delays, or delays differing by a full period (Figure 14.9, Bottom).

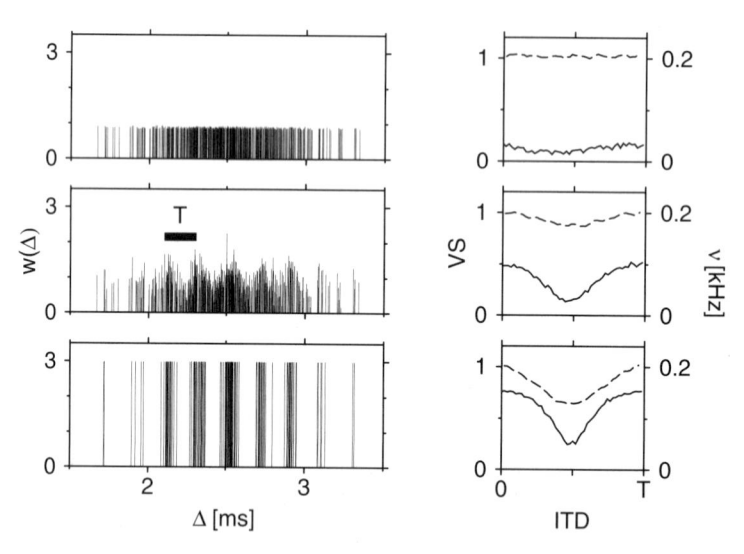

Figure 14.9. Development of tuning to a 5kHz tone. The left column shows the strength of synaptic efficacies w_{ij} of all synapses. Synapses are indexed according to the delay Δ_j of the corresponding transmission line and are plotted as $w_{ij} = w(\Delta)$. On the right, we show the vector strength (vs, solid line) and the output firing rate (ν, dashed) as a function of the interaural time delay (ITD). **Top.** Before learning, there are 600 synapses (300 from each ear) with different delays, chosen randomly from a Gaussian distribution with mean 2.5 ms and variance 0.3 ms. All weights have unit value. The output is not phase-locked ($vs \approx 0.1$) and shows no dependence upon the ITD. **Middle.** During learning, some synapses are strengthened others decreased. Those synapses which increase have delays that are similar or that differ by multiples of the period $T = 0.2$ ms of the stimulating tone. The vector strength of the output increases and starts to depend on the ITD. **Bottom.** After learning, only about 150 synapses (≈ 75 from each ear) survive. Both the output firing rate ν and the vector strength vs show the characteristic dependence upon the ITD as seen in experiments with adult owls [Carr and Konishi, 1990]. The neuron has the maximal response ($\nu = 200$ Hz) for ITD = 0, the stimulus used during the learning session of the model neuron. The vector strength at ITD = 0 is $vs \approx 0.8$ which corresponds to a temporal precision of 25 μs. Taken from [Gerstner et al. 1997.]

The sensitivity of the output firing rate to the interaural time difference (ITD) and the degree of phase locking were tested before, during, and after learning (right column in Figure 14.9). Before learning, the neuron shows no sensitivity to the ITD. This means that the neuron is not a useful coincidence detector for the sound source localization task. During learning ITD sensitivity develops similar to that found in experiments [Carr, 1995]. After learning the output rate is significantly modulated as a function of ITD. The response is maximal for ITD = 0, the ITD used during learning. The form of the ITD tuning curves corresponds to experimental measurements.

To test the degree of phase locking in the output we have plotted the vector strength, vs, as a function of ITD. By definition the vector strength is proportional to the first Fourier component of the histogram of phase distributions; cf. Figure 14.7. It is therefore a suitable measure of phase-locking. The vector strength vs is normalized so that $vs = 1$ indicates perfect phase locking (infinite temporal precision or $\sigma_{\text{out}} = 0$).

Let us focus on the value of vs in the case of optimal stimulation (ITD = 0). Before learning $vs \approx 0.1$, which indicates that there is no significant phase locking. The value of $vs \approx 0.8$ found after learning confirms that after the tuning of the synapses, phase locking is very pronounced.

14.6 Conclusions

In this Chapter we have studied the auditory system of the barn owl as an example of neural pulse coding. In our simplified model, we have seen that the generation of action potentials is very precise, if input spikes *arrive* coherently at the synapses. Coherent input causes large systematic fluctuations of the total input current to the neuron. A temporally modulated input current has also been successfully used in an experimental preparation to generate precisely timed spike output [Mainen and Sejnowski, 1995].

In a general setting, the condition of coherent spike arrival may seem rather artificial. We have seen, however, that a Hebbian learning rule may automatically select and reinforce those synapses which support coherent spike arrival and suppress others.

In the peripheral stages of the auditory system, neurons are extremely fast with an effective membrane time constant in the range of 0.1 ms. In cortex or hippocampus neurons are slower with time constants in the range of 10–50 ms [Bernander et al., 1991]. To translate the results of this Chapter to other areas, we would therefore have to multiply all time scales by a factor of 100. A temporal precision of 20–30 μs for auditory neurons then implies a precision of 2–3 ms for spike timing in other areas. This is still a remarkably fast time scale and would support the idea of synfire chain activity [Abeles, 1991, 1994; Lestienne, 1996].

The spike-based learning rule used in this Chapter is an example of a Hebbian learning rule. Temporal aspects of Hebbian learning have been previously studied in models of sequence learning and completion in associative memory models, for path planning in hippocampal models, and for the development of spatio-temporal receptive fields [Sompolinsky and

Kanter, 1986; Herz et al., 1988, 1989; Abbott and Blum, 1996; Blum and Abbott 1996; Wu et al., 1996; Wimbauer et al., 1994]. The formulation of this Chapter is different since it is based on pulse timing and not on time-dependent firing rates. A related spike-based learning rule has been used for learning of spatio-temporal pulse patterns [Gerstner et al., 1993].

Qualitatively, the form of the Hebbian learning window used in the simulations seems to be in agreement with experimental results [Bliss and Collingridge, 1993; Debanne et al., 1994; Markram et al., 1997] even though the time scale is different. Spike-based Hebbian learning may be seen as a special case of the general problem of synaptic dynamics [Abbott et al., 1997; Nelson et al., 1997; Tsodyks and Markram 1997; Markram and Tsodyks, 1997; Senn et al., 1997]. The next few years will certainly bring a better insight into this fascinating topic.

References

[Abbott and Blum, 1996] Abbott, L. F. and Blum, K. I. (1996). Functional significance of long-term potentiation for sequence learning and prediction. *Cerebral Cortex*, 6:406–416.

[Abbott et al., 1997] Abbott, L. F., Varela, J. A., Sen, K., and Nelson, S. B. (1997). Synaptic depression and cortical gain control. *Science*, 275:220–224.

[Abeles, 1991] Abeles, M. (1991). *Corticonics*. Cambridge University Press, Cambridge.

[Abeles, 1994] Abeles, M. (1994). Firing Rates and Well-Timed Events. In *Models of Neural Networks 2*, E. Domany, K. Schulten, and J. L. van Hemmen, eds., Springer, New York, chapter 3, 121–140.

[Bialek et al., 1991] Bialek, W., Rieke, F., de Ruyter van Stevenick, R. R., and Warland, D. (1991). Reading a neural code. *Science*, 252:1854–1857.

[Bliss and Collingridge, 1993] Bliss, T. V. P. and Collingridge, G. L. (1993). A synaptic model of memory: Long-term potentiation in the hippocampus. *Nature*, 361:31–39.

[Blum and Abbott, 1996] Blum, K. I. and Abbott, L. F. (1996). A model of spatial map formation in the hippocampus of the rat. *Neural Computation*, 8:85–93.

[Carr, 1995] Carr, C. E. (1995). The development of nucleus laminaris in the barn owl. *Advances in Hearing Research*, Manley, G. A., Klump, G. M., Köppl, C., Fastl, H., and Oeckinghaus, H., eds., World Scientific, Singapore, 24–30.

[Carr and Konishi, 1990] Carr, C. E. and Konishi, M. (1990). A circuit for detection of interaural time differences in the brain stem of the barn owl. *J. Neurosci.*, 10:3227–3246.

[Carr, 1993] Carr, C. E. (1993). Processing of temporal information in the brain. *Ann. Rev. Neurosci.*, 16:223–243.

[Chuma and Ohmori, 1998] Chuhma, N. and Ohmori, H. (1998). Postnatal development of phase-locked high-fidelity synaptic transmission in the medial nucleus of the trapezoid body of the rat. *J. Neurosci.*, 18:512–520.

[Debanne et al., 1994] Debanne, D., Gähwiler, B. H., and Thompson, S. M. (1994). Asynchronous pre- and postsynaptic activity induces associative long-term depression in area CA1 of the rat hippocampus in vitro. *Proc. Natl. Acad. Sci. USA*, 91:1148–1152.

[Erwin et al., 1995] Erwin, E., Obermayer, K., and Schulten, K. (1995). Models of orientation and ocular dominance columns in the visual cortex: a critcal comparison. *Neural Computation*, 7:425–468.

[Gerstner and Abbott, 1997] Gerstner, W. and Abbott, L. F. (1997). Learning navigational maps through potentiation and modulation of hippocampal place cells. *J. Comput. Neurosci.*, 4:79–94.

[Gerstner et al., 1993] W. Gerstner, R. Ritz, and J. L. van Hemmen. Why spikes? Hebbian learning and retrieval of time–resolved excitation patterns. *Biol. Cybern.*, 69:503–515.

[Gerstner et al., 1996] Gerstner, W., Kempter, R., van Hemmen J. L., and Wagner, H. (1996). A neuronal learning rule for sub-millisecond temporal coding. *Nature*, 383:76–78.

[Gerstner et al., 1997] Gerstner, W., Kempter, R., van Hemmen J. L., and Wagner, H. (1997). A developmental learning rule for coincidence tuning in the barn owl auditory system. *Computational Neuroscience: trends in research 1997*, J. Bower, ed., Plenum Presss, New York, 665–669.

[Haykin, 1994] Haykin, S. (1994). *Neural Networks*. Prentice Hall, Upper Saddle River, NJ.

[Hebb, 1949] Hebb, D. O. (1949). *The Organization of Behavior*. Wiley, New York.

[Heiligenberg, 1991] Heiligenberg, W. (1991). *Neural Nets in Electric Fish*. MIT Press, Cambridge.

[Hertz et al., 1991] Hertz, J., Krogh, A., and Palmer, R. G. (1991). *Introduction to the Theory of Neural Computation*. Addison-Wesley, Redwood City CA.

[Herz et al., 1988] Herz, A. V. M., Sulzer, B., Kühn, R., and van Hemmen, J. L. (1988). The Hebb rule: Representation of static and dynamic objects in neural nets. *Europhys. Lett.*, 7:663–669.

[Herz et al., 1989] Herz, A. V. M., Sulzer, B., Kühn, R., and van Hemmen, J. L. (1989). Hebbian learning reconsidered: Representation of static and dynamic objects in associative neural nets. *Biol. Cybern.*, 60:457–467.

[Hopfield, 1982] Hopfield, J. J. (1982). Neural networks and physical systems with emergent collective computational abilities. *Proc. Natl. Acad. Sci. USA*, 79:2554–2558.

[Hopfield and Herz, 1995] Hopfield, J. J. and Herz, A. V. M. (1995). Rapid local synchronization of action potentials: towards computation with coupled integrate-and-fire networks. *Proc. Natl. Acad. Sci. USA*, 92:6655.

[Jeffress, 1948] Jeffress, L. A. (1948). A place theory of sound localisation. *J. Comp. Physiol. Psychol.*, 41:35–39.

[O'Keefe amd Recce, 1993] O'Keefe, J. and Recce, M. (1993). Phase relationship between hippocampal place units and the hippocampal theta rhythm. *Hippocampus*, 3:317–330.

[Kempter, 1997] Kempter, R. (1997). *Hebbsches Lernen zeitlicher Codierung: Theorie der Schallortung im Hörsystem der Schleiereule*. Naturwissenschaftliche Reihe, Bd. 17. DDD, Darmstadt.

[Knudsen et al., 1979] Knudsen, E. I., Blasdel, G. G., and Konishi, M. (1979). Sound localization by the barn owl (tyto alba) measured with the search coil technique. *J. Comp. Physiol.*, 133:1–11.

[Kohonen, 1984] Kohonen, T. (1984). *Self-Organization and Associative Memory*. Springer-Verlag, New York.

[Konishi, 1986] Konishi, M. (1986). Centrally synthesized maps of sensory space. *Trends Neurosci.*, 9:163–168.

[Konishi, 1993] Konishi, M. (1993). Listening with two ears. *Scientific American*, 34–41.

[Lestienne, 1996] Lestienne, R. (1996). Determination of the precision of spike timing in the visual cortex of anaesthetised cats. *Biol. Cybern.*, 74:55–61.

[Linsker, 1986a] Linsker, R. (1986). From basic network principles to neural architecture: emergence of spatial-opponent cells. *Proc. Natl. Acad. Sci. USA*, 83:7508–7512.

[Linsker, 1986b] Linsker, R. (1986). From basic network principles to neural architecture: emergence of orientation selective cells. *Proc. Natl. Acad. Sci. USA*, 83:8390–8394.

[Linsker, 1986c] Linsker, R. (1986). From basic network principles to neural architecture: emergence of orientation columns. *Proc. Natl. Acad. Sci. USA*, 83:8779–8783.

[MacKay and Miller, 1990] MacKay, D. J. C. and Miller, K. D. (1990). Analysis of Linsker's application of Hebbian rules to linear networks. *Network*, 1:257–297.

[Mainen and Sejnowski, 1995] Mainen, Z. F. and Sejnowski, T. J. (1995). Reliability of spike timing in neocortical neurons. *Science*, 268:1503–1506.

[Manis and Marx, 1991] Manis, P. B. and S. O. Marx, (1991). Outward currents in isolated ventral cochlear nucleus neurons. *J. Neurosci.*, 11:2865–2880.

[Markram and Tsodyks, 1996] Markram, H. and Tsodyks, M. (1996). Redistribution of synaptic efficacy between neocortical pyramidal neurons. *Nature*, 382:807–810.

[Markram et al., 1997a] Markram, H., Lübke, J., Frotscher, M., and Sakmann, B. (1997). Regulation of synaptic efficacy by coincidence of postsynaptic APs and EPSPs. *Science*, 275:213–215.

[Markram and Tsodyks, 1997b] Markram, H. and Tsodyks, M. (1997). The information content of action potential trains: a synaptic basis. *Artificial Neural Networks - ICANN'97*, Springer, Lecture Notes in Computer Science, 1327.

[Miller and MacKay, 1994] Miller, K. D. and MacKay, D. J. C. (1994). The role of constraints in Hebbian learning. *Neural Computation*, 6:100–126.

[Miller et al., 1989] Miller, K. D., Keller, J. B., and Stryker, M. P. (1989). Ocular dominance column development: analysis and simulation. *Science*, 245:605–615.

[Minai and Levy, 1993] Minai, A. A. and Levy, W. B. (1993). Sequence learning in a single trial. *Proc. World Congress on Neural Networks II*, 505–508.

[Moiseff and Konishi, 1981] Moiseff, A. and Konishi, M. (1981). Neuronal and behavioral sensitivity to binaural time differences in the owl. *J. Neurosci.*, 1:40–48.

[Nelson et al., 1997] Nelson, S. B., Varela, J. A., Sen, K., and Abbott, A. F. (1997). Functional significance of synaptic depression between cortical neurons. In J. Bower, editor, *Computational Neuroscience - Trends in Research 1997*, Plenum Press, 429–434.

[Oertel, 1983] Oertel, D. (1983). Synaptic responses and electrical properties of cells in brain slices of the mouse anteroventral cochlear nucleus. *J. Neurosci.*, 3:2043–2053.

[Oja, 1982] Oja, E. (1982). A simplified neuron model as a principal component analyzer. *J. Math. Biol.*, 15:267–273.

[Reyes et al., 1994] Reyes, A. D., Rubel, E. W., and Spain, W. J. (1994). Membrane properties underlying the firing of neurons in the avian cochlear nucleus. *J. Neurosci.*, 14:5352–5364.

[Reyes et al., 1996] Reyes, A. D., Rubel, E. W., and Spain, W. J. (1996). In vitro analysis of optimal stimuli for phase-locking and time-delayed modulation of firing in avian nucleus laminaris neurons. *J. Neurosci.*, 16:993–1007.

[Rieke et al., 1996] Rieke, F., Warland, D., de Ruyter van Steveninck, R. R., and Bialek, W. (1996). *Spikes – Exploring the Neural Code*. MIT Press, Cambridge, MA.

[Sejnowski, 1989] Sejnowski, T. J. and Tesauro, G. (1989). The Hebb rule for synaptic plasticity: algorithms and implementations. In J. H. Byrne and W. O. Berry, eds., *Neural Models of Plasticity*, Academic Press, chapter 6, 94–103.

[Senn et al., 1997] Senn, W., Tsodyks, M., and Markram, H. (1997). An algorithm for synaptic modification based on exact timing of pre-and postsynaptic action potentials. *Artificial Neural Networks - ICANN'97*, Springer, Lecture Notes in Computer Science 1327:121–126.

[Shadlen and Newsome, 1994] Shadlen, M. N. and Newsome, W. T. (1994). Noise, neural codes and cortical organization. *Curr. Opin. Neurobiol.*, 4:569–579.

[Softky, 1995] Softky, W. R. (1995). Simple codes versus efficient codes. *Curr. Opin. Neurobiol.*, 5:239–247.

[Sompolinsky and Kanter, 1996] Sompolinsky, H. and Kanter, I. (1996). Temporal association in asymmetric neural networks. *Phys. Rev. Lett.*, 57:2861–2864.

[Sullivan and Konishi, 1984] Sullivan, W. E. and Konishi, M. (1984). Segregation of stimulus phase and intensity coding in the cochlear nucleus of the barn owl. *J. Neurosci.*, 4:1787–1799.

[Swindale, 1982] Swindale, N. V. (1982). A model for the formation of orientation columns. *Proc. R. Soc. Lond. B*, 215:211–230.

[Tsodyks and Markram, 1997] Tsodyks, M. and Markram, H. (1997). Neurotransmitter release probability determines the nature of the neural code between neocortical pyramidal neurons. *Proc. Natl. Acad. Sci., USA*, 94:719–723.

[Willshaw and von der Malsburg, 1976] Willshaw, D. J. and von der Malsburg, C. (1976). How patterned neuronal connections can be set up by self-organization. *Proc. R. Soc. Lond. B*, 194:431–445.

[Wimbauer et al., 1994] Wimbauer, S., Gerstner, W., and van Hemmen, J. L. (1994). Emergence of spatio-temporal receptive fields and its application to motion detection. *Biol. Cybern.*, 72:81–92.

[Wu et al., 1996] Wu, X., Baxter, R. A., and Levy, W. B. (1996). Context codes and the effect of noisy learning on a simplified hippocampal CA3 model. *Biol. Cybern.*, 74:159–165.